Architectures, Rules, and Preferences

Lecture Notes No. 184

Architectures, Rules, and Preferences

Variations on Themes by Joan W. Bresnan

edited by

Annie Zaenen, Jane Simpson, Tracy Holloway King, Jane Grimshaw, Joan Maling, and Chris Manning

CSLI
PUBLICATIONS
Center for the Study of
Language and Information
Stanford, California

Center for the Study of Language and Information
Leland Stanford Junior University
Printed in the United States
11 10 09 08 07   1 2 3 4 5

Library of Congress Cataloging-in-Publication Data

Architectures, rules, and preferences : variations on themes by Joan W. Bresnan / edited by Annie Zaenen ... [et al.].

p. cm. – (CSLI lecture notes ; no. 184.)

Includes bibliographical references and index.
ISBN-13: 978-1-57586-560-7 (pbk. : alk. paper)
ISBN-10: 1-57586-560-2 (pbk. : alk. paper)
1. Grammar, Comparative and general—Syntax. I. Bresnan, Joan. II. Zaenen, Annie E. (Annie Else), 1941– III. Title. IV. Series.

P291A73 2007
415–dc22   2007033933
CIP

∞ The acid-free paper used in this book meets the minimum requirements of the American National Standard for Information Sciences—Permanence of Paper for Printed Library Materials, ANSI Z39.48-1984.

CSLI was founded in 1983 by researchers from Stanford University, SRI International, and Xerox PARC to further the research and development of integrated theories of language, information, and computation. CSLI headquarters and CSLI Publications are located on the campus of Stanford University.

CSLI Publications reports new developments in the study of language, information, and computation. Please visit our web site at
http://cslipublications.stanford.edu/
for comments on this and other titles, as well as for changes and corrections by the authors, editors, and publisher.

Contents

Contributors

CYNTHIA L. ALLEN: Australian National University
Cindy.Allen@anu.edu.au.

ALEX ALSINA: Pompeu Fabra University alex.alsina@upf.edu.

ALISON ALVAREZ: Carnegie Mellon University nosila@cs.cmu.edu.

AVERY D. ANDREWS: Australian National University
Avery.Andrews@anu.edu.au.

ASH ASUDEH: Carleton University asudeh@ccs.carleton.ca.

JUDITH BERMAN: Ruhr-Universität
Judith.Berman@ruhr-uni-bochum.de.

KERSTI BÖRJARS: University of Manchester
k.borjars@manchester.ac.uk.

MIRIAM BUTT: Universität Konstanz
miriam.butt@uni-konstanz.de.

HYE-WON CHOI: Ewha Womans University hwchoi@ewha.ac.kr.

YOUNG-MEE YU CHO: Rutgers University yucho@rci.rutgers.edu.

MARY DALRYMPLE: Oxford University
mary.dalrymple@ling-phil.ox.ac.uk.

ABDELKADER FASSI FEHRI: University of Newcastle upon Tyne
a.fassi-fehri@ncl.ac.uk.

Robert Frederking: Carnegie Mellon University
ref+@cs.cmu.edu.

Jeff Good: Max Planck Institute Leipzig good@eva.mpg.de.

Ronald M Kaplan: Powerset kaplan@powerset.com.

Yehuda Falk: The Hebrew University of Jerusalem
msyfalk@mscc.huji.ac.il.

Jane Grimshaw: Rutgers University grimshaw@ruccs.rutgers.edu.

Akira Ishikawa: Sophia University
ishikawa@hoffman.cc.sophia.ac.jp.

Gerhard Jäger: University of Bielefeld
Gerhard.Jaeger@uni-bielefeld.de.

Tracy Holloway King: Palo Alto Research Center
thking@parc.com.

Paul Kroeger: Graduate Institute of Applied Linguistics
paul_kroeger@gial.edu.

Hanjun Lee: Sungkyungkwan University hanjung@skku.edu.

Beth Levin: Stanford University bclevin@stanford.edu.

Lori Levin: Carnegie Mellon University lsl@cs.cmu.edu.

Joan Maling: National Science Foundation jmaling@nsf.gov.

Chris Manning: Stanford University manning@cs.stanford.edu.

Elena Maslova: University of Bielefeld and Stanford University
maslova@jps.net.

Sam Mchombo: University of California, Berkeley
mchombo@socrates.berkeley.edu.

Carol Neidle: Boston University carol@bu.edu.

RACHEL NORDLINGER: University of Melbourne
racheln@unimelb.edu.au.

PETER PETERSON: The University of Newcastle
Peter.Peterson@newcastle.edu.au.

MALKA RAPPAPORT HOVAV: The Hebrew University of Jerusalem
mhovav@mscc.huji.ac.il.

LOUISA SADLER: University of Essex louisa@essex.ac.uk.

MARIKO SAIKI: Kanazawa University
saiki@kenroku.kanazawa-u.ac.jp.

GUIDO SEILER: Universität Zürich gseiler@ds.unizh.ch.

JANE SIMPSON: University of Sydney jhs@mail.usyd.edu.au.

IDA TOIVONEN: Carleton University ida_toivonen@carleton.ca.

NIGEL VINCENT: University of Manchester
nigel.vincent@man.ac.uk.

MARIE-THÉRÈSE VINET: Université de Sherbrooke
marie-therese.vinet@usherbrooke.ca.

ANNIE ZAENEN: Palo Alto Research Center zaenen@parc.com.

Acknowledgements

The vast range of topics dealt with in this volume do credit to the person who inspired them, namely Joan Bresnan. We would like to thank the authors and reviewers, without whom there would be no Festschrift, for all their work on the project.

We would also like to thank Daniela Decheva who standardized and completed the bibliographies and Miriam Butt who helped with the initial latex formatting. Finally, as always, our thanks go to Dikran for being there and giving us CSLI Publications.

Introduction

With affectionate admiration we present these papers to Joan Bresnan.

Joan Wanda Bresnan was born on August 22 1945, and grew up in California. Her first degree (1966) was in philosophy at Reed College in Portland, Oregon, and her interest in philosophy led her to MIT, first to study philosophy and then linguistics. From her interest in philosophy she brought to syntax a concern for testable formalization, and a delight in expressing complex arguments simply and clearly. In 1972 she completed her thesis "Theory of complementation in English syntax", supervised by Noam Chomsky.

She starts her dissertation in grand style:

> "Complementizer", like so many terms in linguistics, is a rebarbative word. A natural suspicion attaches to objects going by such a word. Unlike such weighty and venerable things as predicates, quantifiers, sentences and even conjunctions, the so-called "complementizers" lack ready associations with logic. But therein, perhaps, lies their special interest to syntacticians. What are complementizers? What are they for?

She then takes up her questions:

> "I must confess at once that I cannot answer these questions: without detailed and careful research into many languages, one cannot begin to define "complementizer" in an adequate way."

From the start, we see the features that characterise her later work — the concern with the basic constructs of linguistic theory, the belief that most questions in theoretical linguistics can only be answered by empirical research in lots of languages, and the pleasure in lucid writing. They permeate her later work. Her thesis and much of her major work are grounded in a broad and deep understanding of English grammar, but also show the excitement in hunting down the details of an apparently minor point which is then shown to illuminate aspects of the grammar. The intellectual excitement of discovering what happens in other languages can be seen in her work on Bantu languages with Sam Mchombo (and see his paper in this book), Lioba Moshi and Jonni Kanerva, on Australian languages with Peter Austin, Rachel Nordlinger and Jane Simpson, on Icelandic with Höskuldur Thráinsson, Annie Zaenen and Joan Maling, and on the genesis of new languages (her work on pidgins and creoles with Sarah Roberts).

This book shows how her interests in empirical research on may languages have been transmitted to her colleagues and students. Many papers touch on English, but there are papers on American Sign Language (Neidle), Arabic (Fassi Fehri and Vinet), Bininj Gun-Wok (Nordlinger and Sadler), Catalan (Alsina), Chicheŵa (Mchombo), Chinese (Fassi Fehri and Vinet), German (Berman, Dalrymple, Kaplan and King, Seiler), Hebrew (Falk), Indonesian (Kroeger), Japanese (Cho and Saiki, Ishikawa), Punjabi (Butt), Korean (Choi, Cho and Saiki, Lee), Old English (Allen), Swedish (Asudeh and Toivonen, Vincent and Börjars), and Warlpiri (Simpson).

After Joan finished her thesis, she taught at Stanford University (1972), and at the University of Massachusetts, Amherst (1973–75), before receiving a John Simon Guggenheim fellowship. She returned to MIT (1975–1983). She then took up a chair at Stanford University in 1983, becoming in 1992 the Howard H. and Jessie T. Watkins University Professor, and then in 2000 the Sadie Dernham Patek Professor in Humanities.

During her time at MIT she began developing with Ronald Kaplan a model of grammar that would be both psychologically plausible and computationally tractable, and less abstract than the prevailing theory of grammar. This model was called 'Lexical-Functional Grammar', a name indicating the importance of the lexicon as the repository of information needed by the grammar, and the importance of a level of functional structure as a place for unifying information from the constituent structure and from the lexicon. Thus LFG was built using a parallel architecture. Joan and her students and colleagues developed the ideas of LFG and tested them on a range of languages. The first results appear in a book she edited, *The Mental Representation of Grammatical Relations* (Bresnan 1982).

The constituent structure part of the LFG model relied extensively on the X-bar theory proposed by Ray Jackendoff (1977), with its emphasis on building endocentric phrases as an integral part of the theory. Joan has long been concerned with getting the details of syntactic structure right, and the problem of exocentric phrases, including the clause itself, led her eventually to the more radical proposals of

Bresnan (2001). Several papers explore the internal structure of noun phrases or determiner phrases. Cynthia Allen examines the syntax internal to the noun phrase/determiner phrase to show that, contrary to appearance, in Old English the orders Det Poss and Poss Det are not in free variation and represent different structures. Seiler argues for an apparent preposition in Upper German being a non-projecting prepositional head adjoined to the determiner in a phrase. Yehuda Falk discusses long and short possessor constructions in Hebrew, and makes use of the parallel architecture of LFG to argue against an account based purely on constituent structure. His solution involves taking the feature DEFINITE to have as a possible value an f-structure. The possibilities of counting, partitioning and forming mass and group nouns are discussed from different angles by Grimshaw and Fassi Fehri and Vinet. Grimshaw considers the internal structure of container, portion and picture nouns, and argues for a structural solution involving two extended projections. Fassi Fehri and Vinet consider the interpretation of nominals in Arabic, English and Chinese, and argue for two binary features 'atom' and 'singulative' creating a classification of nouns as individuals, kinds, masses and collectives.

At the level of the clause, Nordlinger and Sadler show that any assumption that verbless clauses should all receive the same syntactic analysis is untenable. Examining a range of copula constructions in a wide range of languages reveals at least two different structural types are needed to represent them: a default one in which the nonverbal predicate is the f-structure PRED of the clause, and another in which the nonverbal predicate is embedded in a higher clause without an overt head in the constituent structure. These structures are needed to account for the fact that some languages allow tense markers on nominals heading clauses, while others have tense on copulas in complementary distribution with nominals heading clauses (zero copula), and still others use zero copula or the pronominal copula to encode a stage-level vs. individual-level distinction.

The parallel architecture of LFG is a metaphor whose power is invoked in many papers. To the original functional structure and constituent structure has been added information structure (King, 1995; Choi, 1999) and this is taken up by Jane Simpson who revisits the work she did with Joan (Simpson, 1983) on non-configurationality in Warlpiri to argue that information structure constrains word order. Neidle's paper extends the parallels into the manual and non-manual domains of signing languages. She shows that a wide range of syntactic information is expressed by non-manual expressions in signed language.

A key feature of the LFG model was the attempt to do away with transformations, movement and traces. One set of structures which apparently required traces were long distance dependencies (*Who did Bill greet t?*). In this festschrift, Kaplan, Dalrymple and King return to the problem, looking at weak crossover data that had been accounted for by positing traces in long distance dependencies. They provide a solution, which does away with traces by making use of the constituent-structure/functional structure correspondence of LFG.

The structures built by unification needed to be constrained. One such constraint proposed in the early LFG model was the Subject condition, that every clause should have a subject. This of course ran into problems with the characterization of null subject languages, such as many of the Romance languages. The paper by Alex Alsina in this book addresses this. He uses copular verb agreement with non-subjects in Catalan to argue that in non-null-subject languages, the subject corresponds to a phrase in the constituent structure with lexically specified features, but in null subject languages there is no such position; subjects either lack a constituent structure correspondent, or appear inside the VP.

One of the innovations of the LFG model was the reliance on the lexicon and on lexical operations, as seen in Joan's work on the passive, control and polyadicity (Bresnan, 1982). Her pioneering work on defining and classifying and representing the kinds of rules that operate on predicate argument structures in the lexicon is extended in several papers. Kroeger shows that the supposed Indonesian valence-increasing suffix *-kan* is polysemous; it can be used in morphosemantic operations to modify lexical conceptual structure, and in morphosyntactic operations as a way of modifying the syntactic expression of arguments. In the late 1980s Lori Levin and Joan among others used hierarchies of semantic roles to develop a theory of the linking of semantic roles, predicate argument structure and grammatical functions (Bresnan, 1990). The basis for such hierarchies is reconsidered here by Malka Rappaport Hovav and Beth Levin, who argue that no single hierarchy can do all that has been demanded of it. This is in part because semantic roles are not primitive constructs, but rather positions in predicate decompositions (structured representations of events), and the hierarchies are actually generalizations over possible event structures, reflecting the relative depth of embedding of semantic roles in the event structures.

The lexicon also provided much of the information about the features of words, which were then passed up the constituent structure tree, and unified in the functional structure. The properties and nature of features are discussed in several papers, those already mentioned

(Falk, Fassi Fehri and Vinet) and others. Vincent and Börjars draw on data from person and gender systems to argue for a constrained account of features, which tries to maintain cross-linguistic constancy in the definition of classes of features. The primes in these definitions may be syntactic or semantic. They further discuss cases where agreement in features does not take place, and suggest that unmarked forms occurring in such contexts be characterized as the null set. They point to consequences for the assumption that for set-valued features, union of the relevant sets is the operator to use. A practical use for features is provided in the paper by Lori Levin, Jeff Good, Alison Alvarez and Robert Frederking. They describe an elicitation tool AVENUE developed in the context of machine translation for discovering which meanings and communicative functions are morphosyntactically marked in a language, that is, for automating morphosyntactic feature detection. The hope is that this will lead to better methods for documenting languages, including endangered languages. They demonstrate an example from Mapudungun (Chile).

Joan built on her original thesis to develop a theory of control within Lexical Functional Grammar (Bresnan, 1982), based on a wide range of data. Asudeh and Toivonen add to this work here, with a discussion of an unusual example of a raising-like phenomenon, "copy raising" as in *Thora seems like she adores popsicles.* They show that its analysis helps understand the way languages encode the source of perceptions and impressions. Crucially, the source of the perception for raising verbs like *seem* are entailed participants, but not arguments of the raising verb. On the basis of German data which suggests that arguments expressed by nominals and sentences have parallel syntactic functions, Berman provides tests for the identification of the grammatical function of complement clauses, and concludes that in German this is crucially determined by structural position.

The work on control and on linking rules led in the 1990s to a flood of work on complex predicates (Alsina, 1997). Here, Ishikawa's paper on honorific verbs in Japanese presents a way of representing the transmission of honorification in complex predicates, and links it to the pragmatics of politeness.

Another major line of inquiry developed from Joan's work with Sam Mchombo on pronouns and agreement markers in Chicheŵa (Bresnan, 1987), which led to the recognition of the importance of information structure in determining the presence of pronouns. It also led to Joan's work with Peter Austin on the relation between pro-drop and other typological properties of languages (Austin, 1996), and this is taken up in Alsina's paper mentioned earlier. Several papers take up the theme of information structure. Sam Mchombo considers the semantic and pragmatic factors that license discontinuous dislocated constituents in Chicheŵa. Miriam Butt examines a puzzling phenomenon of pronominal suffixation/cliticization in Punjabi and argues that they are primarily motivated by discourse considerations.

For LFG to be an adequate model of grammar, the proposed syntactic structures must have an interface with formal semantics. Early work was done on this by Per-Kristian Halvorsen (Halvorsen, 1983). As the LFG model evolved, the demands on the semantic interpretation changed, and glue logic was developed to act as the semantic interpretation (Dalrymple, 1999). However, in turn, as OT-LFG has been developed to capture the insight that variation is an inherent part of language, and that this can be expressed by different rankings of constraints, a semantic interpretation, which is consistent with OT-LFG, is needed. Andrews' paper shows how OT-LFG can be provided with a form of input that has an explicitly specified semantic interpretation by assembling f-descriptions co-generated with sets of meaning-constructors.

While the standard LFG model has been further developed (Bresnan, 2001), in recent years Joan has been considering the place within LFG of ranking constraints, as in Optimality Theory, which has led to the development of OT-LFG. In turn this has allowed the representation of curious morphosyntactic facts, such as those attributed to animacy hierarchies, which have often been dismissed as 'periphery' facts (Bresnan, 2001; Bresnan, 2002). Hanjung Lee draws on earlier work using the CallFriend Korean (CFK) corpus of telephone speech to show frequency effects of the hierarchies of person, animacy and definiteness on case marking in Korean. This is then supported by experiments using eye-tracking to investigate the effects of frequency of case marking and comprehension difficulty in Korean. These are argued to provide new evidence about the active cognitive status of the system of constraint subhierarchies suggested in stochastic OT approaches.

OT-LFG has led to productive work looking at typological variation across languages and dialects, such as Nordlinger and Sadler's work mentioned above. The variation can be matched to variation in other domains. Cho and Mariko Saiki look at variation in the forms of vocative chants in Japanese and Korean, seeing what parts of the underlying system change in order to produce different outputs. They relate this to variation in musical structures. Choi looks at cross-dialect morphological variants of verbs in Korean as to where l-stems are retained, arguing that if constraints are in fact ranked stochastically on a continuous scale, variation phenomena such as the Korean l-verb conjugation can be explained rather easily. Several papers argue that optionality and variation must be derived from the internal structure of the grammar. Seiler looks at Upper German dialects showing different sources of variation: prepositional dative marking varies according to features assigned to the prepositional dative (e.g. does it mark focus or not), while, clause-finally, there is variation in the c-structure, as to whether auxiliary and modal verbs precede the nonfinite complement or not. Peter Peterson examines coordination in English, and shows that there are patterns of choices resulting from a gap in the grammar, i.e. the lack of a way of imposing constraints on lexical items within a coordination. This results in subject-verb agreement being left underspecified. Peterson suggests that, in choosing a form, the speaker bases his choice on factors such as proximity (e.g. "closest conjunct") and semantic salience (e.g. "plural wins").

Two papers consider the foundations of Stochastic Optimality Theory grammars. Elena Maslova examines the general properties of such grammars viewed as parametric statistical models. She shows that while their typological predictions can be determined by the mechanism of constraint interaction, they need not be, depending on the configuration of constraint sets. Gerhard Jäger compares two stochastic generalizations of Optimality Theory, namely Paul Boersma's Stochastic Optimality Theory and Maximum Entropy models. He argues that not only are there provably correct machine learning algorithms for Maximum Entropy models, but also that Paul Boersma's Gradual Learning Algorithm for Stochastic OT can be applied to Maximum Entropy models.

The study of variation naturally leads to the study of historical change, and work has begun in this area (Butt, 2001). In this volume, Cynthia Allen's paper deals with an early stage of English, and considers the loss of the Poss Det construction. Ishikawa considers the replacement of one class of honorific auxiliary verbs by another in Japanese in the last century can be explained using ideas about changes in social attitudes. Butt argues that modeling of the synchronic stages in the reanalysis of a pronoun into an agreement marker is easily expressible in LFG's architecture. Reversing this procedure, Vincent and Börjars show how claims about feature systems can be tested by modelling diachronic changes in such systems.

The papers in this book represent the diversity in advances in understanding language and languages that Joan has been involved in. They also illustrate the fruitful way in which knowledge is created collaboratively. Many of the authors are former students and colleagues of Joan's; many have collaborated with her on papers and projects. Their acknowledgments show how much they appreciate the passion for clear argument, respect for others and desire for co-operative work that she has brought to the field of linguistics. These qualities are now widely recognized; she was elected President of the Linguistic Society of America in 1999, and she became a Fellow of the American Academy of Arts and Sciences in 2004.

Part I

Division of Labor: Phrase Structure and Functional Structure

1

Variation in the NP/DP in Old English: Determiner and Possessive Combinations

CYNTHIA L. ALLEN

1.1 Introduction

This paper[1] investigates the variation in the position of determiners and possessives in Old English (OE) illustrated in (1) and (2):[2]

(1) a. Willaþ ge þæt ic eow agife þysne eowerne cyning
Will ye that I you give this(MAS) your(MAS) king
'Do you wish me to give you your king/this king of yours?'
Vercelli I.135

b. on þære his gebyrde
in that(FDS) his birth(FDS)
'in his birth' Blickling 167.3

(2) a. & heo is þin seo clæneste fæmne
and she is thy(FNS) the(FNS) cleanest virgin
'and she is your purest virgin' Blickling 157.2

[1]The research reported in this paper was partially funded by Australian Research Council Discovery Grant DP0208153.

[2]I use the following symbols, in the order gender, case, number: M=masculine, F=feminine, N=neuter; N=nominative, A=accusative, G=genitive, D=dative. It should be noted that the grammatical features may not be uniquely identified by the suffix as it is glossed, in which case I have glossed them as appropriate for the syntactic context.

Architectures, Rules, and Preferences: Variations on Themes by Joan Bresnan.
Annie Zaenen, Jane Simpson, Tracy Holloway King,
Jane Grimshaw, Joan Maling, and Chris Manning, (eds.).

b. þa cwæð he eft to his þam leofan þegne
then said He after to his the(MDS) dear(MDS) thane(MDS)
'He [Christ] then said to his dear thane [John]'
Vercelli I.231

In the Det(erminer) Poss(essive) construction of (1), the determiner precedes the possessive, while in the Poss Det construction of (2), the order is reversed.[3]

The Det Poss construction is a well-known feature of earlier English, but non-linguist scholars and linguists alike generally[4] do not differentiate this construction from the Poss Det construction. The existence of both constructions has usually been attributed to the freer word order of OE, with the two orders treated as variants of the same construction; for example Bately (1980: cii) gives examples of both Det Poss and Poss Det to illustrate 'the idiom combining the possessive and demonstrative.' Generative linguists who have offered an analysis of Det Poss, such as Haegemann and Guéron (1999: 450-1) and Demske (2001: 190-7), have not usually appeared to be aware of the existence of the Poss Det possibility in OE; an exception is Yoon (2002), whose analysis, however, does not account for the two important characteristics of the Poss Det construction mentioned below.

The general neglect of the Poss Det construction by linguists is particularly surprising given that it is by far the more frequently occurring of the two constructions and is indisputably native, since it occurs in all types of OE texts, including native poetry, while the Det Poss construction is pretty much restricted to translations from Latin (a language which allowed demonstratives and possessives to modify the same N). It is probable that linguists' lack of familiarity with this construction is due to the fact that it is strictly an OE construction, which disappears from all Middle English (ME) texts except some E(arly) ME copies of OE texts. In contrast, the Det Poss construction underwent a revival in Early Modern English under Latin influence, making linguists generally more aware of it. I will therefore focus on the Poss Det construction in this paper, offering an LFG analysis and also presenting hitherto undiscussed facts which any analysis must take into account.

[3]The term 'possessive' in this paper refers only to pronominal possessives, not to genitives in general.

[4]Some scholars working within a traditional framework such as Mitchell (1972: §104-12) make a careful distinction between the two constructions, but their concern is essentially to catalogue the patterns which are found, and they do not attempt an analysis.

1.2 Morphology and Syntax of Possessives and Determiners in OE

1.2.1 Possessives: Morphology

The first and second person possessives differed from the third person possessives in OE in their morphology, but not in their syntax. In the first and second persons, the genitive case of the pronoun was used as a base for further inflection; these possessives agreed with the N they modified, as in (3), where *min* agrees with the neuter accusative singular *lif*, and *minum* agrees with the neuter dative plural *sceapum*:

(3) And ic sylle min agen lif for minum sceapum
And I give my(NAS) own(NAS) life-NAS for my-NDP sheep(NDP)
'And I give up my own life for my sheep' ÆCHI XVII. 9

The suffixes of these possessives follow the 'strong' adjective declension.[5] In contrast, the third person possessives (both singular and plural) did not agree with their heads:

(4) He hylt mid his mihte heofonas
He holds with his might(FDS) heavens
'He holds up the heavens with his strength' ÆCHI I.9

In this example, the indeclinable *his* does not agree with the dative feminine *mihte.* The same lack of inflection in found when the third person possessives co-occur with a determiner, as in (1b) and (2b). The third person possessives are identical in form to the genitive case of the pronoun, and for this reason the possessive forms are traditionally regarded as belonging to distinct word classes of (third person) 'pronouns' and (first and second person) 'possessive adjectives'.[6]

However, all these forms share the same syntactic distribution. This situation is easily captured in LFG by the assumption that although all the possessive forms belonged to the same syntactic category, the first and second person forms were equipped in the lexicon with information that they were the modifiers of something with particular grammatical features. (See Section 3).

[5] OE inherited the Proto-Germanic strong/weak distinction in adjective declensions. Roughly, the strong declension of adjectives was used when an adjective was not preceded by a possessive, genitive NP, or definite determiner, and the weak declension was used when the adjective followed such an element.

[6] Haegemann and Guéron's (1999: 451) statement that 'the Old English possessive pronoun agreed with the head noun' is therefore not accurate for the third person forms, and their proposed analysis incorrectly suggests that the syntax of the third person possessives should be different from that of the other persons, as pointed out by Yoon (2002: 213).

Possessive inflection did not change in the Det Poss construction, e.g. *þysne eowerne cyning* in (1a) has the distinctive strong accusative masculine singular *–ne* suffix on both the determiner and the possessive. This makes the inflecting possessives different from adjectives, which normally had a weak inflection when they followed a definite determiner. Both the Det Poss and the Poss Det construction are found with both the non-agreeing third person possessive and the agreeing possessives. If the determiner were found only co-occurring with the third person possessives, we might suppose that the purpose of the determiner was to supply the possessive with case inflection, but this cannot be.

1.2.2 Determiners: forms and meanings

OE had two demonstratives, SE and ÞES. While ÞES is straightforwardly translated as the demonstrative THIS in Modern English, SE is more complicated. Both the Modern English definite article THE and the distal demonstrative THAT derive from SE.[7] This determiner is sometimes explicitly contrasted with the proximal demonstrative in OE stage, but already at this stage, it is sometimes best translated as 'the', and very often either 'that' or 'the' would serve as a good translation. Both determiners inflected to agree with their N head.

1.2.3 Distribution of Possessives and Determiners

Demske (2001: 190-7) presents five arguments that possessives were adjectives in OE. She assumes that possessives were reanalysed as part of the determiner system in Early Modern English. Space does not allow a refutation of all these arguments, but, it is worth demonstrating that Demske's two strongest syntactic arguments are unconvincing.

Demske suggests that possessives were like adjectives in OE in being able to occur in postnominal position. But while both adjectives and possessives are certainly found in postnominal position in OE poetry, postnominal position is not usual for either simple adjectives or simple possessives in OE prose. Postnominal possessives in the prose are essentially restricted to vocatives, e.g. *fæder ure*, lit. 'father our' in the OE version of the Lord's prayer. Postnominal adjectives are also found in vocative use, but only when accompanied by a determiner, as in the *Men ða leofestan*, 'dearest people', lit. 'people the belovedest', a phrase of commonly used by OE homilists to address their congrega-

[7]Briefly, *se*, the nominative masculine singular form, become *þe* early in ME, and was generalized as an indeclinable form. *That* is the reflex of the neuter nominative/accusative singular form. For details, see Millar (2000).

tions. Furthermore, genitive NP/DPs could generally follow their heads in OE:

(5) SE forma dæg þyssere worulde
the(MNS) first(MNS) day(MNS) this(FGS) world(FGS)
'the first day of this world' ÆCHI VI.150

It is therefore quite possible that the post-head possessives found in poetry and vocatives are best treated as phrasal. At any rate, the facts do not demand an analysis which treats possessives as adjectives. Furthermore, Mitchell (1985: ¶163) notes that postnominal determiners are also sometimes found in OE poetry, a fact which undermines Demske's attempts to show that possessives pattern like adjectives and not like determiners.

The second argument is the existence of the Det Poss construction, where the Poss appears between the determiner and N, the normal position for an adjective. However, such a treatment does not explain the Poss Det construction (which Demske does not mention), since adjectives did not normally occur before determiners in OE.

A systematic investigation (outlined in the Appendix) of the Poss Det and Det Poss constructions has uncovered two principal facts which must be accounted for. First, either SE or ÞES may be used in the Det Poss construction, but only SE is found in the Poss Det construction. Although this restriction is not noted in the few recent works which mention the existence of Poss Det, it appears to be a very solid fact; I have found 250 examples of Poss Det in my investigation, and every one of them has SE, but of the 129 examples of Det Poss, twenty four have ÞES.

Second, the Poss Det construction has an adjective as an integral component. In all the examples which I found of this construction, there is an adjective, as indicated in Table 1.

Poss Det type	N	% of total Poss Det
Poss Det Adj	46	18
Poss Det Adj N	204	82
Poss Det N	0	0
Total	250	100

TABLE 1 Occurrence of Poss Det in corpus

The association of Poss Det with adjectives has not gone entirely unnoticed, but because earlier studies have not adequately discriminated between OE texts which are found in manuscripts which are fairly close to the time of composition of the text and 'OE' texts which are in fact copies found in manuscripts from the Middle English period, there has not been a general recognition of the absolute nature of this restriction on the Poss Det construction in the OE period. For example, Mitchell (1985: §106) cautiously says that the construction is 'rare' without an adjective. In fact he notes that he only knows of one such example:

(6) mid his þæm anwealde
with his the(MDS) power
'with his power' Boethius 69.23

It turns out that although this particular example comes from a text composed in the late ninth century, it in fact is found in a manuscript which was copied long after the text was composed; Ker (1957, art. 305) puts it in the first part of the twelfth century, when the Poss Det construction was dying out (see Section 5). It is possible that the sentence may have had an adjective in it earlier which got omitted in the process of copying at some stage. Another possibility is that an adjective was no longer obligatory in this construction at this late stage. At any rate, a single example in a manuscript at such a remove from the original text cannot be considered a serious counterexample to an otherwise valid generalization.

As indicted in Table 1, in some instances the adjective in question is not followed by an overt N:

(7) & his þone nehstan afrefrige
and his the(MAS) nearest(MAS) comforts
'and comforts his neighbor'

This fact is undoubtedly related to the fact that what are traditionally called 'substantival adjectives' such as *se blinda* 'the blind man' were freely used in OE. A possible approach is to say that in OE, adjectives generally had an alternate lexical entry which supplied the information PRED='PRO' for an unexpressed head N.

In contrast to the Poss Det construction, an adjective is not only optional but infrequent in the Det Poss construction; only 19 of the 130 Det Poss examples in my data have an adjective.

1.3 Proposed Analysis

Before giving an analysis which deals with the facts mentioned above, it is necessary to provide some basic information on adnominal genitives in OE. I will use the term 'genitive' to refer to NP/DPs with a lexical head N in the genitive case. As mentioned in the preceding section, genitives could either precede or follow their heads, depending on various factors, including the 'weight' of the genitive phrase; see McLagan

(2004) for an investigation of these factors in a volume of homilies of the late tenth-century. One fact which will be of relevance concerns the interaction of adjectives and genitives.[8]

An adjective normally directly preceded the head N (Mitchell 1985: ¶172). The adjective could be preceded by another modifier, including genitive a phrase:

(8) mid ðæs folces eorðlican ðeowote
with the(NGS) people(NGS) earthly(NGS) service(NDS)
'with the earthly service of the people' CP(H) 131.14

Examples like (8) are not at all common; when N is modified by both an adjective and a genitive phrase, the genitive phrase is more often in the postnominal position, as in (5). However, examples like (8) occur too frequently to be considered ungrammatical. In contrast to phrasal genitives, possessives normally (in prose, at least) preceded the head N even if it was also modified by an adjective. Genitives of single Ns patterned with the possessives in the respect, as in (9):

(9) on Cristes soþre eaþmodlicre andetnesse
in Crist(MGS) true(FDS) humble(FDS) confession(FDS)
'in the true humble confession of Christ' Blickling 171.9

As in Modern English, prenominal genitives did not normally co-occur with a determiner modifying the head. I will assume that prenominal genitives in OE were Specifiers of DP with a POSS function,[9] and following Bresnan's (2001: 133-41) discussion of the economy of expression and extended heads, I assume that the reason why the head D is not expressed along with the POSS is that its definiteness feature is redundant. I furthermore assume that these phrases were equipped in the phrase structure with a constraining equation specifying that they must have genitive case.

I assume that possessives were determiners already in OE. The treatment of third person possessives is straightforward; they supplied the genitive case demanded of POSS. I assume that first and second person possessive forms, along with all other determiners and also adjectives,

[8]Space does not allow a thorough discussion of the very common construction found in (i), referred to as the Low Prenominal Genitive by Crisma (Forthcoming), where the adjective agrees with the head N, rather than with the genitive N:

(i) seo arlease helwarena stefn wæs gehyred
the(FNS) impious(FNS) hell-dweller(MGP) voice was heard
'the impious voice of the host of Hell was heard' Blickling 87.3

However, an account which treats these as a sort of compound seems promising.

[9]On the POSS function, see Laczkó (1995) and Bresnan (2001). It is irrelevant for our purposes here whether possessives and genitives in OE sometimes had the alternative OBL_{th} function which Laczkó assumes for some *of*-phrases in English.

had lexical entries with statements that they agreed with something in a particular case. For example, the *minum* of (3) would have a lexical entry like (10):[10]

(10)	*min*: D	(↑ PRED = 'PRO')
		(↑ NUM) = SG
		(↑ PERS) = 1
		(↑ CASE) =GEN
	-um:infl$_D$	((POSS ↑) CASE) = DAT
		((POSS ↑) NUM) = PL

This entry uses Inside-Out Functional Uncertainty (Dalrymple 1993, Halvorsen 1988, Bresnan 2001: 65-8) to enforce agreement of the possessive with the N it modifies. Thus, the possessive itself has genitive case, but it also carries the case of the N. It seems reasonable to assume that in the Det Poss construction the determiner is a phrasal demonstrative in a topic-like position in the left periphery of the DP. A similar construction is found in German as discussed by Plank (1992) and it is likely that essentially the same analysis is appropriate for the German and OE facts. The Poss Det construction is typologically more exotic, and it is this construction on which I will focus here.

For reasons which will shortly become clear, I assume an important difference between demonstratives and articles. Giusti (1997) argues that demonstratives are universally phrasal categories, while articles are heads. We can achieve this effect by assuming that ÞES is a determiner which has some sort of PRED. Thus, it can only occur in the Specifier position, as an adjunct to the NP. SE is similar when it means 'that', but is the functional head D, without a PRED, in its article use, where it is a co-head with N or A.

The final assumption, which explains the association of Poss Det with adjectives, is that AP could be the complement of a D head. Thus my suggested analysis for the Poss Det of (2a) is (11):

[10]The entry would in fact be more complex than this, because -um was also the suffix used to agree with neuter and masculine, but not datives in the singular, but adding these details would add nothing to the discussion.

(11)

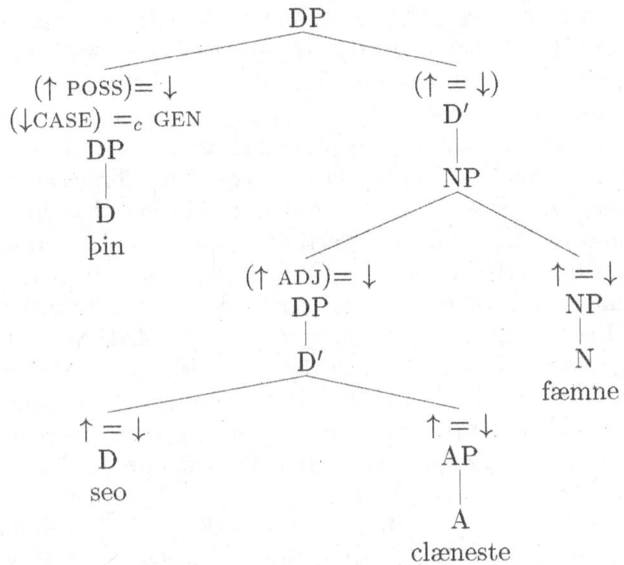

This analysis treats the Poss Det construction as having two determiners in one DP, the first in the Specifier of DP and the second taking AP as its complement in the adjunct of NP. As Giusti (1997) notes, it is not unusual cross-linguistically for adjectives (and prepositions) to be accompanied by articles. A common pattern is that both the noun and the adjective have a determiner:

(12) ha-bayit ha-gadol
the-house the-big
'the big house' (Hebrew, Giusti 1997 ex. 24a)

(13) afto to oreo to vivlio
this the good the book
'this good book' (Greek, Giusti 1997 ex. 41a)

Giusti treats the co-occurrence of an article and an adjective as an instance of a nominal modifier projecting its own extended projection.[11] In an LFG analysis, the AP complement of D in (11) serves the same function as this extended projection. This analysis follows the principle proposed in Bresnan (2001: 101) that complements to functional heads

[11]Kolliakou's (2003: 25, 83) HPSG analysis of Greek is different in that it treats the definite article as a subcategorization requirement of the head N, rather than a head, but it is similar in that she allows for D to select for 'nominal' complements, which include adjectives, in order to account for the ability of determiners to occur freely with adjectives which do not modify an overt head N, such as *ena agliko* 'an English one'.

must have a feature matrix that is equally marked or more marked than that of the functional head; since D is [−transitive, −predicative] and AP is [+predicative], AP may be a complement of D.[12]

Since no modern Germanic language appears to offer evidence for determiners in AP, it may seem surprising to assume this possibility for OE. However, it must also be noted that no modern Germanic language allows the sequence Poss Det, and since the evidence that this combination existed in OE in incontrovertible, it must simply be assumed that OE was different in some important way from all modern Germanic languages. It is of interest in this connection to note that Spamer (1979) and Fischer (2000) argue on separate grounds that weak adjectives (the type of adjective found in these constructions) have nominal characteristics in OE. The nominal characteristics, including the ability to co-occur with a determiner, are not surprising when we realize that the weak adjective declension was originally a nominalization (Curme 1910: 441, Prokosch 1960: ¶89 etc.).

Of most importance is the ability of the analysis to capture the facts. It explains why the Poss Det construction is limited to SE. If ÞES were inserted in D in this construction, it would contribute a second PRED to the DP, which should get its PRED only from the adjective. Thus, the SE of this construction is the article SE. There is interesting support for this analysis from Old Norse, where the Poss Det construction is also found, although apparently much less commonly. Heusler (1962: §410) gives a small number of examples of Poss Det Adj in Old Norse, which differed from OE in already having a definite article INN, distinct from the demonstrative SÁ (cognate with SE). Unfortunately, Heusler was not concerned with the limitations on this construction; he presents the examples in a general discussion of prenominal versus postnominal positioning of possessives. However, it is interesting to note that in all the examples which Heusler gives of the Poss Det combination, it is the definite article which is used. There is furthermore always an adjective, as in the OE examples. Barnes (2001: §3.3.5) also notes that it was common to combine a definite article with a preceding demonstrative in Old Norse when a noun was modified by an adjective, as in *sá (h)inn blindi maðr*, lit. 'that the blind man', but makes no mention of a

[12]However, allowing D to take AP as its complement violates Toivonen's (2001: 73) restrictions on cross-categorial co-head combinations which allow D to take only NP as its complement. Toivonen does not offer any arguments for this stricter requirement, which appears to be motivated mainly by a desire to be as restrictive as possible, nor does she indicate how the more restrictive stipulations will deal with constructions such as English gerunds, which Bresnan (2001: 291) analyzes as nominal phrases with verbal complements.

demonstrative combining with an article when there was no adjective, suggesting that the article was due to the presence of an adjective. The fact that the analysis extends to Old Norse suggests that it is essentially correct, and that already at the OE stage there was a definite article, albeit indistinguishable in form from the demonstrative.

The analysis extends to examples in which a genitive phrase is followed by SE. An unmodified genitive N (usually a proper N) in this construction is not rare:

(14) on Godes þone soþan þeowdom
in God(MGS) the(MAS) true(MAS) service(MAS)
'in the true service of God' Blickling 45.24

Again, simple nouns are similar to possessives, since examples in which a modified N precedes the determiner are uncommon. However, they are found in some texts:

(15) þæs fæder se ancenda sunu
the(MGS) father(NGS) the(MNS) only-begotten(MNS) son(MNS)
'the only begotten Son of the Father' Gregory(C) 261.26

It is not difficult to find an explanation for the fact that examples like (15) are not common. As already noted, the usual position of a phrasal genitive was after the head N when that N was modified by an adjective. This means that we would not expect many examples of a phrasal genitive before a determiner, given our assumption that an adjective was an essential ingredient of the construction. This assumption is given further support by the nature of the few phrasal genitives which do co-occur with a following determiner: they all involve an adjective. Furthermore, the determiner is always SE, as predicted.

1.4 Typological Status and Prehistory of Poss Det

Although it is not typologically unusual for adjectives to co-occur with articles, the particular array of facts found in OE seems to be highly unusual. First, the determiner that accompanies the adjective is optional, making OE quite different from Modern Greek, for example.[13] Second, the association of Poss Det order with adjectives has not been noted in any of the typological literature which I have consulted. It is not unheard of for a language to have a prenominal construction in which a possessive precedes a determiner; this is found for example in

[13]Barnes (2001: §3.3.5) indicates that it is unusual but not impossible for an adjective to following immediately after a demonstrative without an intervening article in Old Norse, suggesting that Old Norse was similar but not identical to Greek in this respect.

Bulgarian where the determiner in question is a enclitic on the first stressed element of NP (Scatton (1984):

(16) mója-ta kníga
my-the book
'my book' Scatton (1984: 316)

Similar facts are found in Macedonian.[14] But the OE construction does not involve an enclitic determiner and it furthermore must always have an adjective, unlike the Slavic constructions. Furthermore, the Slavic construction appears to put emphasis on the possessive — *my* book, not yours (see also Manzelli 1990). This is unlike the OE Poss Det, which seems rather to emphasize the adjective.[15]

In general, any analysis of a dead language which assumes a situation which is not found in any living language must be the subject of skepticism. However, in this instance, the evidence for the association of Poss Det with adjectives in OE is overwhelming because of the large number of examples. It must also be remembered that there is still much that we do not know about the possibilities of the NP/DP universally. It does not appear that the restrictions on the co-occurrence of possessives and determiners is something that typologists have examined very systematically. A language which has a similar construction to the Poss Det construction of OE must have some special characteristics to begin with: it must have possessives which are determiners, rather than adjectives or clitics, and it must allow for determiners to co-occur with adjectives. With such restrictions, we do not expect this sort of Poss Det construction to be at all common.

Furthermore, typologically unusual (but not impossible) constructions can arise when a special set of circumstances combines to bring them about, and it appears that this is what happened with OE. I noted above that weak adjectives started out as nominalizations. I now observe that there is reason to believe that modifiers of N originally had a postnominal position (see Smith 1971). Of particular interest to us here is the fact that the combination Poss + Det + Adj in postnominal position is attested in all the early Germanic languages. Heinrichs (1954) offers examples from all these languages; here, I will present only an illustrative example from Old Saxon and another from OE:

[14] I am grateful to Peter Hill for help with the Bulgarian in particular, and to Liljana Mitkovska for additional information on Macedonian.

[15] It is not obvious what determines the use of Poss Det in all instances. However, it is worth noting that the construction is frequently used when an adjective is contrastive. For example, at Blickling 179.1, the homilist uses *his þone menniscan dæl* 'his human part' when he is making a contrast with Christ's *divine* part.

(17) frô mîn the gôdo
lord my the good
'My good Lord' (Old Saxon, Heliand 2099)

(18) Mattheus, min se leofa
Matthew, my the dear
'Matthew, my beloved...' Blickling 229.30

Heinrichs presents such examples to illustrate articles used as 'linking particles' between nouns and adjectives, and does not differentiate these examples from ones lacking a possessive:

(19) drohtin the gôdo
lord the good
'the good lord' (Old Saxon, Heliand 401)

It seems reasonable to assume, as Heinrichs suggests, that there was still a rather nominal feel to these adjectives; a possible translation for (17) might be 'my Lord, the good one.' A plausible interpretation of examples (17) and (18) is, then, that the possessive modifies the noun it follows,[16] and the following Det + Adj forms a phrase in apposition to the N + Poss, so we have [N + Poss] [Det + Adj].

What makes OE different from most other early Germanic languages is that the combination Poss + Det + Adj is found in the prenominal position also. OE is not quite unique in this respect; at least a few examples are also found in Old Norse, as mentioned above, although they are not likely to be very frequent because the postnominal position for possessives was favored in that language, except when the possessive was emphatic (Barnes 2001: §3.9.6, Heusler 1962: §516.) It would seem that what happened in OE, but not most other Germanic languages, was that the combination Poss + Det + Adj survived the transition to prenominal position, with the Poss moving to the normal position for a prenominal possessive.

1.5 Demise of Poss Det

It is plausible that a marked construction will be vulnerable to loss, and so it is perhaps not surprising that the Poss Det construction did not survive. However, generations of language learners did learn it, since it is found in texts spanning two centuries or so. There is some rather equivocal evidence of a decline in frequency of use in the later

[16]OE texts were not punctuated like Modern English ones, and the comma after Mattheus in (18), added by the editor of the text, is not a reliable guide to the syntax. It is possible, however, that in the OE example, postnominal min is part of the postnominal DP.

OE period, but it is difficult to tell the difference between a diachronic decline here and simple variation in individual taste. What we can say with some certainty, however, is that the Poss Det construction was archaic by the end of the twelfth century. After 1100, there are few original examples (as opposed to examples which are found in copies of texts of OE composition). It can safely be assumed that the Poss Det construction was not really part of the language by the middle of the twelfth century or so, but was copied by scribes in the same way that phrases of the King James Bible are still used today.

It is unclear at this point what triggered the loss of the Poss Det construction, which by the analysis proposed here consists of the loss of the ability for D to select AP complements. The obvious place to look for a cause is in other changes to the determiner and adjectival systems. There are several changes which took place in the ME period in these areas: the emergence of a distinct definite article (possibly assisted by contact with Scandinavian; see Millar 2000), the weakening of the strong/weak distinction, and the general loss of the ability of adjectives to be used 'substantivally', i.e. without a head noun, except in very limited circumstances (e.g. *the poor*), to name a few important developments. The problem with seeing any one of these changes as the 'triggering' event for the loss of Poss Det is that they were all gradual changes which were not very well advanced at the time when Poss Det had apparently vanished as a living construction. The explanation may simply lie in a gradual lessening of the 'nouniness' of the weak adjectives once the prenominal position became regular for them, perhaps aided by a lessening of the deictic effect of SE, which could not have had a PRED in the Poss Det construction by the analysis proposed here but does appear to have had some role in emphasizing an adjective which it preceded. More research is needed into the changing characteristics of adjectives and determiners in ME.

1.6 Conclusion

Laczkó (1995: 78) comments that LFG has so far been mainly focused on sentence-level phenomena and calls for more work on nominal syntax. The present study has attempted to illuminate the structure of the NP/DP in OE. A thorough understanding of the OE stage is an essential base for work on the later development of the NP/DP in English, and although I have only examined one very small part of it here, I hope that my analysis can serve as a start for further work which extends to such things as the interaction between quantifiers and determiners at the OE stage, as well as a small contribution to our knowledge of how determiners can evolve. I have focused on the Poss Det construction in this paper because it is one which has been overlooked for the most part by generative syntacticians, but one which seems to give some particularly useful information about the nature of determiners in OE.

It is clear that English was already a highly endocentric language at the OE stage, despite its case marking system. While there was a certain amount of freedom in the placement of XPs as well as the placement of complements and specifiers within XPs, OE was essentially a configurational language, not a lexocentric one, and the variation between Det Poss and Poss Det order is not due to any general freedom of placement of the constituents of NP/DP, as has so often been assumed. The Det Poss construction, which is found in many languages, needs no special explanation, and the Poss Det construction can be attributed to the fact that D could take AP complements. I have argued that this possibility was the result of the origins of the weak adjectives in Germanic as nominalizations. While the Poss Det construction is typologically unusual, its development can be understood in its historical context. Further research into the question of whether any living languages has a Poss Det construction which is dependent upon the presence of an adjective is needed. Further research is also needed into the reasons for the loss of the ability of D to select for AP complements in EME.

Appendix: Details of the Investigation

The data used in this paper come primarily from the *York-Toronto-Helsinki parsed corpus of Old English prose (YCOE).* I used CorpusSearch (Randall 2000) to find all examples of noun phrases containing both determiners and possessive pronouns in all the texts of the *YCOE* which were assigned a date of xiin (beginning of the eleventh century) or earlier, with two exceptions. First, I excluded coeboeth.o2 (the translation of Boethius's Consolation of Philosophy) because the *YCOE*'s date of s.xmed (middle of the tenth century) is only correct for one of the manuscripts used by the edition which the *YCOE* used; a large portion of this text is edited from a twelfth-century manuscript.. Second, I used cogregdC.o24, which is found in a manuscript of ximed, instead of cogregdH.o23, which is in a manuscript of s.xi1 (first half of the eleventh century). The reason is that the C version is a copy of the earlier version of *Gregory's Dialogues*, while the H version is a copy of a substantially revised version. The C version is furthermore a rich source of Det Poss and Poss Det, confirming already strong generalizations made on the basis of other texts and not offering any counterexamples to those generalizations.

The *YCOE* is a corpus of prose, and to find examples of the Det Poss and Poss Det constructions in verse, I have searched the entire verse OE portion of the Helsinki Corpus, compiled by Rissanen and Ihalainen (1991), for strings which might be used in these constructions.

The factual claims made about Poss Det in the ME period are based on the application of CorpusSearch on the texts designated as 'm1' (i.e. from 1150-1250) in the *Penn-Helsinki Parsed Corpus of Middle English 2* (*PPCME 2*, compiled by Kroch and Taylor 1999), as well as my own reading of some eleventh and twelfth century texts not included in the *PPCME2*. Because the focus of the paper is the syntax of Poss Det in OE, I have not provided the details of these ME texts.

References

Barnes, Michael. 2001. *A New Introduction to Old Norse. Part I: Grammar*. London: Viking Society for Northern Research.

Bresnan, Joan. 2001. *Lexical-Functional Syntax*. Oxford: Blackwell.

Crisma, Paola. 2003. Genitive constructions in the history of English. In G. Banti, P. D. Giovine, and P. Ramat, eds., *Typological Change in the Morphosyntax of the Indo-European Languages*. München: Lincom Europa. To appear.

Curme, George O. 1910. The origin and growth of the adjective declension in Germanic. *Journal of English and Germanic Philology* 9:439–482.

Dalrymple, Mary. 1993. *The Syntax of Anaphoric Binding*. Stanford, CA: CSLI Publications.

Demske, Ulrike. 2001. *Merkmale und Relationen: Diachrone Studien zur Nominalphrase des Deutschen*. Berlin & New York, NY: Walter de Gruyter.

Fischer, Olga. 2000. The position of the adjective in Old English. In R. Bermúdez-Otero, D. Denison, R. M. Hogg, and C. B. McCully, eds., *Generative Theory and Corpus Studies: A Dialogue from 10 ICEHL*, pages 153–181. Berlin & New York, NY: Mouton de Gruyter.

Giusti, Giuliana. 1997. The categorial status of determiners. In L. M. V. Haegeman, ed., *The New Comparative Syntax*, pages 95–123. London & New York, NY: Longman.

Haegeman, Liliane M. V. and Jacqueline Guéron. 1999. *English Grammar: A Generative Perspective*. Oxford: Blackwell.

Halvorsen, Per-Kristian and Ronald M. Kaplan. 1988. Projections and semantic description in Lexical-Functional Grammar. In *Proceedings of the International Conference on Fifth Generation Computer Systems (FGCS'88)*, pages 1116–1122. Tokyo: Japan Institute for New Generation Systems.

Heinrichs, Heinrich M. 1954. *Studien zum bestimmten Artikel in den germanischen Sprachen*. Gießen: W. Schmitz.

Heusler, Andreas. 1962. *Altisländisches Elementarbuch*. Heidelberg: C. Winter.

Ker, Neil R. 1957. *Manuscripts Containing Anglo-Saxon*. Oxford: Clarendon Press.

Kolliakou, Demetra. 2003. *Nominal Constructions in Modern Greek: Implications for the Architecture of Grammar*. Stanford, CA: CSLI Publications.

Kroch, Anothony and Ann Taylor (compiliers). 1999. *The Penn-Helsinki Parsed Corpus of Middle English*. Philadelphia: Department of Linguistics, University of Pennsylvania, 2nd edn.

Laczkó, Tibor. 1995. *The Syntax of Hungarian Noun Phrases: A Lexical-Functional Approach*. Frankfurt am Main & Paris: P. Lang.

Manzelli, Gianguido. 1990. Possessive adnominal modifiers. In J. Bechert, G. Bernini, and C. Buridant, eds., *Toward a Typology of European Languages*, pages 63–111. Berlin: Mouton de Gruyter.

McLagan, Helen R. 2004. *The Syntax of Genitive Constructions in Old English: The Placement of Genitive Phrases in Ælfric's Second Series of Catholic Homilies*. Master's thesis, Australian National University, Canberra.

Millar, Robert M. 2000. *System Collapse, System Rebirth: The Demonstrative Pronouns of English, 900-1350 and the Birth of the Definite Article*. Oxford & New York, NY: P. Lang.

Mitchell, Bruce. 1972. The narrator of the Wife's Lament. *Neuphilologische Mitteilungen* 73:222–234.

Mitchell, Bruce. 1985. *Old English Syntax*. Oxford: Clarendon Press.

Plank, Frans. 1992. Possessives and the distinction between determiners and modifiers (with special reference to German). *Journal of Linguistics* 28:453–468.

Prokosch, Eduard. 1960 [1939]. *A Comparative Germanic Grammar*. Philadelphia, PA: Linguistic Society of America / University of Pennsylvania Press.

Randall, Beth (compilier). 2000. *CorpusSearch: A Java Program for Searching Syntactically Annotated Corpora*. Philadelphia, PA: Department of Linguistics, University of Pennsylvania.

Rissanen, Matti and Ossi Ihalainen (compiliers). 1991. *Helsinki Corpus of English Texts: Diachronic and Dialectal*. Helsinki: University of Helsinki.

Scatton, Ernie. 1984. *A Reference Grammar of Modern Bulgarian*. Columbus, OH: Slavica.

Smith, Jesse R. 1971. *Word Order in the Older Germanic Dialects*. Ph.D. thesis, University of Illinois, Chicago.

Spamer, James B. 1979. The development of the definite article in English: A case study of syntactic change. *Glossa* 13(2):241–250.

Toivonen, Ida. 2001. *The Phrase Structure of Non-Projecting Words*. Ph.D. thesis, Stanford University.

Yoon, Hee-Cheol. 2002. Economy considerations and the derivation of DP in Old English. *The History of English* 13:201–226.

2

Apparent Copular Inversion and the Theory of Null Subjects

ALEX ALSINA

Introduction

The[1] study of copular constructions with an NP complement in Catalan and other Romance languages of the null-subject variety[2] reveals an unexpected situation: although, as a rule, the verb always agrees with the subject in these languages, the copular verb sometimes agrees, at least apparently, with an NP that is not the subject, a phenomenon that I refer to as *Apparent Copular Inversion* (ACopInv). The questions I will address in this paper are:

1. What is the copular verb really agreeing with in ACopInv?
2. Why does ACopInv only occur in languages of the null-subject variety?
3. What distinguishes these languages from non-null-subject languages?

The answers to these questions will be couched in a framework that adopts essential ideas of Lexical-Functional Grammar (LFG) and Optimality Theory (OT). The core of the analysis is the claim that null-

[1]This paper has benefited from comments by Louise McNally, Joana Rosselló and Jane Simpson, which I gratefully acknowledge.

[2]I refer to languages that freely allow the subject to be null and interpreted as a pronoun as *null-subject languages*. The synonymous term *subject pro-drop* or, simply, *pro-drop, languages* is also found in the literature. I refer to languages that always require an overt subject as *non-null-subject languages*.

Architectures, Rules, and Preferences: Variations on Themes by Joan Bresnan.
Annie Zaenen, Jane Simpson, Tracy Holloway King,
Jane Grimshaw, Joan Maling, and Chris Manning, (eds.).

subject languages (as opposed to non-null-subject languages) lack a subject position, which allows subject NPs to be missing and interpreted as pronouns. The coindexing of two expressions, as in the topic-pronoun relation or in the predicative relation, is commonly reflected through agreement (in person, number, and gender) of the expressions involved. However, agreement is overridden by lexically specified features. In null-subject languages, the subject has no lexically specified features and, thus, its features are the result of a competition between the features of the discourse topic coindexed with it and, in copular constructions, the features of the predicative phrase, also coindexed with the subject. ACopInv occurs when the features of the predicative phrase win over the features of the topic. Non-null-subject languages show no sign of this competition, because the subject has its own lexically specified features.

I will first review the evidence that, in Apparent Copular Inversion (ACopInv) constructions, the NP that the copular verb agrees with is not the subject. Once this point has been established, I will propose an analysis that explains why the copular verb can sometimes (apparently) agree with a non-subject, in what cases this happens, and why this phenomenon occurs only in null-subject languages.

2.1 Apparent Copular Inversion

This paper focuses on copular sentences in Catalan in which the predicative complement is an NP.[3] The facts of Catalan that I will present are very similar to the facts of copular sentences in other null-subject languages of the Romance family, such as Spanish and Italian. A copular sentence such as (1a) normally raises no dispute about which of the two NPs involved is the subject and which is the complement. On the other hand, a sentence like (1b), which is truth-conditionally equivalent to (1a), poses serious problems for deciding on the grammatical function of the two NPs.

(1) a. Els impostos {són/*és} la solució.
the taxes are/is the solution
'Taxes are the solution.'

b. La solució {són/*és} els impostos.
the solution are/is the taxes
'The solution is taxes.'

[3] I am not taking a stand in this paper on the issue of whether expressions such as *the problem, the students, I,* or *a mouse* should be classified as NPs or DPs. I will refer to them as NPs, although the term *NP* can be replaced by *DP* without any consequence for the description or the analysis to be given.

The form *són* is the present indicative form of the copula that shows third person plural agreement, whereas the form *és* is the corresponding third person singular form. The fact that *són* is the grammatical form of the copula in both (1a) and (1b) would suggest that the NP *els impostos* (the only plural NP in (1a-b)) is the grammatical subject in both examples. Yet, this conclusion is highly problematic for a sentence like (1b): it is inconsistent with what we know about (a) the position of subjects and complements in Catalan, (b) the possibility of omitting subjects and complements in Catalan, (c) the phenomenon of raising, and (d) the behavior of the verbal clitic *en* in relation to subjects and complements. Examples like (1b), where the phenomenon of agreement seems to diverge from the four other phenomena, as we shall see, with respect to which NP is the subject and which the complement, illustrate the ACopInv construction.[4]

2.1.1 Position of subjects and complements

While subject NPs seem to enjoy a certain freedom of position in Catalan and related languages in that they can appear either in preverbal position or in postverbal position, complement XPs are fairly restricted in their distribution, since they can only appear postverbally as the unmarked option. Pronominal clitics, which can be complements, are subject to different positional restrictions from XPs. In contrast with the acceptable postverbal position of the complement NP *la tempesta* shown in example (2a), any other position of this NP makes the sentence unacceptable, as seen in (2b-d).[5]

(2) a. Els ruixats segueixen la tempesta.
   'The showers follow the storm.'
 b. * Els ruixats la tempesta segueixen.
 c. * La tempesta els ruixats segueixen.
 d. * La tempesta segueixen els ruixats.

Since a preverbal NP cannot be a complement, as shown in (2), we are led to assume that, in (1a), the postverbal NP *la solució* is

[4]In this section, I summarize the evidence presented in Alsina 2004 in favor of the claim that the NP that triggers agreement on the copula in ACopInv is not the subject, but the complement. This claim is by no means generally accepted; see, for example, Hernanz and Brucart 1987 and Fernández Leborans 1999 (for Spanish), Moro 1997 (for Italian), and Ramos 2002 (for Catalan) for the view that (at some level) the NP that triggers agreement on the copula is always the subject.

[5]The examples (2b-d) can be rendered acceptable if the preverbal NP *la tempesta* is pronounced with an intonational peak and is interpreted as a contrastive focus, which characterizes the rhematization construction according to Vallduví 2002 (see Vallduví 2002: 1267-1272 for more examples and discussion). I will not take into account this pragmatically and intonationally marked construction.

the complement and the preverbal NP *els problemes* is the subject, which is consistent with what the agreement facts show. But the same generalization about the position of complements reveals that, in (1b), the postverbal NP *els problemes* is the complement and the preverbal NP *la solució* is the subject, creating a conflict with the conclusion that the agreement facts point to.

2.1.2 Omission of subjects and complements

It is a well-known fact that subjects in Catalan (as in other null-subject languages) can be freely omitted and interpreted as pronouns, provided an appropriate referent is made available in the discourse or in the speech situation. Complements, on the other hand, do not generally have this option. Thus, we have to conclude that the NP that can be left out from examples (1) is the subject. The comparison of (1a) with (3) and of (1b) with (4) shows that, in both cases, only the preverbal NP can be omitted:[6]

(3) a. Són la solució.
are the solution ('They are the solution.')
b. * Els impostos són.

(4) a. Són els impostos.
are the taxes ('It is taxes.')
b. * La solució {són/és}.

If the subject is omitted in these examples, then the overt NP cannot be the subject, but must, instead, be the complement. Thus, we reach the incoherent conclusion that the NP *els impostos* in (4a) is the subject, because it agrees with the verb, and cannot be the subject, because it cannot be left out, as shown in (4b).

While complements cannot generally be omitted with an anaphoric interpretation, and that is particularly the case with the copular verb, as shown in (3b) and (4b), they can be expressed as a clitic that is interpreted anaphorically. For the copular verb, the complement clitic is *ho*, as illustrated in the following examples:[7]

[6] For example, (3a) can be used as a reply to the question *Què tenen de bo els impostos?* 'What is good about taxes?' and (4a) can be used as a reply to the utterance *Tant parlar del problema! I la solució?* 'So much talk about the problem! What about the solution?'

[7] Example (5a) with the overt preverbal NP could be a response to the utterance *M'agradaria saber què és la solució d'aquest problema* 'I would like to know what the solution to this problem is'. The short version of (5a), *Ho són* 'They are', could be used as a reply to the utterance *Tothom diu que els impostos són la solució. Tu què creus?* 'Everyone says that taxes are the solution. What do you think?'. As for (5b), it can be used in the following text: *Si vols saber què és la solució, no ho és*

(5) a. (Els impostos) ho són.
(the taxes) pro are ('Taxes/they are.')

b. Ho són els impostos.
pro are the taxes ('Taxes are.')

The acceptability of examples (4a) and (5b), which appear to be identical except that (4a) lacks the clitic that appears in (5b), would be hard to explain if we assumed that the agreeing NP *els impostos* is the subject in both cases. Why would it be that the complement of *ser*, which appears to be obligatory on the basis of examples like (3b), is optional when the subject is postverbal? However, if we assume that the NP *els impostos* is the subject in (5b), but the complement in (4a), as in (1b), we can maintain the claim that the complement of *ser* is never optional.

2.1.3 Raising

The phenomenon of raising is a well-known subjecthood diagnostic: only the subject of a non-finite clause embedded under a raising verb can be the subject of the matrix raising verb. If a sentence such as (1b) appears as an infinitival clause embedded under a raising verb such as *poder* 'can/may', as in (6), we have to conclude that the subject of the matrix verb is (identified with) the subject of the embedded clause.

(6) La solució poden ser els impostos.
the solution may.3rd.pl be the taxes
'The solution may be taxes.'

The preverbal position of the NP *la solució* in (6) and its omissibility (*Poden ser els impostos* 'It may be taxes') argue for the claim that it is the subject of the matrix clause. Since the matrix verb is a raising verb, its subject must also be the subject of the embedded clause, which leads us to conclude that the subject of (1b) is *la solució*, even though the verb does not agree with this NP. Notice too that the raising verb in (6) does not agree with its subject, but with the complement of the embedded verb.

2.1.4 The verbal clitic *en*

The clitic *en* is required in order to omit the head of an indefinite NP complement of a verb. The missing head is interpreted as identical in meaning to a noun (or nominal group) present in the discourse or inferrable from the speech situation with the same gender feature as the NP. Crucially, the presence of the clitic *en* is only possible, and

pas la borsa. Ho són els impostos 'If you want to know what is the solution, the stock market is not. Taxes are'.

is required, with this function, if the NP with the missing head is a complement of a verb, but not if the NP in question is a subject.[8] The relevant contrast between complement and subject can be illustrated with examples like (7) and (8).

(7) a. Els estudiants llegeixen molts llibres.
'The students read many books.'
b. Els estudiants *(en) llegeixen molts.
the students en read many
'The students read many (of them).'

(8) a. Molts estudiants aprovaran.
'Many students will pass.'
b. Molts (*n') aprovaran.
many en will.pass
'Many will pass.'

The complement (or object) of (7b) is realized as the indefinite NP *molts*, which lacks a head noun: the sentence is grammatical if it includes the clitic *en* and is ungrammatical otherwise (which is what the notation **(en)* signifies). In contrast, example (8b) has the headless indefinite NP *molts* as the subject: in this case, the sentence is grammatical only without the clitic *en*. We can argue that the relevant contrast is due to the difference in grammatical function and not to the difference in position: a headless indefinite NP that is the subject rejects the cooccurrence with the clitic en even when it appears in postverbal position, as in (9):

(9) Aquesta és la novel·la que (*n') han llegit molts.
this is the novel that en have read many
'This is the novel that many have read.'

The clitic *en* can appear in copular sentences, with this function, that is, cooccurring with a headless indefinite complement. The following

[8]With intransitive verbs, particularly unaccusatives, the clitic *en* appears when the sole NP argument of the verb is an indefinite NP with a missing head in postverbal position (or in initial *wh*-phrase position). Even though this NP agrees with the verb, as in (i), I take the generally accepted position that the sole NP argument is a complement (an object) in such cases.

(i) En cauen molts. / *Cauen molts.
en fall.3rd.pl many fall.3rd.pl many
'Many fall.' / 'Many are falling.'

This allows us to maintain the generalization that an NP with a missing head permits and requires the clitic *en* only if it is a complement. The agreement facts in such cases are explained by assuming that there is a non-overt non-thematic subject that shares its agreement features with the complement (see section 3.3; see also Perlmutter 1978, 1983, Burzio 1986, or Alsina 1996, for different formal treatments).

examples show that, although the copular verb agrees with an indefinite NP, the clitic *en* can appear, and is required, in such cases.

(10) Pel que fa a les gasolineres, l'objectiu principal
as for the petrol stations, the objective principal
de la banda *(n') han estat sis a l'Hospitalet
of the gang en have.3rd.pl been six in l'Hospitalet
i Cerdanyola.
and Cerdanyola
'As for petrol stations, the main objective of the gang has been six (of them) in l'Hospitalet and Cerdanyola.'

(11) a. Un euro són 166,386 pessetes.
one euro are.3rd.pl 166.386 pesetas
'One euro is 166.386 pesetas.'

b. I un dòlar, quantes *(en) són?
And one dollar how many en are.3rd.pl
'And one dollar, how many (pesetas) is it?'

c. {En/*∅} són cent seixanta.
en are.3rd.pl a hundred and sixty
'It is a hundred and sixty.'

Sentences like (10) and (11b-c) allow the presence of the clitic *en* and would be ungrammatical without it, since the verb's complement is a headless indefinite NP: *sis* in (10), *quantes* in (11b), and *cent seixanta* in (11c). While the presence of the clitic is evidence that the headless NP in these examples is the complement of the copular verb, the verb agrees with this NP and not with the other NP of the clause, such as *l'objectiu principal de la banda* in (10) or *un dòlar* in (11b). In (11c), the subject is non-overt and can be interpreted as coreferential with *un dòlar*.

2.1.5 Agreement in copular sentences

The agreement facts in copular sentences in Catalan (as in Spanish, Italian and other languages) seem to be describable without specific reference to the subject function. The generalization that accounts for these facts is the following: the copula agrees with its obligatory syntactic dependent (whether subject or complement) that is higher in a person-number hierarchy in which second and first person are above third person, and third person plural is above third person singular. So, if one of the obligatory dependents of the copula is first or second person and the other one is third person, it agrees with the former, regardless of the position (and syntactic function) of the agreement trigger:

(12) a. (L'últim) {sóc/*és} jo.
the last am is I
('The last one is me.'/ 'It is me.')

b. (Jo) {sóc/*és} l'últim.
I am is the last
('I am the last one.')

The fact that one of the two syntactic dependents of the copula is a first person expression forces the copula to agree with it, whether it is the subject or not. In (12a), the subject is presumably the NP *l'últim*, given its preverbal position and given the fact that it can be omitted, as shown by the parentheses around it, and yet the copular verb cannot agree with it, as shown by the unacceptability of the third person singular agreement form *és*. In this case, the verb agrees in first person singular with what otherwise appears to be its complement.

When both syntactic dependents of the copula are third person and one of them is plural, the copula shows third person plural agreement, as illustrated in example (1). Again, the syntactic function and, consequently, the position of the agreement trigger is irrelevant for the choice of agreement form.

It does not seem possible to maintain the claim that the agreement trigger is always the subject NP in copular sentences (see Alsina 2004). If we wanted to maintain this claim, we would have to posit subject selection principles specific to the copula sensitive to the person and number of the NPs involved. But that would make incorrect predictions regarding the position of the NPs involved, the possibility of omitting the subject, the facts of raising constructions, and the occurrence of the clitic *en*.

It seems safe to conclude that, in copular constructions, the verb sometimes agrees with its complement.[9] It is because there is no actual inversion in such cases (understood as a marked alignment of thematic roles and grammatical functions or of grammatical functions and surface positions) that I refer to the construction in which the copula agrees with its complement as *Apparent Copular Inversion* (ACopInv).

[9]The claim that verbs can sometimes agree with a non-subject is by now firmly established on the basis of Icelandic and similar languages. See Andrews 1982 and 1990 for early work in support of this claim. However, in the following sections, I will argue that, in ACopInv, the verb only apparently agrees with a non-subject and that it actually manifests features of the subject.

2.2 A theory of null subjects in OT-LFG

The previous section has established the main facts of copular constructions with a nominal complement in Catalan and has argued that the copula may show agreement with the complement, or, in other words, that the NP that triggers agreement on the copula, in some cases, is not the subject. In the remainder of this paper, I will address the following questions:

1. What does the copula really agree with in ACopInv? (Should the theory allow for agreement with the complement, in a specific set of cases? Or, if the subject is always the agreement trigger, why doesn't the copula show the agreement features of the subject NP in ACopInv?)
2. Why is the phenomenon of apparent inversion (agreement with the complement) restricted to copular constructions?
3. Why does ACopInv only occur in languages of the null-subject variety?
4. What distinguishes these languages from non-null-subject languages?

As for question 3, the connection between the presence of ACopInv in a language and the language being of the pro-drop variety has been proposed by Moro 1997, among others, and can be observed in the examples given in this paper. Catalan is a null-subject language, as we have seen, and has ACopInv; English is a non-null-subject language and the English translations of the ACopInv examples, such as (1b), (4a), (10), (11), (12a), show consistent agreement with the subject, which indicates that English does not have ACopInv. It seems reasonable to assume that this correlation is not accidental and, therefore, to expect the theory to derive it.

In this section, I will address question 4 and propose a theory within the framework of LFG and OT that explains the difference between null-subject languages and non-null-subject languages. The other three questions, 1–3, will be addressed in section 3.

2.2.1 The intuition behind the typological division

Informally speaking, the theoretical difference between the two types of languages is that languages without null subjects have a subject position, whereas languages with null subjects do not have a subject position. The principle that the subject is an obligatory element of the clause, in both types of languages, entails that, in non-null-subject languages, the subject position will have to be filled in every clause, whereas, in null-subject languages, since there is no subject position to fill, the subject may be non-overt, as well as realized in postverbal position.

What is often assumed to be the preverbal subject position in null-subject languages like Catalan is, in fact, a topic position, as has been argued by many authors including Alexiadou and Anagnostopoulou 1998 and Barbosa 2001, for null-subject languages in general, and Bonet 1990, Rosselló 1986, Solà 1992, and Vallduví 1992, specifically for Catalan. An NP in this topic position is entirely optional, since it does not satisfy any obligatory function of the clause, and is connected to the clause through an anaphoric linkage to a pronominal dependent of the clause. This pronominal dependent can be a clitic, in the case of verbal complements, or a null subject, since it is interpreted as a pronoun. All the preverbal "subject" NPs given up to here in the Catalan examples of this paper would have to be analyzed as topics anaphorically linked to null subjects.[10]

It's not that the structural position of subjects in English and other non-null-subject languages — let's call it Spec-IP — does not exist in null-subject languages like Catalan: it's just that it has a different function. Following Vallduví 1992 (see also Bonet 1990 and Solà 1992), we can assume that Spec-IP in Catalan hosts a subset of non-contrastive focus phrases, specifically, *wh*-phrases and a variety of quantified expressions like *ningú* 'no one', *poca cosa* 'not much', *alguna cosa* 'something', etc. Let us say that Spec-IP in null-subject languages is the position of non-contrastive focus. (The topic NP mentioned in the previous paragraph occupies a higher position, such as sister to IP.)

What I want to suggest is that Spec-IP universally can have either of the functions noted: it can host the subject or it can host a focus. The choice of one or the other determines whether we have a null-subject language or a non-null-subject language.[11]

2.2.2 An OT version of LFG

These ideas can best be captured in a framework that separates overt morphosyntactic expressions, syntactic constituents and grammatical categories, such as Spec-IP and the actual words in a phrase, from the grammatical functions and abstract features that correspond to these

[10]The claim that there is no preverbal subject position in null-subject languages is not unanimously accepted (see, for example, Cardinaletti 1997, Costa 2001, Goodall 2001, among others). To the extent that the analysis in this paper is successful in accounting for ACopInv and crucially relies on that claim, it provides evidence in support of the claim that null-subject languages lack a preverbal subject position.

[11]A language in which Spec-IP is a focus position may also have alternative means of expressing focus (perhaps different types of focus), either through intonation, through morphology or syntactic devices.

constituents and words, such as subject or focus. Lexical-Functional Grammar (LFG) is a framework that posits two formally distinct levels of structure to represent these different concepts: c-structure for the former and f-structure for the latter (see Bresnan 1982, Bresnan 2001a, and references cited there). We also need a framework that allows us to capture cross-linguistic variation as different outcomes of competition among constraints. Optimality Theory (OT) does this by allowing the same universal constraints to have different prominence (or ranking) so that the effects of a more prominent constraint may override the effects of a less prominent constraint (Prince and Smolensky 1993, Legendre et al. 1993, Grimshaw 1997a, and many others). I will, therefore, develop these ideas in an OT version of LFG (see Bresnan 1996, 2000, 2001b, Kuhn 2003, among others, for proposals adopting OT in LFG).

The representation of linguistic expressions in LFG is factored out into various structures, or levels of representation, which encode different types of grammatical information by different formal means. In this paper we will be concerned with the two syntactic structures that are traditionally assumed in LFG: c-structure and f-structure.

Both c- and f-structures have their own internal well-formedness conditions (or principles, constraints, rules, etc.), which define a well-formed c- or f-structure in isolation, and the c-to-f-structure mapping constraints, which define a well-formed pairing of c-structure and f-structure. The standard way of interpreting these conditions is to say that a linguistic expression is grammatical if and only if it can be represented by a well-formed pair of c-structure and f-structure, where such a pair is well-formed if and only if both structures satisfy every condition that can apply to them. However, from an OT perspective, it is possible to relativize the application of well-formedness conditions: a linguistic expression is well-formed if and only if it corresponds to the pairing of c-structure and f-structure that *best* satisfies the set of ranked well-formedness conditions applying to these paired structures. Following are some of the constraints applying to c-structure, to f-structure, and to the mapping of c-structure to f-structure, particularly those that will be relevant in this paper.

C-structure is formally modeled as a tree in which the nodes are labeled as grammatical categories and is defined by context-free phrase structure rules, of which the following are relevant examples:

(13) a. IP $\longrightarrow$ XP I′
b. I′ $\longrightarrow$ I VP
c. VP $\longrightarrow$ V XP*

All c-structure nodes are optional: we can assume that all nodes carry some cost (see Bresnan's 2001a Economy of Expression).

F-structure is modeled as a feature structure or attribute-value matrix. Grammatical functions (GFs) are attributes such as SUBJ, OBJ, FOCUS, etc. that take f-structures as values. Other attributes, such as NUM, GEN, etc., take atomic values (for example, PL, FEM, +, etc.). F-structures satisfy the Uniqueness Condition, by which every attribute must take a unique value. Two f-structure well-formedness conditions that we will be concerned with in this paper are the Subject Condition (see Bresnan and Kanerva 1989: 28, Alsina 1996: 20 and references cited there, for precedents) and Completeness (formulated as in Bresnan 2001a: 72):

(14) **SubjCond** (Subject Condition): an f-structure that corresponds to a predicative category (such as a verb or adjective) must include a SUBJ as one of its attributes.

(15) **Compl** (Completeness): every GF designated by a PRED must be present in the f-structure of that PRED.

The c-to-f mapping constraints include the requirement that every c-structure node map onto some f-structure. In what follows, I will notate the mapping between c-structure nodes and f-structures by means of subscripted numbers, so that a c-structure node and an f-structure with the same subscript are understood to be in a mapping (or correspondence) relation. Some of the mapping constraints require a specific correspondence between a particular c-structure node and a particular f-structure attribute, such as the following two mapping constraints:

(16) **SubjPos** (Subject Position): $[_{IP}\ \mathrm{XP}_1\ \mathrm{I}'\ ] \longrightarrow \textsc{subj}\ [\ldots]_1$

(17) **FocPos** (Focus Position): $[_{IP}\ \mathrm{XP}_1\ \mathrm{I}'\ ] \longrightarrow \textsc{focus}\ [\ldots]_1$

These constraints are to be read as conditional statements. (16) should be read as: if there is an XP sister of I′, it maps onto (it is co-subscripted with the f-structure value of) a SUBJ. Likewise, (17) says that an XP sister of I′ maps onto a FOCUS. They are constraints on the mapping between c-structure (a specific phrase-structure configuration — Spec-IP) and f-structure (the SUBJ function or the FOCUS function).

An additional mapping constraint that will be relevant is the idea that features at f-structure must be licensed by c-structure: f-structure features must be provided either by lexical items present at c-structure or by mapping constraints such as (16) and (17). This is a kind of faithfulness constraint (f-structure must be faithful to c-structure) and I will refer to it as F-Faith:

(18) **F-Faith**: at f-structure, atomic features must be lexically specified and GFs must be licensed by a mapping constraint.

According to F-Faith, any atomic feature that is not specified in a lexical item and any GF that is not licensed by the application of a mapping constraint such as (16) or (17) triggers a violation of principle (18).

If we adopt an OT perspective on the application of constraints, it is not necessary for all constraints to be satisfied for a given structure to be grammatical. Given a particular ranking of constraints, it is possible to violate a constraint provided that constraint violation allows the structure to satisfy a higher ranking constraint. Thus, among the set of competing structures, the grammar selects as well-formed the one that best satisfies the set of ranked constraints. In this view, it is important to define the set of competing structures, as well as the ranking of constraints that defines the grammar of a particular language.

I will assume that the INPUT to the GEN component is an underspecified f-structure indicating only semantically and pragmatically relevant features, such as PRED, FOCUS, etc., but not others such as SUBJ, GEN, etc. (See Bresnan 2000 and Kuhn 2003 for similar ideas.) The GEN component maps this input onto fully specified f-structures and pairs them with c-structures. The candidate set consists of all the f-structure/c-structure pairs corresponding to the same input. GEN cannot add or suppress semantically or pragmatically relevant features.

As for the ranking of constraints, we will only be concerned here with those constraints that are relevant for the analysis at hand. It is clear that there are two constraints proposed in this paper that are necessarily in competition — SubjPos (16) and FocPos (17) — since each one specifies a different assignment of grammatical function to the same c-structure position. The different ranking of these two constraints defines the two types of languages that we want to characterize.

2.2.3 The null subject parameter in OT-LFG

In the grammar of a non-null-subject language like English, constraint (16) ranks higher than constraint (17), and, for a null-subject language like Catalan, constraint (17) ranks higher than constraint (16):

(19) a. Non-null-subject language: (16) >> (17)
b. Null-subject language: (17) >> (16)

Let us assume that SubjCond (14) ranks higher than both (16) and (17) for all languages (or, at least, for the languages under consideration). This means that, in both types of languages, the subject is obligatory in all clauses. Let us also assume that, whereas certain c-structure positions require a particular mapping to f-structure because of constraints such as (16) and (17), other c-structure positions are not associated with any specific GF. This is the case of the VP-internal position, the XP sister of V introduced by rule (13c): there is no mapping constraint requiring it to map onto any specific GF. We can think of it as an "all purpose" position, as it can satisfy any GF, such as OBJ, OBL, and, even SUBJ, as we shall see. However, the use of this position carries some cost: since there is no mapping constraint licensing a particular GF mapping onto this position, whatever GF is chosen to map onto this c-structure position will trigger a violation of F-Faith (18). Let us assume that, in the languages under consideration, Completeness (15) outranks F-Faith (18). This means that, in a structure with a predicator (or PRED) that designates a GF such as OBJ that is not licensed by any mapping constraint, a violation of Completeness will be worse than a violation of F-Faith and, so, the c-structure may contain a VP-internal XP mapping onto an OBJ at F-structure. This will satisfy Completeness while violating F-Faith, which, under the proposed ranking of these two constraints, is better than a structure that lacks an OBJ and therefore, violates Completeness while satisfying F-Faith.

This "all purpose" position can in principle also map onto a subject, but, if the language has the option of licensing the subject through a mapping principle such as (16), it will be less costly for the SUBJ to map onto the c-structure position referred to by this principle than for it to map onto an unlicensed position such as the VP-internal position. In a non-null-subject language, where principle (16) outranks (17), the NP daughter of IP is reserved for subjects: this NP must map onto a SUBJ, even if that triggers a violation of principle (17). In this way, the ranking in (19a), together with a high ranking status of SubjCond (14) and the existence of F-Faith (18), explains the fact that, in non-null-subject languages, the subject is obligatorily expressed as an XP daughter of IP in all clauses (except when the subject is supplied by the special clause-initial position that licenses wh-phrases, topics, etc.).

Let us assume four competing candidates for a clause:

1. *no subj*: there is no subject (at f-structure) and, consequently, no corresponding XP at c-structure;
2. *null subj*: there is a subject, but there is no corresponding XP at c-structure;
3. *subj SpecIP*: there is a subject corresponding to an XP daughter of IP;
4. *subj VP-int*: there is a subject corresponding to an XP daughter of VP.

In both types of languages, *no subj* triggers a violation of SubjCond, *null subj* triggers a violation of F-Faith, *subj SpecIP* triggers a violation of FocPos, and *subj VP-int* triggers a violation of F-Faith. On the assumption that null-subject languages and non-null-subject languages have a reverse ranking of SubjPos and FocPos, with F-Faith in between, we derive the correct predictions. As shown in (20), in non-null-subject languages, the optimal structure is *subj SpecIP*, which only violates the lowest of the constraints under consideration.

(20) Subjects in non-null-subject languages:

	SubjCond	SubjPos	F-Faith	FocPos
a. no subj	*!			
b. null subj			*!	
☞c. subj SpecIP				*
d. subj VP-int			*!	

In null-subject languages, the preferred candidates are *null subj* and *subj VP-int*, as they both only violate F-Faith, which is the lowest of the constraints violated by the candidates, as shown in (21).

(21) Subjects in null-subject languages:

	SubjCond	FocPos	F-Faith	SubjPos
a. no subj	*!			
☞b. null subj			*	
c. subj SpecIP		*!		
☞d. subjVP-int			*	

The claim that FocPos (17) ranks higher than SubjPos (16) in null-subject languages means that the Spec of IP can only be used for FOCUS: an XP in this position may, but need not, map onto a SUBJ. Since being a FOCUS is pragmatically different from not being a FOCUS, a structure containing a FOCUS function is in a different candidate set from a structure not containing that function. (20) and (21) illustrate candidate sets in which the SUBJ is not a FOCUS.

In this way, we explain a correlation that has often been observed: languages that allow null subjects also allow postverbal subjects. These languages do not have a subject position (because, in the present theory, SubjPos is below FocPos) and, thus, the subject is free to lack a c-structure correspondent (null subject) or to be realized in the "all purpose" VP-internal position (postverbal subject).

2.3 Why ACopInv occurs only in null-subject languages

Having provided an account of the difference between non-null-subject languages and null-subject languages, we will now address the remaining three questions posed in section 2: what the copula really agrees with in ACopInv, why apparent inversion only occurs in copular constructions, and why ACopInv is restricted to null-subject languages.

2.3.1 The copular restriction on apparent inversion

Explaining why the phenomenon of apparent inversion is restricted to copular constructions must appeal to a property that is unique to the copula. I suggest this property is the function (or meaning) of the copula in the clause:

(22) The copula requires identity of index in its subject and complement.

The index, which can be assumed to be a feature of f-structure, is the linguistic representation of referential dependency (see Bresnan 2001a: 250, Sag and Wasow 1999: 106): two GFs with the same index are coreferential (or referentially dependent). A pronoun and its antecedent are assumed to have the same index, and the same can be said about a predicative expression and its subject. The morphosyntactic manifestation of coindexing (identity of indices) is identity of agreement features:

(23) AgrCoi (Agreement of Coindexed GFs): Two GFs with the same index must have the same agreement features (person, number, and gender).

This can be seen in the choice of pronoun form in English, which has to have the same person, number, and gender features as its antecedent. The effect of this constraint is also visible in the choice of agreement form in predicative adjectives as in the following Catalan examples:

(24) La pel·lícula és {divertida /*divertit
the movie.fem.sg is funny.fem.sg funny.masc.sg
/*divertides}.
funny.fem.pl

This constraint is often violated, particularly when the predicative phrase is not headed by an adjective, but by a noun, as we see in (25).

(25) La pel·lícula és un èxit.
the movie.fem.sg is a success.masc.sg

Nouns and adjectives are all specified for gender and number in Catalan, but they differ in that nouns are lexically marked with one gender feature, whereas adjectives are free to take either value for the gender feature. Thus, we can assume that the various gender and number forms of each adjective are in competition, in the same candidate set, and the form chosen is the one that best satisfies constraints such as (23). In contrast, there is no competition among gender forms in nouns. Therefore, predicative NPs are allowed to violate constraint (23), since there is no competing form that does not violate it.

2.3.2 What the copula agrees with

One of the problems with ACopInv is how to account for the agreement facts without stipulating that the copula agrees with the complement, and not with the subject, in a specific set of cases. However, as we noted in the preceding section, in null-subject languages, there often is no overt subject and what looks like a preverbal subject in most cases (leaving aside focused phrases) is a topic. This topic is coindexed with the null subject, which behaves like a pronoun. So, in copular constructions, the null pronominal subject is coindexed, on the one hand, with a topic and, on the other hand, with the predicative complement. Given this coindexation, it is required by constraint (23) to agree with both the topic and the complement. This requirement can only be satisfied in full if the topic and the complement have the same agreement features. If they do not have the same features of person, number, and gender, one of the two chains of agreement — topic-subject or subject-complement — takes precedence over the other. The choice between the topic and the complement as agreement triggers for the subject of copular sentences is determined by the person and number features of the GFs involved. We can think of person and number features as forming a hierarchy, such that the higher a feature is in this hierarchy the more marked it is:[12]

(26) **Person-Number Hierarchy:**
1st/2nd person > 3rd person plural > 3rd person singular

A violation of AgrCoi is worse the higher the features involved are in this hierarchy. In OT terms, we can view the combination of constraint ArgCoi with the Person-Number Hierarchy as a set of ranked constraints: failure to satisfy AgrCoi is worse when 1st or 2nd person is

[12]The idea that there is a universal hierarchy in which first and second person are more marked than third person and plural is more marked than singular has been argued for by many authors including Greenberg 1966, Grimshaw 1997b, Aissen 1999, Corbett 2000, and Siewierska 2004.

involved than when 3rd person plural is involved, than when 3rd person singular is involved. We can express this idea as follows:

(27) **AgrCoi combined with the Person-Number Hierarchy**:
Assign * for every GF that fails to have the same agreement features as a coindexed GF
which is 1st or 2nd person. ⟶ **AgrCoi-1st/2nd**
which is 3rd person plural. ⟶ **AgrCoi-3rdpl**
which is 3rd person singular. ⟶ **AgrCoi-else(where)**
Ranking: AgrCoi-1st/2nd >> AgrCoi-3rdpl >> AgrCoi-else

Let us illustrate the theory provided so far with the grammaticality contrast given in example (1b), repeated as (28a) and (28b):

(28) a. La solució són els impostos.
b. * La solució és els impostos.

Recall that the initial NP in these examples, *la solució*, is not the subject, but a topic anaphorically linked to the subject. The subject is a pronoun, at f-structure, which corresponds to no constituent at c-structure. Because of the topic-pronoun relation, the subject is coindexed with the topic, and, because of the subject-predicate relation, the subject is also coindexed with the predicative complement *els impostos*. We can assume that the forms *són* and *és*, like all finite verb forms in Catalan, lexically specify the person and number features of the subject. The lexical entry of *són* states that the subject is third person plural and the lexical entry of *és* states that the subject is third person singular. (29) shows the paired c-structure and f-structure for example (28a). The correspondence between the two structures is notated by coindexing the relevant elements of structure.

(29)

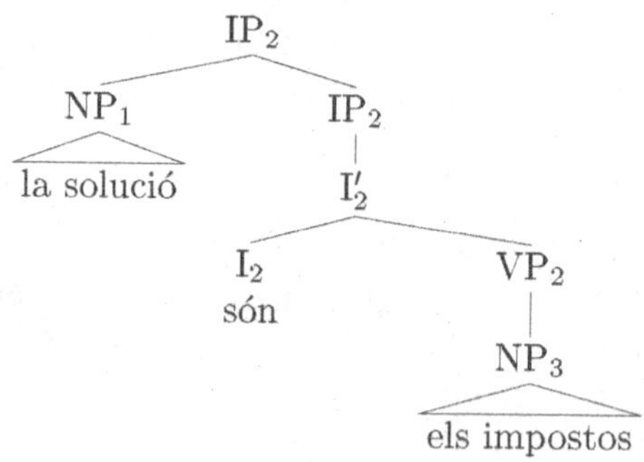

$$\begin{bmatrix} \text{TOPIC} & \begin{bmatrix} \text{PRED} & \text{'solution'} \\ \text{NUM} & \text{sg} \\ \text{PERS} & 3 \\ \text{INDEX} & \text{i} \end{bmatrix}_1 \\ \text{SUBJ} & \begin{bmatrix} \text{PRED} & \text{'pro'} \\ \text{NUM} & \textbf{pl} \\ \text{PERS} & 3 \\ \text{INDEX} & \text{i} \end{bmatrix} \\ \text{PRED} & \text{'be<arg}_3\text{ >'} \\ \text{COMP} & \begin{bmatrix} \text{PRED} & \text{'tax'} \\ \text{NUM} & \textbf{pl} \\ \text{PERS} & 3 \\ \text{INDEX} & \text{i} \end{bmatrix}_3 \end{bmatrix}_2$$

The representation of example (28b) would only differ from (29) in that the c-structure would have the verb form *és*, instead of *són*, and, in the f-structure, the number feature of the subject would have the value sg, instead of pl (see the crucial elements in boldface in (29)). The competition between the structures corresponding to the examples in (28) is resolved in favor of (28a), as shown in the following tableau:

(30) Competition between (28a) and (28b):

	Subj Cond	F-Faith	AgrCoi-1st/2nd	AgrCoi-3rdpl	AgrCoi-else
☞ a. (28a)		***		*	**
b. (28b)		***		**!	*

Both examples have a representation that satisfies the Subject Condition, as in (29). The f-structure in (29), like the f-structure for (28b), fails to satisfy F-Faith three times: a) the subject is not licensed by a mapping principle, b) the PRED feature of the subject is not licensed lexically, if we assume, as I do, that finite verb forms such as *són* and *és* specify the person and number feature of the subject, but not its PRED (see Kuhn 2003: 109) (PRED 'pro' being the least costly of the possible PRED values), and c) the complement is not licensed by a mapping principle. Thus, both representations are equal with respect to constraint F-Faith. AgrCoi-1st/2nd is vacuously satisfied in both cases, as there is no first or second person involved. (29) violates AgrCoi-3rdpl once, as there is one GF, the topic, which is not 3rd person plural, even though it is coindexed with a GF that is 3rd person plural, and it violates AgrCoi-else twice. However, (29) is optimal compared to a structure in which the topic satisfied AgrCoi-3rdpl, as it would violate F-Faith (and Parse, a high-ranking constraint requiring lexically specified features to appear in the corresponding f-structure), since the number feature of the topic is lexically specified. The structure corresponding to (28b) violates AgrCoi-3rdpl twice, as there are two GFs, the topic and the subject, which are 3rd person singular, but are coindexed with a 3rd person plural GF. Therefore, (29) is optimal.

2.3.3 Why there is no ACopInv in non-null-subject languages

The reason why there is no ACopInv, no (apparent) agreement of the copula with the complement, in non-null-subject languages like English is precisely because there is a lexically specified subject in these languages. A sentence like (28a) can be rendered in English as (31a), but not as (31b):

(31) a. The solution is taxes.
b. * The solution are taxes.

Example (31a) has an NP in Spec-IP, which, given the constraint ranking of non-null-subject languages illustrated in (20), is required to map onto a subject. Since this NP has lexically specified person and number features, the failure of any of these features to appear in the subject function would cause a violation of Parse. So, the subject of (31) is specified as third person singular. On the assumption that the verb forms *is* and *are* carry person and number specifications of the subject (third person singular and third person plural, respectively), the choice of *is* will yield a well-formed structure, where the information specified by the lexical items of the NP unifies with the information specified by the verb, whereas the choice of *are* causes a violation of the uniqueness principle, as the f-structure of the subject will have inconsistent specifications for the number feature.

ACopInv crucially depends on there not being a lexically specified subject, but on the subject being a null pronominal (a pronoun at f-structure that corresponds to no constituent at c-structure). In this case the subject lacks lexically specified features and so they are free to be identified with those of the discourse topic (or those of a deictic referent), in order to satisfy AgrCoi. If we are dealing with a copular construction, the subject is also required to agree with the predicative complement, and it is only in this situation that the AgrCoi family of ranked constraints may make it appear as if the verb is agreeing with the complement instead of agreeing with the subject. In fact, the verb is always agreeing with the subject (in the sense that the finite verb always specifies features of the subject); it is just that in copular constructions in null-subject languages the complement sometimes wins over the topic in imposing its features on the subject.

The apparent inverse agreement in ACopInv is similar to the apparent agreement with the complement in unaccusative constructions (also known as brother-in-law agreement) noted in footnote 8. In the present analysis, the similarity is captured by assuming that the verb specifies features of the subject in both constructions, as is the norm, and that the subject and the complement share at least the agreement features. In ACopInv the subject shares its agreement features with the complement, as a result of coindexation; in unaccusative constructions without an overt subject, according to Alsina 1995, 1996, the (nonthematic) subject and the complement are represented as having the same f-structure value, which means they share all features. Consequently, in both constructions, the verb appears to agree with the complement because it really agrees with the subject and the subject and the complement share some (or all) of their features.

2.3.4 ACopInv does not occur only with the copula

The current analysis of ACopInv does not include any principle that makes direct reference to the copula. One of the central elements of the analysis — the family of constraints in (27) that require identity of agreement features of coindexed GFs — appeals to a property found in constructions involving the copula, namely, the coindexation of two GFs of the same clause. If this property is found in constructions involving another verb, depending on what the facts turn out to be, it may provide strong support for the analysis or evidence against it. There is another verb, apart from the copula, that can be argued also to require coindexation of its subject and complement: the verb *semblar* 'seem'. Interestingly, sentences with *semblar* are truth-conditionally equivalent to identical sentences with a positional reversal of preverbal and postverbal NPs:

(32) a. La Maria sembla la noia del paraigua.
the Maria seems the girl of the umbrella
'Maria appears to be the girl with the umbrella.'

b. La noia del paraigua sembla la Maria
the girl of the umbrella seems the Maria
'The girl with the umbrella appears to be Maria.'

In this pair of examples, the two NPs involved have the same agreement features and, so, there is no reason to expect any variation in the form of the verb. However, when the agreement features of the two NPs involved are different, we find that the verb *semblar* has the form that shows agreement with the NP higher in the person-number hierarchy (26), regardless of where this NP appears in the clause:

(33) a. Tu {sembles /*sembla} la noia del
you.2nd.sg seem.2nd.sg seem.3rd.sg the girl of the
paraigua.
umbrella
'You appear to be the girl with the umbrella.'

b. La noia del paraigua {sembles /*sembla}
the girl of the umbrella seem.2nd.sg seem.3rd.sg
tu
you.2nd.sg
'The girl with the umbrella appears to be you.'

(34) a. Les fulles {semblen /*sembla} l' òrgan
the leaves seem.3rd.pl seem.3rd.sg the organ
vital de les plantes.
vital of the plants
'The leaves appear to be the vital organ of plants.'

b. L' òrgan vital de les plantes {semblen /*sembla}
The organ vital of the plants seem.3rd.pl seem.3rd.sg
les fulles.
the leaves
'The vital organ of plants appears to be the leaves.'

The position of the NPs in (33b) and (34b) indicates that the postverbal NP is the complement; however, it is this NP that triggers agreement on the verb. The NP that triggers agreement in (33) and (34) is the same one that would trigger agreement if the verb were the copula, instead of *semblar*. These facts are immediately explained if, as seems reasonable, we assume that *semblar*, like the copular verb, requires coindexing of its subject and complement. These facts would be problematic if the apparent inverse agreement of ACopInv depended on a lexical feature of the copula not shared with any other verb: there would then be no reason to expect apparent inverse agreement with any other verb. In the current analysis, *ser* and *semblar* share the essential property that gives rise to apparent inverse agreement: coindexation of subject and complement.

2.3.5 The asymmetric copula

A problem with the analysis of copular constructions presented here might seem to arise when both the topic and the complement are first and second person. The analysis does not resolve the conflict, as both would be equal in imposing their features on the subject, and yet the data show that, in these cases, the conflict is systematically resolved in favor of the topic:

(35) a. Jo {sóc/ *ets} tu.
I am are.2nd.sg you.2nd.sg
'I am you.'

b. Tu {ets /*sóc} jo.
You.2nd.sg are.2nd.sg am I
'You are me.'

An important difference between these two examples and the examples analyzed so far is that (35a-b) are not truth-conditionally equivalent, unlike what happens in all other cases examined so far, for example, in (1). (35a) means something like 'I play your role' or 'I pretend to be you' and (35b) means something like 'You play my role' or 'You pretend to be me'. It is clear that in (35) the referent of the topic (subject) is not identical to that of the complement: 'you' and 'I' do not refer to the same individual. This is unlike all the other examples considered so far, where there is referential identity between the topic (subject) and the complement.

The explanation I want to propose for cases like (35) is that, although the copula normally imposes coindexing (and referential dependency) between the subject and the complement, the requirement of subject-complement coindexing in some cases is dropped and then the copula has a meaning like "X play the role of Y". This use of the copula is not restricted to situations where both subject and complement are first or second person, although it is the only option in such cases, since it is not possible to interpret a first and a second person in the same utterance as coreferential. It occurs in other cases, as we see comparing (36a) and (36b):

(36) a. El senyor Ramon sóc jo. (*sóc* = am.1st.sg)
'I am Mr. Ramon.'

b. El senyor Ramon és jo. (*és* = is.3rd.sg)
'Mr. Ramon is me/plays my role.'

Example (36a) establishes referential identity between the topic (subject) and the complement. This example could be used when the concept of "el senyor Ramon" is present in the discourse in order to establish the identity of this individual. (36b), on the other hand, keeps the referents of the subject and the complement distinct and could be used to indicate that Mr. Ramon is taking my place, in some sense.

(36a) contains an instance of the "common" copula, which requires coindexing of the subject and the complement: since the features of the complement are "stronger" than those of the topic according to (27), they are imposed on the subject and reflected in the form of the copula. (36b) contains an instance of the "asymmetric" copula: since the subject and the complement are not coindexed, the subject shows the features of the topic. (Italian has another morphological reflex of the difference between the two uses of the copula: there is a contrast between *sono io* 'it is me' and *è me/*io* 'he/she is me' (Moro 1997: 64, 270) (my translations). The difference in meaning between these two uses of the copula in Italian is visible in the translations of the examples in Cecchetto and Oniga 2004: 145–146, although they erroneously attribute the choice of *me* or *io* to case concord.)

2.4 Conclusion

If the claim in this paper is correct, the phenomenon of ACopInv is one of the hallmarks of a null-subject language, together with the possibility of null subjects and postverbal subjects. (Naturally, ACopInv is not visible in null-subject languages that lack a copula, such as Arabic.) These three features of null-subject languages are derived, in the OT-LFG theory proposed here, from the constraint ranking that defines null-subject languages (illustrated in (21)). We can say that what characterizes null-subject languages is the absence of a subject position: a subject can, then, either be null (correspond to no phrase in c-structure) or appear in the "all-purpose" VP-internal position. As a null subject, it is pronominal and constrained to agree with the discourse entity it is coindexed with, like all pronominals. In the copular construction, it is also coindexed with the complement and constrained to agree with it. The potential feature mismatch between the two coindexed elements is resolved by means of a hierarchically ranked family of constraints that favors agreement with the expression containing the more marked features. This hierarchically ranked family of constraints is only visible in null-subject languages, where the subject lacks lexically specified features. In non-null-subject languages, the subject corresponds to a phrase in the c-structure with lexically specified features and preserving these features in the f-structure takes precedence over the constraints that require agreement with coindexed elements.

References

Aissen, Judith. 1999. Markedness and subject choice in Optimality Theory. *Natural Language and Linguistic Theory* 17(4):673–711.

Alexiadou, Artemis and Elena Anagnostopoulou. 1998. Parametrizing AGR: Word order, V-movement and EPP checking. *Natural Language and Linguistic Theory* 16:491–539.

Alsina, Alex. 1995. The fall of function-argument biuniqueness. In G. V. Morrill and R. T. Oehrle, eds., *Formal Grammar: Proceedings of the 7th Conference of the European Summer School in Logic, Language and Information (ESSLLI'95)*, pages 1–16. Barcelona.

Alsina, Alex. 1996. *The role of argument structure in grammar: Evidence from Romance*. Stanford, CA: CSLI Publications.

Alsina, Alex. 2004. La inversió copulativa en català. *Anuari de Filologia* 26:9–44.

Andrews, Avery. 1982. Long distance agreement in Modern Icelandic. In P. Jacobson and G. Pullum, eds., *The Nature of Syntactic Representation*, pages 1–33. Dordrecht: D. Reidel.

Andrews, Avery. 1990. Case structures and control in Modern Icelandic. In J. Maling and A. Zaenen, eds., *Modern Icelandic Syntax*, vol. 24 of *Syntax and Semantics*, pages 187–234. Orlando, FL: Academic Press.

Barbosa, Pilar. 2001. On inversion in wh-questions in Romance. In A. Hulk and J.-Y. Pollock, eds., *Subject inversion in Romance and the theory of universal grammar*, pages 20–59. New York, NY: Oxford University Press.

Bonet, Eulàlia. 1990. Subjects in Catalan. In *MIT Working Papers in Linguistics (Papers on Wh-movement)*, vol. 13, pages 1–26. Cambridge, MA: MITWPL.

Bresnan, Joan, ed. 1982. *The Mental Representation of Grammatical Relations*. Cambridge, MA: The MIT Press.

Bresnan, Joan. 1996. LFG in an OT setting. In M. Butt and T. H. King, eds., *Proceedings of the International Lexical-Functional Grammar Conference 1996 (LFG'96)*. Grenoble: CSLI Online Publications.

Bresnan, Joan. 2000. Optimal syntax. In J. Dekkers, F. van der Leeuw, and J. van de Weijer, eds., *Optimality Theory: Phonology, Syntax and Acquisition*, pages 334–385. Oxford: Oxford University Press.

Bresnan, Joan. 2001a. *Lexical-Functional Syntax*. Oxford: Blackwell.

Bresnan, Joan. 2001b. The emergence of the unmarked pronoun. In G. Legendre, S. Vikner, and J. Grimshaw, eds., *Optimality-theoretic syntax*, pages 113–142. Cambridge, MA: The MIT Press.

Bresnan, Joan and Jonni Kanerva. 1989. Locative inversion in Chichewa: A case study of factorization in grammar. *Linguistic Inquiry* 20(1):1–50.

Burzio, Luigi. 1986. *Italian Syntax: A Government-Binding Approach*. Dordrecht: D. Reidel.

Cardinalettti, Anna. 1997. Subjects and clause structure. In L. M. V. Haegeman, ed., *The new comparative syntax*, pages 33–63. London & New York, NY: Longman.

Cecchetto, Carlo and Renato Oniga. 2004. A challenge to null Case theory. *Linguistic Inquiry* 35(1):141–149.

Corbett, Greville G. 2000. *Number*. Cambridge, UK: Cambridge University Press.

Costa, João. 2001. Marked versus unmarked inversion and Optimality Theory. In A. Hulk and J.-Y. Pollock, eds., *Subject Inversion in Romance and the Theory of Universal Grammar*, pages 91–106. New York, NY: Oxford University Press.

Fernández Leborans, María Jesús. 1999. La predicación: Las oraciones copulativas. In I. Bosque and V. Demonte, eds., *Gramática descriptiva de la lengua española*, pages 2357–2460. Madrid: Espasa Calpe.

Goodall, Grant. 2001. The EPP in Spanish. In W. D. Davies and S. Dubinsky, eds., *Objects and other subjects: Grammatical functions, functional categories and configurationality*, pages 193–223. Dordrecht: Kluwer.

Greenberg, Joseph H. 1966. *Language Universals*. The Hague: Mouton de Gruyter.

Grimshaw, Jane. 1997a. Projections, heads and optimality. *Linguistic Inquiry* 28:373–422.

Grimshaw, Jane. 1997b. The best clitic: Constraint conflict in morphosyntax. In L. Haegeman, ed., *Elements of grammar: handbook of generative syntax*, pages 169–196. Dordrecht, Boston & London: Kluwer.

Hernanz, Maria Lluïsa and José M. Brucart. 1987. *La sintaxis: 1. Principios teóricos. La oración simple*. Barcelona: Crítica.

Kuhn, Jonas. 2003. *Optimality-theoretic syntax: A declarative approach*. Stanford, CA: CSLI Publications.

Légendre, Geraldine, Paul Raymond, and Paul Smolensky. 1993. An optimality-theoretic typology of case and grammatical voice systems. In J. S. Guenter, B. A. Kaiser, and C. C. Zoll, eds., *Proceedings of the 19th Annual Meeting of the Berkeley Linguistics Society (BLS 19)*, pages 464–478. Berkeley, CA: Berkeley Linguistics Society.

Moro, Andrea. 1997. *The Raising of Predicates*. Cambridge, UK: Cambridge University Press.

Perlmutter, David M. 1978. Impersonal passives and the unaccusative hypothesis. In J. J. Jaeger, A. C. Woodbury, and F. Ackerman, eds., *Proceedings of the 4th Annual Meeting of the Berkeley Linguistics Society (BLS 4)*, pages 157–189. Berkeley, CA: Berkeley Linguistics Society.

Perlmutter, David M. 1983. Personal vs. impersonal constructions. *Natural Language and Linguistic Theory* 1:141–200.

Prince, Alan and Paul Smolensky. 1993. Optimality theory: Constraint interaction in generative grammar. Tech. Rep. 2, Rutgers University Center for Cognitive Science, Piscataway, NJ.

Ramos, Joan-Rafael. 2002. El SV, II: La predicació verbal no obligatòria. In J. Solà, M. R. Lloret, J. Mascaró, and M. P. Saldanya, eds., *Gramàtica del català contemporani*, vol. 2, pages 1951–2044. Barcelona: Editorial Empúries.

Rosselló, Joana. 1986. *Gramàtica, configuracions i referències: Per una teoria alternativa del pro-drop romànic.* Ph.D. thesis, Universitat de Barcelona.

Sag, Ivan A. and Thomas Wasow. 1999. *Syntactic theory: A formal introduction.* Stanford, CA: CSLI Publications.

Siewierska, Anna. 2004. *Person.* Cambridge, UK: Cambridge University Press.

Solà, Jaume. 1992. *Agreement and Subjects.* Ph.D. thesis, Universitat Autònoma de Barcelona.

Vallduví, Enric. 1992. A preverbal landing site for quantificational operators. In *Catalan Working Papers in Linguistics 1992*, pages 319–343. Bellaterra: Universitat Autònoma de Barcelona.

Vallduví, Enric. 2002. L'oració com a unitat informativa. In J. Solà, M. R. Lloret, J. Mascaró, and M. P. Saldanya, eds., *Gramàtica del català contemporani*, vol. 2, pages 1221–1279. Barcelona: Editorial Empúries.

3

Copy Raising and its Consequences for Perceptual Reports[1]

ASH ASUDEH AND IDA TOIVONEN

3.1 Introduction

Copy raising is a phenomenon in which a raising verb takes a non-expletive subject and a complement containing an obligatory pronominal "copy" of the subject:

(1) a. Thora seems like she adores popsicles.
    b. * Thora seems like Isak adores popsicles.

English copy raising was initially noticed by Postal (1974, 268, fn.1) and was also touched on by Rogers (1971, 1973) in work that principally concerned what he called *flip perception verbs* (Rogers 1971, 1972, 1973, 1974). The topic has recently received renewed attention in work by Potsdam and Runner (2001) and Asudeh (2002, 2004). The first detailed investigation of copy raising was Joseph's (1976) work on Modern Greek, which was subsequently brought to wider attention by

[1]We would like to thank David Beaver, Dick Crouch, Mary Dalrymple, Jim McCloskey, Line Mikkelsen, Chris Potts, and Peter Sells for invaluable feedback on previous work related to issues discussed here. We also thank Mary, Line, and Chris for helpful discussion of the present work and detailed comments on a previous draft. We are very grateful to Elisabet Engdahl for her constructive comments and suggestions on the penultimate draft. Finally, we would like to thank Marie-Elaine van Egmond and Ilka Ludwig for their comments and discussion in the context of a larger project on comparative Germanic copy raising. We accept sole responsibility for any remaining errors.

Architectures, Rules, and Preferences: Variations on Themes by Joan Bresnan.
Annie Zaenen, Jane Simpson, Tracy Holloway King,
Jane Grimshaw, Joan Maling, and Chris Manning, (eds.).

Perlmutter and Soames (1979). Copy raising is in fact not typologically uncommon and has been attested in a number of unrelated languages, including Samoan (Chung 1978), Hebrew (Lappin 1984), Irish (McCloskey and Sells 1988), Haitian Creole (Déprez 1992), Igbo (Ura 1998), and Turkish (Moore 1998). In this paper, we add to the repository of empirical data on copy raising by giving a characterization of copy raising in Swedish. This has the benefit of allowing us to compare the phenomenon in two closely related Germanic languages, namely English and Swedish. In carrying out the comparison, it becomes evident that copy raising yields insights into the linguistic encoding of the source of perceptual reports, i.e. what it is that gives the speaker the impression that something is the case. We argue that the proper analysis of perceptual sources in copy raising has consequences for linguistic theory, in particular the distinction between arguments/thematic roles and other participants in events and states. The analysis also allows us to solve two empirical puzzles. The first concerns the behaviour of an adjunct encoding the source of perception in Swedish and how this adjunct contrasts with an English adjunct that encodes the goal of perception, i.e. the perceiver. The second puzzle concerns a contrast that holds in both Swedish and English between copy raising and subject-to-subject raising in certain contexts.

3.2 Background

The alternation between infinitival and finite complements of raising predicates has been a central area of investigation in theoretical linguistics for quite some time (Rosenbaum 1967, Postal 1974). The alternation is demonstrated in (2) and (3) for the raising verb *seem* and the raising adjective *certain*:

(2) a. Thora seems to adore popsicles.
    b. Isak is certain to adore popsicles.

(3) a. It seems that Thora adores popsicles.
    b. It is certain that Isak adores popsicles.

The finite complementation pattern is a key piece of evidence that the "raised" subject in the infinitival alternant is not an argument of the raising predicate, since the subject can instead be realized as an expletive.

Copy raising is similar to the finite complementation pattern, since it too apparently involves a finite complement, although one introduced by *like*, *as if*, or *as though*:[2]

(4) a. Thora seems like she adores popsicles.
    b. Isak appears as if / though he has been crying.

Asudeh (2002, 2004) argues that the complement to copy raising is not a finite clause, but rather a predicative prepositional phrase, headed by *like* or *as*, which in turn contains a finite complement. He assimilates the syntax of copy raising to predicative raising:

(5) a. Kim seems crazy / out of control.
    b. Sandy appeared ill / under the weather.

Despite taking a predicative complement, copy raising does exhibit an alternation between a non-expletive and expletive subject, similar to the alternation between subject-to-subject raising and finite complementation in (2) and (3) above:

(6) a. Thora seems like she adores popsicles.
    b. It seems like Thora adores popsicles.

If the possibility of an expletive subject for finite-complement raising verbs in (3) constitutes evidence that a raised subject is not a thematic argument of the raising verb, then the alternation in (6) similarly indicates that a copy raising subject is not an argument of the copy raising verb. We will henceforth refer to examples of a copy raising verb in its expletive-subject alternant, as in (6b), simply as 'expletive examples'.[3] We will take care to distinguish *that*-complement cases like (3) when appropriate. Another note on the terminology: Throughout this paper, we refer to 'raising verbs' and 'copy raising verbs'. The copy raising verbs *seem* and *appear* can also be used as raising verbs, and so the different terms are simply intended to separate the different uses of the verbs.

The fact that copy raising verbs require a pronominal copy of their subject to appear in their predicative complement, as shown in (1) and again in (7), lends further support to the conclusion that a non-expletive copy raising subject is not an argument of the matrix verb.

[2] *As if* and *as though* seem to belong to a slightly higher register than *like*. The latter seems to be preferred in colloquial speech, although there are no doubt also subtle semantic and pragmatic differences between the three forms, which we set aside here. We will principally use only *like* in what follows.

[3] Although we do not discuss them explicitly, we mean remarks about expletive examples to extend to idiom chunk cases like *The cat seems like it's out of the bag* (see Potsdam and Runner 2001, Asudeh 2002, 2004).

(7) a. Thora seems like she adores popsicles.
b. * Thora seems like Isak adores popsicles.

If *Thora* were analyzed as a thematic subject in (7a), the ungrammaticality of (7b) would be mysterious. Asudeh (2002, 2004) provides an analysis of copy raising that assimilates the phenomenon to resumption, as centrally exemplified by resumptive pronouns in unbounded dependencies (McCloskey 1979, Sells 1984). On Asudeh's analysis, the copy raising subject is not licensed by the copy raising verb and must instead compose in place of the copy pronoun, which is removed from semantic composition by a *manager resource* that is lexically contributed by the copy raising verb. Asudeh (2002, 2004) observes that the true copy raising verbs in English are *seem* and *appear*, since these are the verbs that require a copy pronoun in their complements. He contrasts these with *perceptual resemblance verbs* (Rogers's *flip perception verbs*; Rogers 1971, 1972, 1973, 1974): *look*, *sound*, *smell*, *feel*, and *taste*.[4] The latter do not require a pronoun in their complement, as demonstrated by the following contrast:

(8) a. * Thora seems like Chris has been baking sticky buns.
appears as if

b. Thora smells like Chris has been baking sticky buns.
looks
sounds
feels
tastes

Matters are further complicated by the fact that perceptual resemblance verbs may also occur with an expletive subject, thus exhibiting the alternation in (6) above. This is illustrated in (9) with data from English and Swedish:[5]

(9) a. Thora looks / sounds / smells / feels / tastes like Chris has been baking sticky buns.

[4]These verbs occur in various other usages, such as the propositional attitude use of *feel* (*I just feel that they're so uncaring*) or the intransitive use of *smells* (*This shoe smells*). Also, *look* and *sound* can be used with quite bleached meanings in which an appearance or sound is not necessarily involved. In this paper we are only concerned with the uses of these perception verbs with a *like*-complement and in which a sensory modality is involved.

[5]The verbs *feel* and especially *taste* do not allow the expletive variant as easily. Nevertheless, this is not a linguistic constraint, since we have found attested examples in both English and Swedish. The difficulty is rather one of construal, i.e. finding an appropriate context.

b. Thora ser ut / låter / luktar / känns / smakar som om
T. looks out / sounds / smells / feels / tastes as if
Chris har bakat kladdkaka.
C. has baked sticky cake
'Thora looks / sounds / smells / feels / tastes like Chris has baked "sticky cake".'

c. It looks / sounds / smells / feels / tastes like Chris has been baking sticky buns.

d. Det ser ut / låter / luktar / känns / smakar som om
It looks out / sounds / smells / feels / tastes as if
Chris har bakat kladdkaka.
C. has baked sticky cake
'It looks / sounds / smells / feels / tastes like Chris has baked "sticky cake".'

Asudeh concludes that a non-expletive subject of a perceptual resemblance verb is thematic (i.e., it is an argument of the verb), but that a non-expletive subject of a copy raising verb is non-thematic (i.e., it is not an argument of the verb). He treats perceptual resemblance verbs as ambiguous between a thematic subject reading, when they have a non-expletive subject, and a non-thematic subject reading, when they have a expletive subject. The subject of a copy raising verb is always non-thematic, though.

However, other recent literature proposes that a non-expletive copy raising subject is sometimes thematic (Potsdam and Runner 2001) or even always thematic (Matushansky 2002). Matushansky is not primarily concerned with copy raising and does not argue her position, so we will concentrate on Potsdam and Runner's claims. Potsdam and Runner (2001, 456–458) state that a copy raising subject is thematic in cases where the copy pronoun in the complement is not the highest subject or is in non-subject position (Potsdam and Runner 2001):

(10) a. Bill sounds like Martha hit him over the head with the record. (adapted from Rogers 1973, 97)

b. Ermintrude looks like the cat got her tongue. (Rogers 1971, 219, (51))

c. Mary appears as if her job is going well.

This data is partly problematic, since Potsdam and Runner (2001), like most work on English copy raising (e.g., Rogers 1971, 1973, 1974, Heycock 1994), do not distinguish between copy raising verbs and perceptual resemblance verbs. We have already seen that the perception verbs do not require a pronoun in their complement at all. It is therefore irrelevant whether any pronoun that happens to occur in the complement is a subject or not. However, the third example in (10) is an instance of the copy raising verb *appear*.

There are at least two problems with the claim that copy raising verbs can have thematic subjects. The first problem has to do with Potsdam and Runner's (2001, 457) claim that copy raising verbs in their thematic use are "reasonably paraphrased as 'act like' or 'put on the appearance of'". But (10c) is not synonymous with any of the following sentences:

(11) a. Mary acts like her job is going well.
 b. Mary puts on the appearance of her job going well.
 c. Mary puts on the appearance that her job is going well.

First, notice that the most salient readings for these sentences involve a generic/habitual present tense (i.e., *Mary always / usually acts like ...*), whereas the most salient reading of (10c) is a simple present tense in which Mary at this moment appears a certain way. Second, the sentences in (11) entail that Mary is doing something, and perhaps also entail that she is doing it purposefully. However, (10c) does not entail that Mary is actually doing anything that gives off the appearance that her job is going well; she could just be in a state of happiness, for example. Both of these points have to do with the fact that *appear* in (10c) is a stative verb whereas the ones in (11) are not.

Second, the predicates *act like* and *put on the appearance of* require agents capable of intentional action, but copy raising verbs with non-subject copy pronouns do not. Consider the following contrast:

(12) a. The corpse seemed like the coroner had done an exceptionally bad job of dissecting it.
 b. # The corpse acted like the coroner had done an exceptionally bad job of dissecting it.
 c. # The corpse put on the appearance that the coroner had done an exceptionally bad job of dissecting it.
 d. # The corpse put on the appearance of the coroner having done an exceptionally bad job of dissecting it.

The corpse cannot *do* anything to convey the impression that the coroner botched the job. Nonetheless, the copy raising sentence is well-formed and felicitous.

These arguments indicate that the particular semantic sketch that Potsdam and Runner (2001) give of putatively thematic copy raising verbs cannot be right. However, there could still be a thematic use of these verbs with some other, as yet unidentified, meaning. A more pernicious problem with the claim of thematic copy raising verbs is that it erroneously predicts the possibility of copy raising with no copy pronoun whatsoever. Potsdam and Runner (2001, 457–458) cite Heycock (1994) for well-formed examples, but these all involve perceptual resemblance verbs. Copy raising verbs, as we noted above, are in fact ungrammatical without copy pronouns. We have encountered certain speakers who accept some instances of copy raising without any copy pronoun. For these speakers, a thematic analysis may be desirable. However, there are speakers — in fact, the majority of our informants — who reject copy raising without a copy pronoun, although they accept examples where the complement contains a pronominal copy (and the copy pronoun is not necessarily a subject). This pattern of data would be completely unexpected if these speakers had a thematic use of copy raising verbs. We therefore conclude, following Asudeh (2002, 2004), that copy raising subjects are non-thematic.

There is, however, a contrast between copy raising verbs and ordinary raising verbs that is puzzling if both classes of verb have a non-thematic subject and a single, propositional argument. Consider the following context:

(13) A and B walk into Tom's kitchen. Tom is at the stove doing something, but exactly what is a little unclear.

In this context, the following statements by A to B are all felicitous:

(14) a. Tom seems to be cooking.
b. It seems that Tom is cooking.
c. Tom seems like he's cooking.
d. It seems like Tom's cooking.

Now consider the following alternative context:

(15) A and B walk into Tom's kitchen. There's no sign of Tom, but there are various things bubbling away on the stove and there are several ingredients on the counter, apparently waiting to be used.

Given this context, (14a), (14b), and (14d) are still felicitous, but (14c) is odd:

(16) # Tom seems like he's cooking.

If *Tom* is not a thematic subject of *seems*, why is this sentence not felicitous like the infinitival version? We will call this *the puzzle of the absent cook*.

The next section introduces Swedish copy raising, which gives rise to a puzzle of its own. We will show that the two puzzles are connected.

3.3 Copy raising in Swedish

Swedish has only one true copy raising verb, *verka* ('seem'). An example is given in (17), where Maria is the non-thematic subject of *verkar*, and the finite complement clause contains a coreferential pronoun *hon*:[6]

(17) Maria verkar som om hon är glad.
M. seems as if she is happy
'Maria seems as if she's happy.'

As expected of a copy raising verb, the complement clause requires a pronominal copy:[7]

(18) * Maria verkar som om Jonas är glad.
M. seems as if J. is happy

In (18), the complement clause does not contain a pronominal copy of *Maria* and the example is ungrammatical.

Just like English *seem*, *verka* can take an expletive subject and a finite complement, as in (19a). It is also a subject-to-subject raising verb, as illustrated in (19b):

(19) a. Det verkar som om Maria är glad.
it seems as if M. is happy
'It seems as if Maria is happy.'

b. Maria verkar vara glad.
M. seems be.INF happy
'Maria seems to be happy.'

The verb *verka* thus displays the key copy raising characteristics: First, it does not require a thematic subject, as shown in (19a); second, it can take a non-expletive subject and a finite subordinate clause, as shown in (17); and third, when it does take a non-expletive subject and a complement containing a finite clause, a pronominal copy is required in the lower clause. To our knowledge, Swedish copy raising has not previously been discussed in the literature.[8]

[6]In the examples presented in this paper, the complement of *verka* is introduced by *som om*. It should be noted that many speakers can omit *om* and the complement is then introduced by *som* alone. Some speakers also allow *som att* ('as that') and even a plain *att* ('that').

[7]Some speakers find (18) at least marginally acceptable. Those speakers arguably do not have true copy raising, i.e. their grammars treat *verka* as having a thematic subject. As noted above, some English speakers also have a thematic *seem*; see van Egmond (2004) for a discussion of similar dialectal variation in Dutch.

[8]Although a copy raising example is listed in a recent comprehensive reference grammar (Teleman et al. 1999, vol. 4, p.56).

Swedish has other raising verbs that are very similar to *verka* in many respects, but they are not copy raising verbs. These verbs are *förefalla* ('seem'), *tyckas* ('seem') and *se ut* ('look'):

(20) a. Det förefaller / tycks / ser ut som om Maria är glad.
it seems / seems / looks out as if M. is happy
'It seems / looks as if Maria is happy.'

b. Maria förefaller / ser ut att vara glad.
M. seems / looks out to be.INF happy
'Maria seems / looks to be happy'

c. Maria förefaller / tycks vara glad.
M. seems / seems be.INF happy
'Maria seems to be happy'

The verb *se ut* requires an infinitival complement to have the marker *att* ('to'), the verb *tyckas* cannot take *att* and *förefalla* can take a complement with or without *att*. The verbs *tyckas* and *förefalla* can only take a finite complement if the matrix subject is an expletive:

(21) * Maria förefaller / tycks som om hon är glad.
M. seems / seems as if she is happy

The verbs *förefalla* and *tyckas* are thus not copy raising verbs.

The verb *se ut* also has a perceptual resemblance alternant. However, Swedish perceptual resemblance verbs are not true copy raising verbs, because they do not require a pronominal copy in their complement, as shown in (9) above and again here:

(22) Maria ser ut / låter som om Jonas är glad.
M. looks out / sounds as if J. is happy.
'Maria looks / sounds as if Jonas is happy.'

The perceptual resemblance verbs in Swedish are thus parallel to their counterparts in English: Although they can take an expletive subject, as in (9c)-(9d) above, they can also appear with a thematic subject, as in (9a)-(9b) and (22).

3.3.1 A contrast between Swedish and English and a second puzzle

According to the data that has been presented so far, the Swedish verb *verka* is exactly parallel to English *seem*. In examples (23a–23c), the Swedish sentences correspond closely to the English translations. Example (23d) is ungrammatical, as is its English equivalent.

(23) a. Det verkar som om Tom har vunnit.
it seems as if T. has won
'It seems as if Tom has won.'

b. Tom verkar ha vunnit.
   T. seems have won
   'Tom seems to have won.'
c. Tom verkar som om han har vunnit.
   T. seems as if he has won
   'Tom seems as if he has won.'
d. * Tom verkar som om Kalle har vunnit.
   T. seems as if K. has won

Examples shown in previous sections and examples (23a–23d) demonstrate the close similarity between *seem* and *verka*.

However, Swedish *verka* allows a type of expression not available in English:

(24) Det verkar på Tom som om han har vunnit.
     it seems on T. as if he has won
     ∼'Tom gives the impression that he has won.'

Example (24) is close in meaning to example (23c). The *på*-PP specifies that the impression that he (i.e., Tom or someone else) has won originates with Tom. It is not specified how Tom gives off this impression: It could be the way he looks or acts, or it could be something he said.[9] The verb *verka* thus allows for a *på*-PP which specifies the *source* of perception, which we will call the *p-source*. This PP is an adjunct: It is not selected for by *verka*, which only takes a single argument (since it is a raising verb). Moreover, the PP is both syntactically and semantically optional, as is typical of adjuncts. However, a crucial difference between (24) and (23c) is that (24) does not require a copy pronoun in its complement:

(25) Det verkar på Tom som om Kalle har vunnit.
     it seems on T. as if K. has won
     ∼'Tom gives the impression that Kalle has won.'

The *på*-PP thus gives Swedish speakers the capacity to express what (23d) and the following English sentence would arguably express if they were grammatical:

(26) * Tom seems like Kalle has won.

Although the intended meaning of (23d) and (26) is intuitively clear, speakers all but uniformly reject them.

The *på*-PP can be contrasted with the English *to*-PP, which specifies the *goal* of perception (*p-goal*; i.e., the perceiver):

[9] A *på*-PP can also be used with perceptual resemblance verbs such as *se ut* ('look') or *låta* ('sound'). In such cases, the means of conveying the impression is expressed by the verb.

(27) It seemed to me as if Tom had won.

The verbs *verka* and *tyckas* can take a plain NP object with the same interpretation as the English *to*-PP, as exemplified in (28a–28b).

(28) a. % Det verkade mig som om Tom hade vunnit.
it seemed me as if T. had won
'It seemed to me as if Tom had won.'

b. Det tycktes mig som om Tom hade vunnit.
it seemed me as if T. had won
'It seemed to me as if Tom had won.'

The PP *to me* in (27) and the NP *mig* in (28a–28b) do not have the same interpretation as the *på* -PP in (24): In (24), there is something about Tom that makes it seem as if he has won. Examples (27) and (28a), on the other hand, leave unspecified what gives off the impression that Tom has won, but rather express to whom the impression has been given. A note on the Swedish data: The Swedish goal NP illustrated in (28a–28b) does not appear to be as commonly used as the English *to*-PP. Some speakers find (28a) unacceptable. Example (28b) is more generally accepted, although some find it quite formal. In contrast, the *på*-PP is not marginal or particularly formal.

Let us now return to copy raising, which is surprisingly not compatible with *på*-PPs. Compare (23c) above to (29):

(29) * Tom verkar på Lisa som om han har vunnit.
T. seems on L. as if he has won

The ungrammaticality of (29) is unexpected: Why should the PP adjunct be excluded? This is our second puzzle, which we will call *the* på *puzzle*. It is easy to understand what the intended meaning of (29) is: Lisa gives the impression that Tom seems as if he has won. Yet the example is ungrammatical. Example (29) can be contrasted with (30a), which contains a *to*-PP, and Swedish (30b–30c), which contain plain NP objects comparable to the English *to*-NP:[10]

(30) a. Tom seemed to me as if he had won.

b. % Tom verkade mig som om han hade vunnit.
T. seemed me as if he had won
'Tom seemed to me as if he had won.'

c. Tom tycktes mig ha vunnit.
T. seemed me have won
'Tom seemed to me to have won.'

[10]Example (30c) is a raising example instead of a copy raising example, as *tyckas* is not a copy raising verb.

The PP *to me* in (30a) and the NP *mig* in (30b–30c) denote a perceptual goal (the perceiver), not a perceptual source.

We propose that the two puzzles, the puzzle of the absent cook and the *på* puzzle, are connected. The essence of our proposal is as follows. Both puzzles arise due to the linguistic expression of perceptual reports. The examples that led to the puzzle of the absent cook are odd because the subject of the copy raising verb is interpreted as the source of perception when it is unavailable to offer perceptual evidence. The examples that led to the *på* puzzle are ungrammatical because two distinct linguistic expressions specify the source of perception.

3.4 Implications for perceptual reports

We will not present a formal analysis of these facts here, but will instead spell out the proposal in general, but explicit, terms. In copy raising sentences, the subject of the copy raising verb is interpreted as the source of perception (*p-source*). This is why (31a) and its Swedish equivalent (31b) are both odd in a context where the speaker does not have perceptual evidence of Tom, as discussed at the end of section 3.2:

(31) a. # Tom seems like he's cooking.

b. # Tom verkar som om han lagar mat.
T. seems as if he makes food
'Tom seems like he's cooking.'

Examples (31a) and (31b) can be paraphrased as follows: It seems like Tom is cooking and what gives this impression is Tom himself. The example is thus not felicitous in a situation where Tom is not available to be the source of the report. Swedish and English are equivalent with respect to the interpretation of copy raising, and so the Swedish translation of (31a) is equally odd in the given context.

Nevertheless, *p-sources* are not the same as the theta-role *source*. First, the theta-role *source* proto-typically encodes a spatial argument and *p-source* does not. Second, theta-roles are connected to arguments, but the subject of a copy raising verb is not a thematic argument of that verb. Copy raising subjects are licensed only through their connection to the obligatory copy pronoun in the complement. Thus, the subject *Henrika* is not a *thematic* subject of *seem* in (32):

(32) Henrika seems like she's had enough.

We contend that the verbs *seem* and *appear* and their Swedish counterpart *verka* entail a source of perception, but that this source is not connected to an argument. Rather, we analyze p-sources (and p-goals) as entailed participants in the states that these verbs denote. There are thus parallels between perceptual sources/goals and temporal and locative modifiers of eventualities, where we understand the latter to be a cover term for different kinds of events and states (Bach 1981). Eventualities in general entail a time and location, yet these entailments are only sometimes overtly realized. In sum, the solution to the puzzle of the absent cook is that a copy-raised subject is interpreted as the p-source — the source of perception — and ascribing the role of p-source to the subject is infelicitous if the individual in question is not perceivable as the source of the report.

Since we treat the Swedish *på*-PP as contributing a p-source, our analysis treats (33) as synonymous to (34), if *Tom* and *han* are understood coreferentially:[11]

(33) Det verkar på Tom som om han lagar mat.
It seems on T. as if he makes food
'Tom seems like he's cooking.'

(34) Tom verkar som om han lagar mat.
Tom seems as if he makes food
'Tom seems like he's cooking.'

Given our solution to the puzzle of the absent cook, this predicts that (33) is infelicitous in the same contexts as (31b). This prediction is correct. For example, in the scenario where Tom is absent but the kitchen shows signs of cooking, (33) cannot be felicitously uttered.

Let us now turn to puzzle number two, the *på* puzzle, which concerned the ungrammaticality of examples like the following:

(35) * Maria verkar på Per som om hon är glad.
M. seems on P. as if she is happy

In (35), both Maria and Per are specified as the source of perception, and the example is ungrammatical.

Now the question is: Why can't two p-sources be specified? The restriction cannot be due to the state of the world or our knowledge of it. It is after all possible to report that Maria gives the impression that Per gives the impression that she is happy or that Maria and Per together give the impression that she is happy. However, (35) cannot express either of these propositions. We therefore conclude that there is a linguistic constraint against expressing multiple perceptual sources. This can be understood as a generalization of the notion that eventualities have at most one instance of each thematic role (Carlson 1984, Chierchia 1984, 1989, Dowty 1989, Parsons 1990, Landman 2000), which

[11] Note that (34) is grammatical. Recall that the infelicity of (31b) was due to the 'absent cook' scenario.

Carlson (1984, 271) similarly argues cannot be due to "the nature of the world itself". Just as an eventuality cannot have more than one theme, for example, an eventuality cannot have more than one perceptual source. Landman (2000, 38) proposes the following principle for thematic roles:

(36) **Unique Role Requirement**
If a thematic role is specified for an event, it is uniquely specified.

Following Chierchia (1984, 1989), Landman (2000, 44) captures this requirement formally by defining thematic roles as partial functions from eventualities to individuals. Unlike thematic roles, p-sources are not arguments, but we extend the uniqueness requirement to p-sources by similarly defining them as partial functions on eventualities.

The range of the p-source function is however not the set of individuals, but rather the union of the set of individuals and the set of eventualites, thus further distinguishing p-sources from thematic roles. This means that eventualities, in addition to individuals, can be p-sources. For example, a state-as-*p-source* analysis is appropriate for the felicitous expletive-subject sentence in the absent cook scenario:

(37) a. A and B walk into Tom's kitchen. There's no sign of Tom, but there are various things bubbling away on the stove and there are several ingredients on the counter, apparently waiting to be used.
b. It seems like Tom is cooking.

In this case, the p-source is the state of the kitchen. Recall that we refer to examples of a copy raising verb in its expletive-subject alternant simply as 'expletive examples'.

We treat such expletive examples as having an existentially bound p-source. This existential closure is obligatory in English expletive examples, but only optional in Swedish, since Swedish allows a *på*-PP expression of the p-source to co-occur with an expletive subject, as in (33) and the following example:

(38) Det verkar på Per som om Maria är glad.
it seems on P. as if M. is happy
∼'Per gives the impression that Maria is happy.'

However, when the *på*-PP is absent, as in (39), the existential closure is obligatory. Our analysis therefore assigns the following Swedish sentence the same broad interpretation as English (37a) above:

(39) Det verkar som om Tom lagar mat.
it seems as if T. makes food
'It seems like Tom is cooking.'

In sum, expletive examples involve existential closure of the p-source: obligatorily in English and optionally in Swedish.

There is reason to believe that there is also existential p-source closure in Swedish subject-to-subject raising and that in this case it is obligatory. This assumption explains why it is ungrammatical to have a *på*-PP in such cases:

(40) * Maria verkar på Jonas vara glad.
M. seems on J. be happy.

Recall from section 3.2 that in subject-to-subject raising, the subject of the raising verb is not tied to the perceptual source interpretation, since such sentences can be felicitous in the absence of the individual in question (i.e., subject-to-subject raising does not give rise to the puzzle of the absent cook). Example (40) is thus not ruled out because of a p-source clash between *Maria* and *Jonas*. However, if the verb has an existentially bound p-source, the definition of p-source as a (partial) function ensures that there can be no other p-source and as a result there cannot be a *på*-PP contributing a p-source. We do not have direct evidence that English subject-to-subject raising involves an existentially bound p-source, but it is reasonable to assume parity with Swedish, given the lack of evidence to the contrary and given the general similarities between English and Swedish raising.[12] Lastly, let us briefly return to the puzzle of the absent cook and the truth conditions of the perceptual reports we have been discussing. We assume that the result of equating an eventuality p-source with an individual is not false, but rather undefined. We noted that the likeliest p-source in an absent cook scenario, such as (37a), is a state. This means that if a sentence that attributes the p-source to an individual, such as a copy raising example or a Swedish expletive example with a *på*-PP, is used to describe an absent cook situation in which the p-source is actually an eventuality, the equality between the actual p-source and the asserted p-source is undefined. Thus, if sentences like (31a), (31b) or (33) (repeated below) are used in a scenario like (37a), the result is not falsehood, but rather presupposition failure:

---

[12]This leaves the matter of English *seem/appear* with *that*-complements. If arguments that this sort of *seem/appear* is purely epistemic and does not involve a perceptual report are correct (see Matushansky 2002 and references therein), then the *that*-complement cases lack p-sources (and p-goals) entirely. However, we think a more tenable position is that all uses of these verbs involve both an epistemic and a perceptual aspect. It is otherwise unexplained why a PP expressing a p-goal (perceiver) can be used with a *that*-complement:

i It seemed to her that they did not pose a threat.

(41) a. # Tom seems like he's cooking.
b. # Tom verkar som om han lagar mat.
T. seems as if he makes food
'Tom seems like he's cooking.'
c. # Det verkar på Tom som om han lagar mat.
It seems on T. as if he makes food
'Tom seems like he's cooking.'

These sentences involve a conjunction of two propositions: 1) It seems like Tom is cooking and 2) Tom is the p-source. Since the second conjunct is undefined, rather than false, the sentence as a whole cannot be assigned a truth value.

This correctly predicts that the negation of these sentences is equally infelicitous in this scenario:

(42) # Tom doesn't seem like he's cooking.

Our solution to the puzzle of the absent cook thus treats the infelicity of copy raising in the absence of perceptual evidence of the subject as presupposition failure.

This contrasts with a scenario that we have not so far considered in which there is an individual present to serve as a p-source, but it is not the individual named in the sentence (and both A and B know that the two individuals are not the same):

(43) a. A and B walk into Tom's kitchen. Robin is at the stove doing something, but exactly what is a little unclear. A and B recognize Robin and know that Robin is not Tom.
b. A: Tom seems like he's cooking.

In this scenario, our analysis treats A's statement as simply false. The p-source is Robin, not Tom, and since Robin and Tom are both individuals, the result of checking whether the p-source (Robin) is Tom is not undefined, but rather false. This is in turn renders false the larger conjunction representing the sentence as a whole.

3.5 Conclusion

Let us now review our proposal and how it accounts for the English and Swedish data. The key point is that verbs like *seem* and *verka* entail a source of perception, *p-source*, which may or may not be overtly expressed. The p-source is not an argument of the raising verb, and therefore not a thematic role, but rather an entailed participant in its eventuality. A further difference between thematic roles and p-sources is that the latter can be realized by eventualities, in addition to individuals. The pattern of p-source expression in English and Swedish is as follows:

1. English and Swedish copy raising:
   The copy-raised subject is the p-source.
2. English and Swedish subject-to-subject raising:
   The p-source is obligatorily existentially closed.
3. Expletive subjects:
   (a) English: The p-source is obligatorily existentially closed.
   (b) Swedish: The p-source is optionally existentially closed.

We can thus see that one principal typological difference between the two languages with respect to p-source realization lies in whether existential closure of the p-source is obligatory or only optional in expletive-subject examples. The evidence for this difference comes from another typological difference, which is the capacity of Swedish to alternatively express the p-source in a *på*-PP adjunct. We pointed out two puzzles along the way: the puzzle of the absent cook and the *på* puzzle. The first puzzle was solved by the assumption of an obligatory p-source contributed by the copy-raised subject. The attribution of p-source to the subject is infelicitous in a scenario where the subject is not available as the source of perception; it results in presupposition failure. The assumption of a subject p-source in copy raising — along with the extension of the uniqueness requirement on thematic roles to p-sources — also solved the second puzzle. If each eventuality has a unique p-source and the p-source is either filled by the subject (copy raising) or existentially bound (subject-to-subject raising), then the p-source cannot also be realized by a *på*-PP adjunct. However, since existential closure of the p-source is only optional in Swedish expletive examples, a *på*-PP is possible. We have largely set aside the matter of p-goals, but an extension of the account to include these is apparent. P-goals can be defined on a par with p-sources as partial functions on eventualities. The key contrast is that the p-goal function is into individuals, instead of into eventualities or individuals, since only individuals can be perceivers. The definition of p-goal as a function means that p-goals are equally subject to the generalized uniqueness requirement. This correctly predicts that there cannot be multiple instances of English *to*-PP adjuncts expressing p-goals of a single eventuality:

(44) * Tom seems to me to Sara like he is cooking.

We have not formalized our analysis, but we hope that we have been sufficiently explicit that it is clear how a formalization should proceed.

References

Asudeh, Ash. 2002. Richard III. In M. Andronis, E. Debenport, A. Pycha, and K. Yoshimura, eds., *CLS 38: The Main Session*, vol. 1, pages 31–46. Chicago, IL: Chicago Linguistic Society.

Asudeh, Ash. 2004. *Resumption as Resource Management*. Ph.D. thesis, Stanford University.

Bach, Emmon. 1981. On time, tense and aspect: An essay on English metaphysics. In P. Cole, ed., *Radical Pragmatics*, pages 62–81. New York, NY: Academic Press.

Carlson, Gregory N. 1984. Thematic roles and their role in semantic interpretation. *Linguistics* 22:259–279.

Chierchia, Gennaro. 1984. *Topics in the Syntax and Semantics of Infinitives and Gerunds*. Ph.D. thesis, University of Massachusetts, Amherst.

Chierchia, Gennaro. 1989. Structured meanings, thematic roles and control. In G. Chierchia, B. H. Partee, and R. Turner, eds., *Properties, Types and Meaning. Volume II: Semantic Issues*, pages 131–166. Dordrecht: Kluwer.

Chung, Sandra. 1978. *Case Marking and Grammatical Relations in Polynesian*. Austin, TX: University of Texas Press.

Déprez, Viviane. 1992. Raising constructions in Haitian Creole. *Natural Language and Linguistic Theory* 10:191–231.

Dowty, David. 1989. On the semantic content of the notion of 'thematic role'. In G. Chierchia, B. H. Partee, and R. Turner, eds., *Properties, Types and Meaning. Volume II: Semantic Issues*, pages 69–129. Dordrecht: Kluwer.

Heycock, Caroline. 1994. *Layers of Predication*. New York, NY: Garland.

Joseph, Brian D. 1976. Raising in Modern Greek: A copying process. In J. Hankamer and J. Aissen, eds., *Harvard Studies in Syntax and Semantics*, vol. 2, pages 241–281. Cambridge, MA: Harvard University, Department of Linguistics.

Landman, Fred. 2000. *Events and Plurality: The Jerusalem Lectures*. Dordrecht: Kluwer.

Lappin, Shalom. 1984. Predication and raising. In C. Jones and P. Sells, eds., *Proceedings of NELS 14*, pages 236–252. Amherst, MA: GLSA.

Matushansky, Ora. 2002. Tipping the scales: The syntax of scalarity in the complement of *seem*. *Syntax* 5(3):219–276.

McCloskey, James. 1979. *Transformational Syntax and Model Theoretic Semantics: A Case-Study in Modern Irish*. Dordrecht: Reidel.

McCloskey, James and Peter Sells. 1988. Control and A-chains in Modern Irish. *Natural Language and Linguistic Theory* 6:143–189.

Moore, John. 1998. Turkish copy-raising and A-chain locality. *Natural Language and Linguistic Theory* 16:149–189.

Parsons, Terence. 1990. *Events in the Semantics of English: A Study in Subatomic Semantics*. Cambridge, MA: MIT Press.

Perlmutter, David M. and Scott Soames. 1979. *Syntactic Argumentation and the Structure of English*. Berkeley, CA: University of California Press.

Postal, Paul. 1974. *On Raising*. Cambridge, MA: MIT Press.

Potsdam, Eric and Jeffrey T. Runner. 2001. Richard returns: Copy Raising and its implications. In M. Andronis, C. Ball, H. Elston, and S. Neuvel, eds., *CLS 37: The Main Session*, vol. 1, pages 453–468. Chicago, IL: Chicago Linguistic Society.

Rogers, Andy. 1971. Three kinds of physical perception verbs. In *Papers from the Seventh Regional Meeting of the Chicago Linguistic Society*, pages 206–222.

Rogers, Andy. 1972. Another look at flip perception verbs. In *Papers from the Eighth Regional Meeting of the Chicago Linguistic Society*, pages 303–315.

Rogers, Andy. 1974. A transderivational constraint on Richard? In *Papers from the Tenth Regional Meeting of the Chicago Linguistic Society*, pages 551–558.

Rogers, Andrew D., Jr. 1973. *Physical Perception Verbs in English: A Study in Lexical Relatedness*. Ph.D. thesis, UCLA.

Rosenbaum, Peter S. 1967. *The Grammar of English Predicate Complement Constructions*. Cambridge, MA: MIT Press.

Sells, Peter. 1984. *Syntax and Semantics of Resumptive Pronouns*. Ph.D. thesis, University of Massachusetts, Amherst.

Teleman, Ulf, Staffan Hellberg, and Erik Andersson. 1999. *Svenska Akademiens grammatik*. Stockholm: Norstedts.

Ura, Hiroyuki. 1998. Checking, economy, and copy-raising in Igbò. *Linguistic Analysis* 28:67–88.

van Egmond, Marie-Elaine. 2004. Copy raising in Dutch. Honours thesis, University of Canterbury, New Zealand.

4

Functional Identification of Complement Clauses in German and the Specification of COMP*

JUDITH BERMAN

4.1 Introduction

The grammatical function of complement clauses is controversial in LFG. While Kaplan and Zaenen (1989) and Bresnan (2001) assume that in English complement clauses have the grammatical function COMP, Dalrymple and Lødrup (2000) claim that English, German and Swedish are so-called mixed languages, i.e. a complement clause may either be a COMP or an OBJ, depending on the subcategorization requirements of the verb. In Berman (2003a) the traditional view of German syntax is pursued within LFG, according to which nominal and sentential complements (including the subject function) have parallel syntactic functions, i.e. as subjects (SUBJ), accusative objects (OBJ), prepositional objects (OBL_θ) or genitive objects (OBJ_θ). However, while the grammatical function of nominal and prepositional complements is identified by case or preposition and agreement, complement clauses are not morphologically marked in German and do not allow any morphological function specification. This article is especially concerned with the question of how the grammatical function of complement clauses can be identified. Different properties and tests will be discussed and

*For helpful discussions I am grateful to Christian Fortmann and Karin Pittner. Thanks to Steve Berman for correcting my English.

Architectures, Rules, and Preferences: Variations on Themes by Joan Bresnan.
Annie Zaenen, Jane Simpson, Tracy Holloway King,
Jane Grimshaw, Joan Maling, and Chris Manning, (eds.).

it will be shown that the structural position plays a crucial role in determining the grammatical function of complement clauses in German. While identification with SUBJ or OBJ is possible in topic position, in extraposed position they can only be identified as an underspecified complement which I claim to be COMP. The underspecification of COMP allows it to be integrated into the feature specification of the grammatical functions proposed in LFG.

4.2 Function identification in German

In Bresnan (2001) different ways of function specification are proposed. In endocentric organized categories c-structure positions are associated with specific grammatical functions. This correspondence is formulated in the Endocentric Mapping Principles (Bresnan 2001, 119). In exocentric phrases it is assumed that argument functions are identified by means of the morphological features borne by words themselves, e.g. case and agreement. Languages may mix endocentric and exocentric modes of c-structure organization. In German it is generally assumed that the grammatical function of nominal arguments is identified by the morphology. Although nouns are often without case flexives the NP is frequently case-marked by the determiner:

(1) **der** Hund, **den** Hund, **des** Hundes, **dem** Hund
the-NOM dog the-ACC dog the-GEN dog's the-DAT dog

In combination with subject-verb agreement syntactic functions are mainly indicated by the morphology and not determined by structural position.

In Berman (2003a) it is proposed that nominal arguments are adjoined to VP, a position which, according to the Endocentric Mapping Principles, allows morphological function specification. Compare now the formal properties of clausal arguments:

(2) a. Ihn freut, dass sie gewonnen hat.
him-ACC pleases that she won has
'He is pleased that she has won.'

b. Er sagt, dass sie gewonnen hat.
he says that she won has
'He says that she has won.'

c. Er vergewissert sich, dass sie gewonnen hat.
he makes-sure himself that she won has
'He makes sure that she has won.'

d. Er freut sich, dass sie gewonnen hat.
he pleases himself that she won has
'He is pleased that she has won.'

In (2) all clausal complements are formally identical. They are neither case-marked nor do they show agreement with the verb. In traditional German syntax they are nevertheless analyzed as subject clause (a), accusative object clause (b) genitive object clause (c) or prepositional object clause (d). Let us review how this function specification is accounted for.

4.3 Previous Accounts

4.3.1 Traditional German syntax

The main argument for identifying the function of a clause is its alternation with an NP which is related to the same argument position as the complement clause (e.g. Admoni 1982, Helbig and Buscha 2001, Oppenrieder 1991, Berman 2003a).

In German the alternation is possible with all complement clauses.[1]

(3) a. Ihn freut, dass sie gewonnen hat.
 b. Das (that-NOM) freut ihn.

(4) a. Er sagt, dass sie gewonnen hat.
 b. Er sagt das (that-ACC).

(5) a. Er vergewissert sich, dass sie gewonnen hat.
 b. Er vergewissert sich dessen (that-GEN).

(6) a. Er freut sich, dass sie gewonnen hat.
 b. Er freut sich darüber (it-about).

The fact that the clause can be substituted by the NP is taken as evidence of functional identity. The function of the NP can be identified by the morphology.

4.3.2 Dalrymple/Lødrup (2000), Lødrup (2004)

Dalrymple and Lødrup (2000) and Lødrup (2004) claim that UG provides two different functions for clausal complements, namely OBJ and COMP. They assume that if a complement clause can alternate with an NP-OBJ, coordinate with an NP-OBJ[2] or undergo passivization and unbounded dependencies, then it is an OBJ. If not, it has the function COMP. Dalrymple/Lødrup claim German is a mixed language, i.e. complement clauses in German may be either OBJ or COMP.

[1]Since the properties of a subject clause are similiar to complement clauses, e.g. with respect to extraposition and also alternation, I include it under the term complement clause to avoid confusion between argument as syntactic function and argument as θ-role.

[2]This test is not used in Lødrup (2004).

Let us briefly review these tests for German (see also Lødrup 2004 for a general discussion of these tests):

Alternation with an NP-object As we have seen, alternation is also used in traditional German syntax.

However, it is problematic to base function specification on the existence of alternating forms, since some verbs allow different pronominal forms, e.g.:[3]

(7) a. Sie hatte gehofft, dass sie bald fertig ist.
she had hoped that she soon finished is
'She had hoped that she would finish soon.'

b. Sie hatte es/darauf gehofft.
She had it/it-on hoped
'She had hoped so/for it.'

The complement clause of the verb *hoffen* in (7a) can alternate either with an OBJ (*es*) or with an OBL (*darauf*). This shows that function specification can't be based exclusively on alternating forms (see also 4.3.4).

Hence, alternation does not give us a reliable test for functional identity.

Coordination This test is based on the assumption that only phrases with identical function can be coordinated. However it is debatable whether identical functions are an obligatory requirement for coordination. The examples in (8) show that phrases with different grammatical functions can be coordinated as long as they are related to the same argument:

(8) Er erinnerte sich nicht seiner Versäumnisse aber stets
he reminded himself not his-GEN failings but always
an seine Verdienste.
at his merits
'He didn't remember his failings but always his merits'

Although an NP-object may be coordinated with a complement clause in German, the coordination data are not sufficent to determine the grammatical function of complement clauses.

Passivization This test is based on the observation that the SUBJ of the passive clause is the OBJ in the parallel active clause. Hence, by the active-passive diathesis we should be able to determine the grammatical function of the arguments.

Consider, however, the following data:

[3]Cf. Lødrup (2004, 87), who makes the same point with respect to some verbs in Norwegian.

(9) a. Er hat gezweifelt, ob sie kommen wird.
he has doubted if she come will
'He doubted whether she would come.'

b. Immer wieder wurde gezweifelt, ob sie kommen wird.
always again was doubted if she come will
'Again and again it was doubted, if she would come.'

(10) a. Er sagte, dass sie kommen wird.
he said that she come will
'He said that she would come.'

b. Immer wieder wurde gesagt, dass sie kommen wird.
always again was said that she come will
'Again and again it was said that she would come.'

In both cases passivization is possible. However, since German allows impersonal passive we can't conclude that the complement clauses are objects in (a) and subjects in (b). Since the complement clauses are formally identical, passivization does not give us a hint about the grammatical function of the complement clause.[4]

Unbounded dependencies This test is based on the observation that some verbs allow topicalization of the complement clause and some do not (cf. e.g. Webelhuth 1992 for German). Dalrymple and Lødrup (2000) claim that OBJ-clauses can be topicalized, but clauses in the function COMP cannot. According to them, the function of the complement clause is exclusively determined by the subcategorizing verb and is independent of its structural position. Hence, the possibility of topicalization is based on the subcategorization requirements of the verb with the additional assumption - adopted from Kaplan and Zaenen (1989) (cf. 4.3.3) - that COMP can't enter into unbounded dependencies. However, it is unclear how this assumption can be motivated.

In section 4.4 I discuss to what extent the restriction on topicalization gives evidence of the function of the complement clauses in German. But before that, I will briefly contrast the analysis of Dalrymple and Lødrup (2000) with that of Kaplan and Zaenen (1989) and Bresnan (2001), according to which the function of a complement clauses depends on its structural position.

4.3.3 Kaplan/Zaenen (1989/1995), Bresnan (2001)

According to Bresnan (2001):

[4]Only the nominal realizations of the arguments show that the verbs have different subcategorization frames. While *zweifeln* (*doubt*) takes a SUBJ and an OBL_θ (*Er (he-*NOM*) hat an ihm (on him) gezweifelt*), *sagen* (*say*) takes a SUBJ and an OBJ (*Er (he-*NOM*) hat es (it-*ACC*) gesagt*). So we have to refer to the alternating NP or PP to determine the function.

(11) The canonical stuctural realization of subject and object functions is nominal. (Bresnan 2001, 20)

Therefore, in English a complement clause can't be annotated with the SUBJ or the OBJ, but has the grammatical function COMPL.[5] Similarily, Kaplan and Zaenen (1989) propose that in English all extraposed clauses are annotated with COMP.

To account for the restriction on topicalization, Kaplan/Zaenen assume that COMP is excluded from the extractable functions and propose that topicalized complement clauses may be unified by functional uncertainty with e.g. OBJ or OBJ_θ, as long as this is compatible with the subcategorization requirements of the verb. Bresnan assumes that in English a topicalized clause, annotated with the discourse function TOPIC, may be identified with the SUBJ by default (Bresnan 1995, 2001). Topicalized clauses other than subject are associated with an NP-gap. By inside-out functional uncertainty the topicalized clause is identified with the nominal argument function (Bresnan 2001).

The result of both accounts is, on the one hand, that a verb subcategorizes different grammatical functions depending on their categorial realization:

(12) a. I believe it. (OBJ)
b. I believe that this might be true. (COMP)

and on the other hand, that complement clauses have different grammatical functions depending on their structural position, e.g. (Kaplan and Zaenen 1989, 156f. (51)/(52)):

(13) a. Louise told me that Denny was mean to her. (COMP)
b. That Denny was mean to her Louise told me (already). (OBJ_θ)

All of these analyses make use of the complement function COMP. Let us, therefore, take a closer look at the grammatical function COMP.

4.3.4 The complement function 'COMP'

We have seen that in traditional German syntax the substitution of the complement clause with an NP or PP related to the same argument position is taken as evidence of functional identity. Since all complement clauses can be substituted by an NP or a PP there is no need for a further complement function for clausal complements. However, in LFG it is postulated that an NP and a clause related to the same argument may differ functionally, e.g. the NP may be an OBJ while the CP may

[5] Bresnan (2001) uses COMPL, which subsumes the function of finite complement clauses. I will continue to use the term COMP, since I treating the grammatical function of finite complement clauses only.

be a COMP. COMP is taken to be an instance of a complement function like OBJ, OBJ_θ and OBL_θ.[6]

It is well-known that being related to the same argument does not imply functional identity, cf. e.g. passive or locative inversion. In LFG this is captured by the Lexical Mapping Theory. Mapping principles allow an underspecified thematic role to be mapped to different grammatical functions. However it is unclear how the grammatical function COMP could be integrated into Lexical Mapping Theory.[7] Syntactic functions are not taken as primitives, but are defined by the two binary-valued features [+/− restricted] and [+/− objective]. However, this allows the specification of only four argument functions, namely SUBJ, OBJ, OBJ_θ, OBL_θ (cf. the discussion of COMP on the lfg-list initiated by Alsina et al. 1996).

(14)

	−r	+r
−o	SUBJ	OBL_θ
+o	OBJ	OBJ_θ

To date, it is not evident how to integrate COMP into the feature decomposition of argument functions and capture the alternation of OBJ and COMP by the Lexical Mapping Theory.

One possiblity is proposed by Zaenen and Engdahl (1994). They assume that the a-structure of a verb selecting a clausal complement contains a proposition, which is associated with [−o]. According to the mapping principles, the proposition is mapped to the lowest possible function, which, in their analysis, is XCOMP.[8] They assume that XCOMP is a specialization of OBL_θ (Zaenen and Engdahl 1994, 197f.).

In contrast to Zaenen/Engdahl I will assume that the argument structure of a verb is the same regardless of the categorial realization of the complements (cf. Berman et al. 1998, Berman 2003a). So I assume that the θ-roles of the pronoun *es* and the *dass*-clause in (15) are identical.

(15) a. Er glaubt es.
he believes it

[6]COMP is used not only for the grammatical function of finite complement clauses but also for the complement function of other non-nominal categories which are anaphorically controlled (cf. Bresnan 1982, Dalrymple 2001). Again, in this article I confine the discussion to the finite clausal complements.

[7]In early LFG function alternation was captured by lexical rules. In Kaplan/Zaenen extraposition is formulated as a lexical rule which should also be expressible by mapping principles.

[8]Zaenen/Engdahl discuss the mapping of the non-finite complement of the verb *try* as in *John tried to leave.*

b. Er glaubt, dass es so ist.
he believes that it so is

In the following I examine whether there is evidence in German for the claim that nominal and clausal complements have different grammatical functions, hence, whether it is adequate to postulate that finite complement clauses are COMP and, secondly, to what extent structural position plays a role in determining the grammatical function of complement clauses.

4.4 Structural position and functional identification of finite complement clauses in German

4.4.1 German sentence structure

In Berman (2003a) I proposed a c-structure of sentential phrases in German. According to this German clausal structure has one functional projection CP. Left-dislocated phrases are adjoined to CP, topicalized constituents occur in CP-Spec, nominal arguments are left-adjoined to VP, and extraposed constituents are right-adjoined to VP.

4.4.2 Structural positions of complement clauses in German

Complement clauses may occur in different structural positions.[9] They can be left-dislocated, topicalized[10], extraposed and they can occur as a constituent of a topicalized VP.[11] However not every position is open to all complement clauses.

All clausal complements can be left-dislocated. Left-dislocated phrases cooccur with a resumptive pronoun in CP-Spec, e.g.:

(16) a. Dass sie kommen wird, **das** bezweifelt er.
that she come will that doubts he
'That she will come, he doubts.'

b. Dass sie kommen wird, **darauf** freut er sich.
that she come will on-it pleases he himself
'That she will come, he is happy about it.'

In CP-Spec, however, only those clausal complements are grammatical which can be replaced by a nominative or accusative NP, e.g.:

(17) a. Dass sie kommen wird, bezweifelt er.
That she come will doubts he

b. *Dass sie kommen wird, freut er sich.
That she come will pleases he himself

[9] For a more detailed description of the data cf. Berman (2003b).

[10] I confine the discussion to local topicalization.

[11] The occurence of complement clauses in the *Mittelfeld*, i.e. left-adjoined to VP, is generally assumed to be marked.

All complement clauses can be extraposed:

(18) a. Er bezweifelt, dass sie kommen wird.
he doubts that she come will

b. Er freut sich, dass sie kommen wird.
he pleases himself that she come will

Only some complement clauses (see section 4.4.5) may occur as a constituent of a topicalized VP:

(19) Bezweifelt, dass sie kommen wird, hat er nie.
doubted that she come will has he never

The non-uniform distribution of the different types of complement clauses suggests that these structural positions do not behave identically. Since left-dislocated complement clauses occur with a resumptive pronoun, which allows morphological function specification, I will concentrate in the following on the topicalized, extraposed and VP-internal position of complement clauses.

Let us first compare the structural position of topicalized and extraposed constituents. They differ in terms of category as well as function:

In CP-Spec both nominal and clausal phrases can occur, whereas extraposition of nominal phrases is excluded.

In CP-Spec argument as well as adjunct functions can be identified, while attributes and sentential relatives are excluded. In extraposed position all these functions are grammatical.

As far as complement clauses are concerned, we have already seen that in extraposed position all complement clauses may occur, while in topicalized position only some complement clauses are grammatical. Interestingly, extraposed subordinated clauses with the complementizer *wenn* (*if*) or *als* (*when*), which normally indicate adjunct status, can also fill the argument position of the verb. This is not possible if they are topicalized:

(20) a. Ich bedauere (es), wenn Sie nicht kommen können.
I regret (it) if you not come can
'I'll regret it, if you can't come.'

b. *Wenn Sie nicht kommen können, bedaure ich.
if you not come can, regret I
'*If you can't come, I'll regret.'

All these facts suggest that the identification of the grammatical function and the linking to a-structure differ in these two positions.

4.4.3 Functional identification in CP-Spec

Based on data involving weak crossover, it can be shown that in German CP-Spec allows morphological function specification (cf. Berman 2003a).

However, clausal complements don't have any morphological marking. The following examples show how functional identification may work under these conditions.

First, note that German is a Topic Drop language, i.e., a constituent that bears the discourse function TOPIC may be phonetically unrealized in CP-Spec, e.g.:

(21) Kenn ich nicht.
know I not.

As was observed e.g. by Huang (1984), in German Topic Drop is only possible with the SUBJ and OBJ. This means that without any functional marking the identification of grammatical functions in CP-Spec is restricted to SUBJ and OBJ. This can be explained as default identification of the TOPIC with the SUBJ or the OBJ. (Cf. the analysis of Bresnan 2001, 20f. for topicalized subject clauses in English. However, while in English the default identification of the TOPIC is restricted to the SUBJ, in German it includes the SUBJ and the OBJ, both unrestricted grammatical functions.)

Further evidence of the special status of SUBJ and OBJ in CP-Spec is provided by data involving case-ambiguous NPs (examples from Bader et al. 2000, 35f. (2)–(3):

(22) a. Fritz hat die Oma nicht angerufen.
Fritz-SUBJ/OBJ has the grandma-SUBJ/OBJ not called
'Fritz didn't call grandma./Grandma didn't call Fritz.'

b. Fritz hat die Oma nicht geholfen.
Fritz-OBJ_θ has the grandma-SUBJ not helped
'Grandma didn't help Fritz.'

While a SUBJ or OBJ in CP-Spec can be identified without problems even if the NP is case-ambiguous as in (22a), sentences such as (22b) where the case-ambiguous NP in CP-Spec has the function OBJ_θ are difficult to parse.[12]

We can summarize that CP-Spec allows the identification of SUBJ and OBJ without further specifications. However the identification of

[12]As shown by Bader (1996) , different factors have to be taken into account to capture the markedness of (22b), including basic word order, case ambiguity and focus projection. Case ambiguity was shown to be the most important factor. See Bader (1996), Bader et al. (2000) for details.

OBJ$_\theta$ is subject to further restrictions. Parallels can be observed with clausal complements. Clausal complements which occur in CP-Spec are interpretated as SUBJ and OBJ.

In short, my claim is that CP-Spec is annotated with a discourse function. Lacking morphology or further function-specific information, the discourse function is restricted to [−r] arguments, hence in CP-Spec complement clauses are identified with SUBJ or OBJ.

4.4.4 Functional identification of extraposed phrases and the mapping of 'COMP'

We have seen that in CP-Spec morphological function specification as well as default identification of the discourse function with SUBJ or OBJ is possible. The extraposed position, adjoined to VP, is not annotated with a discourse function. Hence default identification is excluded. Morphological identification is done by annotated case conditionals, e.g ($\downarrow$ CASE) = ACC $\Rightarrow$ ($\uparrow$ OBJ) = $\downarrow$, on nominal c-structure positions. Since morphological function specification is generally excluded in extraposed position (NPs can't occur there), and furthermore the specification of SUBJ, OBJ, OBJ$_\theta$, OBL$_\theta$ is mainly tied to morphology in German, I assume that in extraposed position the identification of SUBJ, OBJ, OBJ$_\theta$, OBL$_\theta$ is not possible.

However, as we have observed, all complement clauses can occur in extraposed position and they can fill all (semantically compatible) argument slots of the verb.[13] This contrasts with the behaviour of complement clauses in sentence initial position, where complement clauses which are not related to a [−r] argument are only grammatical if they cooccur with a resumptive pronoun.

Since extraposed complement clauses can be linked to all (semantically compatible) argument positions, they must be compatible with all features these arguments are associated with, e.g. :

(23) a. Er sagt es/dass es stimmt.
he says it-ACC/that it is-right
sagen < θ θ >
[−o] [−r]

b. Er zweifelt daran/dass es stimmt.
he doubts it-on/that it is-right
zweifeln < θ θ >
[−o] [−o]

[13]There are some verbs in German which require an extraposed clause to cooccur obligatorily with a correlative element, especially verbs subcategorizing an OBL$_\theta$.

c. Er vergewisserte sich dessen/dass es stimmt.
he made-sure himself that-GEN/that it is-right.
vergewissern < θ θ >
[−o] [+o]

By principles of the Lexical Mapping Theory the θ-roles are mapped onto grammatical functions, e.g. onto a SUBJ and OBJ with *sagen* or a SUBJ and OBL_θ with *zweifeln*. However, since the grammatical function of extraposed complement clauses is indicated neither by morphology nor by distinct structural position, clausal complements can't be identifed as a specific complement function, as is possible with nominal arguments. The only indication of the grammatical function of the clause is provided by the complementizer, which allows identification as an (unspecific) complement. I suggest, therefore, that in extraposed position complement clauses are identified as underspecified complements.

(24) *glauben* < θ θ >
[−o] [−r]
↓ ↓
PRED SUBJ OBJ

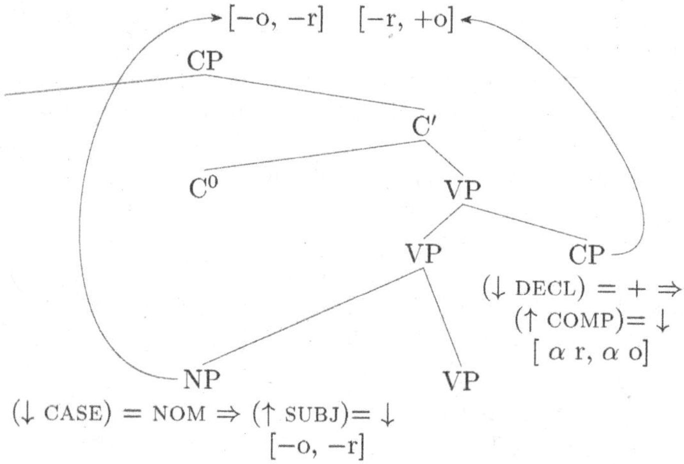

This underspecified complement function is taken to be COMP. So we can assume that in extraposed position, a position where NPs can't occur, conditionals like the following are annotated: (↓ DECL) = + ⇒ (↑ COMP) = ↓.[14] COMP is taken to be underspecified in the sense that the two feature [o] and [r] are not further specified, notated as [α o]

[14]Equivalent conditionals could be formulated for embedded interrogative complement clauses.

and [α r]. Since the features are not specified to a certain value they are compatible with all the feature specifications of the subcategorized functions. The result is that complement clauses are identified as COMP in extraposed position, but being underspecified they are compatible with the subcategorization requirements of the verb.

The underspecification of COMP results in the combination of the categorial status of the clausal complement (lacking morphology) and the special properties of the extraposed position (compatible with all (semantic compatible) argument positions).

In short, my claim is therefore that complement clauses in extraposed position are identified as COMP. COMP is an underspecified complement function [α r, α o] compatible with the feature specification of SUBJ [−o,−r], OBJ [−r, +o], OBL$_\theta$ [−o,+r], OBJ$_\theta$ [+r, +o].

4.4.5 VP-internal topicalization of the complement clause

As shown in section (4.4.2), complement clauses may occur in another structural position, namely as a constituent of a topicalized VP:

(25) Gesagt, dass ich einverstanden bin, habe ich bestimmt nicht.
said that I agreed am have I certainly not
'I certainly did not say that I agree.'

It can be shown that this position is not identical with the extraposed position. Non-integrated subordinated clauses, as well as complement clauses corresponding to the subject-argument are excluded in this position, e.g. :

(26) a. Natürlich hat mich gefreut, dass er einverstanden ist.
Naturally has me pleased that he agreed is
'Naturally I am pleased that he agreed'

b. *Gefreut, dass er einverstanden ist, hat mich schon.
Pleased that he agreed is has me sure

We can conclude that there is a difference in the function identification of complement clauses in extraposed and the VP-internal position. I assume that the VP-internal position is the sister of the verb. I propose that the functional identification of a complement clause which is a sister of the verb is structural. Structural function specification excludes identification as a SUBJ.

In short, my claim is therefore that the function of a VP-internal topicalized complement clause is structurally identified. Being a sister of the verb, identification as SUBJ is not possible.

4.5 Summary

This article was concerned with the question of how the function of complement clauses is identified. Since complement clauses do not have any morphological marking, function identification by case and agreement, as with nominal arguments in German, is not possible. Clausal complements can occur in different structural positions and in agreement with the analysis of Kaplan and Zaenen (1989) and Bresnan (2001) it was claimed that clauses may differ functionally depending on the structural position. The reason for this is that the grammatical function of the complement clause is identified by different means in different structural positions. With left-dislocated clauses the function identification is done by the resumptive proform, i.e. morphologically. Based on data from Topic-Drop and case-ambiguous NPs, it was shown that in CP-Spec there is a preference for identifying morphologically unmarked and case-ambiguous phrases with SUBJ or OBJ. This is in accordance with the fact that the occurrence of complement clauses in CP-Spec is restricted to these two functions. It was assumed that German has a default identification of the Topic with SUBJ or OBJ. With VP-internal topicalization structural function identification is assumed. As sister of the verb the complement clause can't be identified as a SUBJ. In extraposed position neither morphological nor structural function specification is possible. The formal properties of complement clauses allow them only to be identified as a not further specified complement, which was claimed to be COMP. Since extraposed complement clauses can be related to various argument positions and alternate with all nominal argument functions, it was proposed that COMP is an underspecified complement function, compatible with all feature specifications of the argument functions.

References

Admoni, Wladimir. 1982. *Der deutsche Sprachbau.* München: Beck. 4th edition.

Alsina, Alex, KP Mohanan, and Tara Mohanan. 1996. Submission to the LFG list. 3 September 1996. `http://listserv.-linguistlist.org/cgi-bin/wa?A2=ind96&L=lfg&D=1&F=&S=&P=11516.`

Bader, Markus. 1996. *Sprachverstehen.* Opladen: Westdeutscher Verlag.

Bader, Markus, Michael Meng, Josef Bayer, and Jens-Max Hopf. 2000. Syntaktische Funktions-Ambiguitäten im Deutschen. *Zeitschrift für Sprachwissenschaft* 19(1):34–102.

Berman, Judith. 2003a. *Clausal Syntax of German.* Stanford, CA. CSLI Publications.

Berman, Judith. 2003b. Zum Einfluss der strukturellen Position auf die syntaktische Funktion der Komplementsätze. *Deutsche Sprache* 3:263–286.

Berman, Judith, Stefanie Dipper, Christian Fortmann, and Jonas Kuhn. 1998. Argument clauses and correlative *es* in German — deriving discourse properties in a unification analysis. In M. Butt and T. H. King, eds., *Proceedings of the International Lexical-Functional Grammar Conference 1998 (LFG'98)*. Brisbane: CSLI Online Publications.

Bresnan, Joan. 1982. Control and complementation. *Linguistic Inquiry* 13(3):343–434.

Bresnan, Joan. 1995. Category mismatches. In A. Akinlabi, ed., *Theoretical Approaches to African Languages*, pages 19–46. Trenton, NJ: African World Press.

Bresnan, Joan. 2001. *Lexical-Functional Syntax*. Oxford: Blackwell.

Dalrymple, Mary. 2001. *Lexical Functional Grammar*, vol. 34 of *Syntax and Semantics*. New York, NY: Academic Press.

Dalrymple, Mary and Helge Lødrup. 2000. The grammatical functions of complement clauses. In M. Butt and T. H. King, eds., *Proceedings of the International Lexical-Functional Grammar Conference 2000 (LFG'00)*, pages 104–121. Berkeley, CA: CSLI Online Publications.

Helbig, Gerhard and Joachim Buscha. 2001. *Deutsche Grammatik. Ein Handbuch für den Ausländerunterricht*. Leipzig: Langenscheidt, 20th edn.

Huang, C.-T. James. 1984. On the distribution and references of empty pronouns. *Linguistic Inquiry* 15(4):531–574.

Kaplan, Ronald M. and Annie Zaenen. 1989. Long-distance dependencies, constituent structure, and functional uncertainty. In M. Baltin and A. Kroch, eds., *Alternative Conceptions of Phrase Structure*, pages 17–42. Chicago, IL: Chicago University Press. Reprinted in M. Dalrymple *et al.*, eds., *Formal Issues in Lexical-Functional Grammar*, pages 137–165. Stanford, CA: CSLI Publications. 1995.

Lødrup, Helge. 2004. Clausal complementation in Norwegian. *Nordic Journal of Linguistics* 27(1):61–95.

Oppenrieder, Wilhelm. 1991. *Von Subjekten, Sätzen und Subjektsätzen*. Tübingen: Niemeyer.

Webelhuth, Gert. 1992. *Principles and Parameter of Syntactic Saturation*. Oxford: Oxford University Press.

Zaenen, Annie and Elisabet Engdahl. 1994. Descriptive and theoretical syntax in the lexicon. In B. Atkins and A. Zambolli, eds., *Computational Approaches to the Lexicon*, pages 181–212. Oxford: Oxford University Press.

5

The Absence of Traces: Evidence from Weak Crossover

Mary Dalrymple, Ronald M Kaplan, and Tracy Holloway King

5.1 Long-distance dependencies in LFG

Traces were introduced in transformational grammar (Chomsky 1973) in order to give a phrasal account for a wide range of long-distance dependency phenomena: a long-distance dependency between a displaced element in a wh-question or relative clause was assumed to arise by movement of the displaced element, which leaves behind a 'trace' in its original position. The original LFG treatment of long distance dependencies (Kaplan and Bresnan. 1982) was based on an adaptation of the transformational/phrase-structure scheme. The relation between the displaced wh-phrase and its within-clause function was defined in terms of a relation between the wh-word and an empty c-structure constituent, a trace, within the clause. In example (1), the relation between the NP node dominating *who* and the NP node dominating its trace, represented by t, ensures that the wh-phrase *who* is both the FOCUS and the OBJ of the sentence:

Architectures, Rules, and Preferences: Variations on Themes by Joan Bresnan.
Annie Zaenen, Jane Simpson, Tracy Holloway King,
Jane Grimshaw, Joan Maling, and Chris Manning, (eds.).

(1)

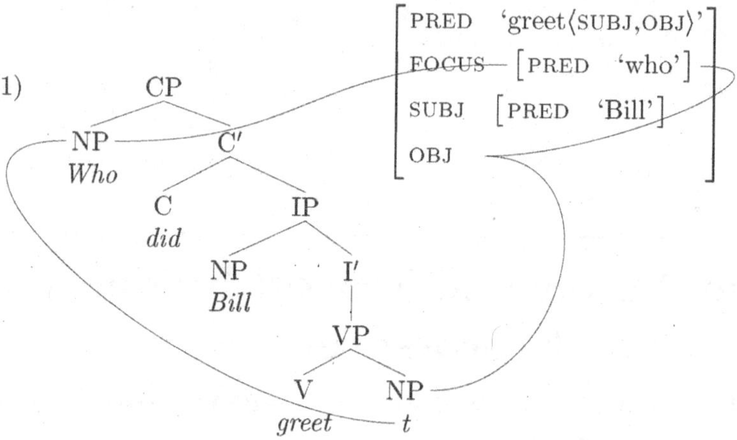

Subsequently, however, Kaplan and Zaenen (1989) proposed that constraints on long distance dependencies are best stated in functional and not phrasal terms, arguing that *functional uncertainty* offers a more accurate and direct characterization of the long distance dependency. A rule like the one in example (2) establishes two roles for the NP daughter of CP: it is the FOCUS, and it plays a grammatical role defined by the functional uncertainty path COMP* OBJ:

(2) CP $\longrightarrow$ NP C′
($\uparrow$ FOCUS) = $\downarrow$ $\uparrow$=$\downarrow$
($\uparrow$ COMP* OBJ) = $\downarrow$

In example (3), the path consisting simply of OBJ is chosen, and the FOCUS f-structure also appears as the OBJ of *greet*:

(3)

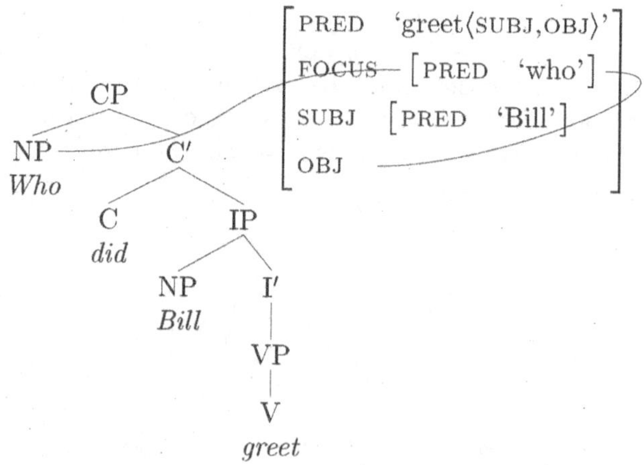

With this account, long distance dependencies no longer provide arguments that trace-like devices are *necessary* in the theory of grammar. And in fact, a traceless theory is preferred for two reasons: it is more adequate descriptively, and it offers theoretical advantages. We outline these reasons below before discussing examples involving weak crossover and how a traceless theory can account for them.

A traceless theory is descriptively more adequate. That is, it can describe data that the traceful theory cannot, as argued in detail by Kaplan and Zaenen (1989). Kaplan and Zaenen (1989) cite evidence from wandering adverbs in Icelandic, cross-categorial dependencies in English, and cross-conjunct relativization constraints in Japanese that can be accounted for naturally in a traceless, but not a traceful, analysis. More recently, Sag (1998) has provided additional evidence against traces in his analysis of the conjunct constraint and of floating quantifiers and adverbs.

For several reasons, a traceless theory is also theoretically preferred. That is, even if the traceless and traceful theories accounted for exactly the same data, the traceless theory is preferable. First, the traceless theory is less redundant in that there is only a single mechanism needed to deal with long distance dependencies. LFG accounts which use the additional device of traces must still rely on functional uncertainty or some other linking device to connect the filler with the gap. It is a general scientific principle that less redundant theories are preferred to more redundant ones. Second, the traceful theory is less tractable mathematically, since it is difficult to constrain how functional uncertainty interacts with the c-structure possibilities of empty trace nodes. This is because subcategorization is the controlling factor in determining how long distance dependencies are resolved, and subcategorization requirements in LFG are stated at the level of f-structure. Further, the listener's perceptual problem is simpler with the traceless theory: the listener must guess only the function of the displaced element, not both a function and a position. Finally, the traceless theory avoids spuriously ambiguous analyses for fillers without 'canonical' phrase-structure positions. For example, in extraction of obliques and adverbs there is more than one possible extraction site, even in a relatively fixed word order language like English, as shown in (4).

(4) a. Oblique extr.: About what did John talk (t) to Mary (t)?
b. Adverb extr.: How often did John talk (t) to Mary (t) about apples (t)?

Thus, there are both empirical and theoretical reasons to prefer the traceless account.

5.2 Weak crossover: A counterexample?

Despite the appeal of a traceless analysis of long distance dependencies, there is evidence that seems to suggest that traces cannot be eliminated: *weak crossover* (Postal 1971, Wasow 1979) seems to indicate that the linear position encoded by a trace does affect grammaticality. The sentence in (5) exemplifies a weak crossover violation:

(5) *Who$_i$ did his$_i$ mother greet *t*?
(cannot mean: Whose$_i$ mother greeted him$_i$?)

The name 'crossover' comes from the transformational analysis of wh-question formation: in a crossover violation, the wh-phrase 'crosses over' a coreferential pronoun when it is moved to the beginning of a sentence. In later analyses, the violation has been reformulated in terms of the position of the trace: a crossover violation ensues when, as in (5), a coreferential pronoun precedes the trace. We concentrate here on *weak crossover* violations, those in which the pronoun precedes but does not c-command the trace. Crossover effects are found in *operator binding*, in particular, binding by WH-operators and quantifiers (Reinhart 1983):

(6) a. *Who$_i$ did his$_i$ mother greet?
b. *His$_i$ mother greeted everyone$_i$.

Our main focus here is on the question of the necessity of traces, and our discussion will center around operator binding in wh-questions. We make only some brief remarks below about quantifier binding in German and English.

Some recent LFG accounts of operator binding and weak crossover propose a return to a theory of long distance dependency with traces (Bresnan 1994, 1995, 1998, 2001, Berman 2000, 2003); these theories adopt the view that the relation between the pronoun and a trace of the displaced wh-phrase is the important one for characterizing weak crossover violations. These theories propose a representation like the one in example (7) for a question like *Who did his mother greet?*, and rule out coreference between the pronoun *his* and the operator *who* by reference to the relation between the position of the pronoun and the position of the trace of *who*:

(7)

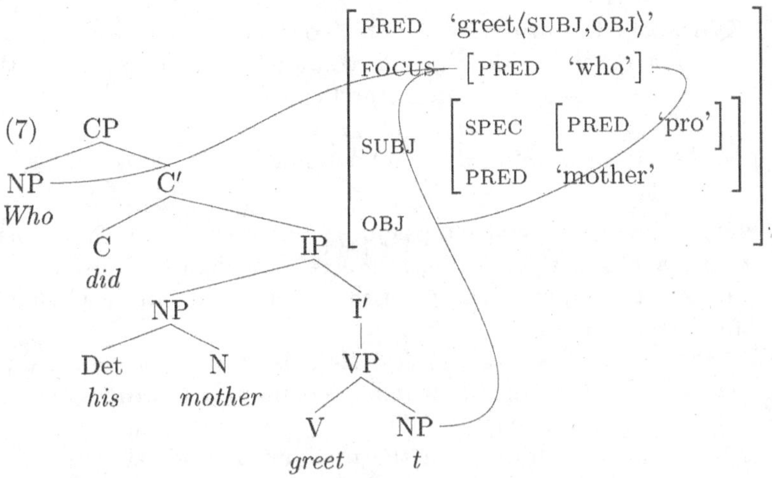

In the following, we provide a reformulation of the constraints on the relation between a pronoun and an operator that allow an account of these examples *without* traces.

5.3 Prominence

Bresnan (1994, 1995, 2001) proposes that operator binding relations are constrained by (at least) two dimensions of *prominence*: syntactic prominence depends on the functional rank of the operator and the pronoun it binds, and linear prominence depends on the linear order between an operator and a pronoun that it binds. We first discuss Bresnan's definitions and then provide a revised set of definitions of these two prominence dimensions.

5.3.1 Syntactic and linear prominence

Bresnan (2001) defines operator binding requirements in the following way:[1]

[1]The definition of Syntactic Prominence in (8) combines Bresnan's Rank Condition (Bresnan 2001, p. 198) with her generalization of that condition to Operator Complexes (Bresnan 2001, p. 204).

(8) **Syntactic Prominence** (A unit containing) the pronoun may not be higher than (a unit containing) the operator on the grammatical function hierarchy:
SUBJ > OBJ > COMP > ...
Linear Prominence The pronoun must not f-precede the operator.

Bresnan further proposes that languages can vary in which of these constraints apply: some languages impose both kinds of prominence constraints, some require only one or the other, some require a disjunction of the two.

We believe that Bresnan's basic insight is correct: prominence requirements between an operator and a pronoun are multifaceted, and different languages can impose different kinds of prominence requirements between an operator and the pronoun it binds. It turns out, however, that a simple redefinition of the linear prominence condition makes many of the same predictions as the definitions above, including for the crucial cases of weak crossover, without assuming traces.

5.3.2 Rethinking linear prominence

The intuition behind our reformulation is that linear precedence requirements between an operator and a pronoun are determined by the overt material which indicates the *syntactic role* of the displaced phrase. This intuition follows the proposal of Sag (1998), though it differs in detail.

A theory with traces accounts for the unacceptability of an example like **Who(m) did Sue talk about his mother to?* by reference to the relation between the pronoun *his* and the trace in the object position of the pronoun *to*, as in (9a). In contrast, our theory (like Sag's) refers to the relation between the position of the pronoun and the position of the stranded preposition *to*. The same results obtain, but without positing a trace, as in (9b).

(9) a. Traces: *Who$_i$ did Sue talk about his$_i$ mother to t_i?
b. No traces: *Who$_i$ did Sue talk about his$_i$ mother [to]?

We first define the notion of *coargument* to encompass the arguments as well as the adjuncts of a single predicate:

(10) **Coarguments**:

the arguments and adjuncts of a single predicate.

We also assume the definition of f-precedence in (11), which follows the original proposal of Bresnan (1984), but differs from some subsequent proposals (e.g., Bresnan 1995, 2001). It is important to note that our proposed redefinition of linear precedence does not depend on adopting this particular formulation of f-precedence as opposed to the more recent proposals.

(11) **F-precedence**:

f_1 f-precedes f_2 if and only if all c-structure nodes corresponding to f_1 precede all nodes corresponding to f_2. (e.g. Kaplan 1989)

We now present our revised prominence requirements:

(12) Let CoargOp and CoargPro be coargument f-structures such that CoargOp contains O and CoargPro contains P. Then:

Syntactic Prominence An operator O is more prominent than a pronoun P if and only if CoargOp is at least as high as CoargPro on the functional hierarchy.

Linear Prominence An operator O is more prominent than a pronoun P if and only if CoargOp f-precedes P.

The most important difference between our revised definitions and those in (8) is that linear prominence depends on the f-precedence properties of *CoargOp*, an f-structure containing the operator, *not* on the operator itself.

5.4 Evaluating the proposal

In this section, we show how our revised definitions can account for weak crossover phenomena in English, German, and Malayalam, without positing traces.

5.4.1 English

Following Bresnan (1995), we assume that in English, the operator must outrank any pronoun it binds in both Linear Prominence and Syntactic Prominence. With this, we correctly predict the unacceptability of example (13):

(13)

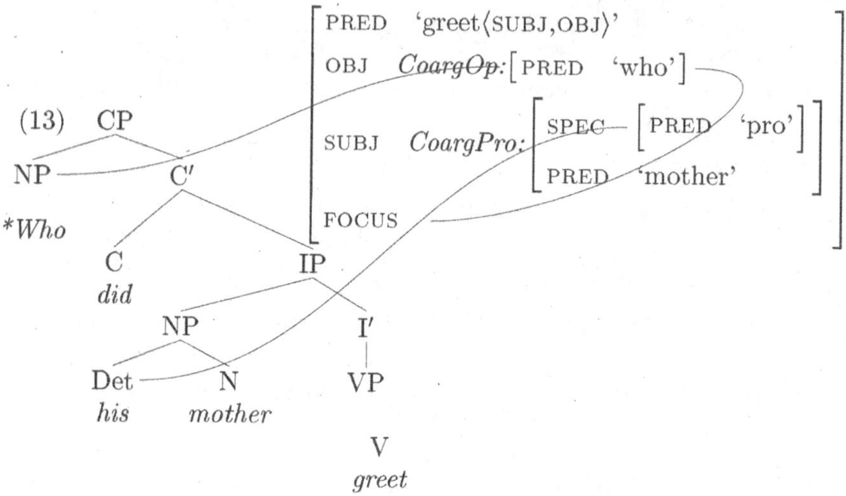

To apply our definitions of prominence, we must first locate the f-structure coarguments that contain the operator and the pronoun. We observe the following:

- SUBJ and OBJ of *greet* are coarguments
- pronoun is *his*
- SUBJ of *greet* contains the pronoun, so it is CoargPro
- OBJ of *greet* contains the operator, so it is CoargOp

On this basis, we check whether both Linear Prominence and Syntactic Prominence are satisfied. In (13), the OBJ *who* f-precedes the pronoun, since every c-structure node corresponding to the OBJ f-structure precedes the pronoun; thus, the Linear Prominence requirement is satisfied. However, the Syntactic Prominence requirement is violated, since CoargPro (SUBJ) outranks CoargOp (OBJ) on the functional hierarchy. This accounts for the unacceptability of the example.

Next, we examine the grammatical sentence *Who$_i$ did Sue talk to about his$_i$ mother?*:

(14) Who$_i$ did Sue talk to about his$_i$ mother?

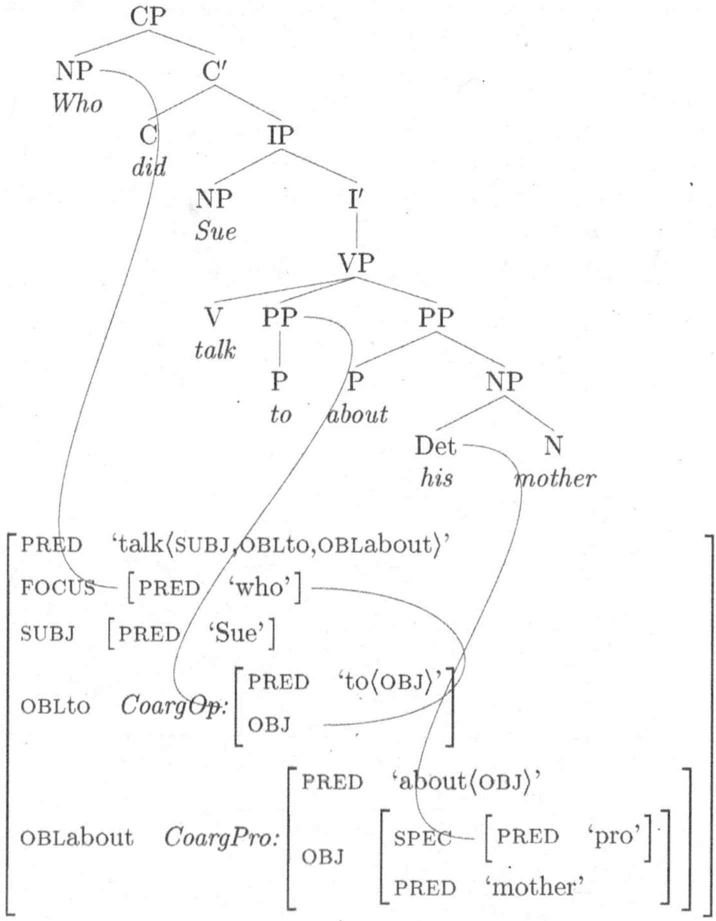

In this example:

- OBLto and OBLabout of *talk* are coarguments
- pronoun is *his*
- OBLabout of *talk* contains the pronoun, so it is CoargPro
- OBLto of *talk* contains the operator, so it is CoargOp

Again, we check to make sure that both Linear Prominence and Syntactic Prominence are satisfied. The syntactic prominence requirement is satisfied: no matter whether we assume that all obliques occupy the same rank on the functional hierarchy or that obliques are ranked relative to each other according to the thematic hierarchy (goal > theme), the CoargOp (OBLto/goal argument) is at least as high as CoargPro (OBLabout/theme argument) on the functional hierarchy. The Linear Prominence requirement is also met. The CoargOp f-structure corresponds to the c-structure nodes PP and P dominating *to*. CoargOp f-precedes the pronoun f-structure, and the Linear Precedence condition is met. Since both requirements are satisfied, the example is correctly predicted to be grammatical.

Finally, we examine the ungrammatical example **Who*$_i$ *did Sue talk about his*$_i$ *mother to?*:

(15) *Who$_i$ did Sue talk about his$_i$ mother to?

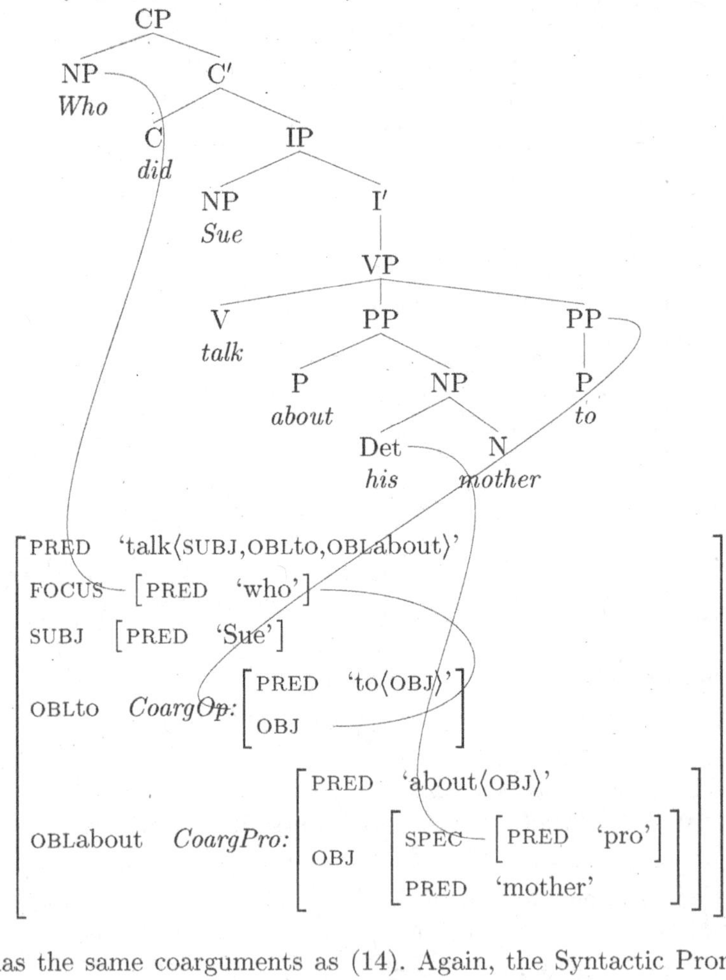

(15) has the same coarguments as (14). Again, the Syntactic Prominence requirement is met. The c-structure nodes corresponding to

CoargOp are the PP and P dominating *to*; these nodes do not f-precede the pronoun, the Linear Precedence requirement is not met, and the example is correctly classified as ungrammatical.

Thus, we have seen that traces are not necessary to account for the weak crossover data in English wh-questions, once coarguments are taken into account. As noted by Joan Bresnan (p.c.) and Ivan Sag (p.c.), some examples involving weak crossover with quantifiers rather than wh-phrases seem to obey less strict binding requirements that the examples examined so far. Sag provides the following example, which he claims is grammatical:

(16) I gave to each$_i$ student a copy of his$_i$ grades.

The binding relation in this example satisfies the Linear Prominence condition, but it violates Syntactic Prominence, since the CoargOp *to each student* is an oblique argument of *gave* and thus lower on the hierarchy than the OBJ CoargPro *his grades*. Bresnan (2001, p. 202, example 52c) points out another sort of example, which she claims is grammatical:

(17) His$_i$ mother, everyone$_i$ should like.

Here, the binding relation obeys Syntactic Prominence, since CoargOp is the SUBJ of *likes*, and CoargPro *his mother* is the OBJ, which is lower than the SUBJ on the hierarchy. However, the relation does not obey the Linear Prominence condition, since the pronoun precedes the CoargOp.

How best to analyze these examples is not clear. We ourselves do not find them fully grammatical, and similar examples have been assigned a question mark or star in previous literature. Therefore, we are reluctant to propose major modifications to our theory on the basis of these relatively shaky judgments. It may be that operator binding for English quantifiers (as opposed to English wh-phrases) is better characterized in terms of a looser, disjunctive set of requirements like those for German, to be discussed in the next section.

5.4.2 German

As stated above, we follow Bresnan (1998, 2001) in assuming that operator binding can obey different constraint in different languages. However, Bresnan (1998, but not 2001) argues that English and German are similar in that they both require Syntactic and Linear Prominence to be satisfied. In contrast, we assume that operator binding in German, unlike English, requires *either* the Linear Prominence *or* the Syntactic Prominence requirement must be met.

First, we consider some patterns of quantifier binding. Both of the examples in (18) are grammatical:

(18) ... dass [jeder] [seine Mutter] mag
that everyone-NOM his mother likes
(CoargOp, SUBJ) (CoargPro, OBJ)

... dass [seine Mutter] [jeder] mag
that his mother everyone-NOM likes
(CoargPro, OBJ) (CoargOp, SUBJ)

'... that everyone$_i$ likes his$_i$ mother'

In example (19), the quantifier *jeder* 'everyone' is the CoargOp SUBJ, and CoargPro is the OBJ:

- SUBJ and OBJ of *mag* 'like' are coarguments
- pronoun is *seine*
- OBJ of *mag* 'like' is CoargPro
- SUBJ of *mag* 'like' is CoargOp

The Syntactic Prominence requirement is met in both examples, since SUBJ outranks OBJ. Since only a single requirement must be satisfied, the Linear Prominence requirement need not hold, and the SUBJ and OBJ may appear in either order.

When the Linear Prominence requirement is met, the Syntactic Prominence requirement need not be met. In example (19), CoargOp is the OBJ *jeden* 'everyone', and CoargPro is the SUBJ *seine Mutter* 'his mother'. Though the Syntactic Prominence requirement is not met, the CoargOp f-precedes the pronoun, and the example is grammatical:

(19) ... dass [jeden] seine Mutter mag
that everyone-ACC his mother likes
(CoargOp)

'... that his$_i$ mother likes everyone$_i$'

- SUBJ and OBJ of *mag* 'like' are coarguments
- pronoun is *seine*
- SUBJ of *mag* 'like' is CoargPro
- OBJ of *mag* 'like' is CoargOp

In example (20), which has the same coargument structure of (19), neither requirement is met, and the sentence is ungrammatical:

(20) *... dass [seine Mutter] [jeden] mag
that his mother everyone-ACC likes
(CoargPro, SUBJ) (CoargOp, OBJ)

'... that his$_i$ mother likes everyone$_i$'

We now turn to examples involving long distance dependencies. In example (21), CoargPro is the SUBJ of 'say', *seine Mutter* 'his mother'. CoargOp is the COMP of 'say'. Since SUBJ outranks COMP, CoargOp is not more syntactically prominent than CoargPro. And since CoargOp does not f-precede the pronoun, the linear prominence requirement does not hold either. Since neither requirement holds, the sentence is classified as ungrammatical. Note that the reason for the ungrammaticality of example (21) is not that there is a trace in the subordinate clause; instead, the subordinate clause itself is treated as the important constituent in determining precedence requirements between the operator and the pronoun.

(21) *jeden/*wen meinte [seine Mutter], [habe sie getröstet]
everyone/who said his mother has she consoled
(CoargPro, SUBJ) (CoargOp, COMP)
'Everyone$_i$, his$_i$ mother said that she consoled./
Who$_i$ did his$_i$ mother say that she consoled?'

- SUBJ and COMP of *meinte* 'say' are coarguments
- pronoun is *seine*
- SUBJ of *meinte* 'say' is CoargPro
- COMP of *meinte* 'say' is CoargOp

In example (22), we evaluate the prominence conditions with respect to the coargument SUBJ and OBJ of *getröstet* 'consoled': the SUBJ *seine Mutter* 'his mother' is CoargPro, and the OBJ is CoargOp. The Syntactic Prominence condition does not hold, since the CoargPro SUBJ outranks the CoargOp OBJ. But the Linear Prominence condition holds, since the CoargOp f-precedes the pronoun. Thus, the operator binding conditions for German are met, and the sentence is predicted to be grammatical:

(22) [jeden/wen] sagte sie, habe seine Mutter getröstet
everyone/who said she has his mother consoled
(CoargOp)
'Everyone$_i$, she said that his$_i$ mother consoled./
Who$_i$ did she say that his$_i$ mother consoled?'

- SUBJ and OBJ of *getröstet* 'consoled' are coarguments
- pronoun is *seine*
- SUBJ of *getröstet* 'consoled' is CoargPro
- OBJ of *getröstet* 'consoled' is CoargOp

Thus, we see that in German simplex and complex clauses, there is no need to posit traces to account for the weak crossover data.

5.4.3 Malayalam

Finally, we briefly examine the behavior of 'null pronouns', phonologically unrealized pronominal elements. As shown by Mohanan (1982) and Bresnan (2001), only the Linear Prominence condition is relevant in Malayalam: the CoargOp must f-precede the pronoun, but no syntactic prominence condition is relevant. Example (23) is ungrammaticalwith an overt pronoun:

(23) *in̲n̲ale awar̄e s̄akaar̄icca st̲riikaḷe in̲n̲ə [oor̄oo kuṭṭiyum]
yesterday they scolded woman today each child (CoargOp)

sahaayiccu
helped
'Today each child$_i$ helped the woman who scolded them$_i$ yesterday.'

- SUBJ and OBJ of *sahaayiccu* 'helped' are coarguments
- pronoun is *awar̄e*
- OBJ of *sahaayiccu* 'helped' is CoargPro
- SUBJ of *sahaayiccu* 'helped' is CoargOp

In this example, CoargOp is the quantifier phrase *oor̄oo kuṭṭiyum*. CoargOp does not f-precede the overt pronoun *awar̄e*, and so the Linear Prominence requirement is not met.

However, with a null pronoun, the sentence is grammatical:

(24) in̲n̲ale ∅ s̄akaar̄icca st̲riikaḷe in̲n̲ə [oor̄oo kuṭṭiyum]
yesterday (they) scolded woman today each child (CoargOp)

sahaayiccu
helped
'Today each child$_i$ helped the woman who scolded them$_i$ yesterday.'

The same coargument information holds for (24) as for (23). However, the null pronoun does not correspond to any c-structure nodes, and so according to the definition of f-precedence in (11), it vacuously f-precedes and is f-preceded by every other f-structure. In particular, it vacuously satisfies the Linear Prominence condition. This explains the difference between the overt and null pronouns in examples (23) and (24).

5.5 Empirical differences between trace and traceless accounts

Though the data from English, German, and Malayalam discussed above are classified correctly by our theory of prominence as well as by theories that assume traces, there are empirically testable differences between the two approaches; in particular, the availability of certain sets of data would allow us to distinguish between our traceless account and the accounts of Bresnan (1994), Bresnan (2001), and Berman (2000, 2003), which assume traces. Though we have not yet been able to find the crucial data that would allow us to decide between the two theories, we provide characterizations of some of these differences in the following, in hopes that some of these crucial data can be found and examined.

5.5.1 Language 1

We first examine what we will call Language 1, a language in which the Syntactic Prominence condition does not apply. More specifically, Language 1 has the following characteristics:

- Fixed word order to encode grammatical functions
- Wh-phrases are displaced to the beginning of the sentence
- Only Linear Prominence is relevant

In Language 1, our theory predicts that an example like (25) would be grammatical, since CoargOp precedes the pronoun, and by hypothesis the Syntactic Prominence condition does not apply:

(25) [who$_i$] did [his$_i$ mother] see (t_i)
(CoargOp, OBJ) (CoargPro, SUBJ)

In contrast, the traceful theory predicts ungrammaticality, since the pronoun outranks the (trace of the) operator in Linear Prominence.

5.5.2 Language 2

We next examine Language 2, a language in which the object precedes the subject. Language 2 has the following characteristics:

- Fixed word order; Object precedes subject
- Wh-phrases are displaced to the beginning of the sentence
- Both Linear Prominence and Syntactic Prominence must hold

In Language 2, our theory predicts grammaticality for example (26):

(26) [who$_i$] saw his$_i$ book (t_i)
(CoargOp, SUBJ) (CoargPro, OBJ)

Here the Syntactic Prominence requirement holds, since CoargOp is SUBJ and CoargPro is OBJ. The Linear Prominence requirement is also met, since CoargOp precedes the pronoun. In contrast, the traceful theory predicts ungrammaticality, since the pronoun precedes the trace.

5.5.3 Language 3

Finally, we examine Language 3, a language in which either prominence requirement must hold. Language 3 has the following characteristics:

- Fixed word order; Subject precedes object
- Wh-phrases are displaced to the beginning of the sentence
- Either Linear Prominence or Syntactic Prominence must hold

Our theory predicts grammaticality for example (27):

(27) [what$_i$] saw its$_i$ owner (t_i)
(CoargOp, OBJ) (CoargPro, SUBJ)

The Syntactic Prominence requirement is not met in this example, since CoargOp is OBJ and CoargPro is SUBJ. However, the Linear Prominence requirement is met, since CoargOp precedes the pronoun. The traceful theory predicts that this example is ungrammatical, however, since once again the pronoun precedes the trace.

5.6 Summary

Our traceless theory accounts for the data on weak crossover that motivated previous researchers to posit traces in long distance dependencies. We accomplished this by providing a new definition of Linear Prominence that applies to f-structure units containing the operator. This exploits the c-structure/f-structure correspondence, a fundamental principle of the formal architecture of LFG. Since we are aware of no other evidence supporting the existence of traces in long distance dependencies, we believe that traces remain unmotivated in the theory of grammar.

Acknowledgments

This paper is based on work previously reported in Dalrymple, Kaplan and King (2001). We are grateful to Joan Bresnan, Yehuda Falk, Ivan

Sag, Annie Zaenen, and the audience at LFG2001 for helpful discussion and comments.

References

Berman, Judith. 2000. *Topics in the Clausal Syntax of German*. Ph.D. thesis, Universität Stuttgart.

Berman, Judith. 2003. *Clausal Syntax of German*. Stanford, CA: CSLI Publications.

Bresnan, Joan. 1984. Bound anaphora on functional structures. Presented at the 10th Annual Meeting of the Berkeley Linguistics Society (BLS 10), February 17, 1984.

Bresnan, Joan. 1994. Linear order vs. syntactic rank: Evidence from weak crossover. In K. Beals, J. Denton, B. Knippen, L. Melnar, H. Suzuki, and E. Zeinfeld, eds., *CLS 30: The main session. Papers from the 30th Meeting of the Chicago Linguistic Society*, vol. 1, pages 57–89. Chicago Linguistic Society.

Bresnan, Joan. 1995. Linear order, syntactic rank, and empty categories: On weak crossover. In M. Dalrymple, R. M. Kaplan, J. T. Maxwell III, and A. Zaenen, eds., *Formal Issues in Lexical-Functional Grammar*, pages 241–274. Stanford, CA: CSLI Publications.

Bresnan, Joan. 1998. Morphology competes with syntax: Explaining typological variation in weak crossover effects. In P. Barbosa, D. Fox, P. Hagstrom, M. McGinnis, and D. Pesetsky, eds., *Is the Best Good Enough? Proceedings from the Workshop on Optimality in Syntax*, pages 59–92. Cambridge, MA: The MIT Press. Invited paper presented at the MIT Workshop on Optimality in Syntax, May 1995.

Bresnan, Joan. 2001. *Lexical-Functional Syntax*. Oxford: Blackwell.

Chomsky, Noam. 1973. Conditions on transformations. In S. Anderson and P. Kiparsky, eds., *A Festschrift for Morris Halle*. New York, NY: Holt, Reinhart, and Winston.

Dalrymple, Mary, Ronald M. Kaplan, and Tracy H. King. 2001. Weak crossover and the absence of traces. In M. Butt and T. H. King, eds., *Proceedings of the International Lexical-Functional Grammar Conference 2001 (LFG'01)*, pages 66–82. Hong Kong: CSLI Online Publications.

Dalrymple, Mary, Ronald M. Kaplan, John T. Maxwell III, and Annie Zaenen, eds. 1995. *Formal Issues in Lexical-Functional Grammar*. Stanford, CA: CSLI Publications.

Kaplan, Ronald M. 1989. The formal architecture of Lexical-Functional Grammar. In C.-R. Huang and K.-J. Chen, eds., *Proceedings of the 2nd ROC Computational Linguistics Conference (ROCLING II)*, pages 3–18. Taipei. Reprinted in Dalrymple et al. (1995, pp. 7–27).

Kaplan, Ronald M. and Joan Bresnan. 1982. Lexical-Functional Grammar: A formal system for grammatical representation. In J. Bresnan, ed., *The Mental Representation of Grammatical Relations*, pages 173–281. Cambridge, MA: The MIT Press. Reprinted in Dalrymple et al. (1995, pp. 29–130).

Kaplan, Ronald M. and Annie Zaenen. 1989. Long-distance dependencies, constituent structure, and functional uncertainty. In M. Baltin and A. Kroch, eds., *Alternative Conceptions of Phrase Structure*, pages 17–42. Chicago, IL: Chicago University Press. Reprinted in Dalrymple et al. (1995, pp. 137–165).

Mohanan, KP. 1982. Grammatical relations and clause structure in Malayalam. In J. Bresnan, ed., *The Mental Representation of Grammatical Relations*, pages 504–589. Cambridge, MA: The MIT Press.

Postal, Paul M. 1971. *Cross-Over Phenomena*. New York, NY: Holt, Rinehart, and Winston.

Reinhart, Tanya. 1983. *Anaphora and Semantic Interpretation*. Chicago, IL: Chicago University Press.

Sag, Ivan A. 1998. Without a trace. Ms., Stanford University.

Wasow, Thomas. 1979. *Anaphora in Generative Grammar*. Ghent: E. Story.

6

Constituent Structure and Grammatical Functions in the Hebrew Nominal Phrase

YEHUDA N. FALK

6.1 Hebrew Nominal Phrases: An Overview

There have been many important transformational studies on the structure of Hebrew nominal phrases.[1] (Representative studies are Ritter 1988, Shlonsky 1988, Hazout 1995, Siloni 1997, Borer 1999, and Engelhardt 2000.) It is striking that, although they agree in broad outline, the details of these analyses vary so widely. The framework in which these analyses have been couched is a constituent-structure-centric theory. It is based on the idea that the various dimensions of syntax are all formalized in terms of a (derivationally related series of) constituent structure(s). A related assumption is that constituent structures essentially look the same in all languages. The undeniable differences between languages are thus a challenge for such a theory, and it is primarily in the formal nature of the devices needed to account for these differences (specifically, the formal motivation for the derivational process of movement) that the analyses that have been proposed differ

[1] This paper is dedicated to Joan Bresnan. Joan's career has exemplified the proper relationship between description and theory, and I feel privileged to have been one of her students. I have benefitted from comments by Miriam Butt, Carmen Dobrovie-Sorin, Edit Doron, Irit Meir, and an anonymous reader. This paper is a follow-up to Falk (2001). Due to space limitations, material from that paper could not be included here.

Architectures, Rules, and Preferences: Variations on Themes by Joan Bresnan.
Annie Zaenen, Jane Simpson, Tracy Holloway King,
Jane Grimshaw, Joan Maling, and Chris Manning, (eds.).

from each other. The alternative is to begin from the assumption that different dimensions of syntax find their representations in different formal objects with distinct properties, which are related to each other by universally constrained language-specific bidirectional principles of mapping or correspondence. The specific model we will assume here is that of Lexical-Functional Grammar (LFG). The previous work which has been carried out in constituent-structure-centric transformational frameworks constitutes a standard analysis against which any alternative must be measured, and we will contrast our proposals which those which have been made in the transformational literature.

One of the central issues in the study of nominal phrases, whether in Hebrew or any other language, is the element which we can informally refer to as the "possessor" (sometimes referred to, somewhat misleadingly, as the "genitive"). It is this question which constitutes the central focus of the present study. In Hebrew, as in English, there are two different possessor constructions: a long one and a short one.

(1) **English**

a. **Long possessor construction**
the old aunt [of [the linguist]]

b. **Short possessor construction**
[the linguist's] old aunt

(2) **Hebrew**

a. **Long possessor construction**
ha- doda ha- zkena [šel [ha- balšan]]
the- aunt the- old [of [the- linguist]]
'the old aunt of the linguist'

b. **Short possessor construction**
doda- t [ha- balšan] ha- zkena
aunt- CONSTR [the- linguist] the- old
'the linguist's old aunt'

Certain similarities and differences between the English and Hebrew constructions are apparent. In both languages, the long construction marks the "possessor" with a preposition, *of* in English and *šel* in Hebrew, and displays a relatively straightforward word order, with the possessor in a normal PP position for the language. The short construction, on the other hand, uses a special morphological form, the genitive form for the possessor in English and the construct form for the possessum in Hebrew, and shows a change in word order. Another difference between the two constructions which is apparent in both languages is the specification of definiteness: in the long construction the main nominal phrase is explicitly marked as definite (by the determiner *the* in English and the prefix *ha-* in Hebrew), while in the short construction such marking is impossible; the definiteness of the nominal phrase is somehow due to the possessor. Another similarity, not evident in these examples, is that when there is another dependent nominal phrase, the possessor outranks it with respect to binding; for example, a possessor can bind an anaphor elsewhere within the larger nominal phrase, but it cannot itself be an anaphor bound from within the nominal phrase. These similarities are striking, and suggest some commonality between the respective English and Hebrew constructions. The differences between the languages are equally interesting, and surface primarily in the short constructions. For instance, while the word order is different from the long construction in both languages, it is different in different ways. The English construction exhibits what appears to be a parallel to the sentential SVO order, with the possessor taking on the appearance of being the "subject" of the nominal phrase. In Hebrew, on the other hand, the nominal phrase is noun-initial, despite the fact that Hebrew clauses are not usually verb-initial. Another difference is the nature of the determination of definiteness of the main nominal phrase in the short construction: in Hebrew the larger phrase inherits the definiteness value of the possessor in what is often referred to as definiteness spreading, while in English the status of definiteness is less clear.

An interesting difference between the two languages which is less discussed in the literature has to do with the use of the two constructions. For relational nouns like 'aunt', both languages use both constructions. However, for true possession, English does not ordinarily use the long construction unless the possessor is also suffixed with *'s*.

(3) a. the linguist's computer
    b. *the/that/a computer of the linguist
    c. that/a computer of the linguist's

In Hebrew, on the other hand, the long construction is the one normally used for true possession; the short construction is typically limited to more formal registers. (We use the symbol '#' to indicate formal register-specific forms.)

(4) a. ha- maxšev šel ha- balšan
       the- computer of the- linguist
       'the linguist's computer'
    b. #maxšev ha- balšan
       computer the- linguist
       'the linguist's computer'

In contrast, for naming places and periods of time, English exclusively uses the long construction and Hebrew the short one.

(5) a. the kingdom of Norway
b. *Norway's kingdom

(6) a. mamlexet norvegia
kingdom.CONSTR Norway
'the kingdom of Norway'
b. *ha- mamlaxa šel norvegia
the- kingdom of Norway
'the kingdom of Norway'

Examples such as these show that the long and short constructions are not mere variants of each other, contrary to what is often assumed. These examples also show that there is cross-linguistic variation in the use of long and short possessor constructions.

6.2 Basic Analysis

6.2.1 Overview

It is the interaction between these various similarities and differences, both within Hebrew and between Hebrew and other languages, that has led to certain aspects of the standard analysis, as well as to differences in formal machinery between the analyses. The basic notions on which there is broad agreement, and on which we concur, seem to be the following:

1. There is a syntactic feature of definiteness which is related to the semantics of definiteness, though not necessarily directly (see Danon 2001 on mismatches between syntactic and semantic definiteness in Hebrew). This formal feature is expressed in English through the definite article *the*, and in Hebrew through a prefix (*ha-*) on the noun.
2. In the short construction, the possessor interacts with the definiteness feature.
3. The short possessor is subject-like in some respects. Many analyses also hold that the long possessor is subject-like.
4. In the Hebrew short possessive construction (the construct state), the head noun is morphologically and/or phonologically dependent on the possessor.

6.2.2 The standard constituent-structure-based analysis

The first three of these properties (which apply in both Hebrew and English) appear to be fairly well accounted for in English by the standard assumptions of constituent-structure-based theories. The definiteness feature is said to reside in the functional category D, which is the functional head of the nominal phrase (thus DP rather than NP). Assuming that the possessor in the short construction occupies the surface position of the specifier of DP, parallel to the clausal subject's position in the specifier of IP, it will have subject-like properties and it will interact (through SPEC-head agreement or Case marking) with the feature of definiteness in D. Finally, since the possessor is an argument of the noun, it originates within the NP, and then raises to [SPEC, DP]. The exact NP-internal position is unclear, since its subject-like properties suggest the specifier but it follows the noun; Giorgi and Longobardi (1991) suggest that it is extraposed by a Heavy-NP-Shift-like operation.[2] Schematically (and ignoring a lot of technical questions):

(7) a.

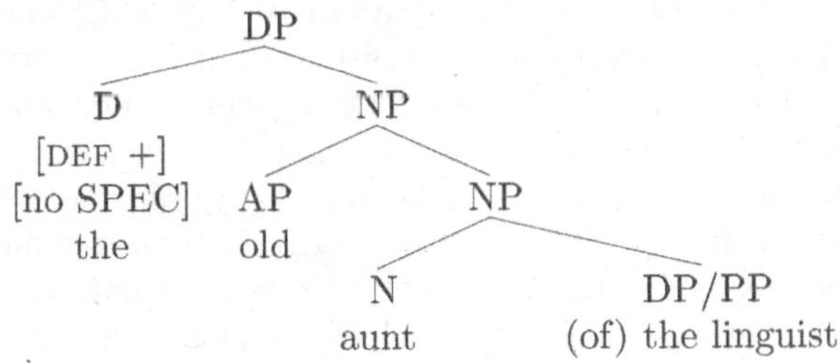

b.

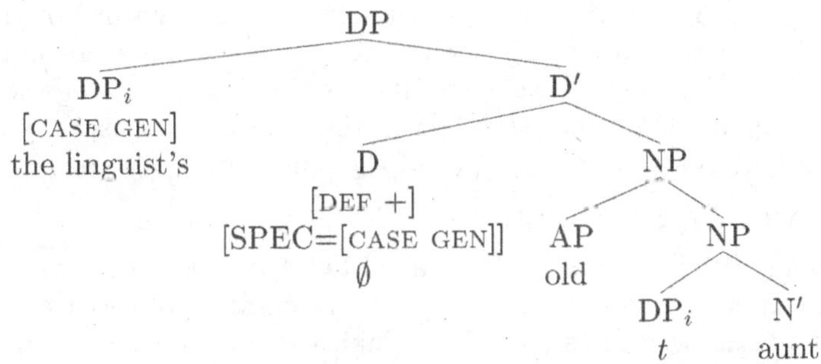

Applying the same analysis to the Hebrew equivalents would result in the wrong word constituent order. In the long possessive, it would result in the adjective preceding the noun, and in the short possessive it would result in the possessor and the adjective both preceding the head noun.

The position of the adjective in the long possessive might be accounted for by a language-specific stipulation specifying that adjectives

[2] Alternatively, it is only the possessor in the short construction that occupies a specifier position, and the long construction involves an adjoined PP. This alternative is adopted for Hebrew by Ritter (1988) and Hazout (1995).

in Hebrew are right-adjoined rather than left-adjoined, but, as noted by Borer (1999), this would not explain the fact that adjectives precede other ("complement") arguments of the noun as well as the long possessor. On the assumption that the iteration and scoping properties of adjectives are represented directly in constituent structure, as is standard in constituent-structure–based accounts, they must be adjoined, and therefore will be structurally higher than complements. On a right-adjunction analysis, they would follow the complements.[3] For this reason, N-to-D movement is often assumed as a way of accounting for the noun-initial order (Ritter 1988, 1991, Siloni 1997). This movement is said to be motivated either by the fact that D (the definite article *ha-*) is phonologically a clitic so the noun needs to raise to it to make cliticization possible (Ritter 1988), or by the fact that it is a prefix on N instead of a separate syntactic entity in D, and therefore must check its features with the empty D (Siloni 1997, Borer 1999).

In the construct, in order to get the right word order, an additional functional category is hypothesized between the D layer and the N layer; while the head noun moves all the way to D, the possessor/specifier only moves to the specifier position of this intermediate functional category, due to language-specific stipulations of features or functional categories.

In summary, in the standard analysis head movement of N to D is generally taken to be a result of the affixal nature of the Hebrew definiteness marker. The height to which various elements raise is a result of language-specific specification of features/categories. There is no explanatory value attached to these specifications; they are simply a stipulation of the grammar of the language.

6.2.3 An LFG analysis

In a multidimensional theory like LFG, facts like these take on a different appearance. C-structure is a representation of the overt expression of syntactic objects and the organization of this overt expression. In addition to c-structure, syntax includes representations of such syntactic relations as grammatical functions and features (f-structure) and predicate-argument relations (a-structure). If we examine the list of agreed-upon aspects of the analysis of Hebrew nominal phrases, none of them relates to overt syntactic expression (i.e. to c-structure). They relate primarily to a feature (definiteness) and grammatical functions (subject and possessor), elements which are represented at f-structure.

[3] At least under standard assumptions. Edit Doron has suggested (personal communication) that right-adjunction to N rather than N′ or NP would derive the right word order.

Much thus hinges on the theory of grammatical functions in general and subjecthood in particular.

We adopt here the analysis of subjects proposed by Falk (2006), under which the familiar "subject" is an amalgam of two distinct grammatical functions: the core function expressing the most prominent argument, termed $\widehat{\text{GF}}$, and a second, "overlay" function.[4] In familiar nominative-accusative languages, these two functions coincide; in typologically different languages they do not coincide, and sentences can have two different elements which share the familiar properties of subjects. Similarly, we take POSS not to be an actual grammatical function, but rather an amalgam of $\widehat{\text{GF}}$ and an overlay function.

The English *the old aunt of the linguist* and the Hebrew *hadoda hazkena šel habalšan* will have approximately the same f-structure.

(8)
$$\begin{bmatrix} \text{DEF} & + \\ \text{PRED} & \text{'aunt<}(\uparrow \widehat{\text{GF}})\text{>'} \\ \text{ADJ} & \left\{ \begin{bmatrix} \text{PRED} & \text{'old'} \end{bmatrix} \right\} \\ \text{GEND} & \text{F} \\ \text{NUM} & \text{SG} \\ \widehat{\text{GF}} & \begin{bmatrix} \text{CASE} & \widehat{\text{GF}} \\ \text{DEF} & + \\ \text{PRED} & \text{'linguist'} \\ \text{NUM} & \text{SG} \end{bmatrix} \end{bmatrix}$$

In the short possessive, since the possessor determines the definiteness of the entire nominal phrase, we hypothesize that the possessor, which functions as the $\widehat{\text{GF}}$, also functions as the value of the attribute DEF.

[4]In the case of subjects, this second function is the function of cross-clausal connection, termed PIV(ot). As we are not dealing with clausal syntax, we hypothesize that the PIV function is irrelevant.

(9)
$$\left[\begin{array}{ll} \text{DEF} & \left[\begin{array}{ll}\text{DEF} & + \\ \text{PRED} & \text{'linguist'} \\ \text{NUM} & \text{SG}\end{array}\right] \\ \widehat{\text{GF}} & \\ \text{PRED} & \text{'aunt}<(\uparrow\widehat{\text{GF}})>\text{'} \\ \text{ADJ} & \left\{\left[\begin{array}{ll}\text{PRED} & \text{'old'}\end{array}\right]\right\} \\ \text{GEND} & \text{F} \\ \text{NUM} & \text{SG}\end{array}\right]$$

This analysis is a formal expression of the idea, discussed in detail by Haspelmath (1999), that the possessor serves the same function as the definite article: to specify the reference of the nominal. The possessor provides information to anchor the reference of the nominal; the definite article is something of a bleached specification, providing no information other than to instruct the hearer to provide a reference.[5] DEF is the overlay function which is part of the traditional POSS; as an overlay function,[6] it is not subcategorizable, but rather must be licensed as sharing a value with a locally licensed function. We will discuss the constraints licensing this structure sharing briefly in §3.

The differences in the overt realization of the nominal phrases in Hebrew and English are a result of language-specific aspects of the f-structure–c-structure mapping. As much as is predictable in constituent-structure–based accounts is predictable here as well: the fact that the Hebrew definiteness marker is a prefix rather than a word belonging to the category Determiner leads to a difference in phrase structure. However, our view of the category D in Hebrew is very different from that taken in constituent-structure–based accounts. Plausible members of the Determiner category in Hebrew are the quantifiers: they are functional noun-like elements which precede NPs which would also be well-formed without them. The presence or absence of a quantifier has no effect on the structure of the rest of the nominal phrase. Therefore, instead of hypothesizing an empty D to which the N moves, the lack of a determiner in unquantified Hebrew nominal phrases (or in

[5]For a similar previous LFG analysis, see Butt, King, Niño, & Segond (1999). This is also similar to the classical analysis (as in Jackendoff 1977), under which determiners and possessors occupy the same structural position.

[6]Under this proposal, the value of the DEF attribute can be either atomic or an embedded f-structure. This seems to me to be the best way to express formally the relationship between "possessors" and definiteness marking. As Joan Bresnan has pointed out (personal communication), nothing in the formal architecture of LFG rules this out; f-structures are not typed feature structures.

the portion of the nominal phrase following the quantifier) is taken to mean that such phrases lack a D and thus are NPs, not DPs. Since the phrases in question are not DPs, there is also no [SPEC, DP] position that the possessor can occupy in the short possessive construction. Under the hypothesis (Bresnan 2001) that lexical categories universally lack specifiers, there is no structural specifier position for the possessor to occupy. This is why short-construction possessors occupy a different position in Hebrew than in English.

Other differences are not predictable under either analysis, but rather are based on language-specific properties. As shown by Falk (2001), for example, the noun + possessor sequence in the construct state does not form a constituent that excludes the adjective(s). The adjective is thus not adjoined to the NP, but rather appears as a daughter of NP and a sister of the possessor in the construct. On the other hand, PPs seem to be adjoined to the NP, even when they are arguments. The Hebrew c-structures thus look very different from those hypothesized in constituent-structure-based theories.[7] [8]

(10) a.

b.

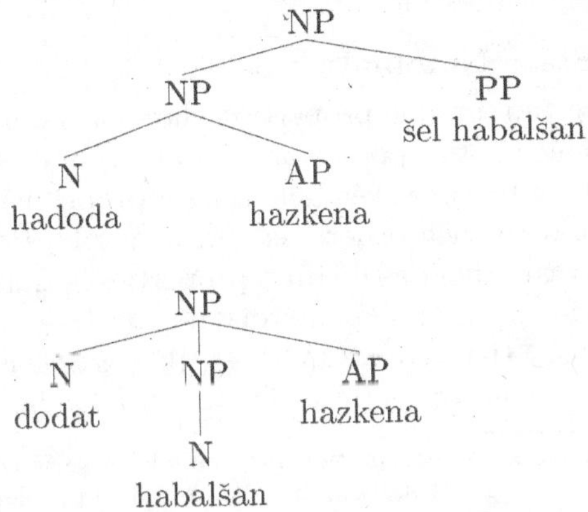

[7] Similar, though not identical, structures are proposed by Dobrovie-Sorin (2001). These structures do not obey the c-structure–f-structure mapping principles proposed by Bresnan (2001). Further cross-linguistic study is necessary to determine the possible parameters of variation.

[8] Binding possibilities are often cited as evidence for the usual structural analysis of Hebrew NPs. Cross-linguistic study of binding (Dalrymple 1993, Bresnan 1995, and others) has shown, however, that c-command is inadequate for accounting for the binding patterns found in the languages of the world. Instead, hierarchies at different dimensions of syntactic structure interact to result in the observed patterns. The thematic hierarchy appears to be relevant here.

Borer (1999) discusses several constituency problems for movement theories. One of them[9] has to do with adjectives in construct state (short possessive) nominals. Adjectives in the construct state, as we have seen, follow the possessor. If both the head and the possessor take adjectival modification, the adjectives must be nested, with the adjective modifying the possessor preceding the adjective modifying the head.

(11) a. dodat ha- balšan ha- generativi ha- zkena
aunt.CONSTR the- linguist the- generative.M the- old.F
'the generative linguist's old aunt'

b. *dodat ha- balšan ha- zkena ha- generativi
aunt.CONSTR the- linguist the- old.F the- generative.M
'the generative linguist's old aunt'

Under a non-movement analysis, there is nothing mysterious about this. The possessor NP is a constituent, and thus coheres in the linear ordering. Since nothing is moved out of this configuration, the constituency is seen transparently in the surface order.

6.2.4 Construct State Nominals

Construct state has certain unique properties: the morphophonological dependence of the head on the possessor, the adjacency of the head and possessor, and definiteness spreading. These properties are often treated as being related to each other (see, for example, Borer 1999), and an analysis that treats them as distinct properties is thus generally considered to be inferior from an explanatory perspective.

However, an analysis that connects these properties is explanatory only if they can be shown empirically to actually be related to

---

[9]Borer devotes an appendix to coordination problems with various movement-based analyses of Hebrew noun phrases, including her own. The problems are complex, involving details of specific analyses, and we cannot go into the specifics here. But it is interesting to note that not one of them is a problem for the present analysis: all involve coordination of an NP constituent, either the possessor in a construct state construction (i) or with further elements adjoined (ii, iii).

(i) beit [[ha- rabi mi- Kiryat Arba] ve [raayat- o]]
house.CONSTR the- rabbi from- Kiryat Arba and wife- his
'the house of the rabbi from Kiryat Arba and his wife'

(ii) [[ha- rabi ha- loxem] ve [raayat- o ha- xasuda]] mi- Kiryat Arba
the- rabbi the- militant and wife- his the- pious from- Kiryat Arba
'the militant rabbi and his pious wife from Kiryat Arba'

(iii) [[dirat ha- rav ha- yafa] u [migraš- av ha- rabim]] b- a- ir
apartment the- rabbi the- pretty and lots- his the- many in- the- city
'the rabbi's pretty apartment and his many lots in the city'

The problems Borer discusses are an artifact of the movement theory.

each other. A cross-linguistic survey, summarized in (12), shows that these are distinct, unrelated facets of the construction. Consider Welsh (Sadler 2000) and Rumanian (Dobrovie-Sorin 2001).

(12)

	Hebrew	Welsh	Rumanian
dependence	+	−	−
adjacency	+	−	+
definiteness spread	+	+	−

While there may be some tendency for these properties to co-occur, having any one of these properties as the source of the other two is clearly inadequate. We will treat these as three independent properties.

The adjacency between the head noun and the element bearing the function DEF under our analysis (i.e. the possessor) is expressed formally in LFG by the annotated phrase structure rule defining the c-structure–f-structure mapping.

(13) $\text{NP} \longrightarrow \underset{\uparrow=\downarrow}{\text{N}} \quad \underset{(\uparrow\text{DEF})=\downarrow}{\text{NP}} \quad \underset{\downarrow\in(\uparrow\text{ADJ})}{\text{AP*}}$

There is clear functional motivation for this position: since the formal purpose of the DEF is to fix the definiteness, and in some sense the reference, of the noun, a position adjacent to the noun is natural. (The English specifier position is natural for different reasons, but, as we have seen, such a position is unavailable in Hebrew.)

The morphological dependence of the head noun on the possessor is often described in terms of de-stressing of the head noun. However, the actual differences in form between free and construct nouns do not support this characterization. There is no phonological justification for the addition of /t/ at the end of feminine nouns or the changing of the masculine plural suffix from *-im* to *-ey*. On the other hand, the construct forms are also used in morphologically bound environments: primarily in compounds, but also with derivational affixes.

(14) a. *bayit* 'house' + *sefer* 'book' ⟶ *beyt sefer* 'school'
safa 'lip, language' + *em* 'mother' ⟶ *sfat em* 'mother tongue'
miflaga 'political party' + *avoda* 'work' ⟶ *mifleget (ha)avoda* '(the) Labor Party'

b. *bayit* 'house' + *-i* adjective ⟶ *beyti* 'domestic'
safa 'lip, language' + *-on* ⟶ *sfaton* 'lipstick'
šana 'year' + *-on* ⟶ *šnaton* '(annual) course catalog'
zayit 'olive' + *-im* plural ⟶ *zeytim* 'olives'

We will represent this semi-formally as a feature [MORPHTYPE BND] at some morphological (or word-structure) projection from c-structure.[10]

(15) NP ⟶ N NP AP*

$\uparrow=\downarrow$ $(\uparrow\text{DEF})=\downarrow$ $\downarrow\in(\uparrow\text{ADJ})$

$(\omega(<*)\ \text{MORPHTYPE})=\text{BND}$

Finally, consider definiteness spreading. The basic fact is that in Hebrew the entire construct noun phrase is definite if the possessor is definite and indefinite if the possessor is indefinite. (An adjective has been included in the Hebrew example to show definiteness agreement, which is a syntactic test for definiteness.)

(16) a. dodat ha- balšan ha- zkena
aunt the- linguist the- old
'the old aunt of the linguist'

b. dodat balšan zkena
aunt linguist old
'an old aunt of a linguist'

This situation, seen also in other Semitic languages (such as Arabic) and in Celtic languages, has been dubbed "definiteness spreading," because it appears that the definiteness value of the possessor has spread to the larger NP. This rather strange state of affairs has led to several lines of analysis in the generative literature. Perhaps the most common is some variant of feature copying, sharing, or percolation. Such analyses have been proposed in various generative frameworks: GB/MP (inter alia Siloni 1997, Borer 1999), LFG (Sadler 2000), HPSG (Wintner 2000). As observed by Dobrovie-Sorin (2001), this analysis is conceptually problematic: this kind of feature sharing is otherwise unheard of. Dobrovie-Sorin's alternative is problematic as well. She assumes that it is only [DEF +] that appears to spread, and attributes this to properties of semantic interpretation rather than to syntax. However, the definiteness of the main NP in Hebrew is syntactic, as shown by adjective agreement. She also proposes that indefinite constructs are not argument constructions, but rather modifier constructions, which are handled differently in her analysis. This is problematic as the same relations can be expressed by both definite and indefinite constructs.

Let us consider the problem of definiteness spread in light of the analysis proposed here. The f-structures are:

[10] The notation '$<*$' refers to the left sister of the node to which is annotated (Dalrymple 2001), and $\omega(<*)$ thus refers to the word structure correspondent of that node.

(17) a.

$$\left[\begin{array}{ll} \text{DEF} & \left[\begin{array}{ll} \text{DEF} & + \\ \text{PRED} & \text{'linguist'} \\ \text{NUM} & \text{SG} \end{array}\right] \\ \text{PRED} & \text{'aunt<}(\uparrow \widehat{\text{GF}})\text{>'} \\ \text{NUM} & \text{SG} \\ \widehat{\text{GF}} & \end{array}\right]$$

b.

$$\left[\begin{array}{ll} \text{DEF} & \left[\begin{array}{ll} \text{DEF} & - \\ \text{PRED} & \text{'linguist'} \\ \text{NUM} & \text{SG} \end{array}\right] \\ \text{PRED} & \text{'aunt<}(\uparrow \widehat{\text{GF}})\text{>'} \\ \text{NUM} & \text{SG} \\ \widehat{\text{GF}} & \end{array}\right]$$

There is no question here of "spreading" or "percolating" the feature DEF: both the main NP and the embedded one have the attribute DEF with a value. However, the value of DEF in the main NP is not a simple '+' or '−', it is a subsidiary attribute-value matrix which has its own DEF attribute. Definiteness spreading can be characterized as involving a path of DEFs terminating in the value + or −.

(18) f is a definite nominal $=_{def}$ $(f\ \text{DEF}^*) = +$
f is an indefinite nominal $=_{def}$ $(f\ \text{DEF}^*) = -$

For example, adnominal adjectives with definite agreement (the prefix *ha-*) can be specified:

(19) $((\text{ADJ}\ \uparrow)\ \text{DEF}^*) =_c +$

The approach to definiteness spreading adopted here accounts for a phenomenon noted by Engelhardt (2000).She notes that there are environments (such as object of the preposition *tox* 'while') which allow indefinite but not definite NPs, yet do allow construct-state NPs with an embedded definite possessor, which are also ostensibly definite.

(20) a. ha- pixut be- šaar ha- dolar tox horada šel
the- devaluation in- rate the- dollar while decrease of
ha- ribit
the- interest
'The devaluation in the exchange rate of the dollar combined with the lowering of interest.'

b. *ha- pixut be- šaar ha- dolar tox ha- horada
the- devaluation in- rate the- dollar while the- decrease

šel ha- ribit
of the- interest

c. ha- pixut be- šaar ha- dolar tox horadat
the- devaluation in- rate the- dollar while decrease.CONSTR
ha- ribit
the- interest

Under the analysis proposed here, the relevant lexical constraint can be expressed in terms of the value of the local DEF.

(21) *tox*: $(\uparrow \text{OBJ DEF}) \neq +$

We need not assume, as Engelhardt does, that such facts force us to say that these nominals are unspecified for definiteness, as a feature copying approach to definiteness spread would lead us to assume.

6.3 Refining the analysis

We turn now to the question of what kind of element can appear as the possessor in the long construction and in the short construction; in the next section we will discuss issues of constituent order.

As noted earlier, not all possessor-like elements are equally grammatical in the short construction and the long one, either in Hebrew or in English. A constituent-structure-based approach, with the standard distinction between external arguments, internal arguments, and adjuncts, cannot make the kind of distinction necessary to account for the various possibilities.

An approach based on grammatical functions provides a more fine-grained approach to the syntactic analysis of arguments. Up to now, we have treated DEF as a second function which can be borne by the $\widehat{\text{GF}}$; while we take it to be universally true that $\widehat{\text{GF}}$ can also function as DEF, we must allow for other, language-specific, identities for DEF. This means that a "possessor" in the short construction bears the function DEF, but may or may not bear the function $\widehat{\text{GF}}$ (it could have some other locally licensed function). Conversely, a "possessor" in the long construction may bear the function $\widehat{\text{GF}}$, but may instead bear some other function which is marked with the same particle (*šel* in Hebrew) that marks $\widehat{\text{GF}}$. In fact, there is reason to believe that not all *šel*-marked elements bear the $\widehat{\text{GF}}$ function. This is because of the existence of what is often described as a third possessor construction in Hebrew: the doubled construction.

(22) #dodat- o šel ha- balšan
aunt- his of the- linguist
'the linguist's aunt'

We follow Engelhardt (2000) in analyzing this construction as agreement (optionally functioning as an incorporated pronoun). The suffix *-o* is an agreement affix for a $\widehat{\text{GF}}$ with the features [PERS 3, NUM SG, GEND M]. Agreement in possessor constructions in Modern Hebrew is stylistically marked, belonging to a higher register than the ordinary possessor constructions. However, speakers of Hebrew have clear intuitions about the grammaticality of the construction, and it can thus be used as a further indication of grammatical functions. Notably, there are some types of possessors which do not allow agreement, even when they allow both long and short constructions.

(23) a. kos kafe
cup coffee
'a cup of coffee'

b. kos šel kafe
cup of coffee

c. *kos- o šel kafe
cup- 3MSG of coffee

Since $\widehat{\text{GF}}$ is the subject-like argument function, it is natural to suppose that agreement on the noun is with its $\widehat{\text{GF}}$. (This is similar to Engelhardt's 2000 analysis, except that she expresses it in terms of a structural metaphor for the grammatical function $\widehat{\text{GF}}$.) We therefore conclude that dependent NPs which are incapable of triggering agreement do not bear the $\widehat{\text{GF}}$ function. Instead, we hypothesize that *kafe* here bears an oblique function used for containers and measures: OBL_{Con}; both Hebrew *šel* and English *of* can be used to mark the OBL_{Con} function. In Hebrew, although not in English, an element bearing the OBL_{Con} function is allowed to serve also as the DEF.

This behavior of container arguments contrasts, as we have seen, with the arguments of relational nouns like *doda*, which allow the full range of possessor constructions. Also allowing the full range of constructions are deverbal action nouns.

(24) a. ha- sgira šel ha- mankal et ha- misrad
the- closure of the- director ACC the- office
'the director's closure of the office'

b. sgirat ha- mankal et ha- misrad
closure.CONSTR the- director ACC the- office

c. sgirat- o šel ha- mankal et ha- misrad
closure- 3MSG of the- director ACC the- office

(25) a. ha- sgira šel ha- misrad alyedey ha- mankal
the- closure of the- office by the- director
'the closure of the office by the director'

b. sgirat ha- misrad alyedey ha- mankal
closure.CONSTR the- office by the- director

c. sgirat- o šel ha- misrad alyedey ha- mankal
closure- 3MSG of the- office by the- director

Under the analysis proposed by Falk (2001), the two variants of action nominals in Hebrew involve, respectively, a verb-like mapping of arguments and a noun-like mapping, mirroring the mixed nominal/verbal properties of these nominals. Under a verbal mapping, the Agent maps to $\widehat{\text{GF}}$ (called SUBJ in Falk 2001) and the Theme to OBJ, while in the nominal mapping, where the OBJ function is unavailable, the Theme maps to $\widehat{\text{GF}}$ and the Agent to an oblique function. In each case, the argument mapped to $\widehat{\text{GF}}$ behaves as expected: allowing agreement and optionally taking on the DEF function.

The most interesting behavior, in both Hebrew and English, is exhibited by what we can call true possessors: NP dependents which bear a semantic relation of possessor to the larger NP. The exact nature of this possessor interpretation depends on the semantics of the head noun: it can be alienable possession, inalienable possession, or the causer of a result. As noted earlier, these arguments do not exhibit the same range of modes of expression as the types of "possessors" we have already discussed. In English, true possessors can be realized either as a prenominal *'s* element, bearing the function DEF, or as a postnominal element bearing double marking: both the particle *of* and the suffix *'s*.

(26) a. the teacher's bag

b. *a/that bag of the teacher

c. a/that bag of the teacher's

In Hebrew, the most natural realization of true possessors is in a *šel* phrase; i.e. the long possessor construction. The short construction (construct state) is associated with higher registers. The agreeing construction is also possible; as always, it too reflects a higher register.

(27) a. (ha-) tik šel ha- mora
(the-) bag of the- teacher
'the teacher's bag'

b. #tik ha- mora
bag the- teacher

c. #tik- a šel ha- mora
bag- 3FSG of the- teacher

In neither English nor casual Hebrew does the possessor display the behavior of a $\widehat{\text{GF}}$ argument. In English, $\widehat{\text{GF}}$ can be marked by *of* alone (without the additional *'s*), and in Hebrew (as in, presumably, every language) $\widehat{\text{GF}}$ can also be DEF. On the other hand, in formal Hebrew true possessors have all the properties of $\widehat{\text{GF}}$: they can be DEF and, crucially, they can trigger agreement. We propose, therefore, that true possessors are arguments which bear the $\widehat{\text{GF}}$ function in formal Hebrew but the OBL_{Poss} function in both English and casual Hebrew. In English, but not in Hebrew, an element bearing the OBL_{Poss} function can also bear the DEF function.

(28) a. English: *the teacher's bag*
Hebrew: not grammatical

$$\begin{bmatrix} \text{DEF} & \begin{bmatrix} \text{DEF} & + \\ \text{PRED} & \text{'teacher'} \\ \text{NUM} & \text{SG} \end{bmatrix} \\ \text{OBL}_{Poss} & \\ \text{PRED} & \text{'bag<}(\uparrow \text{OBL}_{Poss})\text{>'} \\ \text{NUM} & \text{SG} \end{bmatrix}$$

b. English: *the bag of the teacher's*
Hebrew: *hatik šel hamora*

$$\begin{bmatrix} \text{DEF} & + \\ \text{PRED} & \text{'bag<}(\uparrow \text{OBL}_{Poss})\text{>'} \\ \text{NUM} & \text{SG} \\ \text{OBL}_{Poss} & \begin{bmatrix} \text{DEF} & + \\ \text{PRED} & \text{'teacher'} \\ \text{NUM} & \text{SG} \end{bmatrix} \end{bmatrix}$$

c. Formal Hebrew: *tik hamora*
English and casual Hebrew: not grammatical

$$\begin{bmatrix} \text{PRED} & \text{'bag<}(\uparrow \widehat{\text{GF}})\text{>'} \\ \text{NUM} & \text{SG} \\ \text{DEF} & \begin{bmatrix} \text{DEF} & + \\ \text{PRED} & \text{'teacher'} \\ \text{NUM} & \text{SG} \end{bmatrix} \\ \widehat{\text{GF}} & \end{bmatrix}$$

Within the context of an external/internal theory of arguments, this is unexpected. Within the context of the LFG theory of argument mapping (Lexical Mapping Theory or LMT), on the other hand, a $\widehat{\text{GF}}$~OBL alternation is natural: the $\widehat{\text{GF}}$ and OBL functions share the feature specification $[-o]$, and thus form a natural class.

Further study reveals that other types of nominal arguments exhibit other mapping properties. Space limitations preclude a full discussion,[11] but it is clear that the mapping of containers (and of true possessors in English and casual Hebrew) — oblique, not $\widehat{\text{GF}}$ — is mirrored in the mapping of other elements as well, such as Theme arguments of agent nouns and result nouns, Agent arguments of action nominals, and names. This contrasts, as we have seen, with the arguments of relational nouns and the Theme arguments of action nominals, which map as $\widehat{\text{GF}}$ in English and all varieties of Hebrew. As we have already seen, English and Hebrew differ in which nominal arguments (other that $\widehat{\text{GF}}$s) can bear the DEF function. This is what accounts for the contrasts between English and Hebrew in examples like (6)/(7). English allows Agents of action nominals and true possessors to be DEF, while Hebrew eschews those but allows other elements.

(29) a. English:
$(\uparrow \text{DEF}) = (\uparrow \widehat{\text{GF}}) \mid (\uparrow \text{OBL}_{Poss}) \mid (\uparrow \text{OBL}_{Agent})$
b. Hebrew:
$(\uparrow \text{DEF}) = (\uparrow \widehat{\text{GF}}) \mid (\uparrow \text{OBL}_{Con}) \mid (\uparrow \text{OBL}_{Theme}) \mid (\uparrow \text{OBL}_{Name})$

6.4 Constituent Order

We now turn to the ordering of subconstituents of the noun phrase.

The first relevant observation about ordering is that in the short construction the DEF must immediately follow the head noun. As we have seen, this is a natural position for an element determining the definiteness of the head. We will have no more to say about this ordering here. In verbally-mapped action nominals, the element bearing the $\widehat{\text{GF}}$ function must precede all other arguments of the noun.

(30) a. ha- sgira šel ha- mankal et ha- misrad
the- closure of the- director ACC the- office
'the director's closure of the office'
b. *ha- sgira et ha- misrad šel ha- mankal
the- closure ACC the- office of the- director

[11] It is possible that the inherent classification $[+r]$, unused in standard accounts of Lexical Mapping Theory, is used for arguments of nominals which cannot be realized as $\widehat{\text{GF}}$.

This word order matches that found in clauses: the subject must precede the object. In the transformational literature this is taken to be a result of the unique structural position of the $\widehat{\text{GF}}$ in the specifier position of the NP (Siloni 1997) or an embedded VP (Borer 1999). This explanation of the word order is flawed for two reasons. In the first place, as discussed above for underived nouns, the proposed constituent structure is not confirmed by constituency tests. As argued by Falk (2001), both arguments are structurally adjoined to the NP. Secondly, it is not clear that a transformational theory can explain surface order without language-specific stipulations. Specifically, any order can be achieved by movement, and in comparing Hebrew with English it is necessary to account for the absence of movement from [SPEC, NP] to [SPEC, DP] in Hebrew and for its presence in English. (For example, Borer 1999 "assume[s] that Semitic does not have a [Spec, DP] position.") Since movement can be invoked, blocked, or relegated to LF to derive whatever word orders are attested, there is no explanatory value to the proposed configuration. In LFG, constituent order is taken to be a primitive property of constituent structures, one which has a status as a hierarchy defined on c-structure, just as the relational hierarchy is defined on f-structure and the thematic hierarchy on a-structure (Bresnan 1995). The requirement that the $\widehat{\text{GF}}$ precede other arguments is conceptually the alignment of the word-order hierarchy with the relational hierarchy, and is thus a natural requirement. This natural ordering restriction can be expressed in the syntax of Hebrew through the use of functional precedence (Dalrymple 2001): the specification of precedence restrictions by reference to the grammatical functions borne by the constituents.

(31) $\widehat{\text{GF}} \prec_f \text{AF}$ (where AF means "argument function")

Since the linear precedence rules are rules of Hebrew syntax, they apply in clauses as well as in NPs, ensuring that the same order obtains in both.

The ordering of arguments of concrete nouns and of nominally-mapped action nouns is less clear. Consider nominally-mapped action nominals.

(32) a. ha- sgira šel ha- misrad alyedey ha- mankal
the- closure of the- office by the- director
'the closure of the office by the director'

b. %ha- sgira alyedey ha- mankal šel ha- misrad
the- closure by the- director of the- office

The order in which the $\widehat{\text{GF}}$ (Theme) argument precedes the OBL_{Agent} (32a) is unquestionably grammatical. However, there is some disagreement about the status of the other order (32b): it is marked as ungrammatical by Borer (1999), but at least some speakers of Hebrew accept it (Edit Doron, personal communication).

In the case of concrete nouns with a Theme argument and a Possessor argument,[12] the Theme can be realized as the DEF of a construct, as in the following examples from Siloni (1997).

(33) a. tmunat ha- praxim šel ha- yeled
picture.CONSTR the- flowers of the- boy
'the boy's picture of the flowers'

b. *tmunat ha- yeled šel ha- praxim
picture.CONSTR the- boy of the- flowers

(34) a. targumey ha- odisea šel ha- sifriya
translations.CONSTR the- Odyssey of the- library
'the library's translations of the Odyssey'

b. *targumey ha- sifriya šel ha- odisea
translations.CONSTR the- library of the- Odyssey

This follows from our analysis: the Theme is mapped to $\widehat{\text{GF}}$ and the possessor to OBL_{Poss}. Since DEF can be identified in Hebrew with $\widehat{\text{GF}}$ but not with OBL_{Poss}, it is the Theme which appears as the sister of the construct-state head.[13] However, since nothing forces $\widehat{\text{GF}}$ to function as

[12]We assume here that the Agent-like argument of picture nouns is a kind of possessor. Note that in English it is possible to express this as (i).

(i) the picture of flowers of the boy's

Since this double-marked form in English is a realization of the OBL_{Poss} function, we take this to be evidence in favor of such an analysis.

[13]Wintner (2000), in what he admits is a particularly permissive dialect, claims to accept both of the following:

(i) a. tmunat mišmar ha- layla šel rembrandt
picture.CONSTR watch the- night of Rembrandt

b. tmunat rembrandt šel mišmar ha- layla
picture.CONSTR Rembrandt of watch the- night
'Rembrandt's picture of the Night Watch'

The acceptability of (ib), claimed to be ungrammatical in Borer (1999), is unexpected under the analysis outlined here. It is possible that this dialect is more permissive about mapping true possessors to $\widehat{\text{GF}}$. Perhaps related to this is the fact that, when there is only one argument for a picture noun and it is in the construct, some speakers are more flexible than others in what relation they allow the DEF to have: some strongly prefer it to be the depicted entity, as we predict here (Borer 1999, who refers to *tmunat van gox* as "not fully ungrammatical"), while others also allow it to be the artist or the owner (Ritter 1988).

DEF, it should also be possible to have two *šel* phrases. It is here that the data begin to be unclear.

In the first place, double *šel* phrases are awkward at best. (Siloni 1997 marks the examples '?', a practice we will follow here.) This awkwardness renders the judgments less than clear. However, we predict that the order should be the same as in the short possessive, with the Theme ($\widehat{\text{GF}}$) preceding the possessor.

(35) a. ?ha- tmuna šel ha- praxim šel ha- yeled
the- picture of the- flowers of the- boy
'the pictures of the flowers of the boy's'

b. ?ha- targumim šel ha- odisea šel ha- sifriya
the- translations of the- Odyssey of the- library
'the translations of the Odyssey of the library's'

Abstracting away from the awkwardness of the double-*šel*, these appear to be basically grammatical (Siloni 1997 and others). Some speakers, but not all, allow the two arguments to be permuted.

(36) a. %ha- tmuna šel ha- yeled šel ha- praxim
the- picture of the- boy of the- flowers
'the pictures of the flowers of the boy's'

b. %ha- targumim šel ha- sifriya šel ha- odisea
the- translations of the- library of the- Odyssey
'the translations of the Odyssey of the library's'

Such examples are cited as grammatical by Shlonsky (1988), Borer (1999), and Wintner (2000). On the other hand, Siloni (1997) reports that not all speakers accept them.

An order in which an oblique argument (the Agent of nominally-mapped action nominals or the Possessor of a concrete noun) can precede the $\widehat{\text{GF}}$ is unexpected under our analysis as developed to this point, but is actually a natural extension. What distinguishes the constructions in which some speakers find this order possible is a mismatch between the hierarchy at a-structure (the thematic hierarchy) and the hierarchy at f-structure (the relational hierarchy). Speakers who allow both orders thus vacillate between aligning the linear order hierarchy with the f-structure relational hierarchy and aligning it with the a-structure thematic hierarchy. Using the standard LFG notation $\hat{\theta}$ for the most prominent argument at a-structure, and using α for the a-structure–f-structure mapping, the linear precedence rule can be restated:

(37) $\widehat{\text{GF}} \prec_f \text{AF} \vee \alpha(\hat{\theta}) \prec_f \text{AF}$

Using the symbol $\hat{\text{x}}$ as a cover term for an argument which is highest on either the relational hierarchy or the thematic hierarchy (i.e., either $\widehat{\text{GF}}$ or $\alpha(\hat{\ }\theta)$), we can express this as:

(38) $\hat{\text{x}} \prec_f \text{AF}$

Notably, transformational accounts have often resorted to movement to account for these ordering alternations; for example, Borer (1999) suggests that there is an optional reordering rule which operates in noun phrases but not in verb phrases. It is not clear how such a rule would be stated in the framework she assumes. Even if statable, such a rule is arbitrary; the LFG-based approach makes the existence of both ordering possibilities principled.

6.5 Conclusion

We have laid out in this paper an analysis of Hebrew nominal phrases based on the theoretical assumptions of LFG: a parallel constraint-based theory of syntax. We have shown that by shedding the strait-jacket of the assumptions of constituent-structure-based theories we can achieve an analysis which captures the insights of the transformational analyses but is at the same time more faithful to the surface facts of Hebrew and to the cross-linguistic facts.

By adopting a theoretical framework in which grammatical functions are represented as an autonomous dimension of syntax distinct from constituent structure, we have been able to account for both functional and distributional/constituency facts about Hebrew NPs.

References

Borer, Hagit. 1999. Deconstructing the construct. In K. Johnson and I. Roberts, eds., *Beyond Principles and Parameters*. Dordrecht: Kluwer.

Bresnan, Joan. 1995. Linear order, syntactic rank, and empty categories: On weak crossover. In M. Dalrymple, R. M. Kaplan, J. T. Maxwell III, and A. Zaenen, eds., *Formal Issues in Lexical-Functional Grammar*, pages 241–274. Stanford, CA: CSLI Publications.

Bresnan, Joan. 2001. *Lexical-Functional Syntax*. Oxford: Blackwell.

Butt, Miriam, Tracy H. King, María-Eugenia Niño, and Frédérique Segond. 1999. *A Grammar-Writer's Cookbook*. Stanford, CA: CSLI Publications.

Dalrymple, Mary. 1993. *The Syntax of Anaphoric Binding*. Stanford, CA: CSLI Publications.

Dalrymple, Mary. 2001. *Lexical-Functional Grammar*, vol. 34 of *Syntax and Semantics*. New York, NY: Academic Press.

Danon, Gabi. 2001. Syntactic definiteness in the grammar of Modern Hebrew. *Linguistics* 39(6):1071–1116.

Dobrovie-Sorin, Carmen. 2002. From DPs to NPs: A bare phrase account of genitives. In M. Coene and Y. D'Hulst, eds., *From NP to DP. Volume 2: The expression of possession in noun phrases*, pages 75–120. Amsterdam & Philadelphia, PA: J. Benjamins.

Engelhardt, Miriam. 2000. The projection of argument-taking nominals. *Natural Language and Linguistic Theory* 18(1):41–88.

Falk, Yehuda N. 2001. Constituent structure and grammatical functions in the Hebrew action nominal. In M. Butt and T. H. King, eds., *Proceedings of the International Lexical-Functional Grammar Conference 2001 (LFG'01)*, pages 83–103. Hong Kong: CSLI Online Publications.

Falk, Yehuda N. 2006. *Subjects and Universal Grammar: An Explanatory Theory*. Cambridge, UK: Cambridge University Press.

Giorgi, Alessandra and Giuseppe Longobardi. 1991. *The Syntax of Noun Phrases: Configuration, Parameters and Empty Categories*. Cambridge, UK: Cambridge University Press.

Haspelmath, Martin. 1999. Explaining article-possessor complementarity: Economic motivation in noun phrase syntax. *Language* 75(2):227–243.

Hazout, Ilan. 1995. Action nominalizations and the lexicalist hypothesis. *Natural Language and Linguistic Theory* 13(4):355–404.

Jackendoff, Ray. 1977. *$\bar{X}$ Syntax*. Cambridge, MA: The MIT Press.

Ritter, Elizabeth. 1988. A head movement approach to construct-state noun phrases. *Linguistics* 26:909–929.

Ritter, Elizabeth. 1991. Two functional categories in noun phrases: Evidence from Modern Hebrew. In S. D. Rothstein, ed., *Perspectives on Phrase Structure: Heads and Licensing*, vol. 25 of *Syntax and Semantics*, pages 37–62. New York, NY: Academic Press.

Sadler, Louisa. 2000. Noun phrase structure in Welsh. In M. Butt and T. H. King, eds., *Argument Realization*, pages 73–109. Stanford, CA: CSLI Publications.

Shlonsky, Ur. 1988. Government and binding in Hebrew nominals. *Linguistics* 26:951–976.

Siloni, Tal. 1997. *Noun Phrases and Nominalizations: The Syntax of DPs*. Dordrecht: Kluwer.

Wintner, Shuly. 2000. Definiteness in the Hebrew noun phrase. *Journal of Linguistics* 36:319–363.

7

Interplay between Manual and Nonmanual Expressions in American Sign Language (ASL)

CAROL NEIDLE

7.1 Introduction

The distribution of syntactic information across multiple channels in signed languages poses interesting challenges for the choice of appropriate linguistic models.[1] After an overview of organizational differences between languages in the visual-gestural and aural-oral modalities, some recent findings concerning realization of "inflectional" information in American Sign Language (ASL) are summarized. The paper

[1] Acknowledgments: The material presented here is based, in part, upon work supported by the National Science Foundation under Grants No. 9912573, 9809340, 0329009 and 0427988. Any opinions, findings, and conclusions expressed in this material are those of the author and do not necessarily reflect the views of the National Science Foundation. I would like to thank many people who have participated in the research summarized here, including Debra Aarons, Ben Bahan, Dawn MacLaughlin, Norma Tourangeau, and Lana Cook, and especially Robert G. Lee and Michael Schlang. Thanks also to my colleagues Jon Barnes and Paul Hagstrom for interesting discussions that will, I hope, lead to future collaboration on some of the questions raised here in broad terms.

I would also like to take this opportunity to thank Joan Bresnan for her guidance years back as my dissertation supervisor, for her continuing support since that time, and for offering powerful inspiration of many kinds by her own example. I have long admired not only her obvious talents as a linguist, but also her courage in pursuing her own vision of linguistic theory and her sense of adventure in tackling a wide range of real language data and theoretical issues in her work.

Architectures, Rules, and Preferences: Variations on Themes by Joan Bresnan.
Annie Zaenen, Jane Simpson, Tracy Holloway King,
Jane Grimshaw, Joan Maling, and Chris Manning, (eds.).

concludes with a brief discussion of the challenge to find appropriate syntactic models to handle information distributed over the manual and nonmanual channels in signed languages.

7.2 Distribution of information over multiple channels

Although the fundamental linguistic components in signed and spoken languages are comparable, modality has consequences for the "packaging" and distribution of particular types of linguistic information. Whereas speech produces linearly sequenced segments (albeit with significant effects of co-articulation), upon which it is nonetheless possible to superimpose, e.g., variations in fundamental frequency, signed languages involve greater numbers of parallel streams that carry linguistically pertinent information.

7.2.1 Manual channel

Articulation with the hands and arms is the primary means of expression of lexical material in ASL, although some lexical items also have specific nonmanual expressions associated with them (as discussed below).[2]

7.2.2 Nonmanual channel

In parallel with manual signing, facial expressions and gestures of the head and upper body serve a variety of functions, both linguistic and paralinguistic.[3] Potentially competing functions of nonmanual markings include:

(1) *Lexical distinctions.* For example, the signs LATE and NOT-YET, illustrated in Figure 1,[4] are distinguished solely by a mouth gesture: mouth is open and the tongue is sticking out only for the sign meaning 'not yet' but the movement of the hands and arms is otherwise identical for both.

(2) *Affective expressions.* Surprise, pleasure or displeasure, etc., are also expressed on the face; these expressions are sometimes quite similar in appearance to those used for grammatical purposes (although the

[2]We leave aside for the moment the complex relationships and interdependencies between the use of the dominant and nondominant hands. Taking these into account would, however, reinforce the conclusions drawn below.

[3]There is an extensive literature on the use of nonmanual markings for grammatical purposes. See, e.g., Aarons 1994, Bahan 1996, Baker and Padden 1978, Baker-Shenk 1983, Baker and Cokely 1980, Coulter 1979, Liddell 1978, 1980, Neidle et al. 2000. However, there is still further research needed, as many of the linguistically significant nonmanual expressions are not yet fully understood.

[4]The pictures in Figures 1 and 2 are taken from Neidle et al. 2000, ©MIT Press.

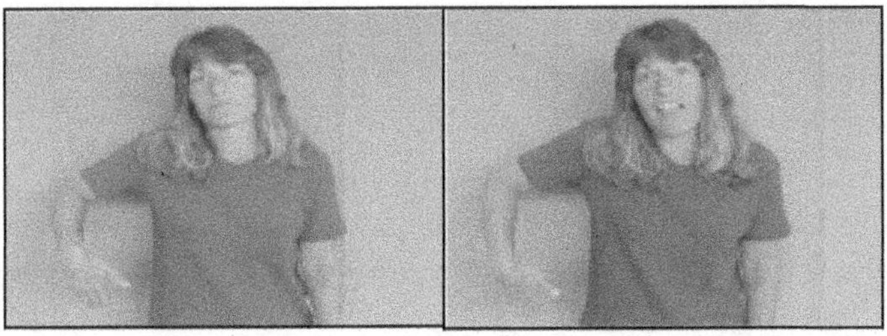

FIGURE 1 LATE (left) vs. NOT-YET (right)

FIGURE 2 CARELESS and WRITE, co-occurring with 'th'

intensity, distribution, and contour differ for affective and grammatical markings; e.g., Baker-Shenk 1983, Corina et al. 1999).

(3) *Adverbial modification.* Mouth gestures frequently co-occur with other signs to provide adverbial information. For example, the gesture glossed conventionally as 'th', which involves the tongue between the teeth, conveys the meaning 'carelessly', as shown in Figure 2 co-occurring with the adjective, CARELESS, and the verb, WRITE. (4) *Syntactic information* about such things as negation; question status and type; reference; subject and object agreement; mood; tense; aspect; definiteness; specificity; and information status (topic, focus) is conveyed by nonmanual signals that occur in parallel with manual signing. The use of these markings for syntactic purposes is the focus of this paper. These syntactically essential nonmanual markings involve head position and (often periodic) head movements (such as nods and shakes), eyebrow height, eye aperture and gaze, mouth movements, and nose wrinkles, among other behaviors. For example, the marking associated with wh-questions involves a cluster of behaviors, normally in-

cluding lowered eyebrows, squinted eyes, and a slight rapid side-to-side head shake.[5]

7.2.3 Syntactic information distributed across channels

We have argued that syntactic nonmanual markings frequently serve as expressions of abstract syntactic features (e.g., [+neg], [+wh], phi-features), and that they occur with a predictable distribution, spreading optionally over manual signs within the c-command domain of the node with which they are associated, diminishing in intensity as distance from that node increases. The optionality of the spread interacts with a strong preference for the nonmanual material to be articulated with manual material; thus, in cases where no manual material is locally available, the nonmanual marking spreads obligatorily. See Neidle et al. 2000, Neidle and MacLaughlin 2002.[6] For example, in the case where a negative sentence includes a manual sign of negation, such as NOT, the nonmanual expression of negation (including a side-to-side head shake) co-occurs with that sign and optionally continues over the rest of the VP. However, a manual sign is not required for negation; the nonmanual marking suffices. In that case, however, it must co-occur with the entire VP.

As in the case just mentioned, the nonmanual marking is sometimes the sole "carrier" of the syntactic information. In many constructions, the nonmanual expression is primary (obligatory), whereas the manual expression is secondary (optional). The range of possibilities is shown in Table 1.

7.3 Expression of various types of syntactic information

The range of grammatical information that is potentially expressed through nonmanual markings is great. It encompasses information about sentence type (e.g., question vs. declarative) of the kind that can be conveyed by intonation in spoken languages. However, a much greater range of syntactic information is expressed by nonmanual expressions in signed language than is normally carried by tone and intonation contours in spoken languages. This includes information about agreement, tense, and aspect. *Specificity*, for example, can be marked by a nose wrinkle (Coulter 1979); this can extend over en-

[5]There is some semantic compositionality, to the extent that the nonmanual 'ingredients' that make up these different syntactic markings have some semantic consistency in their use (Coulter 1979).

[6]Optimality Theoretic constraints would work well in alignment of the lexical (manual) material and the suprasegmental manifestation of syntactic information.

1. *Syntactic information is only marked nonmanually.* "Relative clauses" (really correlatives), "when clauses," certain tense information, specificity.
2. *Nonmanual expression is required; manual sign may also signal this information.* Negation, Yes/No Questions, Conditionals.
3. *Nonmanual marking is required; there is also normally a manual sign.* Wh-questions.
4. *Information can be expressed manually and/or nonmanually.* Expressions of syntactic subject and object agreement in the clause (with parallels in DP).
5. *Information normally expressed manually, can also (or instead) be expressed nonmanually.* Certain aspectual markings.

TABLE 1 Range of possibilities for manual and nonmanual contributions of syntactic information in particular types of constructions.

tire DPs and clauses and is a typical component, for example, of the nonmanual marking of "relative clauses" (really correlatives) in ASL.

7.3.1 Tense and aspect

Certain kinds of *aspectual information* normally expressed through manual reduplicative articulations (as described in Klima and Bellugi 1979) can alternatively involve the same type of repetitive movement being transferred to the head. For example, the verb FLY can be inflected to indicate an iterative action by repetition of the signing along an elliptical path. Under certain circumstances, the hands can remain constant while the head moves in such a way as to convey the same information: the chin traces a kind of elliptical path. This is suggested schematically in Figure 3. Other researchers have also observed this use of the head for displaced motion normally expressed by the hands; it is, nonetheless, somewhat unusual. In addition, however, there are other nonmanual expressions of aspect that are more productive. In fact, further research is needed on a variety of facial expressions (particularly involving the mouth) and periodic head movements that seem to convey aspectual information.

Most recently, collaborative work with Michael Schlang and Robert G. Lee (Neidle and Lee, in preparation) has revealed that grammatical tense information is also expressed on the face. Reduction in eye aperture appears to be used systematically to distinguish non-present from present tenses. Of the non-present tenses, future is normally also marked by a lexical item, sometimes glossed as WILL, which is related to but distinguishable (in terms of articulation and syntactic distribu-

FIGURE 3 Iterativity of the verb FLY expressed alternatively by elliptical motion of the hands and the head

tion) from the adverbial meaning 'in the future' (Aarons et al. 1995, Neidle et al. 2000). Our research thus far indicates that past tense is marked not by a lexical tense marker, but rather, at least in part, by a particular tensing of the muscles of the brow (distinguishable from other kinds of eyebrow gestures). The contrast between present and past is illustrated in Figure 4, by a pair of sentences that are identical in their manual signs but differ only in tense, as indicated by the facial expressions.[7]

7.3.2 Phi-features and syntactic agreement

Movements of the head and directionality of eye gaze are systematically used as expressions of *subject and object agreement*.[8] Points in space are used referentially in signed languages; we have argued that they, in fact, instantiate phi-features (which, in signed languages, include referential information, allowing for referential differentiation of third person referents). Bahan (1996) demonstrated that the same points in space (called "phi-locations" in Neidle and Lee, 2006) that are accessed manually by pronouns, definite determiners, possessive markers, emphatic reflexives and subject and object agreement affixes on verbs

[7]Notice the mouth expression in the bottom sentence. This is very productive and may be aspectual in nature; it is associated with past (completed?) events. We are still analyzing its distribution and meaning. These images are taken from the file "ncslgr10a" on the 2003 CD-ROM, *NCSLGR SignStream Databases Vol. 1*, distributed by C. Neidle (sentences #25, #26).

[8]For details of the analysis and responses to, e.g., Liddell 2000, see Bahan 1996, Bahan et al. 2000, MacLaughlin 1997, MacLaughlin et al. 2000, Neidle et al., 1998, 2000, Neidle and Lee, to appear. The original analysis of the use of subject agreement is recast in Neidle 2002.

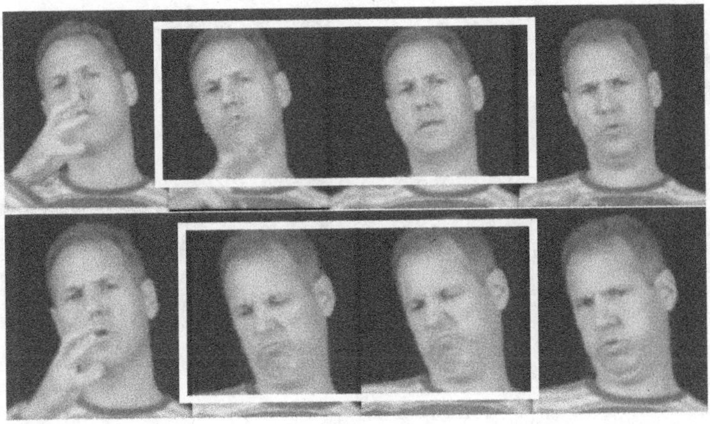

FIGURE 4 Present (top) *vs.* past (bottom): 'Mother [*is/was*] reading a book.' Both sentences involve the signs: 'MOTHER READ-progressive BOOK.' The 1st image in each sequence is captured during the sign MOTHER and the last during the signing of BOOK. The two middle pictures capture the facial expressions during the start frame and the end frame of READ.

are used in the nonmanual realization of subject and object agreement by head tilt and eye gaze. For example, in a transitive sentence, head tilt toward the phi-location of the subject and eye gaze toward the phi-location of the object — when present — mark subject and object agreement, respectively; the articulation of these nonmanual expressions of agreement begin after the subject NP has been signed and extend over the VP. The presence of subject agreement marking in either channel (i.e., marked by either a verbal prefix on a manual sign or by head tilt toward the relevant phi-location) suffices to license null subjects (Bahan 1996). MacLaughlin (1997) demonstrates strong parallels between agreement markings within the clause and DP. In Neidle 2002, it is argued that the head tilt just described, which includes nonmanual expression of subject agreement, actually functions to mark focus.[9] In other words, this marking is present concurrently with the signing of the VP when and only when the VP is in focus (thus resolving the mystery of the apparent optionality of the appearance of nonmanual expression of subject agreement: its appearance is a reflex of the marking of focus). Nonetheless, the syntactic information ex-

[9]There are quite a few distinct nonmanual markings that reflect the information status of a noun or clause in ASL.

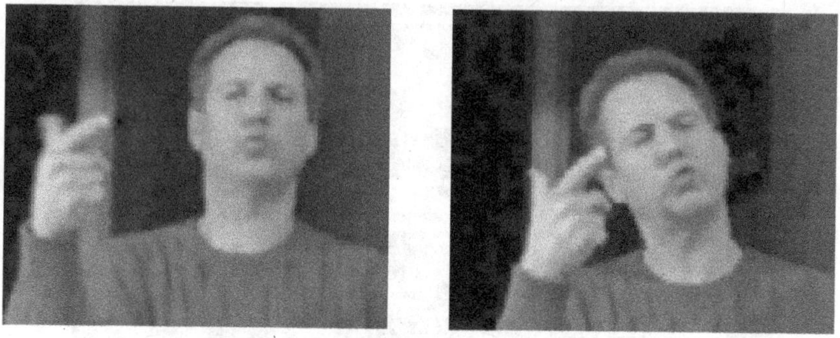

FIGURE 5 The start point of the agreeing verb SHOOT: *with* (on the right) and *without* (on the left) nonmanual expression of subject agreement through head tilt toward the subject's phi-location.

pressed nonmanually has syntactic consequences, e.g., for the licensing of null subjects.

This, information about subject agreement in a clause can be expressed either through prefix (whereby the start point of the articulation of an agreeing verb corresponds to the phi-location of its subject) or nonmanually (when the VP is in focus) by head tilt to that same location. Either overt expression of subject agreement is sufficient to license a null subject. When both manual and nonmanual expressions of subject agreement are present, there is a reduction in the signing space used for both gestures, as the burden of expressing this information is shared between the two channels (Bahan 1996). Compare the two pictures in Figure 5 showing subject agreement (with the same referent) in conjunction with the signing of the agreeing verb, SHOOT. Thus, it is clear that the expression of various kinds of syntactic information is distributed over both the manual and nonmanual channels.

7.4 Annotated video data and tools for linguistic analysis

As part of our recent examination of syntactic constructions in which nonmanual markings play a key role, high-quality synchronized videos of native ASL signers from multiple viewpoints — including a close-up of the face — have been carefully analyzed using SignStream^{TM}, an application that we have developed to facilitate such analysis (illustrated in Figure 6). The SignStream application is distributed on a non-profit basis, and we also have a large annotated corpus of linguistic data from ASL that is publicly available; see `http://www.bu.edu/asllrp/`. For

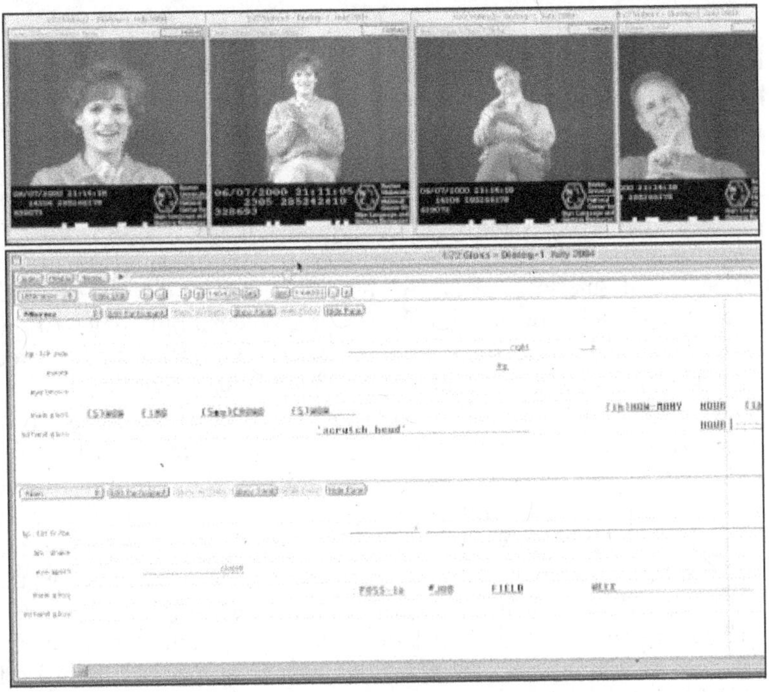

FIGURE 6 SignStream screen shot of two signers engaged in a dialogue, with information about manual and nonmanual behaviors encoded in parallel fields, with vertical alignment of co-temporal events.

further information, see Neidle et al. 2001. This is the first annotated sign language corpus of this kind.

The SignStream application allows for annotation and display of events occurring in multiple parallel fields, with vertical alignment of co-temporal items. Such annotation and display highlight (and have facilitated our study of) the contributions of linguistic information in the various parallel articulatory channels. In addition, these annotations have served as "ground truth" to facilitate computer science research related to recognition of the manual and nonmanual behaviors that carry linguistic information (specifically, for testing and refinement of computer vision algorithms; see, e.g., Neidle et al. 2001, Erdem and Sclaroff 2002, Athitsos et al. 2004, Vogler and Goldenstein 2005, He et al. 2005, Castelli et al. 2006 in press, Tsechpenakis et al. 2006 and to appear).

7.5 Fitting a linguistic model to these data

Ultimately, however, both for purposes of sign language recognition and generation, and for further linguistic research, appropriate syntactic models are needed. For obvious reasons, unification-based frameworks seem ideally suited to integrate the information from the manual and nonmanual channels, but still there is a need to identify the appropriate levels of representation. Of particular interest in comparing signed and spoken languages is the issue of the distribution of various types of linguistic information across multiple (if very different) channels. There have been some interesting recent approaches to integrating information from spoken language prosody (relevant to semantics, information structure, and constituency) with syntactic information (e.g., Asudeh and Mikkelson 2000, Haji-Abdolhosseini 2003, Klein 2000, Steedman 2000, Truckenbrodt 1999). The challenge with respect to ASL and signed languages more generally is that the information conveyed in the manual and nonmanual channels is not totally distinct in kind; syntactic information itself is present in both the manual and nonmanual channels (over and above whatever information normally expressed prosodically in spoken languages may also be carried in both the manual and the nonmanual channels). Further research is clearly needed with respect to integrating syntactic/semantic/prosodic information expressed linguistically in multiple channels. For such research, signed languages — and crossmodal comparisons of syntactic and prosodic structures — offer a particularly fertile terrain for exploration.

References

Aarons, Debra. 1994. *Aspects of the Syntax of American Sign Language.* Ph.D. thesis, Boston University.

Aarons, Debra, Benjamin Bahan, Judy Kegl, and Carol Neidle. 1995. Lexical tense markers in American Sign Language. In K. Emmorey and J. S. Reilly, eds., *Language, Gesture, and Space*, pages 225–253. Hillsdale, NJ: L. Erlbaum.

Asudeh, Ash and Line H. Mikkelson. 2000. Incorporation in Danish: Implications for interfaces. In R. Cann, C. Grover, and P. Miller, eds., *Grammatical Interfaces in HPSG*, vol. 8 of *Studies in Constraint-Based Lexicalism.* Stanford, CA: CSLI Publications.

Athitsos, Vassilis, Jonathan Alon, Stan Sclaroff, and George Kollios. 2004. BoostMap: A method for efficient approximate similarity rankings. In *Proceedings of the IEEE Conference on Computer Vision and Pattern Recognition (CVPR'04)*, pages 268–275. Washington, DC.

Bahan, Benjamin. 1996. *Non-manual Realization of Agreement in American Sign Language*. Ph.D. thesis, Boston University.

Bahan, Benjamin, Judy Kegl, Robert G. Lee, Dawn MacLaughlin, and Carol Neidle. 2000. The licensing of null arguments in American Sign Language. *Linguistic Inquiry* 31(1):1–27.

Baker, Charlotte and Carol A. Padden. 1978. Focusing on the nonmanual components of American Sign Language. In P. Siple, ed., *Understanding Language through Sign Language Research*, pages 27–57. New York, NY: Academic Press.

Baker-Shenk, Charlotte. 1983. *A Micro-analysis of the Nonmanual Components of Questions in American Sign Language*. Ph.D. thesis, University of California, Berkeley.

Cokely, Dennis and Charlotte Baker-Shenk. 1980. *American Sign Language: A Teacher's Resource Text on Curriculum, Methods, and Evaluation*. Washington, DC: Gallaudet University Press, Clerc Books.

Corina, D. P., U. Bellugi, and J. Reilly. 1999. Neuropsychological studies of linguistic and affective facial expressions in deaf signers. *Language and Speech* 42(2-3):307–332.

Coulter, Geoffrey R. 1979. *American Sign Language Typology*. Ph.D. thesis, University of California, San Diego.

Erdem, Ugur M. and Stan Sclaroff. 2002. Automatic detection of relevant head gestures in American Sign Language communication. In *Proceedings of the International Conference on Pattern Recognition (ICPR'02)*, vol. 1, pages 460–463. Quebec.

Haji-Abdolhosseini, Mohammad. 2003. A constraint-based approach to structure and prosody correspondence. In S. Müller, ed., *Proceedings of the 10th International Conference on Head-Driven Phrase Structure Grammar (HPSG'03)*, pages 143–162. Stanford, CA: CSLI Publications.

Klein, Ewan. 2000. Prosodic constituency in HPSG. In R. Cann, C. Grover, and P. Miller, eds., *Grammatical Interfaces in HPSG*, vol. 8 of *Studies in Constraint-Based Lexicalism*, pages 169–200. Stanford, CA: CSLI Publications.

Klima, Edward S. and Ursula Bellugi. 1979. *The Signs of Language*. Cambridge, MA: Harvard University Press.

Liddell, Scott K. 1978. Nonmanual signals and relative clauses in American Sign Language. In P. Siple, ed., *Understanding language through sign language research*, pages 59–100. New York, NY: Academic Press.

Liddell, Scott K. 1980. *American Sign Language Syntax*. The Hague: Mouton de Gruyter.

Liddell, Scott K. 2000. Indicating verbs and pronouns: Pointing away from agreement. In K. Emmorey and H. Lane, eds., *The Signs of Language Revisited: An Anthology to Honor Ursula Bellugi and Edward Klima*, pages 303–320. Mahwah, NJ: L. Erlbaum.

MacLaughlin, Dawn. 1997. *The Structure of Determiner Phrases: Evidence from American Sign Language*. Ph.D. thesis, Boston University.

MacLaughlin, Dawn, Carol Neidle, Benjamin Bahan, and Robert G. Lee. 2000. Morphological inflections and syntactic representations of person and number in ASL. *Recherches linguistiques de Vincennes* 29:73–100.

Neidle, Carol. 2002. Language across modalities: ASL focus and question constructions. *Linguistic Variation Yearbook* 2:71–93.

Neidle, Carol, Benjamin Bahan, Dawn MacLaughlin, Robert G. Lee, and Judy Kegl. 1998. Realizations of syntactic agreement in American Sign Language: Similarities between the clause and the noun phrase. *Studia Linguistica* 52(3):191–226.

Neidle, Carol, Judy Kegl, Dawn MacLaughlin, Benjamin Bahan, and Robert G. Lee. 2000. *The Syntax of American Sign Language: Functional Categories and Hierarchical Structure*. Cambridge, MA: The MIT Press.

Neidle, Carol and Robert G. Lee. 2006. Syntactic agreement across language modalities. In J. Costa and M. C. F. Silva, eds., *Studies on Agreement*. Amsterdam: J. Benjamins. To appear.

Neidle, Carol and Dawn MacLaughlin. 2002. The distribution of functional projections in ASL: Evidence from overt expressions of syntactic features. In G. Cinque, ed., *Functional Structure in the DP and IP: The Cartography of Syntactic Structures*, chap. 7, pages 195–224. Oxford: Oxford University Press.

Neidle, Carol, Stan Sclaroff, and Vassilis Athitsos. 2001. SignStream^{TM}: A tool for linguistic and computer vision research on visual-gestural language data. *Behavior Research Methods, Instruments, and Computers* 33(3):311–320.

Schlang, Mike, Robert G. Lee, and Carol Neidle. 2006. ASL tense and aspect revisited. Ms., Boston University. In preparation.

Steedman, Mark. 2000. Information structure and the syntax-phonology interface. *Linguistic Inquiry* 31(4):649–689.

Truckenbrodt, H. 1999. On the relation between syntactic phrases and phonological phrases. *Linguistic Inquiry* 30(2):219–255.

Vogler, Christian and Siome Goldenstein. 2005. Analysis of facial expressions in American Sign Language. In *Proceedings of the 3rd International Conference on Universal Access in Human-Computer Interaction (UAHCI'05)*. Las Vegas, NV.

8

Verbless Clauses: Revealing the Structure within

RACHEL NORDLINGER AND LOUISA SADLER

8.1 Introduction

In direct contrast to their frequency amongst the world's languages, verbless constructions, such as those illustrated in the following examples (taken from Stassen 1997:62-63), have received relatively little attention in the LFG literature.[1]

(1) Moskva gorod.
Moscow city
'Moscow is a city.' (Russian: Raptschinsky 1946: 11)

(2) Né soldádo.
2SG soldier
'You are a soldier.' (Guaraní: Gregores and Suarez 1967: 158)

(3) John padahk-men.
John teacher-INDEF
'John is a teacher.' (Mokilese: Harrison 1976: 158)

The syntactic analysis of these constructions raises many interesting questions for all theoretical frameworks, for they appear to involve main

[1]Each of us would like to extend our heartfelt gratitude and appreciation for the profound influence that Joan has had on our linguistic careers, as a role model, mentor and colleague. Over the years we have especially valued her insightful criticisms, encouraging remarks and above all the example of her own work, combining detailed empirical discussion with careful theoretical analysis.

Architectures, Rules, and Preferences: Variations on Themes by Joan Bresnan.
Annie Zaenen, Jane Simpson, Tracy Holloway King,
Jane Grimshaw, Joan Maling, and Chris Manning, (eds.).

clause sentences without overt verbs. The existence of a non-verbal but nonetheless sentential c-structure is not in itself at all problematic in LFG, nonetheless the question remains as to what contributes the main PRED of the clausal or root f-structure.

Constructions such as these are closely related to a variety of copula constructions in different languages. These include, for example, languages in which clauses such as those in (1) – (3) contain a *non-verbal* copula element, often deriving originally from a pronoun or demonstrative. Examples include (4) from Maltese and (5) from Hebrew:

(4) Malta hi gzira.
Malta COP/3SG.FEM island
'Malta is an island.' (Borg, 1987/8: 67, cited in Stassen 1997: 78)

(5) Pnina hi nora xamuda.
Pnina PRON.FSG awfully cute
'Pnina is awfully cute.' (Falk 2004: 1)

Technically speaking, such clauses are also 'verbless' in that they do not contain a verbal copula element, and similar issues arise as to their f-structure representation, and in particular, the nature of the clausal PRED. See Falk (2004) for detailed discussion of these issues in Hebrew.

In other languages the sorts of propositions expressed in (1) to (3) make use of a verb, sometimes a 'light' or bleached version of a lexical verb and often a specialized (auxiliary) verb used in a range of copula or predicative constructions.

(6) John is a doctor.
Eve is fond of Mary.
Sandy seems unhappy.
Kim is Mary's friend.

The current paper is intended as a small contribution to the analysis of copula constructions in general by focussing on the analysis of verbless clauses themselves and considering what can constitute evidence in favour of or against a particular syntactic analysis of these clause types. Constructions with overt verbal copulas have received some attention in the LFG literature, as has the related matter of the relational structure of non-verbal predicates dependent on copula verbs (see, for example, Dalrymple et. al. 2004). However, with the exception of Rosén (1996), and some recent discussion in Falk (2004), relatively little attention has been paid to the existence of truly verbless predicative constructions, despite the fact that the study of such constructions may cast light on issues concerning the analysis of copula constructions in general and also of embedded predicational structures.[2] The flexibility of the LFG architecture allows for two quite different approaches to the structure of these clause types. One possibility is that the non-verbal predicate is itself the clausal predicate, selecting in this case for a subject. On this view, a verbless clause such as (7) would have the f-structure given in (8). We refer to this as the 'single-tier' analysis.

(7) Ona vrač.
3SG.FEM.NOM doctor.SG.NOM
'She is a doctor.' (Russian: Fennell 1961: 288, cited in Stassen 1997: 64)

(8)
$$\begin{bmatrix} \text{PRED} & \text{`DOCTOR}\langle\text{SUBJ}\rangle\text{'} \\ \text{CASE} & \text{NOM} \\ \text{NUM} & \text{SG} \\ \text{SUBJ} & \begin{bmatrix} \text{PRED} & \text{`PRO'} \\ \text{NUM} & \text{SG} \\ \text{GEN} & \text{FEM} \\ \text{PERS} & 3 \\ \text{CASE} & \text{NOM} \end{bmatrix} \end{bmatrix}$$

Another possible analysis is that these verbless clauses have a more hierarchical f-structure in which the f-structure of the non-verbal predicate functions as an argument within a higher f-structure which itself has a PRED, but where there is no overt syntactic element corresponding to this predicate in the c-structure. In LFG terms, this means that the clausal PRED information must be contributed to the f-structure via some other means, such as by the phrase structure rules (Rosén 1996) or through information lexically associated with another element in the clause (e.g. Nordlinger and Sadler's (2003) analysis of Tariana verbless clauses). Thus, on this view, the f-structure of (7) would have the sort of structure shown in (9).[3] We refer to this as the 'double-tier' analysis.

[2] Verbless clauses have received some attention in other theoretical frameworks, see for example Avgustinova and Uszkoreit (2003).

[3] There are of course a number of significantly different variants here, differing in terms of the grammatical function assigned to the predicative complement and whether this complement is closed or open (and therefore subject to a functional control analysis). See Dalrymple et al. (2004) for some discussion. For the moment we abstract away from all of these details and simply represent the attribute which corresponds to the predicative element as GF, which may correspond to any of XCOMP, COMP, OBL and PREDLINK.

(9)
$$\left[\begin{array}{ll} \text{PRED} & \text{`BE}\langle\text{SUBJ, GF}\rangle\text{'} \\ \text{SUBJ} & \left[\begin{array}{ll} \text{PRED} & \text{`PRO'} \\ \text{NUM} & \text{SG} \\ \text{PERS} & 3 \\ \text{GEN} & \text{FEM} \\ \text{CASE} & \text{NOM} \end{array}\right] \\ \text{GF} & \left[\begin{array}{ll} \text{PRED} & \text{`DOCTOR'} \\ \text{CASE} & \text{NOM} \\ \text{NUM} & \text{SG} \\ \ldots & \end{array}\right] \end{array}\right]$$

Although most analyses in the LFG literature of *verbal copula* constructions adopt some version of the double-tiered approach shown above it should be noted that the single-tier analysis is also (in theory) appropriate for verbal copula constructions. That is, the copula verb and the non-verbal predicate could be taken to be co-heads of the clause, with the non-verbal predicate providing the lexical PRED and the copula verb providing tense, aspect, mood and other finiteness information.

Despite the possibility of these two quite different approaches, previous discussion of verbless clauses in the LFG literature seems to start off from the implicit premise that all such constructions cross-linguistically should have the same basic analysis (e.g. Rosén 1996 – for a contrary view in which one and the same surface copula form in Hebrew maps to divergent f-structures see Falk 2004 on the Hebrew copula). However, the fact that different possibilities are theoretically possible within the LFG framework suggests that there is no a priori reason why all verbless clauses, or indeed all copula constructions cross-linguistically, should have the same syntactic structure – this is very much an empirical issue. In this paper we discuss and exemplify the wide range of morphosyntactic variation in verbless clauses crosslinguistically, and show how this variation reveals that verbless clauses are not a single structural type at all. We show how the different properties of verbless clause types indicate distinct syntactic structures, which can be given a natural and revealing account by exploiting the two options available within the flexible architecture of LFG. In doing so we relate our discussion both to treatment of copula constructions in LFG, and recent work outside LFG on the descriptive semantic classification of types of predicative constructions.

8.2 Types of Copula Constructions

While our focus is on verbless constructions *per se*, these are generally functionally equivalent (or at least, in functional overlap with) with copula constructions in other languages (or even within the same language), and thus, for the purposes of framing the subsequent discussion, we begin with a discussion of the types of copula constructions more generally.

As noted by Curnow (2000), copula constructions, or those which "encode notions such as identity and classification", are extremely divergent in form (p. 1). In his own study he focusses only on the two core subtypes, which are as follows:

(10) • identity: That man is my father; That woman is Mary.
• group membership or classification: That woman is a doctor; That man is a teacher.

Other types include existence, location and possession, which are often expressed by the same means. Curnow identifies four main strategies for encoding these core subtypes, as follows:

(11) • use of a copula verb
• use of a particle copula
• use of an inflectional copula construction in which a language "treats the copula complement as though it were a verb" - ie the predicate takes some sort of inflection similar to what a verb would normally take
• use of a zero copula, that is, a lack of overt morphological material

This study shows that in very many languages the choice between alternative strategies is often dependent on factors such as tense and aspect, polarity, status of the clause as main or subordinate, person of the subject, and whether the semantic relation expressed is identification or classification. The fact that the choice of strategy in a given language can be influenced by superficial matters of grammatical encoding raises the interesting question as to whether the alternative strategies are externally distinct but correspond to the same f-structure.

In this paper we are concerned primarily with Curnow's latter two strategies, since in these constructions there is no clausal predicate distinct from the non-verbal predicative constituent. The following exemplify the inflectional copula (12) and the "zero copula" (13) respectively.

(12) Ben ğretmen-im.
I teacher-1SG
I am a teacher (Turkish: Curnow 2000: 4)

(13) Pakarli maparnpa.
man.ABS sorcerer.ABS
The man is a sorcerer (Watjarri: Douglas 1981: 238)

In more theoretically oriented work within the framework of HPSG, Avgustinova and Uszkoreit (2003) make much the same descriptive distinctions in their taxonomy of relations holding between a subject and a non-verbal predicate (mediated by a copula verb). Broadly, they distinguish ascriptive predication (with its subtypes as shown, corresponding to Curnow's *classification* subtype) from identificational predication (with its subtypes, corresponding to Curnow's *identity* subtype) from coupling predication, which groups together existential, locative and possessive uses of the copula.

(14) *ascriptive predication*: *attributive*, *classificational*
identificational predication: *equative*, *specificational*

coupling: *existential*, *locative*, *possessive*

Avgustinova and Uskzoreit (2003) observe that in Russian copulaless constructions are permitted in all of these functions – ascriptive, identificational, existential, locative and possessive – where they may alternate with an overt copula verb under certain conditions.[4] Examples include the following, where (15) exemplifies ascriptive clauses and (16) identificational clauses. The ? in (15b.) indicates that the overt present tense copula is possible only with appropriate contextual motivation.

(15) a. On durak/ tolstyj.
he.NOM.SG.M fool.NOM.SG.M /fat.NOM.SG.M
'He is a fool/fat.' (Avgustinova and Uskzoreit 2003: 4)

b. ?On est' durak/ tolstyj.
he.NOM.SG.M is fool.NOM.SG.M /fat.NOM.SG.M
'He is a fool/fat.' (ibid)

[4]For example, Russian short form adjectives such as *gord* 'proud.PRD-ADJ.SG.M' are exclusively predicative and never co-occur with the present tense copula, although they occur with the past tense copula.

(16) a. Boris brat Ivana.
Boris.NOM.SG.M brother.NOM.SG.M Ivan.GEN
'Boris is Ivan's brother.' (Avgustinova and Uskzoreit 2003: 4)

b. Boris est' brat Ivana.
Boris.NOM.SG.M is brother.NOM.SG.M Ivan.GEN
'Boris is Ivan's brother.' (ibid)

What this data demonstrates is that the possibility of the copula being absent, and therefore of non-verbal syntactic predication, is not limited to one particular semantic subtype of copula construction, but is widely available as a syntactic strategy for the expression of predicational structures of a wide variety of types.

8.3 'Single-tier' languages

Returning to the two possible types of analysis for verbless constructions available within LFG, support for the single-tier analysis comes from languages in which non-verbal predicates carry what would otherwise be (intransitive) verbal morphology, just when they function as the clausal predicate. These languages therefore employ Curnow's (2000) 'inflectional copula construction' strategy.[5] In (17a) from Abkhaz, the adjective 'dead' is inflected with subject agreement prefixes and tense/mood suffixes just as the intransitive verb is in (17b):

(17) a. Də-psə́-w-p'.
3SG.SBJ-dead-PRES-DECL
'He is dead.'

b. Də-cŵa-w-p'.
3SG.SBJ-sleep-PRES-DECL
'He is sleeping.' (Abkhaz: Spruit 1986: 97)

Other languages with this type of verbless clause structure include Turkish ((18), also (12) above) and Sirionó (Tupi-Guaraní) (19):

(18) a. Sen genç-sin.
2SG young-2SG
'You are young.'

b. Sen çavuş-sun.
2SG sergeant-2SG
'You are a sergeant.' (Turkish: Lees 1972: 70, cited in Stassen 1997: 46)

[5] In Hengeveld's (1992) typology of verbless clauses, these are referred to as zero-1 constructions.

(19) a. Ñéḍa-he-rae.
road-REFL-FUT
'It will be a road'

b. Kiḅáe-rv.
man-PERF
'It was a man.' (Sirionó: Firestone 1965: 24, 34)

In Bininj Gun-wok (non-Pama-Nyungan, Australia) predicate nominals (including those in 'adjective' function) are inflected for a subset of the regular verbal TAM markers: the past imperfective (which in this context simply marks past tense) and the irrealis mood marker (Evans 2003). Consider the following examples:[6]

(20) Mayh na-mekke nakka bininj-ni.
bird MASC-DEM MASC.DEM human-PAST
'Those birds, they were human then,' (Evans 2003:680, 13.27b)

(21) Na-mak-ni.
MASC-good-PAST
'He was a good man.' (ibid:682, 13.37c)

(22) Yawkyawk bokenh na-wu bene-berd-djenj-ni yimankek
young.girl two MASC-REL 3.DU-tail-fish-PAST CTRFAC
kun-dad-niwirrinj.
NEUT-leg-IRR
'There were two young girls who had tails like fish, they didn't have legs.' [lit. 'there were no legs'] (ibid: 357, 8.96)

As these examples show, nominal predicates in Bininj Gun-wok can be inflected with both tense morphology and agreement morphology (as in (22)) – both of which are usually found only on verbs. The fact that there is no evidence for a verbal head in these constructions, combined with the fact that the nominal predicate itself is inflected with specifically predicate morphology argues strongly for the single-tier analysis of these verbless clauses. This analysis is supported by the fact that the nominal is inflected with the propositional tense/mood marking which is otherwise found on verbs, but *not* on nominals which are arguments or adjuncts of other (verbal) heads. Thus, we represent (20) as (23).[7]

[6] CTRFAC = counterfactual, IRR = irrealis, MASC-DEM = masculine demonstrative, MASC-REL = masculine relative pronoun.

[7] Leaving aside for simplicity's sake the topicalised NP 'those birds', which is the TOPIC.

(23)
$$\begin{bmatrix} \text{PRED} & \text{`HUMAN}\langle\text{SUBJ}\rangle\text{'} \\ \text{TENSE} & \text{PAST} \\ \text{SUBJ} & \begin{bmatrix} \text{PRED} & \text{`THOSE ONES'} \\ \text{SPEC} & \text{DEM} \\ \text{GEN} & \text{MASC} \end{bmatrix} \end{bmatrix}$$

The f-descriptions associated with the tense-inflected nominal are given in (24). We assume that the option for a nominal to behave predicatively and subcategorize for a subject is effected via a lexical rule (or its equivalent):

(24) *bininj-ni*:
$(\uparrow \text{PRED}) = \text{`HUMAN} < \text{SUBJ} >\text{'}$
$(\uparrow \text{TENSE}) = \text{PAST}$

Thus, we generally assume that languages in which non-verbal predicates in verbless clauses are inflected with specifically predicative morphology (such as tense/aspect/mood or subject agreement) provide evidence in favour of the single-tier analysis.[8]

A potentially complicating factor, however, concerns the interaction with the expression of possession in such clause types. Consider the analysis of sentences such as (25) or (26) (repeated from (16) above):

(25) John is Peter's brother.
This is my house.

(26) Boris (est') brat Ivana.
Boris.NOM.SG.M (is) brother.NOM.SG.M Ivan.GEN
Boris is Ivan's brother.

Here we have an identity copula mediating a relation between a SUBJ and a possessed nominal. Suppose that the copula verb, even when it is present in these examples, is a purely functional element expressing tense. These examples would then map to single-tier f-structures as the copula (if present) would not project an f-structure of its own. In this

[8] A subtly different distinction is drawn in Avgustinova and Uszkoreit's (2003) HPSG approach to non-verbal predicates in Russian. They draw a firm distinction between short form predicative adjectives in Russian and the other cases of predication without a copula. In each case, a copula may or may not be present, depending on other factors. But in the case of the short form adjectives, they take the adjective to be the head, with any present copula treated as a specifer of the adjective, because there is morphological evidence of predicate status (it can't be used attributively) and therefore can be the output of a lexical rule adding the relevant information. For all other cases, where the copula is present it is the head (of a headed phrase) and when it is absent they adopt a constructional approach in which "the result is a special type of *non-headed phrase*" (p. 12) (a *silent-copula-phrase*), with two non-head daughters.

case, on current assumptions, nominals such as *house* and *brother* have to be syntactically two-place predicates, subcategorising a SUBJ and a POSS. Although this might appear somewhat unexpected at first sight, we do not think there are grounds for ruling out this possibility. Building on the work of Barker (1995) and others, Laczkó (2000) proposes in connection with Hungarian examples such as (27) that a lexical process may operate on a predicate name and add a POSS function to an argument list.[9]

(27) az én kalap-om
the I hat-1SG
'my hat' (Hungarian: Laczkó 2000: 218)

There is no reason in principle not to expect a predicate nominal in certain languages to also undergo this process producing a two-place predicate that subcategorises for both a SUBJ *and* a POSS:[10]

(28) 'house-π < SUBJ, POSS>'
'brother-π < SUBJ, POSS>'

Interestingly, however, verbless sentences which are potentially analysable along these lines do not seem to occur in Bininj Gun-wok, a language in which, as we saw above, predicate nominals and adjectives appear with subjects in verbless constructions. In Bininj Gun-wok all verbless possessive constructions appear to have the possessor nominal in predicate function, as in the following example, which we assume corresponds to the f-structure in (30). Note that the presence of the past tense marker on the possessor pronoun in this example constitutes evidence that it is functioning as the predicate of the clause.

---

[9]In Nordlinger and Sadler (2003) we suggest that additional support for this account comes from the frequent systematic ambiguity of nominal tense markers which attach to nouns with possessor arguments: in very many languages, the tense marker can temporally locate either the main nominal predicate or the relation of possession. Thus the Guaraní (Tupi-Guaraní) *h-óga-kwé* (his-house-PST) 'his former house' can mean either 'his thing which used to be a house (e.g. it has burned down)', in which the property of being a house is located in the past and the tense marker is interpreted with respect to the nominal itself; or it can mean 'the house which used to be his (but now belongs to somebody else)', in which the possession relation is located in the past, and the tense marker is not interpreted with respect to the nominal 'house'.

[10]Although, of course, this poses a challenge to the standard assumption that POSS is a type of SUBJ function because we would then expect SUBJ and POSS to be in complementary distribution with a single PRED.

(29) Arduk-ni an-ekke modikka.
my-PAST VEG-that car
'That car used to be mine.' (Bininj Gun-wok: Evans 2003:268, 7.32)

(30)

PRED	'MY ⟨SUBJ⟩'
TENSE	PAST
SUBJ	["that car"]

It remains an open question, then, whether there are single-tier languages in which non-verbal predicates can subcategorise for both a subject and a possessor function, although we strongly suspect that such languages exist. In any respect, it is clear that the coexistence of POSS and SUBJ as arguments of the nominal predicate is not necessarily an argument against the single-tier analysis. Clearly, the co-occurence of non-verbal predication with possession throws up a number of complex and interesting issues concerning the representation of possession and the valency of predicates, which we leave for future work.

8.4 Double-tier analysis

As discussed earlier, a double-tier analysis of verbless clauses requires the positing of a 'dummy' predicate – a PRED in the f-structure that does not correspond to anything in the c-structure. It may at first sight seem a little contradictory to suggest that there can be morphological evidence for the existence of this additional layer, since we are essentially looking for overt evidence of non overt structure, but we believe convincing evidence does in fact come from languages in which verbless clauses exhibit 'tense stacking'. It is to these languages that we turn in this section. In Bininj Gun-wok we saw nominals inflected for clause-level tense when functioning as predicates of the clause. In other languages *dependent* nominals (i.e. those functioning as arguments or adjuncts in verb-headed clauses) can also be inflected for tense, in this case a tense which is independent of the tense of the clause. Elsewhere we have referred to this type of tense marking as 'independent nominal tense' (e.g. Nordlinger and Sadler 2004a). In languages with independent nominal tense, nominal tense marking temporally locates the nominal referent independently of the tense of the clause as a whole. This is exemplified in the following example from Tariana (Arawak).[11]

[11]Although relatively unusual this phenomenon is by no means rare. Other languages with this type of nominal tense marking include Halkomelem (Salish) (Galloway 1983), Iate (Macro-Jê) (Lapenda 1968), Kwakw'ala (Northern Wakashan)

(31) Kayu-maka hĩ waripere unyane-pena
so-AFF DEM:ANIM Walipere flood-FUT
di-kakwa-pidana.
3SG.NF-plan=REM.P.REP
'Thus Walipere was planning the future flood.' (Aikhenvald 2003)

In this example the nominal 'flood' is inflected with nominal future tense *-pena* (expressing 'future flood') despite the fact that the clausal tense is remote past, as indicated by the clausal tense/evidentiality clitic *-pidana.*

A language such as Tariana has available two sets of tense affixes – one set occurring on nominals and marking independent nominal tense, and another set marking propositional tense on verbs and predicate nominals (32). The same is true of Guaraní (Tupi-Guaraní), as shown in (33). What is most interesting from the current perspective is that these can combine on the one nominal, as the following examples show:

(32) Pi-ya-dapana-miki-ri-naka.
2SG-POSS-house-PST-NF-PRES.VIS
'This is what used to be your house (I can see it).' (Tariana: Aihkenvald 2003)

(33) Che-roga-rã-ta
1SG-house-FUT$_x$-FUT$_y$
'It will be my future house.' (Guaraní: Dagmar Jung, pc)

Such tense stacking data provides evidence that these verbless predications must be associated with two levels of f-structure: one the locus of the nominal tense and the other the locus of the propositional tense. If this were not the case – if these clauses had the single-tier structure of the Bininj Gun-wok examples above – we would have a clash of tense features, since both the nominal tense and the propositional tense would be unified into the same (clause-level) f-structure. These two possible structures associated with the predicate nominal in (32) are shown in (34) and (35). As is clear in (35), the single-tier analysis is not viable in these tense stacking examples due to the clash of tense features that results.

(Anderson 1985), Nambiquara (Lowe 1999), Potawatomi (Central Algonquian) (Hockett 1958:238), Somali (Cushitic) (Lecarme 1996, 1999): see Nordlinger and Sadler (2004a) for more detail.

(34)
$$\left[\begin{array}{ll} \text{TENSE} & \text{PRES} \\ \text{GF} & \left[\begin{array}{ll} \text{PRED} & \text{`HOUSE}\langle\text{POSS}\rangle\text{'} \\ \text{TENSE} & \text{PST} \\ \text{POSS} & \left[\begin{array}{ll} \text{NUM} & \text{SG} \\ \text{PERS} & 2 \\ \text{PRED} & \text{`PRO'} \end{array}\right] \end{array}\right] \end{array}\right]$$

(35)
$$\left[\begin{array}{ll} \text{PRED} & \text{`HOUSE}\langle\text{POSS}\rangle\text{'} \\ \text{TENSE} & \text{*PRES/PST} \\ \text{POSS} & \left[\begin{array}{ll} \text{NUM} & \text{SG} \\ \text{PERS} & 2 \\ \text{PRED} & \text{`PRO'} \end{array}\right] \end{array}\right]$$

Thus, the presence of the propositional tense marker outside of the independent nominal tense marker in these examples provides evidence for a double-tier analysis of these verbless clauses, in which the nominal predicate has a grammatical function in the clause, rather than serving as the predicate directly (as in Bininj Gun-wok). Otherwise, as we have seen, we would have a clash of tense features in the f-structure of the nominal. If the propositional tense marker is *constructive* however, in the sense that it itself contributes the grammatical function that the nominal stem serves in the clause (Nordlinger 1998b), then the two tense markers contribute information to different f-structures and such a feature clash is avoided. This is shown by the (partial) f-structure for (32) in (34), which is licensed by the following f-descriptions associated with the various tense affixes.[12] The inside-out statement in (36b) specifies that the TENSE = PRES is in the f-structure within which $\uparrow$ (the f-structure of the nominal) appears as the value of the attribute GF.[13]

(36) a. PST-NF: ($\uparrow$ TENSE) = PST
 b. PRES.VIS: ((GF $\uparrow$) TENSE) = PRES

Note that the constructive analysis of propositional tense markers outlined above is needed independently in Tariana (and a number of other languages) because the propositional tense marker can appear on dependent nominals as well as predicative nominals. Aikhenvald (2003)

[12]For simplicity, we have only represented the tense information in the following f-descriptions, and not additional information such as gender and evidentiality. Such information can be incorporated with no impact on the analysis presented.

[13]See Dalrymple 2001 and the references cited therein for a formal definition of inside-out function application and discussion of its application in other grammatical analyses.

states that the propositional tense/evidentiality marker in Tariana appears on any focussed constituent in the clause, including dependent nominals; (37) and (38) are examples and provide further support for the analysis above in which the propositional tense constructs a GF for the nominal to which it is attached (see Nordlinger and Sadler 2004b for further discussion).

(37) Kayu-maka diha nawiki-nha ñamu
SO-AFF he person-PAUS evil.spirit
na-nite nawiki-miki-ri-mha.
3PL.say-TOP.ADV+CL:ANIM person-PST-NF-PRES.NONVIS
'So this man called evil spirit ñamu, they say he is the one who used to be a person (lit. he is an 'ex-person').' (Aikhenvald 2003)

(38) Naha-se-pidana na-inu di-na iniri-nuku
they-CONTR-REM.P.REP 3PL-kill 3PL-OBJ traira-TOP
'They killed the traira fish.' (ibid)

Thus, we take the tense stacking data in Tariana and Guaraní to provide strong evidence that in these languages, nominal predicates are the value of a GF within the clause, as shown in (34). It remains to be explained, however, just what this GF is, and where the PRED of the clausal f-structure comes from in these constructions.

As noted by Rosén (1996), analyses of these clause types in the LFG literature differ as to whether such predicative complements correspond to open or closed functions at f-structure. Andrews (1982), for example, treats them as having the open function NCOMP, while Grimshaw (1982) takes NCOMP itself to be a closed function. Dalrymple et al. (2004) argue that these complements may be open or closed at f-structure – depending on both the language and the particular construction – and follow Butt et al. (1999) in calling the closed function PREDLINK. Unfortunately we don't have the subtle syntactic data required to distinguish between an open or closed function for these predicative nominals in Tariana and Guaraní, and so we will likewise treat them as having the closed function PREDLINK, pending further investigation.[14]

[14]Note that agreement between a SUBJ and a non-verbal predicate just falls out under a single-tier analysis and under a double-tier XCOMP analysis as a case of subject-predicate agreement. However under the PREDLINK analysis it is necessary to state this in some sort of non-standard way (for example, by an additional lexical entry for the predicate adjective which constructs the PREDLINK function and the dummy predicate and states an inside-out constraint over the agreement features of the SUBJ in the f-structure containing the PREDLINK, i.e. ((PREDLINK ↑) SUBJ)).

We assume that a dummy clausal predicate is contributed by the propositional marker itself in these constructions. Thus, the lexical f-descriptions for the tense markers, and the full f-structure for (32) is shown in (40).

(39) PST-NF: $(\uparrow \text{TENSE}) = \text{PST}$
PRES.VIS: $((\text{GF} \uparrow)\ \text{TENSE}) = \text{PRES}$
$((\text{GF} \uparrow)\ \text{PRED}) = \text{'be} \langle\ \text{SUBJ, PREDLINK}\rangle\text{'}$
$(((\text{GF} \uparrow)\ \text{SUBJ PRED}) = \text{'PRO'})$

(40)
$$\begin{bmatrix} \text{TENSE} & \text{PRES} \\ \text{PRED} & \text{'BE}\ \langle \text{SUBJ, PREDLINK}\rangle\text{'} \\ \text{SUBJ} & \begin{bmatrix} \text{PRED} & \text{'PRO'} \end{bmatrix} \\ \text{PREDLINK} & \begin{bmatrix} \text{PRED} & \text{'HOUSE}\langle\text{POSS}\rangle\text{'} \\ \text{TENSE} & \text{PST} \\ \text{POSS} & \begin{bmatrix} \text{NUM} & \text{SG} \\ \text{PERS} & 2 \\ \text{PRED} & \text{'PRO'} \end{bmatrix} \end{bmatrix} \end{bmatrix}$$

On this analysis, the fact that the propositional tense marker in Guaraní constructs a clausal predicate when attached to nominals accounts for the absence of this marker on dependent nominals in verb-headed clauses (since there would then be two clausal PRED values). To account for the occurrence of these affixes with dependent nominals in Tariana, we assume that this part of the f-description is optional in this language.

8.5 Paradigmatic Alternations: Some Issues

We have so far argued in this paper that, in different languages and on the basis of overt morphological evidence, both the single-tier and the double-tier analysis of verbless predicative constructions are motivated. Although we have mentioned in passing some data from languages in which both overt copula and zero (or inflectional) copula constructions exist side by side, we have not yet considered what light these cases shed on the range of possible analyses.

In a reasonably large number of languages it is in fact the case that the absence of an overt copula stands in paradigmatic opposition to the presence of non-present tense copula forms within a particular construction.

For example, in Hebrew the copula-less (41) has a present tense interpretation parallel with the past tense (42) (Falk 2004), and similar facts hold in other Semitic languages such as Arabic.

(41) Pnina nora xamuda.
Pnina awfully cute
'Pnina is awfully cute.' (Hebrew: Falk 2004: 1)

(42) Pnina hayta nora xamuda.
Pnina be.PAST.3FSG awfully cute
'Pnina was awfully cute.' (ibid)

Similarly, in Russian, the present tense copula is ungrammatical in combination with the predicative short adjectives, but is required to encode tense in past and future tense constructions (Avgustinova and Uszkoreit 2003).

(43) On (*est') gord rezul'tatami.
he.NOM.SG.M is proud-PRED-ADJ.SG.M results.INST.PL
'He is proud of the results.' (Russian: Avgustinova and Uszkoreit 2003: 1-2)

(44) On byl gord rezul'tatami.
he.NOM.SG.M was proud-PRED-ADJ.SG.M results.INST.PL
'He was proud of the results.' (ibid:2)

Since the two clause types in (41)–(42) and (43)–(44) respectively are apparently functionally equivalent – differing only in temporal features, it seems correct to propose an analysis under which the predication relations will be the same across both clauses. In principle, of course, the requisite parallelism of analysis can be maintained on either the single-tier or the double-tier approach – in the former the overt copula is simply a tense-marking co-head of the non-verbal predicate, while in the latter a dummy PRED is constructionally or lexically introduced in the absence of the copula. Given that the role of the copula is *solely* functional in these examples, however, we take it that these cases of tense-related paradigmatic alternation are suggestive of a single-tier analysis. In (45) we provide an example of a lexical approach to such cases of paradigmatic alternation, but a constructional approach is also a possibility.[15]

[15]This accords with Falk's (2004) assumption for the alternation in (41)-(42) (although he does not formalise an analysis of the zero copula case), and with the HPSG analysis of Avgustinova and Uzskoreit (2003) for (43) and (44) in which the copula is taken as an optional specifier (i.e. dependent) of the adjectival predicate. It should be noted that both papers take quite different approaches to other copula constructions in Hebrew and Russian respectively.

(45) *gord*
$(\uparrow$ PRED) = 'GORD⟨SUBJ, OBL ⟩'
$(\uparrow$ SUBJ NUM) = SG
$(\uparrow$ SUBJ GEND) = MASC
$((\uparrow$ TENSE) = PRES)

(46) *byl*
$(\uparrow$ TENSE) = PAST

Treating tense as an instantiated feature (e.g. replacing PRES by PRES_ in (45) above) would prevent present tense being contributed by both the lexical equation introduced by the predicative adjective and also by an overt present tense copula. However the issue of how to ensure (for this construction) that the present tense copula is obligatorily absent, remains. On a constructional view it is of course possible to disjoin ϵ with V_{cop} in the relevant phrase structure rule, and then associate $(\uparrow$ TENSE) = PRES with the ϵ disjunct and $\neg$ $(\uparrow$ TENSE) = PRES with the other disjunct. But this in turn would require a "special" c-structure rule. Since our purpose here is not to provide an analysis of Russian copula constructions we leave these matters to one side.

We now turn to a different sort of contrastive opposition which interacts with the means of expression for copula constructions in some languages.

In many Australian languages, such as Wambaya (Nordlinger 1998a) and Martuthunira (Dench 1995), non-verbal predicates form independent propositions, but without any predicate-specific morphology (such as tense marking). Where a copula of sorts is possible, there is a distinct meaning difference between the use and absence of the copula in these constructions. For example, in Martuthunira, Dench (1995) shows that while ascriptive verbless clauses (such as those headed by common nominals in (47) and (48)) are effectively tenseless and imply a characteristic property, the use of a verbal copula allows the setting of temporal bounds on these states, as shown in (49).

(47) Kartungu-ngara pawulu-ngara murtiwarla paju.
2SG.GEN-PL child-PL fast REAL
'Your children are very fast (runners).' (Martuthunira: Dench 1995: 205)

(48) Ngunhaa jami panyu ngurntura-a.
that.NOM medicine good cold-ACC
'That medicine is good for colds.' (ibid: 209)

(49) Pukarti-ngara nyina-marri-nguru jalya-rru.
snakewood-PL be-COLL-PRED rubbish-NOW

'The snakewood trees are all rubbish now (they weren't always).' (ibid: 210)

In Wambaya the verb otherwise meaning 'sit' can be used as a copula, normally with a stage level interpretation, while the non-verbal predication again implies a characteristic property. Consider the following contrast:

(50) Gurijbi/bagijbi ini alaji.
good.I.NOM/bad.I.NOM this.I.SG.NOM boy.I.NOM
'This boy is good/bad.' (Wambaya: Nordlinger 1998a:179)

(51) Alaji gi gurijbi/bagijbi mirra.
boy.I.NOM 3SG.S(PR) good.I.NOM/bad.I.NOM sit
'This boy feels good/bad.' (ibid)

A similar type of distinction is also found in Hebrew. Falk (2004) attributes to Shlonsky (1997) the observation that in the present tense the choice between the zero copula or the pronominal copula can encode a stage-level vs. individual-level distinction, respectively:[16]

(52) Ha-dinozaur hu šikor.
the-dinosaur PRON.MSG drunk.MSG
'The dinosaur is a drunkard.' (Falk 2004: 11)

(53) Ha-dinozaur šikor.
the-dinosaur drunk.MSG
'The dinosaur is drunk.' (ibid)

The question is how this contrast is to be viewed in terms of determining the associated f-structures. Given that non-verbal elements can serve as predicates in these languages, the null hypothesis for the verbless examples would seem to be the single-tier analysis. The question is whether the stage level or temporally bounded/situated examples should be similarly treated as single-tier (with the copula verb taken to be a cohead of the non-verbal predicate), or whether the semantic contrast between the two constructions types should be taken as evidence for them having different syntactic structures – the verbless examples 'single-tiered' and the copula examples 'double-tiered'.

It is beyond the scope of this paper to adequately address this question here, but note that a similar contrast is also found in Bininj Gun-wok (a single-tier language, on our analysis) *in the absence of any overt copulas at all.* In Bininj Gun-wok the choice of subject-coding prefix on some adjectives has a clear semantic effect. Thus in the examples

[16] Falk (2004) treats the zero copula as single-tier and the pronominal copula as double-tier with a PREDLINK.

below, the use of a pronominal prefix gives a situational or eventive (stage-level) reading (54) while the use of the gender marker denotes a long term or characteristic property (individual-level), as in (55) and (56).

(54) Kodjok ka-mak.
(name) 3-good
'Kodjok's OK (e.g. not upset or sick).' (Bininj Gun-wok: Evans 2003: 557)

(55) Kodjok na-mak.
(name) MA-good
'Kodjok's a good/handsome person.' (ibid)

(56) Na-mak-ni.
MA-good-PST
'He was a good man.' (ibid)

Note that this choice of pronominal or gender morphology has no bearing on the ability to combine with tense markers. The root *ngud-jwarre* means 'bad at walking, bad on one's feet'; *al-ngudjwarre-ni* (with feminine gender prefix and past tense) was translated to mean 'she was too old to walk, unable to walk' (i.e. an individual level predicate), while *ba-ngudjwarre-ni* (with the verbal pronominal prefix and past tense) was translated as meaning 'she (felt) too tired to walk' (a stage level predicate) (Evans 2003: 557).

We interpret the Bininj Gun-wok data as showing that both sides of the semantic opposition can be encoded in single-tier f-structures, and can be independent of the use of an overt copula. So there is no reason to expect the verbal copulas above necessarily to be associated with double-tier analyses rather than single-tier co-head analyses.

8.6 Conclusion

While there is much work still to be done on the syntax and semantics of verbless clauses cross-linguistically, it is clear that the standard assumption that verbless clauses should all receive the same syntactic analysis is unfounded. Once verbless clauses are examined in detail, syntactic and morphological differences emerge revealing subtly different syntactic structures. In this paper we have shown that verbless clauses across the world's languages can divided into (at least) two different structural types: one in which the non-verbal predicate is itself the f-structure PRED of the clause (the single-tier analysis); and another in which the non-verbal predicate has a grammatical function within a higher clause with a nonovert head in the c-structure (the double-tier analysis). In the absence of positive evidence to the contrary, the single-tier analysis – which is more economical in assuming less structure – is the default hypothesis for verbless clauses cross-linguistically. However, positive evidence for the double-tier analysis is possible, as for example with the interesting cases of tense stacking in the languages of Tariana and Guaraní. While these clause types raise interesting and challenging issues for all theoretical frameworks, we have shown how these different syntactic structures can be captured naturally within the flexible architecture of LFG. It is hoped that this discussion will prompt further research into the nature of verbless clauses cross-linguistically, and their relationship to copula clauses of all types.

References

Aikhenvald, Alexandra Y. 2003. *The Tariana language of Northwest Amazonia*. Cambridge, UK: Cambridge University Press.

Anderson, Stephen R. 1985. Typological distinctions in word formation. In T. Shopen, ed., *Language Typology and Syntactic Description*, vol. 3, pages 3–56. Cambridge, UK: Cambridge University Press.

Andrews, Avery D. 1982. The Representation of Case in Modern Icelandic. In J. Bresnan, ed., *The Mental Representation of Grammatical Relations*, pages 427–503. Cambridge, MA: The MIT Press.

Avgustinova, Tania and Hans Uszkoreit. 2003. Reconsidering the relations in constructions with non-verbal predicates. In Kosta, P. and Błaszczak, J. and Frasek, J. and Geist, L. and M. Zygis, ed., *Investigations into Formal Slavic Linguistics*, pages 461–482. Frankfurt am Main: P. Lang.

Barker, Chris. 1997. *Possessive Descriptions*. Stanford, CA: CSLI Publications.

Borg, Albert. 1987-8. To be or not to be a copula in Maltese. *Journal of Maltese Linguistics* 17-18:54–71.

Butt, Miriam, Tracy H. King, María-Eugenia Niño, and Frédérique Segond. 1999. *A Grammar-Writer's Cookbook*. Stanford, CA: CSLI Publications.

Curnow, Timothy. 2000. Towards a cross-linguistic typology of copula constructions. In *Proceedings of the 1999 Conference of the Australian Linguistics Society (ALS'99)*, pages 1–9. Perth: Australian Linguistic Society.

Dalrymple, Mary. 2001. *Lexical Functional Grammar*, vol. 34 of *Syntax and Semantics*. San Diego, CA: Academic Press.

Dalrymple, Mary, Helge Dyvik, and Tracy H. King. 2004. Copula Complements: Closed or Open? In M. Butt and T. H. King, eds., *Proceedings of the International Lexical-Functional Grammar Conference 2004 (LFG'04)*, pages 188–198. Christchurch: CSLI Online Publications.

Dench, Alan. 1995. *Martuthunira: A language of the Pilbara Region of Western Australia*. Canberra: Pacific Linguistics.

Douglas, W. H. 1981. Watjarri. In R. M. W. Dixon and B. J. Blake, eds., *Handbook of Australian Languages*, pages 197–272. Canberra: Australian National University.

Evans, Nicholas. 2003. *A Pan-dialectal Grammar of Bininj Gun-Wok (Arnhem Land): Mayali, Kunwinjku and Kune*. Canberra: Pacific Linguistics.

Falk, Yehuda N. 2004. The Hebrew present tense copula as a mixed category. In M. Butt and T. H. King, eds., *Proceedings of the International Lexical-Functional Grammar Conference 2004 (LFG'04)*, pages 226–246. Christchurch: CSLI Online Publications.

Fennell, John L. I. 1961. *The Penguin Russian course*. Harmondsworth, UK: Penguin.

Firestone, Homer L. 1965. *Description and Classification of Sirionó*. London: Mouton de Gruyter.

Galloway, Brent. 1993. *A Grammar of Upriver Halkomelem*. Berkeley, CA: University of California Press.

Gregores, Emma and Jorge Suárez. 1967. *A Description of Colloquial Guaraní*. The Hague: Mouton.

Grimshaw, Jane. 1982. On the Lexical Representation of Romance Reflexive Clitics. In J. Bresnan, ed., *The Mental Representation of Grammatical Relations*, pages 87–148. Cambridge, MA: The MIT Press.

Harrison, Sheldon P. 1976. *Mokilese Reference Grammar*. Honolulu, HI: University Press of Hawaii.

Hengeveld, K. 1992. *Non-verbal Predication: Theory, Typology, Diachrony*. Berlin: Mouton de Gruyter.

Hockett, Charles F. 1958. *A Course in Modern Linguistics*. New York, NY: MacMillan.

Laczkó, Tibor. 2000. Derived Nominals, Possessors and Lexical Mapping Theory. In Miriam Butt and Tracy H. King, ed., *Argument Realization*, pages 189–228. Stanford, CA: CSLI.

Lapenda, Geraldo. 1968. *Estrutura da língua Iatê: falada pelos índios Fulniôs em Pernambuco*. Recife: Unversidade Federal de Pernambuco.

Lecarme, Jacqueline. 1996. Tense in the nominal system. In J. Lecarme, J. Lowenstamm and U. Shlonsky, ed., *Studies in Afroasiatic Grammar: The Somali DP*, pages 159 178. The Hague: Holland Academic Graphics.

Lecarme, Jacqueline. 1999. Nominal Tense and Tense Theory. In F. Corblin, C. Dobrovie-Sorin, and J.-M. Marandin, eds., *Empirical Issues in Formal Syntax and Semantics 2*, pages 333–354. The Hague: Thesus.

Lees, Robert B. 1972. The Turkish copula. In Verhaar, J. W. M., ed., *The verb 'be' and its synonyms*, pages 64–73. Dordrecht: D. Reidel.

Lowe, Ivan. 1999. Nambiquara. In A. Y. Aikhenvald and R. Dixon, eds., *The Amazonian Languages*, pages 269–292. Cambridge, UK: Cambridge University Press.

Nordlinger, Rachel. 1998a. *A Grammar of Wambaya, Northern Territory (Australia)*. Canberra: Pacific Linguistics.

Nordlinger, Rachel. 1998b. *Constructive Case: Evidence from Australian Languages*. Stanford, CA: CSLI Publications.

Nordlinger, Rachel and Louisa Sadler. 2003. The syntax and semantics of tensed nominals. In M. Butt and T. H. King, eds., *Proceedings of the International Lexical-Functional Grammar Conference 2003 (LFG'03)*, pages 328–346. Stanford, CA: CSLI Online Publications.

Nordlinger, Rachel and Louisa Sadler. 2004a. Nominal Tense in Crosslinguistic Perspective. *Language* 80(4):776–806.

Nordlinger, Rachel and Louisa Sadler. 2004b. Tense Beyond the Verb: Encoding Clausal Tense/Aspect/Mood on Nominal Dependents. *Natural Language and Lingustic Theory* 22(3):597–641.

Raptschinsky, Boris. 1946. *Russische Spraakkunst*, vol. I. Groningen: Wolters.

Rosén, Victoria. 1996. The LFG Architecture and "Verbless" Syntactic Constructions. In M. Butt and T. H. King, eds., *Proceedings of the International Lexical-Functional Grammar Conference 1996 (LFG'96)*. CSLI Online Publications, Stanford, CA.

Shlonsky, Ur. 1997. *Clause Structure and Word Order in Hebrew and Arabic: An Essay in Comparative Semitic Syntax*. Oxford: Oxford University Press.

Spruit, Arie. 1986. *Abkhaz Studies*. Ph.D. thesis, Leiden University.

Stassen, Leon. 1997. *Intransitive Predication*. Oxford: Oxford University Press.

Part II

Morpho-syntax: Features of Words and their Syntactic Effects

9

Number and Classifier Distributions in Arabic and Chinese and Their Complementarity

Abdelkader Fassi Fehri and Marie-Thérèse Vinet

9.1 Introduction

It has been observed that languages which exhibit Number (Nb) marking on nouns (tend to) lack classifiers (Cl), and vice versa (cf. e.g. Greenberg (1972)).[1] This has led some authors to postulate a systematic complementary distribution between Nb and Cl, and treat the two markings as discriminately complementary (cf. e.g. T'sou (1976), Chierchia (1998), Borer (2004), among others). Second, the 'count-mass' dichotomy has been thought of in the literature as being the core classification of nouns (Ns), and it has also been associated with a discriminative distribution of Cl and Nb, so that e.g. Chinese Ns are solely thought of as mass, whereas English Ns can be count (in addition to mass, with count as the marked member). Third, (under)specification in interacting Nb and Cl feature values provides an important source of complementarity effects. It involves various parts of the grammar

[1]This paper has been presented namely at the Moroccan 8th LSM meeting (June 2004), and the Linguistics Circle at the University of Surrey, London (June 2004). It builds heavily on Fassi Fehri (2003b). We would like to thank the audiences of these events, and acknowledge helpful discussions and remarks notably by Anne Judge, Alec Marantz, Marie-Claude Paris, Anne Zribi-Hertz, Nadia Amiri, and Huijun Zhou, as well as very fruitful comments by the reviewers of the volume. The usual disclaimers apply.

Architectures, Rules, and Preferences: Variations on Themes by Joan Bresnan.
Annie Zaenen, Jane Simpson, Tracy Holloway King,
Jane Grimshaw, Joan Maling, and Chris Manning, (eds.).

(as conceived e.g. in Bresnan (2001b), extending Jakobson's view of markedness; cf. also Ojeda (1998)), but also provides adequate bases for characterizing parametric variation. In this contribution, we first provide evidence from Arabic and Mandarin Chinese that a systematic complementary distribution between Cl and Nb (and/or plural, Pl) cannot be motivated.[2] Both languages exhibit various forms of classification and plurality, although the first language is thought of as a non-classifier language, and the second one as a general classifier language. Second, we show that N classification cannot be built on a count/non-count (or mass) binary distinction. Such a binary classification obviates the role played by the 'singulative/non-singulative' (or 'individuative/collective') dichotomy in characterizing Pl morphology, typically in e.g. Chinese. It also obviates the role played by singulativity in characterizing integral atomic units (or individuals), or integral kinds, as opposed to non-integral entities such as masses. Partition and integrity will then be shown to be necessary relevant ingredients for defining a classificatory system based on two attribute-value feature pairs: [α atomic] and [β singulative]. The system characterizes four N classes traditionally documented in languages: individuals (Is), kinds (Ks), masses (Ms), and collectives or groups (Gs). Third, various forms and distributions of Pl and Cl are found, including group plural forms in Chinese, quantity plural modifiers in Arabic, and recursive classifiers, all of which point to the inadequacy of the complementarity hypothesis. We show, in particular, that markers of plurality in Chinese are generated either as overt Nb heads (that may move up into determiner D), or as empty Nb heads which are filled by classified Ns, moving to Nb. We claim that values of [α atom] and [β sing] features on Cls may be affected by values of the same features on Nb, e.g. converting a [+ atom] entity to [− atom] or a [∅ atom] entity in the case of set plurals or kinds, respectively, or a [+ sing] entity to a [− sing] or a [∅ sing] in the case of group plurals. Cl and Nb distributions are then not complementary in languages, and they provide no source for defining language types. In 'classifier languages', the [α atom] feature is generally specified at the Cl projection in the grammar, in 'number languages', it is generally specified at the Nb level.[3] Furthermore, the feature [β sing] may also

[2]The article focuses on the standard variety of Arabic, although similar phenomena are productively found in colloquial versions of the language.

[3]As assumed in a number of works, variation is not language specific, but rather to be found in the characterization of functional words and/or features, in the domain of the functional lexicon (see e.g. Chomsky (1999, 2001), Kayne (2003), Holmberg & Sandström (1996), Borer (2004)). Furthermore, overt realization can alternate with overt movement, typically N-to-D, as in e.g. Longobardi (2001 a&b).

be specified at the Nb level, as is the case in Chinese. For concreteness sake, we assume the following DP architecture for nominals:[4]

(1)

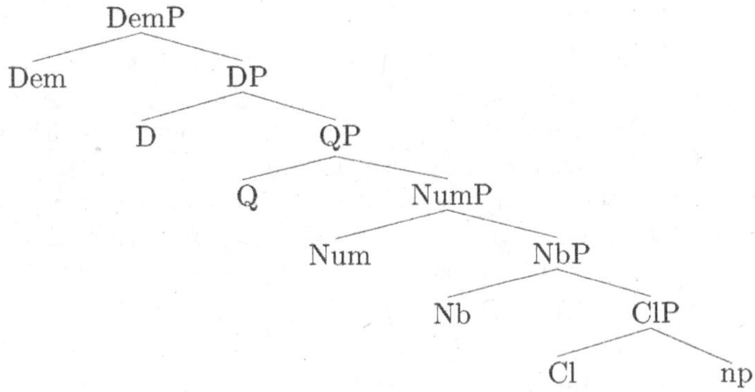

The article is organized as follows. In section 9.2, we provide a brief review of how and why Arabic and Chinese should be both treated (intriguingly) as classificatory systems, and show how Nb does not affect the [β sing] value of the classified noun. We also recapitulate the N classification argued for in Fassi Fehri (2003b). In section 9.3, we argue that the count/non-count distinction is inadequate, and examine why the classificatory system must be rebuilt on atomic and singulative features. In section 9.4, we investigate various forms of pluralities in Arabic and Chinese and show that these uses have no classifier 'flavour'. We then provide reasons why even Chinese pluralities are best thought of as involving Number, rather than Classifier. Moreover, the role played by movement in forming plural 'collectives' is characterized. In section 9.5, we provide an analysis of variation based on 'global' (under)specification (building on Bresnanian insights), rather than inflectional or projectional complementarity of Number and Classifier.

9.2 How different is Arabic from Chinese?

Chinese nouns, which are normally bare, and hence not inflected for Number, can still be interpreted as singular or plural. Moreover, they are not marked for (in)definiteness either. Thus a construction like (2) is four-way (existentially) ambiguous:

(2) wǒ kànjiàn gǒu le
1s see dog Asp
'I see (a/the) dog(s).'

[4] QP might be higher than DemP. The architecture is given for the sake of concreteness, and it does not preclude a more (or less) granular decomposition of DPs.

Second, bare Ns can also be read as generic/kind, as in (3):

(3) wŏ xĭhuan gŏu
1s love dog
'I love dogs.'

Another well-known important property of Chinese is that referents of nouns, whether the counterparts of English count or non-count Ns, need a Cl or a measure phrase to be counted. Thus Cls such as *zhī* are necessarily mediating the counting of individuals, as in (4a & b). Numerals (Num) such as *yī* "one" or *sān* "three" must be followed by a Cl N sequence, otherwise the result is ungrammatical, as in (4c):

(4) a. wŏ kànjiàn yī zhī gŏu
1s see a/one Cl dog
'I saw a dog.'

b. wŏ kànjiàn sān zhī gŏu
1s see three Cl dog
'I saw three dogs.'

c. * wŏ kànjiàn sān gŏu
1s see three dog
'I saw three dogs.'

Consider now Arabic bare Ns. Leaving aside the generic part and the (in)definite part, Arabic bare Ns can behave in essential ways like those of Chinese. First, construction (5) can be interpreted as an eating of one date or more (implying a singular or a plural 'date'):

(5) ?akal-tu tamr-an (* three)
ate-I date-acc
'I ate (one or more) dates (literally 'date').'

Second, this kind of noun cannot occur with a numeral, to count 'dates'. The use of a morphological Cl is needed, to refer to the 'unit' or the 'atomic' date, as in (6), where the Cl *-at* is suffixed to the N:

(6) ?akal-tu tamr-at-an
ate-I date-Cl-acc
'I ate a/one date.'

Note now that Arabic differs substantially from Chinese in that bare Ns are indefinite in both (5) and (6), and a (weak) singular cardinality can be involved in their interpretation. There is an important difference, however, between (5) and (6). In the cardinal reading, (5) counts only kinds, whereas (6) counts only individuals. The introduction of a plural cardinal does not change this state of affairs:

(7) ʔakal-tu ṯalaaṯ-a tamaraat-in
ate-I three-ACC date-unit.pl-GEN
'I ate three (individual) dates.'

(8) ʔakal-tu ṯalaaṯat-a tumuur-in
ate-I three-ACC date.pl-GEN
' I ate three kinds of dates.'

In (7), only the individual reading is available, and in (8) only the kind reading, despite pluralization in both cases. Note that the same contrast is found with singular indefinites above, or duals. In other words, Nb in general (and not just Pl) count units or atoms of different nature, but it has no impact on noun classification. It does not convert a kind to an individual, only a Cl does. Indeed, countability is relevant to Nb, but individuation is not. The similarity between Chinese and Arabic is then that Chinese bare Ns such as 'dog' behave as if referring to kinds in Arabic, and they need a classifier to be individuated. In Fassi Fehri (2003b), four classes of nouns are cross-classified by two feature values: kinds, masses, individuals and groups. Kinds can have integral wholes as their extension (hence their [+ sing] value), but they are unspecified with respect to whether they have singular or plural extensions (hence their [∅ atom] value). Individuals have integral wholes as their extension (they are [+ sing]), and they are atoms (hence [+ atom]), etc. The classification is recapitulated in (9). The examples (10) instantiate Mass and Group in Arabic, and (11) provide the English four counterparts:[5] [6]

(9) N classification
  a. K = [∅ atom, + sing]
  b. I = [+ atom, + sing]
  c. M = [∅ atom, ∅ sing]
  d. G = [+ atom, ∅ sing]

(10) a. štaray-tu zayt-a-n
  bought-I oil-acc-n
  'I bought (some, an) oil.'
  b. laqii-tu fariiq-an
  met-I team-acc
  'I met a team.'

(11) a. I like dates.
  b. I ate a date.
  c. I bought oil.

[5]In Fassi Fehri (2003b), Mass, Kinds, Groups, and Individuals are taken to be 'natural' classes of Ns, with various cross-classifying semantico-syntactic properties, organized through a minimal *mereology.* The latter makes essential use of a *N-part* relation and a *N-integral* property of parts/wholes, thus capturing 'atomicity' and 'integrity/singulativity' of parts and wholes. A [+ atom] is an entity which has no (improper) N-part (which could make the whole-part relation symmetric and reflexive). Individuals and Groups are [+ atom], having no (improper) N-parts. Kinds and Masses, on the other hand, may have N-parts, but are not necessarily specified as such. Vagueness in specification is marked as [∅ atom]. A [+ sing] feature is a property of an entity that is 'N-integral'. Kinds and Individuals are [+ sing] because they have integrity: if they have parts, these parts must be N-integral (i.e. cannot be divided), be they proper or not. If Kind has one or more than an N-integral part, then the part-whole relation will be improper for the first case, and proper for the second. For Individuals, the N-integral part is only improper. What is essential here is that N-integrity is a property of the part (and/or the whole). It is the integrity/singulativity property that unify Individuals and Kinds, which are otherwise different in terms of the atom property. Masses are [∅ sing]: they do not name N-integral wholes or parts. Groups are also conceptually [∅ sing] too: they may apply to a plurality of wholes, including integral wholes, but the latter are not N-integral. A 'team' may be composed of 'John' and 'Mary', but the whole and the parts are not in an N-part-whole relation, nor are they N-integral whole-parts. This system is made available by UG, and distinctions are expected to be manifested either in lexical classes (or roots), or in grammatical f-words (or f-features). Then the question is how much of this system is 'inherently lexical' (or found in the l-lexicon of roots), or functional (carried by f-words or features).

[6]It is important to note that Greenberg's (1972) in his seminal article equates the 'singulative' with the 'noun of unity' in traditional Arabic grammar, i.e. our 'individual', and the 'collective' with our 'kind'. The terms he uses do not have the same contents as Fassi Fehri's (2003b), nor does he build his analysis on a feature system.

d. I met a team.

9.3 Kinds of classifiers and their distribution

Although the term 'classifier' is used quite extensively in the literature, it has no clearly established content, function, or form, nor has it a clear connection to categorization. Allan (1977: 13) takes Cls to denote "some salient perceived or imputed characteristics of the entity to which an associated noun refers". Cl occurrence is claimed to be restricted to classifier constructions "which require the presence of a particular kind of morpheme, the choice of which is dictated by the semantic characteristics of the referent of the head of the noun phrase" (Aikhenvald 2000: 13). Cl then qualifies as the morpho-syntactic mark (or realization) of the 'perceived' semantic characterization. Cl forms often depend on categories (with which they are associated) so that (a) nominal, numeral, and D (article and deictic) Cls (including N class and gender), (b) genitive (possessive) Cls, and (c) verbal (predicate, aspectual) Cls can be distinguishingly identified (cf. Aikhenvald 2000 for discussion). In this article, we concentrate on some kinds of Cls found in the nominal domain, and investigate what could be their (more precise) content, function, and form, and what role is played by Nb (or Pl) in this phenomenology. In fact, we will ultimately limit the term Cl to its narrow sense, namely to markers of individuation, in opposition to measure and similar classifying words and/or phrases.[7]

9.3.1 The count/mass distinction: a misnomer

As mentioned above, *all* Chinese nouns, whether the counterparts of English count or mass Ns, need a Cl or a measure phrase to be counted (see the contrast in (4) above for counting individuals), as also indicated in Krifka (1995). Note that Cl can also occur with quantifiers such as *jǐ* "few", or *měi* "every", as indicated in (12):

(12) a. jǐ gè píngguǒ
few Cl apple
'few apples'

b. měi běn shū
every Cl book
'every book'

[7] As pointed out by a reviewer, the status of classifiers as "markers of individuation" has been formalized in the semantic literature (see e.g. Krifka (1995), among others).

Furthermore, the Cl can occur solely without the Num, as in (3). However, this situation appears to be limited to postverbal positions, and the interpretation is always singular:[8]

(13) wǒ xiǎng mǎi běn shū
1s want buy Cl book
'I want to buy a book.'

On the other hand, referents of mass Ns can be counted or measured through the use of measure or container words, or sorts, as exemplified in (14) and (15):

(14) a. yī bēi kāfēi
one Cl coffee
'a cup of coffee'

b. sān píng jiŭ
three Cl wine
'three bottles of wine'

c. yī piàn miànbāo
one Cl bread
'a slice of bread'

(15) tā kànjiàn sān zhīng yóu
3s saw three sort oil
'S/he saw three sorts of oil (three oils).'

These measure words are also taken to be classifiers in the literature, and the postulated important function of both types of Cls is to *make Ns countable.*[9]

---

[8]Cf. Borer (2004: Chap. 6) for further restrictions in this context. Cls can also be preceded by a demonstrative, with or without a numeral:

(i) (zhèi) sān běn shū
(this) three Cl book
'(these) three books'

(ii) zhèi běn shū
this Cl book
'this book'

When the Cl is necessary, then Q, Num, or Dem may co-occur with it.

[9]As pointed out correctly by a reviewer, mass nouns are not really counted through measure or container words, rather, they can be combined with them to be able to occur with a cardinal numeral. With measure words, the reference is not to counting, but to measuring. Counting quantifies a cardinality of a set, measuring a property other than a cardinality (e.g. temperature or volume). Counting can be applied only to sets, while measuring is applied to sets and non-sets alike. Measures do not partition, although they correlate with a set of measures. Partitioning is only needed in counting. We think that our analysis concurs with this view.

Cls are often divided into two groups. Cheng & Sybesma (1999), inspired by the references cited there, claim that (a) Cls either "create a unit of measure" (they are then called *mass-classifiers* or massifiers), or (b) Cls simply 'name the unit' in which the entity denoted by N naturally occurs (they are then *count-classifiers*). Cheng and Sybesma take it that Chinese makes a distinction between Ns that are inherently/lexically *partitioned* into countable units (count Ns) and those that are not inherently partitioned (mass Ns). The role of the mass-Cl is then to 'create' units by which the amount of the mass is measured/counted. Count-Cls, on the other hand, are associated with already partitioned (countable) units. Following Croft (1994: 162), Cheng & Sybesma (1999:516) appeal to an 'individualizing function' of count-Cls, which enables them to "extract ... distinguished, discrete occurrences" (Iljic (1994: 104)), or to be "a mark of individuation, or singularization" (as Paris (1981: 69) put it).[10] The count/mass distinction, they claim, although inherently present in Ns, is grammatically reflected only at the Cl level (in addition to the role it plays in other parts of Chinese grammar).[11]

Note, however, that the 'counting' function which unifies count-Cls and mass-Cls is still puzzling and obscure. If massifiers operate 'partition' of mass Ns, as it is claimed, to make them countable, why are then already partitioned Ns not countable? Worse, why are supposedly partitioned Ns designated as 'count' in the first place? If partitioning is a distinguishing property between two classes of Ns, as Cheng and Sybesma argue, then it is *not sufficient* for counting, hence the necessary mediation of individuating Cls in the case of (4). Following Fassi

[10] Cheng and Sybesma misleadingly equate this singularization function with that of D, which identifies one instance of what is denoted by N (ibid, p. 517). Croft, Paris and Iljic's intuitions appear to be closer to the view that we adopt here.

[11] Paris (1981) and Cheng & Sybesma (ibid) correctly observe that 'count-classifiers' and 'mass-classifiers' are distinct in two important ways, namely (a) the optional occurrence of *de* (a marker of phrasal boundary inside the DP) with 'mass-classifiers' versus its absence with 'count-classifiers' (cf. (i)), and (b) the modification of the 'mass-classifier' head with a small number of adjectives (*xiǎo* "small", *dà* "big") versus the lack of adjectival modification on 'count-classifier' heads (cf. (iib)) :

(i) a. yī wèi lǎoshī
one Cl teacher
'a teacher'

b. *yī wèi de lǎoshī (Paris 1981)

c. yī kuāng (de) píngguǒ (Paris 1981)
one Cl-basket DE apples
'a basket of apples'

Fehri (2003b), we take 'partitioning' to be *singulativity*. Partitioned Ns are then marked as [+ sing].[12]

On the other hand, Cheng & Sybesma (p. 515) note that massifiers occur not only with 'mass' Ns, but also with 'count' Ns. The examples in (16) illustrate this distribution:

(16) a. yī qún rén
one Cl person
'a group of persons'

b. yī jīn píngguǒ
one pound apple
'a pound of apples'

If the role of mass-Cls is to 'partition', as they claim, how can they be associated with already 'partitioned' Ns (so-called 'count' Ns)? If even inherently partitioned Ns are in need of Cls to be counted (be they interpreted as individual units, or as parts of potentially partitioned entities, or kinds), then the 'counting' function (whatever that is) has to be associated with both 'count-Cls' and 'mass-Cls'. It is not a property of 'count Ns', neither an exclusive property of 'count Cls'. Furthermore, the individualizing/singularizing function which is behind the countability of so-called 'count' Ns remains obscure at best. Indeed, if complementary distribution between the two types of Cls is discriminatory, as is documented in the literature, and exemplified by (17), then that could be an indication that the two Cls share a common property, which enables both to 'create' (rather than 'name', in Cheng & Sybesma's informal terms) the entities to be counted (be they individuals, measures, or amounts, etc.):

(17) a. *sì liàng gè qìchē
four Cl Cl car
'four cars'

b. *yī gè bēi kāfēi
one Cl Cl/cup coffee
'a (unit) cup of coffee'

Cls then serve to count individuals, to measure a portion of a substance, a portion of a collective, or a part of a partitive, as in the following examples:

[12]Note that 'partitioning' is *necessary* for counting only if it is not equated with 'individuating', since kinds and masses can be counted (when partitioned or taxonomized), although they are not taken as individuals (cf. the contrast in (7) and (8) above, as well as Fassi Fehri (2003b) for more details and motivation).

(18) a. yī gè píngzi
one Cl bottle
'a bottle'

b. yī píng jiŭ
one Cl/bottle wine
'a bottle of wine'

c. yī guà zhūzi
one Cl pearl
'a string of pearls'

d. yī dī yǎnlèi
one Cl/drop tear
'a tear'

Their diversity in categorizing objects according to shape, animacy, size, or other perceptual or physical dimensions does not obviate their main role in *counting* (and/or quantifying; cf. e.g. Paris (1981), Krifka (1995), Cheng and Sybesma (1999), among others).[13]

9.3.2 A new classification of classifiers

If both types of Cls are adding extra information to that carried by (bare) Ns, which relates to countability, then the distinction of Cls (examined so far), according to whether they are count-Cls or mass-Cls (or even worse massifiers) cannot be adequate. The classification needed has to take into account the type of information contributed by the Cl (and presumably the N it applies to). If some Chinese bare Ns are interpreted as singular or plural, and others are not (as it is the case for pure mass Ns), then that point to an inherently based distinction of Ns, according to whether they are potentially 'partitionable' or not, basically our [± sing], which cannot be taken as equivalent to 'count' vs. 'mass'.[14] We identify these Ns that can be potentially partitioned and interpreted as plural or singular as *kinds* (Ks), as proposed in Fassi Fehri (2003b). Ks denote potentially an unspecified number of integral wholes or singularities. The unmarked N with respect to singulativity is thought of as being a *mass* M. M has no semantic potential of denoting singulativities (or integral partitions). The contrast at the N level is then not between 'count' and 'mass' Ns, but rather between kinds and

[13]Paris (1981:73) mentions that in the spoken language the 'neuter' classifier *gè* is coming to be used more and more at the expense of other classifiers, a distribution which supports the hypothesis that classifiers are more connected to quantity than to quality or categorization.

[14]This view differs substantially from Chierchia's (1998) proposal that all Chinese Ns are mass (for similar ideas, see also Krifka (1995) and Borer (2004), among others).

masses. Both kinds and masses need a Cl to be counted, but the entities counted are not of the same nature, depending on the nature of the Cl (and the N it applies to). Individual Cls (which are typically characteristic of 'classifier languages') form individuals from kinds, whereas measure (or taxonomic) Cls or words do not operate any ontological change in the nature of kinds or masses.

What the 'counting' Cl does with singulative Ns (or integral partitions) is to make precise whether there is only one integral unit (to be counted), a single atom named an individual I, or an unspecified/non-atomic number of units, a kind K. These two choices of atomization values associated with Cls are exemplified in Arabic and English respectively (cf. Fassi Fehri (2003b) for discussion):

(19) a. samak "fish; kind of fish" ⟶ samak-at "fish-I; an individual fish"

b. apple ⟶ apple-s "apple-K"

In these examples, specified atomization as [+ atom] through the individual Cl is associated with an inherent singularity in the case of Arabic, whereas it is associated with an unspecified Cl atomically (a kind Cl, or a 'kindifier') in English. The Chinese singulativity appears close to the Arabic one, in that no (grammatical) mark is needed to form Kind, which is the unmarked case. Individual Cls are then needed to form individuals, as in Chinese (4) above, much more like what happens with Arabic (19a).

Note now that 'true' mass-Cls (or massifiers) are found in languages. Their role is to remove (or unspecify) the inherently positive singulative value found in Kind (its minimal counterpart), hence converting (a 'lexical') Kind to (a 'grammatical') Mass. This is illustrated in Colloquial Moroccan Arabic, where Mass can be overtly (and grammatically) derived from Kind:

(20) bger "cattle, cows" ⟶ begr-i "cow-M; beef"

Other potential Cls to be found in this system are 'collective' or 'group' Cls, as we will see.[15]

Cls which have been examined so far select nominal entities which involve the singulative and atomic features and rearrange/specify their value. The outcomes may or may not be countable as integral atoms. Kinds and masses, which are unspecified atomically, can also be made countable through Cls of different nature and range. These Cls count 'sorts', 'taxonomies', 'portions' of substance, etc. They tend to be

[15]It will be shown below that at least some Kinds and Groups in Chinese and English are Numbers (with a classifier flavour), rather than Cls.

found cross-linguistically, unlike individual Cls. They are phrasal (and lexical), and they can be easily translated from one language to another. The following Arabic constructions provide examples of counting phrases for kind and mass, respectively:

(21) a. ṯalaaṯat-u ruʔuus-i ġanam-in
three-nom heads-gen sheep-gen
'three heads of sheep'

b. ṯalaaṯ-u qiṭaᶜ-i xašab-in
three pieces wood-gen
'three pieces of wood'

But note that these 'classifiers' are not inflectional, unlike the individual ones. Furthermore, they are used to designate taxonomies, portions, measures, rather than to create atoms or units of some sort. They are then of a different ontological as well as a grammatical nature. Cheng & Sybesma (1999, 1998) note in this respect that even though 'count-Cls' and 'mass-Cls' are both nominals in Chinese, only 'count-Cls' form a closed set, with elements functioning solely as Cls (e.g. *tiáo* for counting long, flexible and narrow objects such as rivers, towels, trousers, streets, etc., *duǒ* for counting flowers, *liàng* for counting different types of vehicles, etc.):

(22) a. yī tiáo hé
one Cl river
'a river'

b. sān duǒ huā
three Cl flower
'three flowers'

c. sì liàng qìchē
four Cl car
'four cars'

'Mass-Cls', however, can occur as Cls as well as independent Ns (e.g. *píng* "bottle" as a unit for measuring wine, and *ping(zi)* "a bottle" as a container), as illustrated in (14) above, repeated here as (23), for convenience:

(23) a. yī bēi kāfēi
one Cl coffee
'a cup of coffee'

b. sān píng jiǔ
three Cl wine
'three bottles of wine'

c. yī piàn miànbāo
one Cl bread
'a slice of bread'

Contrary to 'count-Cls', 'mass-Cls' do not 'categorize'. Moreover, 'mass-Cls' are found in most languages, whereas many fewer languages have 'count-Cls' (so-called 'classifier languages').[16]

Note that this distinction which appears to be at the core of differences between so-called classifier and non-classifier languages can be captured in our classifier system, which makes typically a special room for individual formation, and cannot be so captured in systems based on a count/non-count distinction. As observed, the latter distinction is blind to the individual/non-individual distinction. In the next section, we will see how various forms of pluralities make use of the postulated feature distinctions.

9.4 Kinds of Number

Pl or Nb marking interacts with Cl marking in interesting ways, as widely noticed in the literature, but forms of this interaction need to be more precisely characterized. This section is dedicated to identifying various kinds of Pl/Nb uses in Arabic and Chinese, and to assess naturally expected kinds of interaction. One use of Pl might be termed a *multiplier*. Its function is to multiply individuals or sorts/taxonomies, in the sense that it generates a referential expression from the NP or classifier phrase (ClP) by mapping the nominal expression onto a *multitude* of its realizations. A second use of Pl is found in the context of so-called the 'plural of abundance' or 'the plural of the plural' (or 'double plural'), well-documented in Arabic traditional grammars. The main feature of this kind of Pl is that it applies to masses or kinds without operating a *nominal reference shift* (e.g. from a 'substance' to a 'sort'). It operates on an already formed referential expression (or a nominal term), and it has a *modificational* role of emphasizing the referent's quantity or its high amount. Wiese (1999) conceives it as a mass Nb marker, but we prefer to call it an *amount-Pl*. What is typical of amount-Pl is that it does not apply to countable units, but to amounts of Kind or Mass. A third type of Pl has some flavour of a Cl, being read as a Group or a Kind. We will argue that the latter is another sort of Pl/Nb, 'flavoured' with classification (in a sense to be made precise),

[16]Not all count-classifiers categorize, as pointed out by a reviewer. In some languages (e.g. Persian), a universal Cl can be used with all (transnumeral) nouns. This situation is comparable to that of the neuter classifier *gè* in Chinese (cf. fn. 13).

rather than a true Cl. On the other hand, various forms of pluralization are used in grammars, including not only overt inflectional morphemes or reduplication, but also, as we will argue, overt syntactic movement of classifier phrases to non-overt Nb.

9.4.1 Arabic

Consider first some instances of Pl forms found in Arabic. The following examples instantiate a multiplier Pl of atoms (individuals and groups), as in (24) and (25), and of taxonomies (masses and kinds), as in (26) and (27), respectively:

(24) samak-at "fish-unit; a fish" ⟶ samak-aat "fish-unit-pl; a multitude of integral fish units"

(25) firqat "team" ⟶ firq-aat "teams"

(26) zayt "oil" ⟶ zuyuut "oils; sorts of oil"

(27) samak "fish" ⟶ ʔasmaak "sorts of fish (a multitude of fish)"

In all these cases, we take the Pl to be a multiplier, inputting an atomic individual or sort, and outputting a multitude of these entities.[17]

Another form of Pl in Arabic (Standard Arabic) and Colloquial Moroccan Arabic stands for the amount-Pl variety. In Arabic (28c & d), the 'double Pl' functions as amount-Pl, whereas (28a & b) are multipliers:

(28) a. qawl "saying" ⟶ ʔaqwaal "sayings"
   b. qawl-at "saying-Cl; a saying" ⟶ qawl-aat "saying-Cl-Pl; a multitude of sayings
   c. ʔaqwaal "sayings" ⟶ ʔaqaawiil "a lot of sayings"
   d. farq "difference" ⟶ furuuq "differences" ⟶ furuuq-aat "a lot of differences/ various sorts of differences"

Note that the amount-Pl in (28d) may have a reading of 'double plural', i.e. Pl of sorts of *furuuq* "differences", with *furuuq* itself a Pl. In Moroccan Arabic, similar patterns are found, interacting also with Cls:

[17]Borer (2004) takes the Pl in examples equivalent to (26) to be a 'divider' of mass (a 'partitioner' in Cheng and Sybesma's terms). This then led her to think that the Pl there is a Cl which creates countable units, a view that she generalizes to all Pls. But this view cannot be correct even for (26), given that e.g. the Arabic singular *zayt* "oil" does have the reading of 'one sort of oil', rather than 'oil' (see Fassi Fehri (2003b) for discussion). Consequently, *zuyuut* "oils" is not the Pl of 'oil', but that of 'an oil', an already countable sort. That makes the Pl a multiplier (of sorts), and not a nominal reference shifter from a mass to a non-mass (or count). Note that such a reading is also available for the English Pl 'oils'.

(29) a. bettix "melon, melons" ⟶ bettix-at "melon-Cl; an integral melon"
b. bettix-at "a melon" ⟶ bettix-aat "(many integral pieces of) melons"
c. bettix "melon" ⟶ betatex "a lot of melon; many sorts of melon"
d. šḥam "fat" ⟶ šḥm-ah "fat-Cl; a piece of fat" ⟶ šaḥm-aat "(many) pieces of fat"
e. šḥam "fat" ⟶ šḥum "sorts of fat; a lot of fat" ⟶ šḥum-aat "a lot of fat; many sorts of fat"

Note that (as far as we can tell) the Pl is not used in Arabic as forming a kind, as in the case of English 'apples', where the Pl is close to the Arabic singular K *tuffaaḥ* "apple", rather a multiplier.[18]

These various Pl uses indicate clearly that the functions of Pl are far from being limited to classification, and hence the interactions between Pl/Nb and Cl have to be more carefully examined. In the next subsection, we show that group and kind plurals are Number, rather than Cl.

9.4.2 Chinese

Pl marking in Chinese is not as inflectionally productive as it is in e.g. Arabic, English, or Romance. A bare N may express plurality, without any morphological mark dedicated to it. However, expressed Pls/Nbs are found in Chinese, although they usually carry additional specific information, which then limits the range of their use. Among such information is 'definiteness', which has led some authors to analyze Pl forms such as *-men* as ending in D in syntactic structure, although the latter is chiefly analyzed as a Pl/Nb form (cf. e.g. Li 1999). Second, there is a 'collective' interpretation which has been claimed to be characteristic of the suffix *-men*, and which has led to a dispute on whether the latter must be analyzed as a 'collective'/group marker (cf. Iljic 1994, 2001, Cheng & Sybesma 1999, Norman 1988, Chao 1968, Lü 1947), or just a 'plural' (cf. Li and Thompson 1981, Li 1999). Note that *-men* occurs normally on pronominal forms and animate or human Ns,

---

[18]Wiese (ibid) claims the existence of a multiplier/amount Pl distinction in Persian, but also in Chinese. She illustrates the contrast by (i) and (ii), respectively:

(i) a. ab water "water"
b. ab-ha water-pl "plenty of water"
c. ab-i water-sg "some water"

(ii) a. háizi child "a child; children"
b. háizi-men child-pl "several / a lot of children"

to express a form of plurality, as illustrated in (30). The combination in (31) is not felicitous because it is used with a non-human noun (cf. Iljic (1994, 2001)):

(30) a. wǒ-men
1s-MEN
'we/us'
b. lǎoshī-men
professor-MEN
'professors'

(31) * yǐzi-men
chair-MEN
chairs

The marker *-xiē*, on the other hand, identifies an indefinite plurality, in e.g. *(yī)xiē* in (32a). It is not a classifier, since it can co-occur with other (prenominal) classifiers, as in (32b), where it is suffixed to a demonstrative, and it contributes plural quantity:

(32) a. yī xiē shū
one XIE book
'a few books'
b. zhè-xiē kŭn shū
Dem XIE Cl book
'those piles of books'

Third, classifiers reduplicate to express universal quantification, as illustrated in (33). This indicates also that there is no ban on Cl recursion:

(33) tā gègè xuésheng dōu rènde
3s Cl Cl student all know
'S/he knows all the students'

Fourth, and more productively, group Pls appear to be formed in syntax through a movement process, through which N first moves to the left of the Cl, and the N-Cl sequence is further moved higher to the Nb phrase. The examples in (34) and (35) illustrate the contrast between singular/individual and plural/group readings of the two DPs:

(34) yǒu sān qún rén zài shuōhuà
have three SGCL people at speak
'Three groups of people are speaking.'

(35) rén qùn zài shuōhuà
people GCL at speak
'People are speaking.'

Let us return now to the properties of the suffix *-men*. Although *-men* implies plurality, as is clear with pronouns in (30a), it merely indicates that the members of a particular group should be considered together as a unit, and it "... marks a subjective location: several individuals are grouped together relative to the speaker or some other subjective origin" (as Iljic (1994: 91) put it). In this case, it is best treated as *collective* or a 'group' G, referring to a whole.[19] We think, however, that its grouping function does not obviate the fact that it applies to pluralities, rather than singularities.[20] The specific collective nature of *-men* (as distinct from that of a 'regular' Pl) is further illustrated by the fact that it suffixes to proper Ns, as in (36):

(36) Xiǎo Qiángmen
Xiao Qiang-MEN
'Xiao Qiang's group' (Iljic (1994))

The suffix then serves to identify a group relative to a certain person. It can be read as a sort of an associative plural.[21] If *-men* forms a group Pl in the grammar, under Nb, before getting to D (in the spirit of Li's (1999) analysis, which we concur with in part here), then its grammatical Group nature makes it incompatible with simultaneous counting, as illustrated in (37b):

(37) a. sān gè xuésheng
three Cl students
'three students'
b. *sān gè xuénsheng-men
three Cl students-MEN

[19]Norman (1988: 121) observes that *-men* was originally a compound nominal meaning 'every person'.

[20]The term *collective* has been used in the literature in a variety of ways (Corbett 2000: 117-120, Kemmer 1993: 92-94, Greenberg 1972: 19-25) and this situation has generated a lot of confusion. The internal plural value of collective markers is usually left imprecise, and the term acquires a different content, depending on the language described. Typically, there is a confusion between kinds and groups, as we construe them.

[21]This type of collective reading on proper nouns is far from unique. It is found in other languages, namely Tok Pisin (cf. Mühlhäusler 1981: 43) and Berbice Dutch (Kouwenberg 1994: 238). In Tok Pisin, the form *ol* is an associative or 'group' plural, which is realized in this grammar through the "inversion of N and *ol*". In Berbice Dutch, Kouwenberg (1994: 238) notes that "the plural suffix *-apu* may also be used to mark an associative plural. Cf. also Corbett (2000:102), who discusses associative plural forms added to proper nouns, nouns for kin terms, titles and occupations in Hungarian.

This behaviour is compatible with the fact that the suffix is taken as forming a whole Group, perceived as a singleton atom.[22]

The other marker of plurality, -*xiē* "some, a few", is of different nature, since it identifies with *yi*- an indefinite plural number as in (38a), or an indefinite amount as in (38b):

(38) a. yī xiē shū
one XIE book
'a few books'

b. yī xiē shuǐ
one XIE water
'some water'

Xiē, like -*men*, cannot co-occur with numerals:

(39) * sān xiē shū
three XIE book

It is presumably the case that *yi*- is not a Num in (38), but rather a quantifier, a sort of *some*. Its ambiguity in Chinese recalls that of *waaḥed* 'one, some' in Moroccan Arabic, which can be used either as a Num, or as a sort of 'some', the latter contributing indefiniteness.[23] *Yī* can then be seen as contributing indefiniteness, and *xiē* plurality. The latter expresses in fact a form of a plural (or mass) quantification, which is neutral with respect to (in)definiteness. Support for this treatment comes from the fact that it is possible to express definiteness with *xiē* by using the demonstrative *zhè* (Wu 1999). The outcome is then interpreted as a definite plural:

(40) zhè-xiē xuésheng dōu xǐhuan wǒ
this-number student all like me
'All of these students like me.'

Xiē does not categorize semantically any particular set of Ns, and hence does not behave like classifiers. Furthemore, it can co-occur with other Cls, e.g. *gè* in (41a). With the complex form *hǎo-xiē* "a good number of", various Cls are possible even though they may be left out (the examples are from Iljic 1994: 101):

[22]Iljic (2001: 22) notes in connection with this that "-*men* does not refer to types or groups established on a purely qualitative basis (abstract classes), but to concrete groups of people, delimited in specific situations". He also claims that this suffix crucially "pertains to the grammatical category of person" (Iljic 1994 :91).

[23]In e.g. (i), *waaḥed* contributes indefiniteness, even though it is used with a definite article:

(i) waaḥed r-rajel ja
some the-man came
'Some man came.'

(41) a. Yǒu xiē gè rén bù huì shuō huà
Have XIE Cl man NEG can/know speak word
'There are some people who cannot speak (very well).'

b. hǎo-xiē (jiān) fángzi
a good-number Cl house/room
'plenty of rooms'

c. hǎo-xiē (běn) shū
a good-number Cl book
'plenty of books'

Summarizing, *-xiē* expresses an indeterminate plural number or an indeterminate amount.[24]

A further form of plurality arises through Cl reduplication. In Chinese, Cl reduplication induces universal quantification, which can be viewed as a form of plurality. Universal quantification is often used as a plurality expression (cf. English *you* vs. *you all*; Melanesian Pidgin English *all man*, *all-a man* "the men" (Hall 1943)). Thus Cl reduplication yields a universal reading in (42), or a distributive reading in (43). Paris (1981: 70) points out that the reading is iterative or distributive if the reduplicated classifier is preceded by *yī* "one":

(42) tā gè ge xuésheng dōu rènde
3s Cl Cl student all know
'(S)he knows all the students.'

(43) ... Kānchā-le yī tiáo tiao xīn hángxiàn
... prospect-Asp one Cl Cl new maritime line
'have prospected one after the other the new maritime lines'

Note that the universal reading in (42) is ruled out with an indefinite. In a study on *dōu* quantification, Wu (1999: 113) explains that the role of *dōu* is "to distribute the property of a predicate over an NP", not to measure. An indefinite cannot be quantified by *dōu*:

(44) * yī běn shū Zhangsan dōu dú-le
one Cl book Zhangsan all read Asp

9.4.3 Pluralization through Cl phrase movement

Plural formation in Chinese cannot be characterized solely by identifying morphological inflection (as in the cases of *-men* or classifier

[24]Note that, as mentioned in Chao (1968: 245), *xiē* can co-occur with *-men*, as illustrated in (i) below:

(i) nèi xiē qiángdào-men
dem XIE bandit
'those bandits' (as a group)

Furthermore, *xiē* is incompatible with the kind Cls *zhīng* and *lèi*.

recursion). Its *syntactic* character is even more appealing. As a matter of fact, a general process of Cl phrase movement to Nb can be postulated in connection with the contrast (37a)-(37b) above, not only to account for N-Cl order (which is necessary for the plural reading), but also for the fact that this sequence cannot be preceded by a Num.[25] If the N moves to the left of the Cl, and the whole sequence to Nb, then the sequence which lands in the Nb phrase may or may not be countable, depending on its features. In this context, it is not, due either to (a) the fact that a "collective" entity has been formed in syntax, or (b) to other properties of the sequence, which excludes a Num-Nb co-occurrence. As for (a), it has been repeatedly pointed out in the literature that post-nominal Cl constructions are read as 'collective' (and/or plural), not singular, and (b) they cannot be preceded by a Num. Further examples to illustrate these two properties are provided here:[26]

(45) a. láilái wǎngwǎng de chē-liàng hěn duǒ
arrive-arrive return-return DE car-Cl very many
'Vehicles that come and go are numerous.'

b. láilái wǎngwǎng de (*sān) chē-liàng hěn duǒ
arrive-arrive return-return DE (*three) car-Cl very many
*'Three vehicles that come and go are numerous.'

c. *shū-běn* li de zhishi bù yídìng duì
book-Cl in DE knowledge Neg certainly correct
'The knowledge found in books is not necessarily right.'

d. * wǔ *shū-běn* li de zhishi bù yídìng duì
Five knowledge found in books are not necessarily right

Why is that so? How can a collective reading be correlated with the ban against a preceding Num? Clearly, the answer cannot be a (purely) semantic one. That is, the answer cannot be that groups cannot be counted. Indeed, numerals do appear *after* nouns suffixed with Cls, as in the following examples with *-men* (from Zhang & Sang (1986: 492), after Iljic (2001: 24)), but not before them:

(46) a. tā-men sì gè
3s-MEN four Cl
'the four of them'

[25] For N-Cl movement involved in pluralization, cf. also Li (1999) and Yang (2004).

[26] A suffixing N-Cl sequence can be preceded by other material such as *xiē* and demonstrative in the following example (from Chao 1968: 508):

(i) zhèxiē chē-liàng
demXIE vehicles-Cl
'these vehicles'

b. zhè jiā yǒu gēmenr sān gè
this family have brother+MEN+R three Cl
'In the family, there are three brothers.'

Although these constructions are cases of appositions, they do show that groups are not semantically incompatible with numerals. We think then that the solution must be basically syntactic. The two possibilities in (a) and (b) discussed above are then to explore.

Consider first (a). Suppose that Group formation is the general value of the feature [β singulative], which is marked as [+ sing] with singular individuals. Group formation operates basically on singulative what multiplier (or kind) plurals operate on atomicity, i.e. make the value general, either negative or null, [– , ∅ sing]. If singulative is negative, and it is the higher feature that is manipulated, leaving the atomic feature unchanged (with a positive value), then the non-co-occurrence of Num and Nb can be attributed to a feature value conflict (or absence of agreement). This is so because the Num requires atomic entities to operate on, and the non-singulative provides no such entities. XP movement to form (group) plurals in Chinese can then be motivated by some feature checking in Nb. If Nb is valued as [∅ sing], in the case of Group (much like a [∅ atom] is the value for Kind/generic), then Group formation (through movement) to [∅ sing] in Nb would allow the 'conversion' of the [+ sing] value of the Cl, much in line with the movement of an atomized N to a higher Nb, marked as [∅ atom] would allow the formation of (indefinite) generics in Arabic or Romance (see Fassi Fehri (2003b) for motivation). The structure of *shū-běn* would then appear as follows:

(47)

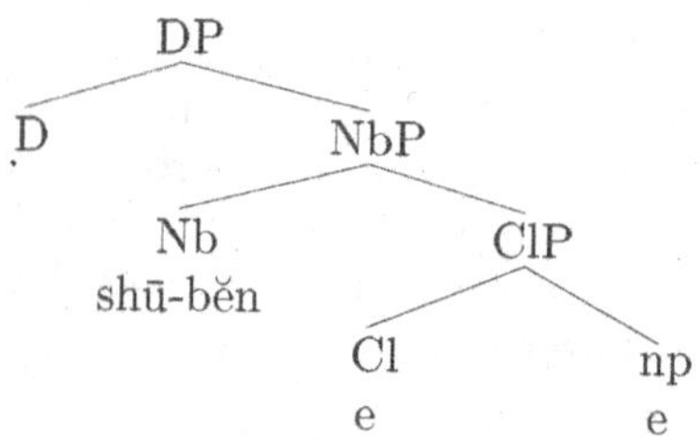

We still have to account, though, for the fact that Num cannot be projected or realized pre-nominally. We assume that cardinals cannot take [∅ Nb] as heads or complements. Zero does not agree with any cardinal, assuming that cardinality starts with 1. The other possibility is that an empty Nb has also an empty D feature, which then triggers necessary movement to D, hence its (in)definite specific reference. An overt Num there would then block movement to D, hence resulting in a non-converging derivation. We leave details of technical choices for further research, highlighting only the syntactic character of plural formation.[27]

9.5 Apparent complementarity of Classifier and Number

In this section, we reexamine the complementarity thesis of Cl and Nb, in the form introduced by Greenberg's (1972), as a base of 'typing' languages, depending on whether they (tend to) express *either* Nb *or* Cl. This complementarity is clearly stated in T'sou (1976), and has inspired Chierchia's (1998) Nominal Parameter, based on the view that Cl and Pl play a parallel role in the grammar. Borer (2004) adopts a slightly weaker position in the sense that she specifically limits the restriction to classifier and plural 'inflection', not to Classifier or Number in general: "Not only is it the case that classifier languages do not (appear to) have plural inflection, but languages which mark plural do not appear to have classifier inflection. In other words, it would appear that

---

[27]Note that the suffix *-men* can co-occur with some Cls, such as *qún* "group", which has a collective G reading, but not a kind Cl, such as *zhǒng* and *lěi*:

(i) a. zhèi qún háizi-men
dem Cl child-MEN
'this group of children' (Yu 1957: 3, after Iljic 2001:21)

b. *zhèi zhǒng háizi-men
dem type child-MEN
'this type of children'

c. *yī lěi lǎoshīmen (Iljic 2001: 21)
one Cl teachers-MEN

Some form of 'agreement' is then going on between the Cl and (the classification flavoured) Nb.

Another property of *-men* is that it is always interpreted as a specific (definite), and never as a generic, hence the contrasts in (ii) and (iii) (Rygaloff 1973):

(ii) a. * yǒu rén-men
have man-MEN
'There are men.'

b. yǒu rén
have man
'There is (are) somebody (some people).'

(iii) a. *tā-men shì lǎoshīmen
they-MEN be teachers
'They are teachers.'

b. tā-men shì lǎoshī
they-MEN be teachers
'They are teachers.'

The specific character of *-men* contrasts with that of English generics/kinds as in *Dogs bark.*

classifier inflection and plural inflection are in complementary distribution". She then goes even further and claims that the latter reflects the *inflectional identity* of plurals and classifiers, which then compete for insertion under the same node: Cl. We first recapitulate some of the firm bases that lead us to think that the complementarity thesis is both empirically illusory, and conceptually inadequate. Furthermore, the inflectional identity thesis can be hardly maintained. Second, we turn to identify what we think is the essential source behind Greenberg's (and others) intuitions of complementarity. We claim that (contra Li (1999)), 'classifier languages' do not lack a projection of Nb, and 'number languages' do not lack a Cl projection, as evidenced by Chinese and Arabic. Rather, the (often manifest) complementarity is to be found in the system of feature (un)specification. Granted that both Nb and Cl may be projected in all languages (and hence be manifest in all of them), we show that if Cls and Pls manipulate values for the same features, namely atomic and singulative, then interactions between valuations of Nb and Cl features are expected, precisely because they occupy different positions in the nominal architecture respectively. Typically, Nb can be thought of as the 'complement' of the Cl in Bresnan's construal of Jakobson's theory of specification and markedness, or its unmarked general realization (cf. also Ojeda (1998)). Overtness of Nb or Cl gives then rise to different configurations of specification in the general case in generalized Nb or Cl language manifestations, although mixed overt systems are not only found (as manifested productively by Arabic, but less so by Chinese), but expected to be found under our theory, but not the identity/complementarity theory.

9.5.1 Confirming the inadequacy of the complementarity/identity thesis

A first clear case of the inadequacy of this thesis is provided by Arabic cases where both Cl and Pl co-occur. This is exemplified by Arabic (28b) and Moroccan Arabic (29b & d) above. In this kind of examples, the Pl is a plural of individuals. Kind undergoes an overt morphological derivation to form Individuals, and Pl applies to the latter to form the individual Pl. The following derivational process accounts for the co-occurrence:

(48) tamr "date K" $\longrightarrow$ tamr-at "an individual date" $\longrightarrow$ tamr-aat "a set of individual dates"

Here the suffix *-at* forms the individual unit from the general kind, and the individual Pl is formed through internal vowel lengthening (*-aa* basically).

That Cl and Pl are not incompatible is also supported by the fact that the Pl of kinds is available as well:

(49) tamr "date K" ⟶ tumuur "kinds/sorts of date"

As pointed out in Fassi Fehri (2003b), Pl formation in these cases is *ontology preserving*, in the sense that it does not operate a classification/reference shift, from a kind/sort to a unit. It is rather a multiplier of 'already' available entities, which are of different nature (sorts, as distinct from individuals). Typically, Pl does not operate classification.

A problematic case for the complementarity thesis is classifier recursion, with a number of Cls co-occurring within the same construction. A Cl construction is then not necessarily limited to one Cl. Various instances of this case are found. For example, the collective marker *qùn* can co-occur with the collective marker *-men* in Chinese, as in fn. 18, repeated here as (50), for convenience.[28]

(50) zhèi qún hàizi-men
dem Cl child-MEN
'this group of children '

Likewise, Cls may reduplicate, as observed earlier with respect to (42) or (43). The following example from Cheng & Sybesma (1999) instantiates this phenomenon:

(51) tiáo tiao dàolù tōng Beijing
Cl Cl road connect Beijing
'All roads lead to Beijing.'

If Cls themselves are not mutually exclusive in the same construction (except when they are semantically incompatible), then there is no reason to think that Pl, even when read as Cl is incompatible with another Cl. The distributions mentioned are then unexpected under the complementarity thesis. They pose no problem for our non-discriminative view.

That Cls are not mutually exclusive can be supported by more subtle evidence coming from comparing Arabic, English, and French. Consider the following contrast in Arabic and English (close to that found in (11) above):

(52) a. talatat-u fuṣuuṣ-i tawm-in
b. three cloves garlic

(53) a. talatat-u ruʔuus-i ʔaǧnam-in

[28]Here *-men* appears to operate more like a 'kindifier' than a 'grouper', close to what happens in the English translation of (50) above, where "children" is a kind , and "group" is a counterpart to the Chinese group Cl.

b. three heads of sheep

In both sets of examples, the measuring words (functioning as Cls) are in the plural form, whereas the head N is in the singular form. But there is reason to think that the Ns are of different classes, the first being Mass, and the second Kind. For example, in French, the difference is manifested through Pl marking in the Kind case, and its absence in the Mass case:[29] [30]

(54) a. trois gousses d'ail

b. trois têtes de moutons (* mouton)

Conceptually, the inadequacy of the complementarity thesis is even more striking. If Pl is of three types at least, as we have seen, and only one of them actively interacts distributively with Cls, then it is hard to see how a strong version of this thesis can be conceived. In the multiplier configuration, the complementary distribution is hardly conceivable on conceptual grounds, given that Cl and Pl are playing distinct roles in the grammar. Second, as in constructions (28c & d) or (29d & e) above, Pl may play the role of *modifier* of the quantity of a Pl (already formed). There is then no unique role of Pl inflection which would parallel the unique role of Cl inflection.

These pieces of evidence combined with previous ones point clearly to the inadequacy of the complementarity thesis. Furthermore, the postulated inflectional identity of Cl and Nb (as in Borer (2004)) is even hardly conceivable. If 'classifier languages' and 'number languages' were indeed to constitute two Greenbergian 'types', then presumably no macro-variation of the sort defined by the complementarity thesis can be justified. What appears to be typical are functions of Nb and Cl in the two types, rather than their existence, along the lines proposed in Fassi Fehri (2003b).

9.5.2 Cross-linguistic instantiations

So far, we have illustrated Cl operations/derivations which form a new Cl ontology from another ontology by changing the value of one of

[29]Compare also with:

(i) trois troupeaux de moutons (* mouton)

(ii) trois têtes de bétail

[30]Further motivation for the empirical inadequacy of the complementarity thesis comes from Pl and Nb distributions in other 'classifier languages'. In his analysis of classifiers in Anamuxra, a language spoken in Papua New Guinea, Ingram (2003:138) argued that in this language nominal classifiers are used with Nb morphological marking for singular, dual and plural. Likewise, Chung (2000) showed that Pl is formed through Cl reduplication in Indonesian, another 'classifier language'.

its features. These derivations operate on one of the two features proposed. They either (by creating atoms, or the reverse, 'de-atomize'), ATOMIZE or SINGULATIVIZE (forming singulative entities, or the reverse, 'de-singulativize'). Here are some of these operations to illustrate:

(55) Atomize
Kind ⟶ Individual
samak "fish" ⟶ samak-at "individual fish"

(56) De-atomize
Individual ⟶ Kind
apple, dog ⟶ apples, dogs

(57) Singulativize
Mass ⟶ Kind
xašab "wood" ⟶ xašab "wood" (xašab-at "wood-unit")

(58) De-singulativize
Kind ⟶ Mass
bger "cows" ⟶ begr-ii "beef"

Note that complex operations which involve changes of the two feature values at the same time are not found (or so it appears):

(59) * Individual ⟶ Mass

(60) * Group ⟶ Mass

(61) * Mass ⟶ Individual

(62) * Mass ⟶ Group

We have found no counterexamples to (60) and (62). That would be examples of groups like "team", converted to the mass "team". Apparent counterexamples to (59) and (61) can be instantiated by 'universal grinder' and 'universal packager' discussed by Pelletier and Schubert (1989) and Jackendoff (1991), as in the following constructions:

(63) There is dog everywhere.

(64) I had three coffees.

If the individual "dog" is 'converted' to a mass "dog" in (63), or the mass "coffee" converted to an individual "coffee" in (64), then these operations, if grammatical, may be potential counterexamples to the claim that only single changes are permitted. We have found, however, no instances of (overt) grammatical Cls that operate these changes. We assume that these conversions operate rather from kinds to individuals. If true, and if ontological classification is limited only to single operations, then the system makes strong predictions, typically with respect to limitations on classification changes.[31]

In Arabic, instances of 'atomic' and 'singulative' ontological classifiers are found, complemented by inherently built-in ontological distinctions at the N level for both features. In Chinese, the only built-in ontological distinction at the N level appears to be 'singulative' (the Kind/Mass distinction), and 'atomic' is left unspecified. As a consequence, an 'atomic' N must be formed through an 'atomizer' (misleadingly named a 'count-classifier'), to enable a singulative N to become an individual I. As for Cheng & Sybesma's 'mass-classifiers', they are not necessarily ontological, since they apply equally to singulative and non-singulative Ns. Though they are necessary for counting, they may introduce units of measures or taxonomies, without affecting the ontology of the N.

If our story is on the right track, then the difference between languages like Chinese and English (or Arabic) is that the former (called a 'classifer language') has only one built-in feature distinction at the N level (the Kind/Mass singulative distinction), but English (and Arabic) has also the 'atomic' distinction built-in (although sometimes quite productively manifested by an atomic Cl in Arabic). Given our classificatory feature system, differences between the two traditional 'types' can then be stated as follows:

(65) In 'classifier languages', only the [β sing] distinction is built-in at the N level; in 'non-classifier languages', the [α atom] feature is also (generally) built-in.

As a consequence of (65), an atomic Cl is needed to form an individual. But note, as observed earlier, that Nb cannot be taken as a Cl in the ontological sense, because Nb is blind to the atomic/taxonomic distinction examined above, although it may also manipulate atomization. Thus although ATOMIZE can be involved both with Cl and Nb, the two atomization processes should not be confused, the first one being more specific, and the second one more general. This view will be more precisely articulated below.

9.5.3 Two levels of atomicity

The difference between Cl and non-Cl languages reflected at the N level correlates with a massive use of Cl in type 1, and a massive use of Nb

[31] A reviewer notes that there seems to be an instance for a derivation in the direction M $\longrightarrow$ I in Kurdish, where *cay* "tea", a mass noun, can be used in restaurant talk constructions like *du (ta) cay* "two CL tea" (with optional Cl), where it refers to portions of tea. We think, however, that this case falls under the 'universal packager' option discussed above.

in type 2, with the apparent complementarity observed above, hence giving the impression that they belong to the same category, or share the same identity. Given that they are not, we still have to explain why Pl tends not to be used with Cl in Chinese, or that the Cl use is less productive in Arabic than that of Nb, or even less so in English.

That Nb and Cl are not in complementary distribution in Chinese is clearly instantiated by the structure of indefinite singulars, as in (18a) above, repeated here as (66), for convenience:

(66) yī gè píngzi
one Cl bottle
'a bottle'

In (66), *yī-* can be taken as overtly realizing Nb, *yī-* being the counterpart to "a" in English, as argued above (see also Chen (2003)). In the singular case then, both Cl and Nb are projected.[32] It is then reasonable to think that ATOMIZE is valued at two different projection levels in the grammar: the Cl level and the Nb level. At the former, the entity formed is (an atomic) individual, and at the latter a singular (or atomic) number of this individual. Note that the [+atom] value for both Cl and Nb is overtly realized (and/or marked), compared to the negative or null values ([∅ atom] or [– atom] for either the Cl or the Nb, which is unmarked and not phonetically realized. The architecture for (66) is then as follows:

(67)

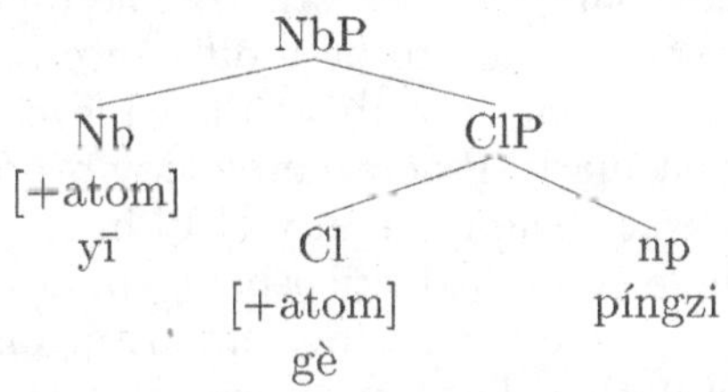

It is then the case that the two kinds of atomiticity can be overtly realized in Chinese, in conjunction with the projection of both Nb and Cl. But such 'double' realization of atomization can be supplemented by only one, as in (13) above, repeated here as (68) for convenience, where only Cl is realized:

[32]If one regards *yi-* as a cardinal numeral in all uses, and rejects Chen's multiple interpretation of it, namely as a singular indefinite (or a number marker), one would not have both Nb and CL in (66). Only a numeral is there, with a Cl (the standard case). We do not think, however, that the unique interpretation option, suggested by a reviewer, is descriptively adequate (see also *yi-xie* interpretation in (38) above).

(68) wǒ xiēng mǎi běn shū
1s want buy Cl book
'I want to buy a book.'

Here *běn shū* is interpreted as a singular (atomic) individual. Cl specification and Nb specification then interact, presumably by some default (percolation) mechanism, to license covert Nb. This situation is close to that of *samak-at-un* 'fish-unit, a fish' in Arabic, where the interpretation is also singular, in the absence of an overt marker of Nb. What is important to observe though is that even in the covert singular Nb, the higher atomicity is still different in nature from the lower one in that it does not form a class (of individuals). It is blind to classification, as illustrated by the Arabic examples (5), (6), and (10), where covert singulars occur for all classes, yet singular number (and/or weak cardinality) is involved in the interpretation.

Consider now the plural case. Pl at first sight appears to be overtly expressed in Chinese (with very specific information, as is the case with *-men*), but not generalized. But a general process of pluralization does exist though, as we have observed in subsection 4.3. It involves Cl phrase movement to Nb. It is also (generally) blind to classes, in comparison with *-men* formation. The Cl-to-Nb movement appears then to be the overt manifestation of plural, compared to singular, where no such a movement takes place, and the number receives its atomic value from that of the Cl, by default (and/or percolation). The difference between Arabic and English then appears to be a difference between languages that mark (specific) atomicity overtly at the Cl level in the form of singulars, and those that mark (general) atomicity overtly (in morphology) in the form of plurals. The generality of Pl in English is manifested by the fact that there is no distinction between 'dogs' and 'oils' in terms of Pl formation, yet the two entities are distinguishable in terms of singulativity interpretation. The same is true of the singular marker *a*, which behaves essentially like *yi-* in Chinese. In Fassi Fehri (2003b), it is proposed that a (vertical) directionality accounts for this variation. In Chinese, the atomic (under)specification appears to be *oriented from bottom to top* (i.e. from Cl to Nb, or from specific to general). In English, it is *oriented from top to bottom* (i.e. from the general Nb atomicity to the specific atomicity of the Cl). Individual units or sorts are then formed at the Cl level, depending on their singulative value. Arabic is a mixed system, although it is closer to English than to Chinese, in that atomicity is of the general type. But when atomicity is expressed overtly at the Cl level, the general atomicity of the Pl overrides that of the Cl. Likewise, movement to Nb of the classifier phrase in Chinese enables the (general) atomic value of the Pl to override the specific atomic value of the Cl. That is to say, Chinese does have a Pl with a (general) content value (as in English), and its 'overt' realization is manifested by movement. It is worth noting that this Pl is often associated with 'specific' definiteness, by default, pointing to the fact that D is projected in the structure (with content), although not phonetically overt.

As for specific plural uses like those of *-men*, typically in the 'collective' reading, so-emphasized in the literature, we assume that plurality formation, when interpreted as a Group, is not manipulating atomize, but rather singulativize. What (general) grammatical group formation does, we assume, is override the specific (positive) value of singulativity, and make it general (or unspecific, hence acquiring a negative or a zero value). The (positive) atomicity of the Cl is left unaffected. This accounts for the fact that the Pl might be a grouper, just as it is a 'multiplier' or a 'partitioner', or even a 'kindifier' or a generic, depending on which of the two features it overrides. We leave unanswered the specifics of the limitations found in Chinese, be they inherently lexical or contextual.

9.6 Summary and conclusion

To sum up, we have shown that Cl and Nb do 'complement' each other, but in ways very distinct from the (inflectional and/or projectional) complementary distribution assumed by some authors, or the shared inflectional identity. Cl and Pl are *both projected* in the languages examined, and they are *both overtly realized*, either via morphology or syntactic movement. The overt morphological realization of either Cl or Nb in the general case, which is basic to 'typing', finds its source in the distinct uses made of the specific vs. general specification of the two features assumed, and the interaction between Nb, Cl, and N projections and specifications (much in line with Bresnan's (2001) insights about 'global' specification, elaborating on Jakobson (1957); cf. also Ojeda (1998)). As far as atomize is concerned, languages (generally) either mark the specific (positive) value via Cl, or the general (negative or zero) value, its 'complement', via Pl, as found in Chinese and English, respectively. Arabic is a mixed system, where both can be marked, the general higher atomicity then overriding the lower one. But Arabic is closer to English in the general case.

Singulativity is assumed to be universally available at the N level, and Cl and Pl concur for valuing the atomic feature. If atomicity is specified at the Cl level, there is no specific need to re-specify it at the

Nb level, if projection interaction is taken advantage of. If it is specified at the Nb level, the same principle applies. The general tendency is then limited to two grammatical options, characterizing the general variation, as stated in (69):

(69) ATOMIZE at the Cl or the Nb level.

Note that (69) is an over-simplification, given not only clear mixed systems like Arabic, but also other forms of micro-variation found in Chinese. It is presumably the case that more micro-variation parameters are involved rather than macro-variation (cf. e.g. Kayne (2003), Homlberg & Sandström (1996), Chomsky (2001), Bresnan (2001 a & b)). Note also that singulativity (vs. collectivity) is in need of more integration in systems of Cl/Nb specification than previously thought. Chinese appears to be a language where such an option is made use of at the Nb level, and a tentative parametrization parallel to (69), is expected to receive wider motivation:

(70) SINGULATIVIZE at the Cl or the Nb level.

Parallelisms between verbal and nominal architectures are presumably helpful in determining precisely how both are structured. It is striking that a similar 'global' system of specification is found in aspectuo-temporal systems, where systems that tend to specify *Aspect* (perfective) do not tend to specify *Tense* (perfect/past), and vice versa (although mixed systems are also found). This distribution has also led some authors to classify languages according to whether they are 'aspect languages' or 'tensed languages' (cf. Fassi Fehri (2003a, 2004) for refutation of this classification, references on this matter, as well as arguments for the directionality of specification). Second, verbs have often been classified in four classes based on two features, another striking parallelism if correct.[33]

References

Aikhenvald, Alexandra Y. 2001. *Classifiers: A Typology of Noun Categorization Devices*. Oxford & New York, NY: Oxford University Press.

Allan, Keith. 1977. Classifiers. *Language* 53(2):285–311.

[33] In Fassi Fehri (in progress), it is shown that the nominal feature system adopted here can be naturally extended to the four Vendlerian verb classes as follows:

(i) V classification

a.	Achievement (= I):	[+ atom, + sing]
b.	Accomplishment (= G):	[+ atom, sing]
c.	Activity (= K):	[∅ atom, + sing]
d.	State (= M):	[∅ atom, ∅ sing]

Astarabaadii, R. 12th c. [1976]. *Šarḥ al-kaafiyyah*. Beyrouth: daar t-tibaacah l-cilmiyyah.

Borer, Hagit. 2004. *Structuring Sense. An Exo-Skeletal Trilogy*. Oxford: Oxford University Press.

Bresnan, Joan. 2001a. Exlaining morphosyntactic competition. In M. Baltin and C. Collins, eds., *The Handbook of Contemporary Syntactic Theory*, pages 11–44. Oxford: Blackwell.

Bresnan, Joan. 2001b. *Lexical-Functional Syntax*. Oxford: Blackwell.

Chao, Yuen R. 1968. *A Grammar of spoken Chinese*. Berkeley, CA: University of California Press.

Chen, Ping. 2003. Indefinite determiner introducing definite referent: A special use of *yi* 'one'+classifier in Chinese. *Lingua* 113(12):1169–1184.

Cheng, Lisa L.-S. and Rint Syberma. 1999. Bare and not-so-bare nouns and the structure of NP. *Linguistic Inquiry* 30(4):509–542.

Cheng, Lisa L.-S. and Rint Sybesma. 1998. 'Yi-wan tang, yi-ge tang': Classifiers and massifiers. *Tsing Hua Journal of Chinese Studies* 28(3):385–412.

Chierchia, Gennaro. 1998. Reference to kinds across languages. *Natural Language Semantics* 6(4):339–405.

Chomsky, Noam. 1999. *Derivation by Phase*. No. 18 in MIT Occasional Papers in Linguistics. Cambridge, MA: MITWPL.

Chomsky, Noam. 2001. *Beyond Explanatory Adequacy*. No. 20 in MIT Occasional Papers in Linguistics. Cambridge, MA: MITWPL.

Chung, Sandy. 2000. On reference to kinds in Indonesian. *Natural Language Semantics* 8(2):157–171.

Corbett, Greville G. 2000. *Number*. Cambridge, UK: Cambridge University Press.

Croft, William. 1994. Semantic universals in classifier systems. *Word* 45(2):145–171.

Fassi Fehri, Abdelkader. 2003a. Arabic perfect and temporal adverbs. In A. Alexiadou, M. Rathert, and A. von Stechow, eds., *Perfect Explorations*. Berlin: Mouton de Gruyter.

Fassi Fehri, Abdelkader. 2003b. Nominal classes and parameters across interfaces and levels, with a particular reference to Arabic. *Linguistic Research* 8(2):9–101.

Fassi Fehri, Abdelkader. 2004. Temporal/aspectual interaction and variation across Arabic heights. In J. Guéron and J. Lecarme, eds., *The Syntax of Time*, pages 235–257. Cambridge, MA: The MIT Press.

Fassi Fehri, Abdelkader. 2006. Verbal and nominal parallelisms. Ms., Mohammmed V University, Rabat. In progress.

Greenberg, Joseph. 1972. Numeral classifiers and substantival number: Problems in the genesis of a linguistic type. In L. Heilmann, ed., *Proceedings of the 11th Congress of Linguists*, pages 17–37. Bologna: Mulino.

Hall, Robert A. 1943. *Melanesian Pidgin English: Grammar, Texts, Vocabulary*. Baltimore, MD: Linguistic Society of America.

Holmberg, Anders and Görel Sandström. 1996. Scandinavian possessive constructions from a Northern Swedish viewpoint. In J. Black and V. Motapanyane, eds., *Microparametric Syntax and Dialect Variation*, pages 95–120. Amsterdam: J. Benjamins.

Iljic, Robert. 1994. Quantification in Mandarin Chinese: Two markers of plurality. *Linguistics* 32:91–116.

Iljic, Robert. 2001. The problem of the suffix *-men* in Chinese grammar. *Journal of Chinese Linguistics* 29(1):11–67.

Ingram, Andrew. 2003. The morphosyntax of classifiers in Anamuxra: Details of a multiple classifier system. *Anthropological Linguistics* 45(2):129–168.

Ishii, Yasuo. 2000. Plurality and definiteness in Japanese. Ms., Kanda University.

Jackendoff, Ray. 1991. Parts and boundaries. *Cognition* 41:9–45.

Jakobson, Roman. 1957. Shifters, verbal categories, and the Russian verb. In R. Jakobson, ed., *Selected Writings II*, pages 130–147. The Hague: Mouton de Gruyter.

Kayne, Richard. 2000. *Parameters and Universals*. Oxford: Oxford University Press.

Kayne, Richard. 2003. Some notes on comparative syntax, with special reference to English and French. Ms., New York University.

Kemmer, Susan. 1993. Verbal and nominal collectives. In *Faits de langues 2*, pages 85–95. Paris: Édition Ophrys.

Kouwenberg, Silvia. 1994. Berbice Dutch. In J. Arends, P. Muysken, and N. Smith, eds., *Pidgins and Creoles: An Introduction*, pages 233–243. Amsterdam: J. Benjamin.

Krifka, Manfred. 1995. Common nouns in Chinese and in English. In G. Carlson and F. J. Pelletier, eds., *The Generic Book*. Chicago, IL: Chicago University Press.

Kurafuji, Takeo. 2001. Plural morphemes, definiteness, and the notion of semantic parameter. Ms., University of Ryukyus.

Kwon, Song-Nim and Anne Zribi-Hertz. 2004. Number from a syntactic perspective: Why plural marking looks 'truer' in French than in Korean. In O. Bonanmi and P. C. Hofherr, eds., *Empirical Issues in Formal Syntax and Semantics 5*, pages 133–158. Paris: Presses de la Sorbonne.

Li, Charles N. and Sandra A. Thompson. 1981. *Mandarin Chinese: A functional Reference Grammar*. Berkeley, CA & Los Angeles, CA & London: University of California Press.

Li, Yen-Hui A. 1999. Plurality in a classifier language. *Journal of East Asian Language* 8(1):75–99.

Longobardi, Giuseppe. 2001a. How comparative is semantics? A unified parametric theory of bare nouns and proper names. *Natural Language Semantics* 9:335–369.

Longobardi, Giuseppe. 2001b. The structure of DPs: Some principles, parameters, and problems. In M. Baltin and C. Collins, eds., *The handbook of contemporary syntactic theory*, pages 562–603. Oxford: Blackwell.

Lü, Shuxiang. 1942. *Zhōngguó wénfǎ yàolüè (Outline of Chinese Grammar) 3 volumes.* Shanghai: Shangwu yinshuguan.

Mühlhäusler, Peter. 1981. The development of the category of number in Tok Pisin. In P. Muysken, ed., *Generative Studies in Creole Languages*. Dordrecht: Foris.

Norman, Jerry. 1988. *Chinese*. Cambridge, UK: Cambridge University Press.

Ojeda, Almerindo E. 1998. The semantics of collectives and distributives in Papago. *Natural Language Semantics* 6(3):245–270.

Paris, Marie-Claude. 1981. *Problèmes de syntaxe et de sémantique en linguistique chinoise*. Paris: Collège de France.

Pelletier, Francis J. and Lenhart K. Schubert. 1989. Mass expressions. In D. Gabbay and F. Guenthner, eds., *Handbook of Philosophical Logic*, vol. 4, pages 327–407. Dordrecht: Kluwer.

Rygaloff, Alexis. 1973. *Grammaire élémentaire du chinois*. Paris: Presses universitaires de France.

T'sou, Benjamin K. 1976. The structure of nominal classifier systems. In P. Jenner, L. Thompson, and S. Starosta, eds., *Austroasiatic Studies II*, pages 1215–1247. Honolulu: University Press of Hawai.

Wiese, Heike. 1999. Two kinds of nominal 'singular' and 'plural' in natural languages: A semantic analysis. Paper presented at the Annual Meeting of the International Linguistic Association, New York. April 18-19.

Wright, William. 1898. *A Grammar of the Arabic Language*. Cambridge, UK: Cambridge University Press, 3rd edn. Translation from Caspari, with edition, corrections and additions.

Wu, Jianxin. 1999. *Syntax and semantics of quantification in Chinese*. Ph.D. thesis, University of Maryland, College Park.

Yang, Henrietta. 2004. Classifiers and plurality in Mandarin. Mimeo. University of Texas, Austin.

10

Boxes and Piles and What's in Them: Two Extended Projections or One?

JANE GRIMSHAW

10.1 Introduction

This paper follows up recent research by van Riemsdijk (1998), Vos (1999), Cardinaletti and Shlonsky (2004), and papers collected in Corver and van Riemsdijk 2001.[1] These works suggest that in addition to the familiar concepts "lexical" and "functional", heads can have an intermediate standing, called "semi-lexical". The present paper presents an analysis of two kinds of DPs which characterize, very roughly speaking, the location or organization of the nominal they are associated with. In *a bottle of wine*, *a pile of pebbles*, *bottle* is a "container" (as in Vos 1999), and *pile* I will call, following the suggestion of Roger Schwarzschild, a "portion". Some of the empirical foundations of work in this area were laid in place in Jackendoff 1977 and Selkirk 1977, Delsing 1993 where the syntax of partitives is a major focus.

The investigation will establish that *boxes* and *piles* are lexical heads. However, this conclusion sets the scene for the analysis of quantity nominals (such as *pound* in *a pound of rice*, and *lot* as in *a lot of rice*.) These turn out, I will show in Grimshaw in prep., *not* to behave as

[1]Thanks are hereby extended to Adrian Brasoveanu, Alan Prince, participants in the Rutgers Seminar in Syntax for 2003, and especially to Roger Schwarzschild for a lot of invaluable discussion.

Architectures, Rules, and Preferences: Variations on Themes by Joan Bresnan.
Annie Zaenen, Jane Simpson, Tracy Holloway King,
Jane Grimshaw, Joan Maling, and Chris Manning, (eds.).

lexical nouns; differing in various ways from the nouns discussed here. The full study covering all of these nouns adds to the evidence that such nouns can be intermediate in status between lexical or functional. The overall conclusion thus supports a version of the "semi-lexical" proposal. Further examples of the DPs under discussion are:[2]

(1) Containers:
  a. A box/basket/case/shelf/ of books
  b. A bottle/glass/cup/flask/bucket of water
  c. A bag/plate of (the) cookies
  d. A scoop of (the) ice cream

(2) Portions:
  a. A ball of (the) clay, wax
  b. A block of wood
  c. A bunch of (the) flowers (not when it means "many")
  d. A wad of (the) paper

An informal characterization of portions is that they describe an arrangement of the material in the second nominal.

10.2 The Independence of the two Phrases

From here on I will refer to the container or portion noun as "N-1" and to the contained or portioned noun as "N-2". The DP headed by N-1 is "DP-1", the DP headed by N-2 is "DP-2". Is N-1 lexical? I will approach the question by trying to decide whether these expressions involve two extended projections or one, following the proposals in Grimshaw 1991, 2001, 2005; van Riemsdijk 1990, 1998. The assumption is that if they clearly contain two extended projections, then they contain two lexical heads, and N-1 must be lexical. If they contain only one extended projection then "N-1" is not truly a noun (i.e. a lexical head) but falls into the more obscure area of "somewhere in between". The evidence shows that they contain two extended projections and hence two lexical heads. The first noun in these structures, N-1, patterns as a noun with respect to numerous syntactic properties, as does the second noun, N-2. N-1s occur in exactly the configurations that nouns like *picture* appear in. N-1 can be preceded by an adjective; N-1 can pluralize; N-1 can be preceded by a determiner, a demonstrative and other prenominal functional elements. This will be illustrated in

[2] Ambiguity is rife within these nouns; "container" nouns can often denote portions, and "portion" nouns can often denote quantities (as in *a pile/piles of money*). The syntax under various meanings is identical as far as the properties examined here are concerned, but not in every respect. See van Riemsdijk 1998 and Vos 1999.

the examples below. It will also be evident from the examples to be cited that N-2 can be shown to be a true nominal for essentially the same reasons.

10.2.1 Elements in DP-1 and elements in DP-2

The load-bearing wall of the lexical-head-analysis of N-1 is the fact that *the syntax of the two DPs is independent.* The syntax of DP-1 and the syntax of DP-2 vary independently. In this respect, containers and portions behave exactly like representational nouns: *pictures of horses, a discussion of DPs.* I assume that these uncontroversially contain two extended projections and two lexical heads. Using "< ... >"to indicate the edge of the lower extended projection, the representations are given in (3).

(3) a. a picture < of horses > (representational noun)
 b. a bottle < of red wine > (container)
 c. a pile < of the pebbles > (portion)

No element inside the angled brackets is part of the higher extended projection, and no element outside the angled brackets is part of the lower extended projection. Material inside the angled brackets and material outside the angled brackets are not locally related, while material within a single extended projection is. The special relationship among elements within the angled brackets motivates the Extended Projection hypothesis (Grimshaw 1991, 2000, 2005; van Riemsdijk 1990, 1998). The grammatical independence of DP-1 and DP-2 manifests itself in several ways. DP-1 and DP-2 can have two of grammatical entities that an extended projection may have only one of, and while determiners and modifiers within each extended projection must be consistent, those of DP-1 and DP-2 need not be. The positioning of adjectives in DP-1 relative to those in DP-2 is unconstrained, while relative positioning of adjectives within a DP (i.e. a single extended projection) is fixed in certain cases. (4) summarizes all of these generalizations, which point to the conclusion that each DP is an extended projection, headed by a lexical noun.[3]

(4) (i) DP-1 and DP-2 can each have a determiner or demonstrative, and the two can be inconsistent.

[3]A more sophisticated theory might allow them to be two extended projections but with a functional item heading the higher, and a lexical item heading the lower. The theory of Extended Projection as presented in Grimshaw 1991, 2000, 2005 does not allow for this possibility. The argument I make here assumes that only lexical heads can be the lowest head in an extended projection.

(ii) They can each have number marking and the number of the two can be inconsistent.

(iii) They can each contain a numeral. A numeral for N-1 is possible even if N-2 is mass, and a numeral for N-2 does not depend on the nature of N-1.

(iv) They can each contain an adjective, and the adjectives can be inconsistent.

The following examples support the claim in (i):

(5) a. **a** box of **the** books; **the** boxes of books
b. **a** ball of **the** clay; **the** balls of clay

(6) a. **this** box of books; **these** cases of wine
(*this books; *these wine)
b. **these** piles of clay; **that** pile of pebbles
(*these clay; *that pebbles)

The determiner or demonstrative on N-1 agrees with N-1, on N-2 it agrees with N-2. The determiners/demonstratives can be inconsistent, one definite and one indefinite, one appropriate for a mass noun and one for a count noun (more on this situation below).

The following examples, and some of those just cited, support the claim in (ii):

(7) a. a **box** of **books**
b. **bottles** of **water**

They show that the number of DP-1 can be singular while the number of DP-2 is plural (7a) and DP-1 can be singular or plural when DP-2 is a mass noun (7b). Examples in (8) show the behavior of numerals:

(8) a. **5** boxes of clay; **1** box of **10** books
b. **300** piles of pebbles; a pile of **20** pebbles; **1** box of **10** books;
c. **5** boxes of **10** books (each); **300** piles of **20** pebbles (each)

If we take the slightly odd interpretations of examples like those in (8b) and (8c) to reflect semantic effects rather than syntactic structure, a matter which needs to be evaluated more carefully, they show that both DPs can contain a numeral and the numeral of DP-1 and DP-2 need not be consistent.

N-2 can be modified by an adjective. When N-1 and N-2 are both modified by adjectives, the adjectives can be contradictory; combinations that can never occur in a single extended projection:

(9) a. a large box of small berries; a small box of large berries
b. *a large small box of berries/a small large box of berries

(10) a. a small pile of large rocks; a large pile of small rocks
b. *a small large pile of rocks/a large small pile of rocks
c. a new bunch of old flowers (newly composed but constructed from old flowers)
d. *a new old bunch/an old new bunch

Surprisingly, an adjective on N-1 sometimes seems to be able to modify N-2, as in *a delicious plate of (the) (ripe) strawberries*; *a fragrant bunch of red flowers*, though this option does not seem to be available for all adjectives: **a ripe plate of (the) strawberries* is marginal, and **a large bunch of flowers* is completely impossible in the reading where it is the flowers that are large.[4]

10.2.2 The Order of Adjectives

Within a single DP, the order of APs is not free (see Sproat and Shi 1991 for extensive discussion). To put it another way, when two adjectives occur in a single extended projection, their relative order can be fixed:

(11) a. a fresh brown egg
b. *a brown fresh egg (except with "comma intonation")

However, the order of the adjective modifying N-1 and the adjective modifying N-2 is unconstrained, as van Riemsdijk (1998) and Vos (1999) point out. An adjective modifying N-1 precedes an adjective modifying N-2 even if the order between the two is disallowed by the ordering restriction that holds within a single extended projection.

(12) a. a fresh basket of brown eggs
b. a brown basket of fresh eggs
c. fresh brown eggs/*brown fresh eggs

(13) a. a red box of big books; a big box of red books
b. a big red box of books; a box of big red books
c. *a red big box of books; *a box of red big books

This shows that any principles organizing adjectives within an extended projection (e.g. size before color) *will fail*, unless DP-1 and DP-2 are two separate extended projections.[5]

---

[4]The analysis of Dutch and German given by van Riemsdijk (1998) and Vos (1999), applied to English, suggests that there might be a difference in grammaticality between examples in which N-2 is preceded by a determiner, and those in which it is not. I am not sure if this effect is found in English.

[5]The same point holds, *mutatis mutandis*, for clausal structures. E.g. *often* can precede *reluctantly* in a single clause, while the reverse order is ungrammatical. Nevertheless, *reluctantly* can precede *often* when they are in different clauses.

There is no constraint regulating the order of an item in one extended projection relative to an item in another extended projection. If DP-1 and DP-2 are separate extended projections the observed freedom of order in adjectives is explained.

10.3 Nouns and Determiner Choice

The independence of DP-1 and DP-2 is supported additionally by another generalization about determiners. *The grammaticality of a DP is never affected by a D which is outside.* D-noun relations in DP-1 are determined by N-1 alone. D-noun relations in DP-2 are determined by N-2 alone. This is as expected. If DP-1 is an independent extended projection, it has N-1 as its lexical head and N-1 determines which determiners may and must occur. The same holds for DP-2: it is N-2 which controls the determiner system of the DP. The evidence for this comes from the well known fact that count nouns and mass nouns, plural nouns and singular nouns, have different determiner possibilities in English. With mass nouns and plurals, the indefinite determiner *a* is impossible. With singular count nouns either the indefinite or the definite determiner is required. The possibility of having a particulardeterminer, and whether it is obligatory or not, depends on the mass/count/plural status of N.

The empirical question is then whether only D-1 can satisfy the requirements of N-1, or whether D-2 can satisfy them. Likewise for D-2 and D-1 with respect to N-2. In fact, N-1 is the "enforcer" for D-1 and N-2 for D-2. We conclude that the potential for a determiner to occur, and the obligatoriness of a determiner, depend on the mass/count/plural status of the lexical head of the DP extended projection, the noun.[6]

If N-1 is a singular count noun, it requires a determiner. If N-1 is plural, it disallows *a*, allows the definite, and is grammatical with no determiner at all. The pattern is just the same for *picture* as for *box* or *pile*: D-1 cannot be absent/covert when N-1 is singular and count:

(14) a. a picture of horses; a box of books; a pile of the books
b. *picture of horses; *box of books;*pile of the books

D-1 can be *a* even when N-2 is plural or mass, but not when N-1 is plural (see note 6 on N-1 as a mass noun):

[6]Certain gaps in the system prevent completion of this paradigm: N-1 can never be mass, and N-2 can never be singular and count (except in examples like *five boxes of an expensive pencil /*expensive pencil* where the interpretation seems to be different: "a pencil of an expensive type", perhaps.) So D-N combinations cannot be evaluated for these N1s and N2s.

(15) a. a picture of (the) horses/snow; a box of (the) pears/hay; a pile of (the) pears/hay
b. *a pictures of (a) horse; *a boxes of (the) pears/hay; *a piles of pears/hay

NP-1 and NP-2 are both grammatical with no determiner provided that N-1 and N-2 are not singular count nouns:

(16) pictures of horses/hay; boxes of books; piles of books

It seems that the ungrammaticality of a D + N-1 combination can never be attributed to the nature of the determiner for N-2. Likewise, the ungrammaticality of D + N-2 combination can never be rescued by the nature of the determiner for N-1. Moreover, the generalizations governing *container* and *portion* N-1s are identical to those governing picture nouns. All cases are explained in the same way if:

(17) (i) Determiner requirements of nouns must be satisfied within the noun's extended projection,
(ii) Container and portion N-1 N-2 configurations contain two extended projections.

To clarify: If N-1 and N-2 were members of the same extended projection (both counting as heads, for example) it would have to be stipulated that N-1 and D-1 are assessed together, and that N-1 and D-2 are assessed as a pair also. However this is done, it seems to inevitably replicate the effect of positing two extended projections, by stipulating special relationships among particular heads in a syntactic structure.

10.4 Conclusion

The two-extended projection-hypothesis explains why N-1 entirely controls the syntax of the higher part of the structure, and N2 entirely controls the syntax of the lower part, with no inter-penetration between them. It follows that each noun can occur with a determiner, and that the two determiners need not be consistent. The implication for adjectives is the same. It follows that each noun can have a number specification which is independent of the number of the other. It follows that the order of adjectives modifying N-1 and those modifying N-2 is unconstrained. Finally, it follows that the determiner requirements of N-1 enforce restrictions on the D system in DP-1 and the determiner requirements of N-2 enforce restrictions on the D system in DP-2.

N-1 and N-2 must be the lexical heads of two different extended projections, just like *picture* and *horses* in *a picture of horses*. This is why DP-1 and DP-2 are self-contained, with no flow of grammatical information between them.

References

Cardinaletti, Anna and Ur Shlonsky. 2004. Clitic positions and restructuring in Italian. *Linguistic Inquiry* 35(4):519–557.

Corver, Norbert and Henk van Riemsdijk, eds. 2001. *Semi-lexical Categories: The Function of Content Words and the Content of Function Words.* Berlin: Mouton de Gruyter.

Delsing, Lars-Olof. 1993. *The Internal Structure of Noun Phrases in the Scandinavian Languages: A Comparative Study.* Ph.D. thesis, University of Lund.

Grimshaw, Jane. 1991. Extended projection. Ms., Brandeis University.

Grimshaw, Jane. 2000. Extended projection and locality. In P. Coopmans, M. Everaert, and J. Grimshaw, eds., *Lexical Specification and Insertion*, pages 115–133. Amsterdam & Philadelphia, PA: J. Benjamins.

Grimshaw, Jane. 2005. Extended projection. In *Words and Structure*, pages 1–73. Stanford, CA: CSLI Publications.

Grimshaw, Jane. 2006. Measure nouns and extended projections. Ms., in preparation.

Jackendoff, Ray. 1977. *X Syntax: A Study of Phrase Structure.* Cambridge, MA: The MIT Press.

Selkirk, Elisabeth O. 1977. Noun phrase structure. In P. Culicover, T. Wasow, and A. Akmajian, eds., *Formal Syntax*, pages 285–316. Orlando, FL: Academic Press.

Sproat, Richard and Chilin Shih. 1991. Prenominal adjectival ordering in English and Mandarin. In *Proceedings of the 18th Annual Meeting of the North Eastern Linguistc Society (NELS 18)*, pages 465–489. Toronto.

van Riemsdijk, Henk. 1990. Functional prepositions. In H. Pinkster and I. Genee, eds., *Unity in Diversity: Papers presented to Simon C. Dik on his 50th birthday*, pages 229–241. Dordrecht: Foris.

van Riemsdijk, Henk. 1998. Categorial feature magnetism: The endocentricity and distribution of projections. *The Journal of Comparative Germanic Syntax* 2:1–48.

Vos, Riet. 1999. *A Grammar of Partitive Constructions.* Ph.D. thesis, Tilburg University.

11

An Analysis of Japanese Honorific Predicates

AKIRA ISHIKAWA

11.1 Introduction

Honorific expressions constitute part of the system known as *verbal treatment*, in which linguistic expressions referring to certain people, their activities, and belongings in an utterance change their forms according to the degree of politeness the speaker wishes to have the utterance imbued with. The degree of politeness is determined by the relative social status of the participants of the utterance situation, i.e., speaker, hearer, the referents of the described event, and the degree of formality called for by the occasion.[1] It is a characteristic of Japanese along with a few other languages such as Korean[2] that expression of politeness is primarily a matter of using specific "grammatical and lexical means" to encode certain kinds of things such as mentioned above rather than the choice of the concepts themselves — what you say matters less than how you say it (Tuzimura 1988). Thus, the same cognitive content can

[1] Nagata (2001) is one of the first studies which deals with the changes of verbal treatment systems over an extended period of the history of the Japanese language. According to this study, the verbal treatment system has been changing more and more in the direction of a hearer-oriented one based on the distinction between within-group and without-group members from a more absolute system reflecting the social ranks of the participants in the early 11th century, at which the period of the study begins.

[2] Hayasi and Minami (1974) deal with different systems of verbal treatment seen in Asian languages and Nahuatl.

Architectures, Rules, and Preferences: Variations on Themes by Joan Bresnan.
Annie Zaenen, Jane Simpson, Tracy Holloway King,
Jane Grimshaw, Joan Maling, and Chris Manning, (eds.).

be encoded as a great number of utterances differing only in the degree of politeness associated with the expressions of the described participants, ranging from very vulgar to super polite. Even if we restrict our attention to honorific predicates, as this paper does, the size of variety due to the kind and degree of politeness is still considerable.[3] Since the problem of the degree of politeness should be treated sociolinguistically, we will only be concerned with the problem of the kinds of politeness relevant for contemporary Japanese honorific predicates as they are lexically and syntactically encoded. The problem of honorification and honorific predicates in Japanese has largely been studied by sociolinguists and traditional Japanese grammarians known as *kokugogakusya* 'national language scholar(s)', as pointed out by Masuko (1992), with the result that some phenomena such as the honorification of complex predicates "have been virtually left untouched". Kuno (1983) is one of the few attempts to analyse the honorification of complex predicates based on aspectual auxiliary predicates such as *hazimeru* 'to begin' and *oeru* 'to finish', using a transformational framework of the most incipient kind. Though very perceptive and interesting even today, his account does not include a principled analysis of Japanese honorification itself which would lead to a classification scheme of various honorific predicates comparable to those proposed by the sociolinguists and traditional grammarians, and which can explain various restrictions associated with specific predicates. So a generative account of Japanese honorific predicates with a proper account of Japanese honorification has not ceased to be a challenge to the generative linguist. In this paper, we will attempt to extend an LFG account of Japanese honorific complex predicates given in Ishikawa (2000) and give an account of the honorification of Japanese complex predicates based on benefactive auxiliary predicates, which is set in a pragmatic account of Japanese honorification using Brown and Levinson (1987)'s theory of politeness in terms of positive and negative faces.

11.1.1 Subject and Nonsubject Honorific Predicates

Honorific predicates in Japanese are basically produced by the following operations in the lexicon.

[3]Asada (1996) shows a list of 21 continuously changing levels of expressions for the imperative of *kuru* 'come' alone. The size of this variety comes from the fact that Japanese predicates are agglutinatively composed of their component morphemes which designate such grammatical categories as tense, aspect, modality, and illocutionary force separately, some of which change form according to the degree of politeness intended, resulting in many combinatory possibilities such as shown in this example.

(1) a. Subject honorific verbs
  i. o-V-ni naru: V takes the so-called 'ren'you' form, which is prefixed with *o*, a nominal honorific marker (this combination is called *honorific gerund* by Martin (1975)), followed by the particle (*zyosi*) *ni*, which in turn is followed by the auxiliary verb *naru*.
  ii. o-V da: the honorific gerund plus a form of the copulative verb, which can change form according to the degree of respect involved.

  b. Non-subject honorific verbs[4]
  o-V suru: the honorific gerund followed by the verb *suru*

(2) a. Tanaka Sensei ga Hanako ni tegami o o-dasi-ni
  Prof. Tanaka Nom Hanako Dat letter Acc o-send-ni
  nat-ta
  naru-Past
  'Prof. Tanaka sent a letter to Hanako.'

  b. Tanaka Sensei wa asita o-tuki da
  Prof. Tanaka Top tomorrow o-arrive da-Pres
  'Prof. Tanaka arrives tomorrow.'

  c. Hanako ga Tanaka Sensei ni o-ai si-ta
  Hanako Nom Prof. Tanaka Dat o-meet suru-Past
  'Hanako met Prof. Tanaka.'

There are also lexical honorific predicates, which are not created by the above lexical operations, but are lexically fixed forms.

(3) a. Subject honorific verbs: *irrassyaru* 'to come', *mesiagaru* 'to eat', etc.

  b. Nonsubject honorific verbs: *ukagau* 'to visit, ask', *mairu* 'to come, go', etc.

11.1.2 Benefactive complex predicates

The benefactive construction in Japanese is based on the three auxiliary verbs *ageru*, *morau*, and *kureru*, which in turn come from the corresponding full verbs *ageru* 'to give', *morau* 'to receive as a gift', and *kureru* 'to (kindly) give to me or somebody within my family circle'. Kuno (1978) gave an analysis of the benefactive construction in terms of empathy, which revealed the pragmatic nature of this construction.

[4]Martin (1975) calls these OBJECT honorific verbs, but since the target of deference is not restricted to OBJECT, we will use the term 'nonsubject' to indicate that SUBJ cannot be the target.

(4) a. Hanako ga Taro kun ni hon o yonde age-ta
Hanako Nom Master Taro Dat book Acc read-Te ageru-Past
'Hanako did Master Taro the favor of reading a book (to him).'

b. Hanako ga Taro kun ni hon o yonde morat-ta
Hanako Nom Master Taro Dat book Acc read-Te morau-Past
'Hanako received the favor from Master Taro of reading a book (to her).'

c. Taro kun ga Hanako ni hon o yonde kure-ta
Master Taro Nom Hanako Dat book Acc read-Te kureru-Past
'Master Taro did Hanako the favor of reading a book (to her).'

In (4a),(4b) and (4c), empathy is associated with Hanako, who is supposedly within the speaker's "family" circle. The three benefactive auxiliary verbs differ in the way that SUBJ and OBL are associated with the benefactor and beneficiary roles and in empathy. These benefactive auxiliary verbs are plain, non-honorific forms, and their honorific counterparts are lexical honorific predicates: *sasiageru*, *itadaku*, and *kudasaru*, respectively. Like the plain forms, these also follow a *te*-gerund to make the benefactive predicate.

(5) a. Hanako ga Tanaka san ni hon o yonde sasiage-ta
Hanako Nom Mr Tanaka Dat book Acc read-Te sasiageru-Past
'Hanako did Mr Tanaka the favor of reading a book (to him).'

b. Hanako ga Tanaka san ni hon o yonde itadai-ta
Hanako Nom Mr Tanaka Dat book Acc read-Te itadaku-Past
'Hanako received the favor from Mr Tanaka of reading a book (to her).'

c. Tanaka san ga Hanako ni hon o yonde kudasat-ta
Mr Tanaka Nom Hanako Dat book Acc read-Te kudasaru-Past
'Mr Tanaka did Hanako the favor of reading a book (to her).'

(5a) and (5b) contain nonsubject honorific predicates, (5c) a subject honorific predicate. The target of empathy remains Hanako in these sentences.

11.2 Lexical Operations for Complex Predicates

In this section, we will introduce the framework we use for specifying the lexical operations involved in producing honorific Japanese complex predicates whereby the components of such a complex predicate can have their semantic contributions specified as they are compositionally combined to form the relevant specifications for the whole predicate.

Since the syntactic behavior of an honorific complex predicate is determined by the respect associated with its arguments, the information about honorification contributed by the components is reflected in the f-structure of the entire complex predicate.

The lexical operations responsible for combining a full verb and an auxiliary verb are based on Bresnan (1982)'s theory of control and complementation. Ishikawa (1985) gives an account of various Japanese complex predicates, especially those involving an XCOMP argument and the XCOMP control relations.

(6) a. Taro ga Hanako ni hon o yom-ase-ta
Taro Nom Hanako Dat book Acc read-saseru-Past
'Taro caused Hanako to read a book.'

b. **saseru** $(\uparrow\text{PRED})=\text{`cause<}(\uparrow\text{SUBJ})(\uparrow\text{OBJ})(\uparrow\text{XCOMP})\text{>'}$
$(\uparrow\text{XCOMP SUBJ}) = (\uparrow\text{OBJ})$

In (6), the causative complex predicate *yom-ase-ta* is made up of a full verb *yomu* 'to read' and the causative auxiliary verb *saseru* 'to cause', which is a bound form requiring an internal sandhi modification when attached to a consonantal verb stem. As shown in (6b), *saseru* takes an XCOMP argument whose subject is controlled by its OBL argument. In terms of the eventualities involved, the causing event is taken to have a causer, a causee, and a caused event, which happens to be a reading event whose agent Hanako is not overtly expressed. (7) is the f-structure of (6a), where $\boxed{1}$ indicates the control relationship between the OBJ and the XCOMP SUBJ.

(7)
$$\left[\begin{array}{ll} \text{SUBJ} & [\text{PRED `Taro'}] \\ \text{OBJ} & [\text{PRED `Hanako'}]\,\boxed{1} \\ \text{XCOMP} & \left[\begin{array}{ll} \text{SUBJ} & [\;\;]\,\boxed{1} \\ \text{OBJ} & [\text{PRED `book'}] \\ \text{PRED} & \text{`read<}(\uparrow\text{SUBJ})(\uparrow\text{OBJ})\text{>'} \end{array}\right] \\ \text{PRED} & \text{`cause<}(\uparrow\text{SUBJ})(\uparrow\text{OBJ})(\uparrow\text{XCOMP})\text{>'} \end{array}\right]$$

As far as the lexical operations for the control and complementation relations are concerned, the benefactive auxiliary verbs, *ageru, morau,* and *kureru,* have the same specifications as those of the causative auxiliary verb *saseru.* The semantic roles associated with the arguments are benefactor, beneficiary, and beneficent act. In order to specify the pragmatic restrictions on the benefactor and the beneficiary arguments, Kuno (1978) uses the concept of empathy, its degree associated with each argument, and the relative strength of the two degrees. Degree of empathy is defined as follows (p. 134):[5]

(8) Degree of empathy: Empathy refers to the state of the speaker identifying himself/herself with the referent x of a noun phrase in a sentence and its degree called the degree of empathy for x is designated by E(x), whose value ranges continuously from 0 (objective description) to 1 (complete identification with oneself).

Using the degree of empathy, we can specify the differences between the benefactive auxiliary verbs.

(9) a. **ageru**
(↑PRED)='do-favor<(↑ SUBJ)(↑ OBL)(↑ XCOMP)>'
(↑ XCOMP SUBJ) = (↑ SUBJ)
(↑ SUBJ BEN-ROLE)=BENEFACTOR
(↑ OBL BEN-ROLE)=BENEFICIARY
(↑ XCOMP BEN-ROLE)=BENEFICENT-ACT
(↑ EMP-COND)='E(↑ SUBJ)>E(↑ OBL)'

b. **morau**
(↑PRED)='receive-favor<(↑ SUBJ)(↑ OBL)(↑ XCOMP)>'
(↑ XCOMP SUBJ) = (↑ OBL)
(↑ SUBJ BEN-ROLE)=BENEFICIARY
(↑ OBL BEN-ROLE)=BENEFACTOR
(↑ XCOMP BEN-ROLE)=BENEFICENT-ACT
(↑ EMP-COND)='E(↑ SUBJ)>E(↑ OBL)'

c. **kureru**
(↑PRED)='do-favor<(↑ SUBJ)(↑ OBL)(↑ XCOMP)>'
(↑ XCOMP SUBJ) = (↑ SUBJ)
(↑ SUBJ BEN-ROLE)=BENEFACTOR
(↑ OBL BEN-ROLE)=BENEFICIARY
(↑ XCOMP BEN-ROLE)=BENEFICENT-ACT
(↑ EMP-COND)='E(↑ OBL)>E(↑ SUBJ)'

From (9a) and (9c), one can see that *ageru* and *kureru* designate the conferring of a benefit in the same direction, i.e. from SUBJ to OBL, but differ in the relative strength of their degrees of empathy, and (9b) shows that *morau* has the opposite directionality in the conferment of a benefit.

[5]All the quotes from Kuno's works including his examples are translated by the current author.

11.3 Japanese Honorifics and their Nature of Politeness

11.3.1 Ontological foundations of Japanese honorific predicates

We will use Brown and Levinson (1987)'s theory of politeness based on negative and positive faces and avoidance of face threatening acts (FTAs) to provide ontological foundations for honorifics.[6] The use of honorific forms to refer to a person to be treated as a superior or an outsider reflects the speaker's adherence to social norms requiring one to know one's station in life and behave accordingly. Such linguistic manifestations of politeness are ontologically motivated by the desire on the part of the speaker to maintain in interacting with others the two kinds of faces which are the two sides of the self-image that every member of a society is supposed to have (Brown and Levinson 1987: 62).

(10) a. negative face: the want of every 'competent adult member' that his actions be unimpeded by others

b. positive face: the want of every member that his wants be desirable to at least some others

In order to say that it is in one's interests to try to maintain these two kinds of wants of every other member of the society, Brown and Levinson introduces the following assumption:

> normally everyone's face depends on everyone else's being maintained, and since people can be expected to defend their faces if threatened, and in defending their own to threaten others' faces, it is in general in every participant's best interest to maintain each other's face (Brown and Levinson 1987: 61)

Masuko (1992) takes issue with the point that defending one's own faces results in threatening those of others, and proposes the following modification:

> Rather, I think that, at least in the Japanese case, people try to defend their faces without threatening others' faces if at all possible: threatening others' faces is a rather serious offence which one does one's best not to commit (Masuko 1992: 75).

This modification to the original assumption makes it possible to view Japanese honorifics as representing such conciliatory moves as mollifying FTAs in both directions. For example, a direct mention of

[6] The term "ontological' is used to refer to this aspect of Japanese honorifics by Masuko (1992).

a volitional act by a superior is taken to threaten the negative face of the superior because its attribution of the volition to the agent delimits the nature of the act as such. If the speaker is to defend the esteemed person's negative face in carrying out his/her own desire to mention the act without making it a FTA, he/she can use an honorific expression which refers to the act but is devoid of the attribution of volition to the agent (= the esteemed person). The use of the honorific expression for the esteemed person's act can also serve to defend the positive face of the person because the honorific expression characterizes the act as an exalted kind of act which corresponds to the person's self-image as someone to be treated deferentially by the speaker, at the same time defending the speaker's positive face by representing him/her as the norm-abiding member of society which he/she wants to have others consider him/her to be.

Thus, for the purpose of the subsequent discussions, we will adopt the above assumptions as the ontological basics. With Masuko, we also consider that Brown and Levinson's FTAs should be augmented by taking the referent(s) in utterances into account in order to be applicable to the analysis of Japanese honorifics. However, we will not attempt to extend their definition of FTAs in this paper, but use their classification of honorifics instead, assuming the necessary changes to the definition can be made. The classification of honorifics is attributed to Comrie (1976), to which Brown and Levinson add the Speaker-Setting axis (Brown and Levinson 1987: 180-81).

(11) a. the speaker-addressee axis: the relation of speaker to hearer (addressee honorifics)
b. the speaker-referent axis: the relation of speaker to things or persons referred to (referent honorifics)
c. the speaker-bystander axis: the relation of speaker (or hearer) to 'bystanders' or overhearers (bystander honorifics)

The speaker-setting axis is considered to be "a socially deictic relation between … social roles assumed by speaker and audience, as partially conditioned by setting and activity type (Brown and Levinson 1987: 181)." These are separately identifiable dimensions along which the relative degrees of strength between the speaker and particular entities on the axes are calculated, but what is more important is that in order to determine a suitable honorific form, all the four axes have to be simultaneously taken into consideration:

> referent honorifics involve the communication of the speaker-referent relation, from which, given the relation between addressee and referent (presumably known to H (hearer)), H may calculate, by triangulation

as it were, what S (speaker) is communicating the speaker-addressee relation to be. Where the referent is directly associated with H (e.g. his house, his possessions, his kin), this will be simple; where the referent is directly associated with S, again the inference will be straightforward, though humbling rather than raising the referent will be appropriate. In either case, the appropriate raising or lowering of the referent by using an honorific or dishonorific label (e.g. 'your palace', 'my hovel') can serve to give deference to H. It is this inferential process that introduces great complexity into the use of reference terms for persons (which are extraordinarily diverse and elaborated in most languages partly for this reason); it is one element, but only one, in the complex process that ethnomethodologists call 'formulation' (Brown and Levinson 1987: 182).[7]

Since an analysis of the process of formulation is not our primary concern, we will specify the information about the relative degree of strength on each axis directly in the form of inequalities similar to those for empathy encoding and identify the set of inequalities characterizing the types of honorific complex predicates seen in Japanese. We will encode relative strength between the relevant entities along the speaker-referent, speaker-addressee, and speaker-setting axes with the features SP-REF, SP-ADD, and REFS, respectively.[8] R(x) is assumed to designate the value of the strength of x along the axis in question.[9] We assume multiple representation of lexical information by which pragmatic information concerning speaker and hearer can be reflected in lexical representations.

(12) subject honorific predicate

a. Tanaka sensei wa sono koto o Tarou kara o-kiki-ni
Prof. Tanaka Top the thing Acc Taro Abl o-hear-ni
natta
naru-Past
'Prof. Tanaka heard about the matter from Taro.'

b. o-kiki-ni naru
(↑ PRED)='hear<(↑ SUBJ)(↑ OBJ)(↑ OBL)>'
(↑ SP-REF)='R(↑ SUBJ)>R(SP)'

[7]Some considerations along the same lines are found in connection with her criticisms of Brown and Levinson's formula for the calculation of the degree of FTAs for Japanese honorifics in Masuko (1992: p. 76-77).

[8]The speaker-bystander axis can be ignored in the analysis of Japanese honorifics. As a case of bystander honorifics, Brown and Levinson (1987) cite Dyirbal 'mother-in-law' language, which is 'a code used in the hearing of certain "taboo" relatives.'

[9]As noted above, we will not go into the problem of 'formulation' in this paper.

c. o-kiki-ni nari-masu
(↑ PRED)='hear<(↑ SUBJ)(↑ OBJ)(↑ OBL)>'
(↑ SP-REF)='R(↑ SUBJ)>R(SP)'
(↑ SP-ADD)='R(HR)>R(SP)'

That the referent of SUBJ is higher in rank than the speaker is a necessary condition for subject honorific predicates. When deference to the hearer must also be expressed, an addressee-oriented honorific auxiliary verb *masu* follows the subject honorific predicate as in (12c).

(13) nonsubject honorific predicate

a. Tarou wa sono koto o Tanaka sensei kara o-kiki
Taro Top the thing Acc Prof. Tanaka Abl o-hear
si-masi-ta
suru-masu-Past
'Taro heard about the matter from Prof. Tanaka.'

b. o-kiki si-masu
(↑ PRED)='hear<(↑ SUBJ)(↑ OBJ)(↑ OBL)>'
(↑ SP-REF)='R(↑ GF)>R(↑ SUBJ)'
(↑ REFS)='R(↑ GF)>R(SP)'
(↑ SP-ADD)='R(HR)>R(SP)'

GF is one of the governed grammatical functions other than SUBJ. Except for rare occasions, nonsubject honorific predicates are used when the hearer is someone to whom the speaker must show deference. This is why only *o-kiki-ni nar-imasu* is given in (13). The other types of honorific predicates, i.e., addressee honorific predicates, humble honorific predicates, and nonsubject humble honorific predicates, can be given similar representations.

11.3.2 Honorific auxiliaries and their characterizations in terms of negative face

In this section, we consider the problem of how *naru* came to replace *nasaru*, and *suru* replaced *itasu* and *mousu* as the representative auxiliary verbs for forming honorific predicates they have been for about a century. Since *naru* and *suru* have full verb counterparts, we will posit the semantic forms of the auxiliary verbs as grammaticalized extensions of those of the corresponding full verbs just as in the case of the benefactive auxiliary verbs *ageru*, *morau* and *kureru*. First, we assume that the honorific gerund *o-V* reflects the promotion of the positive face of the one who is shown deference or the one who shows deference. In either case, the act is raised and treated as fit for the exalted status of the person revered. In the case of subject honorific predicates, since the revered person is the agent of the act, the positive face of the agent is directly promoted. In the case of nonsubject honorific predicates, on the other hand, since the agent is not the one to be revered, it is the speaker's positive face as that of a social norm-abiding member of society that is promoted through the acknowledgement of the positive face of a nonsubject argument. When the referent of the nonsubject argument coincides with that of the addressee, which is most often the case, the sense of abiding by the social rules is most directly conveyed to the hearer.

As for the honorific auxiliaries, we assume that they have to do with the promotion of negative face in the following sense.

(14) a. When the referent of SUBJ is the person to be revered, a plain (as opposed to honorific) mention of the act threatens the negative face of the referent of SUBJ by delimiting his/her willed involvement in the act. This threat to the negative face can be averted to the extent that mention of the willed involvement is hedged by some means.

b. When the referent of a nonsubject argument is the person to be revered, a plain mention of the act threatens the negative face of the referent of the argument because he/she is conceived of as being affected by the act (a kind of impediment to his/her total freedom). This threat can be averted to the extent that mention of the act is so hedged as to affect him/her less.

The change from *o-V nasaru* to *o-V-ni naru*

The change from *o-V nasaru* to *o-V-ni naru* is clearly a case of (14a). The honorific auxiliary verb *nasaru* comes from an honorific full verb of the same form with the meaning 'to do, to perform', whose plain form counterpart is *nasu*. By contrast, *naru* comes from its full verb counterpart with the meaning 'to become, to change into', which designates a change in state.

(15) a. 9 gatu no sue ni naru to daibu
September Gen end Dat become-Pres Cond considerably
suzusiku naru
cool become-Pres
'It gets quite cool towards the end of September.'

b. otamazyakusi ga mina kaeru ni natta
tadpole Nom all frog Dat become-Past
'All the tadpoles transformed into frogs.'

c. gogo kara yuki ni natta
afternoon Abl snow Dat become-Past
'It began to snow in the afternoon.'

When it is used with a deverbal noun, it designates an eventuality without referring to the agency of its effector.

(16) asu wa osoi modori ni naru
tomorrow Top late return Dat become-Pres
'(Mine) is a late return tomorrow (=I will return late tomorrow).'

This makes it possible to refer to somebody's decision without implicating the person's volition. (17a) carries less of an accusing tone than (17b), which uses the verb *modoru*, which designates a volitional act.

(17) a. asu wa osoi o-modori ni nari-masu-ka
tomorrow Top late o-return Dat become-masu-Pres-Interrog
'Will it be a late return tomorrow?'

b. asu wa osoku modor-are-masu-ka
tomorrow Top late return-Hon-masu-Pres-Interrog
'Are you returning late tomorrow?'

When the contemporary subject honorific predicate *o-V-ni naru* first came into use in newspapers, the SUBJ of such a sentence was mostly a governmental office rather than a person (Tuzimura 1968). This shows that the honorific predicate was used in those contexts where the volition of the agent was less obvious than in the case of personal actions. It is not hard to imagine that *o-V-ni naru* was felt to be less threatening to the negative face of the agent because *naru* does not refer to the volition of the agent. Thus, the transition from *o-V nasaru* to *o-V-ni naru* can be taken to be motivated by the speaker's general desire to maintain the negative face of the referent.

In view of the above considerations, we set up the following lexical specifications for the subject honorific auxiliary *naru*.

(18) naru
a. (↑ PRED)='happen-spontaneously<(↑COMP)>'
b. (↑ COMP PRED FORM)=HON-GERUND
c. (↑ COMP SP-REF)='R(↑ COMP SUBJ)>R(SP)'

The transition from *o-V itasu* to *o-V suru*

In the case of the nonsubject honorific predicate *o-V suru*, the transition from *o-V mousu* or *o-V itasu* is equally motivated by the speaker's general desire not to threaten the negative face of the person to be revered, but we also have to take into account the advent of a more egalitarian society prompted by the collapse of the Tokugawa feudalistic regime in 1868 and the establishment of a constitutional government by the new monarchical regime where the four castes of the previous regime were abolished and the people were declared to be equal under the law. In *o-V mousu* or *o-V itasu*, the directionality of honorification (i.e., that they designates an act by an agent who is lower in rank and is taken by the speaker to have to show deference to the referent of a nonsubject argument) is marked by the humbling auxiliary verbs *mousu* and *itasu*, which mitigate the face-threatening nature of an act done for the revered person or with the person as patient because such an act should affect the person less than those where the agent and the revered person are on the same plane. In other words, the lowering effect of humbling verbs derives from the fact that they designate the directionality of an action from the lower plane where the agent belongs to the upper one where the revered person belongs. It is worth noting here that the subject honorific auxiliary *naru* does not contain any element which would produce a comparable raising effect based on the placement of the two parties on different planes.[10] In order to explain the change into *o-V suru*, we argue that placing a person in a higher station is also an act threatening the negative face of the person because it invests the person in a straightjacket of a hierarchical order. In the new society where the people were declared equal, the use of such humbling verbs must be felt to be threatening to the negative face of the revered person who did not subscribe to the retention of the old feudalistic order. In this regard, it is noteworthy that *suru* is the plain verb counterpart of *itasu* which in their full verb capacity mean 'to do'. So *suru* does not carry the directionality of *itasu* itself, but as a direct 'translation' of *itasu*, *o-V suru* can designate the directionality necessary for the nonsubject honorific predicate. For that matter, as we discussed above, *naru* in *o-V-ni naru* does not carry an element indicating the directionality of the honorified act in itself, which is only explainable in terms of the concept of FTAs.

In view of the above considerations, we set up the following lexical specifications for the nonsubject honorific auxiliary *suru*.

(19) suru

a. (↑ PRED)='effect-for-revered-person<(↑SUBJ)(↑XCOMP)>'

b. (↑XCOMP SUBJ)=(↑SUBJ)

c. (↑ XCOMP PRED FORM)=HON-GERUND

[10] It should also be noted that *mousu* involves a further hedge because the meaning of its full verb counterpart is 'to say' rather than 'to do' as in the case of *itasu*. *o-urami mousu* 'to say a grudge' is considerably milder than *uramu* 'to bear a grudge'.

d. (↑ SP-REF)='R(↑ XCOMP GF)>R(↑ SUBJ)'
e. (↑ REFS)='R(↑ XCOMP GF)>R(SP)'
f. (↑ SP-AD)='R(HR)>R(SP)'

11.4 Permeation of honorificity in contemporary Japanese honorific predicates

Explaining the lexical composition of contemporary Japanese honorific predicates in terms of politeness based on Brown and Levinson's theory of FTAs can solve a number of mysteries which have hitherto defied solution by means of purely syntactic mechanisms.

After giving an analysis of the formation of honorific predicates in terms of transformational cycles, Kuno (1982) gives (20) as a possible counterexample to his syntactic approach (Kuno 1982: 63).

(20) a. *terorisuto ga taisi-husai ni isyo o o-kaki-ni
terrorist Nom ambassador-couple Dat will Acc o-write-ni
nar-ase-ta
naru-Caus-Past
'The terrorists made the ambassador and his wife write their wills.'

b. *watasi wa Yamada-san ni niwa no souzi o
I Top Mr Yamada Dat garden Gen cleaning Acc
o-tetudai-ni nar-ase-te simat-ta
o-help-ni naru-Caus-Te blunder-Past
'We inadvertently made Mr Yamada help with the cleaning of the garden.'

But he dismisses this problem as coming from semantic factors by citing sentences as in (21):

(21) wareware wa, Yamada sensei o, o-ibari-ni nari-tai dake,
we Top Prof. Yamada Acc o-lord-ni naru-Desid as=much
o-ibari-ni nar-ase-te o-oki suru koto ni sita
o-lord-ni naru-Caus-Te o-let suru Comp Dat decide-Past
'We decided to let Prof. Yamada lord it over us as much as he likes.'

Instead of a principled explanation, he gives the following four clauses as the reason for the seeming aberration of (20) (Kuno 1982: 64-65).

(22) i. In general, causative sentences (using 'sase') tend to be interpreted in the sense of 'compulsion/interposition' rather than that of 'noninterference'.

ii. A 'compulsion/interposition' causative, but not an 'noninterference' causative, requires that the embedded clause denote an action which can be controlled by the subject of the causative.

iii. The *o-V-ni naru* honorific predicate essentially corresponds to the spontaneous mood in which an action is designated to occur spontaneously without the intervention of the subject's control.

iv. The sense of spontaneity associated with the honorific predicate does not contradict the restrictions of the 'noninterference' causative, but does contradict those of the 'compulsion/interposition' causative.

We have seen how (22iii) can be associated with our principled theory of politeness. (22ii) is not an independent observation, but a restatement of the distinction between the two types of causative. (22i) may be correct, but is irrelevant if the 'noninterference' causative does not always give an acceptable honorific predicate.

(23) a. wareware wa kodomo-tati ni niwa de sukina-youni
we Top child-Pl Dat garden Loc as=they=like
asob-ase-ta
play-Caus-Past
'We let the children play as they liked in the garden.'

b. *wareware wa sensei-gata ni niwa de o-sukina-youni
we Top professor-Pl Dat garden Loc o-as=they=like
o-kuturogi-ni nar-ase-ta
o-relax-ni naru-Caus-Past
'We let the professors relax as they liked in the garden.'

The unacceptability of (23b) shows that (22i) is irrelevant and (22iv) is wrong. According to our FTA account, even the 'noninterference' causative expresses a threat to the negative face of the revered person because it puts the person's act under the authorization of the causer, which is an infringement on the person's total freedom.

In view of the fact that Japanese in the Nara period allowed the corresponding causative (Tuzimura 1988), we are led to the following hypothesis.

(24) Permeation of honorificity
In contemporary Japanese, an honorific predicate must not contain an auxiliary verb which designates a FTA for the revered person.

By this hypothesis, Kuno's (21) can be thought of as a case where the infringement of Prof. Yamada's negative face is only mitigated (but not completely saved) by the following *o-oki suru* 'to let someone do as he/she pleases', which designates noninterference without the sense of authorization. According to our hypothesis, in order to designate the "causative" sense in (23b), we have to use an auxiliary verb which is devoid of a FTA sense such as the English *have V-ing*. The benefactive auxiliary verb *morau* 'to receive a favor' fits the bill most of the time, but it may carry an overtone of implicit imposition in some contexts. So the most usual choice is the honorific benefactive *itadaku* 'to receive a favor (of some revered person)'.

(25) a. wareware wa sensei-gata ni niwa de o-sukina-youni
we Top professor-Pl Dat garden Loc o-as=they=like
o-kuturogi-ni nat-te morat-ta
o-relax-ni naru-Te receive=favor-Past
'We had the professors relaxing as they liked in the garden.'

b. wareware wa sensei-gata ni niwa de o-sukina-youni
we Top professor-Pl Dat garden Loc o-as=they=like
o-kuturogi-ni nat-te itadai-ta
o-relax-ni naru-Te receive=favor-Past
'We had the professors relaxing as they liked in the garden.'

Kuno also takes up the honorification of adversative passives as an apparent counterexample to his transformational analysis, which is claimed to be similarly explained by semantic considerations.

(26) a. *boku wa Yamada sensei ni musuko o o-sikari-ni
I Top Prof. Yamad Dat son Acc o-scold-ni
nar-are-te simat-ta
naru-Pass-Te suffer-Past
'Regretfully I had my son scolded by Prof. Yamada.'

b. *boku wa Yamada san ni ie ni o-ide-ni nar-are-te
I Top Mr Yamada Dat house Dat o-come-ni naru-Pass-Te
simat-ta
suffer-Past
'I suffered from having my home visited by Mr Yamada.'

As to the cause of the unacceptability of these sentences, Kuno cursorily mentions a conflict between the sense of deference associated with the honorific part and the sense of annoyance felt by the subject of the adversative passive, and claims that the solution to this conflict by some means can give rise to an acceptable honorific adversative passive sentence without specifying how. Based on our hypothesis, we can attribute the cause of the unacceptability of (26) to the face-threatening nature of the sense of annoyance of the adversative auxiliary *rare*. In contrast with the causative auxiliary *sase*, *rare* threatens the positive face of the revered person because the act by him/her represented by the honorific part is characterized as undesirable. This reasoning can account for why Kuno's examples of acceptable honorific adversative passives escape being FTAs. The three examples[11] are all cases where the sense of annoyance adds to the positive face of the revered person rather than detracting from it (Kuno 1982: 65).

(27) a. konnani sensei ni hara no soko made
this=much professor Dat belly Gen bottom as=far=as
o-mitoosi-ni nar-arete wa, nani mo kakusidatesuru
o-see=through-ni naru-Pass-Te Cond anything hide
koto wa deki mase-n
Compl Top be=able masu-NEG
'Professor, as you see through to the bottom of our belly this way, we cannot hide anything from you.'

b. watasi-tati gakusei wa sensei ni totuzen o-nakunari-ni
I-pl student Top professor Dat suddenly o-die-ni
nar-are-te simai, kore kara dou sitara ii-ka
naru-Pass-Te suffer-Cond now Abl how do-Cond good-Interrog
tohounikurete i-masu
be=at=a=loss-Te Prog-masu-Pres
'Professor, as you passed away so suddenly on us, we are at a loss what to do from now on.'

In (27a), the professor's perceptibility in seeing through the students' schemes is extolled by describing it as so keen as to annoy them. In (27b), which is supposed to be a memorial address, the deceased professor's leadership is eulogized by describing his loss as so perplexing. In either case, the sense of annoyance, which can lead to an accusation of committing an undesirable act, is turned round, as it were, to emphasize the inherent merits of the revered person, not necessarily the merit of the particular acts.

Thus, we have seen our hypothesis of permeation of honorificity together with our ontological assumptions regarding FTAs can explain the unacceptability of causativized and adversative-passivized honorific predicates in a principled way and predict possible solutions to such

[11]The fourth example is not acceptable to the author.

difficulties by suggesting alternative auxiliaries to express the intended meanings.

11.5 Benefactive Honorific Predicates

The behavior of the benefactive honorific auxiliaries *sasiageru* 'do somebody the favor of Ving', *itadaku* 'receive from somebody the favor of Ving', and *kudasaru* 'do somebody the favor of Ving' can now be explained as the convergent effects of the workings of the empathy and politeness conditions associated with each auxiliary. Their lexical specifications look as follows.

(28) a. **sasiageru**
(↑PRED)='do-favor<(↑ SUBJ)(↑ OBL)(↑ XCOMP)>'
(↑ XCOMP SUBJ) = (↑ SUBJ)
(↑ XCOMP PRED FORM) = (↑ TE-GERUND)
(↑ SUBJ BEN-ROLE)=BENEFACTOR
(↑ OBL BEN-ROLE)=BENEFICIARY
(↑ XCOMP BEN-ROLE)=BENEFICENT-ACT
(↑ EMP-COND)='E(↑ SUBJ)>E(↑ OBL)'
(↑ SP-REF)='R(↑ OBL)>R(↑ SUBJ)'
(↑ REFS)='R(↑ OBL)>R(SP)'

b. **itadaku**
(↑PRED)='receive-favor<(↑ SUBJ)(↑ OBL)(↑ XCOMP)>'
(↑ XCOMP SUBJ) = (↑ OBL)
(↑ XCOMP PRED FORM) = (↑ TE-GERUND)
(↑ SUBJ BEN-ROLE)=BENEFICIARY
(↑ OBL BEN-ROLE)=BENEFACTOR
(↑ XCOMP BEN-ROLE)=BENEFICENT-ACT
(↑ EMP-COND)='E(↑ SUBJ)>E(↑ OBL)'
(↑ SP-REF)='R(↑ OBL)>R(↑ SUBJ)'
(↑ REFS)='R(↑ OBL)>R(SP)'

c. **kudasaru**
(↑PRED)='do-favor<(↑ SUBJ)(↑ OBL)(↑ XCOMP)>'
(↑ XCOMP SUBJ) = (↑ SUBJ)
(↑ XCOMP PRED FORM) = (↑ TE-GERUND)
(↑ SUBJ BEN-ROLE)=BENEFACTOR
(↑ OBL BEN-ROLE)=BENEFICIARY
(↑ XCOMP BEN-ROLE)=BENEFICENT-ACT
(↑ EMP-COND)='E(↑ OBL)>E(↑ SUBJ)'
(↑ SP-REF)='R(↑ SUBJ)>R(SP)'

These honorific auxiliaries are the lexically fixed counterparts of the plain benefactive auxiliaries *ageru*, *morau*, and *kureru*, the first two of which give rise to unacceptable sentences when they undergo the honorific lexical operations in (1).

(29) a. *Hanako ga Tanaka san ni hon o yonde o-age
Hanako Nom Mr Tanaka Dat book Acc read-Te o-ageru
si-ta
suru-Past
'Hanako did Mr Tanaka the favor of reading a book (to him).'

b. *Hanako ga Tanaka san ni hon o yonde o-morai
Hanako Nom Mr Tanaka Dat book Acc read-Te o-morau
si-ta
suru-Past
'Hanako received the favor from Mr Tanaka of reading a book (to her).'

c. Tanaka san ga Hanako ni hon o yonde o-kure-ni
Mr Tanaka Nom Hanako Dat book Acc read-Te o-kureru-ni
nat-ta
naru-ta
'Mr Tanaka did Hanako the favor of reading a book (to her).'

As we saw in (18) and (19f), the SUBJ of *suru* is a conscious effector who regards his act as deferential to the revered person, while that of *naru* is not. This difference leads us to conjecture that those acts which do not affect the revered person enough are not fit for *o-V suru* honorification. (30a) and (30b) are supposed to have roughly the same meaning, but *kangaeru* 'to think' does not carry as fully socialized a sense of having an amorous feeling as *sitau* 'admire'. Our research on verb classes suggests that *o-V suru* honorification goes better with the Attention class of verbs than with the Thinking class of verbs according to Dixon (1991)'s verb classification. As we have no space to go into details, we just leave the conjecture as it is here.

(30) a. ?Hanako wa Yamada san no koto o o-kangae
Hanako Top Mr Yamada Gen matter Acc o-think
si-masi-ta
suru-masu-Past
'Hanako thought of Mr Yamada.'

b. Hanako wa Yamada san no koto o o-sitai
Hanako Top Mr Yamada Gen matter Acc o-admire
si-masi-ta
suru-masu-Past
'Hanako admired Mr Yamada.'

We can also conjecture, more easily this time, that those acts that are inherently disrespectful are not fit for *suru* honorification.

(31) a. ?Hanako wa ayamatte Tanaka sensei ni o-butukari
Hanako Top by=mistake Prof. Tanaka Dat o-bump
si-masi-ta
suru-masu-Past
'Hanako bumped into Prof. Tanaka by mistake.'

b. Hanako wa ayamatte Tanaka sensei o o-uti
Hanako Top by=mistake Prof. Tanaka Acc o-hit
si-masi-ta
suru-masu-Past
'Hanako hit Prof. Tanaka by mistake.'

Since *naru* honorification does not show corresponding semantic restrictions on the lexical classes of the embedded verbs, these restrictions for *suru* honorification can be attributed to the status of the SUBJ of *suru* as the conscious effector of a deferential act. As a result, when *suru* is combined with the honorific gerund of a benefactive auxiliary verb, the resultant complex auxiliary has its SUBJ as the effector of a beneficent act which is expressed as deferential. An act of gift-giving can be seen as an act threatening the negative face of the revered person because it is debt-creating and potentially constrains the freedom of the revered person. On the other hand, an act of gift-receiving can be seen as an act threatening the positive face of the revered person because the person's act is taken to be debt-creating and undesirable. Thus, we can account for the general unacceptability of *o-V suru* honorification of the benefactive auxiliaries, which is further supported by the example in (32).[12]

(32) a. Yamada sensei ga Tanaka san ni hon o yonde
Prof. Yamada Nom Mr Tanaka Dat book Acc read-Te
o-age-ni nat-ta
o-ageru-ni naru-Past
'Prof. Yamada did Mr Tanaka the favor of reading a book (to him).'

[12] According to Kuno (1978)'s theory, there should be a conflict between the empathized arguments and their honorific treatment in this example, which is not felt for some unknown reason. In (29c), the conflict would be felt if we gave the empathized argument *Hanako* honorific treatment.

b. Yamada sensei ga Tanaka san ni hon o yonde
Prof. Yamada Nom Mr Tanaka Dat book Acc read-Te
o-morai-ni nat-ta
o-morau-ni naru-Past
'Prof. Yamada received the favor from Mr Tanaka of reading a book (to her).'

c. *Tanaka san ga Yamada sensei ni hon o yonde
Mr Tanaka Nom Prof. Yamada Dat book Acc read-Te
o-kure si-ta
o-kureru suru-ta
'Mr Tanaka did Prof. Yamada the favor of reading a book (to her).'

11.6 Conclusion

We have shown an LFG account of the lexical composition of Japanese honorific and benefactive predicates, when combined with a theory of politeness based on Brown and Levinson's concept of face threatening acts (FTAs), enables us to have a principled, unified account of how *o-V-ni naru* and *o-V suru* honorification came to replace the previous *o-V nasaru* towards the beginning of the last century, *o-V mousu* and *o-V itasu*, why the causative and adversative passive auxiliaries cannot take *o-V-ni naru* stems, and why the benefactive auxiliaries can undergo only *o-V ni naru* honorification. For reasons of space, we did not discuss the problem of unacceptable **o-V site ageru*, **o-V site morau* and **o-V-ni natte kureru*, but we believe the reader agrees that the hypothesis of permeation of honorificity characterized them as such. A more difficult problem of how we derive the abbreviated forms such as *o-V itadaku* and *o-V kudasaru*, but not **o-V sasiageru*, has to await another paper, but its solution can be glimpsed further up this road.

We would like to thank the Sophia Open Research Center at Sophia University for the grant which supported our current research on Japanese honorifics and systemization of the lexicon and the School of Languages and Comparative Cultural Studies at the University of Queensland for their supportive environment during the final stages of this paper.

References

Asada, Hideko. 1996. *Keigo manyuaru (A Manual for Using Honorifics)*. Tokyo: Nanundo.

Bresnan, Joan, ed. 1982. *The Mental Representation of Grammatical Relations*. Cambridge, MA: The MIT Press.

Brown, Penelope and Stephen C. Levinson. 1987. *Politeness – Some universals in language use*. Cambridge, UK: Cambridge University Press.

Comrie, Bernard. 1976. Linguistic politeness axes: speaker-addressee, speaker-referent, speaker-bystander. Pragmatics Microfiche 1.7:A3, Department of Linguistics, University of Cambridge.

Dixon, Robert M. W. 1991. *A New Approach to English Grammar, on Semantic Principles*. Oxford: Clarendon Press.

Hayasi, Sirou and Huzio Minami, eds. 1974. *Sekai no Keigo (Honorifics and the World's Languages)*. Tokyo: Meizi-syoin.

Ishikawa, Akira. 1985. *Complex Predicates and Lexical Operations in Japanese*. Ph.D. thesis, Stanford University.

Ishikawa, Akira. 2000. Multiple representation of japanese complex predicates–a lexicalist analysis of subject and object honorific forms. In A. Ikeya and M. Kawamori, eds., *The Proceedings of the 14th Pacific Asia Conference on Language, Information and Computation (PACLIC 14)*, pages 131–142. Tokyo: Logico-Linguistic Society of Japan and The Institute of Language Teaching, Waseda University, Media Network Center.

Kuno, Susumu. 1978. *Danwa no Bunpou (The Grammar of Discourse)*. Tokyo: Taisyuukan Syoten.

Kuno, Susumu. 1982. *Sin Nihon Bunpou Kenkyuu (New Studies on Japanese Grammar)*. Tokyo: Taisyuukan Syoten.

Martin, Samuel E. 1975. *A Reference Grammar of Japanese*. New Haven, CT: Yale University Press.

Masuko, Mayumi. 1992. *Referential and Honorific Expressions in Japanese*. Ph.D. thesis, University of Cambridge.

Nagata, Takasi. 2001. *Dai 3sya Taiguu Hyougen-si no Kenkyuu (A Historical Study of the Verbal Treatment of the Third Person Expressions)*. Osaka: Izumi Syoin.

Tuzimura, Tosiki. 1968. *Keigo no Siteki Kenkyuu (Historical Studies on Honrifics)*. Tokyo: Toukyoudou.

Tuzimura, Tosiki. 1988. Keigo to taiguu. In H. Kindaiti, O. Hayasi, and T. Sibata, eds., *Nihongo Hyakka Daiziten (An Encyclopaedia of Japanese)*. Tokyo: Taisyukan.

12

Morphosyntactic vs. morphosemantic functions of Indonesian *-kan*

PAUL KROEGER

Levin and Rappaport Hovav (1998) distinguish two basic types of morphological operations on verbs: those that modify the Lexical Conceptual Structure (LCS, the semantic representation) vs. those that alter the syntactic expression of arguments without changing the semantic roles of those arguments. Locative alternation is an example of the first type; passive and applicative are examples of the second type. Levin and Rappaport Hovav state that the specific affixes used for operations of the first type are frequently the same as those used to mark aspectual distinctions, but are always different from the affixes used for operations of the second type. They know of no language in which the same affix is used to mark alterations to LCS in some forms and changes in the syntactic expression of arguments in other forms. In this paper I will present evidence showing that the Indonesian suffix *-kan* functions in both of these ways. This suffix has been the topic of much discussion over the past 40 years, and a source of considerable confusion. I will argue that in order to understand the various functions of the suffix we must recognize that it has two very different modes of operation in the grammar. These two modes are distinguished by the syntactic (monotransitive vs. ditransitive) and semantic (displaced theme vs. benefactive) patterns that they create. Adopting the terminology of Ackerman (1992) and Sadler and Spencer (1998), I refer to operations

Architectures, Rules, and Preferences: Variations on Themes by Joan Bresnan.
Annie Zaenen, Jane Simpson, Tracy Holloway King,
Jane Grimshaw, Joan Maling, and Chris Manning, (eds.).

that modify LCS as MORPHOSEMANTIC, and to operations that modify only the syntactic expression of arguments as MORPHOSYNTACTIC.[1]

12.1 The problem with lexical classes

The suffix *-kan* has often been described as a "valence increasing" morpheme, or as a marker of increased "transitivity" (Hopper & Thompson 1980). However, as various authors have pointed out (e.g. Dardjowidjojo 1971, 1974; Kaswanti 1995, 1997), the behavior of this suffix is actually quite complex. In some cases, such as (1–2), the suffix does increase the syntactic valence of the verb by promoting an oblique argument or adjunct to Primary Object.

(1) (Kaswanti 1997)

a. John membeli buku itu untuk Mary.
John buy book that for Mary
'John bought that book for Mary.'

b. John membelikan Mary buku itu.
John buy-*kan* Mary book that
'John bought Mary that book.'

c. *John membeli Mary buku itu.
John buy Mary book that

(2) a. Ibu sedang membuat baju untuk adik.
mother PROG make shirt for younger.sibling
'Mother is making a shirt for little brother.'

b. Ibu sedang membuatkan adik baju.
mother PROG make-*kan* younger.sibling shirt
'Mother is making little brother a shirt.'

c. *Ibu sedang membuat adik baju.
mother PROG make younger.sibling shirt

However, with many verbs the suffix triggers no increase in syntactic transitivity or valence, but merely a change in the semantic role of the Primary Object as in example (3). In other cases, the suffix actually appears to reduce the syntactic valence of the verb (4–5).

(3) (Sneddon 1996:79)

a. Perawat membalut luka=nya dengan kain.
nurse wrap wound=3sg with cloth
'The nurse wrapped his wound with a bandage.'

---

[1] I would like to thank David Mead, Wayan Arka, Michael and Alanna Boutin, and the participants at ISMIL (2002) for comments on earlier drafts of this paper.

b. Perawat membalutkan kain ke luka=nya.
nurse wrap-*kan* cloth to wound=3sg
'The nurse wrapped the bandage around his wound.'

(4) (Kaswanti 1997)
a. John memberi Mary buku itu.
John give Mary book that
'John gave Mary that book.'
b. John memberikan buku itu kepada Mary.
John give-*kan* book that to Mary
'John gave that book to Mary.'

(5) (Dardjowidjojo 1971)
a. Dia mengajar saya Inggeris.
3sg teach 1sg English
'He taught me English.'
b. Dia mengajarkan Inggeris kepada saya.
3sg teach-*kan* English to 1sg
'He taught English to me.'

The variable behavior illustrated in (1) through (5) is a problem for traditional analyses of *-kan* which attempt to describe all of these alternations in terms of a uniform syntactic process. Chung (1976) and Vamarasi (1999), for example, assume that all such examples are produced by a syntactic rule that promotes an indirect object or oblique argument to direct object. But in order to make this analysis work, Chung is forced to posit three distinct classes of verbs according to the changes in suffixation which trigger (or indicate) the application of this rule. Chung's classification is presented in (6). Vamarasi presents a very similar analysis, arguing that with some verbs (see examples 1 and 2), *-kan* is used to indicate that the BEN-to-OBJ rule has applied; but with others (examples 4–5) *-kan* is used to indicate that the IO-to-OBJ rule has not applied.[2]

[2] A very recent paper by Cole and Son (2004) suggests that "the role of *-kan* is to indicate the syntactic licensing of an argument in the argument structure that is not licensed syntactically by the base verb." In many cases this means an argument that is present in thematic structure but not expressed in the argument structure of the base verb; in other cases, *-kan* adds an entirely new argument. Crucially, this analysis assumes an independent, optional rule of Dative Shift that is not morphologically marked. Space restrictions do not allow me to address this analysis in the present article.

(6) Chung's (1976) classification of verb roots based on Dative rule

	before Dative	after Dative	sample roots
CLASS I	-∅	*-kan*	*bawa* 'bring', *beli* 'buy', *masak* 'cook', *buat* 'make'
CLASS II	*-kan* ~ -∅	*-i*	*kirim* 'send', *tanam* 'plant', *lempar* 'throw', *tuang* 'pour'
CLASS III	*-kan* ~ -∅	-∅	*bayar* 'pay', *beri* 'give'

One problem for this type of analysis is the fact that for some verbs, the form *meN*-ROOT-*kan* is ambiguous.[3] These roots may follow either of the two basic patterns, as illustrated in (7), and thus must be assigned to two different classes.

(7) (Kaswanti 1995)

a. Ibu menjahit-*kan* saya baju. [Benefactive]
mother sew-*kan* 1sg shirt
'Mother sewed me a shirt.'

b. Saya menjahit-*kan* baju ke tailor. [Causative]
1sg sew-*kan* shirt to tailor
'I had my shirt sewn by a tailor.'

A more serious problem is the issue of markedness reversal. Under the "advancement to object" type of analysis, the most basic form of the verb (the input to the rule) in examples like (4–5) is the one which bears the suffix, while the derived form (the output to the rule) is morphologically unmarked. This counter-intuitive analysis, which violates the spirit if not the letter of the Mirror Principle (Baker 1985), is motivated chiefly by the assumption that the use of *-kan* in (1–5) must be associated with a uniform syntactic process.

In this paper I argue that a more revealing analysis can be achieved by recognizing that the same suffix can trigger two fundamentally different kinds of changes. Adopting a proposal by Kaswanti (1995), I will label the morphosemantic (meaning-changing) uses of *-kan* as $-kan_1$, and the morphosyntactic (meaning-preserving) uses of *-kan* as $-kan_2$. I will argue that the various functions of $-kan_1$ with verbal roots seem to share a component of meaning, or partial LCS, which specifies that one argument causes another argument to change location. This shared component of meaning helps to explain some of the observed constraints on the use of the suffix. Moreover, all uses of $-kan_1$ create syntactically

[3]Transitive verbs normally carry a prefix that indicates their voice category: *meN-* for active, *di-* for passive.

monotransitive verbs; ditransitive verbs marked with -*kan* always involve -*kan*$_2$. Finally, I will argue that most if not all of the category-changing derivational functions of -*kan* should be identified with -*kan*$_1$.

12.2 Meaning-changing vs. meaning-preserving uses

12.2.1 Benefactive applicative (-*kan*$_2$)

All ditransitive uses of -*kan* involve the morphosyntactic operator -*kan*$_2$ functioning as a benefactive applicative, as in (1–2). This form indicates that the primary object is a beneficiary; it is never used for other roles such as goal or recipient. Thus as Sneddon (2000) points out, sentence (8a) can only mean 'He wrote a letter *for* (i.e., on behalf of) his father.' In order to say 'He wrote a letter to his father,' sentence (8b) must be used instead; note that the recipient is marked with a preposition and the verb does not bear a suffix.

(8) a. Dia menulis-*kan* ayah=nya surat.
3sg write-*kan*$_2$ father=3sg letter
'He wrote a letter for/*to his father.'

b. Dia menulis surat kepada ayah=nya.
3sg write letter to father=3sg
'He wrote a letter to his father.'

In this pattern, the suffix does not change the semantic role assigned to any argument and does not alter the inherent semantic content of the root. The second of these points may be illustrated by noting that whenever the suffixed form of the verb can be truly predicated of a given subject, the corresponding base form can also be predicated of that same subject (that is, p-*kan*(x) $\Longrightarrow$ p(x)). Thus an example like (9a), if true, always entails the truth of the corresponding unsuffixed form (9b). With the morphosemantic operator -*kan*$_1$ this is not the case, as illustrated in (10–11).

-*kan*

(9) $_2$: **a implies b**

a. John membeli-*kan* Mary buku itu.
John buy-*kan*$_2$ Mary book that
'John bought Mary that book.'

b. John membeli buku itu.
John buy book that
'John bought that book.'

(10) *–kan*$_1$: **a does not imply b**

a. Saya menjahit-*kan* baju ke tailor.
1sg sew-*kan*$_1$ shirt to tailor
'I had my shirt sewn by a tailor.'

b. Saya menjahit baju.
1sg sew shirt
'I sewed a shirt.'

(11) *–kan*$_1$: **a does not imply b**

a. Buruh itu memuat-*kan* beras ke kapal.
worker that contain-*kan*$_1$ rice to ship
'The workers are loading the rice onto the ship.'

b. ?Buruh itu memuat beras.
worker that contain rice
'The workers contain rice.'

Moreover, as (12) makes clear, *–kan*$_1$ often changes the degree of affectedness implied by the verb, whereas *–kan*$_2$ does not.[4]

(12) a. Ia menembak-*kan* senapang ke kepala orang itu.
3sg shoot-*kan*$_1$ rifle to head person that
'He fired his rifle at that person's head.'
(does not imply that the bullet hit the person)

b. Ia menembak kepala orang itu.
3sg shoot head person that
'He shot that person's head.' (=the bullet hit the person)

A number of authors (e.g., Pinker 1989) have pointed out that the English double object construction can only be used in a benefactive sense if the beneficiary is also interpreted as being a recipient. This constraint has been reported for a number of other languages as well. However, it does not apply to the *–kan*$_2$ construction in Indonesian. Example (13) demonstrates that the beneficiary object of the *–kan*$_2$ verb does not need to be a recipient. Thus while the use of *–kan*$_2$ is restricted to a single very specific semantic role, it does not seem to be subject to any additional semantic constraints and is in fact highly productive.

(13) (Sneddon 2000)
Sopir membawa-*kan* saya koper yang berat.
driver carry-*kan*$_2$ 1sg suitcase REL heavy
'The driver carried the heavy suitcase for me.'

[4]Example (12) was provided by Wayan Arka, p.c.

The benefactive interpretation is never available in monotransitive clauses, e.g., when *–kan* appears on an intransitive root. This fact is illustrated in (14).

(14) a. Murid-murid suka melompat di halaman sekolah.
pupils enjoy jump at yard school
'The pupils enjoy jumping in the school yard.'

b. Guru itu melompat-*kan* murid-murid di halaman sekolah.
teacher that jump-*kan*$_1$ pupils at yard school
'The teacher made/let the pupils jump in the school yard.'
(cannot mean: 'The teacher jumped for the pupils ...')

Wayan Arka (p.c.) notes that the object of the monotransitive verb *men-doa-kan* 'pray for', derived from the intransitive *ber-doa* 'to pray', is a beneficiary in the sense that the object receives some benefit from the action. However, I believe this is an inherent component of the meaning of the root itself, rather than a meaning added by the suffix. The form *mendoakan* never carries the 'in place of' or 'substitute for' meaning which is conveyed by the benefactive applicative construction, as illustrated in (8a) and (13). For example, if someone promises to pray for an hour from 2 to 3 PM and then cannot do it because of a family emergency, he could not use that verb form to ask someone else to take his place on the prayer schedule.

We should note that the beneficiary may be marked with a preposition even when the verb bears the suffix, as shown in (1d) below; compare (1a,b) above. This construction is not allowed in Bahasa Malaysia, and there is some disagreement as to whether it should be considered "proper" Indonesian. Such sentences seem to resist passivization. Several authors have noted that this pattern may be a calque on Javanese.

(1) d. John membeli-*kan* buku itu untuk Mary.
John buy-*kan* book that for Mary
'John bought that book for Mary.'

12.2.2 Locative alternation (*kan*$_1$)

Kaswanti (1995) notes that *–kan*$_1$ frequently alternates with the suffix *–i* whereas *–kan*$_2$ does not. This alternation, which is strongly reminiscent of the English Locative Alternation, is illustrated in (15–17). In these examples, the *–i* suffix indicates that the object is the goal or locus of the action, while *–kan*$_1$ indicates that the object is a displaced theme.[5]

[5]Wolff (1980:201) refers to this as the "conveyance" meaning of *–kan*.

(15) a. Wim menuang-*kan* air ke dalam ember.
Wim pour-kan_1 water to in bucket
'Wim poured water into the bucket.'

b. Wim menuang-*i* ember dengan air.
Wim pour-*i* bucket with water
'Wim filled the bucket with water.'

(16) (Sneddon 1996:96)

a. Buruh itu memuat-*kan* beras ke kapal.
worker that contain-kan_1 rice to ship
'The workers loaded the rice onto the ship.'

b. Buruh itu memuat-*i* kapal dengan beras.
worker that contain-*i* ship with rice
'The workers loaded the ship with rice.'

(17) a. Wim meludah-*kan* biji semangka.
Wim spit-kan_1 seed watermelon
'Wim spat out the watermelon seeds.'

b. Wim meludah-*i* tanah.
Wim spit-*i* earth
'Wim spat on the ground.'

The same alternation is found with many intransitive verbal roots whose basic meaning involves directed motion, as illustrated in (18–19). With these roots, –kan_1 has a causative sense as discussed in section 12.4, but still marks the primary object as a displaced theme.

(18) (adapted from Dardjowidjojo 1971)

a. Air itu sedang meng-alir ke sawah.
water that PROG flow to rice.field
'The water is flowing to the rice field.'

b. Dia meng-alir-*kan* air itu ke sawah=nya.
3sg flow-kan_1 water that to rice.field=3sg
'He caused the water to flow to his rice field.'

c. Dia meng-alir-*i* sawah=nya dengan air itu.
3sg flow-*i* rice.field=3sg with water that
'He flooded his rice field with the water.'

(19) (Dardjowidjojo 1971)

a. Buku saya jatuh.
book 1sg fall
'My book fell.'

b. Dia men-jatuh-*kan* buku saya.
3sg drop-kan_1 book 1sg
'He dropped my book.'

c. Dia men-jatuh-*i* buku saya.
3sg drop-*i* book 1sg
'He fell on my book.'

Levin and Rappaport Hovav (1998:261) propose LCS representations for the Locative Alternation similar to those in (20). Here x represents the agent, y the displaced theme, and z the goal. Notice in particular that the LCS in (20a) contains a substring of the form CAUSE–BECOME–AT, expressing the idea that one participant causes another to undergo a change of location. This seems to be the common semantic core of the primary uses of -kan_1.

(20) a. **Displaced theme as object** (V-kan_1)
[[x ACT]CAUSE [y BECOME P_{loc} z] [$POUR$]$_{MANNER}$]
(= ex. 15a)

b. **Locative object** (V-*i*)
[[x ACT] CAUSE [z BECOME [$FULL?$]$_{STATE}$ WITH-RESPECT-TO y] [$POUR$]$_{MANNER}$]
(= ex. 15b)

Levin and Rappaport Hovav note that, in languages where the Locative Alternation is morphologically marked (like Indonesian but unlike English), the affixes used are frequently also used to mark aspectual distinctions such as telicity. I do not know of any aspectual uses of *-kan*, but the suffix *-i* is sometimes used to indicate iterative aspect as in: *memukul* 'to hit', *memukuli* 'to hit repeatedly'; *mencium* 'to kiss', *menciumi* 'to kiss repeatedly'.

12.2.3 Instrumental -kan_1

Another construction in which a transitive verb root bears the -kan_1 suffix is illustrated in (21–24). This pattern is often referred to as the 'instrumental' use of the suffix. Unlike the benefactive applicative formed with -kan_2, this construction does not increase the valence of the verb because the patient of the base form is expressed as an oblique goal or location argument of the derived verb.

(21) (Sneddon 1996:79)

a. Dia memukul anjing dengan tongkat.
3sg beat dog with stick
'He hit the dog with a stick.'

b. Dia memukul-*kan* tongkat pada anjing.
3sg beat-kan_1 stick to dog
'He used the stick to beat the dog with.'

(22) a. Dia mengikat anjing dengan tali.
3sg tie dog with rope
'He tied up the dog with a rope.'

b. Dia mengikat-*kan* tali ke anjing.
3sg tie-kan_1 rope to dog
'He tied the rope to the dog.'

(23) (Kaswanti 1997)

a. John menikam perut harimau dengan belati.
John stab belly tiger with dagger
'John stabbed the tiger's belly with a dagger.'

b. John menikam-*kan* belati ke perut harimau.
John stab-kan_1 dagger to belly tiger
'John stabbed his dagger into the tiger's belly.'

(24) a. Dia menulis-i ulas meja dengan pensil.
3sg write-*i* cloth table with pencil
'He wrote on the table-cloth with a pencil.'

b. Dia menulis-*kan* pensil pada ulas meja.
3sg write-kan_1 pencil to cloth table
'He wrote with a pencil on the table-cloth.' (cf. ex. 8)

Sneddon (1996:79–80) makes the following very significant comment about this use of *-kan*: "Although these verbs are usually regarded as marking the object as being the instrument with which the action is performed, the object cannot always be so regarded, as shown by the following [ex. 25]. These examples show that what is basically important in these constructions is that the object is something which is handled, manipulated or moved."[6]

(25) (Sneddon 1996:80)

a. Dia memukul-*kan* kepala pada dinding.
3sg beat-kan_1 head to wall
'He beat his head against the wall.'

b. Dia menémpél-*kan* gambar ke témbok.
3sg stick-kan_1 pictures to wall
'He stuck pictures on the wall.'

[6]Sneddon cites Hein Steinhauer (p.c.) as the source of this observation.

In other words, the "instrumental" object must be interpretable as a displaced theme, and need not be an instrument at all. The LCS for this construction must again contain a substring of the form CAUSE–BECOME–AT, and this usage of *-kan*$_1$ will be unavailable for verbs which are semantically incompatible with this component of meaning. This analysis correctly predicts that instruments which are not moved or transferred will be far less acceptable in this construction, as illustrated in (26–28):

(26) a. Dia menulis-*kan* pensil tumpul.
3sg write-*kan*$_1$ pencil dull
'He wrote with a blunt pencil.' (Sneddon 1996:83)

b. *?Dia menulis-*kan* mesin tik.
3sg write-*kan*$_1$ machine type
(intended: 'He wrote with a typewriter.')

(27) (ex. a–b from Kaswanti 1995)[7]

a. ?Jangan membeli-*kan* uang itu buku!
don't buy-*kan*$_1$ money that book
'Don't use that money to buy books!'

b. Jangan sampai uang itu di-beli-*kan* buku!
don't arrive money that PASS-buy-*kan*$_1$ book
'Don't let that money be used to buy books!'

c. *?Jangan sampai kartu Visa itu di-beli-*kan* buku!
don't arrive card Visa that PASS-buy-*kan*$_1$ book
(intended: 'Don't let that Visa card be used to buy books!')

(28) other non-displaced instruments:

a.	**menghitungkan sipoa/sempoa*	'add up with an abacus'
b.	**menimbangkan dacing/neraca*	'weigh with a scale/*dacing*'
c.	**menuangkan corong*	'pour/fill with a funnel'
d.	**memotretkan kamera*	'take pictures with a camera'
e.	**menyalinkan mesin fotokopi*	'make copies with a photocopier'

Notice that movement of certain body parts can be expressed using this construction, as seen in (25a) and in the semi-conventionalized expressions in (29). While the objects in these examples are not instru-

[7]Some speakers reject 27a-b; everyone rejects 27c. The contrast in acceptability seems to be due to the fact that, when paying cash, the ownership of the money changes from buyer to seller. A credit may be handed back and forth during the transaction, but there is no transfer of ownership.

ments in the ordinary sense, they are caused to move toward a specified goal and so are compatible with a displaced theme interpretation.

(29) a. Dia menginjak-*kan* kaki=nya di atas rumput.
3sg tread-*kan*$_1$ foot=3sg on grass
'He set his foot on the grass.' (Sneddon 2000)

b. Dia memandang-*kan* mata ke gunung.
3sg look-*kan*$_1$ eye to mountain
'He turned his eyes to the mountain.'

12.2.4 "Causative" -*kan*$_1$

Examples like those in (30) are often referred to as causatives, but they are peculiar in certain respects. (This pattern, which involves transitive roots, is much less productive than the causative use with intransitive roots, which is discussed in section 12.4.)

(30) a. Saya mencuci-*kan* pakaian pada wanita itu.
1sg wash-*kan*$_1$ clothes to woman that
'I have my clothes washed by that woman.' (Sneddon 1996:75)

b. Saya menjahit-*kan* baju ke tailor.
1sg sew-*kan*$_1$ shirt to tailor
'I had my shirt sewn by a tailor.' (Kaswanti 1995; Verhaar 1980:52)

c. Ibu meminum-*kan* susu pada bayi.
mother drink-*kan*$_1$ milk to baby
'Mother feeds milk to the baby.' (Echols & Shadily 1989:373)

d. Saya memeriksa-*kan* mata saya ke dokter mata.
1sg examine-*kan*$_1$ eye 1sg to doctor eye
'I had my eyes examined by an eye doctor.' (Kaswanti 1995; Verhaar 1980:52)

Baker (1988) points out that there is a very strong correlation between the grammatical relations of causees and recipients. In languages which make the goal or recipient the primary object of a basic ditransitive verb, the causee will almost always be the primary object of a causative verb derived from a transitive root. In languages where the recipient of a basic ditransitive verb is not the primary object, the causee of a causative derived from a transitive root will normally be encoded as an indirect object or oblique argument.

If the sentences in (30) were causative constructions in the normal sense, they would violate this generalization. Basic ditransitive verbs in Indonesian such as *beri* 'give' and *ajar* 'teach' take their goal or recipient as primary object, as seen in examples (4–5). Thus Baker's generalization would predict that the "causees" in (30) should be expressed as primary objects. However, all of them are in fact expressed as oblique (prepositional) arguments. Moreover, they are marked with prepositions that encode locations or goals (*pada* 'at, to', *ke* 'to', *di* 'at'), rather than the agentive preposition *oleh* 'by'. In fact, Sneddon (1996:75) states that with a number of verbs it is more normal in this construction to express the location rather than the actor/causee, as illustrated in (31).[8]

(31) (Sneddon 1996:75)

a. Di mana kau mencuci-*kan* pakaian=mu?
where 2sg wash-kan_1 clothes=2sg
'Where do you have your clothes washed?'

b. Saya mau mencetak-*kan* kartu nama saya
1sg want print-kan_1 card name 1sg
di percetakan baru itu.
at print.shop new that
'I want to get my calling cards printed at that new printery.'

Several authors have suggested that examples like (30a) can be paraphrased as 'I send my clothes to that woman for washing'. I suggest that these examples are created by modifying the basic sense of the root to make it compatible with the semantic core associated with the -kan_1 suffix. The meaning of the derived verb form is something like, "*x* CAUSE *y* BE AT *z* for the purpose of *V*-ing", where *V* represents the basic meaning of the transitive root. This explains why the "causee" phrases in (30) are marked as locations: in this construction their semantic function is that of a location, rather than an agent.

This analysis predicts that the "causative" interpretation will be most acceptable when the sentence can be interpreted as involving a change in location on the part of the patient, and will be much less acceptable when the patient cannot be interpreted as undergoing a change of position. Examples (32–34) provide some confirmation for this prediction.[9]

[8]However, Wayan Arka (p.c.) points out that this goal or location in this construction must be potentially agentive or imply the existence of an agent, as illustrated by the following contrast:

(i) Saya mencucikan pakaian saya di tukang cuci itu/*sungai.
'I have my clothes cleaned at the laundry/*river.'

[9]The following example from Sneddon (2000) represents a possible exception to this generalization: *Saya harus mereparasikan atap rumah.* 'I must get my roof fixed.'

(32) a. Saya memeriksa-*kan* mata saya ke dokter.
1sg examine-*kan*$_1$ eye 1sg to doctor
'I had my eyes examined by a doctor.'

b. ??Gubernur memeriksa-*kan* jembatan itu ke insinyur.
governor examine-*kan*$_1$ bridge that to engineer
(intended: 'The governor had the bridge examined by an engineer.')

(33) Bapak meminum-*kan* air/*sungai pada kerbau.
father drink-*kan*$_1$ water/*river to buffalo
'Father gave the buffalo some water/*the river to drink.'

(34) a. Tetangga saya selalu mereparasi-*kan* mobil=nya pada
neighbor 1sg always repair-*kan*$_1$ car=3sg to
bengkel ini.
workshop this
'My neighbor always has his car repaired at this workshop.'
(Verhaar 1984:39)

b. *?Tetangga saya mereparasi-*kan* rumah=nya pada
neighbor 1sg repair-*kan*$_1$ house=3sg to
tukang.kayu ini.
carpenter this
(intended: 'My neighbor had his house repaired by this carpenter.')

The analysis also predicts that such causatives will not normally be acceptable if the location of the patient is not relevant to the situation described by the verb (e.g. 'hate', 'want'), or if the basic meaning of the verb implies that the actor is moving toward the patient (e.g. 'attack', 'search for', 'visit').

(35) a. *Jangan membenci-*kan* adik pada isteri=nya.
don't hate-*kan*$_1$ younger.sibling to wife=3sg
(intended: 'Don't make our little brother's wife hate him.')

b. *Amerika menyerang-*kan* Pakistan pada India.
America attack-*kan*$_1$ Pakistan to India
(intended: 'America made India attack Pakistan.')

12.2.5 Optional suffixation

The LCS of a monotransitive verb root expressing motion or transfer ('throw', 'send', etc.) already contains a substring of the form CAUSE–BECOME–AT. The root itself satisfies all of the constraints that would be imposed on a derived verb bearing the *–kan*$_1$ suffix. The *–kan*$_1$ suffix may optionally appear with such roots but has no effect on the semantic or syntactic properties of the verb, as illustrated in (36b) and (37b).

Other roots for which *–kan*$_1$ is optional include *lempar* 'throw'; *tuang* 'pour'; *sumbang* 'donate, contribute'; *titip* 'entrust'; *antar* 'send, accompany'; *sebut* 'mention' (Sneddon 1996:84). This pattern of optionality suggests that we might describe the core function of *–kan*$_1$ in terms of unification with the partial LCS "CAUSE–BECOME–AT".

(36) a. Paman mengirim-*i* saya uang tiap bulan.
uncle send-*i* 1sg money every month
'Uncle sends me some money every month.'

b. Paman mengirim(-*kan*) uang kepada saya tiap bulan.
uncle send(-kan$_1$) money to 1sg every month
'Uncle sends some money to me every month.' (Johns 1978:232)

(37) a. Dia menanam-*i* sawah=nya dengan padi.
3sg plant-*i* rice.field=3sg with rice
'He planted his field with rice.'

b. Dia menanam(-*kan*) padi itu di sawah=nya.
3sg plant(-kan$_1$) rice that in rice.field=3sg
'He planted the rice in his field.'

Basic ditransitive roots which select a goal or recipient as primary object, such as *beri* 'give' (4a) and *ajar* 'teach' (5a), may optionally take the suffix *–i* with no change of meaning.[10] But it is important to note that this kind of optional suffixation is impossible with *–kan*$_2$, i.e., *–kan*$_2$ is always obligatory in clauses which match its output structure. In other words, benefactive objects are impossible when the verb carries no suffix, as illustrated above in (1c) and (2c). This fact seems to support the hypothesis that *–kan*$_1$ and *–kan*$_2$ are very different in their modes of application.

12.3 Category-changing derivations

The suffix *–kan* is also used as a category-changing derivational affix. Some examples, mostly from Sneddon (1996), are presented in (38). The roots from which these forms are derived include adjectives (38a), nouns (38b) and even prepositional phrases (38c). In every case, the derived form is a monotransitive verb.

[10]Sneddon (1996:84) argues that *memberi* in examples like (4a) bears the suffix *–i* in underlying form, but that the suffix is deleted by a phonological process of degemination; however, Dardjowidjojo (1971) rejects this idea. Sneddon (1996:92) notes that are also some monotransitive roots which select a goal as object and can optionally take the suffix *–i* with no change of meaning or syntactic properties. These include *menyiram(i)* 'to spray', *menghias(i)* 'to decorate', etc.

(38) a. Adjective roots

ROOT		DERIVED FORM	
bébas	'free'	*membébaskan*	'to liberate'
bersih	'clean (adj.)'	*membersihkan*	'to clean (something)'
habis	'finished, used up'	*menghabiskan*	'to use up'
luas	'broad, spacious'	*meluaskan*	'to widen, cause to spread'
besar	'big'	*membesarkan*	'to enlarge; bring up (a child)'
beku	'frozen'	*membekukan*	'to freeze something'
takut	'afraid'	*menakutkan*	'to frighten'

b. Noun roots

ROOT		DERIVED FORM	
sekolah	'school'	*menyekolahkan*	'send to school'
pasar	'market'	*memasarkan*	'take to market'
makam	'grave, tomb'	*memakamkan*	'bury, entomb'
calon	'candidate'	*mencalonkan*	'to nominate'
hadiah	'gift'	*menghadiahkan*	'give as a present'
nasihat	'advice'	*menasihatkan*	'to advise'
cermin	'mirror'	*mencerminkan*	'to reflect'
saksi	'witness'	*menyaksikan*	'to witness'

c. PP as base (Alwi et al. 1998:121)

BASE		DERIVED FORM	
ke depan	'to the front'	*mengedepankan*	'put in front, put forward, propose'
ke luar	'to the outside'	*mengeluarkan*	'bring out; produce'
ke samping	'to the side'	*mengesampingkan*	'put aside, ignore'

When the base form is an adjective root, as in (38a), suffixation with *–kan* produces an accomplishment predicate: "cause *y* to become STATE". Alwi et al. (1998:128) point out that there is a subtle difference in meaning between these *meN*-Adj*–kan* verbs and similar verbs derived with the causative prefix *per–* (*meN-per*-Adj). The latter forms may express simply an increase in the quality named by the adjective, but the *-kan* verbs must express a true change of state, implying that the object did not have the quality named by the adjective before this event took place. For example, both of these patterns are allowed with the adjective *jelas* 'clear'. The *-kan* verb *menjelaskan* 'clarify, explain' implies that the thing being acted upon or discussed was not clear to begin with. The verb *memperjelas*, on the other hand, means 'increase the clarity of' and could be used for something that was already fairly clear. A similar contrast is found for many other pairs, e.g. *membesarkan* 'make big/great' vs. *memperbesar* 'make bigger', from the root *besar* 'big'.

Jackendoff (1983) and a number of other authors represent change of state predicates as a kind of metaphorical change of location. The LCS representations for the *meN*-Adj-*kan* verbs in (38a) would contain a substring of the form CAUSE–BECOME–AT, with the state named by the base adjective filling the location position. Thus both semantically and syntactically these verbs can be identified as instances of the *-kan*$_1$ suffix. Further evidence for this identification comes from the fact that some of these de-adjectival verbs allow the *-kan* suffix to alternate with *-i*, as in the Locative Alternation pattern discussed in section 12.2.2. Where this is possible, the *-i* suffix marks the object as the goal, source or locus of the action, while *-kan*$_1$ indicates that the object is an entity which undergoes a change of state (metaphorically, the displaced theme).

(39) (cf. Sneddon 1996:87)

panas-*kan*	'make hot'	panas-*i*	'apply heat to'
asin-*kan*	'make salty'	asin-*i*	'apply salt to'
mérah-*kan*	'cause to become red'	mérah-*i*	'apply red stuff to'
kering-*kan*	'cause to become dry'	kering-*i*	'to drain'
takut-*kan*	'make afraid'	takut-*i*	'to fear' (trans.)
jauh-*kan*	'remove/ keep at a distance'	jauh-*i*	'to avoid'
marah-*kan*	'make angry'	marah-*i*	'to be angry at'

When the base form of the *meN*-STEM-*kan* verb is a PP (presumably reinterpreted as a compound stem), as in (38c), the derived verb expresses the meaning CAUSE–BECOME–AT with the PP base expressing the goal. These derivations are clearly compatible with the semantics and syntax of the *-kan*$_1$ suffix.

With noun roots the semantic functions of *-kan* are more varied (Alwi et al. 1998:121–2). If the noun N refers to a location, that location becomes the goal and the derived verb means 'put *y* in the N': *penjara* 'prison', *memenjarakan* 'imprison'; *rumah* 'house', *merumahkan* 'send home; lay off (from work)'; *rumah sakit* 'hospital', *merumahsakitkan* 'hospitalize'; see also the first three examples in (38b). In many other cases, the noun is interpreted as naming a result state and the derived verb is semantically similar to the *-kan* verbs derived from adjective roots. Examples include *raja* 'king', *merajakan* 'make *y* a king; treat like a king'; *anak tiri* 'stepchild', *menganaktirikan* 'treat like a stepchild'; see also the fourth and fifth examples in (38b). It seems natural to identify these kinds of examples as instances of the $-kan_1$ suffix.

There remain other cases, however, where the meaning of the derived verb is harder to relate to the proposed semantic core for $-kan_1$. In many of these examples, the derived verb names a two-place activity predicate, as in the last three examples in (38b). The analysis of activity verbs with *-kan* is an area needing further research.

12.4 Intransitive roots and 'unaccusativity'

The suffix *-kan* can be added to virtually any intransitive verb root to create a monotransitive verb. When it is added to an intransitive verb of motion, the resulting transitive verb has a causative sense as seen in (18b) and (19b). The suffixed form also has a causative sense with intransitive roots that denote a state or change of state, creating an accomplishment predicate like those derived from adjectival roots (38a). In other cases, however, the meaning of the derived transitive form does not include any sense of causation. Some examples of this type are shown in (40–41), adapted from Vamarasi (1999).

(40) a. Anak-anak ber-main di luar.
children play at outside
'The children are playing outside.'

b. Anak itu memain-*kan* piano.
child that play-*kan* piano
'The child is playing the piano.'

(41) a. Kami selalu ber-doa untuk orang tua kami.
1pl.ex always pray for person old 1pl.ex
'We always pray for our parents.'

b. Pendeta itu mendoa-*kan* yang sakit.
pastor that pray-*kan* REL sick
'The pastor prayed for those who were sick.'

Vamarasi uses the contrast between the causative pattern in (18–19) and the non-causative pattern in (40–41) as her primary criterion for distinguishing 'unaccusative' from 'unergative' verbs. She defines unaccusatives as intransitive verb roots which have causative semantics when affixed with *-kan*, and unergatives as intransitive verb roots which do not. Some examples of each type are listed in the following table:

(42) a. 'unaccusatives' (causative sense)

ROOT		DERIVED FORM	
tidur	'sleep'	menidurkan	'put to sleep'
jatuh	'fall'	menjatuhkan	'to drop'
datang	'come, arrive'	mendatangkan	'bring, cause to arrive'
sampai	'arrive'	menyampaikan	'cause to arrive'
timbul	'emerge, arise'	menimbulkan	'cause to emerge'
hilang	'get lost'	menghilangkan	'get rid of'
masuk	'enter'	memasukkan	'put/bring inside'
kembang	'swell'	mengembangkan	'cause to swell'
lahir	'be born'	melahirkan	'to give birth to'
duduk	'sit'	mendudukkan	'to seat, cause to sit'
berhenti	'stop' (intr.)	menghentikan	'cause to stop'
lompat	'jump'	melompatkan	'cause/allow to jump'
renang	'swim'	merenangkan	'cause/allow to swim'
terbang	'fly'	menerbangkan	'cause/allow to fly'
menangis	'cry'	menangiskan	'cause to cry'

b. 'unergatives' (non-causative sense)

ROOT		DERIVED FORM	
berkerja	'work'	mengerjakan	'work at/on, perform'
berpikir	'think'	memikirkan	'think about, ponder'
berdoa	'pray'	mendoakan	'pray for'
bermain	'play'	memainkan	'play (an instrument, etc.)'
berbicara	'converse'	membicarakan	'talk about, discuss'
bernyanyi	'sing'	menyanyikan	'sing (a song)'
(ber)batuk	'cough'	membatukkan	'cough up'
ketawa	'laugh'	mengetawakan	'laugh at'
menangis	'cry'	menangiskan	'weep for, cry over'

Unaccusativity is often associated with a contrast between agentive vs. non-agentive predicates. But agentivity does not appear to be the relevant semantic contrast in (42). Notice that (42a) includes agentive manner of motion verbs like 'jump', 'swim' and 'fly', which are not typically encoded as unaccusatives; and (42b) includes some actions that are far less agentive, such as 'cough' and 'cry'. Moreover, the 'causative' test does not partition the class of intransitive roots neatly, since a few roots (e.g., 'cry') allow both interpretations, as indicated in (42).

I suggest that the causative sense is available primarily for roots whose basic meaning is compatible with the semantic core proposed for *-kan*$_1$, namely CAUSE–BECOME–AT. This would include verbs of motion, such as 'swim' and 'fly', as well as verbs that denote a state or change of state, as discussed in the previous section.

Predicates denoting activities that do not involve motion cannot in general unify with the semantic core CAUSE–BECOME–AT. In the case of *batuk* 'cough', the derived verb *membatukkan* 'cough up' seems very close to the core meaning of the *-kan*$_1$ suffix, but in other cases it is not clear whether the LCS of the suffixed verb is in fact modified or not. In some of these cases, the object of the derived transitive verb is implied by the inherent semantics of the root itself: when we think, we must think about something; when we talk, we must talk about something; when we sing, we must sing something; etc. Levin (1999) suggests that the optional expression of objects of transitive activity predicates need not involve an alternation in the LCS of these predicates. But, as noted above, the function of *-kan* in such forms in a matter for further research.

12.5 Conclusion

We have considered examples demonstrating two fundamentally different uses of *-kan* in Indonesian. One of these (*-kan*$_1$) involves a modification of the semantic structure (LCS) of the verb, while the other (*-kan*$_2$) involves only a change in the syntactic expression of the arguments.

The morphosyntactic operator *-kan*$_2$ is used to form benefactive applicatives, i.e., ditransitive verbs whose primary object is a beneficiary. This construction is highly productive and regular. The morphosemantic operator *-kan*$_1$ has a variety of uses, but we have suggested that its core function is to produce monotransitive verbs whose LCS includes a substring of the form CAUSE–BECOME–AT, and whose object corresponds to the displaced theme. This hypothesis provides an explanation for some of the semantic constraints we have observed on the use of the suffix. The "instrumental" use of the suffix is only acceptable for instruments that are moved to a new location; and provided this condition is met, the pattern is not actually restricted to instruments.[11] The "causative" use of the suffix with transitive roots is only acceptable when the patient is viewed as being taken somewhere to be acted upon; and the prepositional argument in this construction specifies the goal, i.e., the location where the "causee"/agent is located, rather than the causee per se.

The hypothesis also explains why the suffix is optional, and produces no change in meaning or syntax, when the basic LCS of a transitive root already contains a substring of the form CAUSE–BECOME–AT. This is the case for verbs like 'throw', 'send', 'pour', etc. It also helps to explain the split in the behavior of intransitive roots, which does not seem to correspond to standard notions of unaccusativity. The suffix *-kan* has causative semantics precisely where the basic meaning of the intransitive root involves motion, a state, or a change of state. In accounting for this pattern we assumed that changes of state are represented in LCS as metaphorical change of location. The same assumption provides an account for most of the category-changing examples discussed in section 12.3. There remains a residue of lexical idiosyncrasy etc. which this account does not cover, e.g., *me-lukis* 'draw, paint' vs. *me-lukis-kan* 'describe'. Some predicates of emotion take the suffix *-kan*, e.g. *me-rindu-kan* 'miss, long for'; *meng-harap-kan* 'hope for'; *meng-ingin-kan* 'desire'; but most of the predicates in this class take the suffix *-i*.[12] The largest class of data that our analysis currently fails to account for involves intransitive non-motion activity verbs like those listed in (42b). But the vast majority of uses of *-kan* can be assigned to one of the two major types, or modes of application, described above.

One way of treating this dual mode of application is to posit two homophonous *-kan* suffixes, one morphosyntactic and the other morphosemantic. This idea is not a new one in Austronesian linguistics. Sirk (1978) and Mead (1998) have pointed out that two different suffixes, *-*kən* and *-*akən*, can be reconstructed for a very early stage of Malayo-Polynesian. In most modern languages the two forms have merged, but there are a few languages (primarily in Sulawesi) that retain distinguishable reflexes of both forms. I do not know of any phonological evidence to suggest that the two *-kan* suffixes in modern Malay/Indonesian derive from different historical sources. However, if

[11] As we saw in section 12.2.3, in some cases (e.g., money) the relevant constraint is that the instrument must undergo a change of possession.

[12] A few roots can take either suffix, e.g. *ingin* 'desire'. The object-of-emotion use of *-kan* is more common in the passive than the active; see Sneddon 1996:73.

this were indeed the case it could help to explain why we find a single affix marking both morphosyntactic and morphosemantic operations, apparently a relatively uncommon state of affairs.

References

Ackerman, Farrell. 1992. Complex predicates and morpholexical relatedness: Locative alternation in Hungarian. In I. Sag and A. Szabolcsi, eds., *Lexical Matters*, pages 55–83. Stanford, CA: CSLI Publications.

Alwi, Hasan, Soenjono Dardjowidjojo, Hans Lapoliwa, and Anton Moeliono. 1998. *Tata Bahasa Baku Bahasa Indonesia (The standard grammar of Indonesian)*. Jakarta: Balai Pustaka, 3rd edn.

Baker, Mark. 1985. The mirror principle and morphosyntactic explanation. *Linguistic Inquiry* 16(3):373–415.

Baker, Mark. 1988. *Incorporation: a theory of grammatical function changing*. Chicago, IL: University of Chicago Press.

Chung, Sandra. 1976. An object-creating rule in Bahasa Indonesia. *Linguistic Inquiry* 7:41–87.

Cole, Peter and Min-Jeong Son. 2004. The argument structure of verbs with the suffix *-kan* in Indonesian. *Oceanic Linguistics* 43(2):339–364.

Dardjowidjojo, Soenjono. 1971. The *men-*, *men-kan* and *men-i* verbs in Indonesian. *Philippine Journal of Linguistics* 2(2):71–84.

Dardjowidjojo, Soenjono. 1974. The role of overt markers in some Indonesian and Javanese passive sentences. *Oceanic Linguistics* 13:371–389.

Echols, John M. and Hassan Shadily. 1961 [1989]. *Kamus Indonesia-Inggris*. Jakarta: Penerbit PT Gramedia. 3rd edition revised by John U. Wolff and James T. Collins in association with Hassan Shadily.

Hopper, Paul and Sandra A. Thompson. 1980. Transitivity in grammar and discourse. *Language* 56(2):251–299.

Jackendoff, Ray. 1983. *Semantics and Cognition*. Cambridge, MA: The MIT Press.

Johns, Yohanni. 1978. *Bahasa Indonesia: Langkah Baru: A new approach*. Canberra: Australian National University Press.

Kaswanti Purwo, Bambang. 1995. The two prototypes of ditransitive verbs: The Indonesian evidence. In Abraham, Givón, and Thompson, eds., *Discourse Grammar and Typology*, pages 77–99. Amsterdam & Philadelphia, PA: J. Benjamins.

Kaswanti Purwo, Bambang. 1997. The direct object in bi-transitive clauses in Indonesian. In T. Givón, ed., *Grammatical Relations: A Functionalist Perspective*, pages 233–52. J. Benjamins.

Levin, Beth. 1999. Objecthood: An event structure perspective. In S. Billings, J. Boyle, and A. Griffith, eds., *CLS 35: The Main Session. Papers from the 35th Meeting of the Chicago Linguistic Society*, vol. 1, pages 223–47. Chicago, IL: Chicago Linguistic Society.

Levin, Beth and Malka Rappaport Hovav. 1998. Morphology and lexical semantics. In A. Spencer and A. Zwicky, eds., *Handbook of Morphology*, pages 248–271. Oxford: Blackwell.

Mead, David E. 1998. *Proto-Bungku-Tolaki: Reconstruction of its Phonology and Aspects of its Morphosyntax*. Ph.D. thesis, Rice University.

Mohanan, Tara. 1994. *Argument Structure in Hindi*. Stanford, CA: CSLI Publications.

Pinker, Stephen. 1989. *Learnability and Cognition*. Cambridge, MA: The MIT Press.

Sadler, Louisa and Andrew Spencer. 1998. Morphology and argument structure. In A. Spencer and A. Zwicky, eds., *The Handbook of Morphology*, pages 206–236. Oxford: Blackwell.

Sirk, Ülo. 1978. Problems of high-level subgrouping in Austronesian. In S. A. Wurm and L. Carrington, eds., *Proceedings of the 2nd International Conference on Austronesian Linguistics (SICLAC)*, vol. 1, pages 255–273. Pacific Linguistics C-61.

Sneddon, James N. 1996. *Indonesian: A Comprehensive Grammar*. London & New York, NY: Routledge.

Sneddon, James N. 2000. *Understanding Indonesian Grammar: A Student's Reference and Workbook*. St. Leonards, N.S.W.: Allen and Unwin.

Spencer, Andrew and Arnold Zwicky, eds. 1998. *The Handbook of Morphology*. Oxford: Blackwell.

Vamarasi, Marit Kana. 1999. *Grammatical relations in Bahasa Indonesia*. Canberra: Research School of Pacific and Asian Studies, Australian National University. Pacific Linguistics D–93.

Verhaar, John W.M. 1980. *Theori linguistic dan Bahasa Indonesia*. Yogyakarta: Kanisius.

Verhaar, John W.M. 1984. The categorial system in contemporary of Indonesian: Verbs. In B. K. Purwo, ed., *Towards a Description Contemporary Indonesian: Preliminary Studies Part 1 (NUSA 18)*, pages 27–63.

Wolff, John. 1980. *Formal Indonesian*. Ithaca, NY: Cornell University Southeast Asia Program.

13

Automatic Learning of Grammatical Encoding

LORI LEVIN, JEFF GOOD, ALISON ALVAREZ, ROBERT FREDERKING

13.1 Introduction

AVENUE (Probst et al. 2002, Monson et al. 2004, Lavie et al. 2003, Font-Llitjos et al. 2005)[1] is a machine translation system that automatically learns translation rules between two languages. In the AVENUE scenario, one of the languages is a *resource rich language* like English or Spanish, for which there are many human and electronic resources (corpora, morphological analyzers, lexica, etc.). The other is a *resource poor language* with few human and electronic resources. For example, there might be no linguist available to write translation rules and there might not be large enough corpora for automatic machine learning of translation rules. This is true for the vast majority of languages.

Within the current state of the art in commercial machine translation, it is not possible to build machine translation (MT) systems for resource poor languages. However, we have met with indigenous communities (Mapuche, Quechua, and others), who want their languages to be used in jobs, education, government, and health care. Machine translation can be a tool for maintaining functionality in their languages, because it can help them access the Internet and disseminate local culture and information without having to adopt a major national

[1]NSF ITR/PE 0121631. Jaime Carbonell (PI), Ralf Brown, Robert Frederking, Alon Lavie, Lori Levin.

Architectures, Rules, and Preferences: Variations on Themes by Joan Bresnan.
Annie Zaenen, Jane Simpson, Tracy Holloway King,
Jane Grimshaw, Joan Maling, and Chris Manning, (eds.).

language like Spanish or English.[2] The vision of the Avenue project is equal access to information for speakers of all languages.

The steps in building an Avenue system are collection of resources, automated learning of rules and morphology (Probst 2005, Monson et al. 2004) from the collected resources, and translation correction with interactive rule refinement (Font-Llitjos et al. 2005). The Avenue rule formalism and run-time translation system are described in (Lavie et al. 2003).

13.2 Feature Detection: automatic learning of grammatical encodings

Although Avenue has many components, this paper focuses only on one aspect of resource collection, the automatic elicitation of data from bilingual speakers without the help of a human fieldworker. More specifically, this paper is about a process called *Feature Detection*, which learns the morphosyntactic mechanisms that are used for encoding grammatical relations (Bresnan 2001) and some aspects of meaning such as tense and evidentiality. Feature Detection guides a process of Navigation through a typological search space by distinguishing between features that have morph-syntactic consequences, and therefore must be pursued with further questioning, and features that do not have morphosyntactic consequences and can therefore be dropped from further questioning. Although we have used automatic Elicitation and Feature Detection in the development of MT systems, we hope that some of the tools that we have created will be useful in other areas of linguistics. The set of tools includes the Elicitation Tool (Section 13.3), a graphical interface for translating sentences and aligning words and morphemes in two languages, which is simple enough to be used by non-linguists. The elicitation questionnaire is represented internally as a set of feature structures, not as a set of sentences. Elicitation sentences are made by generating English or Spanish sentences that correspond to each feature structure. The same set of feature structures can be used for making corpora in other resource rich languages. Furthermore, the corpus is not fixed. The Feature Specification Schema (Section 13.6) is an XML schema for defining features and values for new corpora. The Multiplier (Section 13.7) allows a linguist to specify combinations of features and values that are of interest. Using these tools, it is possible to create new corpora easily, in any resource rich language (assuming the existence of a feature structure-to-sentence generator), for

[2]Some people are opposed to interference with their language: http://www.clarin.com/diario/2005/08/05/um/m-1027754.htm.

specialized tasks in fieldwork or machine translation. The following set of examples shows typical input to the Feature Detection program. In each example, the first line is a Spanish sentence that was presented to a bilingual native speaker of Mapudungun (Chile). The second line shows a translation into Mapudungun provided by the native speaker and the third line shows word alignments provided by the native speaker. The word alignments are provided graphically (see Section 13.3), but are shown here in their internal representation as indices. The index (3,1) means that the third Spanish word is aligned with the first Mapudungun word. Discontinuous, zero-to-one, many-to-many, and many-to-one alignments are allowed, although not all are illustrated here. The fourth line, in English, is for reference, and may also show some contextual information for the native speaker to take into account, such as whether the hearer is male or female. The contextual information was also presented to the native speaker in Spanish.

(1) a. La piedra cayó.
 b. Ütrünagi ti kura.
 c. ((1,2) (2,3) (3,1))
 d. The rock fell.

(2) a. Una piedra cayó.
 b. Kiñe kura ütrünagi.
 c. ((1,1) (2,2) (3,3))
 d. A rock fell.

(3) a. Caí.
 b. Iñche ütrünagün.
 c. ((1,2))
 d. I fell.

(4) a. Tú caíste.
 b. Eymi ütrünagimi.
 c. ((1,1) (2,2))
 d. You fell. (Hearer is Juan.)

(5) a. Tú caíste.
 b. Eymi ütrünagimi.
 c. ((1,1) (2,2))
 d. You fell. (Hearer is María.)

From these examples, Feature Detection would discover that the gender and animacy of the thing that falls do not have morphosyntactic realizations. The person of the thing that falls is realized on the word that governs it (i.e., agreement). The identifiability/specificity of the thing that falls is realized by a change in word order and a change in a dependent of the thing that falls (determiner). (The observation about identifiability/specificity will turn out not to hold over all Mapudungun examples.)

In carrying out our research program on Feature Detection, we face many of the difficulties faced by field linguistics. The informants might not be consistent in their translations and alignments; we may need to take into account more than one translation of each sentence; it is difficult to elicit phenomena that do not occur in the resource rich language; and the wording of sentences in the resource rich language may influence the translations in the resource poor language, so that some phenomena may be missed.

Most difficult, however, is the size of the search space of features and values. There are millions of possible combinations of feature values (four values for person, multiplied with at least three values for number, multiplied with several temporal and aspectual values, etc.) Informants cannot be expected to translate millions of sentences, and they become bored quickly when faced with irrelevant distinctions. For example, they will not be tolerant of translating masculine and feminine versions of every NP in every sentence if their language does not have morphosyntactic marking for gender. The Avenue system therefore needs to Navigate the search space in a reasonably intelligent way, as human fieldworkers do. Feature Detection (Section 13.9) tracks what has been discovered so far in the process of elicitation. We also propose to build a Navigator (Section 13.11) that makes decisions about what lines of questioning are most likely to be valuable given what has been found so far.

13.3 Elicitation

In the process of elicitation, sentences are presented to informants via the Elicitation Tool (Probst et al. 2001). The informant sees one example at a time (a sentence for elicitation and possibly a disambiguating context for the sentence) and translates it into his/her language. All Unicode fonts are supported, as are right-to-left scripts. The informant uses the mouse to align the words of his/her sentence to the words of the elicitation sentence. Alignments do not have to be one-to-one and may be discontinuous, and some words may remain unaligned. In the elicitation tool, the alignments are shown graphically as lines connecting words and as a list of pairs of numbers such as (7,5) (the seventh Spanish word aligned to fifth Mapudungun word).

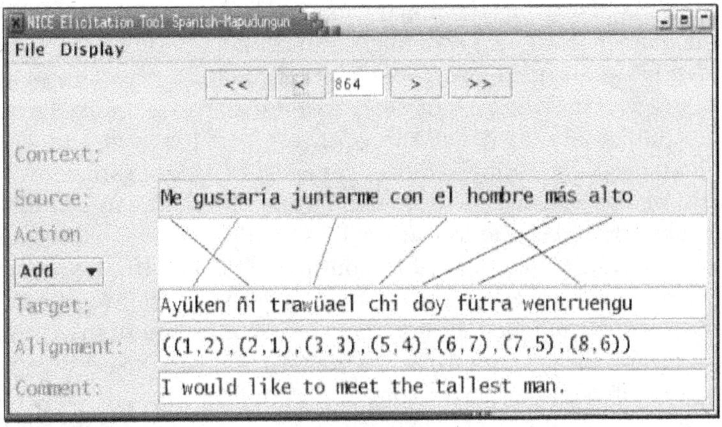

FIGURE 1 The Elicitation Tool

We have used the Elicitation Tool with various small elicitation corpora, between 850 and 2000 phrases and sentences, in several languages, including Hebrew, Mapudungun, Quechua, and Aymara. For some of these languages, several speakers have translated the corpus. We have also used the Elicitation Tool rather extensively for translating around 15,000 sentences and phrases into Hindi (Lavie et al. 2003). Learning to use the Elicitation Tool typically takes only about 20 minutes of training, including the use of the tool itself and the use of keyboard input for non-roman character sets. Informants must be instructed to translate similar sentences similarly. For example, their translations for *He is falling*, *It is falling*, and *She is falling* should be as similar as possible. Most informants can follow this requirement. Some informants like to provide multiple translations for sentences, which is allowed by the Elicitation Tool.

13.4 Underlying ssumptions and definition of the problem

In this section we will explain the basis for two assumptions that underlie our approach: that it should be possible to obtain data from a non-linguist, and that the search for morphosyntactic features should be based on meaning and communicative function.

Eliciting data from non-linguists: Since we cannot count on the availability of a linguist who speaks the resource-poor language we are eliciting, the elicitation process must be simple enough to be carried out by a non-linguist using the Elicitation Tool. Therefore, we do not ask explicit questions about grammar and morphology (in contrast to McShane et al. (2002)); we only ask the informants to translate sentences and align words. We do, however, assume the availability of people who are bilingual and literate in both the resource rich and resource poor language. This may require choosing an orthographic system if the resource poor language does not have a standardized orthography.

We have found some variation in the quality and consistency of translations and alignments from non-linguists. The Hindi speakers we worked with, who were students in college or graduate school, were initially inconsistent in the alignment of closed class items (postpositions and auxiliary verbs), but were able to align consistently with a small amount of supervision from a linguist who did not know Hindi. There is occasionally a problem with an informant missing the point of a sentence, but we hope to reduce the frequency of this problem by providing richer context for each elicitation sentence.

Morphosyntactic vs Functional Approach to Elicitation: Although we are trying to discover morphosyntactic phenomena in the resource poor language, we have organized the search by meaning and communicative function. For example, instead of looking for case markers, we look for noun phrases in different semantic roles and compare their forms. Our search for morphosyntax is organized functionally because we cannot make assumptions about which morphosyntactic mechanisms might be used to express a given function. Definiteness provides a good example of the problems we are trying to avoid by adopting a functional approach in the system. Suppose we want to know how English definite NPs are expressed in another language. We first have to observe that NPs that are marked as definite in English have a variety of functions. Sometimes, determiners mark definiteness as in (6a), but sometimes they do not mark definiteness. In (6b) the definite article marks reference to a species and in (6c) the indefinite article marks a profession in a predicate nominal. Since another language may use different mechanisms for each of these three functions of English determiners, we will only get a clear picture by separating them. What we really want to know is how the semantic components of definiteness are expressed, how references to a species are made, and how predicate nominals are expressed. The portion of the elicitation corpus that covers definiteness will not include uses of *the* that are not related to definiteness, and *the* may even need to be used to mark an NP in parts of the corpus where that NP is intended to be interpreted as indefinite.

This distinction between form and function is very important in our approach.

(6) a. I saw the lion.
   b. The lion is a magnificent beast.
   c. He is a soldier
   (Compare to French *Il est soldat* (Croft 2003).)

The mapping between form and meaning is many-to-many. One form, such as a determiner, may have many functions and one function may have many morphosyntactic realizations. In eliciting the semantic components of definiteness (identifiability, specifiability, uniqueness, familiarity, etc.), we find changes in word order for Chinese definite direct objects, changes in marking for Hebrew definite direct objects, changes in verb agreement for Hungarian definite direct objects, and uses of existential constructions for indefinite subjects in many languages. Since translations are only good when they preserve meaning, we have to be concerned with translating meanings regardless of what forms they take. We have to find definiteness in all of its forms, and cannot focus only on determiners. Our challenge in taking a function-based approach is to find ways of describing linguistic phenomena that are independent of morphosyntax. Comrie et al. (Comrie et al. 1993) advocate a similar split between function and morphosyntax for the production of descriptive grammars, and provide some useful insights into the possible inventory of syntax-independent functional categories.

13.5 The Process of creating an Elicitation Corpus

AVENUE is intended, in principle, to be applicable to any language—including resource poor languages which may be typologically quite divergent from the resource rich languages which serve as elicitation prompts. The elicitation corpus is a search space of communicative functions that might have morphosyntactic realizations in some language. Since this search space is large, and we may want to re-formulate it as we find out more about typological diversity and universals, we have designed a compact and easily modifiable way of characterizing it. In our approach, the elicitation corpus is not represented as a set of sentences, but as a set of feature structures. This is significant because a set of elicitation sentences can be generated from the feature structures (Section 13.8) in any language, for example, English or Spanish. Maintaining consistency between the English and Spanish elicitation sentences is simply a matter of (re)generating them from the same set of feature structures. A sample of a feature structure is shown in Figure 2. The feature structure represents a sentence like *I (masc.) was a teacher* with a masculine singular first person subject and a secondary predication in the past tense indicating a role of the subject. Other types of copular sentences might indicate a property (*I was happy*) or the identity (*I was the teacher*) of the subject. Our feature structures are represented using parentheses as delimiters. Each feature-value pair is enclosed in parentheses, and each (sub)-feature-structure (list of feature-value pairs) is enclosed in parentheses.

```
((actor ((np-general-type pronoun)
         (np-person person-first)
         (np-number num-sg)
         (np-biological-gender gender-male)
         (np-animacy anim-human)))
(predicate ((np-general-type common)
            (np-person person-first)
            (np-animacy anim-human)
            (np-identifiability non-identifiable)))
(c-copula-type role)
(c-secondary-type secondary-copula)
(c-v-lexical-aspect state)
(c-v-absolute-tense past)
(c-v-phase-aspect durative)
(c-imperative-degree imp-degree-n/a)
(c-ynq-type ynq-n/a))
```

FIGURE 2 An AVENUE Feature Structure

The set of feature structures in the Elicitation Corpus is generated automatically from a compact description that is created by a linguist. There are two steps in designing the Elicitation Corpus, Feature Specification and Multiplication. Feature Specification is the process of defining the features and values that will characterize elicitation sentences. A fragment of a Feature Specification is shown in (7) in Section 13.7. Multiplication is the process of describing combinations of features and values to include in the corpus. We have formulated a control language for stating Multiplications, an example of which is shown in Figure 4.

Our approach to corpus creation allows for the corpus to be changed easily for different types of projects by changing the Feature Specification and/or Multiplications. If we decide to make a change in the system of number or tense, it will be changed consistently and automatically in hundreds of related sentences. The system is also flexible enough to be used with any kinds of features and values. For example, even though we have chosen to organize our Feature Specification by communicative function, we could just as easily have created a Feature Specification organized by morphosyntactic features.

13.6 The form of the Feature Specification and Multiplications

Feature Specifications are encoded using an XML-based markup system. Multiplications are partially marked up using XML but also make use of a special syntax optimized for expressing the types of feature and value combinations which need to be Multiplied (Alvarez et al. 2005).

While XML-encoding of Feature Specifications is not crucial for the project at present, it is hoped that this will allow them to more easily interoperate with other relevant XML-based linguistic resources currently under development elsewhere. In particular, the Navigation system of AVENUE should be able to benefit from knowledge encoded in linguistic ontologies, like the General Ontology for Linguistic Description (Farrar and Langendoen 2003), as they begin to encode more and more kinds of linguistic knowledge. Our XML version of (7) is shown in Figure 3.

```
<feature>
    <feature-name>c-causer-intentionality</feature-name>
    <value><value-name>intentional</value-name></value>
    <value><value-name>accidental</value-name></value>
</feature>
<feature>
    <feature-name>c-causee-control</feature-name>
    <value><value-name>in-control</value-name></value>
    <value><value-name>not-in-control</value-name></value>
</feature>
<feature>
    <feature-name>c-causee-volitionality</feature-name>
    <value><value-name>willing</value-name></value>
    <value><value-name>unwilling</value-name></value>
</feature>
<feature>
    <feature-name>c-causation-directness</feature-name>
    <value><value-name>direct</value-name></value>
    <value><value-name>indirect</value-name></value>
</feature>
```

FIGURE 3 XML Version of a Feature Specification

13.7 The Content of the Feature Specification

In this section, we discuss how we determine what features and values need to be covered in the specifications and how we encode them. Achieving broad coverage of the elicitation search space requires relying on available typological models of grammatical variation for essentially any functional feature known to have a coherent morphosyntactic realization in some language. While some functional features—e.g., features for verbal arguments—have well-established models within LFG, others are lacking such models and have required us to adapt models from the descriptive and typological literature and, in a few cases, from other formal frameworks which, for one reason or another, have worked out useful models for a relevant functional domain.

Identifying a Typological Model: As an initial strategy in ensuring that AVENUE has reasonable coverage, we have made use of the Comrie and Smith questionnaire (Comrie and Smith 1977) for linguistic description. While dated in some respects, this questionnaire is one of the few published works which attempts to establish a detailed series of questions to guide a descriptive linguist in writing a complete grammar. Like AVENUE, Comrie and Smith is intended to be of use for any language and, therefore, has served as a useful foundation in building the feature set for the system.

The biggest divergence between work like Comrie and Smith and AVENUE results from AVENUE's reliance on basing the construction of its elicitation corpus on functional features instead of morphosyntactic features. Questionnaires like Comrie and Smith typically contain questions of two distinct types: those relating to functional distinctions which are known to be grammatically marked and those relating to *how* those distinctions are typically marked (as noted by Comrie et al., (Comrie et al. 1993)).

For example, in the domain of questions, Comrie and Smith (page 11) include an enumeration of functionally-oriented question types like *neutral yes-no*, *yes-no expected affirmative*, *yes-no expected negative*, *question-word questions*, etc., and an enumeration of how these types tend to be grammatically marked, for example, with word order changes, particles, tags, intonational patterns, etc. From the perspective of AVENUE, the former type of information is potentially quite valuable in constructing the elicitation corpus, but the latter type is not directly relevant—it is the machine's task to discover how a language marks a given functional feature grammatically.

Not surprisingly, no existing grammatical questionnaire exhaustively lists all of the grammatical features and values needed for AVENUE.

Therefore, in addition to grammatical questionnaires, we make use of a wide range of other sources in determining what features need to be covered by the elicitation corpus. These include: typologically-oriented monographs covering important grammatical domains, for example, Comrie (1985) on tense, Comrie (1976) on aspect, Palmer (2001) on mood, and Aikhenvald (2004) on evidentiality; formally-oriented work with useful discussion of a relevant domain, for example, (McCawley 1998, 692–740) on comparatives and (Foley and Van Valin 1984, 238–320) on clause combing; and descriptions of particular languages which, for one reason or another, serve as useful guides for what distinctions need to be made during elicitation (e.g., Haspelmath (1993), Good (2003)).

Representing the typological model as a Feature Specification: Once we have established a general typological model for a given grammatical domain, we need to encode that model as a set of features and accompanying values which can be used in the construction of the elicitation corpus. This, of course, requires a fair amount of analysis, and it is not always clear that we have hit upon the ideal analysis in a given part of the Feature Specification. It is, therefore, always subject to possible revision. For a project such as this one, the guiding principal is ensuring that functional categories that are known to behave independently of one another with respect to morphosyntactic marking are treated as values for different features so that these values can be independently varied within sets of sentences in the elicitation corpus.

To take a concrete example, consider the features and values used to model the domain of causation given in (7). The selection of these features and values was loosely based on the typology found in (Dixon 2000).

(7) a. **Feature:** Causer intentionality
Values: intentional, unintentional
b. **Feature:** Causee control
Values: in control, not in control
c. **Feature:** Causee volitionality
Values: willing, unwilling
d. **Feature:** Causation type
Values: direct, indirect

The features and values in (7) represent a number of known types of semantic distinctions made in causative constructions. Some of these distinctions are logically dependent on each other—for example, if a causative construction specifically marks that the causer intentionally caused an action to take place then it cannot also mark that the causer acted unintentionally.[3] Other distinctions are logically independent of each other. For example, whether or not a causee performed an action volitionally is independent of whether or not the causation was direct or indirect. In some cases, it might not be completely clear whether or not two values are independent. For example, a causee who is not in control in general would not be expected to willingly do the action. However, since a causee who is in control can act willingly or unwillingly, control and volitionality were separated out as two independent features, as indicated in (7). The specifications have generally been designed to err toward allowing too many independent value combinations, rather than too few.

The Feature Specification is intended to represent the a typological range of distinctions that can be grammatically encoded. It will therefore contain sentences that are intended to elicit causer intentionality, causee control, causee volitionality, and causation type. This does not mean that we expect every language to mark each of these distinctions. It only means that we need to check which of these distinctions are morphosyntactically marked in each language.

The Feature Specification system also allows statements to be made about Restrictions holding among certain features. These are useful when a given feature is only relevant for a feature structure specified for a limited range of feature-value pairs. For example, specifications of values relating to the feature of pronoun inclusivity are restricted to feature structures for pronouns which are first person and plural.

The current Feature Specification is not complete. However, it does have fairly wide-ranging coverage, including, for example, features relating to clause types, discourse settings, agentivity, argument roles, tense/mood/aspect, and adverbial roles—among others.

Multiplications: Choosing combinations of features and values: The problem raised by decomposing functional information into features and values is that logically independent functions may not be treated independently in the morphosyntactic system of a given language. In the case of causation, for example, causative marking may interact with verbal argument structure. In principle, such interactions could be detected by constructing an elicitation corpus where all possible combinations of features and values were represented by some sentence to be translated. In practice, however, this would be a very inefficient way to deal with feature interactions because the attested types

[3] This is not to say that a given construction could not simply be unmarked for whether or not the causer intentionally causes an action—obviously, this can also be the case.

of such interactions are quite limited—causative marking is known to interact with argument structure (Dixon 2000, 43), but it would be unlikely for it to interact with, say, comparative constructions.

AVENUE deals with this problem by explicitly encoding which features and values should be Multiplied together when the feature structures of an elicitation corpus are created. One such Multiplication is given in (8). We have designed a formalism for specifying Multiplications, and have built a GUI to support their formulation. The GUI allows a linguist to browse the Feature Specification and choose feature and value names to include in the Multiplication (Alvarez et al. 2005).

(8) (lexical-aspect #all) ×
(grammatical-aspect #all) ×
(absolute-tense past, present, future)

The Multiplication schematized in (8) encodes a statement that, when feature structures for the elicitation corpus are generated, all of the features for lexical aspect (*state*, *activity*, *accomplishment*, etc.) should be cross-Multiplied with all of the features for grammatical aspect (*perfective*, *imperfective*, etc.) and three features for absolute tense, *past*, *present*, and *future*. This cross-Multiplication is designed to ensure that, if there are critical interactions between tense and aspect in a given language, the corpus will contain sentences in which those interactions can be detected.

Of course, a Multiplication like the one in (8) only specifies a small part of what a feature structure for an entire sentence might look like. Features that are not mentioned in the Multiplication will take a default value. For example, the default value for the polarity feature is *positive*—that is, affirmative, instead of negative, sentences are specified as the default type in the Feature Specification.

While Feature Specification is intended to, ultimately, allow the generation of an elicitation corpus which can uncover most known kinds of morphosyntactically-marked functional features, it is not expected that a "complete" corpus will be generated at any one particular time. Rather, in most cases, a subset of features will be chosen as the basis of a "subcorpus" optimized for the discovery of morphosyntactic marking of those features alone. For example, we have been experimenting with a "copula" corpus, which focuses only on tense, number, gender, person, and predication type (identity, role, attribute) in sentences that are expressed with predicate nominals and predicate adjectives in English.

```
((predicatee
  ((np-general-type pronoun-type common-noun-type)
   (np-person person-first person-second person-third)
   (np-number num-sg num-pl)
   (np-biological-gender bio-gender-male bio-gender-female)))
  {[(predicate ((np-general-type common-noun-type)
                (np-person person-third)))
                (c-copula-type role)]
   [(predicate ((adj-general-type quality-type)
                (c-copula-type attributive)))]
   [(predicate ((np-general-type common-noun-type)
                (np-person person-third)
                (c-copula-type identity)))]}
(c-secondary-type secondary-copula) (c-polarity #all)
(c-general-type declarative)
(c-speech-act sp-act-state)
(c-v-grammatical-aspect gram-aspect-neutral)
(c-v-lexical-aspect state)
(c-v-absolute-tense past present future)
(c-v-phase-aspect durative))
```

FIGURE 4 Multiplication for Copula Sentences

13.8 Making elicitation sentences from feature structures

A Multiplication is expanded into a set of feature structures. For example, the Multiplication in Figure 4 represents 288 feature structures. Each feature structure represents a set of communicative functions or meanings that we want to elicit. However, because informants cannot translate feature structures, we need to represent the feature structures in a form that the informants can understand — sentences in the language of elicitation (e.g., English).

There are two difficulties in representing the meaning of a feature structure in English (or any other language of elicitation). First, some aspects of meaning are not marked in English. So, for example, *I (masc.) fell* and *I (fem.) fell* are the same in English. Second, the feature structures in the elicitation corpus do not contain lexical items. English lexical items therefore must be added.

The GenKit generation system (Tomita and Nyberg 1988) is used for making sentences from feature structures. So far we have only used GenKit to make English elicitation sentences, but the GenKit unification-based formalism is applicable to any language. For the purpose of AVENUE, we do not use a large, comprehensive English generation grammar, but rather several small grammars for generating sub-corpora. For example, the 288 sentences specified in Figure 4 are generated by a small English copula grammar, which covers predication of attributes (*He is happy*), identity (*He is the teacher*), and role (*He is a teacher*). (These sentences may or may not be expressed with overt copulas in other languages.) With the small grammars, we can include small lexicons with semantic features designed to ensure that selectional restrictions are met in the sentences that we generate. The grammars generate comments for features that are not expressed in English, producing strings like *I* ONE WOMAN *fell.* A post-processor prepares the English sentences for presentation in the Elicitation Tool by separating the English sentence *I fell* from the comment ONE WOMAN, which the informant then sees in different fields of the Elicitation Tool.

13.9 Initial experiment with Feature Detection

In this section we will describe a preliminary exercise with Feature Detection. For this experiment we used 48 sentences from the copula sub-corpus, which were translated into Hebrew and Japanese. The sentences included two genders for the subject (masculine and feminine), three persons for the subject (first, second, and third), three tenses (present, past, and future), and two types of predication (role and identity). Identity was only Multplied with third person subjects.

The first step in Feature Detection is identifying minimal pairs of feature structures that differ in only one value of one feature. There will be many minimal pairs for each feature value. For example, positive vs negative polarity will form a minimal pair in each of three tenses.

Each feature structure is associated with a sentence from a resource rich language (from the Elicitation Corpus) and a sentence in the resource-poor one (provided by the informant). Furthermore, in the process of generating the major language sentence, we produce an approximation of the LFG ϕ-inverse mapping from feature structures to constituents. We therefore know which word of the major language is the head of each feature structure and sub-feature structure. Since we also have word alignment, provided by the informant, from the minor to the major language, we indirectly have an approximation of the ϕ mapping from c-structure to feature structure for the minor language. For each minimal pair of feature structures, we want to know whether the corresponding sentences in the elicited language are the same or different. If they are the same, we will conclude that the changing the feature value has no morphosyntactic effect in the context of that particular feature structure.

If there is a difference in the elicited sentences corresponding to a minimal pair of feature structures, we conclude that changing the feature value has a morphosyntactic effect. In this case, we also want to know which part of the sentence is affected. For the purpose of this experiment, morphosyntactic effects are categorized as

- **Substitutions:** different word, including different inflection of the same stem
- **Insertions/Deletions:** one member of the minimal pair contains a word that is not contained in the other.
- **Change in alignment indices:** change in word order

The locations of the morphosyntactic effects are categorized as follows:

- **Me:** The change appears on a word that is the head of the smallest feature structure that contains the minimally different feature-value pair.
- **My Dependent:** The change appears on any dependent of Me.
- **My Governor:** The change appears on the word that is the head of the feature structure that contains the feature structure headed by Me as an argument.
- **Other:** Anything that is not one of the above, for example another dependent of My Governor, such as a secondary predicate.

Figure 5 shows two examples of elicited data for Japanese. The first minimal pair of feature structures differs in the value of tense (past or present). The sentences that correspond to those feature structures differ in one word: *desu* vs. *desita*. These Japanese words are aligned to the English words *is* and *was*. *Is* and *was* are the heads of the smallest feature structures containing the feature value pairs `(tense past)` and `(tense present)`. Therefore, the location of the change is on Me. In other words, the difference in tense is represented on the verb that is the head of the sentence.

The second Japanese example illustrates an interesting point. Japanese is usually classified as having two tenses or aspects, past (or complete) and non-past (or non-complete). However, in this exercise, the informants translated the English future tense with *naru* (become) and a change of mood marked on *desyou*. Feature Detection identifies an extra word aligned to the co-heads (*will be*) of the English sentence, and concludes that future tense in Japanese differs from present tense in an additional word being added. This may be contradicted in other parts of the corpus, for example, if *yomu* appears as both the present and future forms of *read*. We have not yet implemented the final phase

```
1.
Minimal Pair:: (tense past):(tense present)
Comparing:
        He was a teacher.
        kare wa sensei desita    ((1,1 2),(2,4),(4,3))
        He is a teacher.
        kare wa sensei desu      ((1,1 2),(2,4),(4,3))
Type of difference: Substitution
Location of difference: Me

2.
Minimal Pair:: (tense present):(tense future)
Comparing:
        He is a teacher.
        kare wa sensei desu.   ((1,1 2),(2,4),(4,3))
        He will be a teacher.
        kare wa sensei ni naru desyou    ((1,1 2),(2 3,5 6),(5,3))
Type of difference: Insertion/Deletion
Location of difference: Me
```

FIGURE 5 Elicited data from Japanese

of Feature Detection, which will reconcile conflicting findings by identifying the distinguishing circumstances. In this case it may (or may not) turn out that the morphosyntactic consequences of changing tense are different in copular and non-copular sentences.

Figure 6 shows two examples from the Hebrew data. In the first example, a minimal pair of present and past tense, Feature Detection finds an extra word in the past tense, reflecting the fact that there is not an overt copula in the present tense. The second example shows variation based on the biological gender (not grammatical gender) of the subject. Two differences are found, a change on the subject pronoun itself and a change on governor of the subject. The third change, on the predicate nominal (*more* (masc.) versus *mora* (fem.)), was not detected because Feature Detection was actually run on a vowelless script different from the phonemic transcription shown here.

13.10 Remaining issues in Feature Detection

Although we have achieved some basic functionality in Feature Detection, several issues remain to be addressed.

Discovering Case and Voice: Automatic discovery of case and voice systems requires an additional definition of minimal pair. The two feature structures must have the same nominal sub-feature-structure in

```
1.
Minimal Pair:: (tense past):(tense present)
Comparing:
        He was a teacher.
        Hu haya more.     ((1,1),(2,2),(4,3))
        He is a teacher.
        Hu more.          ((1,1),(4,2))
Type of difference: Insertion/Deletion
Location of difference: Me

2.
Minimal Pair::(biological-gender male):(biological-gender female)
Comparing:
        He will be a teacher.
        Hu yihye more.    ((1,1),(2,2),(3,2),(5,3))
        She will be a teacher.
        Hi tihye mora.    ((1,1),(2,2),(3,2),(5,3))
Type of difference: Substitution
Location of difference: Me
Type of difference: Substitution
Location of difference: My governor
```

FIGURE 6 Elicited data from Hebrew

different roles, as in *He hit the ball*, *The ball hit him*, *I threw the ball at him*.

Incomparable Target Language Sentences: As shown in (9) Hebrew predicative sentences do not need an overt copula in the present tense, but they can have a pronominal copula (Doron 1983). In order to detect the morphosyntactic realization of gender, we want to compare(9a) and (9b), or (9c) and (9d). Comparing (9a) and (9d) would give the misleading result that words are added or deleted to express gender. Therefore, when there are multiple translations for the same feature structure, we need to identify the most comparable sentences for Feature Detection.

(9) a. Lea mora.
Leah teacher.FEM
Leah is a teacher.

b. Avi more.
Avi teacher.MASC
Avi is a teacher

c. Lea hi mora.
Leah 3SG.FEM teacher.FEM
Leah is a teacher.

d. Avi hu more.
Avi 3SG.MASC teacher.MASC
Avi is a teacher.

Incomparable Source and Target Language Sentences: In Machine Translation, the term *translation divergence* (Dorr 1994) refers to source and target language sentences that do not translate literally. A typical example of a divergence between English and German is *Ich esse gern* (literally: I eat gladly) and *I like to eat*. These sentences are problematic because the head of the German sentence is *esse* (eat) whereas the head of the English sentence is *like*. Because the head of the German sentence is aligned to the XCOMP of the English sentence, Feature Detection as described above will not find the correct location of morphosyntactic change for this pair of sentences. Divergence detection is therefore a pre-requisite for Feature Detection.

Near Minimal Pairs: Since we may not be able to use the same lexical items throughout the corpus — informants have complained about repetitious vocabulary — we might need to compare sentences such as *He is a teacher* and *She is a firefighter* whose feature structures are a minimal pair except for the lexical items. We must be careful about concluding that gender is marked on the predicate nominal only because *teacher* and *firefighter* are different words. In this case, it would be helpful to combine Feature Detection with the Morphology learning component of AVENUE (Monson et al. 2004) so that we can compare the morphology of the two words instead of just comparing the two strings of characters.

13.11 Navigation

Currently, the size of the Elicitation Corpus is controlled with Multiplications, Restrictions, and Defaults. Multiplications specify exactly which combinations of features and values we are interested in, Restrictions disallow incompatible combinations of features, and Default values of features are used in place of fully multiplying out all values. Eventually we hope to replace these mechanisms with a more intelligent Navigation component.

In the Navigation component we envision, the search for features with morphosyntactic consequences can be directed by explicitly modeling the cost/benefit tradeoff of having the informant translate and align each possible next sentence, using a marginal utility calculation. Marginal Utility (MU) (Wikipedia 2005) is a concept originally from the field of economics/operations research, with applicability to any process of rational decision making under uncertainty. One example of the use of Marginal Utilities in decision making is a paper by Carbonell and Goldstein (Carbonell and Goldstein 1998), where it is used in text summarization. The fundamental idea is to try to decide what to do next, if every choice has possible rewards and costs, and you have imperfect knowledge of what will actually result from your specific action. The MU of a particular choice is defined as:

MU = Expected Value - Expected Cost

The Expected Value is in turn defined as:

EV = Σ (over all outcomes f) P(f)*Value(f)

which is to say it is the sum over all possible outcomes of the value of each of the possible outcomes multiplied by the probability of that outcome. In this system, the EV of a sentence will be the sum of the EVs of all potential facts that might be discovered by Feature Detection from translating/aligning this sentence at this point (i.e., given what has already been translated/aligned), each multiplied by the probability that the result will actually lead to the deduction of a fact. If a feature structure contains values for tense, aspect, and polarity it will have an expected value based on whether or not minimally different feature structures have been observed – feature structures that differs only on the value of polarity, tense, or aspect. If such feature structures have been observed, then it will be possible to make a comparison that might yield a fact. The expected value might also depend on whether tense, aspect, and polarity have been found in previous examples to have morphosyntactic effects. The Expected Cost (EC) represents the expected human cost of translating/aligning the sentence, and may initially be approximated by the number of words in the English sentence plus a term for the number of sentences translated so far; later we may try to empirically determine a more sophisticated formula. For both EV and EC, one essentially gets a weighted average of all possible outcomes from this action, and the MU thus simply reflects the value of the action minus its cost.

The action with the largest MU is thus simply the one that will probably be best. Based on the MU calculation for all remaining Elicitation Corpus sentences, the sentence with the best expected payoff in the current stage of exploring the current language is explored next. The process then repeats until the MU drops to zero, at which point we believe we have learned everything that is reasonable to try to learn from this process: everything likely to be of value that can be learned for a reasonable cost.

As we have just seen, the MU of acquiring a new translation depends in part on the expected value (EV) of any new language facts that might be inferred from the new translation; this inference depends on combining the new facts with previously learned related facts about this language. The EV calculation thus requires a significant amount of linguistic and logical knowledge. This knowledge will be represented in the form of a set of decision graphs that declaratively represent the inference process for each kind of inference that might be made by the Feature Detection system. Describing the detailed design of these decision graphs is beyond the scope of this paper; but in brief, they must be constructed (just once) by computational linguists to encode some of the knowledge used by field linguists, and are used to remember the status of many different partially-completed inferences at run-time, in order to compute EV estimates. A decision graph might for example direct Feature Detection to look at plural number before looking at dual because a language that does not mark plural will also not mark dual.

Each time the informant translates and aligns a new elicitation corpus sentence, the system may learn new facts, and these facts in turn will inform the next MU calculation for all remaining Elicitation Corpus sentences. This is a very large update calculation; it is necessary to update all the affected Decision Graphs in the system. And it must be done quickly, while the informant is waiting, since it determines the next sentence that the informant will translate/align. The design for achieving this is again beyond the scope of this paper, but is related to earlier work by Forgy (Forgy 1982).

13.12 Conclusion

We have presented a framework that uses pairs of translated sentences to discover which meanings and communicative functions are morphosyntactically marked in a language. Although the system has been developed in the context of a Machine Translation project, it has consists of tools for elicitation and corpus creation that may be useful in other areas of linguistics. The true promise of the system, however, is that the development of automated Feature Detection will lead to discoveries about form-function relationships that will give us insight into better methods for the description and documentation of languages, and possibly also insights on which to base linguistic theories.

References

Aikhenvald, Alexandra Y. 2004. *Evidentiality*. Oxford: Oxford University Press.

Alvarez, Alison, Lori Levin, Robert Frederking, Erik Peterson, and Jeff Good. 2005. Semi-automated elicitation corpus generation. In *Proceedings of Machine Translation Summit X*, pages 388–395. Phuket, Thailand: Asia-Pacific Association for Machine Translation (AAMT).

Bresnan, Joan. 2001. *Lexical-Functional Syntax*. Oxford: Blackwell.

Carbonell, Jaime and Jade Goldstein. 1998. The use of MMR, diversity-based reranking for reordering documents and producing summaries. In *Proceedings of Special Interest Group in Information Retrieval (SIGIR)*, pages 335–336. Melbourne.

Comrie, Bernard. 1976. *Aspect*. Cambridge: Cambridge University.

Comrie, Bernard. 1985. *Tense*. Cambridge: Cambridge University Press.

Comrie, Bernard, William Croft, Christian Lehmann, and Dietmar Zaefferer. 1993. A framework for descriptive grammars. In *Proceedings of the XVth International Congress of Linguists*, pages 159–70. Sainte-Foy.

Comrie, Bernard and Norval Smith. 1977. Lingua descriptive studies: Questionnaire. *Lingua* 42(1):1–72.

Croft, William. 2003. *Typology and Universals*. Cambridge, UK: Cambridge University Press.

Dixon, Robert M. W. 2000. A typology of causatives: Form, syntax, and meaning. In R. M. W. Dixon and A. Y. Aikhenvald, eds., *Changing valency: Case studies in transitivity*, pages 30–83. Cambridge, UK: Cambridge University Press.

Doron, Edit. 1983. *Verbless Predicates in Hebrew*. Ph.D. thesis, University of Texas, Austin.

Dorr, Bonnie J. 1994. Machine translation divergences: A formal description and proposed solution. *Computational Linguistics* 20(4):597–633.

Farrar, Scott and Terry Langendoen. 2003. A linguistic ontology for the semantic web. *Glot International* 7(3):97–100.

Foley, William A. and Robert D. Jr. Van Valin. 1984. *Functional Syntax and Universal Grammar*. Cambridge, UK: Cambridge University Press.

Font-Llitjos, Ariadna, Jaime Carbonell, and Alon Lavie. 2005. A framework for interactive and automatic refinement of transfer-based machine translation. In *Proceedings of the 10th Annual Conference of the European Association for Machine Translation (EAMT 10)*. Budapest.

Forgy, Charles L. 1982. RETE: A fast algorithm for the many pattern/many object pattern match problem. *Artificial Intelligence* 19(1):17–37.

Good, Jeff. 2003. Clause combining in Chechen. *Studies in Language* 27(1):113–170.

Haspelmath, Martin. 1993. *A grammar of Lezgian*. Berlin: Mouton de Gruyter.

Lavie, Alon, Stephan Vogel, Lori Levin, Erik Peterson, Katharina Probst, Ariadna Font Llitjós, Rachel Reynolds, and Jaime Carbonell. 2003. Experiments with a hindi-to-english transfer-based MT system under a miserly data scenario. *TALIP (ACM Transactions on Asian Language Information Processing)* 2(2):143–163.

McCawley, James D. 1998. *The Syntactic Phenomena of English,* (Second Edition). Chicago, IL: Chicago University Press.

McShane, Marjorie, Sergei Nirenburg, James Cowie, and Ron Zacharski. 2002. Embedding knowledge elicitation and MT systems within a single architecture. *Machine Translation* 17(4):271–305.

Monson, Christian, Alon Lavie, Jaime Carbonell, and Lori Levin. 2004. Unsupervised induction of natural language morphology inflection classes. In *Proceedings of the 42nd Annual Meeting of the Association for Computational Linguistics (ACL'04), Workshop on Special Interest Group in Computational Phonology (SIGPHON)*, pages 52–61. Barcelona.

Palmer, Frank R. 2001. *Mood and modality*. Cambridge, UK: Cambridge University Press, 2nd edn.

Probst, Katharina. 2005. *Automatically Induced Syntactic Transfer Rules for Machine Translation under a Very Limited Data Scenario*. Ph.D. thesis, Carnegie-Mellon University.

Probst, Katharina, Ralf Brown, Jaime Carbonell, Alon Lavie, Lori Levin, and Erik Peterson. 2001. Design and implementation of controlled elicitation for machine translation of low-density languages. In *Proceedings of Machine Translation Summit VIII, MT-2010 Workshop*. Santiago de Compostela.

Probst, Katharina, Lori Levin, Erik Peterson, Alon Lavie, and Jaime Carbonell. 2002. MT for minority languages using elicitation-based learning of syntactic transfer rules. *Machine Translation* 17(4):245–270.

Tomita, Masaru and Eric Nyberg. 1988. Generation and transformation kit, version 3.2 user's manual. Tech. Rep. CMU-CMT-88-MEMO, Carnegie Mellon University, Pittsburgh, PA.

Wikipedia. 2005. Marginal concepts. http://en.wikipedia.org/wiki/Marginal_-concepts; Wiki of 28 July 2005.

14

Speakers' Choice: Number and Case 'Agreement' in Coordination

PETER PETERSON

14.1 Introduction

Recent accounts of the syntax of coordination (Kaplan & Maxwell 1988, Dalrymple & Kaplan 2000; Huddleston et al 2002; Peterson 2001, 2004) have supported an analysis of coordination in which coordinate structures are not headed but constitute sets. This analysis has been shown to provide a descriptively adequate account of key syntactic properties of coordination, including the distribution of grammatical functions across all conjuncts, and the ability to coordinate unlike categories under certain syntactic conditions.

Within the LFG framework, the c-structure for English coordinate structures would be generated by the following annotated rule schema:

(1) $X \longrightarrow \underset{\downarrow\in\uparrow}{X} \quad C \quad \underset{\downarrow\in\uparrow}{Y}$

A key feature of the c-structure component of this schema is that neither X nor Y on the right hand side of the schema carries the $\downarrow=\uparrow$ notation which is used to convey grammatical information upwards from the head of an endocentric phrase (e.g. from V to its dominating VP). In other words, coordination is not a 'headed' construction; it is not endocentric.[1]

[1] The absence of functional notation on the coordinator in Schema (1) is not an oversight. I assume with Kaplan and Maxwell (1988) that the coordinator is not

Architectures, Rules, and Preferences: Variations on Themes by Joan Bresnan.
Annie Zaenen, Jane Simpson, Tracy Holloway King,
Jane Grimshaw, Joan Maling, and Chris Manning, (eds.).

The f-structure of a coordination is a set of the f-structures of each of the individual conjuncts. Certain grammatical information can pass into the set, but only under very constrained conditions; specifically we can say that grammatical information **distributes** to all members of the set. Consider for example sentence (2):

(2) The children are happy and smiling.

The c-structure and f-structure for this sentence would be as shown in (3) and (4) respectively.[2] The verb *be* has the lexically specified requirement that <↑ SUBJ = ↑ XCOMP SUBJ>. This links the SUBJ of *be* with the SUBJ of each of the conjuncts under a general rule that distributes grammatical functions to all members of the set.

(3)

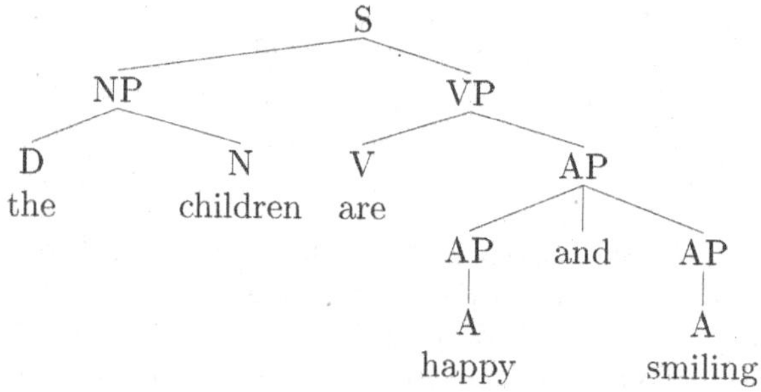

(4)

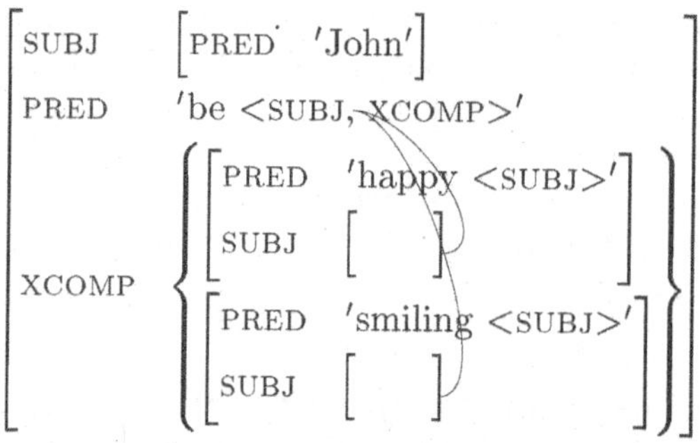

An important consequence of the set-based analysis is that, since coordination is not a headed construction, there is no percolation path for features from individual categories within a coordinate structure to

assigned any functional role, and in particular is not the 'head' of the coordinate construction.

[2] I retain an exocentric analysis of the sentence, using the label S. I do not adopt the currently popular IP analysis which depends on a functional category I (Falk 1984). I treat tensed auxiliary verbs like any other tensed catenative verb in English, with the argument structure <SUBJ, XCOMP>. For arguments in favor of a 'main verb' analysis of auxiliaries, see Huddleston & Pullum 2002 and references therein. However, nothing in the current discussion depends crucially on this decision.

the node dominating the coordination. Therefore lexical properties such as TENSE and NUMBER will not be shared across the coordination as a whole. The lack of distributivity allows individual conjuncts to differ in terms of lexical properties. So for instance it is quite possible for a coordinate NP to contain a singular NP conjoined with a plural NP. Similarly TENSE as a lexical property of verbs does not distribute; it is therefore possible for two coordinated verbs or verb phrases to differ with respect to their value for TENSE, as shown in (5):

(5) John was and is the best bridge player in Newcastle.

Since there is no path allowing information to flow between individual conjuncts and external structures, the coordination as a whole does not inherit lexical properties of the individual conjuncts. A coordination of two singular NPs does not have the property [NUM = SG]. And conversely 'agreement' requirements cannot be distributed within the coordination to individual members of the set. For example, the lexical property [↑ SUBJ NUM = PLU] contained in the lexical entry for *are* does not enforce plurality on the conjoined NPs within the subject NP, as shown in (6):

(6) The ferret and the kitten are chasing each other around the kitchen.

We see then that in this framework the grammar provides no direct means of imposing constraints on lexical items within a coordination.

Note that the same argument holds whether or not we adopt the concept of a 'hybrid' structure for the f-structure of sets (first adumbrated in Bresnan et al 1986; expounded in published form in Dalrymple & Kaplan 1997). This gives an extra layer in the f-structure for attributes of the set as a whole, but it does not thereby provide any mechanism for establishing the values for those attributes from the values of the individual conjuncts, nor for distributing those values downwards to the members of the set. The hybrid f-structure for a coordination of NPs would have the following form:

$$\begin{bmatrix} \text{NUM PLU} \\ \left\{ \begin{matrix} [\quad\;] \\ [\quad\;] \end{matrix} \right\} \end{bmatrix}$$

The question immediately arises: what is the source of the attribute-value pair [NUM PLU]? It cannot be assumed that it has been assigned by a verb with the lexical property [↑ SUBJ NUM = PLU], since that would apply only when the coordination functions as Subject; and of course such NPs can occur in all functions generally available to NPs. Nor is there a straight-forward way of creating the attribute-value pair from the lexical properties of the individual conjuncts; the conjuncts may have values quite independent of the value of the coordination as a whole. Not only does a coordination of two singular NPs produce a plural coordination as in (6), but other coordinations can display singular number or allow a choice, as in the types of examples illustrated in (7) (see Peterson 2004 for further discussion):

(7) i Ham and eggs makes/make a nutritious breakfast.
ii Running five miles and eating fresh fruit is/are good for you
iii John's belligerence and his refusal to accept discipline has/have caused a lot of trouble

Examples such as those in (7) suggest the possibility of a semantic basis for number choice with coordinated subjects: combinations of substances that are considered as one thing are treated as singular; combinations that are considered as two or more (kinds of) things are treated as plural. If this is so, then the determination of number value for coordinated NPs is no longer a syntactic phenomenon.[3]

In the current analysis, the f-structure for a coordination of NPs would have the following form.

$$\left\{\begin{matrix}\left[\quad\right]\\ \left[\quad\right]\end{matrix}\right\}$$

In this case, we must assume that lexical properties such as [↑ SUBJ NUM = PLU] are not used for feature assignment, since there is no site within the f-structure for the establishment of 'new' attribute-value pairs. So the lexical property would be taken as a constraint of the form: 'If SUBJ has a value for NUM, then that value will be PLU.'

Regardless of which particular approach is adopted, there are two important consequences of the set-based analysis of coordination:

(i) there is no syntactic process of subject — verb agreement for coordinate subjects. Either the NUM value for a coordinate subject is semantically determined (under the 'hybrid structure' analysis), or it is left unspecified (under the current analysis). Consequences of this absence of syntactic subject — verb agreement are explored in Section 2 below.

[3]See Reid (1991) for arguments that 'number agreement' is in all cases a purely semantic phenomenon.

(ii) the grammar provides no direct means of imposing constraints on lexical items within a coordination. Thus a condition such as [↑ SUBJ NUM = PLU] cannot apply to individual NPs within SUBJ. Similarly, a condition such as [↑ SUBJ CASE = NOM] cannot permeate the coordinate structure, and therefore cannot apply to individual NPs within SUBJ. The situation with respect to Number is not a problem; in fact, of course, it gives us exactly what we want. We do not want the lexical property [↑ SUBJ NUM = PLU] of the verb *are* in (6) to produce a conflict in values with the singular NPs *the ferret* and *the kitten.* However the situation with respect to Case is less straightforward. If the case requirement [↑ SUBJ CASE = NOM] does not distribute to individual conjuncts, how do we account for observed patterns such as *He and I are going home*? Case assignment is discussed in more detail in Section 3 below.

The position that I am arguing for in this paper is that, since the grammar has no means of imposing constraints on lexical items within a coordination, agreement is left **underspecified**. There is in effect a **gap** in the grammar; the mechanisms provided by the grammatical framework are blocked from applying, and therefore leave some grammatical features unspecified. But there are no actual 'unspecified' forms of verbs or nouns, so the speaker has to choose a form. This choice may be resolved in accordance with what I will refer to as 'speaker strategies', principles of selection which are based on factors such as proximity (e.g. 'closest conjunct') and semantic salience (e.g. 'plural wins').

The key concept here is that of a systemic gap, where the rules of the grammatical system fail to function. Such a gap arises when there is a grammatical principle that applies in general but a particular configuration does not conform to the requirements for its application. For example, agreement applies between a verb and the head of the subject NP; but if the subject has no head, what happens? Reis (1974: 164-166) gives a number of different types of examples where 'the standard rules do not tell the speaker what to do; unless he escapes into an innocuous paraphrase he will have to patch up the hole left by his core grammar.' One method of 'patching up' is to 'establish ad hoc priorities ... by invoking subsidiary principles such as the 'closest conjunct' principle, etc.' (Reis 1974: 166). Reis states very clearly the kinds of differences that may be expected between her 'patch-up rules' (our 'speaker strategies') and 'core rules' of the grammar. Since strategies are not part of the grammatical system, their application will be marked by hesitation, inconsistency and idiolectal variation. And since the strategies are in effect an accumulation of ad hoc solutions to systemic gaps, it is to be expected that they may vary in nature, some being perceptual strategies, others based on semantic principles.

Morgan (1972, 1984b) treats 'patch-up rules' as syntactic principles of the same kind as core grammatical rules. But they do not operate the same way; they are not applied automatically and consistently in the way internalised grammar rules apply. And they are not always, or even usually, syntactically based. Some strategies such as PLURAL WINS are based on semantic principles; others such as FIRST CONJUNCT and NEAREST CONJUNCT seem to have a processing or perceptual basis (see also Pullum 1984).

Two areas in which these strategies can be observed are in the selection of number and case features in English coordinations: the choice of number value for the finite verb will necessarily be independent of the number value of the individual NPs within a coordinated subject; and case requirements such as [↑ SUBJ CASE = NOM] cannot permeate the coordination structure. We therefore predict a high level of idiosyncrasy and variation in number and case marking. The following sections provide extensive data to confirm this prediction and explore in more detail the nature of the strategies available to speakers in the face of grammatical underspecification.

14.2 Agreement

Subject-Verb agreement can be seen as a matching of number values between the subject NP and the finite verb. The number of the subject NP is determined by the number of the lexical head (N) which percolates up to the phrasal (NP) node. So, in *The children were singing*, the noun *children* has the value [NUM = PLU]; hence the NP *the children* has the value [NUM = PLU]. The finite verb *were* is lexically marked for the value [↑ SUBJ NUM = PLU], which agrees with the value for its subject NP and the sentence is therefore grammatical.

When the subject consists of a coordination of NPs, however, this agreement assignment is not available, since as established above, the lexically specified properties of the individual coordinated NPs do not percolate up to the dominating coordinate node, since that is not the head of the construction. Hence the coordinate structure as a whole has no inherent number value, and there is no syntactically determined agreement.

What then happens? In effect, the speaker is 'free' to choose whichever verb form seems appropriate, since there is no possibility of a syntactic clash of Number values. But this freedom does not lead to random selection. The form of the verb is selected in accordance with particular agreement strategies, based either on semantic criteria or on linear order. The semantic basis of choice is illustrated in the sentences in (8):

(8) i Drinking too much and driving too fast are two ways of getting yourself killed.
 ii Drinking too much and driving too fast is a lethal combination.
 iii John's belligerence and his refusal to accept discipline has/have caused a lot of trouble.
 iv *Sally and John has arrived.
 v Sally and John is the best combination.

And-coordination is interpreted as a set, with the individual NP conjuncts enumerating the members of the set. As the sentences in (8) illustrate, the set may be viewed as a collection of two or more individual elements (8i), or as a unified combination (8ii). In many cases, therefore, there is a genuine choice of verb form reflecting the speaker's view of the set of coordinated items, as in (8iii). However, the choice of viewing the set as a unified combination of elements may be ruled out because a 'unified combination' is not seen as a viable option. Hence (8iv) is unacceptable because it is difficult to conceive of two living entities as a single undifferentiated whole; however, as (8v) shows, even this is not always ruled out.

The effect of the linear order of conjuncts on verb choice can be seen most clearly in the examples in (9) (from Morgan 1972):

(9) i There was a man and two women in the room.
 ii There were two women and a man in the room.

The agreement pattern here conforms to what Morgan (1972:281) calls the 'closest conjunct principle', in which the verb 'agrees' in number with the NP which is nearest to it in terms of surface linear order.[4] This pattern seems to be clearest in English in inverted structures where the verb agrees with the first NP conjunct in a following coordinated subject, as in the existential sentences in (9) and in interrogative structures (10):[5]

---

[4] Sadler (2003) provides interesting discussion of single ('asymmetric') conjunct agreement within the LFG framework.

[5] This principle of linear adjacency or 'proximity' applies in other areas of 'agreement' in English as well, such as choice of relative pronoun:

 i the things and people who/*which amuse her most
 ii the people and things which/*who amuse her most

Of course in this case, the choice of *that* would get the speaker off the hook.

(10) (i) Is/are John's brother and his friends downstairs?
(ii) Are/*is John's friends and his brother downstairs?

Johannessen (1996) gives the following example from German which conforms to the same 'closest conjunct principle' (although she has a different explanation):

(11) Aber links war die Binnenalster und
but left was.SG the.NOM.SG inner-Alster.NOM.SG and
die weissen Lichtreklamen.
the.NOM.SG white.PL light-ad.NOM.PL
'But to the left was the inner Alster (lake) and the white light-ads.'

When the subject consists of NPs coordinated with *or*, again subject-verb agreement is blocked. Choice of number with or-coordination is highly variable, with both (12i) and (12ii) accepted by different speakers, and some speakers accepting both at different times (Peterson 1986):

(12) i %Either Kim or Pat is responsible for the damage.
ii %Either Kim or Pat are responsible for the damage.

When the conjuncts differ in number, at least two possible strategies are utilised:[6] the 'closest conjunct principle' (Fowler 1926, Morgan 1972, Quirk & Greenbaum 1973), which gives the agreement patterns in (12); and a 'plural wins' strategy (cf. Partridge 1956: 'if either of the two subjects (sic) joined by *or* is plural, the ensuing verb must be plural'), as in (13):

(13) i Either Harry's parents or his wife is coming
ii Either Harry or his parents are coming
iii Was either your brother or your parents told of your illness?
iv Was the cake or the scones made by Mary?

(14) i Either Harry's parents or his wife are coming
ii Either Harry or his parents are coming
iii Were either your brother or your parents told of your illness?
iv Were the cake or the scones made by Mary?

The survey reported in Peterson (1986) indicates that in declarative structures (i, ii) the 'plural wins' strategy is the more frequently

[6]Peterson (1986) reports the existence of a third strategy, showing agreement consistently with the first conjunct. This strategy conforms to the pattern predicted by Johannessen (1996), in whose analysis it is the first conjunct which determines the features of the coordination. However this pattern was adopted by only six of the 40 informants in Peterson's (1986) survey.

adopted solution. Of the 40 respondents, 25 followed the pattern in (14i,ii) while 15 preferred (13i,ii), the 'closest conjunct principle'. (Note that this preference for (14i) over (13i) is at odds with Morgan, who claims that (14i) is ungrammatical, allowing only (13i).) This preference was maintained in interrogative structures containing *either* (iii), with 22 respondents preferring (14iii) and 14 choosing (13iii). With (iv), however, where the verb is immediately adjacent to the NP, the proximity-based 'closest conjunct principle' regained its strength, with 27 respondents preferring (13iv) over (14iv).

Importantly, as established in Peterson (1986), the choice of verb form by particular speakers is not completely random. Speakers do seem to follow patterns of choice. Speakers who adopt the closest conjunct principle for declaratives also use the same principle for interrogatives; those who use the 'plural wins' choice for interrogatives apply it to declaratives as well. So it is legitimate to refer to these patterns of choice as 'strategies'.

Coordination with *(neither -) (n)or* produces a different pattern of responses again. The figures reported in Peterson (1986) are shown in (15) (figures indicate the number of preferences for plural verb form, out of 40 informants):

(15)	i	Neither Kim nor Pat is/are responsible for this mess	15
	ii	Neither the carrots nor the beans has/have done well	38
	iii	Neither the cake nor the scones tastes/taste fresh	32
	iv	Neither the scones nor the cake was/were made by Mary	30

There is clearly a strong preference for a plural verb form whenever there is at least one plural NP in the coordination, supporting Partridge's (1956) 'plural wins' position that the verb form should be plural if at least one of the coordinates is plural. However, there are 10 votes for a singular verb in (15iv), which suggests that the 'closest conjunct principle' has some support even here. Of particular interest is the vote (15/40) for a plural verb even when both NPs are singular (15i). As Quirk & Greenbaum (1973) point out, the construction *neither X nor Y* is logically equivalent to *X and Y are both not.* It appears that many speakers are using this equivalence as the working principle for determining the appropriate verb form, further support for the claim that verb agreement with coordinate subjects is determined by factors outside of syntax.

These findings strongly support the proposal that speakers are not conforming to an established syntactic 'rule' of verb agreement in these cases. It appears that there are several different kinds of 'strategies' that speakers may choose from to determine verbal number. These 'speaker strategies' (similar in effect to Corbett's 'resolution rules' (Corbett 1991)) are working principles by which speakers can 'patch up' gaps left by the grammar (Reis 1974). In differentiating between 'core rules' of grammar and 'patch-up rules', Reis (1974) shows that the latter are marked by hesitation and inconsistency (idiolectal variation), exactly what Peterson (1986) found with examples of 'agreement' with coordinate subjects. In effect, then, the grammar underspecifies in the area of agreement with coordinated subjects, so speakers resort to various strategies to determine verbal number. Hence we find considerable variability.

Mallinson (1984) finds very similar effects in his study of agreement in Rumanian between predicate adjectives and coordinated subjects. Rumanian has three noun classes, which for the purposes of this discussion we can refer to as MASCULINE, FEMININE and NEUTER 'gender'. If the subject is a coordination of two NPs of the same gender, there is no problem of agreement; a coordination of MASCULINE NPs will require a MASCULINE form of the predicate adjective, etc. If the coordination contains NPs of different genders, the situation becomes very complicated. Mallinson cites the Rumanian Academy Grammar (1963) (RAG) which provides the following 'rules' for the selection of the form for the predicate adjective when the two conjoined NPs are of different gender (adapted from Mallinson 1984: 447):

for animate NPs:
- coordination of MASC and FEM produces MASC plural.

for inanimate NPs:
- coordination of MASC SG and FEM or NEUT produces NEUT PLU agreement
- coordination of MASC PLU and NEUT SG produces MASC PLU agreement
- coordination of MASC PLU and FEM produces agreement with the nearer conjunct
- coordination of MASC PLU and NEUT PLU produces agreement with the nearer conjunct

However, as Mallinson discovered, these rules, besides being extremely complex, do not in fact represent the actual linguistic behaviour of Rumanian speakers. In Mallinson's terms, 'rather than talking about ... competence we should be talking in terms of language incompetence. No two speakers [in Mallinson's survey] achieved precisely the same results and only one speaker produced an agreement pattern that was in accord with the RAG.' Furthermore, 'most of the speakers [were] inconsistent between repeated examples separated by an interval of 20 minutes.' (Mallinson 1984:449). Mallinson does not provide data that could be investigated for the existence of particular speaker strategies such as semantic salience or proximity, but the instability of speaker responses suggests once again a 'gap' in the grammar spawning a set of patch-up strategies.

14.3 Case

Case assignment in English involves assigning nominative case to the Subject by means of a functional equation (↑ SUBJ CASE) = NOM associated with the finite form of the verb. However, if the subject consists of a coordination of NPs, the case assignment is blocked from the individual conjuncts by the functional structure of the coordination; feature value pairs such as (CASE NOM) do not distribute into the set. Similarly, default case assignment in English assigns accusative case to an object NP. But again this case assignment cannot percolate to the individual conjuncts within a coordinated object. Therefore the conjuncts are free to carry either NOM or ACC case marking.[7]

Once again we find that there are several patterns from which speakers can choose. There are in fact four possible patterns: ACC case for both conjuncts; NOM case for both conjuncts; NOM case for first conjunct only; NOM case for second conjunct only. While there are restrictions of choice in formal written registers of Standard English, in everyday spoken English all four patterns are found in coordinations for both subjects and non-subjects. Quinn (1998) reports the following distribution of choices for coordinated pronouns in subject position, from a survey of 90 respondents:

[7] An anonymous referee has raised the common objection that English case marking is too 'impoverished' to reveal anything of general theoretical interest. There are two separate issues here:

(i) English case marking is not impoverished in the pronoun system. There are clearly violable rules of case marking (i.e. English case marking on pronouns is systematic) except within coordinate constructions.

(ii) This exception is what we need to explain.

NOM + NOM	she and we, we and she	12
	he and I, I and he	44
ACC + ACC	her and us, us and her	26
	him and me, me and him	11
ACC + NOM	her and we, us and she	3
	him and I	35
NOM + ACC	she and us, we and her	49
	I and him, me and me	0

Peterson (2004) gives the following examples of coordinations in non-subject positions:

(16) i %Jane invited him and I to the party.
ii %a contract between he and I
iii %An invitation was sent to both she and me.

Results reported from Quinn's survey (Quinn 1998) show that in coordinated non-subject NPs, *I* was used in 46% of all possible occasions; *he*, *she*, *we* and *they* all scored much lower percentages, but were all found.[8]

Two significant points are illustrated by these examples. First, even when both conjuncts have the same case value, that case value does not percolate up to the coordination as a whole. The choice of *her* and *us* as the form of a coordinated subject NP does not impose the value [CASE ACC] on the coordinate subject; that would run into conflict with the functional equation (↑ SUBJ CASE) = NOM associated with the finite form of the verb. The second point to note is the high frequency of examples where the coordinated pronouns do not 'agree' in case with each other. This situation is predicted in the present analysis; since case is not a distributive feature (cf. Dalrymple & Kaplan 2000), there is no expectation of case concord within a coordinate structure.[9]

[8]The reasons for the disparity between first person singular and other pronouns need to be explored further. Quinn attributes it to phonological causes; I suspect the effects of 'hypercorrection', given the almost exclusive focus in classrooms on the use or non-use of *I*.

[9]In languages where case concord is required, such as Standard English or Icelandic, it is possible, as shown in Peterson (2004), to stipulate case agreement by adding a functional equation ↓CASE = ↑CASE to each conjunct in the coordinate structure. This will guarantee that the case of each conjunct matches the case of the coordination as a whole which is assigned by the verb, thus closing the 'gap' in the grammar. Within the present analysis, such stipulation is an 'expensive' addition to the grammar, and no more preferable than stipulation of agreement with only one conjunct (as in the grammaticalisation of 'first conjunct' agreement).

14.4 Conclusion

From the evidence in the preceding sections, it is clear that the speaker of English faces problems with case and number assignment associated with coordinate structures. The LFG account of coordination presented in Peterson (2004) predicts exactly this set of problems. The rules of the grammatical framework do not allow NUM or CASE values to penetrate or escape from the coordinate f-structure, and the speaker is therefore faced with a gap in the grammar which requires the use of 'patch-up rules' (Reis 1974). These 'patch-up rules' conform to the type of 'speaker strategies' suggested by Morgan (1972). The kind of variation we have encountered in this paper is expected if 'agreement' and 'case assignment' are determined on the basis of speaker strategies rather than grammatical principles. And the mixed nature of the system is also expected if the 'system' is an accumulation of workable strategies. (The term 'system' is probably not appropriate here since, as I have argued, agreement and case assignment patterns with coordinate structures are not built into the grammar but are rather a 'patching' mechanism.)

It is worth asking the question whether the range of variation in agreement could be accounted for in terms of Labov-style variable rules or optimality constraints of a kind suggested by Quinn (1998). Corbett (1983) for instance presents an example of agreement in Serbo-Croat, where gender resolution appears to be hierarchically constrained by differing syntactic contexts. So for instance with a coordination of two plural NPs of different gender agreement can be with the 'nearest conjunct only' (our PROX, which Corbett calls 'syntactic') or with 'both conjuncts' (which Corbett calls 'semantic') in which case the default form of MASC PLU is used (even if the conjuncts are feminine and neuter). Corbett states that the choice of resolution strategy is (in part) constrained by a hierarchy of syntactic contexts:

Attributive position	agreement with PROX always
Predicate position	agreement with PROX favoured
Relative pronoun	agreement with PROX favoured
Personal pronoun	agreement with both (MASC PLU) always

It appears, however, that the kind of data presented in Peterson (1986) and Quinn (2002) is much more idiosyncratic and unstable than would be expected from variable rule analysis. The evidence at present suggests support for performance strategies as individual attempts to cope with 'gaps' in the grammar.

References

Alvarez, Gloria, Belinda Brodie, and Terry McCoy, eds. 1984. *Proceedings of the 1st Eastern States Conference on Linguistics (ESCOL'84)*. Columbus, OH: Ohio State University.

Bresnan, Joan, Ronald M. Kaplan, and Peter Peterson. 1986. Coordination and the flow of information through phrase structure. Ms., Stanford University and Xerox PARC.

Corbett, Greville G. 1983. *Hierarchies, Targets and Controllers: Agreement patterns in Slavic*. London: Croom Helm.

Dalrymple, Mary and Ronald M. Kaplan. 1997. A set-based approach to feature resolution. In M. Butt and T. H. King, eds., *Proceedings of the International Lexical-Functional Grammar Conference 1997 (LFG'97)*. San Diego, CA: CSLI Online Publications.

Dalrymple, Mary and Ronald M. Kaplan. 2000. Feature indeterminacy and feature resolution. *Language* 76(4):759–798.

Dalrymple, Mary, Ronald M. Kaplan, John T. Maxwell III, and Annie Zaenen, eds. 1995. *Formal Issues in Lexical-Functional Grammar*. Stanford, CA: CSLI Publications.

Falk, Yehuda N. 1984. The English auxiliary system. *Language* 60(3):483–509.

Fowler, Henry W. 1926. *A dictionary of modern English usage*. London: Oxford University Press.

Huddleston, Rodney D., John Payne, and Peter Peterson. 2002. Coordination and supplementation. In R. D. Huddleston and G. Pullum, eds., *The Cambridge Grammar of the English Language*, pages 1273–1362. Cambridge, UK: Cambridge University Press. Chapter 15.

Johannessen, Janne B. 1996. Partial agreement and coordination. *Linguistic Inquiry* 27(4):661–676.

Kaplan, Ronald M. and John T. Maxwell III. 1988. Constituent coordination in Lexical-Functional Grammar. In *Proceedings of the 12th International Conference on Computational Linguistics (COLING'88)*, vol. 1, pages 303–305. Budapest. Reprinted in Dalrymple et al, 1995: 199–210.

Mallinson, Graham. 1984. Problems, pseudo-problems and hard evidence – another look at the Rumanian neuter. *Folia Linguistica* 18:439–451.

Morgan, Jerry L. 1972. Verb agreement as a rule of English. In *Papers from the 8th Regional Meeting of the Chicago Linguistic Society (CLS 8)*, pages 278–286. Chicago, IL.

Morgan, Jerry L. 1984a. Some problems of agreement in English and Albanian. In C. Brugman and M. Macaulay, eds., *Proceedings of the 10th Annual Meeting of the Berkeley Linguistics Society (BLS 10)*, pages 233–247. Berkeley, CA: Berkeley Linguistics Society.

Morgan, Jerry L. 1984b. Some problems of determination in English number agreement. In G. Alvarez, B. Brodie, and T. McCoy, eds., *Proceedings of the 1st Eastern States Conference on Linguistics (ESCOL'84)*, pages 69–78. Columbus, OH: Ohio State University.

Parker, Frank, Kathryn Riley, and Charles Meyer. 1988. Case assignment and the ordering of constituents in coordinate constructions. *American Speech* 63:214–233.

Partridge, Eric. 1956. *Usage and Abusage: A guide to good English*. London: H. Hamilton. Revised edition.

Peterson, Peter. 1986. Establishing verb agreement with disjunctively conjoined subjects: Strategies vs. principles. *Australian Journal of Linguistics* 6(2):231–250.

Peterson, Peter. 2004. Coordination: Consequences of a Lexical-Functional account. *Natural Language and Linguistic Theory* 22(3):643–679.

Pullum, Geoffrey K. 1984. How complex could an agreement system be? In G. Alvarez, B. Brodie, and T. McCoy, eds., *Proceedings of the 1st Eastern States Conference on Linguistics (ESCOL'84)*, pages 79–103. Columbus, OH: Ohio State University.

Quinn, Heidi. 1998. The distribution of English pronoun forms. Ms., University of Canterbury, New Zealand.

Quirk, Randolph and Sidney Greenbaum. 1973. *A University Grammar of English*. London: Longman.

Reid, Wallis. 1991. *Verb and Noun Number in English: A functional explanation*. London: Longman.

Reis, Marga. 1974. Patching up with counterparts. *Foundations of Language* 12:157–176.

Sadler, Louisa. 2003. Asymmetric coordination and agreement in LFG. In M. Butt and T. H. King, eds., *Nominals: Inside and Out*, pages 85–118. Stanford, CA: CSLI Publications.

15

Feature Resolution and the Content of Features

NIGEL VINCENT AND KERSTI BÖRJARS

15.1 Introduction

The traditional assumption that syntactic features (GENDER, NUMBER, PERSON, etc) have single atomic values (MASC, FEM, SG, PL, 1ST, 2ND, 3RD, etc) is challenged by data of two kinds: INDETERMINACY and CLASH.[1] Indeterminacy occurs when a given item is able to satisfy different feature requirements in different contexts. Clash arises when the

[1] This paper has a somewhat complex pedigree. The first version was prepared and delivered at LFG 2000 at UC Berkeley as a response to some consequences of the model of feature resolution presented in Kaplan & Dalrymple (2000), work which in its turn had originally been presented at LFG 1997 at UC San Diego. We were not able to fix some technical details in time for inclusion in the Proceedings of LFG 2000, and the paper lay dormant for a while thereafter, despite occasional references being made to it in the literature. At LFG 2004 in Christchurch New Zealand the issues the paper addresses arose again in the context of a workshop on agreement and feature resolution led by Mary Dalrymple and Louisa Sadler, and we re-presented our argument, suitably reworked and extended in the light of intervening developments, during that workshop.

We are particularly pleased to be able to offer this revised version of the paper to Joan on the occasion of her 60th birthday since both the original and the later versions gained greatly from her comments and insights. More broadly the genesis of the paper testifies to the strength and collegiality of the LFG community (most obviously but not exclusively evident in the annual LFG conferences) which is a further testament to Joan's inspiration and leadership. Others who have discussed the ideas contained in this paper with us and whom we would like to thank include Grev Corbett, Mary Dalrymple, Ron Kaplan and Louisa Sadler. For current LFG-based work on agreement, co-ordination and

Architectures, Rules, and Preferences: Variations on Themes by Joan Bresnan.
Annie Zaenen, Jane Simpson, Tracy Holloway King,
Jane Grimshaw, Joan Maling, and Chris Manning, (eds.).

context imposes conflicting requirements on a given item so that a resolution must be achieved. Dalrymple & Kaplan (2000) (henceforth D&K) offer an elegant solution to such problems by proposing that features have sets as values. Thus a Latin form such as *bellum* 'war' would have the case value {NOM, ACC}, which makes it compatible with either subject or object function. By contrast the Latin form *miles* 'soldier' has as its value for the case feature the singleton set {NOM}, and is therefore only compatible with subject function. Similarly, an adjective in a context which imposes agreement with conjoined masculine and feminine nouns would have the value {MASC, FEM}, and the grammar of the language would contain a rule stating how such a clash was to be resolved (e.g. by picking one or other of the genders or by a third alternative or not at all; cf Börjars & Vincent 2000, Corbett 1991: Ch 9). D&K go on to argue that the appropriate operation for combining sets and thus achieving the desired resolution is union rather than intersection (contra Sag et al. 1985), and conclude that to the extent that the architecture of LFG favours union over intersection, their analysis in turn provides an argument in favour of LFG as a more restrictive model of grammar.

In this paper we seek to show that D&K are only able to reach their conclusion by virtue of certain arbitrary and not cross-linguistically sustainable definitions of the features that enter into their analyses. When these problems have been remedied it transpires that union is not the only operation required. Furthermore, in other circumstances the sets in question remain uncombined, with the consequence that no form is generated and the relevant morphosyntactic content therefore necessarily goes unexpressed. In §2 we review D&K's proposals in more detail before commenting on their analyses of grammatical person (§3) and gender (§4). In §5 we adduce some new data from Swedish and in §6 we introduce a diachronic perspective into the argument. We draw out our theoretical conclusions in §7.

15.2 Dalrymple & Kaplan's proposal

15.2.1 Set-valued features

As we have noted, the innovative move that D&K make depends on features being able to have sets as values. Set-valued features have been part of LFG since the beginning (Kaplan & Bresnan 1982: 215-

resolution by Mary Dalrymple and Louisa Sadler, see the project described at: http://privatewww.essex.ac.uk/ louisa/agr/NPagreement.html

We are also grateful to Tolli Eythòrsson for his help with the Icelandic data, and to the late Joe Cremona for a valuable and timely conversation on the evolution of gender in Romance.

218), but D&K break new ground by advocating their use in contexts where all members of the set cannot be realised at once and therefore where some resolution mechanism is required. This in turn has the consequence that feature matching will, in some circumstances at least, need to be handled by a different mechanism from simple equality; in particular under their proposal it is necessary to allow union (but not intersection) as a means for combining two sets which are values of the same feature at different locations in a representation. Thus, assume that we have the following f-structures for the pronoun *tu* 'you (SG)' in Spanish and the proper name *José*:

(1) a. José b. tu

$$\begin{bmatrix} \text{PRED} & \text{'José'} \\ \text{PERSON} & \{\} \\ \text{NUM} & \text{SG} \end{bmatrix} \qquad \begin{bmatrix} \text{PRED} & \text{'pro'} \\ \text{PERSON} & \{\text{H}\} \\ \text{NUM} & \text{SG} \end{bmatrix}$$

In (1a) the specification for the person attribute is {}, the empty set, which is a way of saying that the third person is the unmarked person (cf §2.3 below). In (1b) *tu* has a person attribute {H(earer)}. When these are co-ordinated to give *José y tu* 'José and you (SG)', they retain their individual person specifications but the value for the person attribute of the co-ordination is obtained though the union of {H} and {}, which is {H}. In other words second person plus third person equals second person, though of course plural rather than singular. Hence if the conjunction of these two NPs is the subject of a sentence, the verb will be in the second person plural: *cantais* 'you (PL) sing'. The relevant PS rule for co-ordination, with its f-structure inducing annotations, is displayed in (2a) and the resulting f-structure in (2b):[2]

[2]The value for the NUM feature in (2b) is determined semantically, though D&K have nothing explicit to say about the mechanism involved. Features such as PERS and NUM are labelled 'non-distributive' by D&K since they are determined for the conjunction as a whole and are not distributed over each item (compare the values for CASE, which are indeed distributed so that each item in a co-ordination has the case value of the whole co-ordination). We will not discuss this issue further here, but refer to Sadler (1999) for more pertinent data and theoretical reflection. There is also not space here to discuss the proposal by Harley & Ritter (2002) to integrate person and number features into a single geometric representation. This proposal raises the larger theoretical issue of whether features are unstructured bundles as in LFG or have a more complex internal organization. It also makes a number of interesting predictions, not all of which are borne out (Baerman 2004). From this approach, though not only from this approach, it follows that person and number should work together in resolution, which, as Corbett (p.c.) reminds us, is to be expected.

(2) a.NP $\longrightarrow$ NP CONJ NP

$$\begin{array}{lcc} \text{NP} \longrightarrow & \text{NP} & \text{CONJ} & \text{NP} \\ & \downarrow\in\uparrow & & \downarrow\in\uparrow \\ & (\downarrow\text{PERSON}) \subseteq (\uparrow\text{PERSON}) & & (\downarrow\text{PERSON}) \subseteq (\uparrow\text{PERSON}) \end{array}$$

b. José y tu

$$c: \begin{bmatrix} \left\{ \begin{array}{l} t: \begin{bmatrix} \text{PRED} & \text{'Jose'} \\ \text{NUM} & \text{SG} \\ \text{PERS} & \{\} \end{bmatrix} \\ y: \begin{bmatrix} \text{PRED} & \text{'pro'} \\ \text{NUM} & \text{SG} \\ \text{PERSON} & \{\text{H}\} \end{bmatrix} \end{array} \right\} \\ \text{NUM PL} \\ \text{PERSON} \{\text{H}\} \end{bmatrix}$$

The f-structure in (2b) thus satisfies constraints such as:

(3) (t PERS) = {}
(y PERSON) = {H}
(c PERSON) ={} ∪ {H}={H}

15.2.2 Intersection or union?

D&K note (see in particular their §6.5) that the use of the union operator fits nicely with the general principle of LFG that the appropriate f-structure for a given utterance is the minimal f-description consistent with the satisfaction of all the necessary constraints, since union constructs the smallest set which includes all the members of the input sets. Intersection, on the other hand, is an operation which constructs the largest subset consistent with membership of all the input sets. They further point out that De Morgan's laws guarantee that any analysis involving the intersection of two sets can be equivalently reformulated as the union of the complement sets. Hence the fact that the relevant natural language data can be analysed without recourse to intersection provides an argument in favour of LFG as opposed to a less restrictive theory such as HPSG. The danger with this line of argument is that it allows the choice of the requisite formal operation to be determined not by the patterning of the data but by the formal consistency of the theoretical framework, with the attendant risk of putting the analysis beyond empirical verification. It is important to underscore, therefore, that the choice between whether to base an analysis on a feature set A or its complement A′ is not arbitrary if the feature definitions have intrinsic content. Thus, if there are good empirical reasons to believe that we have identified the best set of primitives, then it will not be open to us simply to switch the definitions of the primitives to their opposites in order to ensure the constant use of a given operator such as union or intersection. In what follows, we will argue that as a matter of priority the real world referential basis of the primitives S(peaker) and H(earer) should be maintained in the analysis of all languages, and the formal consequences of that decision should be addressed thereafter. To do otherwise undermines the empirical basis of the research.

15.2.3 The representation of unmarked forms

Just as the substantive content of features has consequences for the kind of operation that will need to be performed on them, so too it affects the way the unmarked member of a system is represented. As we shall see, D&K's person features have the desirable consequence that the third person, which is generally agreed to be the unmarked member of any person system (Benveniste 1946/1966), is represented formally as the empty set {}. The same cannot be said of their analysis of gender. For instance in Hindi they define the feminine as {}, whereas grammarians usually hold that the masculine is the unmarked or neutral form (e.g. Kachru 1992: 126, Mohanan 1994: 229). In what follows we take it as criterial that for whatever morphosyntactic sub-system we examine, we must be able to show by independent tests that the member of that system which is assigned the representation {} acts as the unmarked form.[3] (For further discussion leading to a similar conclusion, see Blevins 2000.) In the remainder of this paper we examine three bodies of data, two drawn from D&K's work and a third of our own choosing. In each case we proceed in three stages. We seek first to establish the relevant system-internal generalizations, including the role of any markedness asymmetries. We next identify the feature characterizations which best capture these generalizations. Only then do we address the question of what formal operations are required and the consequences thereof for the architecture of the grammatical framework.

15.3 Grammatical person

The elements that D&K use to define person systems are S (for Speaker) and H (for Hearer), and the three singular persons are thus characterized set-theoretically as follows:

[3]We leave open the possiblity that in certain sub-systems there may be no discernible markedness relation; cf Trubetzkoy's (1939) classic definition of an equipollent opposition.

(4) {S}: first person
{H}: second person
{}: third person

In a language such as Fula, which distinguishes first person plural inclusive and exclusive, this allows for a straightforward characterization of the plural persons as set out in (5), on the assumption that the plural persons can be obtained by the operation of union on the sets of their constituent singular persons:[4]

(5) {S} ∪ {H} = {S,H} i.e. the 1st person inclusive plural is made up of the speaker and the hearer(s)
{S} ∪ {} = {S} i.e. the 1st person exclusive is made up of the speaker plus one or more others, neither speakers nor hearers
{H} ∪ {H} = {} i.e. two (or more) hearers form the second person plural
{} ∪ {} = {} i.e. two (or more) non-speaker/hearers form the third person plural

The relevant Fula values and forms are set out in the following tables (based on D&K's (79) and (102)), where (6a) contains the pronouns and (6b) the corresponding inflected verb forms of *djod-* 'live':

(6) a.

	SINGULAR			PLURAL	
1ST	*min*	{S}	inclusive	*enèn*	{S, H}
			exclusive	*mènèn*	{S}
2ND	*an*	{H}		*onön*	{H}
3RD	*ö*	{}		*kombè*	{}

[4]It is sometimes claimed that what are traditionally labelled first and second person plurals are not plural in the same sense that *books* is the plural of *book* (e.g. Lyons 1968: 277). The matter is complex; — for excellent discussion see Benveniste (1946/1966: 234-5) and Corbett (2000: Ch 3; 2005) — and we will not delay long over it at this point. In fact, D&K's proposal, once augmented with a mechanism for indicating the number of individuals referred to on any occasion (their NUM feature), appears to be consistent with either side of the debate. The cardinality of the relevant sets for plurals will then always be greater than one, while the set for first person plural will 'include the speaker', which accords with Lyons' assertion that "*we* is not "the plural of *I*": rather, it includes a reference to 'I' and is plural" (1968: 277).

b.

	SINGULAR			PLURAL	
1ST	*mi-djodi*	{S}	inclusive	*djodu-dèn*	{S, H}
			exclusive	*mèn-djodi*	{S}
2ND	*djodu-da*	{H}		*djodu-don*	{H}
3RD	*wo-djodi*	{}		*bè-djodi*	{}

Support for this feature analysis comes too from a property of the paradigm in (6b) that D&K do not mention, namely that it splits between prefixal (1ST SG, 1ST PL EXCL, 3RD SG & PL) and suffixal (2ND SG & PL, 1ST PL INCL) expression of person. Their system allows a very straightforward generalization, namely that whenever the person feature contains the value {H}, either alone or in combination with {S}, the morphology is suffixing; otherwise it is prefixing.[5] The 'elsewhere' or default option includes the 3rd person.

The question that then arises is: how does this system apply to a language like English or Spanish where there is no overtly signalled distinction between first person plural inclusive and exclusive? One possible answer would be that the feature analyses of the grammatical persons displayed in (4) are held constant across languages but that the resulting distinction between two types of first person plural is neutralized in for example the single English pronoun series *we*, *us*, *our*, *ourselves*. D&K take the opposite tack of generating no more feature sets than are realized in a language's overt morphosyntax. This in turn requires them to redefine the first person in English as {S, H}. The union of this set with either the second person or the third person then produces the same outcome, namely {S, H}. In other words the neutralization of a potential contrast is at the level of f-structure rather than in the morphological realization:

(7) 1st person {S, H} $\cup$ 2nd person {H} = 1st person plural {S, H}
1st person {S, H} $\cup$ 3rd person {} = 1st person plural {S, H}

There are several problems with this analysis. In the first place, it implies that different languages have different definitions of first person singular. We know of no evidence to suggest that the concept of personal identity for the speaker varies according to the grammatical system he or she employs, and we suggest that such a Whorfian conclusion is too high a price to pay for formal consistency.[6] Secondly, D&K's analysis

[5] Arnott (1970: 134) argues on the basis of a number of structural properties that the *-en* and *-on* series have more in common than either does with the *men-* series. He therefore concludes that it would be preferable to distinguish two second person forms according to whether the speaker is included or not.

[6] It is interesting to note that Cowper's (2005) critique of the featural characterization of number systems proposed by Harley & Ritter (2002) is based in part on

voids the primitives S and H of any semantic content: H cannot mean 'Hearer' if it is included in the characterization of the pronoun *I*. Since at one level or another the semantic basis of linguistic person will have to be established in order to achieve a proper account of deixis and indexicality (Nunberg 1993), an account like D&K's will require an extra level of structure in which the morphosyntactic features S and H are mapped into semantic ones. Such a mapping will be complicated to a degree which precisely reflects the simplifications introduced into the morphosyntax by D&K's analytical distinction between the roles of S and H in English and Fula. There will therefore be no overall gain in the economy of the general model of language that ensues. D&K try to avoid this charge by suggesting that S and H might have other definitions than simply speaker and hearer, but the problem will not go away this easily. Suppose that H is defined as 'excluding the speaker' along the lines of Sag et al. (1985) or as meaning 'the hearer is *absent* from the reference set' as D&K suggest (D&K: §6.5; Arnott 1970: 134). On either of these interpretations there will still be a conflict between the value of H and the value of S if both are taken to be part of the definition of the pronoun *I*.

The only way to avoid such a conflict would be to say that the characterization of first person singular is {}, which is in fact what Sag et al. (1985: 123) do. This has many other disadvantages. Their analysis is based on two features XSP and THP "whose semantic correlates are "excluding the speaker" and "third person", respectively", and requires the relevant set-combining operation to be intersection. However, as D&K note, this system does not generalise to languages which have an inclusive/exclusive distinction. We share too the reservations that Sag et al. (1985: 154 note 22) attribute to Karttunen (1984), namely that these feature definitions are 'counterintuitive' and do not reflect the unmarked nature of the third person (cf Benveniste 1946).[7] In sum, there seems to be no way to maintain D&K's analysis while at the same time providing direct semantic correlates of the elements S and H.

Finally, their approach ignores the fact that in English there is in any case pragmatic and syntactic (as opposed to morpho-syntactic) evidence for the need to recognise two kinds of first person. Thus in a control context the value of PRO will differ if the antecedent is *you and I* as opposed to *John and I*. This is particularly clear in a context of non-

a similar preference 'that features are used in a cross-linguistically consistent way' (Cowper 2005: 442).

[7]Interestingly, Pollard & Sag (1994) revert to atomic values 1st, 2nd and 3rd for the feature person, and this practice is also adopted in the HPSG account of Serbo-Croatian and other languages proposed in Wechsler & Zlatić (2003).

obligatory or anaphoric control, where split antecedence is permitted, and hence where the value of PRO can be computed with reference to two distinct locations in the clause's f-structure. Consider the following pair of examples:

(8) a. Do you remember that I discussed with you offering ourselves as candidates for the election?
b. Do you remember that I discussed with John offering ourselves as candidates for the election?

In (8a) the subject of *offering* and hence the antecedent of *ourselves* is the combination of you and I, and hence a first person inclusive. (8b) on the other hand is ambiguous in that the subject of *offering ourselves* may be any of you and I, John and I, or John, you and I. This same difference is detectable in different discourse contexts. Thus, compare the two mini-discourses in (9)

(9) a. *A says to B:* I'll buy the food and you get the wine and then we'll (= 'you and I') meet this evening and make dinner together.
b. *A says to B:* I'll collect Bill from the airport and then we'll (= 'Bill and I') see you at the restaurant at 8 o' clock.

Such data suggest that a single cross-linguistic basis for defining grammatical person is preferable even though not all languages express the relevant distinctions in their morphology.

An analogous argument can be constructed with respect to the Italian examples in (10):

(10) a. Io sono contenta/o
I be.PRES.1SG happy.FEM.SG/MASC.SG
'I am happy.' (female speaker vs. male speaker)
b. Tu sei contenta/o
you.SG be.PRES.2 SG happy. FEM.SG/MASC.SG
'You are happy.' (female addressee vs. male addressee)

On the standard assumption that predicative adjectives agree with their subjects, we have to allow for a distinction between a male 'I' and a female 'I', a distinction which is in fact encoded, as is the distinction between a male 'you' and a female 'you', through separate pronouns in certain languages (Corbett 1991: 129-132). Once again there is a distinction within the pronominal system which is available in some languages but not in others, but there is no reason to believe that the underlying categories which the different languages encode are distinct.

We thus propose as a working hypothesis that in grammatical subsystems with a clear referential basis like person, the definitions of the persons should be constant across languages. With the modest change to the D&K system argued for above we can achieve the goal of providing a single system to underlie person across the world. With the primitive properties {S, H}, whose ontological basis is well founded, the appropriate set combining operation is still union, and so we can preserve D&K's appealing argument for the compatibility of choosing union with the existing formal basis of LFG. We now move onto the area of gender where the justification for cross-linguistically invariant definitions is at first sight much more tenuous. Nonetheless, we will try to show that arguments for some degree of cross-linguistic constancy in the definition of classes can be adduced, but at the rather higher cost that union cannot always be preserved as the only operator when the sets come to be combined.

15.4 Gender

For Indo-European gender systems based on the traditional though in large measure contentless labels masculine, feminine and neuter, there is less intuitive difficulty in accepting D&K's conclusion that definitions differ arbitrarily across languages since class membership is also arbitrarily different (French *lune* 'moon' is feminine and *soleil* 'sun' is masculine vs. German *Mond* 'moon' masculine and *Sonne* 'sun' feminine, Meillet 1919: 203).[8] Thus for the three languages they consider they offer the following characterizations of the gender classes:

(11)

	Hindi	Icelandic	Slovene
Masculine	{M}	{M}	{F, N}
Feminine	{}	{F}	{F}
Neuter	–	{M, F}	{N}

In the absence of external correlates, the justification for these features and their assignments is language internal, in particular the way

[8]All the examples of gender that we will discuss in this paper are drawn from different branches of Indo-European: Germanic (Icelandic, Swedish, German), Italic (Latin, French, Italian), Slavic (Slovene), Indic (Sanskrit, Hindi). Here is not the place to go into detail but the general consensus is that in origin there was a two way system based on semantically motivated distinction between animate and inanimate. Subsequently the old animate class split into masculine and feminine, while the inanimate class provides the core of the neuter. Hence the older masc/fem/neuter system of Latin, Sanskrit, Ancient Greek, and its survival through into Modern Greek, Modern German and Icelandic. Elsewhere this three way system collapsed in ways that will be discussed below to give the two genders of modern Romance languages (masc vs. fem) and in a different way the two genders of mainland Scandinavian (common (< masc + fem) and neuter). For discussion see Meillet (1919, 1931, 1948).

the agreement resolution patterns work when noun phrases of differing genders are conjoined. For instance in Hindi, conjoined masculine and feminine nouns trigger a masculine verb (= D&K's (107)).

(12) meraa kuttaa aur merii billii mere saath
 my dog and my cat me with
  MASC   FEM
 ghar mẽ rahte hãĩ
 house LOC live
   SUBJ GEND=MASC.
 'My dog and my cat live with me in the house'

There is no more cross-linguistic validity to the elements {M, F, N} than there is to the traditional labels Masculine, Feminine and Neuter and they might as well be labelled {a, b, c} or {1, 2, 3}. What is consistent about the way D&K set up their analyses is that the feature assignments are chosen in such a way as to permit the use of the union operator. Thus, for the Hindi example in (12), if Masculine was characterized as {} and Feminine as {F}, then we could get the right results with intersection but not with union. The relevant equations would be:

(13) {} (MASC) ∩ {} (MASC) = {} (MASC)
 {} (MASC) ∩ {F} (FEM) = {} (MASC)
 {F} (FEM) ∩ {F} (FEM) = {F} (FEM)

as contrasted with those proposed by D&K (= their (112)):

(14) {M} (MASC) ∪ {M} (MASC) = {M} (MASC)
 {M} (MASC) ∪ {} (FEM) = {M} (MASC)
 {} (FEM) ∪ {} (FEM) = {} (FEM)

In accord with our earlier methodological decision, we suggest that the first step must be to determine the most appropriate generalizations in terms of the structural patterns of the language in question. Only then can the choice be made as to which formal device most adequately models the situation in that language. Now, one consequence of the analysis in (14) as opposed to that in (13) is that it uncouples the concepts of unmarked and unspecified. Thus, in Hindi the unmarked gender is Masculine, as shown precisely by the fact that it appears when there is a conflict of genders to be resolved. Masculine is also the form chosen when there is no gender determined by the structural context, as in the construction exemplified in (15) (= (69) in Mohanan 1994: 229):

(15) ilaa-ne mohan-ko pasand kiyaa
Ila-ERG Mohan-ACC liking.NOM.FEM do.PERF.MASC
'Ila liked (approved of) Mohan'

Commenting on this example and others like it, Mohanan notes that the nominalizations in the nominative such as *pasand* 'liking' and *yaad* 'memory', with which a verb in Hindi would normally agree, are feminine but 'the inflection on the light verbs is that of the masculine singular, indicating absence of agreement' (Mohanan 1994: 229). This yields an argument for saying that just as the impersonal takes the unmarked third person singular form — characterized above as {} — so it takes the unmarked masculine form, also characterized as {} (cf also Andrews & Manning 1999: 21 who refer to the form in question as the 'masculine default form').

Taking our cue from Mohanan, then, what we should look for is other contexts in languages with gender systems where the normal mechanisms of agreement are suspended. Such 'non-agreement' contexts provide us with an insight into the unmarked or default form of the language. If we then say that in such contexts agreement cannot arise, and therefore no features are assigned, it will follow that only members of the system that are characterised by absence of features — formally represented as the empty set {} — can be found.[9] A clear case in point comes from Icelandic. In Icelandic the verb only agrees with the subject if the latter is in the nominative. When the subject is in one of the so-called 'quirky' cases (DAT, GEN or ACC), the verb is always 3rd person singular regardless of the number and person of the subject, just as with the Hindi example:

(16) a. drengina vantar mat
boy.DEF.PL.ACC lack.PRES.3SG food.ACC
'The boys lack food.'

b. Mig/mér vantar hníf
me.ACC/DAT lack.PRES.3SG knife.ACC
'I lack a knife.'

[9] In view of the strictures in Corbett (1991: §9.6.1) against too ready an identification of the unmarked gender with the resolution form, we should emphasise that what we propose is not a blanket cross-linguistic rule whereby unmarked form = resolution form, but rather an account in which the unmarked one is characterized as the empty set. It then depends on the rules of the language in question at what points in the representation the empty set is required in the computation of the morphosyntactic features. In this way we would suggest that our proposal captures the spirit of what is intended by having recourse to unmarkedness in certain resolution contexts without running into the problems identified by Corbett in his discussion. For some further considerations relating to morphosyntactic markedness, see the exchange between Noyer (1998) and Carstairs-McCarthy (1998).

Here, regardless of whether the subject is singular or plural, first or third person, the verb is in the third person singular, generally regarded as the default or non-agreement form (Smith 1996: 174).

Now, simple Icelandic verb forms do not inflect for gender as Hindi verbs do, but certain periphrastic forms contain the neuter or non-agreeing form of the past participle usually referred to as the supine, as in (17):

(17) a. Honum var hjálpað.
he.DAT be.3SG.PST help.PSTPRT.3SG.NEUT
'He was helped.'

b. Henni var skilað
she.DAT be.3SG.PST return.PSTPRT.3SG.NEUT
peningunum.
money.DAT
'She was returned the money.'

c. Það var dansað.
it be.PST.3SG dance.PSTPRT.3SG.NEUT
'There was dancing.'

On D&K's account, in which neuter in Icelandic is characterized as {M, F}, it would just have to be stipulated that the participle is in the neuter, but on a view that says neuter is featureless, this property is what follows from not having a morpho-syntactically accessible subject to provide the necessary gender features. In other words the verb is both 3rd person singular and neuter by default.

A similar situation obtains in Latin. Consider the following examples:

(18) a. pugnabatur
fight.IMPERF.PASS.3SG
'it was being fought', i.e 'there was fighting'

b. pugnatum est
fight.PSTPRT.NEUT.SG be.PRES.3SG
'it has been fought', i.e. 'there has been fighting'

(19) a. me sermonis taedet
me.ACC talk.GEN.SG.MASC tire.PRES.3SG
'the talk tires me'

b. me sermonis taesum
me.ACC talk.GEN.SG.MASC tire.PSTPRT.NEUT.SG
est
be.PRES.3SG
'the talk has tired me'

For the impersonal passive construction (18) and the impersonal (quirky case) verb in (19), the verb form is always third person singular of the appropriate tense, and when the form required is periphrastic, as in the perfect, then the participle is neuter. Both of these properties fall out straightforwardly if we say that in such constructions the verb lacks a nominative subject, the only case that can trigger agreement in Latin, and therefore takes the default person (third), number (singular) and gender (neuter).[10] If then, on the basis of evidence such as this, we take the view that the neuter gender should be represented in Icelandic and Latin as {} rather than as {F, M}, it is a straightforward matter to state the relevant equivalences but only if we make use of intersection rather than union. The resolution rules for Icelandic co-ordination will thus be as follows:

(20) {M} (MASC) ∩ {M} (MASC) = {M}(MASC)
{F} (FEM) ∩ {F} (FEM) = {F} (FEM)
{} (NEUT) ∩ {} (NEUT) = {} (NEUT)
{M} (MASC) ∩ {F} (FEM) = {} (NEUT)
{M} (MASC) ∩ {} (NEUT) = {} (NEUT)
{F} (FEM) ∩ {} (NEUT) = {} (NEUT)

There is now a simple generalization that covers both Hindi and Icelandic: when conjoined nouns differ in gender the adjective goes into the unmarked or default form. The price for making this generalization seems to be the introduction of intersection as a possible set combining operation; or perhaps more conservatively the abandonment of union as the only set operator involved in feature resolution.

Once again the strategy that we have preferred to follow is to define the featural basis of categories in such a way as to maximise cross-linguistic comparability. This turns out to be possible even in such a semantically arbitrary area as grammatical gender,[11] provided one looks for recurrent patterns of default choice or unmarkedness, rather

[10] Incidentally, Latin reminds us that the syntactic default and the resolution form do not have to be the same. Thus with conjoined nouns Latin operates a different strategy and makes the adjective agree with the nearest noun in linear sequence:

(i) cuncta maria terrae-que
all.NEUT.PL sea.NEUT.PL land.FEM.PL-and
'all seas and lands'

(ii) cunctae terrae maria-que
all.FEM.PL land.FEM.PL sea.NEUT.PL-and
'all lands and seas'

[11] Obviously there are also languages in which what is commonly called gender has a natural or semantic basis (Corbett 1991: Ch 2), but they do not present the same challenge to our claim that the characterization of grammatical categories should, wherever possible, be cross-linguistically valid, and we leave them out of

than for direct referential correlates of the kind that are available in the domain of person. It thus appears as if different grammatical subsystems need to have recourse to different means for the combination of set-valued features. It seems that either one has to give up the search for representing markedness values directly in the array of primitives out of which the person, gender or whatever systems are constructed, or else one has to recognise that something more than union is required.

15.5 Adjectives and adverbs

The idea that the non-personal or neuter class is the default, unspecified one is further supported by an additional body of data not considered by D&K, namely the use of the neuter of the adjective as the adverb in Swedish and Danish. Nouns in these languages belong to one of two classes, usually labelled 'Common' and 'Neuter'. Adjectives and determiners in turn agree with the gender of the associated noun as exemplified by Swedish:

(21) a. en vacker sång
a beautiful.COM song(COM)

b. sången är vacker
song.DEF.COM is beautiful.COM

c. ett vackert landskap
a beautiful.NEUT landscape(NEUT)

d. lanskapet är vackert
landscape.DEF.NEUT is beautiful.NEUT

As with many languages there is no formal adverb forming suffix akin to English *ly* or French *-ment*, but rather the *-t* or neuter form of the adjective is used. Thus:

---

account here. On the distinction between semantic and non-semantic gender, see too Wechsler & Zlatić (2003: ch 8). They discuss the instance of Serbo-Croatian, where all co-ordinations involving a neuter resolve to the masculine plural, and have recourse to a distinction between s-gender (semantic gender) and e-gender (empty or expletive gender). On their account the neuter is an e-gender in both Icelandic and Serbo-Croatian (and presumably also Latin), but it is characterised as {} in Icelandic and {N} in Serbo-Croatian. They are then able to exclude the positively characterised Serbo-Croatian neuter from the operation of normal resolution rules. Although, as they note, the Serbo-Croatian pattern does not fall under the mechanism we propose here, nor under the D&K system, it is only for such languages that their special apparatus is required (Wechsler & Zlatić 2003: 184, note 86)). Moreover, it is worth noting that Wechsler & Zlatić's model shares the crucial properties of ours, namely that union is not the required set operation and that the feature definitions should be held constant across languages wherever possible. Moreover, our approach does not suffer from the charge of overgeneration levelled at D&K in Wechsler (in press).

(22) a. Barnet sjunger vackert / *vacker.
child.DEF.NEUT sings beautiful.NEUT beautiful.COM

b. Flickan sjunger vackert / *vacker.
girl.DEF.COM sings beautiful.NEUT beautiful.COM

It is also the *-t* form of the adjective that is used in constructions where the adjective modifies a clause:

(23) a. Att inte kunna gå skulle vara tråkigt.
INF NEG be able go would be boring.NEUT
'Not to be able to go would be boring.'

b. Det skulle vara tråkigt att inte kunna gå.
EXPL would be boring.NEUT INF NEG be able go
'It would be boring not to be able to go.'

What unites the impersonal and the adverbial contexts is that they are contexts of non-agreement. This in turn suggests, following our previous logic, that the *-t* form should be characterized as {}, while for the other class we suggest the characterization {C}.[12] What holds for Latin is then in part also true of Swedish or Danish. The feature basis for the two systems is different — {C} for Swedish/Danish and {M, F} for Latin — but in all three languages what is traditionally called the neuter comes out as {}, i.e. the default or unspecified form which is used in contexts where the remit of agreement rules does not run.

15.6 Diachrony

Another way to test the claims being made here is to look at the way gender systems can change and how these changes can be modelled. We will consider two such situations. The first and simpler concerns the historical origins of the Swedish and Danish system discussed above. This system evolved out of an earlier one in which there was a three way distinction between Masculine, Feminine and Neuter (just as there still is in Modern German, Icelandic, and Faroese) through the conflation of the Masculine and the Feminine into the Common gender. Since this change affects the masculine and feminine we would predict that there should be no essential change in the role and characterization of Neuter; it will continue to function as the default characterized as {}. This prediction is borne out as the examples already discussed from Icelandic and Swedish show.

[12] A natural test at this point would be to ask what form the adjective takes when it is predicated of conjoined nouns from different classes. Unfortunately, adjectives in the plural neutralise the distinction and there is only one form available.

By contrast the Romance development is rather more complex since it is precisely the neuter that is lost. In such a circumstance formerly neuter nouns are re-assigned to the masculine.[13] Since it is the neuter that disappears, the default form having the representation {} has to shift, and it moves to the masculine. Our new system is thus as hypothesised above for Hindi with masc = {} and fem = {F}. Predictably therefore the rules we have developed for dealing with Hindi apply to the choice of a non-agreeing form and also (interestingly since it was not like this in Latin cf note 4) to the gender clash situation.

Let us ask how these changes would be represented on the assumptions made by D&K? In the relevant respects the Latin system with its three genders and its use of the neuter in non-agreeing verb forms is parallel to Icelandic, so we may transpose D&K's characterization of Icelandic gender to Latin gender.[14] The Italian system by contrast shows the same properties as Hindi, with two genders, and with the form that is used for prototypically masculine nouns (i.e those referring to males) also showing up in non-agreement contexts. Thus, on D&K's assumptions, the change in question could be represented as in (24).

(24)	Latin		>	Italian
	Masc	{M}		{M}
	Fem	{F}		{}
	Neuter	{M, F}		–

Here, implausibly, the shift that is consequential upon the loss of the Latin neuter is the change of the feminine from {F} to {}, but as far as we know there is no evidence and no motivation for such a change. On the account we are offering, by contrast, the shift looks as in (25).

(25)	Latin		>	Italian
	Masc	{M}		{}
	Fem	{F}		{F}
	Neuter	{}		–

[13] There are some puzzling exceptions to this rule. Thus, Latin *mare* 'sea' is neuter while its Italian reflex *mare* is masculine and its French reflex *mer* is feminine; again Latin *lac* 'milk' is neuter, but with a masculine descendant in Italian *latte* and a feminine one in Spanish *leche*.

[14] As stated in note 7 the co-ordination facts are not the same in the two languages, but this is for the independent reason that Latin adopts a different strategy thereby forcing agreement even in co-ordination. Icelandic on the other hand treats co-ordination as a context where agreement fails and therefore the same non-agreeing form shows up as in those verb forms which are not able to agree with their structural subjects.

Now the loss of neuter, which must have happened for independent reasons, triggers a shift in the value of masculine. Instead of being simply the category for things that positively are marked as {M}, it is used both for masculine agreement and for the circumstances in which there is no item available to agree with such as past participles of unergative verbs (*Paola ha mangiato/*a* 'Paola has eaten) and occasional adverbs (e.g. *andare piano* 'to go gently' cf the argument in connection with Swedish adverbs above). In other words, there is independently a requirement on gender systems that there be an unmarked member of the opposition; if the unmarked member falls away, then that role is inherited by another term. The system that D&K propose, on the other hand, makes the change look as if it affects the feminine, when in fact the feminines remain by and large constant over time.[15]

Interesting confirmation of our analysis comes from a residue of the Latin neuter which survives in some Central and Southern Italian dialects. Such dialects have a contrast between nouns used in a mass and a count sense (Maiden 1997: 73-4), leading to pairs as in (26):

(26) a. *lu ferru* 'the iron (implement)' vs. *lo ferro* 'iron (substance)'
b. *lu friddu* 'the cold one' vs. *lo friddo* 'the cold' (opposite of 'heat')

The mass forms are the continuers of Latin neuters, but this distinction only exists for nouns and determiners and not for adjectives. Hence agreements in coordinated cases of the past participle in non-agreeing contexts have the masculine form. In other words, the unmarked member of the system here, as elsewhere, is the masculine, which therefore will be characterized as {}, while we shall have to postulate some other property — say {N} or {mass} — to characterize the residual and now marked neuters. This in turn argues against the original Latin neuter being characterized positively, as we would then not be able to account for the change of status of the neuter even in those Romance varieties where it does, residually, survive.[16]

15.7 Theoretical consequences

The data and analyses presented in this paper point in a number of interesting directions from a theoretical point of view.

[15]There are some changes from feminine to masculine but the motivation in such cases is different. For instance names of fruit trees were feminine in Latin but belonged to the predominantly masculine second declension, so that a shift in gender class for these items restored a missing link between form and content. Thus, Lat *pirus* 'pear tree' (f.)> Italian *pero* 'pear tree' (m.)

[16]On a similar development in Spanish, see Harris-Northall (2005).

a) The primes used in describing grammatical systems like person and gender should be held constant across languages.

b) The basis for such primes can be either semantic (as in the case of person) or structural (as in the case of gender).

c) There are, in different places in different languages, contexts in which agreement does not take place. We have called this 'non-agreement', and in such circumstances an unmarked or default form occurs.[17] We have proposed that cross-linguistically such default forms be characterized as {}.

d) The principles (a)–(c), which we believe to be empirically and methodologically well founded, when applied in the context of D&K's idea of set-valued features, have the consequence that union of the relevant sets is not always the right operator to invoke.

e) This in turn raises the question of whether intersection might also be necessary. At first sight the answer to this is yes. Recall that we argued for the three genders of Icelandic to be characterized respectively as {M}, {F}, {}. Intersecting {M} and {F} would then yield {}, which is the desired outcome in the case of agreement of an adjective with a co-ordination of a masculine and a feminine noun. Intersection, however, has the undesirable consequence that it is at odds with the basic architecture of LFG, which is built on the assumption that we always take the smallest set consistent with a given f-description. Moreover, as Mary Dalrymple has pointed out to us (p.c.), our analysis does not imply intersection in any cases except where the aim is to yield the empty set. Suppose instead that the node annotations for non-distributive features were reversed so that in place of (27a) we had (27b).

(27) a. NP $\longrightarrow$ NP CONJ NP

	NP	CONJ	NP
	$\downarrow\in\uparrow$		$\downarrow\in\uparrow$
	$(\downarrow\text{GEND}) \subseteq (\uparrow\text{GEND})$		$(\downarrow\text{GEND}) \subseteq (\uparrow\text{GEND})$

b. NP $\longrightarrow$ NP CONJ NP

	NP	CONJ	NP
	$\downarrow\in\uparrow$		$\downarrow\in\uparrow$
	$(\uparrow\text{GEND}) \subseteq (\downarrow\text{GEND})$		$(\uparrow\text{GEND}) \subseteq (\downarrow\text{GEND})$

This would work well in the case under discussion, since the empty set is the only one which is a subset of both {M} and {F}. However, as Mary points out, on standard LFG assumptions it would also yield {} even when like genders were co-ordinated, since the empty set is the

[17] For a similar concept see the discussion of 'neutral agreement' in Corbett (1991: Ch 7.2). As Grev Corbett points out (p.c.), conjoined defaults will also yield a default, so that in Icelandic, conjoined 'quirky' subjects also trigger default singular verb forms. This provides a further argument for {} as the representation of the default.

smallest set which is a subset of both {M} and {M}. This is clearly a very undesirable result.

Some other route to the null set therefore needs to be found. One such is proposed by Blevins (2000). This account is a lexeme-and-paradigm based solution which has entries expressed in a way very similar to that proposed by D&K though with values that are nearer to what is advocated here. The paradigm of the Icelandic adjective *svart* 'black', for example, would look as follows:

(28)

	Masculine	Feminine	Neuter
GENDER	{M}	{F}	{}

The matching of such entries to structures required in particular contexts depends on the Paradigmatic Blocking Principle formulated by Blevins as (29) (= his (19)):

(29) PARADIGMATIC BLOCKING PRINCIPLE
A structure S in a syntagmatic context C realises an entry E iff S is the minimal solution sanctioned by E in C that conflicts with each paradigmatic opponent of E.

This principle ensures that only if the context requires an entry with specifically defined values — for instance a masculine adjective to agree with one or more masculine nouns — is the paradigm of the lexeme in question searched for the appropriate form. Otherwise, the null features of the syntactic context — that is in LFG terms the f-structure representation — force the selection of the most unmarked lexical entry. Space does not permit us to go into further details (for which see Blevins 2000), but his model provides a formal mechanism which represents the unmarked member of a paradigm as {}, and which inserts the 'minimal solution' from the lexicon into a morphosyntactically defined context. It thus allows us to retain the desiderata of the original D&K proposal while admitting the data and solutions outlined in the present paper.

(f) Let us finally turn to another class of data which also constrain the use of union as the sole set operator. These are circumstances in which no resolution of the conflicting feature values is achievable within the language in question and therefore certain logically possible combinations have no acceptable expression. This phenomenon was called STALLING in Börjars & Vincent (2000). Corbett (1991: 269-70) gives the example of agreement with conjoined nouns in Tamil, which has a three-way, semantically based gender system: 'masculine (for nouns denoting male rationals), feminine (for female rationals) and neuter (for non-rationals)'. In the plural the distinction between masculine and feminine is neutralized so that there is a rational plural form and a non-rational one. Conjoined masculine and feminine nouns thus take rational plural agreement. Corbett goes on to note, however, that 'the rules do not allow for the combining of rationals and non-rationals; an alternative must be used such as "Raman came and the dog came" or "Raman came, with the dog".' The existence of this phenomenon provides a valuable yardstick by which to judge our conclusions so far. We have argued for the null set as the characterization of the unmarked form, which we have said arises in contexts where the normal processes of agreement do not reach, and we have shown how an account along the lines of Blevins (2000) can provide a solution to this problem without an undesirable extension of D&K's original model to include set intersection. What the data from stalling show is that in addition there must be the possiblity for the grammar of a natural language to include a statement to the effect that certain logically possible patterns must go unexpressed. Even where a default solution is available, in some contexts it is simply not used, and the grammar will somehow have to represent that fact. This is a syntactic analogue to morphological defectivity (Börjars, Vincent & Chapman 1997: 176, note 7; Morin 1996; Vincent 2003, 2005), and both are — from an acquisitional and conceptual view — equally puzzling. The highly frequent Italian verb *rimanere* 'to remain' has a past participle *rimasto*, but the somewhat rarer verb *permanere* 'to persist' simply has no past participle even though two perfectly good candidates exist, namely **permanuto* by the regular rule for that conjugation class and **permasto* by analogy with *rimasto*. Such gaps, when rule-governed forms are available, remain an unexplained conundrum within linguistic theory. Our discussion here shows that they can arise in syntax as well as morphology.

References

Andrews, Avery and Christopher D. Manning. 1999. *Complex predicates and information spreading in LFG*. Stanford, CA: CSLI Publications.

Arnott, David W. 1970. *The nominal and verbal systems of Fula*. Oxford: Clarendon Press.

Baerman, Matthew. 2004. Directionality and (un)natural classes in syncretism. *Language* 80(4):807–827.

Benveniste, Émile. 1946/1966. Structure des relations de personne dans le verbe. *Bulletin de la société linguistique de Paris* 43(1):21–12. Reprinted in E. Benveniste, 1966, Problèmes de linguistique générale 1, Paris, Gallimard, 225–236.

Blevins, James P. 2000. Markedness and agreement. *Transactions of the Philological Society* 98(2):233–262.

Börjars, Kersti and Nigel Vincent. 2000. Multiple case and the 'wimpiness' of morphology. In M. Butt and T. H. King, eds., *Argument Realization*, pages 13–37. Stanford, CA: CSLI Publications.

Börjars, Kersti, Nigel Vincent, and Carol Chapman. 1997. Paradigms, periphrases and pronominal inflection: a feature-based account. In *Yearbook of Morphology 1996*, pages 155–180.

Carstairs-McCarthy, Andrew. 1998. Comments on the paper by Noyer. In S. Lapointe, D. Brentari, and P. Farrell, eds., *Morphology and its relation to phonology and syntax*, pages 286–301. Stanford, CA: CSLI Publications.

Corbett, Greville G. 1991. *Gender*. Cambridge, UK: Cambridge University Press.

Corbett, Greville G. 2000. *Number*. Cambridge, UK: Cambridge University Press.

Corbett, Greville G. 2005. Suppletion in personal pronouns: Theory versus practice, and the place of reproducibility in typology. *Linguistic Typology* 9(1):1–23.

Cowper, Elizabeth. 2005. A note on number. *Linguistic Inquiry* 36(3):441–455.

Dalrymple, Mary and Ronald M. Kaplan. 2000. Feature indeterminacy and feature resolution. *Language* 76(4):759–98.

Harley, Heidi and Elizabeth Ritter. 2002. Person and number in pronouns: A feature geometric analysis. *Language* 78(3):482–526.

Harris-Northall, Ray. 2005. The count/non-count distinction in castilian: Evidence for its place and function in the medieval language. In R. Wright and P. Ricketts, eds., *Studies on Ibero-Romance linguistics dedicated to Ralph Penny*, pages 167–185. Newark, DE: Juan de la Cuesta.

Kachru, Yamuna. 1992. Hindi. In W. Bright, ed., *International Encyclopaedia of Linguistics*, vol. II, pages 123–127. Oxford & New York, NY: Oxford University Press.

Kaplan, Ronald M. and Joan Bresnan. 1982. Lexical-functional grammar: A formal system for grammatical representation. In J. Bresnan, ed., *The mental representation of grammatical relations*, pages 173–281. Cambridge, MA: The MIT Press.

Karttunen, Lauri. 1984. Features and values. In *Proceedings of the 10th International Conference on Computational Linguistics (COLING'84)*, pages 28–33. Stanford, CA.

Lapointe, Steven, Diane Brentari, and Patrick Farrell, eds. 1998. *Morphology and its relation to phonology and syntax*. Stanford, CA: CSLI Publications.

Lyons, John. 1968. *Introduction to theoretical linguistics*. Cambridge, UK: Cambridge University Press.

Maiden, Martin. 1997. Inflectional morphology of the noun and adjective. In M. Maiden and M. Parry, eds., *The dialects of Italy*, pages 68–74. London: Routledge.

Meillet, Antoine. 1919. Le genre grammatical et l'élimination de la flexion. *Scientia* 25(86, 6). Reprinted in A. Meillet, 1948, Linguistique historique et linguistique générale, Paris, Champion, 199–210.

Meillet, Antoine. 1931. Essai de chronologie des langues indo-européennes: La théorie du féminin. *Bulletin de la société linguistique de Paris* 32:1–28.

Meillet, Antoine. 1948. La catégorie du genre et les conceptions indo-européennes. In A. Meillet, ed., *Linguistique historique et linguistique générale*, pages 211–229. Paris: Champion.

Mohanan, Tara. 1994. *Argument structure in Hindi*. Stanford, CA: CSLI Publications.

Morin, Yves-Charles. 1996. The simplicity and acquisition of defective paradigms: A historical perspective. Paper presented at the 7th International Morphology Meeting, Vienna, 16-18 February 1996.

Noyer, Rolf. 1998. Impoverishment theory and morphosyntactic markedness. In S. Lapointe, D. Brentari, and P. Farrell, eds., *Morphology and its relation to phonology and syntax*, pages 264–285. Palo Alto, CA: CSLI Publications.

Nunberg, Geoffrey. 1993. Indexicality and deixis. *Linguistics and Philosophy* 16(1):1–43.

Pollard, Carl and Ivan Sag. 1994. *Head-driven Phrase Structure Grammar*. Chicago, IL & London: Chicago University Press.

Sadler, Louisa. 1999. Non-distributive features in Welsh co-ordination. In M. Butt and T. H. King, eds., *Proceedings of the International Lexical-Functional Grammar Conference 1999 (LFG'99)*. Manchester: CSLI Online Publications.

Sag, Ivan, Gerald Gazdar, Thomas Wasow, and Steven Weisler. 1985. Coordination and how to distinguish categories. *Natural Language and Linguistic Theory* 3:117–171.

Smith, Henry. 1996. *Restrictiveness in case theory*. Cambridge, UK: Cambridge University Press.

Trubetzkoy, Nikolai. 1939. *Grundzüge der Phonologie*, vol. 7. Prague: Travaux du Cercle Linguistique de Prague.

Vincent, Nigel. 2003. Defectiveness and the limits of the paradigm. Paper delivered at a workshop on paradigmatic irregularities, University of Manchester.

Vincent, Nigel. 2005. Suppletion and defectiveness: The verb 'to be' in Latin and Romance. Paper delivered at the Workshop on Morphological Interfaces, Schloss Freudental, 10–12 February 2005.

Wechsler, Stephen. in press. 'elsewhere' in gender resolution. In K. Hanson and S. Inkelas, eds., *The Nature of the Word — Essays in Honour of Paul Kiparsky*. Cambridge, MA: The MIT Press. To appear.

Wechsler, Stephen and Larisa Zlatić. 2003. *The Many Faces of Agreement*. Stanford, CA: CSLI Publications.

Part III

Meaning: Semantics and Information Structure

16

Input and Glue in OT-LFG*

AVERY D. ANDREWS

In glue logic (Dalrymple 1999, 2001, Asudeh 2004), LFG has found a reasonably stable but developing method for connecting syntactic structures to formal semantic intepretation. However current formulations of glue logic make the rather unsatisfactory move of divorcing grammatical features from any intrinsic connection with what are usually regarded as their meanings. Rather than directly connecting a grammatical feature attribute-value combination such as [NUM PL] to a meaning-constructor that produces a plurality meaning, current glue simply co-introduces a grammatical feature and any associated meaning constructors in the entries of all lexical items introducing the feature. Not only does this lose any account of important traditional observations about how morphology and semantics are related, it also creates an incompatibility with current OT-LFG, which depends on the idea of f-structures having intrinsic semantic content (Kuhn 2003, pp. 64–65,74). The lack of a means to connect OT-LFG to a formal semantics leaves it incomplete not only in comparison with its contemporary competitors, such as Categorial Grammar, HPSG, and conventional LFG, but even in its own terms, in that there are significant constraints which can't be formulated without explicit semantics, most noticeably scope-based ones such as Bresnan's (2001b) FAITH^{NEG}, or the 'respect-the-tree' constraints that one would plausibly use to ac-

* I would like to acknowledge the useful and instructive comments of an anonymous reviewer, which I have not always fully heeded. Errors are of course my own.

Architectures, Rules, and Preferences: Variations on Themes by Joan Bresnan.
Annie Zaenen, Jane Simpson, Tracy Holloway King,
Jane Grimshaw, Joan Maling, and Chris Manning, (eds.).

count for scoping modifier and light verb constructions such as those discussed by Andrews (1983), Alsina (1997), and Andrews and Manning (1999). In this paper I will develop a proposal to add glue-logic based semantic interpretation to OT-LFG, and show how it supports formulations of scope-based constraints, as well as a better account of the relationship between grammatical features and meanings. The basic idea is that an input will consist of two components, an f-description delimiting a range of potential candidate feature-structures, and an assembled collection of meaning-constructors determining a meaning. The f-description determines the candidate-set in the same way that an underspecified f-structure does in conventional OT-LFG,[1] while the meaning-constructors specify the semantic content that is associated with the structure. In conventional glue, a lexical item has a single lexical entry which specifies its morphological, c-structural, f-structure and semantic (glue) information all at once. For example, assuming a simple operator semantics for the past tense, the entry for a verb form such as *went* might be:

(1) *went*:V, PRED 'Go$_{motion}$<(↑SUBJ)>', TENSE PAST,
$\lambda x.go(x) \quad : \quad (\uparrow \text{SUBJ})_e \multimap \uparrow_t,$
$\lambda P.Past(P) \quad : \quad \uparrow_t \multimap \uparrow_t$

Here both the TENSE and PRED-features are stipulatively co-introduced with appropriate meaning-constructors, the format in which meaning-contributions are specified in glue semantics. Since this format is likely to be unfamiliar to many readers, I'll make some explanatory remarks, although space prohibits giving a thorough treatment (see Andrews (2004) for more details). In the constructors, to the left of the colon, on the 'meaning-side', appears a statement of the semantic contribution made by the item, in a lambda-calculus based format. On the right, on the 'glue side', appear the 'assembly instructions', which constrain the possibilities for combining the meaning given on the meaning-side with the meanings provided by other constructors. We will have a bit more to say about how assembly works later on. A treatment along the lines of (1) can't be used in OT-LFG, because we need to associate a feature-structure with a meaning independently of its morphological realization (at least if we want to apply the ideas of OT to any aspects of the latter). In order to produce an input that specifies a feature-structure and a meaning, but not a morphological realization, it is necessary to split the lexicon into two components, a 'Semantic

[1]There is no substantive consequence to using descriptions rather than structures, although they keep the formalism simpler and closer to the description-based tendency in LFG formalization.

Lexicon' connecting features to meaning, and a 'Morphological Lexicon' connecting features to pronunciations and other morphologically relevant information, such as inflectional diacritics (conjugation and declension classes). The Semantic Lexicon will then be used to generate the inputs, and the Morphological Lexicon to produce the alternative realizational candidates. In addition to allowing OT-LFG to have a formal semantics at all, the splitting of the lexicon will be seen to have some desirable properties in accounting for certain properties of the interface between semantics, syntax and morphology.

In the first section below, I will provide some general motivation for the split lexicon, and in the second, I will make a specific proposal for using it to generate inputs for OT-LFG. In the third section I will show how the proposal supports the formulation of scope-based constraints such as Bresnan's FAITH^{NEG} and other 'tree-respecting' constraints. This may seem like a somewhat disjointed collection of topics, but I believe that they pose the most important issues that an explicit account of the syntax-semantic relationship in OT-LFG has to deal with.

16.1 The Split Lexicon

LFG and virtually all other grammatical theories have a reasonable account of the one-to-many paradigmatic relations between features and their morphological spellings (alternations, usually conditioned but sometimes free), as well as many-to-one syntagmatic relations (fusional/portmanteau realizations). But LFG in its various forms has tended not to provide a clean and explicit account of the similar properties of the features-to-meaning relationship.

Consider for example the morphological and semantic properties of the verb *go*. We find what appears to be a single morphological unit, with conditioned alternate spellings /gow/, /wɛnt/, /gɔ/, but quite a wide range of meanings, partially dependent on what other morphological units *go* appears together with. Here some uses of the past tense form /wɛnt/ are illustrated:[2]

(2) a. Mary went to the store
 b. The milk went off
 c. The alarm went off
 d. Susan went off at the children about the state of the kitchen
 e. Mike went 'what on earth is going on here??'

[2] A rather puzzling gap in my dialect at least is *forego*, which appears to have the nonfinite past *foregone*, but note the finite **forewent* (which does however appear in the dictionary).

f. Joe went nuts

g. Fred underwent an unpleasant operation

The shared morphological irregularity is evidence that all of these forms involve some sort of common feature, but this clearly cannot be a meaning as such, since the meanings are quite different, ranging from somewhat related to apparently completely distinct.

In standard LFG, the meanings are coded into different PRED-features. The morphological relationships are not represented in any theoretically explicit way, although perhaps alluded to by using subscripted variants of 'Go' as the PRED-values, such as 'Go$_{say}$' for the *go* of (e). Lacking an explicit formal semantics, OT-LFG would appear to be stuck with the classic treatment, but with standard LFG plus glue-logic, things are potentially better. Most of the constraints involving the PRED-features can be taken over by the meaning-constructors (Completeness, Coherence, perhaps even Predicate Uniqueness (Dalrymple (2001, pg. 220), Kuhn 2001), which leaves the PRED-feature with no clear function other than to interface with the morphology.[3] If the PRED-feature is no longer tied to the meaning, it becomes possible for all of the uses of *go* to introduce the same PRED-feature. The morphology can then be arranged to spell this out in different ways in different situtations, such as /wɛnt/ when in combination with a [TENSE PAST] feature. However LFG+glue has a difficulty with another aspect of the feature-to-meaning interface, due to its failure to directly express generalizations relating the presence of features to the presence of meanings. Since features and meaning-constructors are stipulatively co-introduced in the lexical entries of words or formatives, it is an accident that there are any general correlations between the presence of features and the presence of meanings, independently of the morphological expressions of the features. Of course the association between features and meanings is not a simple one-to-one or even one-to-many relationship, as witnessed by phenomena such as *pluralia tanta* (non-compositional interpretation of lexical stems and the plural feature), the rise of 'preterite present' verbs (non-compositional interpretation of past tense verb forms as present time reference), and idiomatic/quirky case-marking. Nonetheless, the association of features with meanings is quite pervasive, and any theory which does not express it is severely deficient.

To address this issue, we need to do something to associate meaning-constructors in some direct way with the features that they tend to

[3]Therefore it might be better to replace PRED-features with FORM-features, although we won't do this here.

cooccur with. In a conventional LFG architecture, this could be accomplished with a fairly low level splitting of the lexicon whereby the meaning-constructors would be attached at a late stage in the construction of lexical entries, on the basis of what features those entries contained.[4] But this won't work for OT-LFG, where we need to attach meanings to structures which lack information about morphological realization. So we propose a deeper split, where the Semantic Lexicon is used to produce interpreted feature-structures, and the Morphological Lexicon to produce morphologically spelled-out realizations.

The Morphological Lexicon presents no novelties; it looks like a conventional LFG-lexicon, except for the removal of subcategorization information from the PRED-values. The Semantic Lexicon will however need some kind of new formal device, in order to connect features to meaning constructors. Since OT-LFG wants an underspecified feature-structure to constrain the possible morphosyntactic realizations of the meaning of an utterance, a reasonable thing to try for would be a device that co-generated f-descriptions (which can do the work of underspecified f-structures) with sets of meaning-constructors. Using a '$\Leftrightarrow$' connective to pair f-structural and semantic information with the former on the left and the latter on the right, we can formulate some sample Semantic Lexical Entries (SLEs) as follows, where $\mathcal{G}$ is a convenient abbreviation for a functional uncertainty expression ranging over the grammatical functions that may be universally used to express arguments:

(3) a. $(f\,\text{TENSE}) = \text{PAST} \;\Leftrightarrow\; \lambda P.Past(P) : f_t \multimap f_t$

b. $(f\,\text{PRED}) = \text{`Go'},\ (f\,\mathcal{G}) = g \;\Leftrightarrow\; \lambda x.Go(x) : g_e \multimap f_t$

In the next section we will see why only f-structure variables, not GF-application terms, appear on the glue-side of the meaning constructors.

Although we assume f-descriptions as the underlying formalization of the f-structural component of an SLE, it is sometimes more readable to present it as a structure; when we do this, we'll use the standard GF_i notation for underspecified term grammatical functions:

(4) a. $f{:}\begin{bmatrix}\text{TENSE} & \text{PAST}\end{bmatrix} \;\Leftrightarrow\; \lambda P.Past(P) : f_t \multimap f_t$

[4] A morphological component along the lines of Stump (2001), as adapted to LFG by Sadler and Nordlinger (2004, 2005) could also be adapted to co-introduce features with meaning-constructors in a reasonable way, although not as required by OT-LFG.

b. $f{:}\begin{bmatrix} \text{PRED} & \text{`Go'} \\ \text{GF}_1 & g{:}[\ \ ] \end{bmatrix} \Leftrightarrow \lambda x.Go(x) : g_e \multimap f_t$

But this should be understood as an informal version of a description-based formulation using functional uncertainty.

SLEs in the format of (3) clearly express facts about the connections between features and meanings. In the next section we will present a mechanism for using them to produce inputs which are in effect underspecified f-structures correlated with meanings; in the remainder of this section I will discuss how they accomodate two further aspects of the relationships between features and meanings.

One important complexity of this relationship is that it is possible for a feature to have multiple meanings; this is rather obviously the case for the PRED-features of lexical items such as *go*, and also occurs with grammatical features, such as for example semantic cases, which typically express similar but significantly different ranges of meanings in different languages. This can be straightforwardly accomodated by having multiple SLEs associating different meanings with the same feature. For example, alongside of SLE (3b) for the motional interpretation 'Go' feature, we can have (5) for the quotative:

(5) $(f\,\text{PRED}) = \text{`Go'},\ (f\,\mathcal{G}) = g,\ (f\,\mathcal{G}) = h$
$\Leftrightarrow \lambda y.\lambda x.Say(x, y) : h_t \multimap g_e \multimap f_t$

The second complexity I'll consider is non-compositional interpretation, whereby several different features are interpreted together way to give an 'idiomatic' meaning. Conventional LFG manages non-compositional interpretation in a somewhat clunky but workable way with FORM-features and constraining equations (Kaplan and Bresnan 1982, pp. 213–214), but I am aware of no proposals for it in standard OT-LFG. In our present approach, we can accomodate it by referring to multiple features in the SLE. For example, following Toivonen's (2001) treatment of verb-particle constructions, we can propose an entry such as this for one of the noncompositional interpretations of *go off*:

(6) $f{:}\begin{bmatrix} \text{PRED} & \text{`Go'} \\ \text{GF}_1 & g{:}[\ \ ] \\ \text{XCOMP} & [\text{PRED} \ \ \text{`Off'}] \end{bmatrix}$

$\Leftrightarrow \lambda x.become\_unpalatable(x) : g_e \multimap f_t$

This mechanism seems appropriate for what Egan (2004) describes as the 'CHUNKS' style of noncompositional interpretation, in which an arrangement of co-occurring overt lexical items seem to constitute a 'chunk' whose meaning must simply be listed. If the chunks are defined over f-structure, a certain amount of syntactic manipulation can also be accomodated, but not some of the more complex phenomena discussed in the literature, such as by Nunberg et al. (1994). However SLEs may well be sufficient to account for idioms whose interpretation is accomplished by strictly grammatical means.

An intriguing feature of the split lexicon is that it produces a certain amount of symmetry between the workings of spellout of features in overt morphology, and their semantic interpretation as meanings. Corresponding to the phenomenon of variant morphological realization of the same feature (such as for example *-īs*, *-ibus*, etc. expressing the feature combination [CASE DAT/ABL, NUM PL] in Latin), we have multiple meanings for the same feature, and corresponding to the phenomenon of portmanteau realization of multiple features as a single morphological form, we have noncompositional interpretation of multiple features as a single semantic unit. But there are major differences, most importantly, we'll see in the next section that 'semantic spellout' is resource-sensitive, while morphological spellout isn't. Freely variant realization furthermore seems to be rather less common than its interpretational counterpart, multiple meanings.

A final point is that the present proposal can be seen as an extension of the thesis of van der Beek and Bouma (2004) that the lexicon should be seen as a language-specific parameter to **Gen**. The morphological lexicon indeed does function here as a language-specific parameter to **Gen**, but the semantic lexicon goes a bit further in being a language-specific parameter to the specification of the input. Such a parameter could be seen as a substantial violation of the principle of the Richness of the Base, that all constraints on the input should be produced by constraint rankings, but this could be challenged on the basis that RotB was originally proposed as a principle to rule out language-particular but systematic constraints, such as morpheme structure constraints. The semantic lexicon on the other hand is unsystematic, and it is difficult to see how to get it to emerge from constraint interactions; the absence of semantic information from the output being not the least of the obstacles. In the next section we shall impose some further conditions on the input, which RotB can be claimed not to forbid on the basis that they are universal and unviolated, rather than unsystematic.

16.2 Generating and Using the Input

We now describe a process for generating the inputs. The basic idea is to take a multiset of SLEs, replace their variables, and see if the resulting f-description is satisfiable and meaning-constructors assemblable. If so, then the pair $<F, M>$ is an input, where F is the f-description and M the assembled set of meaning constructors. The principle of the Richness of the Base provides a reason to challenge the requirements of satisfiability and assembleability, but because these constraints are taken to be universal and unviolable, this objection is not compelling, and they make it easier to see how proposed analyses will behave. Perhaps future work will support a different view.

For a concrete illustration of how inputs are supposed to be produced, suppose we add to the Semantic Lexicon an entry for the proper name *Marvin*:

(7) $(f\,\text{PRED}) = \text{`Marvin'} \;\Leftrightarrow\; \textit{Marvin} : f_e$

If we leave the variables of the SLEs in (3) untouched and replace f with g in (7), we get the following f-description and meaning-constructor set:

(8) a. $(f\,\text{TENSE}) = \text{PAST}$
$(f\,\text{PRED}) = \text{`Go'}$
$(f\,\mathcal{G}) = g$
$(g\,\text{PRED}) = \text{`Marvin'}$

b. $\lambda P.\textit{Past}(P) \;:\; f_t \multimap f_t$
$\lambda x.\textit{Go}(x) \;:\; g_e \multimap f_t$
$\textit{Marvin} \;:\; g_e$

The f-description is satisfiable,[5] and the meaning-constructors are assembleable, so we have an input that is roughly equivalent to a conventional OT-LFG input such as:

$$(9)\quad \begin{bmatrix} \text{GF}_1 & \begin{bmatrix} \text{PRED} & \text{`Marvin'} \end{bmatrix} \\ \text{TENSE} & \text{PAST} \\ \text{PRED} & \text{`Go'} \end{bmatrix}$$

but with the significant improvement that it comes with a precisely specified formal semantic interpretation, *Past(go(Marvin))*, provided by the assembled meaning-constructors. Readers unfamiliar with glue might find it useful to have a brief discussion of what assembly involves. Most presentations of glue for LFG assemble meaning-constructors using deductions (see Asudeh (2004) for a very perspicuous presentation

[5]Satisfiability will be decideable as long as the SLEs don't introduce any inside-out functional uncertainty (Backofen 1994).

of this approach), but for beginners, and for our present purposes, I think it is more helpful to use a different technique, proof-nets, especially as developed by de Groote (1999) and Perrier (1999), and applied to LFG (with notational streamlining) by Andrews (2004).

The basic idea of proof-nets is to connect the literals (the f-structure designators, subscripted by their semantic type)[6] on the glue-side with links, in accord with certain constraints, which, among other things, specify how to construct a logical form for the whole utterance on the basis of the meaning-sides of the assembled constructors.

The first point is that the '$\multimap$' connective used on the glue-side is linear implication, a connective of linear logic,[7] so that the material to its left is called the antecedent of the formula it serves as connective of, the material to the right, the consequent. The technique of assembly used here, proof-nets, depends on the idea of connecting the literals (non-implicational (sub)formulas) of the glue-sides with links, subject to certain constraints. These literals consist of an f-structure designator, which can be intuitively thought of as a location to which content can be delivered, or from which it can be collected, and a type-symbol, initially assumed to be e or t as in basic categorial grammar, although what types are really necessary could be debated.

One important constraint on linking is a notion of polarity, whereby the formulas and subformulas have positive or negative polarity, and content is seen as flowing along the links from positive to negative. The relevant polarity rules are as follows:[8]

(10) a. The polarity of an entire glue-side is positive
b. The polarity of the antecedent of a positive implication is negative
c. The polarity of the consequent of a positive implication is positive

Given polarity, we can formulate some basic hookup rules as follows:

(11) a. Every negative literal must be connected to a single positive one with the same f-structure location and semantic type
b. Every positive literal but one (the final output) must be connected to a negative literal

[6] They're called 'literals' because, in the logical interpretation of the notation, they are atomic formulas and negations of atomic formulas, as discussed in Fry (1999).

[7] See Andrews (2004), Asudeh (2004), Dalrymple (2001), and the papers in Dalrymple (1999) for further discussion.

[8] Unfortunately, de Groote (1999) and Perrier (1999) adopt the opposite polarity convention; here I've followed some LFG work that uses polarity.

On the basis of (10,11), (12) is the only well-formed hookup for the constructors of (8):

(12) $\lambda P.Past(P) \; : \; f_t \multimap f_t$

$\lambda x.Go(x) \; : \; g_e \multimap f_t$

$Marvin \; : \; g_e$

To get a logical form for the sentence, we then assign content to all of the formulas and subformulas in accord with the following rules

(13) a. The content of an entire glue-side of a constructor is the meaning-side of that constructor.

b. The content of a positive literal is propagated along the link to a negative to which it is connected.

c. If a positive-polarity implication has content α, and its antecedent has content β, then the content of the consequent of the implication is $\alpha(\beta)$.

There are additional constraints and content-flow rules, as discussed in the present approach in Andrews (2004), but this will do for our present needs.

The mechanics of how assembly works is the reason why we want only f-structure variables, not functional application terms, to appear in the meaning-constructors, as mentioned in the discussion of (3). With only variables in the glue terms of the meaning-constructors, it will be the case that a subsititution of variables for variables determines a range of possibilities for semantic assembly, as illustrated for example in (8b). But if the glue term for *go* were for example $(f\,\text{SUBJ})_e \multimap f_t$, then some other technique would be needed to control assembly.

There are at least two constraints I will impose on this procedure. The first is that substitutions won't merge variables in a single meaning-constructor. For example we will not allow both f and g in (3b) to be replaced with f. The effect of this constraint is to thin out the candidate set a bit, and to require f-structure fusions between predicates and arguments, such as occur with complex predicates, to involve faithfulness violations. This may turn out not to be necessary, but I think it makes the system easier to work with.

The second, and more essential, constraint is that the f-descriptions must be able to be satisifed without merging atomic values. Suppose there were no such constraint. Then we could select the SLE (3a) for the past tense feature any number of times, stacking up the tense operator with no limit. It might be possible to avoid specific instances of this kind of problem with clever formulations of the associated meaning-constructors (perhaps the t type could be split into tensed and tenseless events, with *Past* mapping the latter onto the former), but we clearly want to prevent this for any feature without needing to engage in delicate engineering with the type system, which a general prohibition of atomic value merger achieves.

There are various ways in which the constraint could be implemented; an approach with properties that will be useful later is to assign to each meaning-constructor a unique index when it is selected from the lexicon, and mark this index on each of the atomic feature-values introduced in the f-descriptional component of the SLE-instance. The index will then keep features associated with different constructor instances from merging, thereby implementing the constraint. We will see later that the indexes and the relations they define will also be useful for stating constraints connecting constituent structure to semantic relationships.

A more general perspective on the non-merger constraint is that it is a kind of resource sensitivity (Asudeh 2004, pp. 87–99): under semantic interpretation, a feature can only be used once, and all features must be used. This is a major difference between the semantic interpretation of features and their morphological spellout, since the latter is clearly not resource-limited: one feature in the syntactic structure can be spelled out many times, or not at all.[9] This second form of resource-sensitivity in the grammar is inherently simpler than the one involved in semantic assembly, since it doesn't involve any assembly of the feature resources, merely their conversion into meaning-constructors.

But leaving this issue for now, we can state the proposed definition of how an arbitrary input is generated from the Semantic Lexicon as follows:

(14) 1. Select a multiset of Semantic Lexical Entries from the Semantic Lexicon.
2. Assign to each entry instance (in the multiset) a unique index, and attach that index to each atomic feature value in the f-descriptional component of the entry.
3. Rename the f-structure variables in each entry instance, subject to the constraint that distinct variables within an entry

[9]One might think that the use of glue-logic for semantic interpretation already captures the resource-based nature of the intepretation of features, but this isn't really the case in current LFG, since lexical entries merely stipulate the co-introduction of meaning-constructors together with feature values.

don't merge (of course, merger of variables across different entry instances is essential).

4. Check that the resulting f-description F is satisfiable.
5. Try to find a way to assemble the meaning-constructors to produce a meaning M.
6. If 4 and 5, succeed, return the resulting pair $<F, M>$ as an input.

Although this is a technique for defining a set, rather than a practical computational procecudure, it should be clear that it occasions no extraordinary computational difficulties for dealing with the set it defines. The two tasks we might wish to undertake are comprehension and generation. For comprehension, a method similar to the restriction-based analysis-by-description technique of Wedekind and Kaplan (1993) could be used, whereby features would be removed from a provisional copy of the structure as meaning-constructors were added. Production is a much deeper matter; it is in general quite unclear how we come up with coherent semantic representations which fulfill whatever purposes we might be attempting to achieve by producing language. But it should be obvious that formulating the problem as that of picking a set of SLEs from the Semantic Lexicon that can be assembled, and assembling them, adds no gratuitous difficulties. Although (14) will suffice as a basic input-generation scheme, there is at least one elaboration that would be worth considering. Dalrymple (2001, pp. 265–269) shows that in order to capture some results originally due to Kasper (1995), 'intersective' and 'gradable' adjectives will have to have two meaning-constructors, one specifying the distinctive meaning of the adjective, the other combining this intersectively with the meaning of the rest of the nominal that the adjective appears in. Having most adjectival lexical entries contain copies of the same 'intersective' meaning-constructor is rather awkward, and can be avoided by the suggestion of Asudeh and Crouch (2002) and Asudeh (2004) that certain meaning-constructors might be introduced by the phrase-structure rules. This possibility is not available in OT-LFG, but two alternatives are.

The first, and formally least problematic, is to suppose that there are constructors that introduce features that are frequently not spelled out in the morphology of languages. For example the constructor (14) below for intersective and gradable adjectives would be (Dalrymple 2001, pg. 266):

(15) $g \in (f\,\text{ADJUNCT}) \Leftrightarrow \lambda P.\lambda Q.\lambda x.P(x) \wedge Q(x)$:
$((g\,\text{VAR})_e \multimap g_t) \multimap ((f\,\text{VAR})_e \multimap (f\,\text{RESTR})_t) \multimap$
$(f\,\text{VAR})_e \multimap (f\,\text{RESTR})_t$

This could be co-introduced with a feature such as MOD +, which would be unexpressed in English, but perhaps spelled out as the *ezafet* of Farsi and similar languages. An alternative might be to have a small list of universally available meaning-constructors that aren't associated with atomic feature-values, but can be freely added to the multiset of SLEs selected by step 1 of (14). The nature of these freely available 'syncategorematic' constructors would have to be constrained in some manner in order to avoid undecidablility, a matter I won't go into there. Now that we have our inputs, the next step is to use them in OT-LFG. The main thing we have to do is modify the Restricted definition of **Gen** (Kuhn 2003, pg. 74), where Φ_{in} is the underspecified input f-structure:

(16) *Restricted definition of* ***Gen***:
$Gen_{G_{inviol}}(\Phi_{in}) = \{<T, \Phi'> \in L(G_{inviol}) \mid \Phi_{in} \sqsubseteq \Phi'$, where Φ' contains no more semantic information than $\Phi_{in}\}$

Obvously, we need to replace the reference to subsumption with satisfaction, since the input is now an f-description rather than an (underspecified) f-structure (although we will continue to represent it as Φ_{in}, due to the minimal substantive difference between f-descriptions and f-structures). A more obscure question is what to do about the requirement that the candidate not contain more semantic information than the input.

The problem is that it is not clear what it would mean for the candidate to contain additional semantic information: the semantic content of something is dependent on how it is used and reacted to by the agents that encounter it, as much as by its intrinsic properties. If the candidate is taken as a representation of what is to be performed, as opposed to how that is to be understood, how could it have additional semantic content?

I think this can be seen as an unclarity flowing from the absence of an explicit account of semantics in standard OT-LFG. Kuhn acknowledges 'some leeway' in the definition of semantic information, but suggests that it can be specified by 'declaring particular features or feature-combinations as contributors to semantic information' (2003, pp. 74–75). An obvious response, the one most in accord with the spirit of OT, would be to simply drop the requirement, and allow the candidates to freely overparse the input by adding additional features. There is however a difficulty with this in the present framework, which is that OT-LFG already includes a facility for overparsing in the mechanism for lexical insertion: not all the specifications in a (in our framework, morphological) lexical entry need to be used to build the candidate f-structure (Bresnan 2001b, Kuhn 2003, pp. 106–108). Perhaps the lexical overparsing mechanism could be retired in favor of a structural one, but to achieve maximum compatibility with previous work we will for the present retain the former, and prohibit the latter in order to avoid redundancy in the theory.

One way to do this would be to recognize a set of semantically interpretable feature-values as opposed to uninterpretable ones (mainly, if not exclusively, structural case), and require that the candidate not contain any interpretable features not required by the input. This would appear to be Kuhn's suggestion. A problem with it is that syntactic cases are frequently fully homophonous with semantic cases, indicating that they involve the same feature, which must therefore sometimes be semantically interpretable, and sometimes not. An easy solution to this would be to have a list of features which can fail to be semantically interpreted, and allow overparsing of the input only for features that appear on this list. This leads to the following Revised restricted definition of **Gen**:

(17) *Revised restricted definition of* ***Gen***:
$Gen_{G_{inviol}}(\Phi_{in}) = \{<T, \Phi'> >\in L(G_{inviol}) \mid \Phi'$ satisfies Φ_{in}, and all features in Φ' that aren't required to satisfy Φ_{in} are on the list of features that don't require a semantic interpretation}

Given (17), the rest of OT-LFG, including both the generation and evaluation of candidates, can now procede as conceived by Bresnan and formulated by Kuhn, except for the difference that we how have an explict level of compositional semantics that can be used for the formulation of constraints. Before developing this further, I'll make one final remark about the proposed form of the inputs, which is their lack of a 'semantic projection' as standardly assumed in LFG-with-glue (Dalrymple 2001, Asudeh 2004). As discussed in Andrews (2004), the semantic projection does not appear to have any clear function, so it is omitted here. Many earlier proposals for semantic interpretation in LFG made essential use of a semantic projection, such as those of Halvorsen (1983) and Wedekind and Kaplan (1993), but in glue-logic, the meanings are contained within the meaning-constructors, and all the syntax has to provide is locations where they can be connected to each other. F-structures can do this job as well as objects on a semantic projection, so the latter should be eliminated, unless some substantial arguments for it are produced.

16.3 Scope-based Constraints

We have now developed a conception of how formatives can contribute to meaning in OT-LFG; the other topic we will consider is how arrangement does, in the form of constraints on scope.

An example of such a constraint in current OT-LFG literature is Bresnan's (2001b) $\text{FAITH}^{\text{NEG}}$, which imposes restrictions on the ordering of negative markers and other material in the clause. For example the form *cannot* can have the *not* taking scope over the negative, while the separated *can not* requires the auxiliary to outscope the negative:

(18) a. John cannot leave
b. John can not leave

Bresnan proposes that the difference between (a) and (b) in (18) is the result of a structural difference, whereby in (a), the Neg is adjoined to the auxiliary's I, while for (b) it is to be adjoined to VP, yielding a structure such as this:

(19)

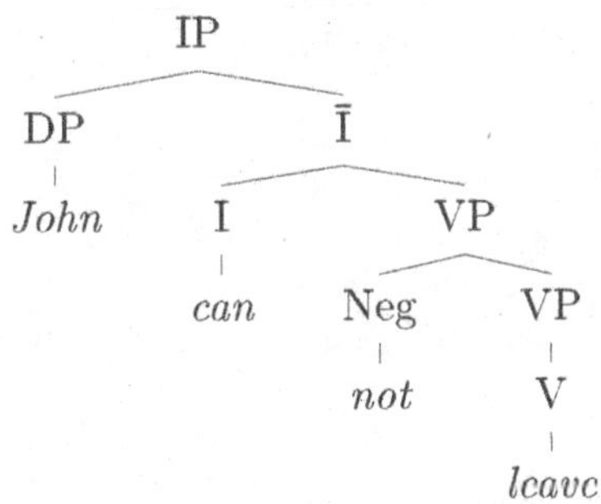

Inflectional and I-adjoined negatives appear to take scope with respect to the auxiliary in a manner determined by the lexical choice of the auxiliary; for *must not* and *mustn't* are interpreted as NEC NEG, while *need not* and *needn't* are NEG NEC (see de Haan (1997) for literature survey and discussion).

The VP-adjoined negative seems to scope consistently under the auxiliary in affirmative clauses. That a violable constraint is involved is indicated by the fact that a Q NEG POSS reading becomes possible in the stilted question form where the interrogative appears in C but the negative is left behind:[10]

(20) Can we not help them?

Another example is provided by the difference between:

[10] This sentence-form could perhaps be obtained in the registers where it occurs, by penalizing inflected negatives in C (or perhaps everywhere), although one would need to make sure that this constraint wouldn't cause trouble elsewhere.

(21) a. John often hasn't paid taxes

b. John hasn't often paid taxes

(a) might be true and (b) false, if John's taxable income is 0 half the time on average.

Other potential applications would include the 'tree-respecting' constraints governing complex predicates (Alsina 1997) and 'scoping modifiers' (Andrews 1983), and the iconic ordering of markers in 'case-stacking' (Dench and Evans 1988). Here, scope-sensitive constraints might be able to replace complex alternative mechanisms that have been proposed to account for the data, such as multiple projections for complex predicates and scoping modifiers (Andrews and Manning 1999, Andrews 2004).

To develop any such constraints, we need to establish some connections between scope in the semantic representation, and the arrangements of formatives in the syntactic tree, and proof-nets as presented above turn out to be quite useful for this. In this format, the two readings of (18) would be represented as the following patterns of linkage:

(22) a. *not* outscopes *can*:

$\lambda S.not(S) \;:\; f_t \multimap f_t$

$\lambda S.can(S) \;:\; f_t \multimap f_t$

$\lambda x.leave(x) \;:\; g_e \multimap f_t$

$John \;:\; g_e$

b. *can* outscopes *not*:

$\lambda S.not(S) \;:\; f_t \multimap f_t$

$\lambda S.can(S) \;:\; f_t \multimap f_t$

$\lambda x.leave(x) \;:\; g_e \multimap f_t$

$John \;:\; g_e$

There is a straightforward definition of relative scope in terms of hookup patterns: the lower scoped element has an output that feeds into the higher one. Complex configurations involving quantifiers and certain control verbs have rather complicated hookups with inputs and outputs being traded between pairs of constructors, but we can formulate a definition that copes with these complexities by means of a notion of 'Final Output', which amounts to the last positive polarity to be assigned by (22):

(23) a. The Final Output of an implication is the Final Output of its consequent.
b. The Final Output of a literal is the output of that literal.

We can now define 'Outscopes' recursively, with the aid of the concept 'Feeds Into':

(24) a. A meaning-constructor B Feeds Into a meaning-constructor A iff the final output of B is an input to A.
b. A meaning-constructor A Outscopes a meaning-constructor B if there is a sequence of meaning-constructors $C_1, \ldots, C_n$ such that $C_1 = A$, $C_n = B$, and for $1 \leq i < n-1$, C_i Feeds Into C_{i+1}.

The conditions on well-formed hookups will guarantee that Outscopes is an asymmetric relation (Lemma 4.6, de Groote 1999). This Outscopes relation will apply in the expected way to quantifiers, as well as negatives and similar $t \multimap t$ operators, and would also be relevant to formulating constraints to capturing the 'respect of the tree' and iconic ordering of stacked cases phenomena mentioned above.

The next thing we need is some way to connect c-structure nodes to meaning-constructors, so that the c-structural relations between the former can be linked to the Outscopes relations between the latter. This can be done with the aid of the indexes that were originally introduced to impose resource-sensitivity on feature-interpretation. We can provide that, when a candidate is checked for satisfying the input f-description, the feature-values in the candidate f-structure acquire the indexes from their correspondents in the input. The next step is to connect the features to c-structure nodes, in particular the preterminals where the feature are spelled out. In conventional LFG, there is no a formalized relationship between features and preterminals (although some principles, such as the Morphological Blocking Principle of Andrews (1990), do make at least implicit use of such a relation), but in OT-LFG there is, in the form of the 'λ-projection' introduced by Bresnan (2001a) to support OT-based accounts of morphosyntactic competition. The λ-projection assigns to each preterminal in the c-structure a mini-f-structure assembled on the basis of the f-description of the word introduced under this preterminal (Kuhn 2003, pp. 111–113). Therefore we can transmit indexes from the features of the full candidate f-structure to the matching ones in the mini-f-structures of the λ-projection, and thence, finally, to the preterminals themselves.

So now we have a many-to-many relationship between c-structure nodes and meaning-constructors, which can be used in various ways to formulate constraints. The approach I will take is to project c-structure relationships between preterminals back onto meaning-constructors, reminiscently of how the c-structure precedence relationships between c-structure nodes are projected back onto f-structures to give the 'f-precedence' relationship (Kaplan 1995, 21). The c-structure relationship I will use is the one called 'm-command': a node A m-commands node B iff every maximal category dominating A also dominates B. Note that the relation is formulated in such as way that a negative or negatives cliticized or otherwise adjoined to an auxiliary will not m-command it, and will therefore not be required to take scope over it by a constraint formulated in terms of m-command. We can project m-command back to the meaning-constructors with the following definition:

(25) Meaning-constructor M m-commands meaning-constructor N iff every preterminal linked to M m-commands every preterminal linked to N.

We can use this in a preliminary formulation of FAITH^{NEG}:

(26) If a negative meaning-constructor M Outscopes a meaning-constructor N, it must m-command N.

Various issues arise in refining this formulation.

Perhaps the most important one is how to count multiple violations of the constraint (Kuhn 2003, pp. 89–90). Kuhn proposes that constraints contain a special metavariable, $*$, such that one violation is accrued for each instantiation of the metavariable that falsifies the constraint (whereas there is no counting of the number of ways in which the so-instantiated constraint is violated). For a constraint such as (26), which regulates the relationships between two elements, I think the most plausible treatment would be to have two metavariables, one for each of the elements. As before, one violation mark will be accrued for each instantiation for which the constraint is not satisfied, but the instantiations will specify pairs of elements rather than singletons. Since the meaning-constructors are the unique elements being related, it seems best to take them to be the things represented by the metavariables, so we reformulate (26) as (27):

(27) If $*_1$ is a sentential negative meaning-constructor (one with glue term $f_t \multimap f_t$, which introduces the negation operator), and $*_2$ a meaning-constructor, and $*_1$ Outscopes $*_2$, then $*_1$ m-commands $*_2$.

(27) is formulated in terms of specifically negative constraints due to some puzzling data whereby adverbs can reorder freely around positive auxiliaries but not negative ones:

(28) a. John probably can file his return in June
b. John can probably file his return in June
c. John certainly must file his return by June 15
d. John must certainly file his return by June 15

If the auxiliary is negated, the scoping becomes rigid, with post-auxiliary orderings become unacceptable:[11]

(29) a. John probably can't file his return in June
b.*John can't probably file his return in June
c. John certainly mustn't file his return after June 15
d.*John mustn't certainly file his return after June 15

One puzzling aspect of this data is what the c-structures should be. The post-modal orderings can be treated as adjoined to the following VP (Sells 2001, 61), but the restrictive and well-motivated phrase-structure theory of Toivonen (2001) doesn't seem to provide an easy answer to the pre-modal ordering, since (a) adjunction to $\bar{\mathrm{I}}$ is not permitted by the theory (b) adjunction to I is not an option either, since the adverbs can be phrasal: *John almost certainly can('t) file in June.* So it remains to be seen how adverb-modal ordering facts will integrate with other scoping effects in the formulation of constraints related to (27). Nonetheless, it seems plausible that constraints connecting Outscopes to m-command would be effective in controlling the c-structure arrangements of scoping modifiers and light-verbs that appear in VP-nests, as argued by Alsina (1997) and (Manning 1992, Manning 1996).

16.4 Conclusion

We have shown how f-descriptions can be co-generated with sets of meaning-constructors, which can then be assembled, to provide OT-LFG with a form of input that has an explicitly specified semantic interpretation rather than merely an intuitively interpreted feature-structure. Such a proposal is particularly important for constraints related to scope, which is not well represented by LFG f-structures, due to their characteristically flat organization. But there are other kinds of meaning-related constraints that the proposal should be able to accomodate, such as for example Linking Theory constraints. It remains

[11] See Nilsen (2002) for discussion of a semantic constraint that would rule out (b, d) above, as long as something will fix the scope of the adverb below the negative.

to be seen whether these can be accomodated without further modifications of the approach.

References

Alsina, Alex. 1997. A theory of complex predicates: Evidence from causatives in Bantu and Romance. In A. Alsina, J. Bresnan, and P. Sells, eds., *Complex Predicates*, pages 203–246. Stanford, CA: CSLI Publications.

Alsina, Alex, Joan Bresnan, and Peter Sells, eds. 1997. *Complex Predicates*. Stanford, CA: CSLI Publications.

Andrews, Avery D. 1983. A note on the constituent structure of modifiers. *Linguistic Inquiry* 14:695–697.

Andrews, Avery D. 1990. Unification and morphological blocking. *Natural Language and Linguistic Theory* 8:507–557.

Andrews, Avery D. 2004. Glue logic vs. spreading architecture in LFG. In C. Mostovsky, ed., *Proceedings of the 2003 Conference of the Australian Linguistics Society (ALS2003)*. Newcastle, Australia. `http://www.newcastle.edu.au/school/-lang-media/news/als2003/proceedings.html`.

Andrews, Avery D. and Christopher D. Manning. 1999. *Complex Predicates and Information Spreading in LFG*. Stanford, CA: CSLI Publications.

Asudeh, Ash. 2004. *Resumption as Resource Management*. Ph.D. thesis, Stanford University.

Asudeh, Ash and Richard Crouch. 2002. Coordination and parallelism in glue semantics: Integrating discourse cohesion and the element constraint. In M. Butt and T. H. King, eds., *Proceedings of the International Lexical-Functional Grammar Conference 2002 (LFG'02)*, pages 19–39. Athens: CSLI Online Publications.

Backofen, Rolf. 1994. Regular path expressions in feature logic. *Journal of Symbolic Computation* 17(5):421–455.

Bresnan, Joan, ed. 1982. *The Mental Representation of Grammatical Relations*. Cambridge, MA: The MIT Press.

Bresnan, Joan. 2001a. Explaining morphosyntactic competition. In M. Baltin and C. Collins, eds., *Handbook of Contemporary Syntactic Theory*, pages 11–44. Oxford: Blackwell.

Bresnan, Joan. 2001b. *Lexical-Functional Syntax*. Oxford: Blackwell.

Dalrymple, Mary, ed. 1999. *Syntax and Semantics in Lexical Functional Grammar: The Resource-Logic Approach*. Cambridge, MA: The MIT Press.

Dalrymple, Mary. 2001. *Lexical Functional Grammar*, vol. 34 of *Syntax and Semantics*. New York, NY: Academic Press.

Dalrymple, Mary, Ronald M. Kaplan, John T. Maxwell III, and Annie Zaenen, eds. 1995. *Formal Issues in Lexical-Functional Grammar*. Stanford, CA: CSLI Publications.

de Groote, Philippe. 1999. An algebraic correctness criterion for intuitionistic multiplicative proof-nets. *Theoretical Computer Science* 224(1–2):115–134.

de Haan, Ferdinand. 1997. *The Interaction of Modality and Negation*. New York, NY & London: Garland.

Dench, Alan and Nicholas Evans. 1988. Multiple case-marking in Australian languages. *Australian Journal of Linguistics* 8(1):1–47.

Egan, Andy. 2004. Pretense for the complete idiom. Under review; `http://www.geocities.com/eganamit/papers.html`.

Fry, John. 1999. Proof nets and negative polarity licensing. In M. Dalrymple, ed., *Syntax and Semantics in Lexical Functional Grammar: The Resource-Logic Approach*, pages 91–116. Cambridge, MA: The MIT Press.

Halvorsen, Per-Kristian. 1983. Semantics for Lexical-Functional Grammar. *Linguistic Inquiry* 14(4):567–615.

Kaplan, Ronald M. 1995. The formal architecture of LFG. In M. Dalrymple, R. M. Kaplan, J. T. Maxwell III, and A. Zaenen, eds., *Formal Issues in Lexical-Functional Grammar*, pages 7–27. Stanford, CA: CSLI Publications.

Kaplan, Ronald M. and Joan Bresnan. 1982. Lexical-Functional Grammar: A formal system for grammatical representation. In J. Bresnan, ed., *The Mental Representation of Grammatical Relations*. Cambridge, MA: The MIT Press. Also in Dalrymple *et al.* (eds.) 1995; page number references to 1982 version.

Kasper, Robert T. 1995. Semantics of recursive modification. Handout for Head-driven Phrase Structure Grammar (HPSG) Workshop Tübingen, June 1995, `ftp://ling.ohio-state.edu/pub/-HPSG/Workshop.Tue.85/Kasper/`.

Kuhn, Jonas. 2001. Resource sensitivity in the syntax-semantics interface and the german split NP construction. In W. D. Meurers and T. Kiss, eds., *Constraint-Based Approaches to Germanic Syntax*. Stanford, CA: CSLI Publications.

Kuhn, Jonas. 2003. *Optimality-Theoretic Syntax – A Declarative Approach*. Stanford, CA: CSLI Publications.

Manning, Christopher D. 1992. Romance is so complex. Tech. Rep. CSLI-92-168, Stanford University, Stanford, CA.

Manning, Christopher D. 1996. Romance complex predicates: In defence of the right-branching structure. Paper presented at the 8th European Summer School on Logic, Language and Information (ESSLLI'96), Workshop on Surfaced-Base Syntax and Romance Languages.

Nilsen, Oystein. 2002. Domains for adverbs. Paper submitted to *Lingua* for special edition on adverbs, edited Artemis Alexiadou. `http://www.let.uu.nl/Eoystein.nilsen/personal/domains.pdf`.

Nunberg, Jeff, Ivan Sag, and Thomas Wasow. 1994. Idiom. *Language* 70(3):491–538.

Perrier, Guy. 1999. Labelled proof-nets for the syntax and semantics of natural languages. *Logic Journal of the IGPL* 7(5):629–655.

Sadler, Louisa and Rachel Nordlinger. 2004. Relating morphology to syntax. In L. Sadler and A. Spencer, eds., *Projecting Morphology*, pages 159–185. Stanford, CA: CSLI Publications.

Sadler, Louisa and Rachel Nordlinger. 2005. Case-stacking in realizational morphology. To appear in *Linguistics*.

Sadler, Louisa and Andrew Spencer. 2004. *Projecting Morphology*. Stanford, CA: CSLI Publications.

Sells, Peter. 2001. *Structure, Alignment and Optimality in Swedish*. Stanford, CA: CSLI Publications.

Stump, Gregory. 2001. *Inflectional Morphology: A Theory of Paradigm Structure*. Cambridge, UK: Cambridge University Press.

Toivonen, Ida. 2001. *The Syntax of Non-Projecting Words*. Ph.D. thesis, Stanford University.

van der Beek, Lenoor and Gerlof Bouma. 2004. The role of the lexicon in optimality-theoretic syntax. In M. Butt and T. H. King, eds., *Proceedings of the International Lexical-Functional Grammar Conference 2004 (LFG'04)*, pages 60–79. Christchurch: CSLI Online Publications.

Wedekind, Jürgen and Ronald M. Kaplan. 1993. Type-driven semantic interpretation of f-structures. In *Proceedings of the 6th Conference of the European Chapter of the Association for Computational Linguistics (EACL'93)*, pages 404–411. Utrecht.

17

The Role of Pronominal Suffixes in Punjabi

MIRIAM BUTT

17.1 Introduction

It is well known that languages will incorporate pronouns into the verbal system and that these incorporated pronouns tend to give rise to agreement inflection via intermediate stages of cliticization (e.g., Givón 1976).[1] It is less well known that such pronomimal clitics/suffixes are also part of the areal characteristic of South Asian languages. Despite a claim to this effect by Emeneau (1956) and isolated work on languages such as Kashmiri (e.g., Hook and Kaul 1987, Wali and Koul 1994, 1997, Bhatt 1999), Poguli (Hook 1987) or Maithili (Bickel, Bisang and Yādava 1999), pronominal cliticization is not generally considered to be a typical property of South Asian languages. Masica (1976, 1991), for example, makes no mention of pronominal incorporation in his highly regarded and extremely useful survey of South Asian languages.

This paper examines a hitherto puzzling phenomenon of pronominal suffixation/cliticization in Punjabi and relates it to a wider areal and crosslinguistic perspective on pronominal incorporation, particularly by taking into account the Lexical-Functional Grammar (LFG) perspective on the interaction between pronominal incorporation, agreement and discourse factors that has been developed over the years (e.g., Bres-

[1] See Corbett 1995 for a comprehensive overview of the issues.

Architectures, Rules, and Preferences: Variations on Themes by Joan Bresnan.
Annie Zaenen, Jane Simpson, Tracy Holloway King,
Jane Grimshaw, Joan Maling, and Chris Manning, (eds.).

nan and Mchombo 1987, Austin and Bresnan 1996, Bresnan 2001).[2] The analysis proposed here also builds on Butt and King's (1996, 1997) analysis of Urdu information structure. The Punjabi pronominal clitics are analyzed as being primarily motivated by discourse considerations in that they are used to background referential information. This analysis also picks up on Givón's (1976) original idea that one source for pronominal agreement is the *after-thought* structure by which known topics/information are repeated via right dislocation.[3]

17.2 Some Initial Data

In this section, I introduce the relevant Punjabi data as it was introduced to me, namely, as a puzzle seemingly without a coherent or natural explanation. Before proceeding on to the data, a few general remarks on Punjabi and South Asian languages in general are in order.

Punjabi is an Indo-Aryan language spoken mainly in Pakistan and North India (in the Punjab provinces). There are several different dialects within Punjabi, so the situation is potentially quite complicated. The data reported on here have been provided by speakers from Lahore, Pakistan. Punjabi is closely related to Urdu/Hindi. Some differences between the two languages are that Punjabi is a tone language while Urdu/Hindi is not (only some of the examples include tonal markings—this is due to differing transcription practices in the sources), and that

[2]At this point, I would like to thank Joan Bresnan for the linguistic guidance she has provided me with over the years. I first encountered Joan in the late 1980s at a conference in Worcester, Massachusetts just after I had graduated from college and when I already knew that I would be going to Stanford as a graduate student. The conference presented "Women at the Frontiers of Science" and I found Joan's talk on linking galvanizing. I knew then and there that I had made the right decision to go to Stanford. While life as a graduate student was often frustrating, it was more than compensated by those days when one had been in Joan's office, presented one's ideas more or less incoherently, had them impatiently sorted through, partly destroyed and then shown how to make a watertight case for what one thought the analysis should be. On those days I knew that **this** is what linguistics was about — sorting through data and arguments to come to an analysis that rang so true it could not but stand the test of time, as has the bulk of Joan's work over the decades.

[3]Further thanks for feedback and comments are due to an anonymous reviewer, Elena Bashir, Balthasar Bickel, Dan Everett, Peter Hook and the audiences at the workshop on *Case, Valency and Transitivity* held in June 2003 in Nijmegen as well as the workshop on *Evolution of Syntactic Relations* held in February 2004 as part of the annual DGfS (German Linguistics Society) meeting. In particular, I would like to thank Helen de Hoop and Christan Lehman and Stavros Skopeteas for organizing these workshops, respectively, and inviting me to participate in them. Nayyara Karamat not only checked the data presented in this paper, but also came up with additional data and generalizations that shed further light on the underlying Punjabi system. I would like to thank her for her valuable linguistic insights.

the split-ergative pattern in Punjabi is confined to third person subject pronouns and nouns, whereas it encompasses all subject pronouns and nouns in Urdu/Hindi.

South Asian languages include the Indo-Aryan, Dravidian and Tibeto-Burman language families. These languages are genetically unrelated but have entered into a regional *Sprachbund* or linguistic area (Masica 1976). Some (relevant) well known areal characteristics are: non-nominative subjects, split-ergativity, complex predicates, object agreement and rampant pro-drop.

In investigating the nature of complex predicates and linking in Punjabi, Akhtar (1997, 1999) came across some verbal morphology that he could not place and finally categorized as "argument replacing morphemes", because these morphemes seem to cooccur with pro-drop in Punjabi. Some examples are shown in (1).

(1) a. xɑt lɪkʰɪa=**i**?
letter.M.Sg.Nom write.Past=2.Sg
Have you written the letter?' (Akhtar 1999:282) Punjabi

b. jɑndra kʰʊl gɪ-a=**je**?
lock.M.Sg.Nom open go-Past.3.Sg=2.Pl
'Has the lock been opened by you?' (Akhtar 1999:284) Punjabi

c. pʊtɑr=ne koṭiã pejɪã=**je**
son.M=Erg jumper.M.Pl.Nom send-Past.M.Pl=2.Pl
'(Your) son has sent jumpers for you (plural).'
(Akhtar 1999:284) Punjabi

d. fɑwɑd=ne dɪtti–**s(u)**
Fawad.M.Sg=Erg give.Past.F.Sg=3.Sg
'Fawad gave this to her.' (Akhtar 1997:3) Punjabi

e. xɑt lɪkʰia=**ne**
letter.M.Sg.Nom write.Past=3.Pl
'They wrote a letter.' (Akhtar 1999:283) Punjabi

Akhtar observes that these morphemes are not restricted to core arguments, but can also refer to adjuncts ((1b)) or beneficiaries not specified by the subcategorization frame of the verb ((1c)). Furthermore, they do not account for all of the arguments that are dropped ((1d)). Data from the interaction with negation suggests that these morphemes are in fact clitics which cannot form a prosodic word on their own, but must cliticize onto a preceding prosodic word. This is demonstrated by a comparison of the data in (1d) and (2), which show that the *=s(u)* can either appear on the main verb, or on the negative element preceding the main verb.

(2) fawad=ne nɛ=**s(u)** dɪtti
Fawad.M.Sg=Erg not=3.Sg give.Past.F.Sg
'Fawad did not give this to her.' (Akhtar 1997:7) Punjabi

There seems to be no clear reason for the existence of these clitics. That is, none of the generally established ideas on the close link between pro-drop and agreement, pro-drop and pronominal incorporation, and case and agreement can account for the distribution of the Punjabi pronominal clitics (see section 17.3). Furthermore, while the generalizations with respect to pro-drop, agreement and case assignment are entirely parallel in Punjabi and Urdu/Hindi, Punjabi sports a set of these pronominal clitics, but Urdu/Hindi does not. It is therefore not clear what these pronominal clitics in Punjabi really are good for.

Very little information about the clitics is available in the literature. They have gone unreported in modern descriptions of Punjabi (e.g., Bhatia's 1993 reference grammar or Masica's 1991 overview of the Indo-Aryan languages).[4] One has to reach back to Bailey's (1912:82–86) grammar of Punjabi before coming upon an in-depth discussion of pronominal clitics in standard Punjabi. Before moving on to discuss the relevant data, I briefly summarize the currently available analyses as to pro-drop, agreement and case which were alluded to above, and then introduce the basic LFG approach employed in this paper.

17.3 Pro-Drop, Agreement, Case and Pronominal Incorporation

In a classic paper, Rizzi (1986) suggested a correlation between pro-drop and rich verb agreement. This correlation was shown not to hold exactly, but the general idea that agreement licenses pro-drop is still generally accepted in the literature. For example, Alexiadou and Anagnostopoulou (1998) link pro-drop to the feature [+D], which allows agreement affixes to have independent entries in the lexicon. The postulation of independent lexical entries for agreement affixes is correlated with the idea that these affixes stem from pronominal incorporation, and therefore had been associated with independent lexical entries in the past.

The original pro-drop proposal was made for Italian, a language in which only subjects can be dropped. Given subject agreement on verbs, the correlation is therefore clear. However, the correlation cannot be

[4] Bhaṭia (1993:228–229) does report on a secondary pronoun system of clitics, but only for the Shahpur Doabi dialect of Punjabi (spoken in India, east of Amritsar). The forms he gives are *=s*, *=m*, *=se*, *=ẽ*, *=ũ*, *=ne* and *=r*. He denies the existence of pronominal clitics in the standard Majhi form of Punjabi, spoken in Lahore and Amritsar.

upheld for South Asian languages in even a weak form. Consider the Punjabi data in (3), which is representative of the broader South Asian pattern (see (4)–(6)). Generally, every single argument in the sentence can be dropped. In (3a), the object agreement would only license the dropping of the object.[5] In (3b), no argument is licensed to be dropped. Nevertheless, all of the arguments can be omitted and no correlation between agreement and pro-drop can be established.

(3) a. o=ne nadya=nũ roṭi dıtti?
Pron.3=Erg Nadya.F=Dat bread.F.Sg.Nom give.Perf.F.Sg
'Did he give Nadya (some) food?' Punjabi
ji, dıtti
yes.Polite give.Perf.F.Sg
'Yes, gave.' Punjabi

b. o=ne nadya=nũ vek^{h}ea?
Pron.3=Erg Nadya.F=Acc see.Perf.M.Sg
'Did he see Nayda?' Punjabi
ji, vek^{h}ea
yes.Polite see.Perf.M.Sg
'Yes, saw.' Punjabi

(4) ji, di-ya
yes.Polite give-Perf.M.Sg
'Yes, gave.' Urdu

(5) ho, dila
yes.Polite give.Perf.M.Sg
'Yes, gave.' Marathi

(6) a. hæ̃, di-e-tʃ^{h}-e
yes give-Part-Perf-3
'Yes, (he) gave. Bengali

b. hæ̃, di-e-tʃ^{h}-i
yes give-Part-Perf-1 Bengali
'Yes, (I) gave.

Punjabi, Urdu and Marathi are ergative languages, Bengali is not. In addition, Bengali has lost any form of gender agreement. Despite

[5]In both Urdu/Hindi and Punjabi, the verb agrees with the nominative (unmarked) argument. If the subject is nominative, the verb agrees with the subject. But if the subject is ergative, as in (3), then object agreement becomes possible as in (3a). If neither the subject nor the object are nominative/unmarked, then the verb shows default masculine singular agreement, as in (3b) (for Hindi, see Mohanan 1994; for Punjabi, see Bailey 1912, Bhatia 1993). Punjabi shows an additional ergativity split according to person (only the 3rd person is marked overtly with an ergative case clitic) that is irrelevant for the purposes of this paper.

these differences in the case and agreement systems of the languages, the possibilities for pro-drop (namely, everything) are the same. No immediate connection between pro-drop and agreement can therefore be established for Punjabi and South Asian languages in general. But how about a more complex variant that was also part of Rizzi's original proposal? The more complex formulation includes a role for abstract case in that the licensing of *pro* is considered to be coextensive with nominative Case assignment (Rizzi 1986), which in turn is related to agreement. With the advent of Agr nodes, structural Case and verbal agreement could be intimately connected because structural Case could be assigned via Agr positions (see Mahajan 1989, 1992 for a detailed proposal for Hindi in particular). In a more modern proposal, Alexiadou and Anagnostopoulou (1998), for example, formulate conditions on EPP checking as parasitic on Case checking.

However, this more complex correlation between agreement and case and the licensing of arguments cannot be upheld either (Butt and King 1997). The monologue in (7) is taken from the Hindi movie *Dilwale Dulhania Le Jayenge.* The current topic in (7a) has nominative case ('they') and refers to some pigeons the narrator has been observing in Trafalgar Square. The verbal morphology agrees with this nominative subject.

(7) a. [**ye**]$_T$ b^{h}i mer-i=ki tərã **hẽ**
Pron.3 also I.Gen-F.Sg=Gen.F.Sg like be.Pres.Pl
'They$_{topic}$ are also like me.' Hindi

b. jahã **dana** dek^h-**a**
where seed.M.Sg.Nom see-Perf.M.Sg
'where (they$_{cont.topic}$) see a seed' Hindi

c. ʊdɑr ga-**ye** or peṭ bɑr kɑr
there go-Perf.M.Pl and stomach.M.Sg.Nom fill having
ʊṛ ga-**ye**
rise go-Perf.M.Pl
'there (they$_{cont.topic}$) go and having filled (their) stomach (they$_{cont.topic}$) fly away.' Hindi

The narration is continued in (7b), with the current, continued topic dropped. In (7c), the continuing topic would be realized as a nominative subject and the verb shows agreement with this unrealized subject. However, in (7b), the overt realization of 'they'(=pigeons) would be ergative and the verb does not show subject agreement, but object agreement. Thus, the verbal morphology is not licensing pro-drop, nor is structural nominative Case being licensed via any sort of agreement. Note that while I have used a Hindi example here, the corresponding

Punjabi monolog would be structurally exactly parallel to the Hindi one in (7). The correlation between case, agreement and pro-drop therefore cannot be used to account for pro-drop in Hindi and in South Asian languages in general (see Butt and King 1997 for more discussion).

A somewhat different perspective on pro-drop has recently been proposed by Neeleman and Szendrői (2005), who argue that attempts at associating pro-drop directly with licensing via case and/or agreement represents a misunderstanding of the phenomenon. They instead seek to explain the presence of pro-drop via heuristics for the spell-out of the morphological features associated with the pronominal paradigm of a language. By invoking Kiparsky's (1973) Elsewhere Principle, they are able ensure that some feature bundles may be realized as a zero spell-out of the pronoun, thus giving rise to what looks like pro-drop. Their focus on the pronominal paradigm of a language predicts that rampant pro-drop as in South Asian languages or Chinese, another well known case which does not allow for an direct association of case, agreement and pro-drop (Huang 1984), can only occur if: 1) case morphology in the pronominal paradigm is agglutinating (i.e., as in Turkish); 2) the pronominal forms do not vary for case (i.e., as in Chinese or Japanese). Neeleman and Szendrői (2005) analyze the pronominal paradigm of Urdu/Hindi as fundamentally agglutinative for case and so the possibility of pro-drop in Urdu/Hindi follows from their account. If one accepts their argumentation for Urdu/Hindi, then, given that the pronominal paradigms of Urdu/Hindi and Punjabi are fairly close (see Butt and King 2005 for an in-depth discussion of case and the Urdu/Hindi pronominal paradigm), their analysis can also be extended to Punjabi. The core Punjabi pronominal paradigm is shown in (8).

(8)

	NOM	ERG	ACC/DAT	GEN
1.Sg	mɛ̃	mɛ̃	mɛ=nũ	mer-a/i/e
1.Pl	asĩ	asã	sa=nũ	saḍḍ-a/i/e
2.Sg/Disresp.	tũ	tũ	tɛ=nũ	ter-a/i/e
2.Pl/Resp.	tusĩ	tusã	tuha=nũ	tʊhaḍḍ-a/i/e
3.Prox.Sg	e	es=ne	es/e=nũ	es/e=d-a/i/e
3.Prox.Pl	e	enã=ne	enã=nũ	enã=d-a/i/e
3.Dist.Sg	o	os=ne	os/o=nũ	os/o=d-a/i/e
3.Dist.Pl	o	onã=ne	onã=nũ	onã=d-a/i/e

However, the Punjabi data presented in section 17.2 falls out of the scope of Neeleman and Szendrői's (2005) account. For one, they do not address the interaction of pronominal cliticization with pro-drop. For another, they explicitly state that adjuncts are not assumed to be part of the phenomenon, but as the Punjabi data in (1) showed, adjuncts and arguments seem to behave alike with respect to pronominal cliticization and pro-drop.

Another interesting proposal with respect to pro-drop and pronominal incorporation goes back to Jelinek (1984), who suggested that prononimal incorporation into the agreement system gives rise to the ability of agreement morphology to satisfy a predicate's argument slots. The idea is that the agreement morphology retains the ability of the former pronouns to satisfy the predicate's argument slots. Overt NPs, which are in a sense "doubling" the pronouns/agreement morphology, are analyzed as adjuncts. Under this analysis, missing or omitted NPs are therefore not a case of pro-drop, but represent situations in which syntactically unnecessary adjuncts are not expressed (the adjuncts may be expressed for semantic or discourse purposes). This analysis is particularly attractive for languages with relatively free word order: if the NPs are actually adjuncts, then their relatively free distribution in the clause follows automatically.

However, Austin and Bresnan (1996) show that despite the initial attractiveness of this proposal, it need not be right for all languages. They focus particularly on Warlpiri and Jiwarli and show that despite a wide spread acceptance of Jelinek's initial proposal for Australian languages, the correlation does not hold up in light of a closer look at the facts. It should also be clear from the South Asian facts discussed so far that the pronominal argument hypothesis cannot account for all of the Punjabi data.

17.4 The LFG Perspective

Austin and Bresnan (1996) propose an alternative analysis that is embedded in a more differentiated view of the interaction between phrase structure properties, predicate-argument structure and discourse considerations (see Bresnan 2001 for a comprehensive discussion). Free word order characteristics are taken to be independent of whether or not incorporated pronouns can satisfy the argument slots of a predicate. The synchronic distribution of incorporated or bound pronouns vs. independent NPs is considered to be governed by discourse factors such as topic or focus. As per Givón's (1976) original idea, verbal agreement morphology in languages can be derived from initial pronominal incorporation, which in turn is fed by the discourse backgrounding of full pronouns. In particular, several stages of historical change can be differentiated and modeled quite cleanly.

Full pronouns, like full NPs, are subject to word order variation due to discourse factors: topicalization, afterthought backgrounding, etc. When pronouns are positioned immediately adjacent to the verb, cliticization often results because of the generally unstressed nature of pronouns, compounded with discourse considerations such as de-emphasis, etc. Cliticization in turn can give rise to incorporation, which feeds into a potential reanalysis of these pronouns as "mere" agreement inflections.

The reanalysis of a pronoun with referential force into agreement morphology entails the loss of the referential contribution of the pronoun. A logical step on the path of this reanalysis is that the referential contribution of the pronoun be realized *optionally* before being lost altogether. And indeed, the full range of possibilities have been attested crosslinguistically.

In Navajo, for example, the incorporated pronouns satisfy the argument positions of the verb, as well as indicating topicality (Bresnan 2001). In Warlpiri and Jiwarli, on the other hand, the former incorporated pronominals no longer have a function that goes beyond verb agreement. In Chicheŵa, the subject and object markers can both be shown to be descended from former incorporated pronouns. However, there is an asymmetry between the behavior of the subject vs. the object marker. The subject marker is functionally ambiguous in that it can either serve as a "mere" agreement marker, or as a referential predicate that satisfies the verb's argument slot. The object marker, on the other hand, is always referential and cannot be used in conjuction with an overt NP object. The presence of an NP that is coreferential with the object marker triggers an adjunct interpretation of that NP. The distribution of object marker vs. object NP is governed by the discourse factors of topicality or contrastive focus (Bresnan and Mchombo 1987, Bresnan 2001).

An example illustrating the functional ambiguity of the subject marker in Chicheŵa is shown in (9). In (9a), there is an NP subject, as well as an agreement marker (10.SM, where SM stands for subject marker). In (9b), there is no subject NP and as Chicheŵa is not a rampant pro-drop language like Punjabi or Urdu/Hindi, the subject marker must be supplying the referential argument that satisfies the predicate's argument slot.

(9) a. Njûchi zi-ná-lúm-a a-lenje
10.bee 10.SM-Past-bite-FV 2-hunter
'The bees bit the hunters.' Chicheŵa

b. Zi-ná-lúm-a a-lenje
10.SM-Past-bite-FV 2-hunter
'They bit the hunters.' Chichewâ

Under Bresnan and Mchombo's (1987) analysis, the subject marker contributes subject agreement features to the functional analysis of the clause. This is shown in (10). The subject marker also optionally contributes a PRED 'PRO'. When there is an overt NP subject, this option is not realized. This is because PRED features in LFG are not subject to unification and so the PRED feature contributed by the subject marker would clash with the PRED supplied by the full NP. The referential option is therefore only realized when there is no overt NP subject.

(10)

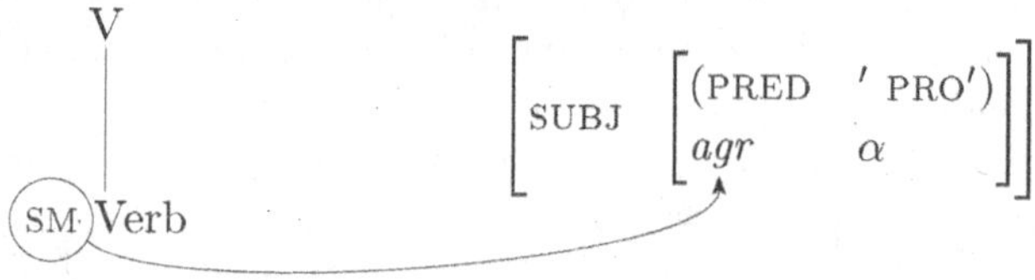

LFG's architecture thus allows an exact modeling of each of the synchronic stages in the diachronic process of the reanalysis of a pronoun into an agreement marker. It implicates discourse factors in the reanalysis, but separates these out from the language particular realization of word order. Neither is structural case necessarily implicated in the formation of new agreement morphemes (in contrast to some of the proposals surveyed in the previous section, for example). The established LFG perspective on pronominal cliticization and pronominal incorporation therefore emerges as a promising framework for developing an understanding of the pronominal clitics found in Punjabi.

The next sections present a closer look at the data available with respect to Punjabi pronominal clitics. Section 17.5 seeks to establish that these clitics indeed show some pronominal behavior. Evidence in favor of a pronominal status of these clitics is adduced from both synchronic patterns of distribution and diachronic data. Section 17.6 discusses data which point to an analysis by which discourse backgrounding has led to pronominal cliticization and, in some cases, an absorption of the former pronouns into the verbal paradigm as agreement morphemes.

17.5 Pronominal Clitics in Punjabi

This section takes a closer look at the form of the clitics and their synchronic distribution. The synchronic data in section 17.5.1 reveal some pronominal behaviour, as well as indications that a progressive reanalysis into the verbal paradigm may indeed be under way. The diachronic and comparative evidence discussed in section 17.5.2 serves to strengthen the synchronic evidence.

17.5.1 Synchronic Form and Distribution

Akhtar (1997, 1999) describes four suffixes/clitics for Punjabi ((1)). The dialect he describes is spoken in the Gujrat District of the Punjab in Pakistan. He had his data confirmed by 3 native speakers from Lahore, Pakistan where standard Punjabi is spoken. The *-u* of the *-su* form is optional. Akhtar claims that the *su* form is predominantly used in Lahore, the *-s* form in Gujrat. Generally, though, the *-s* seems more common.

(11)

Form	Person/Number	Tense
=i	2.Sg	
=je	2.Pl	
=s(u)	3.Sg	
=ne	3.Pl	Past

Bailey (1912:82–86) in his grammar of Punjabi includes an explicit discussion of "pronominal suffixes" and provides the forms in (12).

(12)

	Number	
Person	Singular	Plural
2	-ũ, -i, -a, -ĩ	je
3	s-, -sũ	ne, ṇe

The older data from Bailey and the newer data provided by Akhtar show some overlap, as well as some differences. It seems clear that there are no first person pronoun clitics in Punjabi. But where Akhtar provides only one form for the 2nd person singular, Bailey has four. Some checking in Lahore yielded the information that the forms *-a* and *-ũ* are still attested, though infrequent.[6] In general the use of these pronominal clitics tends to be associated with older speakers and the Punjabi spoken in rural villages.[7]

Bailey further provides some nasalized and retroflex forms and notes that the *ne* is used when it forms a separate "word". Bailey also sees the *je* and *su* forms as acting non-affixally in certain contexts, but the others as generally acting affixallly, thus indicating a possible progressive process of cliticization. The retroflex and nasalized forms no longer seem to be part of the Punjabi reported on here. An exception is the

[6]These and other supplementary data were provided by Nayyara Karamat, who lives in Lahore and comes from a Punjabi speaking family originally from Hafizabad.

[7]Thanks to Elena Bashir and Nayyara Karamat for this information.

future tense, where the pronominal clitics appear to be infixed (used as affixes under Bailey's analysis), as shown in (13).

(13) a. mẽ mar-ũ-g-a
I beat-2.Sg-Fut-M.Sg
'I will beat you.' (Bailey 1912:82) Punjabi

b. mẽ tənũ mar-ã-g-a
I you.Acc beat-1.Sg-Fut-M.Sg
'I will beat you.' (Bailey 1912:82) Punjabi

c. *mẽ tənũ mar-ũ-g-a
I you.Acc beat-2.Sg-Fut-M.Sg
'I will beat you.' (Bailey 1912:82) Punjabi

The *-ũ* in (13a) is analyzed as a pronominal infix and indicates the 2nd person object.[8] In (13b), in contrast, the infixed morphology is that of the regular future paradigm, which shows simple agreement with the subject.[9] This contrast is established quite clearly by the unacceptability of (13c), where the pronominal infix could only be understood as doubling the overt pronominal object. This is not permitted in Punjabi, showing that the pronominal clitics/infixes have referential force and are not functioning as simple agreement markers.

Another example along the same lines taken from modern Punjabi is shown in (14), where the *s* could refer to the subject or object (preferentially the subject), but since its referential contribution would then clash with one of the full pronouns, the sentence is ungrammatical.

(14) *o=ne o=nũ akʰe=s
Pron.3=Erg Pron.3=Acc say.Past=3.Sg
'He/She told him/her.' Punjabi

However, it is difficult to find/construct such examples because the pronominal clitics could actually refer to all sorts of other non-argument participants as well. An example is shown in (15), where the verb is intransitive and the *je* points to the non-argument addressee. The plural form is used because plurals generally also double as polite forms in the language.

(15) mẽ aea je
I come.Past 2.Pl
'(I say to you) I have come/am coming.' (Bailey 1912:85) Punjabi

[8] Bhatia (1993:248) lists the *ũ* form as a dialectal variant.

[9] Since the inflectional future *-g* in Urdu and Punjabi is derived from a former *go* (Sanskrit *gam*) auxiliary, the "regular" future agreement morphology may actually also be derived from former pronominal clitics. This remains to be investigated in more detail, but see Butt and Lahiri (2003) for some discussion of the Urdu facts.

Interestingly, in modern Punjabi, it is possible to double the *je* form with a full pronoun, as shown in (16), where the *je* is interpreted as referring to the 2nd person subject.

(16) tʊsi$_i$ kɑm karya je$_i$
you work.Nom do.Imp.Pol 2.Pl
'Could you please do the work.' Punjabi

An initial hypothesis (due to Nayyara Karamat) is that the *je* may actually be in the process of being reanalyzed as a polite form of the regular present tense auxiliary *e* 'is'. This conforms with intuitions of native speakers and is also very likely under a scenario of historical change in which these former pronouns are gradually absorbed into the verbal paradigm in one form or another.

One final point to address is Akhtar's confinement of *ne* to the past tense. This observation has not been confirmed by further checking, but Bailey's list of when to use the pronominal clitics, rendered here in (17), perhaps provides a useful clue to why Akhtar classified it as such.

(17) **Use of Pronominal Clitics** (Bailey 1925:82):
(i) to indicate the object, direct or indirect
(ii) to indicate possession or connection
(iii) with the past tenses of transitive verbs to indicate the agent or subject of the verb
(iv) for the second person, singular and plural, to indicate the person addressed

We had so far established that the pronominal suffixes can be used to "replace" or refer to any argument or adjunct (section 17.2). Bailey (1912) provides a more differentiated picture in that he confines the usage to objects in general ((17i)) and to subjects in the past tense ((17iii)). However, Bailey is careful to note that these rules are not inviolable, but must be seen as governing the "regular usage" of these clitics. An example of (17iv) has already been presented in (15), some examples of (17ii) are shown in (18).

(18) a. mɛ̃ kɑm ne=s kita
I work.M.Sg.Nom not=3.Sg do.Past.M.Sg
'I didn't do his work.' Punjabi

b. mʊnḍe kɑm kɑrde=s(u)
boy.M.Pl.Nom work.M.Sg.Nom do.Pres.M.Pl=3.Sg
'His/her sons work.' (based on Akhtar 1997:4) Punjabi

In section 17.6, this and the other established properties of pronominal clitics are analyzed as being due to the discourse backgrounding of former full pronouns. Before moving on to an analysis, some diachronic evidence in favor of progressive pronominal incorporation is adduced in the next section.

17.5.2 Historical Origin — Pronominal Incorporation

Emeneau (1965) provides a survey of languages he was aware of that showed pronominal suffixes. They include Pashto, Balochi, Brahui (a Dravidian language pocket in an otherwise Indo-Aryan area), Sindhi, Lahanda, Kashmiri, Shina, Shumashti, Pasahi, Bashgali (Kati), Waigali, Ashkun.[10] Emeneau concludes that pronominal suffixation is in fact an areal characteristic. He sees the origin of pronominal suffixation as being due to language contact with neighboring Iranian languages. However, he believes that the ground for this ready borrowing must already have been structurally inherent in the languages.

A different perspective is taken by Grierson (1895a), whose investigation of the Kashmiri pronominal clitic system led him to accumulate comparative evidence from other languages and attempt to find a language internal explanation for the phenomenon by tracing the possible origin of the construction.[11] Some examples from Kashmiri, Lahanda and Sindhi[12] are given in (19)–(21) by way of comparison with the Punjabi data.

(19)	tsɨ	chu-h-**an**	vucha:n	
	you-NOM	be-2.SG.NOM-3.SG.ACC	see-PRES.PPL	
	'You are looking at it.'			Kashmiri
	(Sharma 2001:226, with correction by Peter Hook)			

(20) a. kitu-**s**`
do.Part-3.Sg.Obl
'It was done by him.' (Grierson 1895a) — Lahanda

a. kitō-**vē**
do.Part-2.Obl
'It was done by you.' (Grierson 1895a) — Lahanda

(21) a. chaḍḍiā̃-**ī̃-se**
left-3.Sg.Obl-3.Sg
'He gave him up.' (Grierson 1895a) — Sindhi

b. chaḍḍiā̃-**ī̃-va**
left-3.Sg.Obl-2.Pl
'He gave you up.' (Grierson 1895a) — Sindhi

---

[10] For a discussion of Siraiki see Shackle (1976:101–107).

[11] Among others, see Hook and Kaul 1987, Wali and Koul 1994, 1997, Bhatt 1999, Sharma 2001 for some modern work on Kashmiri.

[12] Lahanda and Sindhi are languages of Pakistan, the province of Kashmir is divided between India and Pakistan.

The table in (22) reproduces the full set of forms as recorded by Grierson (1885a:345) (as well as I can read them) for these three languages.[13] Grierson traces the pronominal clitics/suffixes to *enclitic* pronouns in Sanskrit and some pronouns Prākrit. This reconstruction is of interest for the purposes of this paper because it fits in with the idea that pronominal clitics are derived from deemphasized and therefore generally also destressed pronominal forms. As indicated by the name, Sanskrit enclitic pronouns could not stand alone, but cliticized onto another prosodic word.

Grierson (1895b) reconstructs pronominal incorporation of the same type for Nepali, Maithili, Assamese, Bengali, Oṛiya and Marathi. Present day Marathi, Bengali, Assamese and Oṛiya show no signs of pronominal clitics as far as I am aware, indicating that in these languages the former pronominal clitics may have been entirely absorbed into the verbal paradigm. Maithili, in contrast, still has a flourishing system of pronominal suffixes/clitics (Bickel, Bisang and Yādava 1999).

(22)

	Kashmiri		Lahanda		Sindhi	
	Pron.	Suffix	Pron.	Suffix	Pron.	Suffix
1.Sg.Dir	*bo*	*m* or *s*	*mã:ĩ:*	*m* or *s*	*ã:ũ:*	*se* or *me*
1.Sg.Obl	*me*	*m*	*mai*	*m*	*mũhũ*	*me*
1.Pl.Dir	*asi*		*assã:*	*sē*	*asĩ:*	*sĩ:, sũ:*
1.Pl.Obl	*asi*		*assā*	*sē*	*asã:*	*ũ:, sũ:*
2.Sg.Dir	*tsa*	*h*	*tũ:*	*vẽ:* or *ō*	*tũ:*	*ẽ:*, e
2.Sg.Obl	*tse*	*t* (dat *y*)	*tai*	*ēī* (dat *ī*)	*tō*	e, (*ēī*)
2.Pl.Dir	*tohi*	*vạ*	*tussã:*	*vē*	*tavhĩ:*	*u, va*
2.Pl.Obl	*tohi*	*vạ*	*tussã:*	*vẽ* or *o*	*tavhã:*	*va*
3.Sg.Dir.M	*su*	*u*	*ū, sō*	*s*	*ū, sō*	(*se*)
3.Sg.Obl.M	*tạmi* (inst) *tas* (dat)	*n̲* (dat *s*)	*ū:, taĩ:*	*s*	*una, tãhẽ*	*se* (inst *ĩ:*)
3.Pl.Dir.M	*tim*	*h*	*ũ, sō*		*hū, sē*	(*ne*)
3.Pl.Obl.M	*timau* (inst)	*h*	*ũ:hã:, tinhã:*	*hẽ:* or *ni*	*hune, tane*	*ne* (inst *ũ:*)

The particular reconstructions Grierson proposed are as follows. The first person forms are derived from original Sanskrit enclitic pronouns *mā* (acc, sg), *me* (dat/gen, sg). These correspond to Prākrit *mã* and *me*. The *s* forms are traced to the oblique forms of full plural pronouns

[13] Peter Hook notes that some of the Kashmiri forms must be wrong, however, in the context of this discussion, I cannot do more than provide Grierson's original data.

in Prākrit.[14] For the second person, the Sanskrit enclitics are *tvā* (acc, sg), *te* (dat/gen, sg), *vas* (acc/dat/gen, pl). The corresponding Prākrit is *te* (sg), *vo* (pl). The forms in *t-* and some of the *v-* forms are derived from these. The *h*, *ī*, *eī* and some of the *v-* forms are traced back to the Prākrit second person pronouns *bhē* and *uyhē*, which relate to old dual forms (see Pischel 1955:§420 for a complete list of second person pronouns in Prākrit, Whitney 1889:§491 for Sanskrit). Finally, for the third person, the forms in *n* are derived from a defective Sanskrit pronominal which had *ena* as a stem. The forms in *s* are derived via Sanskrit *asya* (3sg, gen) and Prākrit *sē*. The *u* forms may be associated with an instrumental version.

Ascertaining whether Grierson's reconstructions are indeed correct would take us well beyond the scope of this paper. However, his ideas are usefully suggestive. Grierson himself does not investigate Punjabi,[15] but we can reasonably pose the question whether the pronominal clitics found in Punjabi could be amenable to Grierson's reconstruction. It is quite clear that the set of pronominal clitics in Punjabi cannot be related directly to the current set of full pronouns: 2nd person singular *tũ, tẽ* vs. *ũ, a, i, ĩ*; 2nd person plural *tusĩ, tuha* vs. *je*; 3rd person singular *e, o, enā̃, onā̃* vs. *s(u), ne.*

However, in analogy to the Lahanda *ī*, *eī* forms, the Punjabi *i* and *je* forms could be traced back to the Prākrit second person pronouns *bhē* or *uyhē*, as Grierson has suggested. The third person forms *ne* and *s(u)* also seem to be amenable to the type of reconstruction Grierson proposes: they could be related to defective Sanskrit *ena* and a locative form in *-u*. Though these reconstructions await confirmation via serious historical work, they provide, at the very least, a suggestive and interesting clue towards their synchronic analysis.

Finally, as to the absence of first person pronouns in Punjabi, this could be attributed to a more general trend within South Asian languages. Bickel, Bisang and Yādava (1999) note that there are no first person pronominal suffixes in Maithili and attribute this to the pressure on self-effacement in the social context. In terms of an information-structural analysis, as presented in the next section, the pressure to omit first person pronouns makes sense: first persons tend to be topical and therefore prone to be dropped entirely, rather than backgrounded postverbally.

---

[14]The Prākrit pronouns are derived from Sanskrit *aṣmad* (e.g. **assahũ*, **assahĩ*). The derivations proposed by Grierson are quite intricate and involve complex arguments by Hoernle and Brugmann (Grierson 1895a:345).

[15]Grierson treats Lahanda as a form of Punjabi, namely Western Punjabi. Whether this is a correct classification continues to be a matter of some dispute.

17.6 An Analysis in Terms of Information Structure

This section first presents Butt and King's (1996, 1997) analysis of the interaction between discourse functions and word order in Urdu/Hindi (section 17.6.1) and then applies it towards motivating pronominal postverbal cliticization. The idea is that information-structural backgrounding (Givón's 1976 afterthought backgrounding) accounts for the postverbal placement of pronouns. Because these pronouns represent backgrounded information, they also tend to be destressed and therefore also tend to cliticize (cf. the Sanskrit enclitic pronouns). Over time, this cliticization can feed into a further reanalysis of the pronouns into the verbal paradigm (e.g., as agreement morphology).

Section 17.6.2 presents some more synchronic evidence in support of an information-structural analysis. Taken together with the synchronic and diachronic data discussed in the previous sections, the picture that emerges fits in nicely with Bresnan's (2001) analysis of pronominal incorporation.

17.6.1 Discourse Functions and Word Order

Butt and King (1996, 1997) investigate the relatively free word order of the SOV language Urdu/Hindi from an information-structural perspective (cf. Vallduví 1992) and conclude that Urdu/Hindi must be classified as a *discourse configurational* language along the lines of Hungarian (É Kiss 1995). That is, while the main constituents of a sentence can be scrambled quite freely from a syntactic perspective, the placement of the constituents relative to one another makes a difference as to the information-structural content of the utterance (see Gambhir 1981, Kidwai 2000 for similar ideas on Hindi, but in different frameworks, also cf. King 1995 for Russian).

Butt and King assume a four-way distinction for discourse functions that is based on two features: [±New] and [±Prom(inent)]. This four-way distinction is inspired and adapted from Choi 1999—Vallduví 1992, for example, only assumes a three-way distinction.

(23) Discourse Functions

[+New] =	focus [+Prom]
	completive information [−Prom]
[−New] =	topic [+Prom]
	background information [−Prom]

Butt and King use the terms *topic* and *focus* in a way that is presumably familiar to the reader: topics indicate prominent but old information, focus is used for information that is both new and prominent. It can be shown that these information-structural notions find a rough positional correlation in Urdu/Hindi (again, cf. Gambhir 1981, Kidwai 2000). Topics tend to be clause initial, while focus tends to be immediately preverbal. This positional placement is typical of discourse configurational languages (cf. É Kiss 1995).

The terms *completive information* and *background* are not as widely used in the literature as topic and focus. Backgrounded information is taken to be both old and non-prominent. It could in principle be left out of the sentence altogether, hence the sense that this information has the nature of an *afterthought* (cf. Givón 1976). Backgrounded information occurs postverbally and tends to be preceded by an intonational break (this break occurs after the verbal complex). Finally, Butt and King coined the term *completive information* for the material that is not prominent, but new. In a sense, this is the "other" category, i.e., material that is included in the clause because it is new and furthers an understanding of the situation, but one which is neither foregrounded nor backgrounded in any special way. This information occurs between the clause-initial topic and the preverbal focus.

The constructed example in (24) illustrates all four types of discourse functions. Urdu/Hindi *to* 'indeed' has a general emphasizing function and a specific function as a topic marker (see Kidwai 2000). The focus in this sentence, 'market', is marked by a high tone in the immediately preverbal position, the backgrounded information is deemphasized and has falling intonation.

(24) [nadya]$_T$ (to) [ɑb^{h}i]$_{CI}$ [ṭɔfi]$_{CI}$ [bazar=se]$_F$
Nadya.F.Nom indeed just now toffee.F.Nom market.M=from
xɑrid rɑh-i t^h-i [mere=liye]$_B$
buy stay-Perf.F.Sg be.Past-F.Sg I.Gen.Obl=for
'Nadya was just buying toffee at the market for me.' (Urdu)

Butt and King's (1997) particular interest lay in uncovering the conditions for pro-drop in Urdu/Hindi. Since pro-drop in Urdu/Hindi and other South Asian languages is not licensed by agreement or case, Butt and King (1997) explored a discourse driven hypothesis for the rampant pro-drop found in South Asian languages. Based on a study of Hindi movie discourses, Butt and King (1997) found that a discourse-based hypothesis is indeed plausible in that only old information is dropped. In particular, continuing topics or backgrounded information were good candidates for pro-drop. Butt and King's general findings have been confirmed by a more extensive corpus study conducted by Prasad (2000), who furthermore showed that it is mainly subjects which are pro-dropped.

From an information-structural point of view, backgrounding and pro-drop thus both emerge as a method of dealing with old and non-prominent information. One difference between backgrounding and pro-drop lies in the degree of (de)emphasis. Backgrounded information is still recoverable within the clause, pro-dropped information is wholly context-dependent. A reasonable hypothesis would be that subjects are more prone to pro-dropping, because these tend to be easy to recover from the context.[16]

Backgrounding thus emerges as a good strategy to deemphasize non-subjects. Given the hypothesis that the pronominal clitics are originally backgrounded information, two observations about the data fall out immediately. For one, it would be expected that the clitics are oblique (non-nominative) forms of the pronouns. Recall that Grierson's (1895a) reconstruction of the pronominal forms involved only oblique forms. For another, it would be expected that first person pronouns are generally absent from the paradigm, since a first person reference is generally eminently recoverable from the discourse context and would therefore tend to be pro-dropped, rather than being backgrounded.

17.6.2 Information Structure and Pronominal Clitics

This section applies the information-structural analysis towards an explanation of the distribution and properties of Punjabi pronominal clitics. For the sake of clarity and completeness, I first provide a sample analysis of the interplay between word order, grammatical relations and information structure. Butt and King (1997) provide an analysis of this interplay in terms of LFG's projection architecture. In addition to the usual f(unctional) structure, an i(nformation)-structure is assumed to project from the c(onstituent)-structure. This allows a clean separation of predicate-argument information from information structure and predicts that any grammatical function or adjunct could in principle take on any of the available discourse functions.

Furthermore, it allows an account of verbal or predicate focus, which is problematic in an account that integrates discourse functions directly into the f-structure (e.g., Bresnan 2001). In such an account, when the main predicate of the sentence is focused, it is impossible to represent just the focusing of that element. Instead, the nature of the f-structure

[16]Subjects are often also topics and in some languages this connection is made very explicitly. One prominent analysis within LFG has therefore been to integrate the discourse functions TOPIC and FOCUS with the grammatical functions (Bresnan 2001:94–96) and represent them as part of the f-structure. Butt and King do not favor such an analysis, preferring instead to keep distinct levels of representation for functional and information structure, see the discussion in section 17.6.2.

representation entails that when the main predicate is identified with the focus discourse function, the entire f-structure must be interpreted as being focused: because the main predicate heads the f-structure, anything contained as part of that f-structure is automatically in focus as well (King 1997). Thus, there is no way to distinguish between predicate and sentential/clausal focus, an embarassment which is avoided in a clean representational distinction between i-structure and f-structure.

The representations in (26) and (27) provide analyses of the sample monolog in (25) (these utterances precede the pigeon utterances in (7) above). Utterance (25b) has a pro-dropped subject. In this case, it is a continuing topic from the previous utterance. This is indicated by coreference in the i-structure in (27).

(25) a. mɛ̃ bais bɑrs=se yahã rɑh rɑh-a hũ
I.Nom twenty-two year=from here live Prog-M.Sg be.Pres.1.Sg
'I_{topic} have been living here for 22 years.' Hindi

b. rozana ɪs hi sɑrɑk=se gʊzɑr-ta hũ
daily this Emph street.F=from pass-Impf.M.Sg be.Pres.1.Sg
'Daily ($\text{I}_{cont.topic}$) go through this street.' Hindi
(Dilwale Dulhania Le Jayenge)

(26) **Functional-structure** for (25a):

$$\begin{bmatrix} \text{PRED} & \text{' live<SUBJ,OBL> '} \\ \text{SUBJ} & \begin{bmatrix} \text{PRED} & \text{' PRO '} \\ \text{NUM} & \text{sg} \\ \text{PERS} & 1 \end{bmatrix} \\ \text{ADJUNCT} & \left\{ \begin{bmatrix} \text{PRED} & \text{' TWENTY-TWO YEARS '} \end{bmatrix} \right\} \\ \text{OBL} & \begin{bmatrix} \text{PRED} & \text{' HERE '} \end{bmatrix} \end{bmatrix}$$

Functional-structure for (25b):

$$\begin{bmatrix} \text{PRED} & \text{' pass<SUBJ> '} \\ \text{SUBJ} & \begin{bmatrix} \text{PRED} & \text{' PRO '} \end{bmatrix} \\ \text{ADJUNCT} & \left\{ \begin{matrix} \begin{bmatrix} \text{PRED} & \text{' STREET '} \end{bmatrix} \\ \begin{bmatrix} \text{PRED} & \text{' DAILY '} \end{bmatrix} \end{matrix} \right\} \end{bmatrix}$$

(27) **Information-structure** for (25a) and (25b):

$$\left[\begin{array}{l}\left[\begin{array}{ll}\text{TOPIC} & \left\{\left[\begin{array}{ll}\text{PRED} & \text{'PRO'}\\ \text{NUM} & \text{sg}\\ \text{PERS} & 1\end{array}\right]\right\}\\ \text{FOCUS} & \left\{\left[\begin{array}{ll}\text{PRED} & \text{'HERE'}\end{array}\right]\right\}\\ \text{COMP.INF} & \left\{\left[\begin{array}{ll}\text{PRED} & \text{'TWENTY-TWO YEARS'}\end{array}\right]\right\}\end{array}\right]\\ \left[\begin{array}{ll}\text{TOPIC} & \left\{\left[\ \right]\right\}\\ \text{FOCUS} & \left\{\left[\begin{array}{ll}\text{PRED} & \text{'STREET'}\end{array}\right]\right\}\\ \text{COMP.INF} & \left\{\left[\begin{array}{ll}\text{PRED} & \text{'DAILY'}\end{array}\right]\right\}\end{array}\right]\end{array}\right]$$

There is no backgrounded (postverbal) information in these utterances, so this discourse function is absent from the reprsentation in (30).[17] If there were any backgrounded information, it would be represented as part of the i-structure on a par with the other discourse functions that are assumed.

Turning back to the main proposal of this paper, I propose that the Punjabi pronominal clitics should be analyzed as backgrounded material. The information-structural analysis of (28), for example, would thus include the clause initial subject as a topic, the immediately preverbal object as a focus, and the postverbal pronominal clitic as backgrounded information.

(28) [sʊmbɑl=nũ]$_T$ [kɑtab]$_F$ dɪtti=[s(u)]$_B$
Sumbal.M.Sg=Dat book.F.Sg.Nom give.Past.F.Sg=3.Sg
'S/he gave the book to Sumbal.' (Akhtar 1997:2) Punjabi

The following sections provide some evidence for this view; however, as the anonymous reviewer rightly points out, a full discussion of the discourse conditions which result in the use of full pronouns vs. pronominal clitics vs. pro-drop needs to be presented. Sadly, such a discussion goes well beyond the scope of this paper and will have to be the subject of another paper.

[17]The i-structure and f-structure are related to each other via LFG's projection architecture. The fact that 'here' is both an adjunct and a focus is thus recoverable from the representation.

Supporting Synchronic Evidence

Akhtar (1997:6) notes that the arguments *s(u)* stands for are unstressed and not the focal part of the sentences. He also shows that the pronominal clitics cannot stand for *wh*-words ((29)–(30)). This makes sense under the information-structural analysis since *wh*-words tend to be in focus and are therefore not candidates for backgrounding.

(29) a. fɑwɑd=ne kɪs=nũ mɑria?
Fawad.M.Sg=Erg who.Obl=Acc beat.Past
'Whom did Fawad beat?' (based on Akhtar 1997:5) Punjabi

b. fɑwɑd=ne mɑria=s(u)
Fawad.M.Sg=Erg beat.Past=3.Sg
'Fawad beat him/her.' Punjabi
but not 'Whom did Fawad beat?' (based on Akhtar 1997:6)

(30) a. kɪs=ne mʊnḍe=nũ mɑria?
who.Obl=Erg boy.Obl=Acc beat.Past.M.Sg
'Who beat the boy?' (based on Akhtar 1997:5) Punjabi

b. mʊnḍe=nũ mɑria=s(u)
boy.Obl=Acc beat.Past.M.Sg=3.Sg
'S/he beat the boy', not 'Who beat the boy?' Punjabi
(based on Akhtar 1997:5)

The clitics also cannot stand for nominative arguments ((31)). This fact seems odd at first sight, but again receives a straightforward explanation under the analysis proposed here. Butt and King (1997) note that nominative arguments tend to be semantically incorporated or focused (see Mohanan 1995, Dayal 2003 for further discussion and motivation), both of which makes them unavailable for discourse backgrounding and therefore unavailable for pronominal cliticization.

(31) a. fɑwɑd=ne kɑtab pɑṛi
Fawad.M.Sg=Erg book.F.Sg.Nom read.Past.F.Sg
'Fawad read the/a book.' (based on Akhtar 1997:5) Punjabi

b. fɑwɑd=ne pɑṛi=s(u)
Fawad.M.Sg=Erg read.Past.F.Sg=3.Sg
'Fawad read (his/her something).'
but not 'Fawad read it.' Punjabi
(where it=book, based on Akhtar 1997:5)

Finally, recall that pronominal clitics can refer to possessive specifiers as well ((18)). This property again falls out from general considerations of word order and discourse. Given that genitive specifiers are in principle able to scramble independently (cf. Mohanan 1994 for Hindi), they can also be placed in the postverbal backgrounding position and there become candidates for pronominal cliticization and incorporation.

The currently available synchronic data thus more than supports an information-structural analysis of pronominal cliticization. The next section turns to a discussion of the diachronic predictions that go along with the information-structural analysis.

Supporting Diachronic Evidence

Recall that according to Givón's (1976) original suggestions and according to LFG's view on pronominal incorporation (section 17.4), several stages of historical change are predicted:

(32) i. Pronouns are backgrounded for discourse reasons.
ii. These pronouns could either be full pronouns and then develop cliticized forms, or they could already be enclitics.
iii. The cliticized forms are reanalyzed as part of the verbal paradigm. This can include a stage in which the referential content of the pronoun is optional.

With respect to (32ii), Grierson's (1895a) reconstructions seem to suggest that a majority of the backgrounded pronouns have been enclitics at least since Sanskrit: the ancestors of the current forms are often traced to old accentless enclitic pronouns. Consider Whitney's (1889:§500) description of *ena*, one of the possible ancestors of the current forms: "There is a defective pronominal stem, *ena*, which is accentless, and hence used only in situations where no emphasis falls upon it." This indicates that the pronouns the modern Punjabi clitics were derived from already served a deemphasizing (non-focal) function.

With respect to (32iii), there is some evidence that the Punjabi pronominal clitics are beginning to be absorbed into the regular verbal paradigm. Consider the observation that the 2nd plural *je* can cooccur with overt full pronouns in situations of polite requests ((16)). Given the paradigm for the present tense of the 'be' auxiliary (Bailey 1912:50) in (33), it is highly plausible that both the 2nd person plural *je* and the third person plural *ne* could be assimilated into this paradigm. The *je* would extend the paradigm as a polite form, whereas the *ne* could be reanalyzed as being part of this paradigm. Note that the pronominal clitic *ne* is not nasalized, whereas the 3rd person plural in (33) is.

(33)

Present of Punjabi *be* (Bailey 1912:50)		
	Singular	Plural
1st	ã	ã
2nd	ẽ/ɛ̃	o
3rd	e/ɛ	nẽ

Interestingly, Bhatia (1993:243) in his grammar of Punjabi provides a non-nasalized form as the third person plural of 'be'. Given that nasalization in both Punjabi and Urdu/Hindi also serves as a marker of politeness, it is entirely plausible that the pronominal clitic *ne* has recently been collapsed with auxiliary *nẽ*, whereby the nasalization has been reanalyzed as part of the politeness marking. This scenario is accordance with native speaker intuitions, who, when first confronted with the pronominal clitic *ne*, assume that it is part of the paradigm in (33).

Finally, recall that Grierson (1895b) reconstructed pronominal incorporation for a number of other languages besides Kashmiri, Lahanda and Sindhi. Some of these other languages are Bengali, Oṛiya, Assamese, and Maithili. In their current form, Bengali, Oṛiya, and Assamese do not employ pronominal clitics: the former pronouns have been entirely absorbed into the verbal paradigm as agreement markers. For Maithili, Bickel, Bisang and Yādava (1999) also argue that the pronominal suffixes are on their way to being integrated as agreement morphemes.[18] Given these data and observations, I propose that the singular *i* (also *ĩ*, *ũ*, *a*) and *s(u)* forms be analyzed as enclitic pronouns with referential force. They contribute a PRED 'PRO' and are incompatible with full pronouns or NPs that designate the same grammatical function. In contrast, the plural forms *je* and *ne* are in the process of being absorbed into the verbal paradigm. Their referential force is optional, that is, they only optionally contribute a PRED 'PRO'. This is entirely in parallel with the situation described for Chicheŵa in section 17.4. A diachronic prediction is that the *je* and *ne* are currently at an intermediate stage and that they will lose their referential force entirely. The singular pronominal clitics will presumably also be absorbed into the verbal paradigm via an intermediate stage, however, at the moment they retain their full referential force.

[18]Some intriguing historical data remains to be uncovered with respect to the behavior of the future, cf. (13), however, a discussion of these data would lead us too far afield.

17.7 Conclusion

In conclusion, this paper has tried to establish that standard Punjabi shows pronominal cliticization as part of an areal phenomenon (Emeneau 1965). The presence of pronominal clitics is related to pro-drop in that both are discourse strategies. The evidence suggests that pronominal cliticization is the result of postverbal discourse backgrounding, while pro-drop applies to old information that is wholly recoverable from the context.

The synchronic and diachronic evidence furthermore points to a gradual absorbtion of these clitics into the verbal paradigm, a process whose successive synchronic stages can be accounted for elegantly under an analysis which combines the standard LFG account of pronominal incorporation (Bresnan 2001) with the information-structural analysis proposed by Butt and King (1996, 1997). In particular, the data and analyses put forward in this paper lend support to Givón's (1976) original idea that discourse backgrounding can feed into the development of a verbal agreement system.

References

Akhtar, Raja Nasim. 1997. Affix-*s(uu)* constructions in punjabi. In *Essex Graduate Working Papers in Linguistics*, vol. 2, pages 1–18. Colchester: University of Essex.

Akhtar, Raja Nasim. 1999. *Aspectual Complex Predicates in Punjabi*. Ph.D. thesis, University of Essex.

Alexiadou, Artemis and Elena Anagnostopoulou. 1998. Parametrizing AGR: Word Order, V-Movement and EPP-Checking. *Natural Language and Linguistic Theory* 16(3):491–539.

Austin, Peter and Joan Bresnan. 1996. Non-configurationality in australian aboriginal languages. *Natural Language and Linguistic Theory* 14(2):215–268.

Bhatia, Tej. 1993. *Punjabi: A cognitive-descriptive grammar*. London: Routledge.

Bhatt, Rakesh M. 1999. *Verb Movement and the Syntax of Kashmiri*. Dordrecht: Kluwer.

Bickel, Balthasar, Walter Bisang, and Yogendra P. Yādava. 1999. Face vs. empathy: the social foundation of maithili verb agreement. *Linguistics* 37(2):359–364.

Bresnan, Joan. 2001. *Lexical-Functional Syntax*. Oxford: Blackwell.

Bresnan, Joan and Sam A. Mchombo. 1987. Topic, pronoun, and agreement in Chicheŵa. *Language* 63(4):741–782.

Butt, Miriam and Tracy H. King. 1996. Structural topic and focus without movement. In *Proceedings of the International Lexical-Functional Grammar Conference 1996 (LFG'96)*. Grenoble: CSLI Online Publications.

Butt, Miriam and Tracy H. King. 1997. Null elements in discourse structure. In K. V. Subbarao, ed., *Papers from the NULLS Seminar*. Delhi: Moti Lal Banarsi Das. To appear.

Butt, Miriam and Tracy H. King. 2003. Case systems: Beyond structural distinctions. In E. Brandner and H. Zinsmeister, eds., *New Perspectives on Case Theory*, pages 53–87. Stanford, CA: CSLI Publications.

Butt, Miriam and Tracy H. King. 2005. The status of case. In V. Dayal and A. Mahajan, eds., *Clause Structure in South Asian Languages*, pages 153–198. Dordrecht: Kluwer.

Butt, Miriam and Aditi Lahiri. 2003. Verbal passepartouts. Ms., Universität Konstanz.

Choi, Hye-won. 1999. *Optimizing Structure in Context: Scrambling and Information Structure*. Stanford, CA: CSLI Publications.

Corbett, Greville. 1995. Agreement. In J. Jacobs, A. von Stechow, W. Sternefeld, and T. Vennemann, eds., *Syntax: An International Handbook of Contemporary Research*, vol. 2, pages 1235–1244. Berlin: Walter de Gruyter.

Cummings, Thomas and Thomas G. Bailey. 1912. *Panjabi Manual and Grammar: A guide to the Colloquial Panjabi of the Northern Panjab*. Calcutta: Baptist Mission Press.

Dayal, Veneeta. 2003. Bare nominals: Non-specific and contrastive readings under scrambling. In S. Karimi, ed., *Word Order and Scrambling*, pages 67–90. Oxford: Blackwell.

É. Kiss, Katalin. 1995. *Discourse Configurational Languages*. Oxford: Oxford University Press.

Emeneau, Murray. 1956. India and linguistic areas. In *India and Historical Grammar, Publication No. 5*, pages 25–75. Annamalai: Department of Linguistics, Annamalai University. Republished 1980 in Anwar S. Dil, ed., *Language and Linguistic Area: Essays by Murray B. Emeneau*, pages 126–166, Stanford University Press.

Gambhir, Vijay. 1981. *Syntactic Restrictions and Discourse Functions of Word Order in Standard Hindi*. Ph.D. thesis, University of Pennsylvania.

Givón, Talmy. 1976. Topic, pronoun, and grammatical agreement. In C. Li, ed., *Subject and Topic*, pages 149–188. New York, NY: Acadmic Press.

Glassman, Eugene H. 1977. *Spoken Urdu*. Lahore: Nirali Kitaben.

Grierson, George A. 1895a. On Pronominal Suffixes in the Kāçmīrī Language. *Proceedings of the Royal Asiatic Society, Calcutta* 64(1):336–351.

Grierson, George A. 1895b. On the Radical and Participial Tenses of the Modern Indo-Aryan Languages. *Proceedings of the Royal Asiatic Society, Calcutta* 64(1):352–375.

Hook, Peter E. 1987. Poguli Syntax in the Light of Kashmiri: A Preliminary Report. *Studies in the Linguistic Sciences* 17:63–71.

Hook, Peter E. and Vijay K. Kaul. 1987. Case Alternation, Transitionality and the Adoption of Direct Objects in Kashmiri. *Indian Linguistics* 48:52–69.

Huang, C.-T. James. 1984. On the distribution and reference of empty pronouns. *Linguistic Inquiry* 15(4):531–574.

Jelinek, Eloise. 1984. Empty categories, case and configurationality. *Natural Language and Linguistics Theory* 2(1):39–76.

Kidwai, Ayesha. 2000. *XP-Adjunction in Universal Grammar: Scrambling and Binding in Hindi-Urdu*. Oxford: Oxford University Press.

King, Tracy H. 1995. *Configuring Topic and Focus in Russian*. Stanford, CA: CSLI Publications.

King, Tracy H. 1997. Focus domains and information structure. In M. Butt and T. H. King, eds., *Proceedings of the International Lexical-Functional Grammar Conference 1997 (LFG'97)*. San Diego, CA: CSLI Online Publications.

Kiparsky, Paul. 1973. 'Elsewhere' in phonology. In S. R. Anderson and P. Kiparsky, eds., *A Festschrift for Morris Halle*, pages 93–106. New York, NY: Holt, Rinehart and Winston.

Mahajan, Anoop. 1989. Agreement and agreement phrases. In *MIT Working Papers in Linguistics*, vol. 10, pages 217–252. Cambridge, MA: MITWPL.

Mahajan, Anoop. 1992. The specificity condition and the CED. *Linguistic Inquiry* 23(3):510–516.

Masica, Colin. 1976. *Defining a Linguistic Area: South Asia*. Chicago, IL: The University of Chicago Press.

Masica, Colin. 1991. *The Indo-Aryan languages*. Cambridge, UK: Cambridge University Press.

McGregor, Ronald S. 1968. *The Language of Indrajit of Orchā: A Study of Early Braj Bhasa Prose*. Cambridge, UK: Cambridge University Press.

Mohanan, Tara. 1994. *Argument Structure in Hindi*. Stanford, CA: CSLI Publications.

Mohanan, Tara. 1995. Wordhood and lexicality: Noun incorporation in Hindi. *Natural Language and Linguistic Theory* 13(1):75–134.

Neeleman, Ad and Kriszta Szendrői. 2005. Radical pro drop and the morphology of pronouns. To appear in *Linguistic Inquiry*.

Payne, John R. 1995. Inflecting postpositions in Indic and Kashmiri. In F. Plank, ed., *Double Case: Agreement by Suffixaufnahme*, pages 283–298. Oxford: Oxford University Press.

Pischel, Richard. 1955. *A Grammar of the Prākrit Languages*. Delhi: Motilal Banarsidass. First published in German 1900, current edition was reprinted in 1981.

Prasad, Rashmi. 2000. A corpus study of zero pronouns in hindi: An account based on centering transition preferences. In *Proceedings of the Discourse Anaphora and Reference Resolution Conference 2000 (DAARRC'00)*, pages 66–71. Lancaster University.

Rizzi, Luigi. 1986. Null objects in Italian and theory of *pro*. *Linguistic Inquiry* 17(3):501–557.

Shackle, Christopher. 1976. *The Siraiki Language of Central Pakistan: A Reference Grammar*. Oxford: School of Oriental and African Studies.

Sharma, Devyani. 2001. Kashmiri case clitics and person hierarchy effects. In P. Sells, ed., *Formal and Empirical Issues in Optimality Theoretic Syntax*, pages 225–256. Stanford, CA: CSLI Publications.

Subbarao, Karumuri V. 1999. Agreement in south asian languages and minimalist inquiries: The framework. In *Proceedings of the International Symposium on Language Contact, Convergence and Typology in South Asia*. Tokyo: The Institute for the Study of Language and Cultures of Asia and Africa (ILCAA).

Vallduví, Enric. 1992. *The Informational Component*. New York, NY: Garland.

Wali, Kashi and Omkar N. Koul. 1994. Kashmiri Clitics: The Role of Case and CASE. *Linguistics* 32(6):969–994.

Whitney, William D. 1889. *Sanskrit Grammar*. Cambridge, MA: Harvard University Press. 9th Issue of the 2nd Edition (1960).

18

Dislocation and Split NPs in Chicheŵa

SAM MCHOMBO

18.1 Introduction

The morphological structure of the verb in Chicheŵa, (and other Bantu languages), comprises a verb root (VR) to which verbal extensions such as causative, applicative, reciprocal, passive, stative, etc. are suffixed, and to which prefixes are added.[1] The prefixes, analyzed as clitics in some studies (cf. Allan, 1983; Mchombo 2002a, 2002b, 2004b) include, *inter alia*, a Subject Marker (SM) that agrees in ϕ-features with the grammaticized (internal) TOPIC (ordinarily assumed to be the subject), and an Object Marker (OM), analyzed as an incorporated pronominal argument, agreeing with a discourse licensed (external) Topic NP (cf. Baker 2003; Bresnan & Mchombo 1986,1987; Demuth & Johnson 1989; Morimoto 2000). This is illustrated in (1) below:

[1] I am grateful to Eyamba Bokamba, Mary Dalrymple, Cécile De Cat, Lisa Cheng, Kamil Ud Deen, Laura Downing, Gisbert Fanselow, Caroline Féry, Pascal Kishindo, Rose Letsholo, Victor Manfredi, Lutz Marten, Setumile Morapedi, Yukiko Morimoto, Al Mtenje, Andreas Nolda, and an anonymous reviewer, for comments and discussions that greatly influenced the shape and contents of this paper. None of them shares the blame for any errors. The paper gained considerably from presentations to audiences at the School of Oriental & African Studies (University of London), at Zentrum für Allgemeine Sprachwissenschaft and The Univesity of Potsdam in Germany, at the 35th Annual Conference on African Linguistics at Harvard University and, at La Universidad de Sonora in Hermosillo, Mexico.

Architectures, Rules, and Preferences: Variations on Themes by Joan Bresnan.
Annie Zaenen, Jane Simpson, Tracy Holloway King,
Jane Grimshaw, Joan Maling, and Chris Manning, (eds.).

(1) Mkángo u-da-wá-ómb-án-íts-á alenje ndí asodzi[2]
3-lion 3SM-pst-2OM-hit-recip-caus-fv 2-hunter and 2-fishermen
'The lion made them hit each other, the hunters and the fishermen.'

In this sentence, the SM *u* in the verbal morphology agrees with the nominal *mkángo* 'lion.' With respect to word order, the nominal agreeing with the SM need not appear initially, although that is the preferred position in discourse-neutral contexts or when there is need for disambiguation. In the absence of the OM, the object NP *alenje ndí asodzi* 'hunters and fishermen' in the example above must maintain string adjacency with, and appear after, the verb. When the OM is included, the word order is relatively free, with the NP cross-referenced by the OM appearing in dislocated position and functioning as TOPIC (cf. Bresnan & Mchombo 1987; Deen 2004; Letsholo 2002).

The dislocated NP agreeing with the OM may also have its constituents discontinuous or split (Mchombo 2003; Mchombo & Morimoto 2004). There are also cases when the components associated with the object NP are non-contiguous in the absence of the OM but so not appear to constitute discontinuity in the canonical sense.

This paper will focus on such split NPs in Chicheŵa, with comment on the relations that hold between the discontinuous components. In the case of split NPs not induced by the presence of the OM, specific semantic relations hold between the discontinuous constituents, such as anaphoric or super-ordinate/hyponym relation between the fronted

---

[2]The acute accent on a vowel e.g., é indicates a high tone. The rising tone and falling tone are indicated, respectively, as follows: ä, û. Low tones are unmarked. The following abbreviations are used in the glosses:

Appl	applicative
AssocM	associative marker
Caus	causative
Fv	final vowel
OM	object marker
Perf	perfective aspect marker
Poss	possessive
Prox.dem	proximal demonstrative
Pst	past tense marker
Recip	reciprocal
SM	subject marker

and the remnant nominal in the clause.[3] Cases where the NP cannot be discontinuous, either because of semantic consideration or for structural reasons, even in the presence of the OM, will be considered too.

18.2 Verbal Morphology in Chicheŵa

As noted, the morphological organization of the verb includes an obligatory SM, and a Tense/Aspect marker, among other things. This is exemplified by the following sentence:

(2) a. njuchí zi-na-lúmá alenje
10-bees 10SM-pst-bite 2-hunters
'The bees bit the hunters'

The object NP *alenje* 'hunters' is required to appear in post-verbal position, maintaining string adjacency with the verb while the subject could appear after the Verb Phrase (VP) as shown below.[4]

(2) b. Zi-na-lúmá alenje njûchi.
10-SM-pst-bite 2-hunters 10-bees
'The bees bit the hunters.'

If the verb object sequence is disrupted, as when the subject NP *njûchi* 'bees' appears between the verb and the object NP *alenje* 'hunters', the sentence is ungrammatical (see Bresnan & Mchombo 1986, 1987, for details).

(2) c. *Zi-na-lúmá njûchi alenje
10-SM-pst-bite 10-bees 2-hunter

The presence of the SM and OM also licenses the omission of the NPs that are in agreement with them. The expression below is grammatical despite the absence of the NPs.

(2) d. Zi-na-wa-luma
10SM-pst-2OM-bite
'They bit them.'

[3]It is arguably the case that some of the constructions dealt with cannot be taken to be bona fide 'split NPs.' This is because in some cases, as in the case in super-ordinate/hyponym relation, the parts do not form constituents at any level of syntactic representation. The anonymous reviewer has brought to my attention that in Warlpiri and many Australian languages the generic and the super-ordinate can form a constituent — as can the whole together with a part. Naturally, this does rely on language particular constituency tests.

[4]Word order does contribute towards disambiguation when the object marker (OM) is included in the verbal morphology and the NPs are from the same gender class. The NP closest to the SM, or in preverbal position, is construed as cross-referenced by the SM or as the subject.

The possible omission of the nominal expressions that are supposed to 'discharge the argument variables' (cf. Neale 1996), has raised interesting questions concerning the analysis of the SM and OM in Bantu and their relation to the nominal expressions in agreement with them.

18.3 The Pronominal Argument Status of the OM

Current analyses have converged on the treatment of the object marker as a pronominal argument. The presence of the NP that is cross-referenced by the OM is not demanded by aspects of grammatical structure. Originally suggested in Mchombo (1984), the analysis received its clearest and detailed articulation in the work of Bresnan & Mchombo (1986, 1987), conducted with the theory of Lexical Functional Grammar (LFG). The analysis has been extended to other Bantu languages (cf. Demuth & Johnson 1989; Letsholo 2002; Omar 1990; Rubanza 1988; Sabimana 1986, to cite a few). The NP cross-referenced by the OM is a TOPIC, part of discourse structure, appearing in a dislocation construction (cf. De Cat 2002; Morimoto 2000).

The fact that the SM is obligatory appears to point to its status as an agreement marker (cf. Deen 2004). Bresnan & Mchombo analyzed the SM as functionally ambiguous between a pronominal argument and an agreement marker. The functional ambiguity of the SM further suggests the status of the NP that it agrees with as a grammaticized TOPIC or Internal Topic (I-TOP) (cf. Baker, 2003; Morimoto 2000).

The suggested treatment of the SM and OM as pronominal arguments argues for subsuming Chicheŵa to the pronominal argument hypothesis (Jelinek 1984). According to this view the arguments required by the predicator are filled by the pronominal arguments in the verbal morphology. The NPs cross-referenced by these pronominal arguments are in adjunct positions, licensed by information or discourse structure (see Austin & Bresnan 1996 for more discussion).

Jelinek's analysis of pronominal affixes as arguments got extended to account for the property of non-configurationality in polysynthetic languages. As outlined by Hale, such languages have the following properties:

(i) free word order,
(ii) syntactically discontinuous expressions, and
(iii) null anaphora.

By "null anaphora" Hale referred to "the situation in which an argument (e.g., subject, object) is not expressed by an overt nominal expression in phrase structure" (Hale 1983:40). The expression 'syntactically discontinuous expressions' refers to the situation where non-adjacent constituents may correspond to a single argument of the verb, or a single adjunct, resulting in discontinuous expressions (cf. Hale, 1981).

Languages such as English do not exhibit any of these traits. In English grammatical relations are signaled in part by word order, constituents resist discontinuity, and nominal arguments are not optional. The analysis of morphological elements marked on the head as satisfying argument structure, making the nominal expressions unnecessary for grammatical structure is applicable to Bantu.

The analysis of the SM and OM as incorporated pronominal arguments that satisfy lexical structure accords with the 'syntactic analysis' of the subject clitic in French, as noted by De Cat (2002). The question for French is, what is the status of *il* and what is the status of the nominal *un enfant* in a sentence such as the following?

(3) Un enfant, il arrive pi il te pose une question
a child, he arrives then he to-you asks a question
'A child arrives and he asks you a question'

According to De Cat, the subject clitic *il* is a syntactic entity, effectively fulfilling the requirements of argument structure. The nominal expression that it agrees with is interpreted as a topic of that sentence. She notes that "...peripheral topics are dislocated by base-generated adjunction to a sentential maximal projection (TP or CP)" (De Cat 2002: 3). Such peripheral XPs are "dislocated phrases" (ibid.) They are subject to omission without inducing ungrammaticality and are base generated in Topic positions. De Cat adopts the definition of Topic proposed by Reinhart (1981) as "what the sentence is about." She observes, further, that indefinites like *un enfant*, can indeed receive a topic interpretation when they have a generic reading, noting that "it is only under their existential reading that they are incompatible with a topic interpretation" (ibid: 4).

Letsholo, commenting on the Bantu language Ikalanga, maintains that "...topicalization in Ikalanga does not involve movement. A topicalized NP in Ikalanga is base generated in its surface position..." (Letsholo 2002: 33).

The syntactic analysis of subject clitics in French is partially applicable to Bantu languages. The difference lies in the obligatoriness of the SM in Bantu, in contrast to the subject clitic in French.

18.4 Discontinuous NPs in Chicheŵa

The OM in Chicheŵa is a necessary condition for discontinuity of the constituents of an internally complex dislocated NP (Mchombo 2001,

2004a, 2003). Chicheŵa is a head initial language and, within a Noun Phrase (or Determiner Phrase (DP)), the modifiers are ordered after the head noun and agree with it in number and gender. Consider the following:

(4) a. Njuchí izi zi-ná-**wá**-lúm-á **álenje**
10-bees 10prox.dem 10SM-pst-2OM-bite-fv 2-hunter
awa **ópúsa**
2prox.dem 2SM-foolish

b. **Awa** njuchí izi zi-ná-**wá**-lum-a
2-prox.dem 10-bees 10prox.dem 10SM-pst-2OM-bite-fv
alenje **ópúsa**
2-hunters 2SM-foolish

c. **Alenje** zi-ná-**wá**-lum-a njuchí izi
2-hunters 10SM-pst-2OM-bite-fv 10-bees 10-prox.dem
awa **ópúsa**
2-prox.dem 2SM-foolish

d. Izi **awa** **ópúsa** zi-ná-**wá**-lum-a
10-prox.dem 2prox.dem 2sM-foolish 10SM-pst-2OM-bite-fv
alenje njûchi
2-hunters 10-bees
'These bees bit these foolish hunters.'

Th intimate connection between the presence of the OM and the discontinuity of the constituents of the NP is illustrated by the ungrammaticality of sentences (5b and 5c) below. In these examples, the OM is absent.

(5) a. Njúchí izi zi-ná-lúmá **alenje** **awa**
10-bees 10proxdem 10SM-pst-bite 2-hunters 2proxdem
ópúsa
foolish
'These bees bit these foolish hunters.'

b. ***Awa** njúchí izi zi-ná-lúmá **alenje**
2proxdem 10-bees 10proxdem 10SM-pst-bite 2-hunters
ópúsa
foolish

c. ***Awa** **ópúsa** njúchí izi zi-ná-lúmá
2proxdem foolish 10-bees 10proxdem 10SM-pst-bite
alenje
2-hunters

While the presence of the OM may be a necessary condition for discontinuity of the constituents of the nominal expression in anaphoric relation with it, it is not a sufficient condition. This will be shown below.

18.5 Semantic Relations Governing Linearization

Chicheŵa provides instances of non-canonical split NPs that are not induced by the presence of OM. These require certain semantic relations to hold between the components. In the first case the remnant must be in an appositional relation to the dislocated or fronted head noun. Significantly, the word order must be such that the head noun is in left-dislocated position, on the left periphery of the clause. The remnant must maintain an anaphoric (appositional) relation with the dislocated NP. Consider the following:

(6) a. *Makású* anyání a-na-**í**-gúl-íl-á *awa*
6-hoe 2-baboons 2SM-pst-4OM-buy-appl-fv 6-these
óbúntha **mikángó yókálamba**
6SM-blunt 4-lion 4SM-aged
'(As for) hoes, the baboons bought the aged lions these blunt ones.'

In this example, the OM *i* cross-references *mikángó yókálamba* 'aged lions,' not *makású awa óbúntha* 'these blunt hoes.' The split NP has its head noun *makásu* 'hoes' appearing sentence-initially with its modifier remaining in post-verbal position. Such constructions are possible when the remnant is anaphoric. That the remnant must be construed as anaphoric to the fronted noun is further exemplified by the following:

(6) b. *Mbûzi* atsíkáná á mfúmu a-a-gul-á
10-goats 2-girls 2-AssocM 9-chief 2S-perf-buy-fv
zákúd-a
10SM-black
'Goats, the chief's girls have bought black (ones)'

c. *Mikánda*, anyaní ópúsa a-na-b-á *yófiíla*
4-beads 2-baboons 2SM-silly 2SM-pst-steal-fv 4SM-red
'Beads, the silly baboons stole red ones.'

The constraints on word order, requiring the modifier to be the remnant and not precede the head noun, is shown by the ungrammaticality of the following:

(7) a. *awa óbúntha anyání a-na-**í**-gúl-íl-á
6-these 6SM-blunt 2-baboon 2SM-pst-4OM-buy-appl-fv
makásu **mikángó yókálamba**
6-hoe 4-lion 4SM-aged

b. **zakuda* atsíkáná á mfúmu a-a-gul-á
10SM-black 2-girls 2AssocM 9-chief 2SM-perf-buy-fv
mbûzi
10-goats

c. **yofiila* anyaní ópúsa a-na-b-á *míkánda*
4SM-red 2-baboons 2SM-silly 2SM-pst-steal-fv 4-beads

The linearization strategy employed with split NPs not induced by OM appears to require preservation of the 'base' order. Possibly, this may be part of a general constraint on linearization in natural language. Comparable restrictions have been noted in the Algonquian language of Ojibwe (cf. Kathol & Rhodes 1999). The word order seems to be sensitive to semantic factors. Syntactically, the preservation of the base ordering relations in the output (split) structure undermines a movement analysis of split NPs. The movement would need to be sensitive to the order of the moved constituents, giving the movement rule global power.

The linearization of the split NPs in Chicheŵa could equally be dealt with in terms of constraints on anaphoric linkage. In view of the anaphoric nature of the remnant, it could be claimed that the linear order reflects preservation in the c-structure representation of f-command relations (cf. Bresnan 2001; Dalrymple 2001) with the ordering restriction deriving from the appositive nature of the remnant.

18.6 Semantic Relations

Another situation obtains when the dislocated NP specifies a super-ordinate term and the remnant denotes a subset or hyponym. In these cases, it is arguable that the two nominals do not constitute "discontinuous constituents," as they do not seem to comprise a constituent in the standard sense (cf. Nolda, 2000, for some observations from German). The situation is exemplified by the following:

(8) a. *Nsomba*, anyání ópúsa a-na-gúl-á *milämba*
10-fish 2-baboon 2SM-foolish 2SM-pst-buy-fv 4-mudfish
'(As for) fish, the foolish baboons bought mudfish'

b. *Miténgo*, njovu z-anu zi-ku-gwéts-á
4-trees 10-elephants 10SM-your 10SM-pres-fell-fv
milámbe
4-baobabs
'(As for) trees, your elephants are pulling down (the) baobabs.'

In these cases, the super-ordinate term appears in a left-dislocated position while the hyponym appears in the post-verbal position. The structure is ungrammatical if the hyponym precedes the super-ordinate term even when the construction involved is, arguably, a right dislocation. Consider the following:

(9) a. **Milămba* anyaní ópúsa a-na-gúl-á *nsomba*
4-mudfish 2-baboon 2SM-foolish 2SM-pst-buy-fv 10-fish

b. *Anyaní ópúsa a-na-gúl-á *milămba nsomba*
2-baboon 2SM-foolish 2SM-pst-buy-fv 4-mudfish 10-fish

The situation that obtains between the left-dislocated antecedent and the remnant also holds for quantified NPs. In a split NP, the Topic head noun must precede the quantifier and it must be in a left dislocation position:

(10) a. Zisakasa anyaní ópúsa a-na-máng-á zi-sanu
8-grass-huts 2-baboons 2SM-silly 2SM-pst-build-fv 8SM-five
z-ókha
8SM-only
'Grass huts, the silly baboons built only five.'

b. Zisakasa anyaní ópúsa a-na-máng-á zó-chépa
8-grass-huts 2-baboons 2SM-silly 2SM-pst-build-fv 8SM-few
'Grass huts, the silly baboons built a few.'

As in previous examples, the head noun must precede the remnant or the quantifier:

(11) a. *Zi-sanu z-ókha anyaní ópúsa a-na-máng-á
8SM-five 8SM-only 2-baboons 2SM-silly 2SM-pst-build-fv
zisakasa
8-grass huts

b. *Zó-chépa anyaní ópúsa a-na-máng-á zisakasa
8SM-few 2-baboons 2SM-silly 2SM-pst-build-fv 8-grass-huts

These facts indicate the relevance of linear precedence relations to semantic interpretation and the need for articulation of linearization principles. Alternatively, this can be viewed as a constraint on the preservation or transparency in c-structure of f-structure relations. For instance, while command relations are stated in f-structure, the mapping of the elements in c-structure should make those relations transparent, facilitating the computation of the construal of the expression. In brief, the linearization principle is regulated by semantic factors that require giving the set before the subset. This means that the information in the component that is construed a the whole precedes that of the parts. Thus, the super-ordinate is given in front of the hyponym, and the whole in front of the quantifier.

18.7 On NPs that cannot be Discontinuous

There are cases where discontinuity of the constituents of the NP is not possible. Two cases will be examined here. In the one case, the OM is present, yet there are constraints on how constituents of the NP could be split. Among the cases where discontinuous constituents are not possible are relative clauses (cf. Mchombo 2003, 2004). These will be avoided here. More illustrative are recursive constructions involving associative phrases. This is exemplified by NPs with a head noun and a complement introduced by the associative marker *-a* 'of' as shown below:

(12) a. chipanda chá kazitápe
7-calabash 7AssocM 1a-spy
'The spy's calabash.'
Lit. 'calabash of spy.'

This construction allows for recursion, shown in the following construction:

(12) b. chipanda ch-á kazitápé w-á alenje
7-calabash 7SM-AssocM 1a-spy 1SM-AssocM 2-hunters
'Calabash of the spy of the hunters.'

This nominal has its ϕ-features duplicated by the OM in the verbal morphology in sentence (13) below.

(13) Anyaní á mísala a-ku-**chí**-phwány-a
2-baboon 2AssocM 4-madness 2SM-pres-7OM-smash-fv
chipanda chá kazitápé wá alenje
7-calabash 7AssocM 1a-spy 1AssocM 2-hunter
'The mad baboons are smashing the calabash of the hunters' spy.'

In this case, re-ordering the major nominal constituents of the sentence does not pose any problems. However, discontinuity of the constituents of the nominal expressions is tolerable only within limits, as illustrated below:

(14) a. **Chá kazitápé wá alenje** anyaní
7AssocM 1a-spy 1AssocM 2-hunter 2-baboon
á mísala a-ku-**chí**-phwány-a **chipanda**
2AssocM 4-madness 2SM-pres-7OM-smash-fv 7-calabash
'Of the spy of the hunters the mad baboons are smashing the calabash.'

However, when it is the more deeply embedded associative phrase 'of the hunters' that is displaced, the result is ungrammatical.

(14) b. ***Wá** **alenje** anyaní á misala
1AssocM 2-hunter 2-baboon 2AssocM 4-madness
a-ku-**chí**-phwány-a **chipanda chá** **kazitápe**
2SM-pres-7OM-smash-fv 7-calabash 7AssocM 1a-spy

A relevant consideration here could be that there is a clash in the ϕ-features of the displaced constituent and the OM. That turns out to be irrelevant, as demonstrated by the example below where the ϕ-features are controlled for through selection of nominals from the same gender class.

(14) c. Anyaní á mísala a-ku-**chí**-phwány-a
2-baboon 2AssocM 4-madness 2SM-pres-7OM-smash-fv
chipanda chá **chiphadzúwá chá** **alenje**
7-calabash 7AssocM 7-beauty-queen 7SM-AssocM 2-hunter
'The mad baboons are smashing the calabash of the hunters' beauty-queen'

Moving the Associative Phrase 'of the hunters' as in (14b) still yields ungrammatical results, despite the agreement between the OM and the moved Associative Phrase.

(14) d. ***Chá** **alenje** anyaní á misala
1AssocM 2-hunter 2-baboon 2AssocM 4-madness
a-ku-**chí**-phwány-a **chipanda chá** **chiphadzúwa**
2SM-pres-7OM-smash-fv 7-calabash 7AssocM 7-beauty-queen

The ungrammatical sentence involves discontinuity of constituents of a complement of a noun that is itself a complement of a higher noun. This could be handled through appeal to island effects perhaps along the lines of the A-over-A constraint or, possibly, a modified version of the Left Branch Condition of Ross (1967). Alternatively, as noted by Dalrymple (p.c), the extraction is eliminated by general restrictions on constructions involving non-branching dominance.

Notable from these considerations is the fact that discontinuous constituents in Chicheŵa and the limits on them do not straightforwardly provide motivation for accounts of information structure grounded in movement rules. Conversely, information structure does not motivate the need for such devices in grammatical theory. This has already been foreshadowed by the observations above concerning constraints on linear precedence. It was noted that the requirement that split NPs preserve the 'base' linear order undermines the motivation for a movement analysis of discontinuous elements (cf. Dahlstrom 1987; Kathol & Rhodes 1999; Mchombo & Morimoto 2004). The movement rule would involve the stipulation that independently moved elements must retain the same ordering relation between the base and derived positions. As noted by Sells (2001), this is a recurrent problem for transformational approaches to phenomena like multiple wh-questions and object shift.

18.8 Semantic Restrictions on Discontinuity

A case where discontinuous constituents are disallowed on semantic grounds involves what may be called intersective modifiers,[5] also known as 'intensional adjectives' (cf. Andrews & Manning 1999). These are illustrated by such NPs as 'the alleged criminal,' 'the promised land,' 'my ex-wife' etc. In Chicheŵa, such NPs cannot be split. Consider the following:

(15) a. mkází w-angá wá kále
1-woman 1SM-1st poss 1SM-AssocM old
'my ex-wife' (lit: my woman of old)

b. dzíkó ló-lónjéz-dw-a
5-country 5SM-promise-passive-fv
'(the) promised land'

These NPs can appear in sentences such as the following:

(16) a. mkángó wókálamba u-ku-fún-á mkází w-angá
3-lion 3SM-aged 3SM-pres-want-fv 1-wife 1SM-1st poss
wá kále
1SM-AssocM old
'The aged lion wants my ex-wife.'

b. ***mkázi w-ánga** mkángó wókálamba
1-wife 1SM-1st poss 3-lion 3SM-aged
u-ku-fún-á **wá** **kále**
3SM-pres-want-fv 1SM-AssocM old

In (16b) the NP 'my ex-wife' is split, with 'my wife' appearing on the left periphery of the clause, typical of left dislocation. The sentence is ungrammatical and remains marginal even with the OM. It is worse if the head noun *mkázi* 'woman, wife' is fronted alone, and *w-angá wá kale* 'my ex' is the remnant. This is shown in (16c) below:

(16) c. ***mkázi** mkángó wókálamba u-ku-fún-á
1-wife 3-lion 3SM-aged 3SM-pres-want-fv
w-ánga **wá** **kále**
1SM-1st poss 1SM-AssocM old

d. ***mkázi** mkángó wókálamba u-ku-mú-fún-a
1-wife 3-lion 3SM-aged 3SM-pres-1OM-want-fv

[5] Thanks to Caroline Féry and Andreas Nolda for pointing out this fact to me.

w-ánga **wá** **kále**
1SM-1st poss 1SM-AssocM old

The ungrammaticality shown by the sentences with split NPs indicates the role that semantic considerations may play in syntactic structure. This raises again the perennial questions concerning syntax/semantics interface. It is a matter of fact that there is an intimate connection between syntax and semantics, and between information structure and morphosyntax. Commenting on the grammatical level of representation called logical form (LF) Chomsky claims that LF is the contribution that grammar makes to semantic structure (cf. Chomsky 1987) The issue here is whether there are aspects of syntactic organization that are determined by semantic considerations. If linearization is sensitive to semantic aspects, then the relation between syntax and semantics, as well as between information structure and morphosyntactic organization merits sustained investigation.

18.9 Conclusion

The issue of how information structure notions such as topic and focus are integrated into grammatical structure, and associated with syntactic arguments, involves examination of the relation between syntax and pragmatics. The involvement of the dislocation construction is indicative of that. It has been claimed that "...dislocated constructions are licensed at the syntax/pragmatics interface..." (De Cat 2002; 99). The issues raised in this paper highlight the intricacies in the relations between information structure and morphosyntactic organization. The involvement of semantic factors in linearization, and constraints on discontinuity imposed by intersective modifiers, among other things, indicate a rather intricate relation between syntax and semantics on the one hand, and between information structure and morphosyntactic organization on the other. This is a situation where the relations could be brought into sharp focus in a theory where the informational structures are factored out, with explicit linking principles to capture the connections between the various components, as advocated within the theory of LFG.

References

Allan, Keith. 1983. Anaphora, cataphora, and topic focusing: Functions of the object prefix in Swahili. In I. Dihoff, ed., *Current Approaches to African Linguistics*, vol. 1, pages 323–335. Dordrecht: Foris.

Andrews, Avery D. and Christopher D. Manning. 1999. *Complex Predicates and Information Spreading in LFG*. Stanford, CA: CSLI Publications.

Austin, Peter and Joan Bresnan. 1996. Non-configurationality in Australian aboriginal languages. *Natural Language and Linguistic Theory* 14(2):215–268.

Baker, Mark. 1990. Pronominal inflection and the morphology/syntax interface. In *CLS 26: The main session. Papers from the 26th Meeting of the Chicago Linguistic Society*, pages 25–48. Chicago, IL: Chicago Linguistic Society.

Baker, Mark. 2003. Agreement, dislocation, and partialconfigurationality. In A. Carnie, H. Harley, and M. Willie, eds., *Formal Approaches to Function in Grammar: In honor of Eloise Jelinek*, pages 107–134. Amsterdam: J. Benjamins.

Bresnan, Joan and Sam Mchombo. 1986. Grammatical and anaphoric agreement. In *CLS 22: Papers from the Parasession on Pragmatics and Grammatical Theory*, vol. 2, pages 278–297. Chicago, IL: Chicago Linguistic Society.

Bresnan, Joan and Sam Mchombo. 1987. Topic, pronoun and agreement in Chichewa. *Language* 63(4):741–82.

Chomsky, Noam. 1987. *Generative Grammar: Its basis, development and prospects*. Kyoto: Kyoto University of Foreign Studies.

Dahlstrom, Amy. 1987. Discontinuous constituents in Fox. In P. Kroeber and R. E. Moore, eds., *Native American Languages and Grammatical Typology*, pages 53–73. Bloomington, IN: Indiana University Linguistics Club. Papers form a conference at the University of Chicago.

De Cat, Cécile. 2002a. *French Dislocation*. Ph.D. thesis, University of York.

De Cat, Cécile. 2002b. On the status of French subject clitics and their impact on the information structure of the sentence. Ms., University of York.

Deen, Kamil U. 2004. Let's build some agreement: The status of the subject prefix in Nairobi Swahili. Paper presented at the 35th Annual Conference of African Linguistics, Harvard University.

Demuth, Katherine and Mark Johnson. 1989. Interaction between discourse functions and agreement in Setawana. *Journal of African Languages and Linguistics* 11:21–35.

Hale, Kenneth L. 1981. Preliminary remarks on the grammar of part-whole relations in Warlpiri. In J. Hollyman and A. Pawley, eds., *Studies in Pacific languages and cultures: In honour of Bruce Biggs*, pages 333–344. Auckland: Linguistics Society of New Zealand.

Hale, Kenneth L. 1983. Warlpiri and the grammar of non-configurational languages. *Natural Language and Linguistic Theory* 1:5–47.

Jelinek, Eloise. 1984. Empty categories, case, and configurationality. *Natural Language and Linguistic Theory* 2:39–76.

Jelinek, Eloise. 1996. Topic and focus in Navajo inverse. In *Proceedings of the 15th West Coast Conference in Formal Linguistics (WCCFL 15)*, pages 241–255. Stanford, CA: CSLI Publications.

Kathol, Andreas and Richard A. Rhodes. 1999. Constituency and linearization of Ojibwe nominals. In M. Caldecott, S. Gessner, and E.-S. Kim, eds., *Proceedings of the Workshop on Structure and Constituency in Languages of the Americas (WSCLA 4)*, pages 75–91. Vancouver: Dept. of Linguistics, University of British Columbia.

Letsholo, Rose. 2002. *Syntactic Domains in Ikalanga*. Ph.D. thesis, University of Michigan.

Letsholo, Rose. 2004. WH constructions in Ikalanga: An alternative analysis. Paper presented at the 35th Annual Conference of African Linguistics, Harvard University.

Matthewson, Lisa and Charlotte Reinholtz. 1996. The syntax and semantics of determiners: A comparison of Salish and Cree. In H. Davis, ed., *Papers from the 31st International Conference on Salish and Neighbouring Languages (ICSNL 31)*, pages 211–237. Vancouver: University of British Columbia Press.

Mchombo, Sam. 1984. The non-existence of verb-object agreement in Bantu. Ms., Massachusetts Institute of Technology and University of Malawi.

Mchombo, Sam. 2001. Effects of head-marking on constituent order in Chichewa. Paper presented at the 6th International Lexical Functional Grammar Association conference, June 25-27, 2001. The University of Hong Kong.

Mchombo, Sam. 2002a. Affixes, clitics and Bantu morphosyntax. In M. Amberber, ed., *Perspectives on Cognitive Science 3. Language Universals and Variation*. Westport, CT: Greenwood.

Mchombo, Sam. 2002b. Argument structure, functional structure, and the split morphology hypothesis. In Z. E. Fernández and R. M. O. Ciscomani, eds., *VI Encuentro International de Linguistica en el Noroeste*, pages 29–53. Hermosillo: Université de Sonora.

Mchombo, Sam. 2003. On discontinuous constituents in Chichewa. In A. Zribi-Hertz and P. Sauzet, eds., *Typologie des langues d'Afrique et universaux de la grammaire*, pages 141–167. Paris: L'Harmattan.

Mchombo, Sam. 2004a. Head-marking, agreement and partial configurationality in Chichewa. In I. B. Aguilar and M. C. Llamas, eds., *VII Encuentro Internacional de Linguistica en el Noroeste*, pages 431–444. Hermosillo: Université de Sonora.

Mchombo, Sam. 2004b. *The Syntax of Chichewa*. Cambridge, UK: Cambridge University Press.

Mchombo, Sam and Yukiko Morimoto. 2004. Local constraints on Chichewa discontinuous constituents. Paper presented at the 8th International Lexical Functional Grammar Association conference, New York, NY.

Morimoto, Yukiko. 2000. *Discourse Configurationality in Bantu Morphosyntax*. Ph.D. thesis, Stanford University.

Morimoto, Yukiko. 2002. From synchrony to diachrony: Topic salience and cross-linguistic patterns of agreement. Ms., Heinrich-Heine Universität Düsseldorf.

Neale, Stephen. 1996. Prolegomena to a 'variable-driven' syntax: reflections on logical form and Chomsky's minimalist program. Ms., University of California, Berkeley.

Nolda, Andreas. 2000. Split topicalization in German. In R. Sackmann, ed., *Studies in Integrational Linguistics*. Amsterdam: J. Benjamins. To appear.

Omar, Alwiya S. 1990. Grammatical and anaphoric relations in Kiswahili: Functions of the subject and object prefixes. Unpublished paper, Indiana University.

Reinhart, Tanya. 1981. Pragmatics and linguistics: An analysis of sentence topics. *Philosophica* 27:53–94. Special Issue on Pragmatic Theory.

Ross, John R. 1967. *Constraints on Variable in Syntax*. Ph.D. thesis, Massachusetts Institute of Technology.

Rubanza, Yunus Ismail. 1988. *Linear Order in Haya Verbal Morphology: Theoretical Implications*. Ph.D. thesis, Michigan State University.

Sabimana, Firmard. 1986. *The Relational Structure of the Kirundi Verb*. Ph.D. thesis, Indiana University.

Sells, Peter, ed. 2001. *Formal and Empirical Issues in Optimality Theoretic Syntax*. Stanford, CA: CSLI Publications.

19

Deconstructing Thematic Hierarchies*

MALKA RAPPAPORT HOVAV AND BETH LEVIN

This paper aims to deepen our understanding of a widely adopted theoretical construct: the thematic hierarchy (TH). A TH is a ranking of a set of semantic roles, intended to reflect precedence relations among them. THs are adopted by proponents of many major theoretical frameworks, including Lexical Functional Grammar, Functional Grammar, Government-Binding and descendants, and Role and Reference Grammar, and they figure in accounts of a considerable range of linguistic phenomena in many languages, including subject and object selection, applicativization, causativization, and serialization, as well as in the statement of typological implicational generalizations.

Despite the frequent appeals to the TH, there is a lack of agreement concerning its formulation. The literature contains a plethora of

*We dedicate this paper to Joan Bresnan, with whom we were both fortunate to study syntax. Over the years several strands of our work have been indebted to hers; in fact, her writing on the thematic hierarchy played an important part in the development of our own thinking about it.

This paper draws on Chapter 6 of Levin and Rappaport Hovav (2005). We thank John Beavers, Ivy Sichel, and Shiao Wei Tham, and the audience at the Hebrew University English Department Linguistics Seminar for fruitful discussion of the issues in this paper. Fellowships at the Center for Advanced Study in the Behavioral Sciences provided us with time to develop these ideas; financial support for Levin's stay at the Center was provided by the Center's general funds and for Rappaport Hovav's stay by the Andrew W. Mellon Foundation Grant 29800639. The preparation of this paper was supported in part by Israel Science Foundation grant 806-03 to Rappaport Hovav.

Architectures, Rules, and Preferences: Variations on Themes by Joan Bresnan.
Annie Zaenen, Jane Simpson, Tracy Holloway King,
Jane Grimshaw, Joan Maling, and Chris Manning, (eds.).

instantiations of the TH, which differ in the semantic roles composing the hierarchy and the ranking of these roles. An implicit working hypothesis is that one TH is valid for all languages and all relevant phenomena, and the "right" TH will emerge from empirical investigation. Critics, however, take this variety of THs as evidence that it is impossible to arrive at a single TH and that, therefore, it makes no sense to posit such a construct.

After providing some background on the appeal and limitations of the TH in sections 1 and 2, we examine the ways in which THs should be understood. We argue that it is impossible to formulate a single TH that will cover all the generalizations that THs have figured in, since these generalizations are heterogeneous in nature. Often a TH is best understood as providing a notation—a ranking of semantic roles—for stating a generalization. This notation has been used to state a variety of generalizations, leading to different THs, but such THs do not explain the generalizations they capture, nor can they be primitive linguistic constructs. In most instances, the generalizations captured by proposed THs arise from several interacting factors, and the key to understanding the relevant THs lies in teasing apart these factors. In fact, some generalizations which appear to implicate THs actually turn out to be more accurately stated in terms of other properties, such as animacy, which are aligned in systematic ways with semantic roles.

In this context, we turn to the most widespread use of the TH: constraining the basic realization of the arguments of a verb. We suggest that in this domain there is indeed a universal ranking of semantic roles; however, the TH which expresses this ranking is epiphenomenal and not an independent, primitive construct. Rather, this TH can be derived from the more basic elements of the lexical semantic representation of verbs. We uncover the sources of TH effects in argument realization by examining two understandings of the TH that have figured in accounts of this phenomenon, showing that each uses a distinct notion of prominence to rank semantic roles—notions that are related to two views of the nature of semantic roles themselves. We demonstrate that both notions of prominence have a part to play in subject and object selection.

19.1 Problems with thematic hierarchies

Although THs are often used to account for robust linguistic generalizations, there is some skepticism regarding the status of the TH as a linguistic construct, stemming largely from the bewildering number of formulations in the literature. We present a small sample to illustrate their variety. (In the THs below, "Agt" is agent, "Assoc" is associative, "Ben" is benefactive, "Eff" is effector, "Exp" is experiencer, "G" is goal, "Inst" is instrument, "L" is location, "Mann" is manner, "Rec" is recipient, "S" is source, "Temp" is temporal. Roles ranked together are separated by a slash. Dik's "goal" and Fillmore's "objective" are relabelled "patient" to conform to more established usage and facilitate comparison.)

(1) a. Agt > Th/Pat > G/S/L (Baker 1997)
    b. Agt > Exp > Th (Belletti and Rizzi 1988)
    c. Agt > Ben > Rec/Exp > Inst > Th/Pat > L (Bresnan and Kanerva 1989)
    d. Agt > Pat > Rec > Ben > Inst > L > Temp (Dik 1978)
    e. Agt > Exp > Inst > Pat > G/S/L > Time (Fillmore 1971)
    f. Agt > Dat/Ben > Pat > L > Inst/Assoc > Mann (Givón 1984)
    g. Act > Pat/Ben > Th > G/S/L > Ben (Jackendoff 1990)
    h. Agt > Eff > Exp > L > Th > Pat (Van Valin 1990)

These and other THs differ along several dimensions. First, they may include alternate relative rankings of certain pairs of roles; for example, Fillmore ranks patient below instrument, while Givón does the opposite. Second, some THs use finer-grained roles than others. Van Valin distinguishes between agents and effectors and between patients and themes, while others do not. Some THs rank non-cooccurring roles (e.g., goal and experiencer) with respect to each other, while others do not. Some THs include only roles associated with arguments, while others also include those associated with adjuncts.

There are two reactions to this diversity. Some researchers assume that a closer scrutiny of the empirical evidence will provide arguments in favor of a particular TH (cf. the exchange between Bresnan and Kanerva (1989, 1992) and Schachter (1992)). Others merely dismiss the TH. Newmeyer, for example, concludes that "There is reason for strong doubt that there exists a Thematic Hierarchy provided by UG. That seems to be the best explanation for the fact that after over three decades of investigation, nobody has proposed a hierarchy of theta-roles that comes close to working" (2000:65).

It is necessary, however, to determine what counts as a working TH. Proposed THs can be meaningfully compared only if they are interpreted in the same way and are meant to account for the same range of phenomena. Existing THs differ in both respects. Once the interpretation given to prominence is made explicit and tied in an explanatory way to the phenomena a given hierarchy is meant to account for, it should be possible to answer questions such as whether or not a TH should only rank semantic roles of co-arguments of a verb and what the appropriate grain-size of the roles constituting a TH is. As we discuss, once the various uses of the TH notation are appropriately understood, no single TH may turn out to cover the entire range of generalizations that appeal to a TH. This conclusion, however, does not mean that a particular TH may not accurately capture the generalizations motivating it.

19.2 Context dependence: One motivation for a thematic hierarchy

We begin our close scrutiny of the TH by reviewing a major motivation for positing it: "context dependence" in the realization of arguments. There often is no one-to-one correspondence between an argument's semantic role and its morphosyntactic realization; its realization often depends on the roles of cooccurring arguments. As we show, the TH is well-suited for capturing such context dependence.

This point can be illustrated with the widely-cited paradigm in (2), which is the basis of Fillmore's (1968) subject selection rule in (3), subsequently reformulated in terms of a TH.

(2) a. The door opened.
    b. Dana opened the door.
    c. The chisel opened the door.
    d. Dana opened the door with a chisel.

(3) If there is an A [=Agent], it becomes the subject; otherwise, if there is an I [=Instrument], it becomes the subject; otherwise, the subject is the O [=Objective, i.e., Patient/Theme]. (Fillmore 1968:33)

These data illustrate context dependence as the expression of *the door* depends on whether there is a cooccurring agent or instrument role and, similarly, the expression of the instrument depends on whether there is a cooccurring agent. These observations are naturally captured by the TH in (4) together with a subject selection rule that states that the argument of a verb bearing the highest-ranked semantic role is its subject.

(4) Agent > Instrument > Patient/Theme

TH-based accounts, then, allow reference to arguments in terms of the relative ranking of their semantic roles, obviating the need to refer explicitly to specific semantic roles. This property facilitates more general accounts of various linguistic phenomena. In fact, the just-posited subject selection rule in conjunction with the TH in (5) will account for Speas's (1990:73) observation that recipients can be subjects only when not in the presence of an agent, as shown in (6).

(5) Agent > Recipient > Theme

(6) a. Alex received a package.
b. Sam sent Alex a package.

A somewhat different form of context dependence is found in Polinsky and Kozinsky's (1992) study of applicatives and causatives in Kinyarwanda. They note that whether an "oblique" argument or a causee can be the first of two objects of an applicative or causative verb depends on cooccurring "oblique" arguments (the second object is the verb's "own" object). They propose that in instances of cooccurrence, the argument ranked higher in the TH in (7) is expressed as the first object.

(7) recipient > benefactive > possessor > causee > instrument > comitative (Polinsky and Kozinsky 1992: 440, (40))

This hierarchy, for instance, captures the observation that a benefactive has priority over an instrument for expression as first object, with the instrument expressed as an oblique PP.

Context dependence also has prompted reference to THs in the statement of crosslinguistic generalizations about argument realization (Dik 1978, 1997; Givón 1984). "Deep" ergative languages aside, all languages allow a verb's agent to be expressed as subject, but differ as to whether other arguments may be expressed as subject in the absence of an agent. Similarly, all languages allow patient/themes as objects, but vary as to which other non-agent arguments can also be objects. Dik (1978) and Givón (1984) propose that the constraints on variation can best be described through reference to a TH. Languages choose semantic roles that can be realized as subjects or objects from a continuous portion of the TH starting with the agent for the subject and the second-highest role for the object and working downwards—what Dik calls the Continuity Hypothesis (1978:76). As Dik illustrates, languages may differ in their choice of cut-off points for subjecthood or objecthood on the TH. Thus, assuming the TH in (8), all languages have agent subjects, some might have agent and patient subjects, others agent, patient and recipient subjects, and so on. None, however, would have patient, recipient, and instrument subjects only. Similarly, according to (8) a language would allow benefactive objects only if it allows patients and recipients also to be objects.

(8) Agt > Pat > Rec > Ben > Inst > Loc > Temp
(Dik 1978: 70, (3))

These typological generalizations apply across languages, defining a set of possible languages with respect to the options for the realization of various semantic roles as subject and object. In contrast, the instances of context dependence discussed earlier involve priorities among a verb's co-arguments with respect to their potential realization as subject or (applied) object. So, while Dik's generalization states that a language only allows recipient subjects, if it also allows agent and patient subjects, the other type of generalization involves whether a recipient may be realized as the subject of a particular verb in a language which allows such subjects. The ranking of semantic roles relevant for one purpose may not be relevant for the other. Recognizing that different kinds of generalizations capture context dependence over distinct domains is crucial for understanding why various THs have been proposed.

19.3 Deconstructing thematic hierarchies

The key to understanding the myriad instantiations of the TH lies in teasing apart the factors which underlie the generalizations captured by particular hierarchies, as we show in this section and the next. Before attempting to show this, we mention some complicating issues that must be recognized in any comparative evaluation of THs, so they can be set aside. First, two THs can be compared only if any semantic roles they both include have the same extension, yet this is often not the case. One theory of semantic roles may use a particular label more broadly than a second; differences in grain-size are particularly prevalent with the notions "goal", "theme", and "patient". Second, a TH interacts with other constructs and assumptions of the larger linguistic theory it is integrated into. Some variation in the placement of a particular semantic role across THs might be traced to such interactions and may lack empirical consequences. For instance, whether the TH is used with a monostratal or multistratal syntactic theory can have repercussions for role ranking, as we mention below. Furthermore, the choice of semantics-to-syntax mapping algorithm and the ranking of semantic roles in a TH are mutually dependent, and some disagreements about the statement of the TH may stem from this interdependence. Fuller discussions of these issues is found in Levin and Rappaport Hovav (2005).

Sometimes THs simply provide a concise way of stating a particular generalization which arises from a conspiracy of independent factors and should not be confused with the explanation for the generalization. For instance, Polinsky and Kozinsky (1992:440) write that their TH, cited in (7) "is simply a generalization of the empirical regularities discussed". To illustrate this we scrutinize hierarchies which differ as to whether or not benefactives and recipients are ranked together and as to whether these roles are ranked above or below patient/theme. These differences can be understood in the context of a survey of the expression of these roles in and across languages. Many languages allow recipient and benefactive arguments to be expressed not only as adjuncts, but also via a "core" grammatical relation, e.g., as first object in a double object construction (e.g., English) or as a dative case-marked NP (e.g., German). Since they both show the same core expression, a recipient and a benefactive cannot cooccur (**I mailed Mom Pat the letter*), so a statement about the ranking of these roles relative to, say, patient/theme does not have to distinguish between them. Other generalizations, however, must treat them differently. One example is Polinsky and Kozinsky's (1992) generalization about which role has precedence in access to direct object expression in applicatives; a second is Dik's (1978, 1997) generalization about the likelihood that NPs bearing particular roles will be subjects or objects crosslinguistically (see section 2).

Turning now to the ranking of recipient and benefactive with respect to patient/theme, Dik (1978, 1997) ranks these two roles below patient/theme to capture the generalization that all languages allow patient/theme direct objects, but only some allow recipient or benefactive objects (at least in terms of surface "coding" in the sense of Keenan (1976)). Furthermore, patient/themes are typically the subjects of unaccusative intransitive verbs, but no language allows recipient or benefactive subjects of "unaccusatives" (Baker 1996, 1997). Since Dik wishes to capture the likelihood of a semantic role being associated with both subject and object in a single TH within a monostratal framework, patient/theme needs to be ranked above recipient or benefactive, since subject and object are chosen working down from the top of the TH.

In contrast, Givón (1984) posits the reverse ranking: recipient (his "dative") and benefactive are higher than patient/theme. This ranking reflects a concern with language-internal interactions in the realization of arguments bearing particular semantic roles. It is well-known that recipients and benefactives often usurp from patient/themes certain of the coding properties of direct objects, such as control of object agreement on the verb, closeness to the verb, and promotion to subject under passive. Givón's ranking appears to express the likelihood that NPs bearing these semantic roles show these properties. When a patient/theme and a recipient or benefactive both bear core grammatical relations, the recipient or benefactive is more likely to show these coding properties. For example, in the English double object construction the recipient or benefactive appears immediately after the verb and is the derived subject in the related passive.

The point to stress is that the facts that Dik is interested in and those that Givón is interested in cannot be captured by a single TH, although specific THs can be formulated to express each generalization. Such THs, however, must be considered convenient shorthands for stating the relevant generalizations; they are not primitive constructs which figure in the explanation of the phenomena. In the final analysis, a deeper explanation for the range of facts must be found; we now speculate on what it might be.

Recipients and benefactives have coding properties that motivate Givón to rank them together and above patient/theme. The reason, probably, is that recipients and benefactives are typically animate, while patient/themes are not. Animates are more likely to be topical than inanimates, and it is topical NPs that tend to show these coding properties. In fact, crosslinguistically, there are various factors which determine which of two objects in a double object construction have these coding properties, including animacy and definiteness. Thus, ultimately the observations underlying Givón's ranking have their source in animacy considerations, and semantic roles and—hence, the TH—are only indirectly implicated (cf. Evans 1997). Why do Dik's and Polinsky and Kozinsky's generalizations rank recipient above benefactive? Perhaps, they distinguish recipients from benefactives because recipients, but not benefactives, are arguments of their verb (cf. Polinsky and Kozinsky 1992:440) and, hence, more likely to become objects. We speculate that the ranking of patient/theme above recipient and benefactive in Dik's hierarchy for the purposes of subject and object selection has its roots in the fact that recipients and benefactives are usually expressed with dedicated "semantic cases", while patient/themes are not. Hence, patient/themes are more likely to be basic direct object across languages, and only languages which have some means of "advancing" recipients and benefactives to direct object will have them as objects.

19.4 The thematic hierarchy in argument realization

The assumption that the TH is a primitive linguistic construct is most often made in conjunction with TH-based accounts of how the arguments of a given verb can be syntactically realized—perhaps, the best known use of the TH. The TH is used to define constraints on argument realization, allowing attested and precluding unattested pairings of semantic roles with grammatical relations. However, in most recent work semantic roles are taken to be derived notions, so that a TH, as it is composed of semantic roles, should also be derived. Semantic roles are essentially labels for classes of arguments; there are two major approaches to defining these classes in terms of basic elements of the lexical semantic representations of verbs. These two approaches to understanding semantic roles dovetail with two distinct understandings, pointed out by Bresnan and Kanerva (1989:23-24), of what the ranking of roles in a TH represents. We show each understanding of the ranking derives from the associated understanding of semantic roles. The TH, then, turns out to be epiphenomenal, derived from the basic elements of lexical semantic representation; nevertheless, these elements should, in principle, give rise to a clear ranking of semantic roles.

One way of understanding the derivative status of semantic roles takes them to be labels for positions in an "event structure"—a structured representation of an event, usually taking the form of a predicate decomposition. Prominence relations among arguments, defined in terms of positions in the predicate decomposition, induce a ranking of the corresponding semantic roles and, thus, give rise to a TH. The TH, then, reflects the relative depth of embedding of semantic roles in the event structure (e.g., Jackendoff 1990). There is a second instantiation of the idea that prominence relations reflect the internal "structure" of a verb's own meaning, which is cited by Bresnan and Kanerva (1989) in introducing the two conceptions of the TH: the TH reflects the order of composition of arguments with their verb (e.g., Larson 1988). In fact, order of composition is meaningful only if it reduces to depth of embedding. The reason, as Kratzer (1996) points out, is that alternative orders of composition of the arguments of a single predicate have no detectable semantic effect. Therefore, it is not surprising that some researchers suggest that the TH reflects both depth of embedding and order of composition of arguments (Kiparsky 1987, based on Wunderlich 1977).

A TH thus defined is not an independent construct, but a generalization over possible event structures. Each event structure defines a set of semantic roles that may cooccur as arguments of verbs—one of the pluses of defining roles over event structures. The inventory of event structures, then, determines the possible sets of cooccurring roles, and, thus, what sets of roles may be ranked. Roles that do not cooccur as arguments of a verb do not appear in the same event structure and, thus, cannot be ranked with respect to each other. Since semantic roles name argument positions in an event structure and there are taken to be fairly few event structures involving a small set of rather general predicates, the posited semantic roles are fairly coarse-grained. For example, a frequently posited predicate is CAUSE, and its first argument is taken to define a semantic role. Although this role is usually identified as "agent" (e.g., Jackendoff 1972), it is probably more accurate to label it "causer" since the first argument of this predicate is not filled only by agents in a strict sense; for some verbs, it could also accommodate natural forces and certain instruments (Baker 1997; Van Valin and Wilkins 1996). The label "agent" in THs of this type is then best viewed as a stand-in for all the "roles" which can appear as first argument of CAUSE. More generally, any semantic role figuring in such a TH may be a stand-in for what are several related finer-grained roles in other types of THs.

Structurally-based THs are usually appealed to by researchers who assume that the semantics-to-syntax mapping "preserves" prominence relations between arguments: "Constituent structure at D-structure represents (the) semantic compositionality (of events)", to quote Marantz (1993:143). Such THs figure in generalizations about the relative prominence of arguments in the syntax, as in Larson's statement that "the lowest role on the Thematic Hierarchy is assigned to the lowest argument in constituent structure, the next lowest role to the next lowest argument, and so on" (1988:382).

If "order of Th-roles is a reflection of their semantic depth" (Kiparsky 1997:484), then an independent criterion is needed to establish when one argument of a multiargument verb is more embedded than a second. Clearly, when such a verb has a complex event structure, comprised of one event embedded in a second, then an argument of the higher event is less embedded than an argument of the lower event and should outrank it in the TH. A range of evidence has been adduced for attributing a complex event structure to causative verbs, such as *break* or *kill* (Dowty 1979; McCawley 1973; Morgan 1969; von Stechow 1995, 1996). In such an event structure the caused event containing the patient is embedded under the predicate CAUSE, which also takes the causer as an argument, justifying the ranking of causer over patient.

However, there is no independent way to establish the relative ranking of arguments of a multiargument verb with a simple event structure, including the two arguments of non-causative verbs like *have, love, see, want, scratch,* and *wipe.* One argument of such verbs is realized as subject and the other is not, suggesting a prominence relation between them, yet their relative ranking cannot be established independent of their morphosyntactic realization, which is what the ranking is supposed to predict. For example, this understanding of the TH cannot explain why it is the experiencer rather than the stimulus argument of verbs like *see* or *love* that is realized as subject, since there is no embedding relation between these two arguments in a typical event structure, and, thus, in this and comparable examples there is no way to rule out certain unattested pairings of semantic roles with grammatical relations. Although the inability to handle such examples proves a serious limitation of the structural understanding of the TH, there is a second way of understanding the derived status of semantic roles, which can be used to supplement the first, as it can impose a ranking on arguments when event structure position fails to. The second approach to semantic roles takes them to be defined in terms of sets of lexical entailments imposed by verbs on their arguments by virtue of the parts they play in the events the verbs describe. Dowty's notion of proto-role is perhaps the best-known instantiation of this approach (Dowty 1991; Ackerman and Moore 2001; Primus 1999). Semantic roles, then, represent clusters of "event-based" properties of arguments, with each of these properties contributing in its own way to the ranking of arguments, and, hence, to the place of the semantic roles defined over them in a TH. For instance, as some researchers (Dowty 1991:574; Croft 1998:37; Koenig and Davis 2001:83; Primus 1999:52–53) have noticed, several of the entailments included under Dowty's Agent and Patient Proto-roles come in pairs: the Agent Proto-role entailment "causing an event or change of state in another participant" can be paired with the Patient Proto-role entailment "undergoes change of state" and the Agent Proto-role entailment "movement (relative to the position of another participant)" can be paired with the Patient Proto-role entailment "stationary relative to movement of another participant". These paired entailments arise because of asymmetric relations between participants in certain types of events, and, thus, they implicitly define a ranking of arguments (Primus 1999). Lexical entailments, then, may be involved in defining prominence relations, and, consequently, the TH may be seen as the "cumulative result of interacting relative prominence relations among semantic entities" (Mohanan 1994:28). This idea finds its roots in the work of Fillmore (1977:102), who suggests that the TH he proposed in earlier work (Fillmore 1968, 1971) should be replaced by the following series of rankings.

(9) a. An active element outranks an inactive element.
    b. A causal element outranks a non-causal element.

c. A human (or animate) experiencer outranks other elements.

d. A changed element outranks a non-changed element.

e. A complete or individuated element outranks a part of an element.

f. A 'figure' outranks a 'ground'.

g. A 'definite' element outranks an 'indefinite' element.

The properties of arguments that Fillmore recognizes, as well as a comparable set proposed by Mohanan (1994:28), overlap considerably with the entailments that constitute Dowty's (1991:572) Agent and Patient Proto-roles. This overlap suggests that there is agreement concerning the semantic elements that matter most for argument realization.

The question is what "prominence" means in statements such as those in (9). Fillmore (1977) sees such statements as specifying the relative "salience" of various event participants. Thus, on the view that semantic roles are defined by sets of lexical entailments, a TH made up of such roles would represent a conflation of the effects of such statements. That is, roles would be ranked not in terms of their position in an event structure, but rather in terms of the semantic components that contribute to "salience" or perhaps "topicworthiness". In fact, Givón (1984) and Hawkinson and Hyman (1974), among others, see the TH "as representing a scale of discourse topicality of argument types rather than an order of semantic composition" (Bresnan and Kanerva 1998:23-24). On this understanding, the TH is seen as similar to various natural prominence scales, such as those in (10), which have been appealed to in accounts of a wide range of linguistic phenomena, including coding properties of arguments, such as word order and morphological case.[1]

(10) a. PERSON: first, second > third

b. REFERENTIALITY: pronoun > proper name > common noun

c. ANIMACY: human > animate > inanimate

d. DEFINITENESS: definite > specific > non-specific

[1]The natural prominence scales in (10) rank properties of the NPs that fill semantic roles (or what Evans (1997) calls the "cast"); in contrast, a TH ranks semantic roles, which involved "event-based" properties of NPs—properties entailed by the event described by the verb. It is perhaps for this reason that these natural prominence scales figure in accounts of somewhat different phenomena than the TH; see Levin and Rappaport Hovav (2005). Furthermore, one reason why the semantic properties referred to in Fillmore's statements in (9) do not all find analogues in Dowty's and Mohanan's work is that Fillmore makes reference to properties of the fillers of semantic roles, as well as to event-based properties.

In the scales in (10), prominence is understood as akin to "cognitive salience" (McCarthy 2001; Newmeyer 2000) or "topicality" (Givón 1984), where these are determined on the basis of some semantic properties of NPs. We have introduced two conceptions of semantic roles, reflecting two perspectives on the lexical semantic representation of verbs, each of which allows a ranking to be imposed on semantic roles. We have already shown that semantic roles cannot be exhaustively ranked for purposes of argument realization solely on the basis of the "structure" of event structure. We now consider whether semantic roles can be ranked for these purposes by the event-based entailments that underlie them. We show that these entailments do have a contribution to make, but that argument realization also requires reference to the geometry of event structure.

As noted above, there is considerable agreement concerning the event-based entailments that figure in argument realization. However, a careful consideration of the entailments making up Dowty's Agent Proto-role (1991:572) reveals that not all of these entailments are equally important. Specifically, causation outranks Dowty's other Agent Proto-role entailments in determining subjecthood (Davis and Koenig 2000:75-76). For example, in languages with productive morphological causativization, the introduced causer invariably becomes the subject of a complex causative event, regardless of the number of Agent Proto-role entailments carried by the causee—the base verb's subject argument. Specifically, the new causer is the subject, even if the base verb requires that its subject be sentient, as in the Hebrew example (11a) or, even sentient and volitional, as in the Finnish example (11b).

(11) a. Ha-b'dixa hicxika oti.
the-joke laugh.CAUS I.ACC
'The joke made me laugh.'

b. Uutinen puhu-tt-i nais-i-a
news.item talk-CAUS-PAST woman-PL-PART
pitkään.
long-ILL
'The news made the women talk for a long time.'
(Davis and Koenig 2000: 75, (26))

And, as the pair in (12) shows, causation also takes priority over another Agent Proto-role entailment, motion: a moving participant is the subject only when there is no causer (Dowty 1991).

(12) a. The train passed/crossed the border.

b. The wind blew the napkin off the table.

This data suggests that causation outranks all the other Agent Proto-role entailments in subject selection. We now propose an explanation for this observation.

Among Dowty's Agent Proto-role entailments, causation is the only one that corresponds to a notion that is readily definable in most proposed event structures. We suggest its importance to subject selection follows if prominence relations in the event structure are preserved in argument realization. A causer argument, being the least embedded in a typical causative event structure, would always take precedence over any other argument, no matter what its semantic properties, for the purposes of subject selection. In this way, the relative embedding relations between arguments in a valid event structure are preserved in the syntactic realization of the arguments of a verb; in the syntax the relations could be defined by c-command in a constituent structure or by a hierarchy of grammatical relations.

Although event structure plays an important role in subject and, most likely, object selection,[2] other event-based statements of prominence come into play where event structure is inadequate. For instance, when two arguments are at the same level of embedding in the verb's event structure, as with *see* or *love*, semantic prominence, as defined by a set of statements such as Fillmore's in (9), determines their relative syntactic prominence. Many of the properties identified by Dowty, Fillmore, and Mohanan lack analogues in typical event structures; they often differentiate among the finer-grained instantiations of the coarse-grained roles defined by positions in event structure. The use of such event-based properties allows semantic roles to be broken down into smaller components that interact in argument realization. In this section we have shown that a TH used for determining the options for realizing the arguments of a given verb can be derived from more basic properties of the lexical semantic representation of verbs; it should not be considered a primitive construct. Presumably, such a hierarchy should be universal, with languages agreeing on the relative ranking.[3]

[2]Dowty proposes a set of Patient Proto-role entailments relevant to object selection. Although we do not go into detail here, there is evidence that of these entailments, "changes state" outranks the others. Interestingly, this entailment too has a place in most proposed event structures, as they typically include a predicate such as BECOME or CHANGE.

[3]It is possible that crosslinguistic differences in the options for the morphosyntactic expression of arguments may suggest that languages have different rankings; however, we suggest that the rankings are the same, but the differing morphosyntactic options available may obscure this. See Levin and Rappaport Hovav (2005) for discussion.

However, as discussed in previous sections, other posited THs, used as statements of various generalizations over semantic roles, may rank roles in a different way.[4]

19.5 Conclusion

We conclude by returning to the TH posited to account for Fillmore's well-known subject selection paradigm, 'Agent > Instrument > Patient', and show that it too cannot be a universal primitive construct. First, a purely "structural" interpretation is inappropriate for this TH, as it does not capture the syntactic c-command relations among the NPs bearing the roles included in this TH. Sentences with a morphologically basic verb that include an agent, an instrument, and a patient never have the instrument structurally more prominent than the patient. Yet, this TH does not qualify as a natural prominence scale either as instruments are almost always taken to be less "cognitively salient" than agents and patients.

Most likely, this TH conflates two distinct semantic criteria. The verb *break*, used to exemplify Fillmore's subject selection paradigm, is a dyadic change of state verb, taking causer and patient arguments. The causer argument can be "filled" by an agent, instrument, or natural force (see section 4). The ranking of agent over instrument indicates that when the causer argument is instantiated with an instrument, the expression of an agent is not possible, while the choice of agent as the causer argument does not preclude the expression of an instrument. The ranking of agent and instrument above patient could be given a structural prominence interpretation, by stipulating that causers are always more prominent than patients in syntactic structure. In sum, this TH aptly captures the generalizations behind Fillmore's paradigm, but is not a primitive linguistic construct. This case study highlights once again the major points of this paper. Every posited TH is worthy of serious scrutiny since it represents an attempt to capture a linguistic generalization. Although a range of generalizations are statable with the same TH notation, these generalizations fall into quite different types. They neither can, nor should, be given a single explanation. Yet, taken individually each generalization and, concomitantly, each

[4] Almost without exception, THs, no matter what generalization they are intended to capture, rank agent highest—a ranking which surely requires an explanation. We speculate that every TH, in the final analysis, encodes some form of prominence and that agents, which are defined by a convergence of many of the properties contributing to high prominence (e.g., Givón's (1984) cluster concept definition of agency), will necessarily be ranked highest in any hierarchy.

proposed TH, has much to contribute to our effort to understand how language works.

References

Ackerman, Farrell and John Moore. 2001. *Proto-properties and Grammatical Encoding: A Correspondence Theory of Argument Selection*. Stanford, CA: CSLI Publications.

Alsina, Alex, Joan Bresnan, and Peter Sells, eds. 1997. *Complex Predicates*. Stanford, CA: CSLI Publications.

Baker, Mark C. 1996. On the structural positions of themes and goals. In J. Rooryck and L. Zaring, eds., *Phrase Structure and the Lexicon*, pages 7–34. Dordrecht: Kluwer.

Baker, Mark C. 1997. Thematic roles and syntactic structure. In L. Haegeman, ed., *Elements of Grammar. Handbook of Generative Syntax*, pages 73–137. Dordrecht: Kluwer.

Belletti, Adriana and Luigi Rizzi. 1988. Psych-verbs and θ-theory. *Natural Language and Linguistic Theory* 6(3):291–352.

Bresnan, Joan and Jonni M. Kanerva. 1989. Locative inversion in Chicheŵa: A case study of factorization in grammar. *Linguistic Inquiry* 20(1):1–50. Reprinted in T. Stowell and E. Wehrli, (eds.), 1992, pages 53–102.

Bresnan, Joan and Jonni M. Kanerva. 1992. The thematic hierarchy and locative inversion in UG: A reply to Paul Schachter's comments. In T. Stowell and E. Wehrli, eds., *Syntax and the Lexicon*, vol. 26 of *Syntax and Semantics*, pages 111–125. New York, NY: Academic Press.

Davis, Anthony and Jean-Pierre Koenig. 2000. Linking as constraints on word classes in a hierarchical lexicon. *Language* 76(1):56–91.

Dik, Simon C. 1978. *Functional Grammar*. Amsterdam: North-Holland.

Dik, Simon C. 1997. *The Theory of Functional Grammar. Part 1: The Structure of the Clause*. Berlin: Mouton de Gruyter, 2nd edn. Edited by Kees Hengeveld.

Dowty, David R. 1979. *Word Meaning and Montague Grammar*. Dordrecht: Reidel.

Dowty, David R. 1991. Thematic proto-roles and argument selection. *Language* 67(3):547–619.

Evans, Nicholas R. D. 1997. Role or cast. In A. Alsina, J. Bresnan, and P. Sells, eds., *Complex Predicates*, pages 397–430. Stanford, CA: CSLI Publications.

Fillmore, Charles J. 1968. The case for case. In E. Bach and R. T. Harms, eds., *Universals in Linguistic Theory*, pages 1–88. New York, NY: Holt, Rinehart and Winston.

Fillmore, Charles J. 1971. Some problems for Case Grammar. In R. J. O'Brien, ed., *Report of the 22nd Annual Roundtable Meeting on Linguistics and Language Studies*, pages 35–56. Washington, DC: Georgetown University Press.

Fillmore, Charles J. 1977. Topics in lexical semantics. In R. W. Cole, ed., *Current Issues in Linguistic Theory*, pages 76–138. Bloomington, IN: Indiana University Press.

Givón, Talmy. 1984. *Syntax: A Functional-Typological Introduction*, vol. 1. Amsterdam: J. Benjamins.

Hawkinson, Annie K. and Larry M. Hyman. 1974. Hierarchies of natural topic in Shona. *Studies in African Linguistics* 5(2):147–170.

Hopper, Paul J. and Sandra A. Thompson. 1980. Transitivity in grammar and discourse. *Language* 56(2):251–295.

Jackendoff, Ray S. 1972. *Semantic Interpretation in Generative Grammar*. Cambridge, MA: The MIT Press.

Jackendoff, Ray S. 1990. *Semantic Structures*. Cambridge, MA: The MIT Press.

Keenan, Edward L. 1976. Towards a universal definition of 'subject'. In C. N. Li, ed., *Subject and Topic*, pages 303–333. New York, NY: Academic Press.

Kiparsky, Paul. 1997. Remarks on denominal verbs. In A. Alsina, J. Bresnan, and P. Sells, eds., *Complex Predicates*, pages 473–499. Stanford, CA: CSLI Publications.

Koenig, Jean-Pierre and Anthony Davis. 2001. Sublexical modality and the structure of lexical semantic representations. *Linguistics and Philosophy* 24(1):71–124.

Kratzer, Angelika. 1996. Severing the external argument from its verb. In J. Rooryck and L. Zaring, eds., *Phrase Structure and the Lexicon*, pages 109–137. Dordrecht: Kluwer.

Larson, Richard K. 1988. On the double object construction. *Linguistic Inquiry* 19(3):335–391.

Levin, Beth and Malka Rappaport Hovav. 2005. *Argument Realization*. Cambridge, UK: Cambridge University Press.

Marantz, Alec. 1993. Implications of asymmetries in double object constructions. In S. A. Mchombo, ed., *Theoretical Aspects of Bantu Grammar*, pages 113–150. Stanford, CA: CSLI Publications.

McCarthy, John J. 2002. *A Thematic Guide to Optimality Theory*. Cambridge, UK: Cambridge University Press.

McCawley, James D. 1973. Syntactic and logical arguments for semantic structures. In O. Fujimura, ed., *Three Dimensions of Linguistic Theory*, pages 259–376. Tokyo: TEC Company.

Mohanan, Tara. 1994. *Argument Structure in Hindi*. Stanford, CA: CSLI Publications.

Morgan, Jerry L. 1969. On arguing about semantics. *Papers in Linguistics* 1:49–70.

Newmeyer, Fritz. 2002. Optimality and functionality: A critique of functionally-based optimality-theoretic syntax. *Natural Language and Linguistic Theory* 20(1):43–80.

Polinsky, Maria and Isaac Kozinsky. 1992. Ditransitive constructions in Kinyarwanda: Coding conflict or syntactic doubling? In G. C. C. Canakis and J. M. Denton, eds., *CLS 28: The main session. Papers from the 28th Meeting of the Chicago Linguistic Society*, vol. 1, pages 426–442. Chicago, IL: Chicago Linguistic Society.

Primus, Beatrice. 1999. *Cases and Thematic Roles: Ergative, Accusative and Active*. Tübingen: M. Niemeyer.

Rooryck, Johan and Laurie Zaring, eds. 1996. *Phrase Structure and the Lexicon*. Dordrecht: Kluwer.

Schachter, Paul. 1992. Comments on Bresnan and Kanerva's 'Locative inversion in Chicheŵa: A case study of factorization in grammar'. In T. Stowell and E. Wehrli, eds., *Syntax and the Lexicon*, vol. 26 of *Syntax and Semantics*, pages 103–110. New York, NY: Academic Press.

Speas, Margaret J. 1990. *Phrase Structure in Natural Language*. Dordrecht: Kluwer.

Stowell, Tim and Eric Wehrli, eds. 1992. *Syntax and the Lexicon*, vol. 26 of *Syntax and Semantics*. New York, NY: Academic Press.

Van Valin Jr., Robert D. 1990. Semantic parameters of split intransitivity. *Language* 66(2):221–260.

Van Valin Jr., Robert D. and David P. Wilkins. 1996. The case for 'effector': Case roles, agents, and agency revisited. In M. Shibatani and S. A. Thompson, eds., *Grammatical Constructions*, pages 289–322. Oxford: Clarendon Press.

von Stechow, Arnim. 1995. Lexical decomposition in syntax. In U. Egli, P. E. Pause, C. Schwarze, A. von Stechow, and G. Wienold, eds., *Lexical Knowledge in the Organization of Language*, pages 81–118. Amsterdam: John Benjamins.

von Stechow, Arnim. 1996. The different readings of *wieder*: A structural account. *Journal of Semantics* 13(2):87–138.

20

Expressing Pragmatic Constraints on Word Order in Warlpiri

JANE SIMPSON

20.1 Introduction

In this paper I discuss word order in one Australian language, Warlpiri, with respect to information packaging.[1] Recent papers (Austin and Bresnan 1996, Laughren 2000, 2002, Legate 2002) have suggested that topic and focus in Warlpiri can be represented as constituent structure positions in an extended left periphery. I shall argue that the left periphery does need to be enriched, and that modifications to the phrase structure are needed to account for some properties of what can occur in initial position in Warlpiri. However, I shall argue that focus is not neatly representable in terms of constituent structure, and that it is probably necessary to represent information structure as a separate dimension (Choi 1999, King 1997, King and Zaenen 2004, Mohanan and Mohanan 1994). I shall also argue, following Choi and Butt and King (Butt and King 1996); that topic and focus are better analysed in terms of features of relative prominence and relative newness.

[1]It is a great pleasure to dedicate this paper to Joan Bresnan. Working with her on an ancestor of this paper, I first learned the pleasure of sustained linguistic argument, and admired her generosity and respect for colleagues and students, an admiration which continues. My thanks to the participants in the 2004 LFG Conference in Canterbury, to Fiona Napaljarri Gibson, who checked examples in this paper in 2004, Ilana Mushin, Mary Laughren, David Nash, the participants in the Blackwood Conference on Australian languages in 2005, and an anonymous reviewer.

Architectures, Rules, and Preferences: Variations on Themes by Joan Bresnan.
Annie Zaenen, Jane Simpson, Tracy Holloway King,
Jane Grimshaw, Joan Maling, and Chris Manning, (eds.).

A reason for examining Warlpiri data is that, at 600,000 words, the machine-readable corpus of Warlpiri material is one of the largest available for an Australian language, and this enables us to make a start on examining information structure.

20.2 Warlpiri word order

In this section I shall examine some properties of Warlpiri, and show how they can be accounted for in modern theories of syntax. The groundwork for understanding word order in Warlpiri was laid by Ken Hale in papers published between 1973 and 1983 (Hale 1973, 1976, 1981, 1982, 1983). Five observations relevant to this paper are:

A. The word order of major constituents is not determined by grammatical function. although when a proposition is negated or questioned, there are further restrictions on the word order.

B. A complex consisting of propositional particles, complementisers, aspect and clitic pronouns occurs usually in second position, but also in first or third position in the sentence. Hale called this complex the "AUXiliary". These are the underlined elements in 1. The clitic pronouns are obligatory and double noun phrases. (Free pronouns are optional and often have an emphatic meaning). If the clause consists only of a verb and an AUX which for morpho-phonological reasons cannot occur initially, then the verb must appear initially, as in (2).[2] Laughren notes that in the context for (2), the only new information is that the proposition is true.

(1) Yapa-ngku ka=ju=lu ngaju-ku murdukayi wirrja.pi-nyi[3]
person-ERG PRES=1O=333S 1-DAT car covet-NPST
'People covet my car.' [Hale 1966:0381]

---

[2]If the AUX appears before the verb, as in the unusual example below, Laughren et al. (2005) state that this results in emphasis on the tense/aspect component of the AUX.

(i) Ka=rna=jana || wangka-mi.
PRES=1S=333O talk-NPST
'I **am** (going to) talk to them.' (in reply to 'You should/must talk to them.') (Laughren 2005: ex 30b).

Out of context, a younger speaker in 2004 wanted to paraphrase this sentence so that the AUX was not initial.

[3]Sources for examples in square brackets are from the Warlpiri corpus. FNG refers to data collected by Jane Simpson in 2004. Abbreviations used in glosses include:

(2) Wangka-mi ka=rna=jana.
talk-NPST PRES=1S=333O
'I'm talking to them/I talk to them.' (e.g. in reply to 'Do you talk to them?') (Laughren et al. 2005: ex 30a)

C. The sentence negating word **kula** (which appears initially in the AUX) can never be preceded by the main predicator (whether noun or verb):

(3) **Kula**=rna=ngku yi-nyi miyi=ji.
not=1S=2O give-NPST good=KN
'I'm not going to give you food.' [Hale 1959:27]

D. WH words normally appear initially, unless they are acting as indefinites.

(4) **Nyarrpara**=ka=npa ya-ni?
where=PRES=2S go-NPST
'Where are you going?' [Hale 1959:25]

E. The AUX can follow a verb but not a verb together with its complement(s). Hence there is no evidence for a surface VP in Warlpiri. A similar argument has been made for Wambaya (Nordlinger 1998).

The relation between word order and information structure is illustrated in the dialogue in (5).

(5) Ai. "Lakurru ngurrju=wiyi=nya yiri=nya ka=npa
axe good=before=question sharp=question PRES=2S
marda-ni nyuntu=ju?"
hold-NPST 2S=KN
'Do you have a good sharp axe?'

FUT:	Future		
KN:	Known		
NOM:	Nominaliser		
O:	Object	NPST:	Nonpast
S:	Subject	PAST:	Past
DAT:	Dative	PRES:	Present
ERG:	Ergative	PASTPROG:	Past progressive
LOC:	Locative		
1	first person		
11	1 dual exclusive	111	1 plural exclusive
12	1 dual inclusive	122	1 plural inclusive
2	second person		
22	2 dual	222	2 plural
3	third person		
33	3 dual	333	3 plural

B. "Yuwayi, ngurrju ka=rna marda-ni; kala nyuntu?"
yes good PRES=1S have-NPST but 2S
'Yes, I have a good one; how about you?'

Aii. "**Ngaju ngurrju=yijala** ka=rna marda-ni;"
I good=also PRES=1S have-NPST
'I have a good one also.' [Hale 1966: 949: Tape 2.15]

Although the auxiliary cannot follow a VP, it can follow a complex noun phrase as in (5Ai). More than one constituent can precede the AUX in some contexts, as in the contrastive context in (5Aii), *Ngaju ngurrju=yijala*. The first element *ngaju* is old information carried over from the previous sentence. It is the response to the hook, 'how about you?' The speaker chooses to represent this prominent topic as a full pronoun, not just as the bound pronoun in the AUX, and it appears in initial position. Following it is part of the new information, 'good'; the speaker also has a 'good' one. The axe is carried-over old information which is not explicitly mentioned. Thus the two different positions have different discourse functions, prominent old information, followed by new information. In this contrastive context, the order of information borne by the two constituents is 'Prominent topic, new information', as Laughren has pointed out.

In the 1980s the lack of restriction on placement of grammatical functions was captured by postulating rules that generated free word order with a special position for the AUX (Simpson 1991). Semantico-pragmatic constraints were invoked to describe the position of the negative *kula* and of WH words.

A problem with the free word order rule is that it provides no explanation for the fact that not all orders of grammatical functions are equally likely. Swartz noted that where S(ubject) or O(bject) are expressed overtly by a noun or free pronoun, there is a strong preference for S preceding Verb and a less strong preference for O preceding Verb[4] (Swartz 1988, 1991). Of course the substantial use of zero anaphora results in there being only a small number of clauses in which S and O are realised overtly.

Another problem is that it does not describe the discourse salience of initial position, noted by Swartz for Warlpiri and for other Australian languages (Blake 1979, Donaldson 1980, Mushin and Simpson submitted). Phrases denoting discourse entities that the speaker wants

[4]Swartz's 1988 count of 5 oral texts (344 clauses) in Warlpiri produced a preference for SV over VS, and for VO over OV. Swartz's 1991 count of 3 oral texts (312 clauses) showed a stronger preference for SV, but a preference for OV over VO.

to make prominent relative to other entities appear initially. This can be diagrammed as follows:

Discourse prominent element		Less prominent
XP	AUX	ZP...

FIGURE 1 Swartz's information structure division

The discourse salience of initial position provided an important device for expanding the coverage of word order. In 1996 Austin and Bresnan proposed an enriched left periphery making use of the functional categories, I and I′ (Austin and Bresnan 1996).

$[_{IP}$ SpecIP $[_{I'}$ I $[_S$ XP...]

By making the leftmost element SpecIP and restricting it to grammaticalised discourse functions, they expressed the connection of initial position with discourse salient positions. These included TOPIC or FOCUS, and SUBJECT, which is also treated in LFG as a grammaticalised discourse function, since subjects are, as a reviewer points out, default topics in many languages (King and Zaenen 2004). Thus the preference for S V order was captured in part by the attraction to initial position of discourse functions. The initial position of WH words and the answers to constituent questions could also be captured since they represent FOCUS, a grammaticalised discourse function.

AUX is generated in I, and follows SpecIP; this allows for the normal case of AUX in second position, since it is assumed that specifiers cannot be multiply filled in Warlpiri. Austin and Bresnan also assumed that there is no need for a special Complementiser or CP phrase in Warlpiri, since the elements that have similar meanings to complementisers appear adjoined to the aspect and pronominal clitics in the AUX word. The fact that there is no VP constituent possible in initial position is captured by adopting the exocentric category S which contains no VP constituent that includes complements of the verb (Bresnan 2001). An important feature of this analysis is that the pre-AUX position is not restricted to either TOPIC or FOCUS. Instead, the locus of the AUX in I acts as a beacon indicating that what precedes it is discourse salient.[5] However, in the version of X′ theory Austin and Bresnan used, Spec IP is not available for lexical categories, and hence for verbs. This meant that they needed to invoke a prosodic inversion rule to account for verb-initial clauses. The discourse salience of the pre-AUX position also laid

[5]The use of pronominal clitics as the right edge marker of what is discourse salient is noted for other Australian languages (Mushin and Simpson, submitted, Rose 2001).

the way for accounting for a curious difference of scope with inversion and AUX placement with preverbs such as *puta* which have a negative element in their meaning (Nash 1986).

(6) **Puta**=rna nya-ngu.
some=1S see-PAST
'I saw some of it.' [translation: Nash 1986];
'I didn't really see it.' [translation: FNG 13/8/04]

(7) Nya-ngu=rna **puta**.
see-PAST=1S some
'I saw it some more, again.' [Nash 1986, FNG 13/8/04]

The difference in interpretation between (6) and (7) can be attributed to what is made prominent in the discourse, the verb or the preverb.[6]

Austin and Bresnan's approach provided explanations for several of the earlier problems, and formalised the connection of word order with information structure. But it left several other problems unresolved, as observed by Laughren and Legate (Laughren 2002, Legate 2002). These problems included the appearance of more than one element before the AUX, the status of verb-initial clauses, and the placement of the negative complementiser *kula*. In this paper I shall attempt to address these problems.

20.2.1 More than one element before the AUX

While Austin and Bresnan's account does not allow for more than one phrase preceding the AUX, it can be easily modified to allow for the common Warlpiri topicalization construction in which a constituent, a topic, appears to the left of the clause to which it relates, the comment (Hale, et al. 1996), and intonationally separated from it.

(8) **Walyka**, ngula ka=rlipa ngarri-ni pirriya.
cool.weather that PRES=122S call-NPST winter
'Walyka', that is what we call winter. [Hale 1966:741]

Laughren (2002) and Legate (2002) enriched the left periphery to accommodate this. In the LFG framework, this can be captured by using King's representation of hanging topics (King 1995) using an Expression node (originally derived from Banfield (Banfield 1973), as a reviewer points out).

Further evidence for the information order 'topic – new information' is provided by an example discussed by Legate and Laughren. M's

[6]The normal order is Preverb Verb. Verb Preverb structures are rare in the corpus.

question in (9) contains the sequence 'question word *nyarrpara=wiyi* topic *pangurnu=ju*', which is carried over from A's suggestion.

(9) A: Pangurnu-rlu=rlupa pangi-ni?
shovel-ERG=122S dig-NPST
'Let's dig with a shovel?'

M: **Pangurnu=ju** **nyarrpara=wiyi** ka=nkulu marda-ni?
shovel=KN where=before PRES=222S hold-NPST
TOPIC FOCUS AUX
'Where have you got a shovel?' [Hale 1959:8.78]

(10) and (11) show NPs expressing new information in front of the AUX, as well as a different kind of element in initial position, an evidential Speech Act particle *karinganta.*

(10) Q. Nyarrparla ka=npala yula-mi?
why PRES=22S cry-NPST
'Why are you two crying?'

A. **Karinganta wangumarnanypa=lku waja**=npa nyuntu=ju.
I.assert orphan=now I.say=2S 2S=KN
'It's that you are now an orphan.' [Warlpiri Dictionary *karinganta*]

(11) Q. Nyarrpa-jarri-mi waja - nyampu-rla=ju?
how-become-NPST I.say this-LOC=KN
'What is going on here?'

A. **Karinganta yantarli** ka=rna nyina
I.assert behind PRES=2S sit.NPST
ngurlupardu kuja=ka=rna yurrpa-rni.
seed that=PRES=1S grind-NPST
'Well I am staying here and am grinding seeds.' [Darby 1978/9. Text 3]

Laughren extends the left periphery to include a complementiser phrase CP. The C position provides a place for the generation of the sentence negator *kula.* SpecCP provides a place for the Focus phrase. Above these she introduces a Force phrase, which provides a place for the Topic, and also for the speech act evidentials. Thus the ordering of Topic and Focus is built into the left periphery. Below this, to account for the internal structure of the AUX, Laughren splits the AUX into aspect marker (AS), and pronominal clitics, which appear to be generated in agreement phrases. The splitting off of a C position revolves around a division between AUX bases as to whether they can intrude between a Preverb and a Verb or not. The proposed complementiser *kula* hardly ever intrudes between a preverb and a verb.

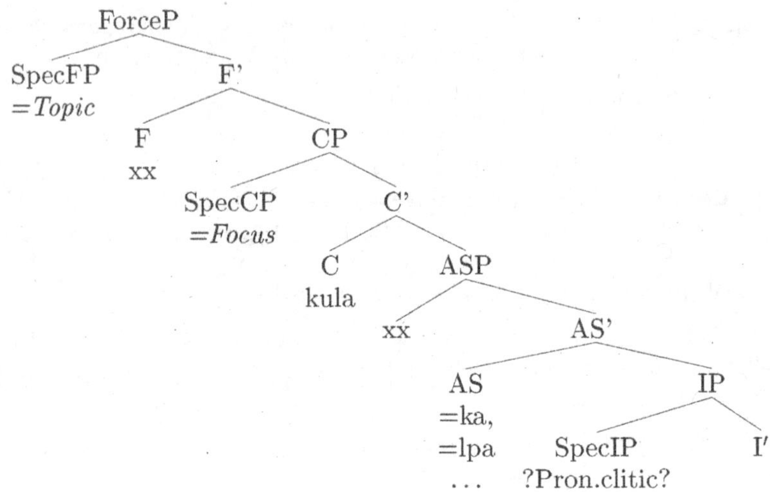

The places marked with xx are places where C, ASP and Pronominal clitics can move as a group.

FIGURE 2 Laughren's extended left periphery: ForceP

Even this extended left periphery is not generous enough, since, as example (12) shows, three elements can occur before the AUX, and appear to be in the same intonation unit.

(12) Q. Yuwa nyarrpa-ma-nu=ngku=lu yalumpu=ju?
hey what-cause-PAST=2O=333S there=KN
Nyiya-rlu=ngku nya-ngu?
What-ERG=2O see-PAST
'Oh, what did they do to you there? What happened to you?'

A. **Karinganta** **ngaju=ju** **yinya-patu-rlu** =ju=lu
I.say 1O=KN those-mob-ERG =1O=333S
EVIDENTIAL TOPIC FOCUS

ngarrka-patu-rlu jiily-ngarru-rnu mardukuja-ngurlu-kula –
man-mob-ERG point-tell-PAST woman-from-it.was
FOCUS

ngarrka-patu-rlu.
man-mob-ERG
?FOCUS
'I'm telling you that I was fingered by those men there over the woman, by the men.'
[Winnie Nangala, Yuendumu 1981 Wiinywiinypakurlu]

Hence we must allow at least three expressions in front of the AUX, in the order: Evidential particle, Topic, Focus. We defer consideration of this until we have considered the position of the sentence negator *kula*.

20.2.2 The problem of verbs

Using X′ theory current at the time, Austin and Bresnan were forced to propose that the only times V can precede an AUX is when the AUX is prosodically inverted over the verb in initial position, to express the morphological requirement that certain elements of the AUX must be hosted by overt material.

However, as Mary Laughren (Laughren 2002) points out, Verbs can appear before the AUX even if the AUX is heavy enough (i.e. the left-most element in the AUX is a morpheme with more than one syllable) to stand on its own sentence-initially. In (13) the AUX *kaji=ka=npa* occurs in second position, even though the AUX base *kaji* can occur sentence initially in other contexts.

(13) **Yaany-pardi-mi** kaji=ka=npa nyuntu ngula=ji ngari
take.personally-NPST if=PRES-=2S 2S that=KN just
ka=rna wangka-mi yapa panu-kurra.
PRES=1S talk-NPST person all-to
'You are taking it personally, but I'm just talking to everyone.'
[Warlpiri Dictionary: PPJ 6/84]

Laughren and Legate (Legate 2002) have various syntactic solutions to this, either generating a lexical V directly in a Specifier position, or having a VP which excludes the complements of the V. Laughren provides information structure motivation for such initial Vs, arguing that, sentence-initially, the verb may have discourse salience equivalent to that which a nominal in such a position has. She notes that verbs cannot generally be topicalised in Warlpiri, and suggests that the relevant information structure relation for verbs appearing before the AUX is 'focus' (Laughren 2002). Her illustrations follow:

(14) **Wangka-mi** ka=rna=jana kurdu-kurdu-ku.
talk-NPST PRES=1S=333O child-child-DAT
'I am talking to the children.' (in reply to 'What are you doing?')

(15) **Kurdu-kurdu-ku** ka=rna=jana wangka-mi.
child-child-DAT PRES=1S=333O talk-NPST
'I am talking to the children.' (in reply to 'Who are you talking to?') (Laughren et al. 2005: ex 30c, d)

(14) suggests that, when the predicator constitutes new information as the answer to a question, it is likely to appear in initial position. We return to this later.

20.2.3 The use of C

How is the V generated in the pre-AUX position? Here we can make use of the possibility of generating Verbs in C positions, following Grimshaw's extended projections (Grimshaw 2005). Austin and Bresnan did not have a Complementiser Phrase. But, as Laughren and Legate show, a CP is useful for expressing the appearance of more than one element in front of the AUX. We can adapt the Austin and Bresnan tree to accommodate the possibility of three elements preceding the AUX by introducing a Complementiser phrase, CP, as in Figure 3. We will also need the Expression Node to express the evidential/speech acts and the hanging topics.

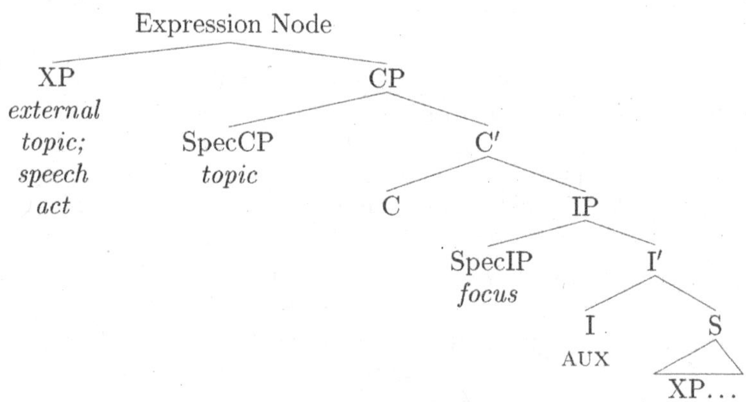

FIGURE 3 Adding a CP to an LFG constituent structure

The speech act markers *karinganta* 'I say', *kulanganta* 'I thought counterfactually', *kala* 'but' are generated here as alternatives to the hanging topic. However, they are not intonationally distinct in the same way that hanging topics are, and so this positioning is tentative. This complementary distribution is based on a preliminary examination of the corpus, and requires further testing with native speakers.

If we assume that Warlpiri has no VP, then we need to say something about why the verb can appear in the pre-AUX position at all. It is clearly more restricted than other XPs appearing before the AUX, as Laughren has shown. So we do not wish to generate V freely in Spec CP position. But if we assume a C position, and also that V is a lexical V^0, then V can be generated under C. This predicts that topicalised NPs such as temporal topics can precede sequences of V (questioned or not) AUX. And they can, as in example (16).

(16) M: **Ngula-jangka=ju nyarrpa-jarri-ja**=lku=nkulu?
that-from=KN what-become-PAST=now=222S

A: Warrki-kirra=lku=rnalu jukurra ya-nu –
work-to=now=111S later go-PAST
'After that what did you do?' 'We went later to work.' [Hale 1959:7.147]

(17) Paka-rnu=lu=nyanu. **Ngula-jangka=ju ya-nu=rni=li**
hit-PAST=333S=REFL that-from=KN go-PAST=hither=333S
Kurra-ngka=lku.
Kurra-LOC=now
'They hit each other. After that they came to Kurra now.' [P. Rockman Napaljarri, Wawurlja, (Napaljarri and Cataldi 1994)]

Can we motivate the C complementiser position? Yes. Laughren observes that the positioning of the sentence negator *kula* can be best accommodated by assuming that it is a complementiser and appears in C. As in many other Australian languages, *kula* mostly occurs sentence initially, although occasionally it occurs following a topic.

(18) Ngaju kula ka=rna ya-ni
1.ABS not PRES=1S go-NPST
TOPIC New information
'I'm not **going**.'

(19) Kula ka=rna ngaju ya-ni
not PRES=1S I.ABS go-NPST
New information
'**I'm** not going.' (Laughren 2002:28a, c)

The fact that *ngaju* in (19) carries contrastive new information despite the fact that it does not precede the AUX will be discussed in the next section. If *kula* is generated in the C position, then it will always follow the TOPIC.[7] If both the verb and *kula* can be base-generated in C, and if we assume that they cannot co-occur in C, then we can represent the fact that the verb cannot precede *kula*: **V kula AUX*. If we assume that *kula* is a function word and cannot bear a discourse function, then it cannot appear in SpecIP. As a lexical category, V cannot occur in Spec IP and so **Kula V AUX* is blocked.

Kula normally acts like an AUX base attached directly to the AUX. The question then arises of whether the sequence Verb/*kula* XP AUX is possible, that is, when the C is filled and an XP is generated in Spec IP. The sequence 'Verb XP AUX' has been claimed to be ungrammatical (Hale et al. 1996). The lack of syntactic coding in the Warlpiri corpus does not permit for easy searching for verbs in this position, and native speaker intuitions need to be tested. We discuss possible information structure reasons for this gap in the next section.

But there are one or two examples of an NP appearing between the *kula* and the AUX, and these are in focus (20), as our structure predicts. Since negation is often itself an important piece of new information, it will only rarely co-occur with a pre-AUX focus.

(20) **Mawarna, kula milpirri** ka=lu ngarri=rni
cloud.type, not cloud.type PRES-333S call-NPST
wulurarri-wulurarri, kala kajara yangka kuja
cloud.type but cloud.type the that
ka nguna-mi-rni.
PRES lie-NPST=hither
'White clouds, not heavy rain clouds, are what they call wulurarri-wulurarri, rather they are the wispy thin clouds.' [Hale 1966:0275, translations from Warlpiri Dictionary][8]

---

[7]Laughren also places the complementiser *kaji* in C. I assume it is generated along with Aspect particles in AUX, since question words can precede this complementiser, as in Laughren's example:

(17f) Nyarrpara-kurra kaji=ka=rna ya-ni?
where-to if=PRES=1S go-NPST
'Where am I likely to go to?'

[8]A younger speaker (FNG) had difficulty with this sentence in 2004, perhaps because of the obsolete words for clouds. But when asked to translate 'It wasn't a big kangaroo that I shot, it was a small one', she produced a sentence with a similar kula XP predicator structure:

(i) **Kula wirijarlu=wiyi**=rna luwa-rnu, ngula=ju wita pardu
not big=before=1S shoot-PAST, that=KN small dear.one

It seems sensible to assume that when in C the verb and *kula* receive the same kind of prominent discourse function that we have otherwise associated with the element appearing in Spec IP.

20.3 Information structure in Warlpiri

The discussion in the previous section has relied heavily on information structure in order to express the constituent structure of Warlpiri. Discourse information provides the potential for explaining the interactions of word order with questions and negation. As Figures 2 and 3 show, discourse information is built into the phrase structure rules for both the LFG and Minimalist accounts, including Swartz's claim about the discourse salience of initial position. This claim has been expanded to accommodate the pre-AUX ordering 'Topic ... Focus' by Legate and Laughren.

A somewhat different claim was made by Hale, when he distinguished the use of word order to express grammatical functions from pragmatically determined word order, and noted the importance of pre-verbal position:

> I will use the term 'expression in focus' (EIF) to refer to a constituent (argument, direct or oblique, etc.) which is, relatively speaking, 'in focus'. This is the expression whose referent is taken by the speaker to be 'new' to the audience, or 'new' in relation to the discourse — 'newsworthy', in the terminology of Mithun (1987). It includes what Swartz (1985: passim) calls the 'sentence topic' and what Payne (1987: 786) refers to as 'non-identifiable information', for which 'the hearer is instructed to open a new active discourse file', as well as 'pragmatically markers' information (e.g. content-question words). The notion 'in focus' here is a relative one. An argument, the object, for example, is relatively more, or less, 'in discourse focus' by comparison with some other argument, the subject, say. If an expression is not an EIF, then it can be said to be an 'expression out of focus' (EOF), again, in a relative sense. Given this terminology, the discourse principles governing word order and elision in the two 'free word order' languages under consideration here [Walpiri and Papago JHS] can be expressed in preliminary fashion as follows:
>
> (3) Ordering principles in discourse:
> 1. EIF precedes the predicator (e.g. the V):
> 2. EOF follows the predicator, or it is elided. (Ken Hale 1992: 66–67)

He illustrates this with a question-answer pair from Warlpiri:

(21) Q. **Nyiya** ka karla-mi karnta-ngku
what PRES dig-NPST woman-ERG
'What is the woman digging?'

A. **Yarla** ka karla-mi
yam PRES dig-NPST
'She is digging yams.' [Hale's (4)]

Of this example Hale writes:

> In the question, the question word is the EIF, and consequently precedes the verb. The subject being relatively 'out of focus', follows the verb. In the answer, the answer to the question, i.e., the object, is the EIF and, accordingly, precedes the verb. By contrast, the subject is the EOF and, in this case, is elided. Certain marked constructions (e.g., clefting for focus, dislocation for topic) are only partially accommodated by (3)... [pp. 67–68]

Notice that Hale's attribution of newness to the pre-verbal position is attested in Laughren's example (19), in which *ngaju* follows the AUX and appears immediately before the verb, and is treated as new information.

Hale's discussion is brief, concentrating only on arguments, and not on what happens when, say, the AUX or the main predicator are made prominent. His claim is diagrammed below:

Element in focus	PREDICATOR	Element out of focus
XP...	V or N	ZP...

FIGURE 4 Hale's information structure division

Example (21) does not distinguish Hale's and Swartz's claims, since the new information occurs simultaneously before the AUX and before the verb. To test it, I examined the claim in the Warlpiri corpus, looking at 101 constituent questions and answers, which occurred in natural speech, and which did not have single word answers. Table 1 shows the results:

pre-AUX	post-AUX before Verb	post verb	**ngari** 'just' in pre-AUX position	TOTAL
77	4	9	13	103

TABLE 1 Position of new information in answers to constituent questions in the Warlpiri corpus

Thus the normal place for both WH words and for new information in response to a question is in initial position. This is compatible with

Verb-initial Imperative	Verb-initial, short AUX	Verb following AUX	Other verb-initial	TOTAL
1	3	32	1	37

TABLE 2 Verb as new information in answer

both Swartz's and Hale's claims, since Swartz emphasises the initial position, and Hale emphasises the preverbal position. The fact that more new information occurs following the verb than occurs between the AUX and the verb is not predicted on Hale's account.

Now, the salience of initial position together with Laughren's discussion of the motivation for putting verbs in initial position suggests that, when the predicator constitutes new information as the answer to a question, it is likely to appear in initial position. To test this, I examined 37 question and answer pairs from the Warlpiri corpus which could be interpreted as questioning predicators and events. Apart from yes-no questions, predicators and events are questioned in Warlpiri, by using the interrogative pronoun *nyarrpa* (how, which) with the intransitive verb marker *-jarrimi* (what is happening? what are you doing?) or the transitive verb marker *-mani* (what is happening to someone/something? what are you doing to someone/something?). The answers to such questions are likely to provide us with examples of the normal structures used to express the situation in which the subject is the topic and the predicator expresses some new information about this topic (Vallduví's 'link-focus' = Lambrecht's 'predicate-focus'), and perhaps of those in which the entire sentence reports an event, (Vallduví's 'all-focus' = Lambrecht's 'sentence-focus') (Lambrecht 1994, Vallduví 1992). In 32 of these cases, contrary to the 'new information initial' prediction, the verb followed the AUX. Table 2 presents the results: Here are some examples where the verb is not initial. Sometimes what precedes the AUX is a repeated temporal topic.

(22) M: **Tina-jangka**=pa=nkulu nyarrpa-jarri-ja?
dinner-from=PASTPROG=222S what-become-PAST
'What did you do after dinner?'

(23) A: **Ngula-jangka=ju** =lpa=rnalu=jana
that-from=KN =PASTPROG=111S=333S
Old information Old information

yarda ya-nu jangkardu.
again go-PAST against
New information
'After that we went after some more.' [Hale 1959:8.202-3os]

Or the material before the AUX can be part of the new information.

(24) M: Nyarrpa-jarri-ja=lku=ngulu?
what-become-PAST=then=222S
'What did you do then?'

A: Tawunu-kurra=lku =rnalu yarnka-ja=rni –
town-to=then =111S set.out-PAST-hither
New information Old info. New information
'We came to town then.' [Hale 1959:7.150]

Thus when a verb is part of the new information resulting from questioning the predicator or the sentence, there's no necessity for it to appear initially. This contrasts with case-marked noun phrases acting as the answers to constituent questions, where there is a strong preference for the new information to appear in initial position before the AUX. Predicator focus does not result in verbs appearing preferentially in initial position.

But the verb can occur initially in other situations, when the verb itself is questioned, when it is what is being defined or illustrated, when there is a strong contrast, when the verb is imperative or in the present tense used as a strong suggestion as in (25).

(25) "**Nyarrpa-ma-ni**=rli=jana?"
what-cause-NPST=12S=333O
'What shall we do?' [about this meat which the dogs are taking]
Ngula kuja wangka-ja jinta-kari kuja=ju.
then thus speak-PAST one-other thus=KN
'Then one of them said thus:'
"**Yirra-rni** =rli kuyu walya-kurra."
put-PRES =12S meat ground-to
New info. Old info. Old info. New information
'Let's put the meat on the ground.'
[Malikijarra Purunjunjujarrakurlu]

This suggests that newness of information alone is not enough to license the verb appearing before the AUX. There must be some other prominence given to the verb. In this the verb differs from NPs. This difference in ability to appear in the pre-AUX position between arguments and predicators means that we must look beyond simple ideas of prominence and newness for an explanation.

20.3.1 Reconciling Hale's and Swartz's positions

We turn now to ways of reconciling Hale's and Swartz's accounts of information structure. Swartz's (1988) position can be extended and interpreted as follows:

What precedes the AUX *is more prominent than what follows the* AUX.

If the Verb is generated in C and followed by an AUX, it will be interpreted as either the default or as having a prominent Verb. If the Verb is generated under S, then something else will be prominent, an NP or the negative complementiser.

Swartz's position also allows a partial account of some of the possible orderings in sentences with complex predicates consisting of Preverb and Verb. In the order 'Preverb Verb AUX', Preverb and Verb are generated together as a lexical verb inside C. In information structure terms, they are treated as prominent because they precede the AUX. In the order 'Preverb AUX Verb', the Preverb is generated in C, and the Verb in S. Since the Preverb precedes the AUX, it is more prominent than the Verb, and so in example (6) the readings "I saw some of it; I didn't really see it" are generated. When the Verb precedes the AUX, it is more prominent than the Preverb, and so in example (7) the reading "I saw it some more" is generated.

The order 'Verb Preverb AUX' is only rarely attested. It would be produced by generating Verb in C, and Preverb in Spec IP. If we just look at prominence there would be no reason for blocking it, since two prominent elements can precede the AUX. A similar problem is shown by the rarity of the order 'Verb NP AUX' (claimed to be ungrammatical in Hale et al. (1996)). This contrasts with the possibility of hanging topics or temporal topics preceding Verbs, 'NP V AUX' of which we have seen examples.

I suggest that the rarity of 'Verb NP AUX' and 'Verb Preverb AUX' relates to the information structure property that Hale observed, namely that the position preceding the Verb is new information. From the Prominence of AUX, it would follow that both the Verb and the NP or Preverb must be prominent. From Hale's pre-Verb Newness condition, it would follow that both the NP and the Preverb must be less New than the Verb in the order 'Verb NP/Preverb AUX'. We have seen elsewhere that the preferred order of Old and New before the AUX is 'Older Newer AUX'. This would be a reversal, 'Newer Older AUX'.

The importance of distinguishing prominence from newness allows for the reconciliation of Hale's and Swartz's observations. Hye-Won Choi has suggested that discourse functions should be resolved into general information features: relatively new information in the clause [NEW], and relatively prominent information in the clause [PROM] (Choi 1999). Choi's account allows for two kinds of focus, and two kinds of topic, prominent and non-prominent. Sentential topics can be linked with prominent focus by sharing the feature [PROM].

How does this play out for Warlpiri? Figure 5 presents this schematically. Relatively prominent information, whether topical or new information, occurs in the position before the AUX, as Swartz suggests — but the span of words up until the AUX can be considered prominent. The attachment of the AUX to a constituent signals the prominence of that constituent, but also signals the transition to less prominent information. The AUX contains pronominals which indicate continuing topics. The constituent to which the AUX attaches may or may not be new information. Relatively new information, as Hale suggests, precedes the verb — but the whole preverbal area can be considered new, the leftmost limit being the C position.

←	Prominent	Transition	Less prominent →		Not specified
Topic	Focus Contrast				
XP	V or YP	AUX:	ZP ...		WP
	C			V	
Less new	**New** →		**New** ←	**New** ←	**Not specified**

FIGURE 5 Prominence and Newness in Warlpiri

Something which is both prominent and new has the AUX attached to it. WH words are new, and most likely to be prominent. Hence they normally occur in pre-AUX position. The verb is itself assumed to be new. If it appears in the C position in front of the AUX and there is an NP following the AUX, then the verb is prominent, e.g. an imperative or a suggestion. Otherwise it appears in pre-AUX position only when there is nothing else that the AUX can attach to. In that case, the

Verb is prominent only in so far as it is more prominent than the AUX. The discourse status of the right periphery — what follows the main predicator — is not specified under either account. This requires much more detailed investigation.

20.4 On extended new information

In the previous section, we have illustrated Swartz's claim that discourse-prominent information precedes the AUX, and Hale's claim that new information precedes the verb. We have argued that prominence and newness apply to spans within a clause, rather than to single phrase structure positions. We have also claimed that prominence and newness are relative notions. If one piece of new information is to be made prominent vis à vis another, then the prominent information precedes the AUX, and the non-prominent information follows it. This predicts that some non-prominent new information can follow the AUX and precede the verb, as in (26), when a WH word follows the AUX, and in (27) when a verb occurs in C position, and the WH word actually occurs following the AUX rather than in Spec IP. (28) and (29) show that even an NP with contrastive focus can appear following the AUX.

(26) Pikirri=ji=npa **nyarrpara-rla** warungka.ma-nu=rnu?[9]
spearthrower=KN=2S where-LOC forget -PAST=hither
TOPIC AUX FOCUS
'Where did you inadvertently leave the spear-thrower on your way here?' [Laughren, 2002 (31) a.]

(27) Langakari-langakari-jarri ka=npa **nyarrpa-rla**, Nampijinpa?
think.about.NPST PRES=2S how-LOC NAME
[Context: define langakari-langakari-jarri] 'What are you thinking about, Nampijinpa?' [ppj]

(28) Kula=rna **ngajulu-rlu** jukurrpa nya-ngu.
not−IS I-ERG dreaming see-PAST
Nyurnu.patu-rlu –jukurrpa.
ancestor-ERG dreaming
'I didn't see the dreaming. Our ancestors [did see] the dreaming.' [Ngarlkirdi-kirli, Paddy Sims Japaljarri]

(29) Larrwa, larrwa kula=ka=lu
pipe, pipe not=PRES=333S
TOPIC NOT-AUX

[9] Laughren's structure is:
[$_{FP}$ Pikirri=ji=npa$_i$ [$_{CP}$ nyarrpara-rla t$_i$ [$_{IP}$ t$_i$ [warungka.ma-nu=rnu]]]]

nyampu-rla=jala wurduju.ma-ni kala
here-LOC=indeed manufacture-NPST but
FOCUS
wurnturu=jala, larrwa=ju.
far=indeed pipe=KN
'Larrwa pipes are not manufactured here but rather a long way off.' [Hale 1966:02226]

Legate handles examples such as (26) and (27) by proposing that more focus phrases would be needed in front of the verb. She has a complex set of movement and licensing procedures to account for these and for Focus occurring on elements between the AUX and the verb (Legate 2002:280):

[(Top*HTLD*) [ForceP [(TopP*) [(FocP) [(FocP$_{wh}$) [FinP]]]]]]

In these cases two Focus phrases are plausible, because the entities in focus are distinct from each other. But there are a number of examples where the entities are not distinct. Warlpiri has so-called discontinuous NPs, in which nominals referring to the same entity and bearing the same grammatical function (as indicated by case-marking) occur in different parts of the clause (Nash 1986, Simpson 1991). (30) contains a Question word *nyajangu* following the AUX (Legate's FocP*wh*), while *karnta*, construed as part of the same function, precedes the AUX.

(30) M: **Karnta** ka=lu **nyajangu** jilimi-rla=ju
woman PRES=333S how.many single.women's.camp-LOC=KN
nyina?
be.NPST
'How many women are in the single women's camp?' [or perhaps 'As for women, how many are in the single women's camp?']

A: Panu ka=lu nyina.
many PRES=333S be.NPST
[Context: appears to be discourse initial] 'There are many.' [Hale 1959:VII 7.51-4]

Notice that FocP*wh* must be able to precede the other FocP as well, since in (31) and (32) the WH word precedes the AUX, while another nominal referring to the same entity follows the AUX.

(31) **Nyarrpara-ngurlu** ka=nkulu **ngapa-ngurlu=ju** wapa-mi?
which-from PRES=222S water-from=KN walk-NPST
[Context: The people from that place laughed at it when it asked them] 'Hey you people! Which water-source do you walk from?' [= are you using] [Warlpiri Dictionary nyinnga: krn]

(32) A. **Nyajangu=ngku karli** yu-ngu nyuntu-ku;
how.many=2O boomerang give-PAST you-DAT
kirdana-rlu nyuntukupalangu-rlu?
father-ERG your-ERG
'How many boomerangs did he give you, your father?'

B. **Panu=ju** yu-ngu **karli**; **panu** nganta=ju yu-ngu
many=1O give-PAST boomerang; many seems=1O give-PAST
kirdana-rlu ngajukupalangu-rlu **karli** ngaju-ku.
father-ERG my-ERG boomerang me-DAT
[Context: define nyajangu] 'He gave me many boomerangs; my father gave me many.' [Hale 1966 1-1101.TEXT :791:]

(32) shows that a modifier can be split by the AUX in this way from its head. The newer information **panu** is put in front of the AUX and its head (which is topical from the previous sentence) follows the verb. Splitting a constituent in this way is thus comparable to the use of focal stress in English: *He gave me MANY boomerangs.* (33) shows that split modifiers can occur even when both express new information.

(33) A: Nyiya ka=npa wardu.pi-nyi nga-rninja-ku=ju?
what PRES=2S prefer-NPST eat-NOM-DAT=KN
[Context: offering B a choice of meat] 'What do you want to eat?'

B: **Nyampu** ka=rna **marlu** wardu.pi-nyi
this PRES=1S kangaroo prefer-NPST
ngurrju=ju kuyu=ju.
good=KN meat=KN
'I prefer [this JHS] kangaroo which is the best meat.' [PPJ 10/87, translation Warlpiri Dictionary]

Another striking example is (34), in which the new information is represented by two constituents, one of which is quantified with the clitic *=mipa* meaning 'only' preceding the AUX.

(34) M: Karnta=ngku=lu rdanpa-rnu
woman=2O=333S accompany-PAST
[context, discussing what A. did while hunting] 'Did any women accompany you?' [Warlpiri Dictionary translation]

A: Lawangarra. **Kuyu mipa=rna jinta** pinja-nu
none.at.all meat only-1S one hit.go-PAST
ngula=ju =pa=ju=lu jurnta parnka-ja panu=ju.
that=KN =PAST=1O=333S away run-PAST many=KN
'None at all. All the meat I got was one and the rest got away from me.' [Hale translation - [H50:7.45]]

Both words denoting the entity in focus appear before the verb, thus supporting Hale's idea of the importance of the pre-verbal position. However, they are separated by the AUX. Hale's translation of (34) suggests that the most prominent element is the initial element kuyu 'meat' — contrasting with the answer to the question 'no women' given in the previous clause. Intuitively, the AUX acts as a marker, saying 'What precedes me is prominent'. Thus both Hale's observation about the discourse salience of pre-verbal position, and Swartz's observation of the discourse prominence of initial position are simultaneously true. Two distinct phrase structure constituents, separated by the AUX, jointly provide the answer, or the questioned element of the clause, the new information. We are a long way from a full understanding of information structure possibilities in Warlpiri, and much of what I have written here is tentative and requires serious investigation of the Warlpiri corpus and Warlpiri speakers' intuitions for confirmation or disconfirmation. However, I think that the interactions of the use of the AUX position to show relative prominence, and the use of the Verb position to show relative newness must make us suspicious of a simple one-to-one mapping between information structure constructs and phrase structure position. In fact, it complements the argument made by Mohanan and Mohanan that focus should not be reduced to a position in a constituent structure representation (Mohanan and Mohanan 1994). They showed that the focus marking in Malayalam allows simultaneous focusing of more than one element (for example, the theme and recipient of a ditransitive verb) which do not constitute a single unit in phrase structure representations. They used this to argue for a multi-dimensional view of grammar, in which information structure, constituent structure and functional structure are separate dimensions. Tracy Holloway King made a related argument for independent information structure based on scoping of discourse functions in Russian (King 1997). The Warlpiri data provides additional support for this approach, by providing evidence of the complementary situation, when two constituents separated by the AUX represent new information and express the same grammatical function, but only one of them is made prominent.

20.5 Conclusion

I have argued that the asymmetry between nouns and verbs as to their freedom to precede the AUX can be expressed by maintaining the position that there is no VP in Warlpiri and by assuming that there is a C position in which a lexical V can be generated under restricted discourse prominence conditions.

Pragmatic conditions on word order in Warlpiri involve both the position of new information (Hale's idea of preverbal salience), and the prominence of that information (Swartz's idea about the importance of initial position). Expressing information structure order constraints cannot be straightforwardly derived from phrase structure constituency, since the AUX can intervene between elements which both represent new information, and since it is not possible to limit one position or the other to a particular kind of focus, for example WH-words. Hence this provides some support for the proposal for a separate dimension of information structure.

References

Austin, Peter and Joan Bresnan. 1996. Non-configurationality in Australian Aboriginal languages. *Natural Language and Linguistic Theory* 14(2):215–268.

Banfield, Ann. 1973. Narrative style and the grammar of direct and indirect speech. *Foundations of Language* 10:1–39.

Blake, Barry J. 1979. *A Kalkatungu grammar*. Canberra: Pacific Linguistics.

Bresnan, Joan. 2001. *Lexical-Functional Syntax*. Oxford: Blackwell.

Butt, Miriam and Tracy H. King. 1996. Structural topic and focus without movement. In M. Butt and T. H. King, eds., *Proceedings of the International Lexical-Functional Grammar Conference 1996 (LFG'96)*. Grenoble: CSLI Online Publications.

Choi, Hye-Won. 1999. *Optimizing Structure in Context: Scrambling and Information Structure*. Stanford CA: CSLI Publications.

Donaldson, Tamsin. 1980. *Ngiyambaa: The Language of the Wangaaybuwan*. Cambridge, UK: Cambridge University Press.

Grimshaw, Jane. 2005. *Words and Structure*. Stanford, CA: CSLI Publications.

Hale, Kenneth L. 1973. Person marking in Walbiri. In S. Anderson and P. Kiparsky, eds., *A Festschrift for Morris Halle*, pages 308–344. New York, NY: Holt, Rinehart and Winston.

Hale, Kenneth L. 1976. The adjoined relative clause in Australia. In R. M. W. Dixon, ed., *Grammatical Categories in Australian Languages*, pages 78–105. Canberra: Australian Institute of Aboriginal Studies.

Hale, Kenneth L. 1981. *On the position of Walbiri in a typology of the base*. Bloomington, IN: Indiana University Linguistics Club.

Hale, Kenneth L. 1982. Some essential features of Warlpiri main clauses. In S. Swartz, ed., *Papers in Warlpiri grammar: in memory of Lothar Jagst*, pages 217–315. Berrimah: Summer Institute of Linguistics.

Hale, Kenneth L. 1983. Warlpiri and the grammar of non-configurational languages. *Natural Language and Linguistic Theory* 1(1):5–47.

Hale, Kenneth L. 1992. Basic word order in two 'free word order' languages. In D. Payne, ed., *Pragmatics of Word Order Flexibility*, pages 63–82. Amsterdam & Philadelphia, PA: J. Benjamins.

Hale, Kenneth L., Mary Laughren, and Jane Simpson. 1996. Warlpiri syntax. In J. Jacobs, ed., *Handbook of Syntax*, pages 1430–1451. Berlin & New York, NY: Walter de Gruyter.

King, Tracy H. 1995. *Configuring Topic and Focus in Russian*. Stanford, CA: CSLI Publications.

King, Tracy H. 1997. Focus domains and information structure. In M. Butt and T. H. King, eds., *Proceedings of the International Lexical-Functional Grammar Conference 1997 (LFG'97)*. San Diego, CA: CSLI Online Publications.

King, Tracy H. and Annie Zaenen. 2004. F-structures, information structure, and discourse structure. Paper presented at Christchurch, New Zealand, extended abstract available at http://cslipublications.stanford.edu/LFG/9/lfg04kingzaenen-abs.html.

Lambrecht, Knud. 1994. *Information Structure and Sentence Form: A Theory of Topic, Focus, and the Mental Representations of Discourse Referents*. Cambridge, UK: Cambridge University Press.

Laughren, Mary. 2000. Constraints on the pre-auxiliary position in Warlpiri and the nature of the auxiliary. In J. Henderson, ed., *Proceedings of the 1999 Conference of the Australian Linguistic Society (ASL1999)*. Perth. Available on-line.

Laughren, Mary. 2002. Syntactic constraints in a 'free word order' language. In M. Amberber and P. Collins, eds., *Language Universals and Variation*, pages 83–130. Westport, CT: Praeger.

Laughren, Mary, Rob Pensalfini, and Tom Mylne. 2005. Accounting for verb initial order in an Australian language. In A. Carnie, H. Harley, and S. A. Dooley, eds., *Verb First: On the syntax of verb-initial languages*, pages 367–401. Amsterdam & Philadelphia: J. Benjamins.

Legate, Julie A. 2002. *Warlpiri: Theoretical Implications*. Ph.D. thesis, Massachusetts Institute of Technology.

Mohanan, KP and Tara Mohanan. 1994. Issues in word order in South Asian languages: enriched phrase structure or multidimensionality? In M. Butt, T. H. King, and G. Ramchand, eds., *Theoretical perspectives on word order in South Asian languages*, pages 153–184. Stanford, CA: CSLI Publications.

Mushin, Ilana and Jane Simpson. 2006. Discourse prominence in four Australian languages. In B. Baker and I. Mushin, eds., *Discourse and grammar in Australian languages*. Amsterdam: J. Benjamins. To appear.

Napaljarri, Peggy Rockman and Lee Cataldi. 1994. *Warlpiri Dreamings and Histories: Yimikirli*. San Francisco, CA & London & Pymble: Harper Collins.

Nash, David. 1986. *Topics in Warlpiri Grammar*. New York, NY & London: Garland.

Nordlinger, Rachel. 1998. *A grammar of Wambaya, Northern Territory (Australia)*. Canberra: Pacific Linguistics.

Rose, David. 2001. *The Western Desert code: An Australian cryptogrammar*. Canberra: Pacific Linguistics.

Simpson, Jane. 1991. *Warlpiri Morphosyntax: A Lexicalist Approach*. Dordrecht: Kluwer.

Simpson, Jane and Joan Bresnan. 1983. Control and obviation in Warlpiri. *Natural Language and Linguistic Theory* 1(1):49–64.

Swartz, Stephen M. 1988. Pragmatic structure and word order in Warlpiri. In *Papers in Australian Linguistics*, vol. 17, pages 151–166. Canberra: Pacific Linguistics.

Swartz, Stephen M. 1991. *Constraints on Zero Anaphora and Word Order in Warlpiri Narrative Text*. Darwin: Summer Institute of Linguistics.

Vallduvì, Enric. 1992. *The Informational Component*. New York, NY & London: Garland.

Part IV

Variation

21

Melody, Rhythm, and Prosodic Structure in Linguistic Chants

YOUNG-MEE YU CHO AND MARIKO SAIKI

21.1 Introduction

The area of intersection between music and language that is often manifested in linguistic chants provides an invaluable window through which one can investigate the nature of the prosodic structure of a language as well as the musical structure of chants in general. It is often noted that there is a hierarchy of melodic forms that ranges 'from the least formalized (normal speech intonation) to the most formalized (accompanied singing)' (Gardiner, via Ladd 1978: 525) with the intermediate forms utilized by rap musicians, talking blues performers, street vendors, auctioneers, train conductors, etc.

This paper focuses on *vocative chant*, one of the most studied of the intermediate forms, where level pitches and durational specifications of stylized intonation clearly beg for both musically and linguistically based interpretations. Vocative chant is a term commonly used to refer to tunes for calling people, often from a distance (e.g. Liberman 1975 and Leben 1976). It is also known as the 'calling contour' of Gibbon (1976), the 'stylized fall (associated with routineness)' of Ladd (1978, 1996), and 'the chanted call' of Hayes and Lahiri (1992) and Gussenhoven (1993). During the past decade or so, important cross-linguistic

Work on this paper was supported by a Grant-In-Aid for Scientific Research (#17520255) from the Japan Society for the Promotion of Science.

Architectures, Rules, and Preferences: Variations on Themes by Joan Bresnan.
Annie Zaenen, Jane Simpson, Tracy Holloway King,
Jane Grimshaw, Joan Maling, and Chris Manning, (eds.).

generalizations have emerged concerning the nature of the tunes and the role of lexical and musical prominence.

For instance, Ladd (1978, 1990) associates a stepping-down sequence of two level tones with the semantic implication of 'stereotyped,' 'stylized,' and 'routine,' rather than with the calling per se. One of the most salient linguistic characteristics of this sequence is the change from a higher steady level pitch to a lower one, and the function of this intonation is "to signal a certain element of predictability or stereotype in the message" (Ladd 1978: 520). In the repertoire of stylized intonation, vocative chant, then, occupies a place closer to music, with its characteristics of fixed intonation, highly exaggerated voice quality, melody and rhythm. One important generalization of English vocatives noted by Leben (1976) is their tendency to change pitch only on rhythmically strong syllables, while other chants are less musically constrained with less formalized rhythms and melodies.

Moreover, it is sometimes noted that music and language intersect even at the most formalized end of the hierarchy. For instance, the matching between the linguistic tone and the musical melody in tonal languages (e.g. Cantonese (Yung 1991) and Mandarin (Wee 2002)) is not random but quite systematic. In Cantonese opera, the linguistic tones of the text serve in effect as a form of musical notation, in the absence of conventional western-style notation; an actual performance is constructed through the mental compositional process of matching linguistic tones with a somewhat limited repertoire of available tunes by each performer (Yung 1991). For Mandarin folksongs, Wee (2002) demonstrates how the preservation of contrasts is accomplished between two distinct elements of prominence in music and language. The conflicts that arise when the linguistic tone is articulated in the context of the prescribed musical melody are resolved by preserving the tonal integrity of the head syllable, whereas the conflicts in non-head syllables are tolerated and disambiguated by syntactic and semantic cues.

Similarly, intonation patterns of normal speech have been successfully described in terms of aligning a sequence of H and L pitch contours with segmental material (Pierrehumbert and Beckman 1988), although in speech the tones are not sustained (or terraced) throughout the syllables that bear a certain pitch as in music. In addition, intonation contours of normal speech are also characterized by rhythmic organizations that we often associate with music. In this paper, we first sketch how the texts and the tunes are related by examining a range of vocative chants in Korean and Japanese. We then analyze the rhythm of the vocative chant in Japanese, based on the metrical analysis of duration presented in Hayes and Lahiri (1992), as well as on the notions of linguistic head assumed in Wee (2002).

Note that in our description of the tunes observed in vocative chant, we use the notation **L**, **M** and **H** in bold face. They stand for three different tunes or notes on the musical score, and should be interpreted so that there is a minor interval by three degrees between **L** and **M**, and a major interval by two degrees between **M** and **H**. Accordingly, **L**, **M** and **H**, for instance, designate the musical tunes that correspond to E, G and A on the major scale in Western music.

21.2 Vocative Chant in Korean

Vocative chant in Korean and its relevance in identifying lexical prominence were first discussed by Ko (1999), where the differences between the Seoul dialect and the Chŏnnam dialect are derived in terms of lexical pre-specification.

Korean Vocative chant is realized on the sequence of a name (which is usually disyllabic) and a vocative suffix (*-a* after a consonant-final name and *-ya* after a vowel-final name). The same melody is repeated on the word, *nolca* ('let's play!').

The following three subsections sketch the vocative chant patterns in the Seoul, Chŏnnam and South Kyŏngsang dialects, where we see a systematic relationship between the musical tunes and linguistic specification in Korean.

21.2.1 Seoul

In Seoul Korean vocative chant, all names plus the vocative suffix (*-a* or *-ya*) are invariably realized as **MHM**.

(1) Seoul Vocative Chant
Segments: <u>Name-suffix</u>, nol-ca 'Name, let's play!'
Melody: **M H M** **MHM**

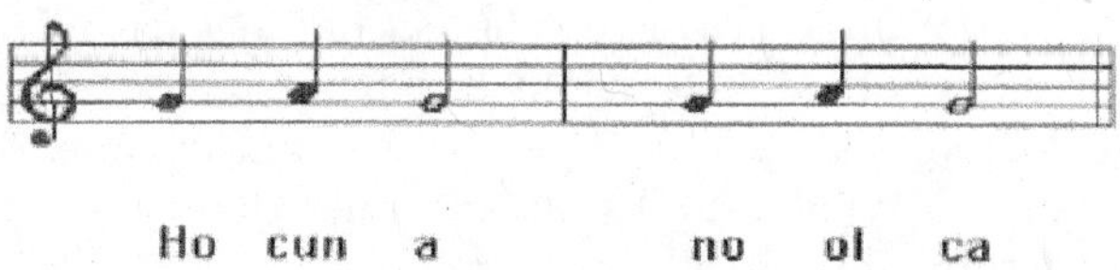

In Cho and Saiki (2003), we correlate the lack of lexical prominence in Standard Korean with the uniformity of the vocative melody, in contrast to the other two dialects to be discussed next.

21.2.2 Chŏnnam

While the sequence name+vocative suffix in Seoul Korean invariably surfaces as **MHM** in vocative chant, tunes for the same sequence in Chŏnnam Korean exhibit two different types.

One type applies to the names which are pronounced with the H tone on the second syllable, and as illustrated in (2.a), the sequence of the two syllables which constitute a name, and the vocative suffix surfaces as **MHM** in vocative chant.

The other type is for initially accented names as exemplified in (2.b). Unlike the unmarked case in (2.a), the lexical H is preserved in terms of the **H** tune for the vocative melody.

(2) Chŏnnam Vocative Chant

a. (M)H+M (names with H on the 2nd syllable + vocative suffix):

```
ən-suk-a   ən-a-ya   saŋ-wən-a
 \  /  /    |  |  |   \  /  /
MHM        MHM       MHM
```

b. HM+M (initially accented names + vocative suffix):

```
yəŋ-sən-a,   hyən-chəl-a   ho-cun-a
 |  /  /       |  /  /      /  /  /
HHM          HHM          HHM
```

We conclude that the vocative melody in Chŏnnam is sensitive to linguistic tone specification. We also assume that the vocative chant in Chŏnnam is **HM** and it is right-aligned. In the first type of vocative chant, as shown in (2.a), default **M** is assigned to syllables other than the last two syllables. This type of vocative chant is the unmarked (default) case, given that it selects the same tune sequence as Seoul Korean, which lacks underlying pitch assignment.

This edge-alignment is best argued for when we observe the vocative tune assignment to non-disyllabic names. Regardless of the number of syllables in a name, or the presence or the absence of the vocative suffix, the association always proceeds from right to left, assigning **H** to the penultimate syllable, followed by **M** assigned to the final syllable. When there are more than two syllables, all syllables other than the last two are assigned the **M** tune. This is all illustrated in (3).

(3) Align **HM** to the right edge of a name

```
acəs'i   tulumiya   cʰoloŋ cʰoloŋ pitnali-ya
/ | \    V  /  /     \    \ | /  /    /  /
MHM      MHM                M         HM
```

21.2.3 South Kyŏngsang

Whereas the Chŏnnam dialect, which does not exhibit a clear pitch-accent system in ordinary speech, shows a rather simple two-way system in the chant, the contrast in the tone-melody association between Seoul Korean on the one hand, and such pitch-accent systems as South Kyŏngsang on the other hand, is quite remarkable.

As shown in (4.a)–(4.c), there are three classes in South Kyŏngsang names depending on their linguistic pitch specification: atonic names (MH), initially accented names (HM), and doubly accented names (HH). They exhibit three different patterns in the selection of the tunes for the vocative chant (see Cho 2002 for details).

This is all expected, given that South Kyŏngsang is a pitch accent language and that the underlying pitch is preserved for the vocative melody. Moreover, just like the first type of vocative chant in Chŏnnam, as shown in (2.a), the tune selection in (4.a) is the unmarked (default) case in South Kyŏngsang, in that it shares the same melody as Seoul Korean.

(4) South Kyŏngsang Vocative Chant (p.c. Y-H Cho)

a. MH+M (atonic name + vocative suffix):

ho-cun-a   pyəŋ-chəl-a   ən - a - ya

M H M   **M H M**   **M H M**

b. HM+M (initially accented name + vocative suffix):

yəŋ-sən-a   hyən-chəl-a   sən-suk-a

H M M   **H M M**   **H M M**

c. HH+M (doubly accented name + vocative suffix):

saŋ-wən-a   hi-myəŋ-a   kuk-wən-a

H H M   **H H M**   **H H M**

To summarize, the dialect differences regarding the melody selection in Korean vocative chant depends on the underlying tone specification on the linguistic level. When there is no underlying tone, **MHM** surfaces, as in Seoul Korean and default cases in Chŏnnam and South Kyŏngsang. For initially accented names, the vocative melody selects the **H*M** sequence, and for doubly accented names in South Kyŏngsang, **HHM** tunes are selected, preserving the underlying pitches.

21.3 Vocative Chant in Japanese

Segments for vocative chant in Japanese usually consist of a name, or a sequence of a name and a vocative suffix (*-tyaN*, *-kuN*, or *-saN*), followed by the expression *asobo* or *asobimasyo* ('Let's play!'). An answer to this invitation may follow in the form *hai* ('yes') or *(mata) atode* ('later'). This is shown in (5).

(5) Name (+vocative suffix), asobo/asobimasyo 'Name, let's play'!
Hai! 'Yes!'or (Mata) Atode! 'Later!'

The melody associated with the vocative chant in Japanese is perceived in the three tunes **L**, **M** or **H**. They reflect the three notes that form a *tetra cord* for Japanese folk melody, as Fumio Koizumi pointed out in his ground breaking work from 1958. Not only the vocative chant, but also the other chants in Japanese are tuned based on the tetra cord. As we mentioned in section 1, these tunes are interpreted so that there is a minor interval by three degrees between **L** and **M**, and a major interval by two degrees between **M** and **H**. For example, (6) shows two sets of tetra cords for Japanese folk music.

(6) Two Instances of Tetra Cord for Japanese folk Melody:

A-C-D E-G-A
L-M-H L-M-H

In Japanese vocative chant, we observed that there are two patterns in the melody. One is clearly dependent on the highs and lows of the lexical pitch, while the other is independent of lexical specification. The first pattern is observed among more than half of the Tokyo dialect speakers whom we interviewed (henceforth *Tokyo 1* speakers), while the second is observed among the rest of the Tokyo dialect speakers (*Tokyo 2* speakers) as well as the speakers of the *Fukui* dialect. Note that in the Fukui dialect of Japanese, the distinctive pitch is totally missing, which will be discussed in more detail below.

21.3.1 Tokyo 1

The following regularities are observed in Tokyo 1 vocative chant (Cho and Saiki 2003). First, the L and H in unaccented names occur as **L** and **M**, respectively. Second, for initially accented names, the initial H and the other lexical pitches are sung to the tunes **H** and **L**, respectively. Third, in medially accented names, the accented mora (H*) is realized as **H**. Finally, all through the data, the vocative suffix and the penultimate mora are assigned the **H** and **M** tunes respectively, regardless of the kind of lexical pitches they bear.

If we take the sequence of 3-mora name and a vocative suffix, for instance, the case with an unaccented name (e.g. *Mayumi-tyaN*, pronounced as LHH+H,) and the other with an accented name (e.g. *Máriko-tyaN*, pronounced as H*LL+L) are chanted to the tunes **LMH** and **H*MH**, respectively. In both cases, *asobo* ('let's play!', pronounced as LHH) is sung to the melody **LMH**, as illustrated in (7).

If we refer to the major scale in Western music, the initial moras for *Mayumi-tyaN* and *Mariko-tyaN* are likely to be sung to the notes, for example E and A, respectively, while the second mora and the vocative suffix for both examples, to the notes G and A, respectively. This clearly shows that the linguistic prominence as well as the contrast is preserved both in language and in the vocative melody.

(7) Mayumi-tyaN asobo vs. Máriko-tyaN asobo

L M H L M H H*M H LM H

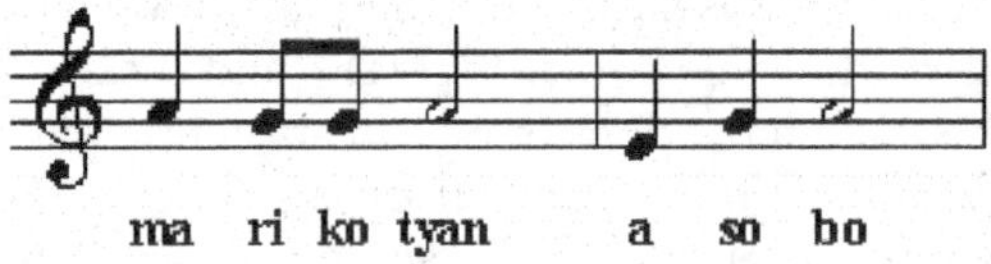

Moreover, the vocative chant in Tokyo 1 is **MH**, and the assignment of these tunes to the words proceeds from right to left. Thus, for example, the assignment of tunes to the segments *KeNichi-kuN* (4 mora unaccented name + vocative suffix, pronounced as LHHH+H) show the three patterns shown in (8), which reflect logically viable linking possibilities between the segments and the vocative tunes.

(8) 1. KeNichi-kuN 2. KeNichi-kuN 3. KeNichi-kuN

L M H L M H L M H

21.3.2 Tokyo 2 and Fukui

Unlike Tokyo 1, Tokyo 2 and Fukui vocative chants disregard lexical pitch distinction. In these dialects, all names with the vocative suffix are realized with the **HMH** tune sequence. Moreover, the **HMH** melody is repeated all through the chant, of course including the *asobo* 'let's play!' part. Compare (9) with (7).

(9) Mayumi-tyaN asobo vs. Máriko-tyaN asobo

H M H H M H H*M H HM H

Furthermore, in Tokyo 2 and Fukui, there is a systematic variation in melody association. For example, the vocative melody for *KeNichi+kuN* varies in three ways which are obtained by assuming logically possible multiple linkings of the first two tunes of the **HMH** melody, as illustrated in (10). Note that the association of the **HMH** chanting tunes with the segments is again from right to left. Compare (10) with (8).

(10) 1. KeNichi-kuN 2. KeNichi-kuN 3. KeNichi-kuN

H M H **H M H** **H M H**

We argue that Tokyo 2 and Fukui vocative chant is the case where the melody overrides lexical pitch specification. In other words, in this variety of vocative chant, music is overriding language. The Fukui dialect of Japanese does not have a distinctive pitch. Thus, it naturally follows that the chanting of Fukui speakers is not constrained linguistically. It automatically takes up the melody determined by music. Likewise, Tokyo 2 vocative chant allows music to take over linguistic specifications. We have observed similar cases in other kinds of chanting in Tokyo Japanese. For example, in the counting chant (*ichi, nii, san,...* 'one, two, three,...'), numbers are invariably chanted to the **HM** melody up to ten, ignoring the lexical pitch specification, while afterwards, chanting tunes reflect the lexical pitches assigned to the number words. Also, in the Tokyo teasing chant (*Mityatta. Mityatta. Sensei-ni itte-yaroo!* 'I saw it. I saw it. I'll tell the teacher!'), **HM** recurs throughout the chant, again despite the linguistic pitch.

21.3.3 Rhythm in Japanese Vocative Chant

Pyongko is a rhythm that has been adopted for a vast range of Japanese traditional folk songs as well as chants. This rhythm is characterized by two musical notes, where the durational ratio between the first and the second ranges from 3:1 to 1:1, with 2:1 intervening in between (Mitsui and Takahira 2001), as illustrated in (11).

(11) Pyongko variants:

	1st note		2nd note
a. 3 : 1	dotted eighth-note	+	sixteenth-note
b. 2 : 1	quarter-note	+	eighth-note (triplet)
c. 1 : 1	eighth-note	+	eighth-note

Pyongko variants mentioned above occur for the vocative chant in Japanese. For example, it is observed that the name part of *Yuri+tyaN* 'accented 2-mora name + vocative suffix' and *Koga+saN* 'unaccented 2-mora name + vocative suffix' are chanted to the rhythms described in (12.a)–(12.c), where the numbers indicate the durational ratio for the three syllables *Yu*, *ri* and *tyaN*, and *Ko*, *ga* and *saN*. Notice that Pyongko in (11.a)–(11.c) occurs for the first two moras in (12).

(12)

	Yu	ri	+	tyaN
	Ko	ga	+	saN
a.	3 :	1	:	4
b.	2 :	1	:	3
c.	1 :	1	:	2

As pointed out in sections 3.1 and 3.2, vocative chant in Japanese is **MH**, and the assignment of these tunes to the words proceeds from right to left. Regardless of the kind of lexical pitches, the vocative suffix and the penultimate mora are assigned the tunes **H** and **M**, respectively. Moreover, in Tokyo 1, the other lexical pitches are faithfully reflected in the vocative melody. This is illustrated in (13), for *Yuri-tyaN* (2 mora accented name + vocative suffix), and in (14), for *Koga-saN* (2 mora unaccented name + vocative suffix).

(13)

vocative melody:	**H**	**M**	**H**
lexical pitch:	H	L	L
	Yu	ri +	tyaN

(14)

vocative melody:	**L**	**M**	**H**
lexical pitch:	L	H	H
	Ko	ga +	saN

In order to account for the occurrence of Pyongko in Japanese vocative chant, we follow Hayes and Lahiri's (1992) representation called *rhythmic structure*, where horizontal and vertical grids refer to 'the salience of individual beats' and 'beat sequences at varying intervals,' respectively, and argue for the following organization of Japanese rhythmic structure.

First, Japanese is a mora-timed language. In speech and perception, a Japanese mora takes approximately an equal duration of time (Kubozono 1999, and Kubozono and Homma 2002). It follows then, that on the linguistic level, Japanese has a rhythmic structure in which every horizontal grid carries the same duration in time.

Second, Japanese has a contrast between an accented word and an unaccented word, where the former contains a 'pitch fall' after the accented H (H*), while the latter does not. Hence, assuming Wee's (2002) notion of *linguistic head*, namely, the phonologically most salient unit under contrast, H* is identified as a linguistic head. Furthermore, the linguistic head is captured on the rhythmic structure of Hayes and Lahiri (1992), with the vertical grid higher than the non-head elements. Thus, incorporating the level of representation, rhythmic structure (henceforth, rhythmic tier), the vocative chants for *Yuri-tyaN* in (13) and *Koga-saN* in (14) are analyzed as shown in (15) and (16), respectively.

(15) Accented name (Yuri) + vocative suffix (-tyaN)

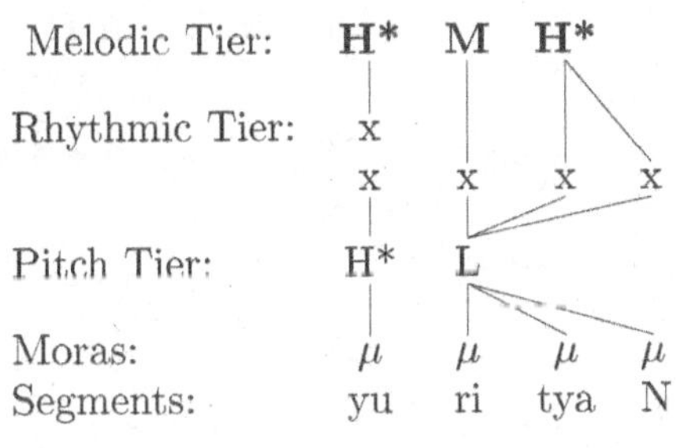

(16) Unaccented name (Koga) + vocative suffix (-saN)

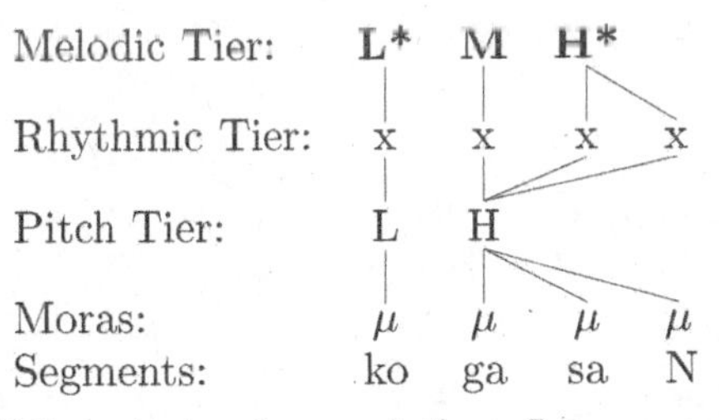

In addition, it is observed that Japanese vocative chant is most frequently sung to the 4/4 time signature, where the first beat and the third beat are accented. Thus, in (15) and (16), the accented beats are expressed with an asterisk (*) on the vocative melody (on the melodic tier).

Notice that the Pyongko variant in (11c) is a natural consequence of the analysis shown in (15) and (16), since the durational ratio between the first and the second mora is explicitly captured as 1:1 on the rhythmic tier, in terms of a single occurrence of x for both of them. The other Pyongko variants, i.e. those in (11a) and (11b) also follow, given the process of *beat splitting*, 'whereby a variable number of weak beats are inserted after the strong beats,' and *tone sharing* that follows, guaranteeing that the beat retains the original tone, as discussed in Hayes and Lahiri (1992). Thus, the two outputs of beat splitting shown in (17) are possible for *Yuri-tyaN* and *Koga-saN*. (17a) and (17b) are instantiated in (18a) and (18b) for *Yuri-tyaN*, and in (19a) and (19b) for *Koga-saN*, respectively. In (17)–(19), the weak beats inserted after the strong beats by beat splitting are indicated in bold face (**x**).

(17)

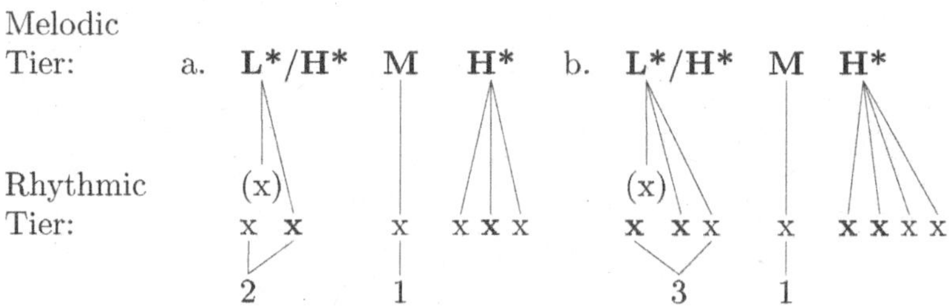

(18) a. Accented name (Yuri) + vocative suffix (-tyaN)

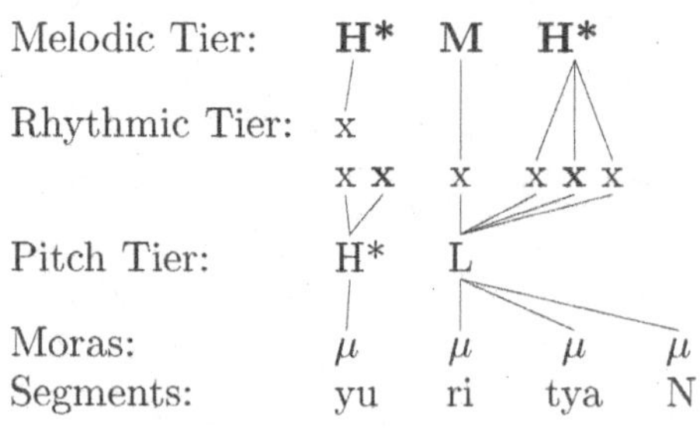

b. Accented name (Yuri) + vocative suffix (-tyaN)

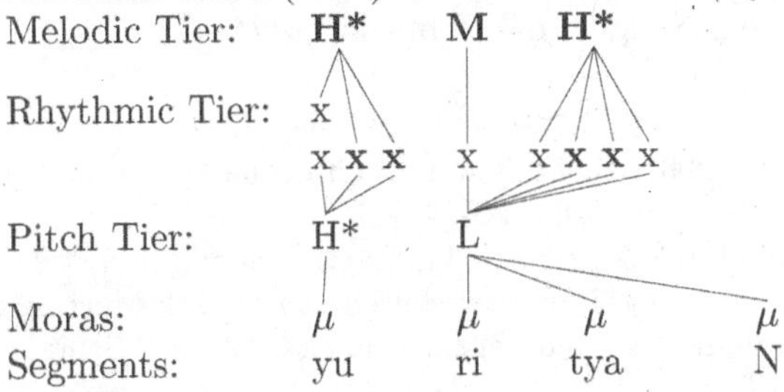

(19) a. Unaccented name (Koga) + vocative suffix (-saN)

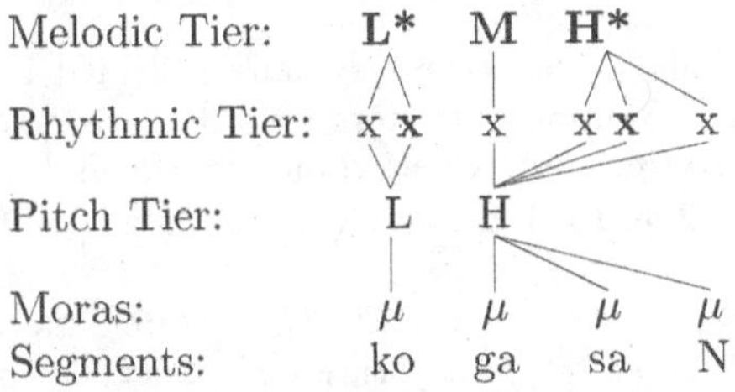

b. Unaccented name (Koga) + vocative suffix (-saN)

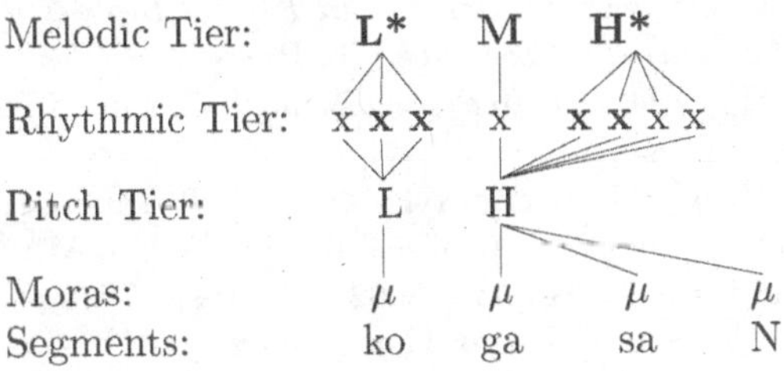

We do not have space to discuss Korean rhythmic behavior, but our initial investigation confirms the hypothesis that the rhythmic tier should be motivated in Korean and must be part of the universal music-language interface.

21.4 Conclusion

We have shown how linguistic structure such as lexical prominence and metrical organization interacts in meaningful ways with musical structure of melody and rhythm in Korean and Japanese vocative chant. The text-melody association and the rhythmic lengthening we have discussed clearly demonstrate that the intersection of music and language involves a common vocabulary. Cross-dialectal and cross-linguistic variations, then, result by employing a set of well-defined parameters universally available in language and music interface.

References

Cho, Young-mee Y. 2002. Syllable weight and tone in Korean. *Japanese and Korean Linguistics* 12(2):104–116.

Cho, Young-mee Y. and Mariko Saiki. 2003. Preservation of lexical prominence in vocative chant. Paper presented at the 13th Meeting of Japanese and Korean Linguistics Conference, August 2, 2003, Michigan State University.

Gibbon, Dafydd. 1976. *Perspectives of Intonation Analysis*. Bern: H. Lang.

Gussenhoven, Carlos. 1993. The Dutch foot and the chanted call. *Journal of Linguistics* 29:37–63.

Hayes, Bruce and Aditi Lahiri. 1992. Durationally specified intonation in English and Bengali. In J. Sundberg, L. Nord, and R. Carlson, eds., *Music, Language, Speech and Brain*, pages 78–91. London: Macmillan.

Inkelas, Sharon and Draga Zec. 1988. Serbo-Croatian pitch accent. *Language* 64(2):227–48.

Kim, No-Ju. 1996. *Tone, Segments and Their Interaction in North Kyungsang Korean*. Ph.D. thesis, Ohio State University, Columbus.

Ko, Eon-Suk. 1999. Interaction of tone and stress in Seoul and Chonnam Korean. In S. Bird, A. Carnie, J. D. Haugen, and P. Norquest, eds., *Proceedings of the 18th West Coast Conference in Formal Linguistics (WCCFL 18)*, pages 246–259. Tucson, AZ: Cascadilla Press.

Koizumi, Fumio. 1958. *Nihon Dentoo Ongaku no Kenkyuu*. Tokyo: Ongaku no Tomo-sya.

Kubozono, Haruo. 1999. Mora and syllable. In N. Tsujimura, ed., *The Handbook of Japanese Linguistics*, pages 31–61. Malden, MA: Blackwell.

Kubozono, Haruo and Takeru Honma. 2002. *Onsetsu-to Moora*. No. 15 in Eigogaku Monograph Series. Tokyo: Kenkyuusya.

Ladd, D. Robert. 1978. Stylized intonation. *Language* 54(3):517–39.

Ladd, D. Robert. 1996. *Intonational Phonology*. Cambridge, UK: Cambridge University Press.

Leben, Will. 1976. The tones in English intonation. *Linguistic Analysis* 2:69–107.

Liberman, Mark. 1975. *The Intonational System of English*. Ph.D. thesis, Massachusetts Institute of Technology.

Mitsui, Toru and Nozomi Takahira. 2001. 'Pyongko' rhythm as Japan's other within. *The Bulletin of the Faculty of Education, Kanazawa University, Humanities and Social Sciences* 51:27–36.

Pierrehumbert, Janet and Mary E. Beckman. 1988. *Japanese Tone Structure*. Cambridge, MA: The MIT Press.

Wee, Lian H. 2002. Unraveling the relation between Mandarin tones and musical melody. Ms., Rutgers University.

Yung, Bell. 1991. The relationship of text and tune in Chinese opera. In J. Sundberg, L. Nord, and R. Carlson, eds., *Music, Language, Speech and Brain*, pages 78–91. London: Macmillan.

22

Morphological Variation of *l*-Verbs in Korean: An OT Account

HYE-WON CHOI

22.1 Introduction

Variation is a difficult problem for any theory of linguistics; it often leads to optional application of rules or principles of the theory, which could in essence bring unpredictability to grammar. Variation has also been a problem for Optimality Theory, which was originally based on strict ranking of constraints, but recently various attempts have been made to resolve the issue within the theory (Anttila 1997, 2002, Boersma and Hayes 2001, Bresnan et al. 2001, Legendre et al. 1999, Nagy and Reynolds 1997).

Korean shows a morphological variation in the conjugation of *l*-"irregular" verbs.[1] Presented below in (1) are a few examples that illustrate this variation (which were found via internet search). In standard dialect, the *l*-verbs presented in (1) such as *phal* 'to sell', *yel* 'to open', *al* 'to know', *pel* 'to earn', *sal* 'to live', and *mal* 'to roll', should conjugate like the first forms given in (1): *phal-myen, yel-lako, a-n,*

[1]A preliminary version of this paper was presented at the Summer Conference of the Korean Society for Language and Information in June, 2004. I thank the audience, especially Hee-Rak Chae, Yong-Beom Kim, Yongkyoon No, Byong-Rae Ryu, and Hae-Kyung Wee, for their valuable questions and comments. I am also grateful to an anonymous reviewer for his or her insightful comments. Any errors or misinterpretations are of course mine.

Architectures, Rules, and Preferences: Variations on Themes by Joan Bresnan.
Annie Zaenen, Jane Simpson, Tracy Holloway King,
Jane Grimshaw, Joan Maling, and Chris Manning, (eds.).

pe-nikka, sa-seyyo, and *ma-pnita*.[2] However, quite a few speakers conjugate them as in the second variants: *phal-ɨmyen, yel-ɨlako, al-ɨn, pel-ɨnikka, sal-ɨseyyo,* and *mal-ɨpnita.*

(1) Examples of *l*-Verb Variation

a. *phal* 'to sell': phal-myen ~ phal-ɨmyen
ceke wenlay phanmay kakyek-i elma-eyo? kuliko, ceke, han kay-ssik **phal-ɨmyen** an toy-yo?
'What is the original price of those? Can you **sell** them by singles?'
<www.simsimi.com/simsimi/sim_event_view.php?uid=56&start=1>

b. *yel* 'to open': yel-lako ~ yel-ɨlako
Cangayin Itongkwen Yentay Park Kyengsek tayphyo-ka hanguy sehan-ul huntul-e poi-mye kwutkey tathi-n Seoul-si Tosi Chelto Kongsa mwun-ul **yel-ɨlako** yokwuha-ko iss-ta.
'Park Kyengsek, president of Alliance for the Rights of the Handicapped, requested to **open** the tightly-shut door of Seoul Railroad Co., while waving (to the public) the petition letter.'
<www.withnews.com/print.php3?no=521>

c. *al* 'to know': a-n ~ al-ɨn
kulemyense ku keleka-nun kwaceng-eyse kyeysok sentong-ul han keya. salam-tul-un choylwuthan-man sso-n cwul **al-ɨn** keya, silthan-ul sso-n key anila.
'Then, I continued to rally people as I walked along. People **knew** (thought) that they only shot tear gas, not real bullets.'
<altair.chonnam.ac.kr/~cnu518/data/data3_4302.html>

d. *pel* 'to earn (money)': pe-nikka ~ pel-ɨnikka
sutha-tul-un caki kayseng-i-ko ton-ul **pel-ɨnikka** sangkwan-i eps-ciman ai-tul-eykey-nun khun chwungtongkam-ulo sutha-tul-i ha-ko iss-nun akseyseli tung-i sa-ko sipheci-ese...
'It doesn't matter to the stars (celebrities) because it's their style and they **earn** (make) money, but to the kids, it's a big temptation and they simply want to buy the stuff like the accessories that the stars are wearing...'
<okgu-e.cein.or.kr/home/home/graduate/graduate84//.htm>

[2]This paper uses the Yale Romanization System when transliterating Korean letters into Roman alphabet except for the case of vowel *u*. Instead of the Yale representation *u*, the phonetic symbol *ɨ* is used throughout the paper.

e. *sal* 'to live': sa-seyyo ~ sal-ɨseyyo
Toksantong-ila hasi-ess-na-yo? kyellon-un pilla sal-ko siphusi-myen censey-lo **sal-ɨseyyo.**
'Did you say it is Toksan-dong? The conclusion is, if you want to live in a villa, then rent one (Lit: **live** in one by renting one).'
<www.r114.co.kr/z/order/community/04.asp?F4=1&F7=1324>

f. *mal* 'to roll': ma-pnita ~ mal-ɨpnita
kimpali-uyey kim-ul kkal-ko ku-uyey pap-ul phye noh-ko, kim-pap caylyo-lul hana-ssik kacilenhi noh-ko kkokkkok kimpap-ul **mal-ɨpnita.**
'Place the seaweed sheet on the bambooroll, put rice on top, put each ingredient one by one, and you **roll** (the whole thing) tightly.'
<www.cjfood.com/life/life_03_b_view.asp?part=spring&idx=43>

Although prohibited by prescriptive grammar of Korean, this type of "wrong" conjugation examples are quite common in casual spoken language and they are not so rare in the written language also. Therefore, they should not be discounted as accidental mistakes made by some small number of (less educated) speakers. For example, *sal-ɨ-*, an impossible sequence according to the prescriptive grammar, alone marks 1,510 hits in the *google* search (www.google.co.kr), which includes not only casual chats but also more serious registers like news reports.

This paper examines this variation of *l*-verbs illustrated in (1) above in Optimality Theory. The variation will be explained in relation to the standard form such that the variants result from a slight change in the ranking of the same set of constraints. It will be argued that promotion of ranking of some faithfulness constraints brings about the variation.

22.2 Conjugation Patterns of *l*-Verbs

The *l*-verbs are not a small closed group of verbs that are used only scarcely in the language. They include most common verbs such as *nol* 'to play', *pel* 'to make money', *sal* 'to live', *al* 'to know', *wul* 'to cry', and *phal* 'to sell'. (2) is a list of *l*-verbs including adjectival verbs in (2b).

(2) List of *l*-Verbs

a. *kal* 'to change, grind'; *kel* 'to hang'; *kkul* 'to drag'; *nel* 'to hang'; *nol* 'to play'; *tal* 'to hang'; *tol* 'to turn'; *tul* 'to carry, enter'; *mal* 'to roll, quit'; *mil* 'to push'; *mol* 'to drive' *nal* 'to fly'; *ppal* 'to wash (clothes), lick'; *pel* 'to earn'; *sal* 'to live'; *ssul* 'sweep'; *al* 'to know'; *yel* 'to open'; *wul* 'to cry'; *cel* 'to limp'; *col* 'to doze'; *cwul* 'to shrink'; *phal* 'to sell'; *phwul* 'to solve, untie'; *hemwul* 'to demolish'

b. *kil* 'to be long'; *tal* 'to be sweet'; *mel* 'to be far'; *cal* 'to be tiny'

l-verbs are morpho-phonologically determined in that any verb whose stem ends in an *l* belongs to this group, and that they all, adjectival or not, behave the same way morpho-phonologically in conjugation. We will see their morpho-phonological characteristics in this section.

22.2.1 *l*-Verbs in Standard Form

l-verbs are "irregular" along with six other groups of irregular verbs in Korean in that the stem changes in some way or other when combined with verbal suffixes; in contrast, regular verbs do not change any part of their stems when followed by suffixes. *l*-verbs have two distinguishable characteristics.

First of all, the initial vowel *ɨ* in *ɨ*-initial suffixes gets dropped after the stem-final *l* in *l*-verbs. Therefore, the sequence of *l-ɨ* is not possible for *l*-verbs.[3] The *ɨ*-deletion is, in fact, observed quite often in the verbal morphology of the language: the *ɨ* in *ɨ*-initial suffixes is always dropped if the verb stem ends in a vowel; on the other hand, the *ɨ* is retained if the verb stem ends in a consonant.[4] See the contrast between the consonant-final verbs in (3a) and the vowel-final verbs in (3b) below. Interestingly, *l*-verbs pattern with vowel-final verbs in this respect, as

[3]In fact, we see some cases of *l-ɨ* sequence, not in *l*-verbs but in *t*-verbs. The *t* in *t*-verbs turns to an *l* when followed by a vowel; for example, *ket-ɨnikka* becomes *kel-ɨnikka*, hence an *l-ɨ* sequence.

[4]Some might think of this as a case of insertion instead of deletion: that is, an *ɨ* is inserted if the verb ends in a consonant rather than the *ɨ* being deleted if the verb ends in a vowel. However, this epenthesis view is problematic. First of all, if we took the view that an *ɨ* was inserted, then we should explain why an *ɨ*, not another vowel, say an *e* ([ə]), is inserted, knowing that quite a few verbal suffixes start with an *e* in Korean (see (4) for reference). If we take the deletion view, then we can say that vowel-initial suffixes start either with an *e* or with an *ɨ* and that only the *ɨ*-initial suffixes drop the initial vowel *ɨ* after the stem-final vowel, the reason being that *ɨ* is the weakest vowel in Korean. Second, not all verbal suffixes in Korean are vowel-initial; therefore, to sustain the epenthetic view, one would have to say that only a subset of verbal suffixes allow ɨ-insertion while others do not. For example, the interrogative suffix *-ni* never allows the *ɨ* before it, while the subordinator suffix *-ni* 'because' does. If we took the insertion view, we would have no way of explaining why only the subordinator *-ni* allows the insertion. If we take the deletion view, we can say that the interrogative *-ni* is originally *-ni* without the *ɨ*, while the subordinator *-ni* is *-ɨni* originally and the *ɨ* is deleted after a stem-final vowel.

shown in (3c); the *ɨ* in the suffix is deleted after an *l* just as it is deleted after a vowel in the stem. For reference, verbal suffixes are listed in (4), classified by their initial sound.

(3) *ɨ* drops after *l*
  a. C-final verbs: mek-ɨmyen, wus-ɨlako
  b. V-final verbs: ca-myen, po-lako
  c. *l*-final verbs: sal-myen, phal-lako

(4) Verbal Suffixes (Sohn 1999, 231-240)
  a. V-initial Suffixes:
  -e/a, -e/a la, -e/a se, -e/a taka, -e/a to, -e/a yo; -(ɨ)lla, -(ɨ)llay(-yo), -(ɨ)l, -(ɨ)lkey(yo), -(ɨ)lyeko, -(ɨ)m, -(ɨ)ma, -(ɨ)msey, -(ɨ)myen, -(ɨ)myense, -(ɨ)n, -(ɨ)na, -(ɨ)ni, -(ɨ)nikka, -(ɨ)o, -(ɨ)psita, -(ɨ)sipsio
  b. C-initial Suffixes:
  -ca, -ci (Neg), -ci(yo), -ciman, -ktun, -key (Fam.), -key, -ki, -ki wihayse, -ki ttaymwuney, -ko(Inf.), -ko, -ko(se), -kwun(-yo), -na, -ney (Fam.), -ney(-yo), -ni, -nula(ko), nula-myen, -nun, -(nu)nka, -(nun)ta, -(nu)ntey, -nunya, -nya, -pnikka, -pnita, -sey, -so, -supnita, -ta, -taka, -telato, -tolok, -tunci

This indicates that speakers of (standard) Korean perceive of *l* more like a vowel than a consonant, which is not so inconceivable given that liquid sounds have a vowel-like quality and hence do not always pattern with other hard consonants cross-linguistically (e.g. syllabic *l* of *bottle* or syllabic *r* of *water* in English).

The other important characteristic of *l*-verbs is that the stem *l* is dropped when the following sound is *n*, *s*, or *p*.[5] This is illustrated in (5).

(5) *l* drops before *n*, *s*, or *p*
  a. *n*-initial suffixes: sa-ney, *sal-ney; pha-ney, *phal-ney
  b. *s*-initial suffixes: sa-sey, *sal-sey; pha-sey, *phal-sey
  c. *p*-initial suffixes: sa-pnita, *sal-pnita; pha-pnita, *phal-pnita

For example, the final *l* in the *l*-verb *sal* 'to live' is deleted when the suffix starts with an *n* as in *-ney* ('Familiar'-style ending), thus *sa-*

[5] It is not clear why *l* is dropped before *n*, *s*, or *p* especially when these sounds do not form a natural class. Since the focus of this paper is not on the phonological phenomenon itself but rather on the variation, we will just take it as a fact. Also, one might argue that the *p*-initial suffixes given in (5c) are in fact *ɨ*-initial and the *ɨ* is dropped as explained in (3). The current analysis is compatible with this view too.

ney, not **sal-ney*, as illustrated in (5a). Similarly with the *s*-initial and *p*-initial suffixes in (5b) and (5c) respectively.

Note that the stem-final *l* in *l*-verbs is retained if the suffix starts with a consonant other than *n*, *s*, or *p*. See (6) below.

(6) *l* is retained before other C-initial suffixes

a. sal-ko, *sa-ko; phal-key, *pha-key

b. sal-ciman, *sa-ciman; phal-ca, *pha-ca

c. sal-taka, *sa-taka; phal-tolok, *pha-tolok

As shown in (6), the stem *l* should not be deleted before the suffixes that begin with a consonant other than *n*, *s*, or *p*, such as *-key*, *-ko*, *-ciman*, *-ca*, *-taka* and *-tolok*; the *l*-dropped forms such as **sa-ko*, **pha-ca*, and **pha-tolok* are ungrammatical.

Also, we can see the combination effect of the *ɨ*-drop and the *l*-drop when the suffix starts with an *ɨ* which is followed by an *n*, *s*, or *p*. This is demonstrated in (7).

(7) Both *ɨ* and *l* drop before *ɨ*-initial suffixes with *n*, *s*, or *p*

a. *-ɨn*: sa-nikka,*sal-ɨnikka,*sal-nikka; pha-nikka,*phal-ɨnikka, phal-nikka

b. *-ɨs*: sa-seyyo,*sal-ɨseyyo,*sal-seyyo; pha-seyyo,*phal-ɨseyyo, phal-seyyo

c. *-ɨp*: sa-psita,*sal-ɨpsita,*sal-psita; pha-psita,*phal-ɨpsita, phal-psita

In this case, both *ɨ* and *l* are dropped: the *ɨ* in the suffix is dropped because it follows an *l* in the stem; the stem *l* is dropped too because the *l* is now followed by an *n*, *s*, or *p* after the *ɨ* disappears. Neither the *ɨ*-retained form such as **sal-ɨnikka* nor the *l*-retained from such as **phal-nikka* is grammatical in standard dialect.

To summarize, *l*-verbs in the standard dialect have two distinctive characteristics: the *ɨ*-drop in the suffix and the *l*-drop in the stem in proper environments.

22.2.2 *l*-Verbs in Variation

As introduced in (1), speakers show variation for *l*-verbs. The examples in (1) are repeated below in (8), stripped of the contexts they appear in.

(8)

a. *phal* 'to sell': phal-myen ~ phal-ɨmyen

b. *yel* 'to open': yel-lako ~ yel-ɨlako

c. *al* 'to know': a-n ~ al-ɨn

d. *pel* 'to earn (money)': pe-nikka ~ pel-ɨnikka
e. *sal* 'to live': sa-seyyo ~ sal-ɨseyyo
f. *mal* 'to roll': ma-pnita ~ mal-ɨpnita

One obvious feature we notice in the variation examples, i.e. the second forms in (8), is that the suffix *ɨ* is not dropped throughout. Recall that in the standard dialect, as shown in the first forms above, the *ɨ* never follows an *l*. Yet, here the *l*-*ɨ* sequence is allowed. Additionally, since the *ɨ* is not dropped in this variant, the *l* in the stem is not adjacent to an *n*, *s*, or *p* in the suffix either, as can be seen in the last four examples (8c, d, e, f). Take (8d) for instance. Since the initial *ɨ* in the suffix *-ɨnikka* is not deleted in this variant of the language, the *l* in the stem will never be adjacent to the *n* in the suffix; therefore, the *l* cannot be deleted, and hence it appears in the output form. Likewise with the *s* in (8e) or the *p* in (8f).

(9) summarizes the variant behavior of the *l*-verbs.

(9) Conjugation Pattern in *ɨ*-Retention Variant
a. sal-ɨmyen, phal-ɨlako (cf. sal-myen, phal-lako)
b. sal-ɨnikka, phal-ɨseyyo, pel-ɨpsita (cf. sa-nikka, pha-seyyo, pe-psita)
c. sa-ney, pha-sey, pe-pnita; *sal-ney, *phal-sey, *pel-pnita
d. sal-ko, phal-ca, pel-tolok; *sal-ɨko, *sal-ɨca, *sal-ɨtolok

As shown in (9a), an *l*-verb, e.g. *sal*, in this variant, does not have the *ɨ* deleted in the *ɨ*-initial suffixes unlike in the standard dialect, hence *sal-ɨmyen*, not *sal-myen*. This means that *l*-verbs in the variant behave like consonant-final verbs (e.g., *mek-ɨmyen*), unlike in the standard dialect where they behave like vowel-final verbs (e.g., *ca-myen*). Recall our discussion around (3). In other words, speakers of the variant seem to treat *l* more like a regular consonant. Moreover, because of the ɨ-retention, *l*-drop does not happen before the *ɨ*-initial suffixes with *n*, *s*, or *p*, as demonstrated in (9b). However, this should not be interpreted such that *l*-drop never takes place in the variant. If the suffix originally starts with *n*, *s*, or *p* without the interruptive *ɨ*, that is, if the suffix is not *ɨ*-initial, as in (9c), *l* does get dropped, just as in the standard dialect. This shows that *l*-drop exists for the variant speakers also, but that the environment for the *l*-drop is met less often due to the absence of *ɨ*-drop. Finally, if the suffix starts with a consonant other than *n*, *s*, or *p*, as in (9d), *l* is retained, just as in the standard dialect. To summarize, unlike the speakers of the standard dialect who have both the *ɨ*-drop and the *l*-drop, the speakers of this variant seem to have only the *l*-drop but not the *ɨ*-drop.

In addition to the pattern of variation that was shown in (9), which will be called the 'ɨ-retention variant' for convenience, we also see a slightly different variant, a much rarer one. We will call the latter the 'ɨ-insertion variant'.[6] See examples in (10) below, which show conjugations with an *n*-initial suffix, *-ney(yo)*.

(10) Examples of ɨ-Insertion Variant

a. phwu-neyyo ~ pwul-ɨneyyo
cham, kuliko Senwu-ka cakkwuman meli-lul phwul-eyo. emma-ka yeyppukey hay cwusin meli-lul kunyang pangwul cap-ko ssuk **pwul-ɨneyyo**.
'Ah, also, Senwu continues to undo her hair. She holds the hair string, which mom did her hair so beautifully with, and just **unties** it.' <www.hanil90.co.kr/madang/citybbs.html?table=hanilki&request=1136&last=-50&mode=>

b. tu-neyyo ~ tul-ɨneyyo
annyenghaseyo? 'mydoll1218'-ipnita. Shinbi aylpem-ey 1 penc-cay nolay 'Sepangnim'-ilan nolay-ka cham mam-ey **tul-ɨneyyo.**
'Hi. I am "mydoll1218." Lit: The first song "Husband" in Shinbi's album has **entered** my heart (I like the song).' <music.puckii.com/artist/ artist_albumreview_content.asp?album_code=143&review_code=706>

c. ki-neyyo ~ kil-ɨneyyo
haciman cen panphwum-ul halye-ha-pnita. waynyahamyenyo, cey khi-nun 163 intey. sayngkak-pota kicang-i cham **kil-ɨneyyo**. cey tali-ka ccalp-ase kulenci-nun moll-ato.
'However, I'm gonna return it. Because I am 163 (cm) and its length is unexpectedly **long**. Maybe my legs are too short.' <shop15.daum.net/jsp/front/prodeval/ProdEvalRelList.jsp?CID=C11231&PID=A191_515016>

In the ɨ-retention variant shown in (9), *l* is deleted when the suffix is *n*-initial, as illustrated in (9c); in contrast, in this more radical variant, i.e the ɨ-insertion variant, an ɨ, which was absent in the original suffix, is inserted into the suffix, and therefore creates an environment which retains the *l*. As a result, we end up with no cases of *l*-drop in this radical

[6] This type of examples shown in (10) are in fact much harder to come by, compared with the type illustrated in (1). Taking the example of *phwul* 'to solve, untie', the verb *phwul* marks 1,060 hits in the *google* search for the kind of examples shown in (1); however, it marks only one hit, which is example (10a), for the kind in (10). This indicates that while the absence of ɨ-drop (or the ɨ-retention) is quite common, the ɨ-insertion exists only for a small number of speakers.

variant. Recall that (9c) was the only environment that forces an *l*-drop in the *ɨ*-retention variant. Now, the *l*-verbs in this radical variant are not "irregular" verbs any more because the stem *l* never drops. In other words, the speakers of the radical variant have completely "regularized" the *l*-"irregular" verbs at the expense of modifying the *n*-, *s*-, or *p*-initial suffixes a bit by means of ɨ-insertion. We should note here that even these radical speakers do not insert an *ɨ* for non-*n,s,p*-initial suffixes: the pattern in (9d) obtains for these speakers as well, thus *sal-ko, phal-ca, pel-tolok*. That is, an *ɨ* is inserted exactly to avoid the *l*-drop, not to simply avoid consonant clusters. The conjugation pattern of the radical variation is summarized in (11).

(11) Conjugation Pattern in *ɨ*-Insertion Variant

a. sal-ɨmyen, phal-ɨlako (cf. sal-myen, phal-lako)

b. sal-ɨnikka, phal-ɨseyyo, pel-ɨpsita (cf. sa-nikka, pha-seyyo, pe-psita)

c. sal-ɨney, phal-ɨsey, pel-ɨpnita (cf. sa-ney, pha-sey, pe-pnita)

d. sal-ko, phal-ca, pel-tolok; *sal-ɨko, *sal-ɨca, *sal-ɨtolok

In short, both of the variants share the property that the *ɨ* of the *ɨ*-initial suffixes is not dropped, as illustrated in (9a,b) and (11a,b). On the other hand, the difference between the *ɨ*-retention variant and the *ɨ*-insertion variant lies in the contrast between (9c) and (11c), i.e. the conjugation before the *n,s,p*-initial suffixes: only the *ɨ*-insertion variant inserts an *ɨ* in this situation, by which it avoids the *l*-drop completely.

22.3 An OT Analysis of *l*-Verbs

In this section, we will explore to account for the three different patterns of conjugation of *l*-verbs in terms of Optimality Theory. It will be argued that the variants are also governed by the same set of constraints as the standard form but that only a slight change in the constraint ranking generates the alternative variants.

22.3.1 OT Constraints for *l*-Verb Conjugation

In Optimality Theory, as is well known, grammar consists of violable constraints, which are ranked: a violation of higher-ranking constraints is more costly. Therefore, the candidate that does not violate a higher-ranking constraint than any other candidates is the optimal and grammatical output. The constraints relevant to the conjugation patterns of *l*-verbs are presented in (12).

(12) Constraints

a. *l-{nsp}: the *l* in *l*-verbs is deleted before *n*-, *s*- or *p*-initial suffixes.[7]
b. *{Vl}-ɨ: the vowel ɨ cannot follow a [-Obs] sound, i.e., a vowel or a liquid *l*.[8]
c. F(ɨ): the vowel ɨ should not be deleted from nor added to the suffix.
d. F(*l*): the *l* in *l*-verbs should be maintained in the output.[9] (*l* should not be deleted.)

The first constraint *l-{nsp} in (12a) is a markedness constraint that states the condition for the *l*-drop. The second constraint *{Vl}-ɨ in (12b) states that the suffix vowel ɨ cannot follow a non-obstruent sound, i.e. a vowel or a liquid *l*. This constraint captures the generalization that the liquid sound *l* patterns with vowels, not with consonants; hence, it motivates the ɨ-drop in the standard form. These markedness constraints may conflict with the faithfulness constraints. For example, F(ɨ) states that the vowel ɨ should not be deleted from nor added to the suffix, but *{Vl}-ɨ would motivate the ɨ to be deleted from the suffix. Similarly with F(*l*) and *l-{nsp}: F(*l*) prohibits *l*-deletion, whereas *l-{nsp} prompts it.

The resolution of these conflicts between the constraints comes in the form of ranking in Optimality Theory. When two constraints are in conflict, the higher-ranking constraint is stronger so that a candidate that violates the higher-ranking constraint loses to a candidate that satisfies it. The ranking of the constraints for *l*-verbs is suggested below:

(13) Constraint Ranking

a. Common:	*l-{nsp}	≫ F(l)	
b. Standard:		≫ *{Vl}-ɨ	≫ F(ɨ), F(l)
c. ɨ-Retention Variant:		≫ F(ɨ)	≫ *{Vl}-ɨ, F(l)

[7]Kim (2003) makes a similar proposal, actually in two separate constraints: CSS (Coronal Sonorant Sequences), which has the effect of prohibiting the sequence of *ln*; No-*l*]vs *s (*ls)*, which prohibits the sequence of *ls*. In fact, Kim does not have a constraint that prohibits the sequence of *lp*, probably because she does not deal with the examples that contain such a sequence. See footnote 5 again.

[8]The constraint *{Vl}-ɨ covers Kim's (2003) No-*r*]vs ɨ *(*rɨ)*, which prohibits the sequence of *rɨ* (i.e. *lɨ* in our case).

[9]Kim's (2003) two faithfulness constraints, MAX-IO ("A segment in the input has a correspondent in the output") and RM ("Morphemes should be realized phonetically in the output"), ensure the same effect as F(ɨ) and F(*l*) have that no deletion from or addition to the input should take place. In addition, Kim has more *l*-specific constraints, MAX-IOstem ("A segment of the stem in the input has a correspondent in the output") and MAX(cont) ("The [+continuant] feature of the input segment must be preserved in the output"), which further guarantee the retention of *l* in the stem.

d. ɨ-Insertion Variant: ≫ F(*l*) ≫ F(ɨ), *{V*l*}-ɨ

First of all, both the standard form and the variant forms share the ranking given in (13a). We never see the sequences of *ln*, *ls*, *lp* in any of these variants, which means that between **l*-{*nsp*} and F(*l*), **l*-{*nsp*} is stronger, i.e. **l*-{*nsp*} ≫ F(*l*).

What is not shared among the three variants is the ranking among the three remaining constraints, *{V*l*}-ɨ, F(ɨ), and F(*l*). As we have seen above, in the standard form, the sequence of *lɨ* is never allowed, which indicates that the markedness constraint *{V*l*}-ɨ is ranked higher than the faithfulness constraints F(ɨ) and F(*l*), as summarized in (13b). In contrast to the standard form, the markedness constraint *{V*l*}-ɨ is not always ranked higher than the faithfulness constraints in the variant forms. In the ɨ-retention variant, the moderate variant, the faithfulness constraint F(ɨ) is ranked higher than *{V*l*}-ɨ and F(*l*), whereas in the ɨ-insertion variant, the radical variant, the faithfulness constraint F(*l*) is ranked higher than F(ɨ) and *{V*l*}-ɨ. The promotion of a faithfulness constraint over the markedness constraint *{V*l*}-ɨ in the variant forms leads to the retention of ɨ and also of *l* in the *lɨ* sequence, and even to the addition of ɨ in the radical variant to further retain *l*. We will see this effect in detail in what follows.

22.3.2 Deriving Variation in Optimality Theory

Standard Form

Let us first look at the standard form. As outlined in section 2.1, *l*-verbs in the standard form have the ɨ-drop and the *l*-drop, and if the conditions are met properly, both ɨ and *l* may drop altogether. Let's look at the case of ɨ-drop first. Recall the examples in (3c). We will take the example where the verb stem *sal* 'to live' is followed by an ɨ-initial suffix, *-ɨmyen* 'if'. The OT evaluation is represented in Tableau 1 in (14).

(14) Standard: ɨ-drop from ɨ-initial suffixes

T1	sal-ɨmyen	*l-{nsp}	*{Vl}-ɨ	F(ɨ)	F(l)
	a. salɨmyen		*!		
☞	b. salmyen			*	
	c. samyen			*	*!
	d. saɨmyen		*!		*

First of all, the input in this case is *sal-ɨmyen*, the combination of the base verb *sal* and the suffix *-ɨmyen*. The constraints are positioned left to right according to the ranking for the standard form given in (13b).

We have four possible candidates to evaluate: candidate (a) *salɨmyen* is the output that is identical to the input, where both the stem *l* and the suffix *ɨ* are retained; candidate (b) *salmyen* is the one where the suffix *ɨ* is dropped; candidate (c) *samyen* has both the stem *l* and the suffix *ɨ* dropped; finally, candidate (d) *saɨmyen* has the stem *l* dropped but the suffix *ɨ* retained.

Note that the highest constraint **l*-{*nsp*} does not play any role in this competition because the input has no *n*, *s*, or *p* in the suffix, so that the constraint is vacuously satisfied by all the candidates. Remember that the *lɨ* sequence is not allowed in the standard form. Now, candidate (a) violates constraint *{V*l*}-*ɨ*, the next highest constraint, because it contains the *lɨ* sequence. This candidate is the most faithful candidate by retaining everything in the input, thus satisfying F(*ɨ*) and F(*l*). Yet, since *{V*l*}-*ɨ* is higher-ranking than F(*ɨ*) and F(*l*), candidate (a) loses to candidate (b) or candidate (c). One possible way to avoid the sequence is to drop the *l* in the stem, which is candidate (d). However, after dropping the *l*, candidate (d) still violates *{V*l*}-*ɨ*; without the stem *l*, the vowel *a* in the stem is followed by the suffix vowel *ɨ*. Violating this high-ranking constraint, this candidate falls out of competition too. Candidate (b), on the other hand, satisfies constraint *{V*l*}-*ɨ* by dropping the *ɨ* in the suffix, and thus violates constraint F(*ɨ*). Candidate (c) also satisfies constraint *{V*l*}-*ɨ* by dropping not only the suffix *ɨ* but also the stem *l*, and therefore violates one more constraint, F(*l*), in addition to F(*ɨ*). Therefore, candidate (b), which drops the *ɨ* only, wins this competition and thus becomes the optimal candidate.

Note that the ranking between F(*ɨ*) and F(*l*) does not matter to the optimality of candidate (b); either ranking will yield the same result because the remaining two candidates (b) and (c) both violate F(*ɨ*), and only (c) further violates F(*l*). In essence, this competition shows that the most optimal way to avoid the *lɨ* sequence is to drop the suffix *ɨ* (candidate (b)), not the stem *l* (candidate (d)), due to the higher ranking of *{V*l*}-*ɨ* over F(*ɨ*).

Now, we will see the case of *l*-drop. See the examples in (5) again. Let's look at the case where the verb is combined with a suffix that starts with an *n*, *s*, or *p* without the preceding *ɨ*, e.g. *-neyyo*. The input for this evaluation then will be *sal-neyyo*. See Tableau 2 in (15).

(15) Standard: *l*-drop before *n/s/p*-initial suffixes

T2	sal-neyyo	*l-{nsp}	*{Vl}-ɨ	F(ɨ)	F(l)
	a. salɨneyyo		*!	*	
	b. salneyyo	*!			
☞	c. saneyyo				*
	d. saɨneyyo		*!	*	*

The most faithful candidate in this competition is candidate (b), which is the same as the input, thus satisfying the faithfulness constraints F(ɨ) and F(*l*). This candidate, however, violates the highest-ranking constraint *l-{*nsp*} because of the *ln* sequence in it. Candidate (c), on the other hand, violates constraint F(*l*) by dropping the *l* in the stem, but instead satisfies *l-{*nsp*} by doing so. Candidate (c) wins over candidate (b) exactly because the markedness constraint *l-{*nsp*} is ranked higher than the faithfulness constraint F(*l*). The other candidates, which have an ɨ in them, i.e. candidate (a) and candidate (d), violate F(ɨ) because the ɨ, which was not in the suffix originally, is inserted here, modifying the original suffix. The insertion of ɨ actually brings a more serious consequence to these candidates because it makes the candidates violate a higher-ranking constraint, *{V*l*}-ɨ. The violations of this high-ranking constraint of course drives them out of competition. Therefore, candidate (c) with the *l*-drop is the optimal output.

We have seen in the above two examples that the ɨ-drop and the *l*-drop are encouraged due to the higher ranking of markedness constraints *l-{*nsp*} and *{V*l*}-ɨ over the faithfulness constraints. Now, let us see if this set-up gets us the combination effect as well. We will examine the case where the suffix begins with an ɨ, followed by an *n*, *s*, or *p*. Take the example of *sal-ɨnikka*. Recall similar examples of this kind in (7).

(16) Standard: ɨ-drop and *l*-drop before ɨ-*n/s/p*-initial suffixes

T3	sal-ɨnikka	*l-{nsp}	*{Vl}-ɨ	F(ɨ)	F(l)
	a. salɨnikka		*!		
	b. salnikka	*!		*	
☞	c. sanikka			*	*
	d. saɨnikka		*!		*

Unlike in (15), the ɨ-containing candidates, i.e. (a) and (d), do not violate F(ɨ) because the ɨ was originally in the suffix. Yet, they are knocked out of competition because they violate the higher-ranking constraint *{V*l*}-*ɨ*; for the stem *l* and the suffix *ɨ* compose the unallowable sequence *lɨ*. Now, candidate (b), without the suffix *ɨ*, violates the highest-ranking constraint **l*-{*nsp*} because without the *ɨ*, the *l* in the stem is followed by an *n* in the suffix. Therefore, candidate (c), which has lost both *l* and *ɨ* and consequently violates F(*ɨ*) and F(*l*), becomes the optimal output in this competition.

The most faithful candidate with no *ɨ*-drop or *l*-drop can win too in the standard form. It happens when the suffix begins with a consonant other than *n*, *s*, or *p*. Look at the case of *sal-ko* in Tableau 4 in (17). Recall similar examples in (6).

(17) Standard: No *l*-drop before C-initial suffixes

T4	sal-ko	**l*-{*nsp*}	*{V*l*}-*ɨ*	F(*ɨ*)	F(*l*)
	a. salɨko		*!	*	
☞	b. salko				
	c. sako				*!
	d. saɨko		*!	*	*

The most faithful candidate (b) violates no constraints in this competition: it does not violate **l*-{*nsp*} because the suffix contains no such consonant, nor does it violate *{V*l*}-*ɨ* because *ɨ* was not present in the original suffix. The less faithful candidates, (a) with an ɨ-insertion, (c) with an *l*-drop, and (d) with an ɨ-insertion and an *l*-drop, only aggravate the situation. Therefore, in this competition, the input-like candidate (b) is the optimal candidate.

Variants

The variants, both *ɨ*-retention and *ɨ*-insertion, differ from the standard form in that the stem *l* is retained in more environments. Recall their variation patterns in (9) and (11) respectively. One way to retain the stem *l* is to allow the *lɨ* sequence. In the *ɨ*-retention variant, this is accommodated by not dropping the *ɨ* in the suffix, which means in the current framework that the ranking of F(*ɨ*) is raised so as to outrank *{V*l*}-*ɨ*. On the other hand, the *ɨ*-insertion variant, which is much rarer, retains the stem *l* more aggressively: it even has an *ɨ* inserted for non-*ɨ*-initial suffixes, in addition to not dropping the *ɨ* in the *ɨ*-initial suffixes. The latter can be accounted for by raising the ranking of F(*l*) higher than *{V*l*}-*ɨ* and F(*ɨ*). We will see how the alternative rankings work below.

Let us look at the *ɨ*-retention variant first. Recall the ranking for the *ɨ*-retention variant in (13c). Let us start with *sal-ɨmyen.* Compare Tableau 5 in (18) with Tableau 1 in (14).

(18) *ɨ*-Retention Variant: No *ɨ*-drop from *ɨ*-initial suffixes

T5	sal-ɨmyen	*l-{*nsp*}	F(ɨ)	*{V*l*}-ɨ	F(*l*)
☞	a. salɨmyen			*	
	b. salmyen		*!		
	c. samyen		*!		*
	d. saɨmyen			*	*!

The major difference in the *ɨ*-retention variant is the higher ranking of F(*ɨ*) over *{V*l*}-*ɨ*; namely, keeping the suffix *ɨ* is more important than avoiding the *lɨ* sequence in this variant. Hence, candidate (a), which used to lose to candidate (b) or candidate (c) in the standard form, now wins over them. Candidate (d) also loses to candidate (a) since it violates F(*l*) additionally. Therefore, candidate (a) is the optimal output in the *ɨ*-retention variant.

The same thing happens for the competition of *sal-ɨnikka.* The suffix *ɨ* is retained and consequently the stem *l* is retained as well. See Tableau 6 in (19) and compare it with Tableau 3 in (16).

(19) *ɨ*-Retention Variant:
No *ɨ*-drop and thus no *l*-drop before *ɨn/s/p*-initial suffixes

T6	sal-ɨnikka	*l-{*nsp*}	F(ɨ)	*{V*l*}-ɨ	F(*l*)
☞	a. salɨnikka			*	
	b. salnikka	*!	*		
	c. sanikka		*!		*
	d. saɨnikka			*	*!

The *ln* sequence (also, the *ls* or *lp* sequence) is not allowed in this variant too; the ranking of *l-{*nsp*} is still the highest. So, candidate (b), violating *l-{*nsp*}, falls out of competition. Now, due to the new ranking, i.e. the reverse ranking of F(*ɨ*) over *{V*l*}-*ɨ*, candidate (c) loses to candidate (a) or (d). In fact, candidate (a) wins over candidate (d) because (d) further violates F(*ɨ*). This way, the *l*-drop does not take place, and hence the stem *l* as well as the suffix *ɨ* is retained in this variant form.

Now, what will happen if the suffix does not begin with an *ɨ*? Without the intervening *ɨ*, candidate (c) with the *l*-drop is the optimal output just like in the standard form (recall Tableau 2 in (15)). Take the case of *sal-neyyo* again, whose evaluation is illustrated in Tableau 7 in (20).

(20) ɨ-Retention Variant: *l*-drop before *n/s/p*-initial suffixes

T7	sal-neyyo	*l-{nsp}	F(ɨ)	*{Vl}-ɨ	F(l)
	a. salɨneyyo		*!	*	
	b. salneyyo	*!			
☞	c. saneyyo				*
	d. saɨneyyo		*!	*	*

As seen above, candidate (b) is easily knocked out; it violates the highest-ranking constraint **l*-{*nsp*}. Also, the ɨ-containing candidates. (a) and (d), are out of competition, violating F(ɨ) because the vowel ɨ is inserted and thus modifies the original form of the suffix. Therefore, the *l*-dropped candidate (c) is the optimal candidate in the variant as well as in the standard form. In other words, unless the suffix contains an ɨ originally, the stem *l* still gets dropped to obey **l*-{*nsp*}.

Finally, the stem *l* does not drop before a regular consonant-initial suffix in the ɨ-retention variant, just as in the standard form. See Tableau 8 in (21).

(21) ɨ-Retention Variant: No *l*-drop before C-initial suffixes

T8	sal-ko	*l-{nsp}	F(ɨ)	*{Vl}-ɨ	F(l)
	a. salɨko		*!	*	
☞	b. salko				
	c. sako				*!
	d. saɨko		*!	*	*

Just as in the standard form discussed around Tableau 4 in (17), the faithful candidate (b) violates no constraints; hence, with the new variant ranking, it still wins, and it will win with any other ranking.

We will move on to the ɨ-insertion variant now. What makes the ɨ-insertion variant distinct from the ɨ-retention variant is the fact that the stem *l* is retained even in the case where the suffix does not begin with an ɨ: this is done via ɨ-insertion. As a result, the stem *l* is never dropped in this radical variant, which shows that the faithfulness constraint F(*l*) is higher-ranked, higher than *{V*l*}-ɨ and F(ɨ). See the example of *sal-neyyo* again, now in Tableau 9 in (22) below.

(22) *ɨ*-Insertion Variant: No *l*-drop and *ɨ*-insertion before *n/s/p*-initial suffixes

T9	sal-neyyo	*l-{*nsp*}	F(*l*)	*{V*l*}-*ɨ*	F(*ɨ*)
☞	a. salɨneyyo			*	*
	b. salneyyo	*!			
	c. saneyyo		*!		
	d. saɨneyyo		*!	*	*

The highest-ranking constraint removes candidate (b) out of competition first. Note that the *ln* sequence is not allowed in this variant either. The next high-ranking constraint F(*l*) would penalize any remaining *l*-less candidates, (c) and (d); in fact, candidate (c) *saneyyo*, which used to be the optimal output in the standard form and the *ɨ*-retention variant, violates this constraint and thus loses to candidate (a). Candidate (a) managed to retain the stem *l* by inserting an *ɨ* into the suffix. This insertion leads to a violation of F(*ɨ*) as well as of *{V*l*}-*ɨ*, yet helps satisfy F(*l*). Now that the ranking of F(*l*) is higher than *{V*l*}-*ɨ* and F(*ɨ*), candidate (a) is the optimal candidate in the *ɨ*-insertion variant.

We should note, however, that this ɨ-insertion is motivated to retain *l*; the *l*-drop would be forced if the *ɨ* were not inserted. This can be attested in the example of *sal-ko*. Here, the *l* need not drop because the next sound is not *n*, *s*, or *p*. Therefore, the *l*-retained candidate (b), *salko*, not the *ɨ*-inserted candidate (a), *salɨko*, is the optimal candidate in the *ɨ*-insertion variant also. See Tableau 10 below.

(23) *ɨ*-Insertion Variant: No *l*-drop before C-initial suffixes

T10	sal-ko	*l-{*nsp*}	F(*l*)	*{V*l*}-*ɨ*	F(*ɨ*)
	a. salɨko			*!	*
☞	b. salko				
	c. sako		*!		
	d. saɨko		*!	*	*

Due to space limitations, we will skip the discussion of the tableaux for *sal-ɨnikka* and *sal-ɨmyen* for the *ɨ*-insertion variant. As expected, an *l*-retaining candidate is always a winner. In (24), the *ɨ*-retaining candidate (a) is the optimal candidate just as in the *ɨ*-retention variant; in (25), on the other hand, both candidate (a) and candidate (b) can be winners due to the tied ranking between *{V*l*}-*ɨ* and F(*ɨ*).

(24) ɨ-Insertion Variant: No ɨ-drop and no *l*-drop before *ɨn/s/p*-initial suffixes

T11	sal-ɨnikka	**l-{nsp}*	F(*l*)	*{V*l*}-*ɨ*	F(*ɨ*)
☞	a. salɨnkka			*	
	b. salnikka	*!			*
	c. sanikka		*!		*
	d. saɨnikka		*!	*	

(25) ɨ-Insertion Variant: No *l*-drop before ɨ-initial suffixes

T12	sal-ɨmyen	**l-{nsp}*	F(*l*)	*{V*l*}-*ɨ*	F(*ɨ*)
☞	a. salɨmyen			*	
☞	b. salmyen				*
	c. samyen		*!		*
	d. saɨmyen		*!	*	

22.4 Conclusion

To summarize, the variants (both the ɨ-retention and the ɨ-insertion) differ from the standard form in that they retain the stem *l* in more occasions than the standard form does: among the four examples we have seen, i.e. *sal-ɨmyen*, *sal-neyyo*, *sal-ɨnikka*, and *sal-ko*, the standard form retains the *l* only in two examples (*salmyen*, *salko*), the ɨ-retention variant in three examples (*salɨmyen*, *salɨnikka*, *salko*), and the ɨ-insertion variant in all four examples (salɨmyen, *salɨneyyo*, *salɨnikka*, *salko*). The ɨ-retention variant achieves the *l*-retention by not dropping the suffix ɨ, while the ɨ-insertion variant does so more aggressively even by inserting an ɨ. In a sense, the variant forms are more "regular" than the standard form in conjugating the "irregular" *l*-verbs; in fact, the ɨ-insertion variant is the most "regular" since it treats the consonant *l* just like any other consonants in the language. In other words, the variations around the *l*-verbs appear to be motivated by the underlying desire to regularize the irregularity in the language.

In the theoretical perspective, the variations can be systematically accounted for by the variable ranking among the three constraints, *{V*l*}-*ɨ*, F(*l*), and F(*ɨ*): in the standard form, the markedness constraint *{V*l*}-*ɨ* is ranked higher than the faithfulness constraints F(*l*) and F(*ɨ*); in the ɨ-retention variant, the faithfulness constraint F(*ɨ*) is ranked higher than *{V*l*}-*ɨ* or F(*l*); finally, in the ɨ-insertion variant, the other faithfulness constraint F(*l*) is ranked higher than the others. The relative promotion of the faithfulness constraints in the variant forms reflects the speakers' desire to stick to the more "regular" form (the *l*-retaining form), i.e. the form that is closer to the input.

Although the idea of variable ranking of constraints is not a standard assumption of Optimality Theory, it is not novel either: the ideas such as 'partial constraint ordering', 'stratified partial ordering', 'multiple ranking', or 'floating constraints' have been entertained to explain synchronic, diachronic, or acquisitional variation phenomena (Anttila 1997, 2002, Nagy and Reynolds 1997, Legendre et al. 1999). While all these ideas are based on the discrete ranking of constraints, it is recently suggested that constraints may not be ranked discretely, but rather ranked on a continuous scale and in a stochastic manner (Boersma and Hayes 2001, Bresnan et al. 2001). That is, each constraint has a range of values (with standard deviation) instead of a single fixed value, and the constraints are positioned continuously on a scale at varying distances. Therefore, some constraint is ranked distant enough with the neighboring constraints so that the ranking between them is always the same (one dominating the other), whereas other constraints are ranked closer so that the ranking between them can sometimes be reversed.

If constraints are in fact ranked stochastically on a continuous scale, such variation phenomenon as the Korean *l*-verb conjugation can be explained rather easily. That is, the ranking distance between the highest constraint **l*-{*nsp*} on one hand and the lower constraints *{V*l*}-*ɨ*, F(*l*), and F(*ɨ*) on the other is big enough; thus the ranking between **l*-{*nsp*} and the rest will never get reversed. However, the ranking distances among the lower three constraints *{V*l*}-*ɨ*, F(*l*), and F(*ɨ*) are so close to one another that there are overlaps; these overlaps generate the reverse rankings, so all three constraints each can be ranked higher than the other two. Hence, we get three different rankings and therefore three different variant forms.

In addition to being able to explain the variable rankings among the three constraints, this stochastic model has another advantage, namely, that it can capture the fact that the three variants are not equally distributed in terms of frequency. As mentioned earlier, the standard form is the most dominant form, the *ɨ*-retention variant is the next, and the *ɨ*-insertion variant the least. While the discrete ranking model that allows partial or multiple rankings basically predicts equal distribution of each ranking, the stochastic model can take care of the unequal distribution by means of unequal distances (or overlaps) between the involved constraints.

Although the preliminary internet search showed the general picture of the distribution of the three variants, a full-scale corpus-based research should be conducted to show exactly how far or close the constraints are distanced on the continuous ranking scale. I leave this for future study.

References

Albright, Adam. 2005. The Morphological Basis of Paradigm Leveling. In L. Downing, T. A. Hall, and R. Raffelsiefen, eds., *Paradigms in Phonological Theory*, no. 8 in Oxford Studies in Theoretical Linguistics, pages 17–43. Oxford: Oxford University Press.

Anttila, Arto. 1997. *Variation in Finnish Phonology and Morphology*. Ph.D. thesis, Stanford University.

Anttila, Arto. 2002. Variation and Phonological Theory. In J. K. Chambers, P. Trudgill, and N. Schilling-Estes, eds., *The Handbook of Language Variation and Change*, Blackwell Handbooks in Linguistics, pages 206–243. Oxford: Blackwell.

Boersma, Paul and Bruce Hayes. 2001. Empirical Tests of the Gradual Learning Algorithm. *Linguistic Inquiry* 32:45–86.

Bresnan, Joan, Shipra Dingare, and Christopher D. Manning. 2001. Soft constraints mirror hard constraints: Voice and person in English and Lummi. In M. Butt and T. H. King, eds., *Proceedings of the International Lexical-Functional Grammar Conference 2001 (LFG'01)*, pages 13–32. CSLI Online Publications.

Kim, Gyung-Ran. 2003. /l/-deletion in Korean: A problematic case for an OT-based account. *Studies in Phonetics, Phonology, and Morphology* 9:17–35.

Legendre, Géraldine, Paul Hagstrom, Anne Vainikka, and Marina Todorova. 1999. Partial constraint ordering in child French syntax. Tech. Rep. JHU-CogSci-99-11, Johns Hopkins University, Baltimore, MD.

Nagy, Naomi and Bill Reynolds. 1997. Optimality Theory and Word-final Deletion in Faetar. *Language Variation and Change* 9:37–55.

Sohn, Ho-Min. 1999. *The Korean Language*. Cambridge, UK: Cambridge University Press.

23

Maximum Entropy Models and Stochastic Optimality Theory

GERHARD JÄGER

23.1 Introduction

In a series of recent publications (most notably Boersma 1998; see also Boersma and Hayes 2001), Paul Boersma has developed a stochastic generalization of standard Optimality Theory in the sense of Prince and Smolensky 1993. While a classical OT grammar maps a set of candidates to its optimal element (or elements), in Boersma's Stochastic Optimality Theory (StOT for short) a grammar defines a probability distribution over such a set. Boersma also developed a natural learning algorithm, the **Gradual Learning Algorithm** (GLA) that induces a StOT grammar from a corpus. StOT is able to cope with natural language phenomena like ambiguity, optionality, and gradient grammaticality, that are notoriously problematic for standard OT.

Keller and Asudeh 2002 raise several criticisms against StOT in general and the GLA in particular. Partially as a reaction to that, Goldwater and Johnson 2003 point out that maximum entropy (ME) models, that are widely used in computational linguistics, might be an alternative to StOT. ME models are similar enough to StOT to make it possible that empirical results reached in the former model can be transferred to the latter, and these models have arguably better formal properties than StOT. On the other hand, the GLA has a higher cognitive plausibility (as can be seen from Boersma and Levelt 2000) than the standard learning algorithms for ME models.

Architectures, Rules, and Preferences: Variations on Themes by Joan Bresnan.
Annie Zaenen, Jane Simpson, Tracy Holloway King,
Jane Grimshaw, Joan Maling, and Chris Manning, (eds.).

In this paper I will argue that it is possible to combine the advantages of StOT with the ME model. It can be shown that the GLA can be adapted to ME models almost without modifications. Put differently, it turns out that the GLA is the single most natural on-line learning algorithm for ME models. Keller and Asudeh's criticism, to the degree that it is justified, does not apply to the combination of ME evaluation with GLA learning, and the cognitive advantages of the GLA are maintained.

23.2 Stochastic OT and the Gradual Learning Algorithm

I will give only a brief sketch of Boersma's model here — the interested reader is referred to Boersma and Hayes 2001 for a more thorough introduction.

StOT shares the generator component with standard OT. It also uses a set of ranked and violable constraints as the basis for grammatical evaluation. The constraints are not ranked on an ordinal scale though, but each is assigned a real number on a continuous scale, its *rank*. This way it is possible to speak of the distance between two constraints in a meaningful way. In each evaluation event, some random noise is added to each constraint rank. The ranking of a constraint after adding the noise is called the *selection point*. The constraints can be ordered according to the value of their selection points, and this ordering can be used as ranking in the standard OT sense. However, adding the noise value to the ranks of the constraints may change their ordering, so the ranking of selection points may differ from evaluation to evaluation. In this way the ranking on the continuous scale defines a probability distribution over ordinal rankings. This in turn defines a probability distribution over the set of candidates — the probability of a candidate to be optimal is the sum of the probabilities of all ordinal rankings that make it optimal.

The noise that is added to each constraint rank is a normally distributed random variable with mean 0 and standard deviation 1. The probability of a constraint ranking $C_1 > C_2 > \cdots > C_n$ can thus be given by the following formula (where r_i is the rank of constraint C_i and N is the standard normal distribution):

$$P(C_1 > \cdots > C_n) = \int_{-\infty}^{+\infty} dx_1 N(x_1 - r_1) \int_{-\infty}^{x_1} dx_2 N(x_2 - r_2) \cdots \int_{-\infty}^{x_{n-1}} dx_n N(x_n - r_n)$$

A StOT grammar adequately describes a language if it assigns probabilities to the linguistic signs (sentences, syllable structures or whatever) in the corpus that match with their empirical relative frequencies in this language.

If the distances between the ranks of the constraints are very high, the probability of the ordinal ranking that matches the ordering of the ranks converges towards 1. Standard OT, where there is only one ranking, can thus be seen as a borderline case of StOT.

The GLA is an algorithm that takes an analyzed corpus as input and returns a rank for each constraint. Learning is successful if the acquired ranking adequately describes the language from which the corpus was drawn. The generator and the constraint set are known by the learner in advance. By analyzed corpus I mean that both the input and the output (underlying form and surface form for production and conversely for comprehension) are visible to the learner. Likewise, the degree of violations that each constraint incurs on each observation are accessible to the GLA. Each observation thus assigns a natural number to each constraint (the number of stars, so to say), and this is the only information that the GLA needs.

Each constraint is a function from candidates to natural numbers (the number of violations it incurs). I'll write these functions as c_1, c_2 etc. to distinguish the function from the name of the constraints. A ranking is a vector of real numbers (the ranks of the constraints). Observations — input-output pairs — are fed to the GLA in a sequence $(i_1, o_1), (i_2, o_2), (i_3, o_3), \ldots$ of independent trials. At each point in the learning process, the learner assumes some hypothetical ranking vector $\vec{r}$ that is possibly adjusted in each step. A ranking vector defines a probability distribution over output candidates. For each observed output o_n, the learner hypothesizes an output h_n for the input i_n that is drawn according to the probability distribution that corresponds to $\vec{r}_n$. (i_n, h_n) is compared to the observation (i_n, o_n), and the adjustment of $\vec{r}$ depends on this comparison. All constraints that favor the observation over the hypothesis receive a higher rank and vice versa. There is a positive constant η, the learning rate or *plasticity*, that determines the impact of a single learning event. So the update rule for the GLA is

$$(\vec{r}_{n+1})_i = (\vec{r}_n)_i + \eta \cdot \mathrm{sgn}(c_i(i_n, h_n) - c_i(i_n, o_n))$$

(The sign operator "sgn" maps positive numbers to 1, negative numbers to -1, and 0 to itself.) The initial grammar of the learner, $\vec{r}_1$, has to be given *a priori*. If we simplify things further by stipulating that constraints are binary, the sign operator can be omitted.

This formula involves two random variables that are drawn from different distributions. (i_n, o_n) is drawn according to the empirical probability distribution p_{emp}. The probability of a learner's hypothesis depends on two independent distributions — the empirical probability of an input follows from the empirical distribution over input-output pairs and the structure of **GEN**:

$$p_{emp}(i) = \sum_{o:\mathbf{GEN}(i,o)} p_{emp}(i, o)$$

Each $\vec{r}$ defines a probability distribution over the possible outputs for a given input, written as the conditional probability $p_{\vec{r}}(\cdot|i)$.

(i_n, h_n) is drawn from the product of these two distribution $p_{\vec{r}_n}$. To keep notation simple, I'll use the convention

$$p_{\vec{r}}(i, o) = p_{emp}(i) \cdot p_{\vec{r}}(o|i)$$

The expectation values under the distributions p_{emp} and $p_{\vec{r}}$ are written as E_{emp} and $E_{\vec{r}}$ respectively. As long as all constraints are binary, the expected adjustments of the constraints is then

$$(\vec{r}_{n+1})_i \quad = \quad (\vec{r}_n)_i + \eta \cdot (E_{\vec{r}_n}[c_i] - E_{emp}[c_i]) \qquad (23.1)$$

So in effect the GLA compares the average degree of violations of each constraint in the training corpus with its expected degree of violations according to the current grammar of the learner. The algorithm converges if these two values coincide for each constraint.

There is, however, no general proof that the GLA will always converge towards a correct constraint ranking, even if the training corpus is generated by some StOT grammar, and the correct set of constraints is available to the algorithm.[1] This is a serious drawback, and it seems worthwhile to consider alternative models of probabilistic generalizations of OT.

23.3 The maximum entropy approach

Goldwater and Johnson 2003 compare StOT with Maximum Entropy models (or, as they are sometimes called, log-linear models) that are

[1]Keller and Asudeh 2002 criticize several aspects of StOT and the GLA. The fact that there is no proof of convergence is the only serious one, I think. They give some examples for languages that the GLA is unable to learn, but these cases involve harmonically bounded candidates with a non-zero probability. It is a general feature of OT that harmonically bounded candidates are always ungrammatical, and it is thus no defect of the GLA that it is unable to learn languages which behave otherwise. Also, I do not think that testing the GLA on unseen data would reveal much about the GLA as such. Testing on unseen data is important to detect over-training. Whether or not training a StOT grammar with some corpus using the GLA leads to over-training depends mainly on the set of constraints and the size of the training corpus; the training algorithm as such has little bearing on that.

state of the art by now in computational linguistics (see for instance Berger et al. 1996 or Abney 1997). Let me briefly explain what "maximum entropy" means.

Suppose we know that a certain experiment has two possible outcomes, A and B, but we don't know anything else about it. Which probability should we assign to A and B? The best answer seems to be: 50% probability for each. Likewise, if there are five possible outcomes, A, B, C, D and E, the best estimate is to assign 20% to each if we don't have further information. Every other distribution of the probability mass would represent a bias which is not supported by knowledge. And if we also know that the outcome will be A or B with a probability of 70%? Then the least biased estimate is to assign 35% to both A and B, and 10% to each of the three other events. There is a clear intuition that the least biased hypothesis is the most parsimonious one.

The information theoretic notion of *entropy* quantifies the bias of a probability distribution. The entropy H of a probability distribution p is defined as

$$H(p) = \sum_{x} p(x) \log \frac{1}{p(x)}$$

The least biased distribution has the highest entropy, and vice versa. If we have partial knowledge about a stochastic process and we have to estimate the underlying probability distribution, the best guess is to choose among all distributions that are compatible with our knowledge the one with the highest entropy.

Let us assume that the unknown probability distribution is a language L in the StOT sense, i.e. a probability distribution over a set of input-output pairs. We know the set **GEN** of possible elements of the language (the generator) and a set of constraints. We also know how many violations each constraint incurs on each candidate, the marginal probabilities of the different inputs, and — crucially — we know how often each constraint is on average violated in the language in question. This may be the result of investigating a large sample of L, but the only empirical facts we are able to observe are the inputs and the number of constraint violations of each observation. So we are looking for a relative probability distribution over the potential output for each input which predicts the correct average degree of violation of each constraint, and among all distributions with this property, we will choose the one with the highest entropy. It can be shown (see Della Pietra et al. 1995 for a proof) that this distribution takes the following form:

$$p_{\vec{r}}(o|i) = \frac{1}{Z_{\vec{r}}(i)} \exp(\sum_{j} r_j c_j(i, o))$$

where $Z_{\vec{r}}(i)$ is a normalization constant which ensures that the probabilities of all candidates sum up to 1. It holds that

$$Z_{\vec{r}}(i) = \sum_{o:\mathbf{GEN}(i,o)} \exp(\sum_j r_j c_j(i,o))$$

Taking the logarithm on both sides yields

$$\log p_{\vec{r}}(o|i) = \sum_j r_j c_j(i,o) - \log Z_{\vec{r}}(i)$$

So the logarithm of the probability of a candidate is a linear function of its constraint violations. (Therefore these probability distributions are called "log-linear".) Of course there are infinitely many log-linear distributions, depending on the values of the rank parameters r_j. Della Pietra et al. 1995 also show that among all these log-linear distributions, the one which maximizes the likelihood of the language L is the one which assigns the correct average degree of violations to each constraint. In other words, the unique log-linear distribution which assigns maximal likelihood to L is at the same time the unique distribution with the empirically correct predictions of average constraint violations that maximizes entropy. There are several learning algorithms available for ME models. Della Pietra et al. 1995 developed *improved iterative scaling* specifically for this application. Besides, standard machine learning algorithms like *gradient ascent* or *conjugate gradient ascent* are applicable as well and guaranteed to converge towards the correct distribution.

The general setup of a maximum entropy model is very similar to a StOT grammar. The main difference between StOT and ME is the evaluation component, i.e. the way in which constraint ranks are interpreted as a probability distribution. Like StOT, ME models can be seen as a generalization of standard OT. (In the ME context, constraint violations have to be interpreted as negative numbers in the ME context and as positive integers in StOT to facilitate comparison. I will tacitly do this from now on.) If the ranks (or "weights", as the parameters $\vec{r}$ are usually called in the ME tradition) of the constraints are very high and spread far apart, the probabilities of candidates that would be sub-optimal in classical OT converge towards 0 in the ME interpretation.

The models differ slightly in their treatment of cumulativity of constraint violations. Both StOT and ME diverge from classical OT in admitting *ganging-up effects.* By this I mean that violations of several lower-ranked constraints may jointly outweigh a violation of a higher ranked constraint. ME furthermore predicts *counting cumulativity.* This means that a higher degree of violations of one constraint always reduces probability, no matter what other constraints and other candidates do. In StOT only the relative strength of a constraint violation of a candidate in comparison with other candidates matters. In the present paper I will restrict attention to binary constraints, and thus such effects are excluded by definition.

Goldwater and Johnson 2003 repeat all experiments from Boersma and Hayes 2001 but use ME and conjugate gradient ascent instead of StOT and GLA. They show that the results of both approaches are very similar. So for all we know, there are no clear empirical reasons to favor the one model over the other. From a theoretical point of view ME seems to be superior though because the available learning algorithms are guaranteed to converge. On the other hand, Paul Boersma (personal communication) mentions two advantages of StOT/GLA over the standard learning algorithms for ME models. First, all these algorithms are off-line algorithms, while the GLA works on-line. This means that improved iterative scaling or (conjugate) gradient ascent needs to "know" the average degree of violation of each constraint *before* the actual learning starts. In practice this means that first the training corpus has to be analyzed in its entirety before learning can take place. The GLA, on the other hand, works gradual. It processes the observations one at a time and gradually approaches the target distribution. Human language acquisition obviously works on-line. Therefore the GLA is *prima facie* cognitively more plausible. Furthermore, the study Boersma and Levelt 2000 demonstrates for a certain empirical domain that the GLA actually predicts the correct order of acquisition. An off-line algorithm is by its very nature unable to make predictions about acquisition order.

23.4 GLA = Stochastic Gradient Ascent

One of the standard machine learning algorithms that is applicable to ME models is *Gradient Ascent.* This algorithm finds a local maximum of a real-valued function f in an n-dimensional vector space provided f is continuous and differentiable. For ME learning, we have to find the ranks that maximize the likelihood of the training corpus. Since the logarithm is a monotonically increasing function, we can as well maximize the average log-likelihood, i.e. we have to find the parameters $\vec{r}$ that maximize the empirical average of the log-likelihood according to $p_{\vec{r}}$. It is given by the formula

$$f(\vec{r}) = E_{emp}[\log p_{\vec{r}}(i,o)]$$

which is a continuous and differentiable function of the rank vector $\vec{r}$. The log-likelihood has the desirable property of being convex, which means that it does not have non-global local maxima. Gradient Ascent is thus guaranteed to find the global maximum. The gradient of a function f at a point $\vec{r}$ is the vector pointing from $\vec{r}$ in the direction where f grows steepest. Gradient Ascent is an iterative algorithm that, starting from some initial point $\vec{r}_1$, moves small steps in the direction of the local gradient. Since each step increases the value of f, this process is bound to approach the global maximum.[2]

The jth component of the gradient of a function $g(\vec{r})$ is the partial derivative $\frac{\partial}{\partial r_j} g(\vec{r})$. For log-likelihood in a ME model it holds that

$$\frac{\partial}{\partial r_j} f(\vec{r}) = E_{emp}[c_j] - E_{\vec{r}}[c_j] \tag{23.2}$$

Note that this gradient is exactly the direction of the update in the GLA (23.1), modulo the convention that constraint functions take non-negative values in StOT and non-positive values here. The update rule for gradient ascent is thus identical to the expected effect of the GLA update rule.

Gradient ascent is still an off-line algorithm though. The expectation values of the constraints have to be known in advance. However, it can easily be transformed into an on-line algorithm. The on-line version is known as *Stochastic Gradient Ascent* (SGA for short) and is a standard technique for training connectionist networks. Here one observation is processed at a time, and the empirical expectation value of each constraint is replaced by the observed value. Adapted to ME, the update rule thus is

$$(\vec{r}_{k+1})_j = (\vec{r}_k)_j + \eta \cdot (c_j(i_k, o_k) - E_{\vec{r}}[c_j])$$

Recall that the distribution $p_{\vec{r}}$ is a product of the theoretical conditional probability distribution $p_{\vec{r}}(o|i)$ and the marginal empirical probabilities of the inputs $p_{emp}(i)$. The latter cannot be calculated analytically. Therefore $E_{\vec{r}}[c_j]$ has to be estimated as well. We thus replace it by a random variable that has $E_{\vec{r}}[c_j]$ as its expected value. This can be done by drawing a sample h_k from the distribution $p_{\vec{r}}(\cdot|i)$ corresponding to the current rankings $\vec{r}$. This leads us to the revised update rule

$$(\vec{r}_{k+1})_j = (\vec{r}_k)_j + \eta \cdot (c_j(i_k, o_k) - c_j(i_k, h_k))$$

For the special case that all constraints are binary, this *is* the Gradual Learning Algorithm, and for the general case it is very closely related to it.

[2]Provided the function is convex. In the general case only convergence towards a local maximum is guaranteed.

Let us consider the consequences of this finding. Both the GLA for StOT and SGA for ME are on-line algorithms. They both converge iff the empirical and the acquired expectation value for each constraint coincide, i.e. if for all constraints C_j:

$$E_{emp}[c_j] - E_{\vec{r}}[c_j] = 0$$

Under the ME interpretation, among all distributions sharing this property, the learning algorithm finds the one with the highest entropy. If the GLA under the StOT interpretation converges towards a different distribution for the same training corpus, it will be one with lower entropy, i.e. a less parsimonious hypothesis.

23.5 Order of acquisition

Boersma and Levelt 2000 report an experiment where the acquisition of Dutch syllable structures was simulated using StOT and the GLA. I repeated the experiment with a ME model and SGA and obtained almost identical results.

The attested frequency of Dutch syllable types in child-directed speech is as in table 1 (taken from Boersma and Levelt 2000 who attribute it to Joost van de Weijer, personal communication).

CV	44.81%	CCVC	1.98%
CVC	32.05%	CCV	1.38%
VC	11.99%	VCC	0.42%
V	3.85%	CCVCC	0.26%
CVCC	3.25%		

TABLE 1 Frequency of syllable types in Dutch

Following the optimality theoretic acquisition study Levelt and van de Vijver 1998, Boersma and Levelt 2000 assume the following five constraints pertaining to syllable structure:

- *CODA: "don't produce codas" (violated by -C and -CC syllables)
- ONSET: "don't produce vowel-initial syllables" (violated by V- syllables)
- *COMPLEXCODA: "don't produce complex codas" (violated by -CC syllables)
- *COMPLEXONSET: "don't produce complex onsets" (violated by CC- syllables)
- FAITH: "don't add or delete material"

The set-up is speaker oriented. Both input and output are assumed to be (or to specify) syllables structures. The first four constraints are markedness constraints and only apply to the output. The last constraint is violated whenever input and output differ.

Boersma and Levelt's experimental setup is as follows. Each of the nine syllable types can be both input and output. There are thus 81 potential input-output pairs. FAITH is never violated in the adult language — in the training corpus input and output always coincide. The corpus frequencies given above are taken to represent the empirical probabilities.

In the initial state FAITH is ranked low and the markedness constraints high (a standard assumption in the OT literature). The GLA gradually lowered the markedness constraints and simultaneously raised FAITH until it became the strongest constraint. The algorithm converges towards the following ranking:

FAITH ≫ *COMPLEXONSET ≫ *COMPLEXCODA ≫ ONSET ≫ *CODA

The final relative ranking of the markedness constraints emerges early during the learning process. FAITH outranks the markedness constraints thus not all at once but one by one, starting with *CODA and ending with *COMPLEXONSET. The intermediate stages correspond to rankings where the learner would produce some, but not all syllable types faithfully. Furthermore, during the phases where FAITH and some markedness constraint have similar ranks, the learner would assign different outputs for the same input substantial probabilities, i.e. the learner is predicted to pass stages of optionality before complex syllable types are firmly acquired. This effect does in fact occur during human language acquisition.

In Boersma and Levelt's simulations, the GLA learned the Dutch syllable types most of the time in the following order:

CV < CVC < VC < CVCC < CCVC < CCVCC

In about 30% of the experiments, the order of CCVC and CVCC was reversed. The author report no results on the other three syllable types.

According to Levelt and van de Vijver 1998, Dutch children acquire the syllable types in one of the following two orders, where types enclosed in curly brackets are acquired more or less simultaneously.

- CV < CVC < V < VC < {CVCC, VCC} < {CCV, CCVC} < CCVCC

- CV < CVC < V < VC < {CCV, CCVC} < {CVCC, VCC} < CCVCC

The simulation results do in fact fit rather well with the empirical acquisition data.

I repeated Boersma and Levelt's experiment using a ME model and Stochastic Gradient Ascent (SGA). I used a learning rate $\eta = 0.1$. In the initial state, FAITH had a rank of 0.0, and all other constraints a rank of 10.0. The constraint rankings as a function of time is given in figure 1.

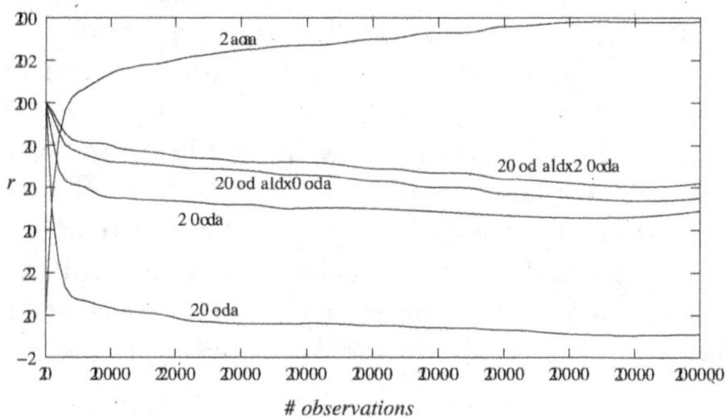

FIGURE 1 Learning of constraint ranks

The ME learning algorithm acquires the same constraint ranking as the GLA, and it does so with a qualitatively similar trajectory. This fact, as well as the order of acquisition to be reported shortly does not depend on the learning rate and the precise initial ranking of the markedness constraints as long as they are initially ranked above FAITH and the latter is initially ranked at 0.

Since the probability of a candidate is a continuous function of the constraint rankings both in Boersma's and in the ME model, the ac quisition of syllable types is predicted to be gradual in both theories.

In the experiments I conducted, the syllable types where consistently acquired in the following order:

CV < CVC < V < VC < CVCC < {CCV, CCVC} < VCC < CCVCC

This is very close to the empirically observed acquisition orders, except that CVCC is acquired too early or VCC too late. It is also consistent with Boersma and Levelt's results. From the available information it is hard to tell whether or not their results are closer to the empirical data than mine, but the difference is certainly small.

23.6 Conclusion

In this article I compared two stochastic generalizations of Optimality Theory, namely Paul Boersma's Stochastic Optimality Theory and Maximum Entropy models that are frequently used in machine learning contexts. As pointed out by Goldwater and Johnson 2003, the empirical predictions of the two models are rather similar. The latter is advantageous from a formal point of view because there exist provably correct learning algorithms for Maximum Entropy models while the learnability problem for Stochastic OT is still open. On the other hand, Boersma's Gradual Learning Algorithm for Stochastic OT has been successfully applied in many contexts, and it is arguably a better model of human language acquisition than the off-line training algorithms for ME models that are standardly used.

I demonstrated that the Gradual Learning Algorithm is not confined to StOT. It can be applied to ME models as well. In this context it is actually a variant of the Stochastic Gradient Ascent training algorithm that is well-established for other machine learning problems. The insights about language acquisition that the GLA offers are maintained if it is combined with the Maximum Entropy approach to constraint evaluation.

References

Abney, Steven. 1997. Stochastic attribute-value grammars. *Computational Linguistics* 23(4):597–618.

Berger, Adam, Stephen Della Pietra, and Vincent Della Pietra. 1996. A maximum entropy approach to natural language processing. *Computational Linguistics* 22(1):39–71.

Boersma, Paul. 1998. *Functional Phonology*. Ph.D. thesis, University of Amsterdam.

Boersma, Paul and Bruce Hayes. 2001. Empirical tests of the gradual learning algorithm. *Linguistic Inquiry* 32(1):45–86.

Boersma, Paul and Clara Levelt. 2000. Gradual constraint-ranking learning algorithm predicts acquisition order. In *Proceedings of Child Language Research Forum 30*, pages 229–237. Stanford, CA: CSLI Publications.

Della Pietra, Stephen, Vincent Della Pietra, and John Lafferty. 1995. Inducing features of random fields. Tech. Rep. CMU-CS-1995-144, Carnegie Mellon University, Pittsburgh, PA.

Goldwater, Sharon and Mark Johnson. 2003. Learning OT constraint rankings using a maximum entropy model. In J. Spenader, A. Eriksson, and Ö. Dahl, eds., *Proceedings of the Stockholm Workshop on Variation within Optimality Theory*, pages 111–120. Stockholm University.

Keller, Frank and Ash Asudeh. 2002. Probabilistic learning algorithms and Optimality Theory. *Linguistic Inquiry* 33(2):225–244.

Levelt, Claartje and Ruben van de Vijver. 1998. Syllable types in cross-linguistic and developmental grammars. Ms., Rutgers Optimality Archive.

Prince, Alan and Paul Smolensky. 1993. Optimality theory: Constraint interaction in generative grammar. Tech. Rep. 2, Rutgers University Center for Cognitive Science, Piscataway, NJ.

24

Constraint Subhierarchies as Syntactic Universals: Evidence from Variation and Processing

HANJUNG LEE

24.1 Introduction

Optimality Theory is a grammar formalism developed by Prince and Smolensky in the early 1990s.[1] This new framework brings certain general connectionist computational principles into generative grammar. The connectionist concept of intuitive knowledge as a set of conflicting soft constraints, interacting via optimization of well-formedness, combines with linguistic representations and universal constraints from generative grammar.

According to Optimality Theory (henceforth OT), a grammar is a system of conflicting universal constraints which are violable and ranked in a dominance hierarchy. Variation across languages reflects the resolution of conflicts among violable universal constraints. A surface

[1] Versions of this paper were presented at the 38th Meeting of the Chicago Linguistic Society, University of Chicago (April 2002), the Gradedness Conference, University of Potsdam (October 2002), the 17th Annual CUNY Conference on Human Sentence Processing, University of Maryland (March 2004), the Pionier Workshop on Differential Case Marking, University of Nijmegen (July 2004), and at the 9th International Cognitive Linguistics Conference, Yonsei University (July 2005). I'd like to thank the audiences at all occasions of presentation. Parts of the research presented here were supported by the US National Science Foundation (BCS-0112231) and by the Korea Research Foundation (KRF-2005-A00076).

Architectures, Rules, and Preferences: Variations on Themes by Joan Bresnan.
Annie Zaenen, Jane Simpson, Tracy Holloway King,
Jane Grimshaw, Joan Maling, and Chris Manning, (eds.).

form is 'optimal' in the sense that it incurs the least serious violations of a set of violable universal constraints, ranked in a language-specific hierarchy. Although it was originally applied to phonology, the relevance of OT to morphosyntax, semantics, computational linguistics and psycholinguistics has become increasingly apparent. One significant advance in recent studies in OT syntax is the emergence of a novel way of dealing with variation that has been proposed in (functional) stochastic OT approaches (Aissen and Bresnan 2002), which incorporate probabilities into the grammar component. In particular, Aissen and Bresnan employ hierarchies well-known from the functional/typological literature, such as the animacy and definiteness hierarchies, to account for both grammaticalized patterns crosslinguistically as well as language-internal quantitative variation. Their analysis very insightfully shows that recasting these hierarchies within OT as subhierarchies of universal constraints which are violable and may be overridden by conflicting constraints solves the basic problem of the softness of markedness hierarchies as universals in syntax.

The present paper is an attempt to contribute to this line of ongoing research by presenting experimental evidence for the universal status of the markedness constraints suggested in recent stochastic OT approaches to morphosyntactic variation. Specifically, I will discuss results from a corpus study and two experiments investigating how the relative markedness of argument NPs as a subject and an object influences the frequency of case marking and comprehension difficulty in Korean. The experiments provide new evidence about the active cognitive status of the system of constraint subhierarchies suggested in recent (stochastic) OT approaches (e.g., Aissen 1999, 2003, Aissen and Bresnan 2002).

24.2 Markedness Hierarchies and Differential Case Marking

It is well-known that hierarchies of person, animacy and definiteness are important properties in the systems of voice and case marking of a number of languages. In particular, they have effects on case marking has been demonstrated by work on split case marking phenomena in various languages, where certain classes of subjects and objects are marked, but not others. The standard example of a subject marking split is from Dyirbal, in which first and second person are overtly case-marked when they function as objects, but are not overtly marked as subjects (Dixon 1972, 1979; Silverstein 1976). Conversely, third persons are overtly case-marked when they function as subjects (of transitive clauses), but are not overtly case-marked as objects. Aissen (2003), following Bossong (1985), refers to splits in subject and object marking as differential subject marking (DSM) and differential object marking (DOM) respectively.

An intuition which recurs in the literature on DOM and DSM is that they arise from the need to maximally differentiate subject and object. In other words, as emphasized by the functional approach of Silverstein (1976), subjects prototypically have features that are high on the hierarchies of person, animacy and definiteness, while objects prototypically have low features. When objects have high features, they need to be marked as atypical, because they are the ones most likely to be confused with subjects if left unmarked. Conversely, subjects which have low features are the ones most in need of being distinguished from objects because they are the ones most likely to be confused with objects if left unmarked.

Dyirbal and other Australian languages exhibit both DSM and DOM. It is also common for languages with overt case marking to exhibit either DSM or DOM, but not both. The former possibility is realized in languages like Fore, where neither personal pronouns nor names may be marked in subject function, but inanimates must be (Scott 1978; Donohue 1999). Case marking systems which exhibit DOM only are found in a wider range of languages. In DOM languages, the split is very often triggered along the lines of animacy and definiteness. These dimensions are often given on referentiality scales, where the cut-off point is taken to vary from language to language:

(1) a. Animacy hierarchy: Human > Animate > Inanimate
    b. Definiteness hierarchy: Personal pronoun > Proper noun > Definite NP > Indefinite specific NP > Non-specific NP (Aissen 2003: 437; cf. Silverstein 1976)

The general pattern, observed in a number of languages, can be summarized as the following implicational universal: if a given object O can be case-marked in language A, then objects which are more prominent than O on one or both of the hierarchies in (1) can also be marked in A.

Working within the framework of Optimality Theory (OT; Prince and Smolensky 1993), Aissen (2003) formalizes this generalization using markedness constraints resulting from the operation of hierarchy alignment[2] in conjunction with iconicity and economy constraints per-

[2] Harmonic alignment is an operation which combines two scales to form a universally impermutable constraint hierarchy. It was introduced originally by Prince and Smolensky (1993) to express the relation between syllable position and sonority (the

taining to case. The constraint hierarchies which form the basis for her analysis of animacy-sensitive DOM are given in (2):

(2) a. *SUBJ/INAN(IMATE) >> *SUBJ/ANIM >> *SUBJ/HUM(AN)
b. *OBJ/HUM(AN) >> *OBJ/ANIM >> *OBJ/INAN

The high-ranking constraints in (2a,b) penalize inanimate subjects and human objects respectively. Crucially, constraint hierarchies derived by hierarchy alignment, including (2a,b), are universal subhierarchies, which are hypothesized to be present in every grammar in the same relative order and must be interleaved with other constraints.

In DSM/DOM languages, marked configurations like those penalized by the high-ranking constraints in (2a,b) are marked or flagged as atypical, but not excluded entirely. Aissen (2003) implements this flagging by the formal operation of constraint conjunction. Conjunction of the iconicity constraint *ZERO$_C$ ("Avoid null expression of case feature") with the subhierarchies in (2) results in two new subhierarchies of iconicity constraints, which have the effect of favoring case marking:

(3) Iconicity constraints:
a. *SUBJ/INAN & *ZERO$_C$ >> *SUBJ/ANIM & *ZERO$_C$ >> *SUBJ/HUM & *ZERO$_C$
b. *OBJ/HUM & *ZERO$_C$ >> *OBJ/ANIM & *ZERO$_C$ >> *OBJ/INAN & *ZERO$_C$

The subhierarchy in (3a) penalizes null expression of an inanimate referring subject over null expression of an animate or human referring subject. The effects of the subhierarchy in (3a) can be clearly seen in a DSM system like that of Fore, where only inanimate subjects must be case-marked, while case marking of animate subjects is (sometimes) possible but not obligatory and human subjects are rarely marked (Scott 1978; Donohue 1999).

---

more prominent position (the nucleus) attracts segments which are more sonorous, while less prominent positions (the margins) attract less sonorous segments) and later applied to morphosyntax in Aissen's influential work (Aissen 1999, 2003). The formal definition of harmonic alignment is given below (Prince and Smolensky 1993: 136):

Harmonic Alignment: Suppose a binary dimension D_1 with a scale X > Y on its element X, Y, and another dimension D_2 with a scale a > b > ... > z on its elements. The harmonic alignment of D_1 and D_2 is the pair of Harmonic scales:
HX: X/a > X/b > ... > X/z
HY: Y/z > ... > Y/b > Y/a

The *constraint alignment* is the pair of constraint hierarchies:
CX: *X/z >> ... >> *X/b >> *X/a
CY: *Y/a >> *Y/b >> ... >> *Y/z

The subhierarchy in (3b) penalizes null expression of a human referring object over null expression of an animate or inanimate referring object. The subhierarchies in (3) logically entail implicational universals. That is, they predict that if a human referring subject is case-marked, inanimate or non-human subjects must also be case-marked; and if an inanimate referring object is case-marked, so must human or non-human animate objects be case-marked. In a stochastic OT framework (to be discussed in section 4), this property of the constraint subhierarchies in (3) is generalized to predictions of relative frequency: if case marking occurs with some frequency for a given nominal argument, it must occur with equal or higher frequency for any more marked types of argument. A strong piece of evidence for this generalization comes from variable case marking in Korean, which we will discuss in detail in section 3.

A wide typological range of object marking splits is also surveyed in Aissen (2003). Her survey includes DOM systems which are predicted by interactions of iconicity constraints including those in (3a,b) and the economy constraint in (4). See Aissen (2003) for a detailed discussion.

(4) Economy constraint: *STRUCT(URE)$_C$ ("Avoid case structure")

In sum, fundamental patterns and limits of variation found in DSM and DOM systems across languages can be accounted for in terms of interactions between two kinds of markedness constraints in OT that are in conflict: (i) the iconicity constraints which can be motivated in terms of maximization of contrasts for ease of comprehension from the point of view of the hearer, and (ii) the economy constraint, which embodies minimization of effort from the point of view of the speaker.

24.3 Active Cognitive Status of Constraint Subhierarchies: Evidence from Variation

Lee (2002, 2003, 2006, to appear) presents evidence of frequency effects of the hierarchies of person, animacy and definiteness on case marking in Korean. Korean has been described as a language in which all subjects and objects are case-marked, and in which case marking is optional in colloquial speech. Ellipsis of the accusative case marker, which normally indicates the object of canonical transitive verbs, is illustrated in (5):[3]

[3]The abbreviations used in the glosses are as follows: ACC 'accusative', AUX 'auxiliary verb', COND 'conditional', LK 'linker', NEG 'negation particle', NOM 'nominative', TOP 'topic marker'.

(5) Onul-un swul masi-myen an toy.
Today-TOP alcoholic drink(-ACC) drink-COND NEG AUX
'(I) shouldn't drink today.'

However, it is not fully informative to say that use of case markers is optional. When data from naturally-occurring colloquial speech are taken into account, it becomes obvious that variability in case marking in Korean is not random.

Lee (2002) conducted an extensive analysis of the ellipsis of case markers (CE), as found in the CallFriend Korean (CFK) corpus of telephone speech collected by the Linguistic Data Consortium (LDC). The 1996 release used in this study consists of 60 unscripted telephone conversations spoken by 200 native speakers of Korean, lasting between 5 and 30 minutes. Of 60 telephone conversations, 35 conversations were transcribed by two native speakers of Korean. Each transcript was then scanned for all instances of overt subject and object NPs regardless of whether or not they occurred with a case marker. For each token, factors that have been claimed in the literature to affect case marking patterns crosslinguistically were coded (person, animacy and definiteness), in addition to the grammatical function of the NP (subject and object).[4] These factors are listed in (6). The reliability of coding indicated by the kappa statistic (Carletta 1996) greater than 0.80 was achieved for all these dimensions (See Lee (2002, 2006, to appear) for discussion of methodological issues).

(6) a. Grammatical function: subject or object
b. Person: first, second or third
c. Animacy: human, animate or inanimate
d. Definiteness: personal pronoun, proper name or other[5]

The sampling method yielded a total of 1956 overtly expressed subject and object NPs. The breakdown of NPs by the presence and ab-

[4]In the present work we examine CE only in subjects and direct objects of transitive verbs which are usually marked with nominative and accusative case markers respectively. These are the two grammatical functions which exhibit the highest rates of CE in the CFK corpus (28.1% and 46.8%, respectively). More oblique functions (e.g., indirect objects of ditransitive verbs, experiencers, goals, and sources) and adjuncts (e.g., expressions of time) were not considered because there are too few cases of CE in our annotations to allow us to make statistically meaningful generalizations about the condition under which CE is most likely to occur.

[5]In contrast to English, Korean does not possess articles which grammatically encode the (in)definiteness of nouns. Due to the difficulty of automatically determining the definiteness and specificity of nouns, we did not attempt to differentiate the various kinds of noun phrases which do not belong to the two most definite NP categories, i.e., personal pronouns and proper nouns.

sence of following case markers is given in Table 1. CE indicates the ellipsis (or absence) of case markers (nominative and accusative) following nouns; N-CASE and N-~CASE refer to nouns that are marked by case markers and other particles that are not case markers (e.g., focus and discourse markers) respectively.

(7) Table 1. Frequency of tokens by the presence and absence of case markers

	Subject	Direct object
CE	355 (28.1%)	326 (46.8%)
N-CASE	489 (38.9%)	175 (25.2%)
N-~CASE	416 (33%)	195 (28%)
Total	1260 (100%)	696 (100%)

Now let us see whether person, animacy and definiteness correlate with CE in subjects and direct objects in the CFK data. Table 2 shows the effect of person on CE. The leftmost column gives the three categories of person. We calculated the number of times each person was expressed in non-case marked and case-marked forms. These numbers are given with the rates of CE and case marking.

(8) Table 2. Interaction of case marking and person in CFK

	Subject		Direct object	
Person	CE	N-NOM	CE	N-ACC
1	47 (52.2%)	43 (47.8%)	11 (55%)	9 (45%)
2	51 (46.8%)	58 (53.2%)	16 (53.3%)	14 (46.7%)
3	257 (39.8%)	388 (60.2%)	299 (66.3%)	152 (33.7%)

Although the percentage of first and second person pronouns in spoken conversational Korean is very small,[6] the person/subject marking effects are significant. In particular, the rate of CE for third person subjects is significantly lower than the rate for local person (first and second person) subjects ($\chi^2 = 6.11$, df = 2, p = 0.047). In the case of direct objects, the CE rate for third person objects is higher than the rate for local person objects, although this difference is not significant ($\chi^2 = 3.01$, df = 2, p = 0.22). Now let us turn to animacy. As Table 3 shows, human and (non-human) animate subjects exhibited a higher rate of CE than inanimate subjects.

[6]This is due to the strong tendency to omit first and second person references in Korean.

(9) Table 3. Interaction of case marking and animacy in CFK

	Subject		Direct object	
Animacy	CE	N-NOM	CE	N-ACC
Human	221 (52.7%)	224 (47.3%)	88 (54.7%)	73 (45.3%)
Animate	68 (36%)	126 (64%)	35 (50.7%)	34 (49.3%)
Inanimate	66 (28%)	170 (72%)	203 (74.9%)	68 (25.1%)

Once again, the results for direct objects are the converse: human and animate objects are overtly marked by the accusative case marker more often than inanimate objects. For both argument roles, the interaction of case marking and animacy was significant in the CFK data. In particular, the rate of CE for human and animate subjects is significantly higher than the rate for inanimate subjects (χ^2 = 33.26, df = 2, p = 0.00). Conversely, in the case of direct objects, the CE rate for human and animate NPs is significantly lower than the rate for inanimate NPs (χ^2 = 25.47, df = 2, p = 0.00). However, there was no statistically significant difference in the behavior of human arguments and non-human animate arguments for both argument roles. In other words, the data suggest that the distance between elements on the animacy hierarchy (Human > Animate > Inanimate) is not equal; the rate of CE for human NPs is far closer to that of non-human animate NPs than that of inanimate NPs.

These results are consistent with the findings of Fry's (2001) study of CE in Japanese. Fry found that subject marking and object marking in Japanese exhibit a reversed pattern with respect to animacy, although in his data the animacy effect is significant in subjects but not in objects. We also found that definiteness interacts with the choice of case-marked and unmarked forms of subjects and direct objects in the CFK data. As Table 4 shows, the CE rate for strongly definite subject NPs (pronouns and names) is significantly higher than the rate for other low definite NPs (χ^2 = 6.98, df = 2, p = 0.03). Turning to direct objects, we find stronger results in the opposite direction. In particular, the CE rate for strongly definite object NPs is significantly lower that the rate for other object NPs (χ^2 = 53.72, df = 2, p = 0.00).

(10) Table 4. Interaction of case marking and definiteness in CFK

	Subject		Direct object	
Definiteness	CE	N-NOM	CE	N-ACC
Pronoun	129 (47.6%)	142 (52.4%)	24 (32.4%)	50 (67.6%)
Name	36 (46.8%)	41 (53.2%)	15 (42.9%)	20 (57.1%)
Other	190 (38.3%)	306 (61.7%)	287 (73.2%)	105 (26.8%)

In sum, the relative frequency of the choice of unmarked forms over case-marked forms in the CFK data increases with subjects high in person, animacy and definiteness[7] and objects low in those dimensions, and decreases with low prominence subjects and high prominence objects. These results strongly suggest that the tendency to case-mark non-canonical argument types is not specific to split ergative/accusative languages and that it is also present in the grammars of pure nominative-accusative languages like Korean. Moreover, the fact that we find similar DSM/DOM effects in Korean bolsters Aissen's claim that her iconicity constraints represent universal linguistic constraints within OT.

But how exactly can probabilities be incorporated into the grammar component of OT? Quantitative variation is problematic for the standard OT architecture because the (standard) OT grammar is deterministic, in the sense that each input is mapped onto a single output. An alternative that is being actively pursued is to replace the strict ranking system with a stochastic evaluation system in which constraints are weighted numerically, and in which these numerical weights have uncertainty (Boersma 1998, Boersma and Hayes 2001). For example, in the system of Boersma and Hayes (2001), probabilistic noise at evaluation time allows multiple outputs. So closely ranked constraints can give variable outputs. Pioneering work in this direction within the area of OT syntax has been done by Bresnan, Dingare and Manning (2001), who present an interesting application of stochastic OT to person/voice interaction in English and Lummi. They demonstrate convincingly that in stochastic OT, frequential preferences in usage and categorical grammatical rules can be explained in a unified way in terms of the same typologically motivated constraint system. In the following section I will show that the statistical patterning of the CFK data discussed

[7]We can determine the relative weights of each of these three factors by using logistic regression (an excellent explanation of logistic regression is given in Paolillo (2002)). However, I will not discuss a logistic regression analysis because the primary issue here is to investigate factors that correlate significantly with case ellipsis and not to determine the relative strength of their influence.

above can be analyzed within the stochastic OT framework in a way analogous to Aissen's account of the categorical DSM and DOM: non-categorical, quantitative variation follows when the same iconic and economy constraints that are motivated for an account of crosslinguistic DSM/DOM are ranked closely on a continuous ranking scale with stochastic evaluation.

24.4 A Unified OT Account of CE and DCM

Stochastic OT (StOT), pioneered by Boersma (1998), is one of a family of probabilistic OT frameworks that can provide a unified account of categorical and variable data (see Boersma and Hayes (2001) for reviews). It differs from standard OT in that it presupposes a continuous scale of constraint rankings rather than a discrete ordinal scale. That is, constraints are not simply ordered, but they have a value on the continuous scale of real numbers. Hence, constraints differ not only in dominance but in distance. Also, in StOT evaluation is stochastic. At each evaluation the value of each constraint is perturbed by temporarily adding to its ranking value random noise drawn from a normal distribution. The value permanently associated with a constraint is called a *ranking value*, while a constraint's value in any given evaluation is called the *selection point*.

Boersma and Hayes (2001) exemplify StOT with various empirical testcases of phonological variation, and recently it has been increasingly applied to the study of syntactic variation as well (see Bresnan and Deo 2001, Bresnan et al. 2001, Bresnan and Nikitina 2003, Clark 2004, Dingare 2001, Koontz-Garboden 2001, among others). Below, I will illustrate how the StOT model can be used to describe the patterns and limits of variation in case marking through the analysis of CE in Korean and DOM in Sinhalese (Gair 1970).[8] The StOT analysis throughout incorporates the constraints of Aissen (2003). For reasons of space limitation, I will focus only on the animacy effect on case marking in Korean and Sinhalese.

Recall from section 3 that animacy-conditioned DOM is a statistical tendency in colloquial Korean: the relative frequency of the choice of unmarked forms over case-marked forms in the CFK data increases with objects that are low in prominence on the animacy hierarchy (see Table 3). In contrast, in Sinhalese, animate referring objects are optionally case-marked, while inanimate objects may not be case-marked (Gair 1970). The comparison of these two languages is very useful because it

[8]The discussion in this section draws analyses from Lee (2002, 2006, to appear).

shows that a stochastic OT grammar based on the constraints laid out above can account for CE and categorical DOM in a unified way.

We used the Praat system (Boersma and Weenink 2000), which includes an implementation of the Gradual Learning Algorithm (GLA; Boersma 1998; Boersma and Hayes 2001), to determine the constraint ranking values and output distribution of grammars. The GLA is able to approximate the frequency distributions present in the learning data. For Korean, the GLA was confronted with a frequency distribution shown in (11). Since there is no evidence from the CFK data that there are significant differences between human and non-human animates (see the discussion in section 3), they were collapsed into a single category 'Hum-Anim' for simulation purposes. Correspondingly, the two high-ranking iconicity constraints in the subhierarchy in (3b), i.e., *OBJ/HUM & *ZERO$_C$ and *OBJ/ANIM & *ZERO$_C$, were collapsed into a single constraint, *OBJ/HUM-ANIM & *ZERO$_C$.

(11) Simulated Korean input/output distribution

Input:	% OBJ	% OBJ-CASE
Hum-Anim	53.5	46.5
Inanimate	74.9	25.1

Starting from an initial grammar in which all constraints had the same ranking values (=100.00), the GLA assigned the ranking values in (12).[9] Observe that the ranking value of the economy constraint *STRUCT$_C$ is close enough to the ranking values of the two iconicity constraints (within the near-categorical distance of 10; see fn. 9) to predict variable outputs for both inputs.

(12) Ranking values for constraints (Korean)

*STRUCT$_C$	100.782
*OBJ/HUM-ANIM & *ZERO$_C$	100.430
*OBJ/INAN & *ZERO$_C$	98.782

The output distributions of the learned grammar closely matched the frequency distributions in the CFK data shown in (13):

(13) Output distributions of grammar (Korean)

Input:	% OBJ	% OBJ-CASE
Hum-Anim	54.99	45.01
Inanimate	74.1	24.3

[9]The standard deviation of ranking variation here is fixed at 2.0. When the ranking distance between two crucial constraints is 10 units (=5 standard deviations), the outputs are near-categorical; when the distance is 18 units (=9 standard deviations), reversal of constraint dominance reduces to 1 in 10 billion (less than once in a lifetime) (Boersma and Hayes 2001: 50).

For Sinhalese, the GLA was presented with the frequency distribution given in (14). (This is not based on real data.) We assume 0%/100% frequency for humans and inanimates and 50%/50% frequency for non-human animates. That is, in the learning data 100% of the outputs for the [human] input were case-marked; 100% of the outputs for the [inanimate] input were non-case-marked; and 50% of the outputs for the [animate] input were case-marked (the other 50% were not).

(14) Simulated Sinhalese input/output distribution

Input:	% OBJ	% OBJ-CASE
Human	0	100
Animate	50	50
Inanimate	100	0

The GLA assigned the ranking values in (15). Observe that the iconicity constraint *OBJ/HUM & *ZERO$_C$, penalizing the non-case marked form of a human-referring object, is more than 10 units above the economy constraint *STRUCT$_C$. This ranking yields the obligatory case marking of a human-referring object. In contrast, the iconicity constraint for a non-human animate object is ranked very close to *STRUCT$_C$. The close ranking distance between these two constraints yields the alternative outputs (unmarked and case-marked forms of an animate object) through frequent constraint dominance reversal under stochastic evaluation. Sinhalese also differs crucially from the partial Korean grammar in (13) in that the *STRUCT$_C$ is more than 10 units above *OBJ/INAN & *ZERO$_C$. This ranking yields the (near)-categorical unmarked output for the [inanimate] input, capturing the categorical influence of animacy on object marking.

(15) Ranking values for constraints (Sinhalese)

*OBJ/HUM & *ZERO$_C$	114.059
*OBJ/ANIM & *ZERO$_C$	99.481
*STRUCT$_C$	99.354
*OBJ/INAN & *ZERO$_C$	87.107

Once again, the output distributions of the learned grammar approximate the frequency distributions present in the learning data:

(16) Output distributions of grammar (Sinhalese)

Input:	% OBJ	% OBJ-CASE
Human	0	100
Animate	48.6	51.4
Inanimate	100	0

In sum, OT grammar with stochastic evaluation can provide a unifying account for variable case marking in Korean and crosslinguistic categorical DSM/DOM phenomena in terms of the same system of iconicity and economy constraints that are typologically motivated.

Further evidence for the active cognitive status of the constraint subhierarchies comes from psycholinguistic experimentation. A great deal of research has already shown that the definiteness of NPs in a sentence influences sentence processing. The following section reviews two explanations that have been offered for effects of NP types on sentence processing.

24.5 Definiteness Effects on Sentence Processing

Understanding the difficulties involved in processing complex sentences may provide insight into the nature of mental processes underlying language comprehension. Sentences with restrictive relative clauses (RCs) are a type of complex structure that has proven very useful for studying language processing. This is particularly so for subject-extracted and object-extracted RCs, as illustrated below.

(17) The lawyer that irritated the banker filed a hefty lawsuit.

(18) The lawyer that the banker irritated filed a hefty lawsuit.

In a subject-extracted RC, like (17), the extracted element (e.g., *lawyer*) serves as the unexpressed logical subject of the verb in the embedded clause (i.e., *irritated*). In an object-extracted RC, like (18), the extracted element is understood to function as the unexpressed logical object of the verb in the relative clause. Although subject-extracted RCs are generally easier to comprehend than object-extracted RCs (Ford 1983; King and Just 1991; King and Kutas 1995), there are cases where this difference in difficulty is significantly reduced. Bever (1974) noted that double-center embedded sentences (e.g., (19)), which are usually nearly impossible to understand, appear to become much more intelligible when they have a mixture of different types of NPs (e.g., (20)).

(19) The reporter the politician the commentator met trusts said the president won't resign.

(20) The reporter everyone I met trusts said the president won't resign.

Greatly decreased difficulty in the processing of center-embedded structures has been attributed to the non-similarity of the two critical NPs and the accessibility/definiteness of the embedded NP. In what follows, I will consider each of these explanations in turn.

Similarity-based interference account

The similarity-based interference account (Gordon et al. 2001) is based on the idea that the syntactic complexity of object-extracted RCs is compounded by the confusability of the entities represented by the NPs. That is, in (18), the representation of *lawyer* and *banker* are quite similar. Interpreting object-extracted RCs like (18) requires comprehenders to maintain distinct representations of the two and this task is made more difficult by the relatively complex syntax. In a series of self-paced reading experiments, Gordon et al. (2001) tested sentences where the first (modified) NP was a description and they varied the type of the second NP, using descriptions, the pronoun *you*, and short, common proper names as illustrated in (21) and (22).

(21) The banker that the judge/you/Bob praised climbed the mountain.

(22) The banker that praised the judge/you/Bob climbed the mountain.

They found greatly decreased difficulty in object-extracted RCs when the second NP was the pronoun *you* or a proper name. Because they found the greatest decrease in difficulty when the two critical NPs came from dissimilar types, they concluded that their results provided support for the view of Bever (1974) that mixing different types of NPs in a sentence reduces the processing complexity associated with center-embedded structures.[10]

Since the focus of the present study is markedness, I will not discuss similarity effects in any further detail here. The issue of how markedness and similarity interact in comprehension is discussed in Lee, Lee and Gordon (2004, 2006) and Lee (2005).

Accessibility-based account

The accessibility-based account suggested by Gibson (1998) and colleagues (Warren and Gibson 2002) views the effects of NP types on processing difficulty in a different way. On this account, the number of discourse referents that intervenes between a filler and the site where it is attached determines how difficult it will be to integrate the filler, and hence how much disruption comprehenders will experi-

[10]Additional experiments that Gordon, Hendrick and Johnson (2004) have conducted have shown that no reduction in the difference in processing difficulty between object-extracted and subject-extracted RCs occurs when (i) the second NP is an indefinite expression, (ii) differs in number from the first expression, (iii) is a generic expression, or (iv) is always the NP *the person*. The difference between object-extracted and subject-extracted RCs is significantly reduced when the second NP is the quantified expression *everyone*.

ence. The account proposes further that local person pronouns such as *you*, *me*, *I* and *us* represent a special class of referring expressions. Essentially, because local person pronouns refer to entities that are immediately available in the comprehender's environment, they impose less of a load on working memory than referring expressions such as *the lawyer* whose meaning must be retrieved from long-term memory. Gibson (1998) found that the rated complexity of object-extracted RCs decreases when local person pronouns replace other types of referring expressions.

More recently, Warren and Gibson (2002) found that sentence complexity is more closely related to gradations of the accessibility of the embedded subject, such as proposed in the definiteness hierarchy (23) (Aissen 2003) or in the givenness hierarchy (24) (Gundel et al. 1993; Ariel 1991) than to whether the embedded subject was a local person pronoun or not.

(23) Aissen's definiteness hierarchy:
Pronoun > Name > Definite > Indefinite

(24) The Gundel et al. (1993) givenness hierarchy:
Central   Peripheral
in focus > activated > familiar > uniquely identifiable > referential

The use of particular referring expressions such as pronouns, proper nouns, definites and indefinites is a strategy for marking the accessibility of the mental representation of discourse referents. Ariel (1991) argues that all referring expressions in all languages are arranged on a scale of accessibility, and the use of high accessibility referring expressions implies that the discourse referent has high accessibility to the addressee, while the use of low accessibility referring expressions implies that it has low accessibility to the addressee. Thus, the definiteness hierarchy can be interpreted as a ranking of accessibility markers from high accessibility markers (e.g. pronouns) to low accessibility markers (e.g. indefinites).

Warren and Gibson (2002) conducted a complexity rating study in which they varied the type of the subject NP in the object-extracted RCs across six levels of the givenness hierarchy: (1) first-/second-person pronouns; (2) third-person pronouns; (3) first names; (4) full names; (5) definite descriptions; (6) indefinite descriptions. Because they found that complexity was increasingly reduced as the definiteness of the embedded NP increases from least definite/accessible to most definite/accessible, they concluded that their findings support a referential processing theory based on accessibility and NP type, consistent with referent access models proposed by Garrod et al. (1994) and Myers and O'Brien (1998).

Warren and Gibson's (2002) study is of special interest here, as their finding is strikingly consistent with Aissen's constraint subhierarchy for subject definiteness: the cost associated with the processing of referential expressions differs in the direction predicted by Aissen's definiteness constraint subhierarchy (25a):

(25) Definiteness constraint subhierarchy (Aissen 2003: 445)

a. *Subj/Nonspecific >> *Subj/Specific >> Subj/Definite >> *Subj/Name >> *Subj/Pronoun

b. *Obj/Pronoun >> *Obj/Name >> *Obj/Definite >> *Obj/Specific >> *Obj/Nonspecific

However, most experiments that found the effect of NP types on processing difficulty focused on showing the effect of different types of (embedded) subjects. So little is known about how the definiteness of *objects* affects processing difficulty. To address this question, I report two eye-tracking experiments investigating how the relative prominence of a subject and an object in definiteness influences the processing of Korean center-embedded complement clause structures (Experiment 1) and double-object causative constructions (Experiment 2).

As emphasized by typologists, the definiteness hierarchy in (23) must be understood in connection with the grammatical function hierarchy (Subject > Non-subject). In other words, these hierarchies do not express markedness *per se*, but a ranking. Thus, pronouns are not inherently less marked than names and other referring expressions: they are less marked *qua* (transitive) subjects and more marked *qua* objects. Conversely, non-pronouns are not inherently more marked than pronouns: they are more marked as subjects but less marked/more natural as objects.

A substantial literature indicates that pronouns are unmarked as subjects but marked as objects whereas descriptions are unmarked as objects but marked as subjects (Givn 1984, Croft 1990, Aissen 1999, 2003). Given the cross-linguistic tendency that less definite elements are encoded in object position, one can expect that there is a stronger tendency to prefer descriptions as the object over pronouns. As we will see in sec. 6.2, this tendency is confirmed by the result of experiment 2.

24.6 Active Cognitive Status of Constraint Subhierarchies: Evidence from Sentence Comprehension

The experiments reported in this section are designed to determine whether the relative markedness of a subject and an object in definiteness affects processing difficulty. We used an eye-tracking method that gives us an excellent chance of detecting subtle, early processing effects (Rayner 1998; Rayner and Pollatsek 1989).

24.6.1 Experiment 1

Experiment 1 tested the hypothesis that more definite referents which have appeared in the prominent syntactic position (pronoun subjects) are easier to process than less definite referents which have appeared in the same position (common noun or description subjects).

Materials and Design Experiment 1 tested center embedded complement clause structures in Korean to determine how the definiteness and similarity of two adjacent *subject* NPs affect processing difficulty. We varied whether the matrix subject NP and the embedded subject NP were pronouns or descriptions. The nouns were matched for length and frequency. The four conditions are illustrated in (26)-(29). Forty eight sentences were created with different matrix verbs and embedded verbs, and the test sentences were mixed with an equal number of unrelated filler sentences to form a single list of 96 sentences. Participants saw each experimental sentences only in one condition; across participants, all sentences occurred in all conditions. Eye movements were recorded as subjects read the experimental sentences using an SMI EyeLink system. Twenty four native speakers of Korean were tested in the experiment. They had gone to the United States as adults and were residents in the Chapel Hill area at the time of the experiment. All had normal or corrected to normal vision.

(26) Matched (Pronoun-Pronoun)
Kutul-i **wuli-ka** silhum-ul haysstako malhayssta.
3.PL-NOM 1.PL-NOM experiment-ACC ran said
'They said that we ran experiments.'

(27) Matched (Description-Description)
Uysa-ka **haksayng-i** silhum-ul haysstako malhayssta.
doctor-NOM student-NOM experiment-ACC ran said
'The doctor said that the student ran experiments.'

(28) Non-matched (Pronoun-Description)
Kutul-i haksayng-i silhum-ul haysstako malhayssta.
3.PL-NOM student-NOM experiment-ACC ran said
'They said that the student ran experiments.'

(29) Non-matched (Description-Pronoun)
Uysa-ka wuli-ka silhum-ul haysstako malhayssta.
doctor-NOM 1.PL-NOM experiment-ACC ran said
'The doctor said that we ran experiments.'

Center-embedded complement clause structures illustrated above are locally ambiguous in a head-final language like Korean.[11] The sequence of the two nominative NPs is compatible with an analysis, consisting of a nominative subject followed by a nominative object, because Korean stative verbs and nonagentive verbs may assign nominative case to their object. The two nominative NPs may also be analyzed as subjects of different verbs. This is illustrated in (30):

(30) a. Coargument analysis
[NP_{nom} (SUBJ) NP_{nom} (OBJ) ...
b. Two-clause analysis
[NP_{nom} (SUBJ) [NP_{nom} (SUBJ) ...

[11] Several properties of Korean grammar (the fact that it allows empty pronominals and sequences of identically case-marked nominal expressions, and is head-final) make this language highly locally ambiguous. As a result, assumptions about ambiguity resolution play a central role within any analysis of sentence processing that attempts to account for Korean data. There are three main issues relevant to ambiguity resolution: (i) what constraints affect the initial interpretation of an ambiguous input; (ii) how many representations can be followed initially: one or more than one; (iii) how reanalysis take place. With respect to the first issue, I assume that multiple constraints interact to to determine the preferred reading(s) at points of ambiguity, as argued for in Crain and Steedman (1985), Altmann and Steedman (1988), Gibson (1991) and MacDonald et al. (1994), among others. The interacting constraints that I assume include plausibility, lexical/morphological frequency, markedness of argument types, interference, semantic and formal similarity and syntactic complexity. With respect to the second issue, my assumption is that the parser can retain multiple representations in parallel up to memory limitations (Gibson 1991, Trueswell et al. 1994, among others). Analyses that receive little support will no longer be worked on, and their activation in the competition set will decrease. Although they are not being actively worked on, these representations remain in the representation space with a low activation, so that a later incoming element may reactivate one of them. Reanalysis consists of (1) the parser reactivating a representation whose activation has dropped below threshold previously, (2) returning to the point in the structure where the activation has dropped below threshold, and then (3) parsing left-to-right from this point in the same way as in the first analysis, if necessary reparsing material that was processed and misattached earlier.

However, as the accusative-marked NP is read, a clause boundary is created between the two nominative NPs. When the next word, the embedded form of transitive verb, is encountered, the bi-clausal analysis is confirmed and a matrix verb is predicted:

(31) [NP_{nom} (SUBJ) [NP_{nom} (SUBJ) NP_{acc} (OBJ) V_1] V_2]

There is not yet strong empirical evidence relevant to whether the Korean parser's preferred interpretation of the locally ambiguous part of the center-embedded complement clause structure is (30a) or (30b) (cf. Kim 2000). The co-argument analysis (30a) is syntactically simpler, and requires fewer head-argument relations. But lexical and morphological frequencies strongly bias the initial interpretation towards the two-clause analysis (30b), because the nominative marker *-ka* is much more frequent as a subject marker than as an object marker. It is also possible that readers do not commit themselves to an analysis of the structure before they read the word after the sequence of nominative NPs. Though this is an interesting issue in its own right, it goes beyond the focus of the present study.

Results We used two measures of eye movement. The first was the first-pass reading time, which is the sum of the duration of the first fixation on a word plus any subsequent fixations on that word that occur before a successive word is fixated. This provides a good measure of the initial processing of a region. The second measure was the rereading time, which is the sum of the duration of any fixations made on a region after subsequent regions have already fixated. For each of the five word positions of the test sentences, two analyses of variance were computed, one with participants (F_1) and one with items (F_2) as a random variable. The factors included in the analyses were the types of the two nominative NPs (pronoun vs. description) and their similarity (matched vs. non-matched). In the following the results for first-pass reading times and rereading times will be presented separately.

First-pass reading times The means by subjects of the first-pass reading times as a function of NP type and similarity are presented in Table 5.

(32) Table 5. First-pass reading times (ms) in Experiment 1

	Matched		Non-matched	
	Pron-NP1 Pron-NP2	Desc-NP1 Desc-NP2	Pron-NP1 Desc-NP2	Desc-NP Pron-NP2
Main clause				
NP1 (SUBJ)	260	270	247	272
Embedded clause				
NP2 (SUBJ)	274	282	263	306
NP3 (OBJ)	249	241	232	242
V1 (verb)	333	359	333	353
Main clause				
V2 (verb)	224	242	215	268

The first-pass data produced a significant main effect of the type of NP1, the subject of the main clause, demonstrated by the fact that the description NP1 condition took longer to read than the pronoun NP1 condition ($F_1(1,23)=9.98$, $p<.05$; $F_2(1,47)=20.62$, $p<.01$). Readers continued to have difficulty in the description NP1 condition while processing NP2, NP3 and V1 (NP2: $F_1(1,23)=3.35$, $p=.080$; $F_2(1,47)=7.13$, $p<.01$, NP3: $F_1(1,23)=9.1$, $p<.01$; $F_2(1,47)=10.11$, $p<.01$, V1: $F_1(1,23)=4.42$, $p=.05$; $F_2(1,47)=6.89$, $p<.05$).

In addition, the first-pass data also produced a robust effect of the type of NP2, the subject of the embedded clause, at NP2 and V1, demonstrating that readers had greater difficulty in the pronoun NP2 condition than the description NP2 condition (NP2: $F_1(1,23)=14.15$, $p<.01$; $F_2(1,47)=2.23$, $p<.01$, V1: $F_1(1,23)=6.01$, $p<.05$; $F_2(1,47)=27.87$, $p<.01$). These data indicate that sentences in which the main clause subject is a description and the embedded subject is a pronoun were the most difficult to process in initial processing.

Rereading times The means by subjects of the rereading times as a function of NP type and similarity are presented in Table 6.

(33) Table 6. Rereading times (ms) in Experiment 1

	Matched		Non-matched	
	Pron-NP1 Pron-NP2	Desc-NP1 Desc-NP2	Pron-NP1 Desc-NP2	Desc-NP Pron-NP2
Main clause				
NP1 (SUBJ)	502	425	366	417
Embedded clause				
NP2 (SUBJ)	480	422	313	435
NP3 (OBJ)	286	228	182	248
V1 (verb)	198	207	146	190
Main clause				
V2 (verb)	79	111	65	115

As in the first-pass data, the pronoun NP2 condition had significantly longer rereading times at NP1, NP2 and NP3 than the description NP2 condition (NP1: $F_1(1,23)=8.96$, $p<.01$; $F_2(1,47)=4.85$, $p<.05$, NP2: $F_1(1,23)=9.22$, $p<.01$; $F_2(1,47)=7.56$, $p<.01$, NP3: $F_1(1,23)=8.34$, $p<.01$; $F_2(1,47)=7.85$, $p<.01$). The data therefore demonstrate that more definite referents which have appeared in the prominent syntactic position (pronoun subjects) are easier to process than less definite referents which have appeared in the same position (common noun or description subjects).[12]

Discussion One interesting aspect of the results is differential difficulty of the two non-matched conditions: on the first-pass reading time measure, sentences with description main clause subjects (NP1) and pronoun embedded subjects (NP2) were more difficult to process than any other kinds of sentences, while sentences with pronoun main clause subjects (NP1) and description embedded subjects (NP2) were the easiest on both reading time measures.

The similarity-based account of Gordon et al. (2001) offers no reason why there should be such a difference. Warren and Gibson's accessibility-based account allows for a decrease in processing difficulty when the subject is a pronoun, but it does not explain why the

[12]Subject similarity effects were not detectable in first-pass reading times but were significant in rereading times: reading time for NP1, NP2 and NP3 was elevated when the NP1 and NP2 was of a matched type as compared to non-matched type (NP1: $F_1(1,23)=5.75$, $p<.05$; $F_2(1,47)=14.71$, $p<.01$, NP2: $F_1(1,23)=7.69$, $p<.05$; $F_2(1,47)=18.66$, $p<.01$, NP3: $F_1(1,23)=8.53$, $p<.08$; $F_2(1,47)=4.57$, $p<.05$). This result demonstrates that the definiteness effect is detectable very early but similarity-based interference occurs later in comprehension. The early occurrence of the definiteness effect is likely due to the fact that readers use the definiteness cue early in the assignment of syntactic functions of NPs.

pronoun NP1-description NP2 condition is easier than the description NP1-pronoun NP2 condition. According to this account, the number of discourse referents that intervenes between a head and its dependent(s) determines how difficult it will be to integrate these elements, and this process is less costly when the integration step crosses more accessible or more definite elements. If this is the case, the pronoun NP1-pronoun NP2 condition should be the easiest, and the description NP1-description NP2 should be the most difficult. However, our data is clearly inconsistent with this prediction.

The relative difficulty of the description NP1-pronoun NP2 condition can be accounted for by proposing that syntactic embedding correlates with the low degree of topicality. It has been observed that non-pronominal lexical NPs strongly tend to have referents whose topic status is low, and they often occur in backgrounded portions of a discourse. Lambrecht (1986: 317) enumerates five parameters associated with the higher and lower degree of topicality of a NP referent:

(34)	High Topicality:	Low Topicality:
	more salient referent	less salient referent
	more anaphoric referent	less anaphoric referent
	more specific referent	less specific referent
	higher transitivity of clause	lower transitivity of clause
	little or no syntactic embedding	frequent syntactic embedding

The quantitative study of spoken French corpuses by Lambrecht (1986) shows that lexical subject NPs tend to appear more frequently in embedded clauses than other referential expressions of higher topicality. Of the 83 non-topicalized lexical subject NPs in the three corpuses Lambrecht analyzed, 22 (26.5%) are embedded. But only 10 out of the 102 occurring topicalized NPs (9.8%) are found in embedded clauses.

A relatively strong correlation among syntactic embedding, low topicality and coding as a lexical NP is also found in the CFK data. In the annotated part of the corpus, there were 138 utterances that are center-embedded complement clause structures, and 77 (56%) out of these contain overt main and embedded subject NPs. Table 7 shows the distribution of pronoun and description subject NPs in main and embedded clauses.

(35) Table 7. Distribution of pronoun and description subject NPs in CFK

	Main clause	Embedded clause
Pronoun Subject	25 (32%)	9 (12%)
Description subject	7 (9%)	30 (39%)
Other (Name, quantifying expression, etc.)	45 (59%)	38 (52%)

The results in Table 7 show that the Korean data are similar to the French data Lambrecht (1986) analyzed. In Korean too, pronoun subjects have a strong preference to appear in main clauses, whereas description subjects have a frequency bias toward occurring in embedded clauses.

The comparison of the results of the corpus analysis and Experiment 1 shows clearly that the preference for a pronoun as a main clause subject observed in the corpus is visible in comprehension: sentence types that are more frequent in the corpus (i.e., sentences that contain pronoun main clause subjects and description embedded subjects) are also easier to understand.

Given the asymmetry between main and embedded subjects in coding preference, a question arises as to why the pattern in English object-extracted RCs is the reverse of that for Korean center-embedded complement clause constructions. Why is it that in English object-extracted RCs with a pronoun embedded subject are easier than the ones with a description RCs? We suggest that this difference we observe between English and Korean is due to the independent functional difference between RCs and complement clauses. As Francis et al. (1999) point out, an important function of object-extracted RCs is to anchor to the previous discourse the modified head of the RC, which tends to denote an unestablished topic that is new to discourse (see also Fox and Thompson (1990)). This is illustrated in the following example from Francis et al. (1999: 94).

(36) Our friend, the President, right now, says no new taxes. We should and especially, if anything, be cutting taxes now because of the recession and at the same time, **the budget he sent to Congress** has tax and fee increases, so, uh, I know the politicians, uh, aren't straightforward.

In (36) the discourse new *budget* is anchored to *the President.* Note that the pronominal reference to *the President* in the RC guides the hearer to relate *the budget* to the referent which has already been evoked in the discourse. This function of object-extracted RCs in discourse may provide a possible explanation for why English object-extracted RCs with a pronoun embedded subject are easier than the ones with a description embedded subject.

24.6.2 Experiment 2

As an alternative to the accessibility-based account proposed in Warren and Gibson (2002), we considered the prediction of an account based on the notion of markedness. In particular, we tested the prediction that more definite referents which have appeared in less prominent syntactic positions (pronoun objects) are more difficult to process than less definite referents which have appeared in the same position (description objects).

Materials And Design In Experiment 2, we used a different kind of complex sentence, double object causative constructions, to examine how different types of objects affect processing difficulty. Double object causative constructions contain two objects that are accusative-marked. We varied whether the first object NP (causee) and the second object NP were pronouns or descriptions, as illustrated in (37)-(40).

(37) Matched (Pronoun-Pronoun)
Yumi-ka **kutul-ul wuli-lul** manna-key hayssta.
Yumi-NOM 3.PL-ACC 1.PL-ACC meet-LK made/let
'Yumi made them meet us.'

(38) Matched (Description-Description)
Yumi-ka **uysa-lul haksayng-ul** manna-key hayssta.
Yumi-NOM doctor-ACC student-ACC meet-LK made/let
'Yumi made the doctor meet the student.'

(39) Non-matched (Pronoun-Description)
Yumi-ka **kutul-ul haksayng-ul** manna-key hayssta.
Yumi-NOM 3.PL-ACC student-ACC meet-LK made/let
'Yumi made them meet the student.'

(40) Non-matched (Description-Pronoun)
Yumi-ka **uysa-lul wuli-lul** manna-key hayssta.
Yumi-NOM doctor-ACC 1.PL-ACC meet-LK made/let
'Yumi made the doctor meet us.'

Forty-eight sentences were created with different verbs, and the test sentences were mixed with an equal number of unrelated filler sentences to form a single list of 96 sentences. Twenty-four native speakers of Korean from the same population as in Experiment 1 participated in the study. The design and procedure were the same as in the preceding experiments.

Like the experimental sentences tested in Experiment 1, the input string used in Experiment 2 is locally ambiguous. Specifically, after processing the first two NPs, the input string is consistent with either a single clause analysis, as in (41a), or a two-clause analysis, as in (41b).

(41) a. Single-clause analysis
[NP_{nom} (SUBJ) NP_{acc} (OBJ) ...
b. Two-clause analysis
[NP_{nom} (SUBJ) [NP_{acc} (OBJ) ...

The single clause analysis in (41a) would be preferred as the initial interpretation because it is syntactically simpler. The reader may project a prototypical transitive verb with two arguments before the verb is actually read (Boland et al. 1995, Altmann and Kamide 1999). At the next word, the second accusative NP, a clause boundary between the two accusative NPs becomes necessary, but the single clause analysis in (41a) can be retained. However, when the next NP is posited, it is clear from the form of the word that this verb is a part of a causative verbal complex and reanalysis must take place in order to switch from the initially favored structure (a) to a different one. At this point, the parser returns to the first accusative NP, the misanalyzed point, and proceeds to parse the structure again, this time pursuing the analysis of the first accusative NP as a cause argument of the causative verb, which is predicted to follow. Note that in causative constructions, the first accusative NP has a dual role: it serves semantically as the missing logical subject of the first verb (*key*-form verb) and at the same time as the syntactic object (cause argument) of the second verb (causative verb) (Bratt 1995). Accordingly, at the first verb readers have to build a new representation associating the first accusative NP with it and with the following causative verb. Hence, a slow down is predicted at this point.

Results For each of the five word positions of the test sentences, two analyses of variance were computed, one with participants (F_1) and one with items (F_2) as a random variable. The factors included in the analyses were the types of the two accusative NPs (pronoun vs. description) and their similarity (matched vs. non-matched). In the following the results for first-pass reading times and rereading times will be presented separately.

First-pass reading times The means by subjects of the first-pass reading times as a function of NP type and similarity are presented in Table 8.

(42) Table 8. First-pass reading times (ms) in Experiment 2

	Matched		Non-matched	
	Pron-NP2 Pron-NP3	Desc-NP2 Desc-NP3	Pron-NP2 Desc-NP3	Desc-NP2 Pron-NP3
NP1 (SUBJ)	258	245	259	249
NP2 (OBJ1)	330	260	332	279
NP3 (OBJ2)	312	252	278	301
V1 (*key*-verb)	520	438	517	440
V2(causative verb)	180	142	152	125

The first-pass data produced a significant main effect of the type of NP2, the first accusative NP (causee), demonstrated by the fact that the pronoun NP2 condition took longer to read than the description NP2 condition ($F_1(1,23)=6.65$, $p<.017$; $F_2(1,47)=7.97$, $p<.01$). Readers continued to have difficulty in the pronoun NP2 condition while processing NP3, V1 and V2: these three regions were read significantly slower in the pronoun NP2 condition than in the description NP2 condition (NP3: $F_1(1,23)=5.44$, $p<.05$; $F_2(1,47)=7.57$, $p<.01$, V1: $F_1(1,23)=8.54$, $p<.01$; $F_2(1,47)=9.06$, $p<.01$, V2: $F_1(1,23)=5.94$, $p<.05$; $F_2(1,47)=4.97$, $p<.05$). At none of the five regions were there significant effects of the type of NP3 and similarity of NP2 and NP3.
Rereading times The means by subjects of the rereading times as a function of NP type and similarity are presented in Table 9.

(43) Table 9. Rereading times (ms) in Experiment 2

	Matched		Non-matched	
	Pron-NP2 Pron-NP3	Desc-NP2 Desc-NP3	Pron-NP2 Desc-NP3	Desc-NP2 Pron-NP3
NP1 (SUBJ)	192	177	201	149
NP2 (OBJ1)	730	638	751	601
NP3 (OBJ2)	630	468	688	473
V1 (*key*-verb)	572	395	574	416
V2(causative verb)	98	46	91	52

As in the first-pass data, significant effects of the type of the first object were found in the four critical regions from NP2 until V2: NP2, NP3, V1 and V2 were read significantly slower in the pronoun NP2 condition than in the description NP2 condition (NP2: $F_1(1,23)=10.22$, $p<.01$; $F_2(1,47)=9.52$, $p<.01$, NP3: $F_1(1,23)=9.29$, $p<.01$; $F_2(1,47)=10.33$, $p<.01$, V1: $F_1(1,23)=4.22$, $p=.051$; $F_2(1,47)=$

4.18, $p<.05$, V2: $F_1(1,23)=8.54$, $p<.01$; $F_2(1,47)=9.06$, $p<.01$). No other significant effect was found in this experiment.

Discussion Both reading time measures revealed a significant effect of the markedness of the first object NP (causee): first-pass reading times in the four critical regions were slower in the pronoun OBJ1 condition than in the description OBJ1 condition. The rereading times give additional evidence that the pronoun OBJ1 condition caused more difficulty than the other three. The data therefore demonstrate that it is the relative markedness as an object, not the definiteness of an NP itself, that affects the processing of complex sentences. The theories of sentence processing discussed in section 5 do not predict the effect of NP markedness. In particular, the similarity-based account (Gordon et al. 2001) predicts that the two matched conditions cause more difficulty than the non-matched conditions. However, no similarity effect was found in both first-pass reading times and rereading times. Instead, the greatest difficulty was observed when the first object was a pronoun. The absence of similarity effects in Experiment 2 is likely due to the serial position of the second object and the first verb, which conforms to the canonical object-verb order in Korean. Thus readers should have less difficulty assigning the appropriate semantic role (theme) to this object, as evidenced by the shorter reading times at the object position in Experiment 1 compared to the position of the two preceding nominative NPs and also by the shorter reading times at the second object position in Experiment 2 compared to the first object position. It is likely, therefore, that the ease of the OBJ1-V1 integration significantly decreases confusability between the two adjacent accusative NPs, reducing (or eliminating) similarity-based interference. The pattern of results in Experiment 2 is not consistent with predictions of the accessibility-based account (Warren and Gibson 2002). This account predicts that the OBJ1-V1 integration and the OBJ1-V2 integration is less costly when OBJ1 is a pronoun than when it is a description, but the greatest difficulty was observed when OBJ1 was a pronoun.[13]

In light of these findings, one way to improve Warren and Gibson's formulation of integration cost is to assign each referent a graded cost

[13]Warren and Gibson (2002: 86) mention that not all new referents are difficult to process and not all old referents are easy to process. In fact, extensive evidence suggests that old referents which have appeared in prominent syntactic positions are more accessible than old referents which have appeared in less prominent positions (Arnold 1998, Ariel 1991, Gordon et al. 1993, Gundel et al. 1993). The effort required to process a new referent into discourse is also variable, as discussed by Garrod and Sanford (1982) and Tanenhaus and Carlson (1990). However, Warren and Gibson's model of integration cost does not take into account the syntactic function of referential expressions as a factor contributing to integration cost.

based on its relative markedness and then use those graded cost in calculating integration costs. Less marked NPs will have lower costs than more marked ones, leading to lower cost for the integrations which cross them.

Regardless of the issue of how integration cost can be best formulated, the results of the current experiments show that the relative markedness of nominal arguments affects processing difficulty. The data show that processing costs associated with referential expressions differ in the direction predicted by the subhierarchies of markedness constraints suggested in recent (stochastic) OT approaches to morphosyntactic variation (e.g., Aissen 1999, 2003; Aissen and Bresnan 2002).

24.7 Conclusion

The present study has presented results from a corpus study and two experiments investigating how the relative markedness of argument NPs as a subject and an object influences the frequency of case marking and comprehension difficulty in Korean. In the corpus study of Korean case ellipsis, we have shown that quantitative patterning found in Korean case ellipsis can be analyzed within the stochastic OT framework in a way analogous to an account of the categorical differential case marking phenomena proposed by Aissen (2003). In this analysis, categorical split case marking found in various languages is viewed as conventionalization of the same universal pragmatic tendency to mark disharmonic elements (e.g., high-prominence objects and low-prominence subjects), which is also present in the variable case-marking systems of languages like Japanese and Korean. In the two eye-tracking experiments, we found that the same hierarchies that play a role in the categorical structure of some languages and in the frequency of variable outputs in Korean influence comprehension difficulty in Korean. The results of these studies provide new evidence about the universal status of the system of constraint subhierarchies suggested in recent (stochastic) OT approaches (e.g., Aissen 1999, 2003; Aissen and Bresnan 2002). Further the experiments show that the markedness effects over the time course of comprehension can be measured using eye-tracking under natural reading conditions.

References

Aissen, Judith. 1990. Markedness and subject choice in Optimality Theory. *Natural Language and Linguistic Theory* 17(4):673–711.

Aissen, Judith. 2003. Differential object marking: Iconicity vs. economy. *Natural Language and Linguistic Theory* 21(3):435–483.

Aissen, Judith and Joan Bresnan. 2002. Optimality theory and typology. Course taught at the DGfS/LSA Summer School 'Formal and Functional Linguistics', Heinrich-Heine Universität Düsseldorf.

Altman, Gerry and Yuki Kamide. 1990. Incremental interpretation at verbs: Restricting the domain of subsequent reference. *Cognition* 73(3):247–264.

Altmann, Gerry and Mark Steedman. 1988. Interaction with context during human sentence processing. *Cognition* 30(2):191–238.

Ariel, Mira. 1991. *Accessing Noun-Phrase Antecedents*. London: Routledge.

Arnold, Jennifer. 1998. *Reference Form and Discourse Patterns*. Ph.D. thesis, Stanford University.

Bever, Thomas G. 1974. The ascent of the specious, or there's a lot we don't know about mirrors. In D. Cohen, ed., *Explaining Linguistic Phenomena*, pages 173–200. Washington, DC: Hemisphere.

Boersma, Paul. 1998. *Functional Phonology*. The Hague: Holland Academic Graphics.

Boersma, Paul and Bruce Hayes. 2001. Empirical tests of the gradual learning algorithm. *Linguistic Inquiry* 32(1):45–86.

Boersma, Paul and David Weenink. 2000. Praat computer program. Online, Institute of Phonetic Sciences, University of Amsterdam.

Boland, Julie, Michael Tanenhaus, Susan Garnsey, and Greg Carlson. 1995. Verb argument structure in parsing and interpretation: Evidence from wh-questions. *Journal of Memory and Language* 34:774–806.

Bossong, Georg. 1985. *Differentielle Objektmarkierung in der Neuiranischen Sprachen*. Tübingen: G. Narr.

Bratt, Elizabeth O. 1995. *Lexical and Periphrastic Causatives in Korean*. Ph.D. thesis, Stanford University.

Bresnan, Joan and Judith Aissen. 2002. Optimality and functionality: Objections and refutations. *Natural Language and Linguistic Theory* 20(1):81–95.

Bresnan, Joan and Ashwini Deo. 2001. Grammatical constraints on variation: 'be' in the survey of English dialects and (stochastic) Optimality Theory. Ms., Stanford University.

Bresnan, Joan, Shipra Dingare, and Christopher D Manning. 2001. Soft constraints mirror hard constraints: Voice and person in English and Lummi. In M. Butt and T. H. King, eds., *Proceedings of the International Lexical-Functional Grammar Conference 2001 (LFG'01)*, pages 13–32. Hong Kong: CSLI Online Publications.

Bresnan, Joan and Tatiana Nikitina. 2003. On the gradience of the dative alternation. Ms., Stanford University.

Carletta, Jean. 1996. Assessing agreement on classification tasks: The kappa statistic. *Computational Linguistics* 22(2):249–254.

Clark, Brady. 2004. *A Stochastic Optimality Theory Approach to Syntactic Change*. Ph.D. thesis, Stanford University.

Crain, Stephen and Mark Steedman. 1985. On not being led up the garden path: The use of context by the psychological parser. In D. Dowty, L. Karttunen, and A. Zwicky, eds., *Natural Language Processing: Psychological, Computational and Theoretical Perspectives*, pages 320–358. Cambridge, UK: Cambridge University Press.

Croft, Wiliam. 1990. *Typology and Universals*. Cambridge, UK: Cambridge University Press.

Dingare, Shipra. 2001. *The Effects of Feature Hierarchies on Frequencies of Passivization in English*. Master's thesis, Stanford University.

Dixon, Robert M. W. 1970. Ergativity. *Language* 55(1):59–138.

Dixon, Robert M. W. 1972. *The Dyirbal Language of Northern Queensland*. Cambridge, UK: Cambridge University Press.

Donohue, Cathryn. 1990. Optimizing Fore case and word order. Ms., Stanford University.

Ford, Marilyn. 1983. A method for obtaining measures of local parsing complexity throughout sentences. *Journal of Verbal Learning and Verbal Behavior* 22:203–218.

Fox, Barbara A. and Sandra A. Thompson. 1990. A discourse explanation of the grammar of relative clauses in english conversation. *Language* 66(2):297–316.

Francis, Hartwell S., Michelle L. Gregory, and Laura A. Michaelis. 1990. Are lexical subjects deviant? In S. Billings, J. Boyle, and A. Griffith, eds., *CLS 35: The Main Session. Papers from the 35th Meeting of the Chicago Linguistic Society*, vol. 1, pages 85–97. Chicago, IL: Chicago Linguistic Society.

Fry, John. 2001. *Ellipsis and 'wa'-Marking in Japanese Conversation*. Ph.D. thesis, Stanford University.

Gair, James W. 1970. *Colloquial Sinhalese Clause Structures*. The Hague: Mouton de Gruyter.

Garrod, Simon C. and Anderson Sanford. 1982. The mental representation of discourse in a focused memory system: Implications for the interpretation of anaphoric noun phrases. *Journal of Semantics* 1:21–41.

Garrod, Simon C. and Anderson Sanford. 1994. Resolving sentences in a discourse context: How discourse representation affects language understanding. In M. A. Gernsbacher, ed., *Handbook of Psycholinguistics*, pages 675–698. San Diego, CA: Academic Press.

Gibson, Edward. 1991. *A Computational Theory of Human Linguistic Processing: Memory Limitations and Processing Breakdown*. Ph.D. thesis, Carnegie Mellon University.

Gibson, Edward. 1998. Syntactic complexity: Locality of syntactic dependencies. *Cognition* 68(1):1–76.

Givón, Talmy. 1984. *Syntax: A Functional-Typological Introduction*, vol. 1. Philadelphia, PA: J. Benjamins.

Gordon, Peter C., Barbara Grosz, and Laura Gilliom. 1983. Pronouns, names and the centering of attention in discourse. *Cognitive Science* 17(3):311–347.

Gordon, Peter C., Randy Hendrick, and Markus Johnson. 2001. Memory interference during language processing. *Journal of Experimental Psychology: Learning, Memory and Cognition* 27(6):1411–1423.

Gordon, Peter C., Randy Hendrick, and Markus Johnson. 2004. Effects of noun phrase type on sentence complexity. *Journal of Memory and Language* 51:97–114.

Gundel, Jeanette, Nancy Hedberg, and Ron Zacharski. 1993. Cognitive status and the form of referring expressions in discourse. *Language* 69(2):274–307.

Kim, Youngjin. 2000. Resolving grammatical marking ambiguities in Korean: An eye-tracking study. Ms., Ajou University.

King, Jonathan and Marcel A. Just. 1991. Individual differences in syntactic processing: The role of working memory. *Journal of Memory and Language* 30:580–602.

King, Jonathan and Marta Kutas. 1995. Who did what and when? Using word- and clause-level ERPs to monitor working memory usage in reading. *Journal of Cognitive Neuroscience* 7(3):376–395.

Koontz-Garboden, Andrew. 2001. A stochastic OT approach to word order variation in Korlai Portuguese. In M. Andronis, C. Ball, H. Elston, and S. Neuvel, eds., *CLS 37: The Main Session. Papers from the 37th Meeting of the Chicago. Linguistic Society*, vol. 1, pages 395–208. Chicago, IL: Chicago Linguistic Society.

Lambrecht, Knud. 1986. *Topic, Focus, and the Grammar of Spoken French.* Ph.D. thesis, University of California, Berkeley.

LDC. 1996. *CallFriend Korean corpus*. University of Pennsylvania: Linguistic Data Consortium.

Lee, Hanjung. 2002. Referential accessibility and stylistic variation in OT: A corpus study. In M. Andronis, E. Debenport, A. Pycha, and K. Yoshimura, eds., *CLS 38: The Main Session. Papers from the 37th Meeting of the Chicago. Linguistic Society*, vol. 1, pages 361–378. Chicago, IL: Chicago Linguistic Society.

Lee, Hanjung. 2003. Parallel optimization in case systems. In M. Butt and T. H. King, eds., *Nominals: Inside and Out*, pages 15–58. Stanford, CA: CSLI Publications.

Lee, Hanjung. 2005. Effects of noun phrase type on sentence processing. *Discourse and Cognition* 12(1):105–129.

Lee, Hanjung. 2006a. Parallel optimization in case systems: Evidence from case ellipsis in Korean. *Journal of East Asian Linguistics* 15(1):69–96.

Lee, Hanjung. 2006b. Quantitative variation in Korean case ellipsis: Implications for case theory. In H. de Hoop and P. de Swart, eds., *Differential Case Marking (Studies in Natural Language and Linguistic Theory)*. Springer. To appear.

Lee, Hanjung, Yoonhyoung Lee, and Peter Gordon. 2004. Noun phrase type and referential processing in Korean: An eye-tracking study. Paper presented at the 17th Annual CUNY Conference on Human Sentence Processing.

Lee, Yoonhyoung, Hanjung Lee, and Peter Gordon. 2006. Linguistic complexity and information structure in Korean: Evidence from eye-tracking during reading. To appear in *Cognition*.

Myers, Jerome and Edward O'Brien. 1998. Accessing the discourse representation during reading. *Discourse Processes* 26(2):137–157.

Paolillo, John C. 2002. *Analyzing Linguistic Variation: Statistical Models and Methods*. Stanford, CA: CSLI Publications.

Prince, Alan and Paul Smolensky. 1993. Optimality theory: Constraint interaction in generative grammar. Tech. Rep. 2, Rutgers University Center for Cognitive Science, Piscataway, NJ.

Rayner, Keith. 1998. Eye movements in reading and information processing: 20 years of research. *Psychological Bulletin* 124(3):372–422.

Rayner, Keith and Alexander Pollatsek. 1980. *The Psychology of Reading*. New York, NY: Prentice-Hall.

Scott, Graham. 1978. *The Fore Language of Papua New Guinea*. Canberra: School of Pacific Studies, Australian National University.

Silverstein, Michael. 1976. Hierarchy of features and ergativity. In R. M. W. Dixon, ed., *Grammatical Categories in Australian Languages*, pages 112–171. Canberra: Australian Institute of Aboriginal Studies.

Tanenhaus, Michael and Greg Carlson. 1990. Comprehension of deep and surface verb-phrase anaphors. *Language and Cognitive Processes* 5(4):257–280.

Trueswell, John, Michael Tanenhaus, and Susan Garnsey. 1994. Semantic influences on parsing: Use of thematic role information in syntactic disambiguation. *Journal of Memory and Language* 33:285–318.

Warren, Tessa and Edward Gibson. 2002. The influence of referential processing on sentence complexity. *Cognition* 85(1):79–112.

25

Stochastic OT as a model of constraint interaction

ELENA MASLOVA

25.1 Introduction

Stochastic OT is a set of specific assumptions about the mechanism of interaction between universal linguistic constraints: the choice of optimal candidates is determined by the rankings of constraint weights, but the rankings can be "perturbed" by a normally distributed "evaluation noise" (Boersma and Hayes 2001); the combined weight of a set of cooperating constraints is thus assumed to equal the maximum of their own weights.[1] This implies that the combined effect of a set of cooperating constraints is only slightly stronger than the effect of the strongest constraint in this set. An interesting question is whether this hypothesis is correct, i.e., whether (and to what extent) it accurately predicts the universal properties of grammatical variation. Whereas this paper does not presume to answer this question, it provides necessary computational tools and defines a minimal condition on StOT grammars under which the StOT assumptions about the mechanism of constraint interaction can be tested against cross-linguistic data.

[1]This paper has its origin in discussions I have had with Joan Bresnan over the last couple of years and would hardly have been written without her interest and encouragement. It is not only with greatest respect, but also with deepest gratitude that I dedicate this paper to her on this occasion: her mesmerizing intellectual openness — so rare in presentday linguistics — helped me enormously in putting together two disconnected (descriptive and mathematical) parts of my linguistic self.

Architectures, Rules, and Preferences: Variations on Themes by Joan Bresnan.
Annie Zaenen, Jane Simpson, Tracy Holloway King,
Jane Grimshaw, Joan Maling, and Chris Manning, (eds.).

Section 2 examines the general properties of StOT grammars viewed as parametric statistical models. Knowledge of these properties considerably facilitates all StOT-related computations (Section 3) and will, I hope, be useful independently of the theoretical agenda of this paper. Section 4 returns to the problem of typological predictions entailed by StOT grammars and shows that they can but need not be determined by the specific properties of the StOT mechanism of constraint interaction, depending on the configuration of constraint sets. Obviously, the plausibility of this mechanism can be corroborated or falsified by cross-linguistic evidence only insofar as StOT grammars do entail StOT-specific linguistic predictions. Finally, Section 5 establishes a minimal condition that must be satisfied by a StOT grammar in order to have this property and the corresponding criterion of linguistic plausibility of the StOT mechanism of constraint interaction.

25.2 Stochastic OT as a parametric statistical model

A StOT model M can be represented as a pair $< C, \mu >$, where C is a vector of constraints and μ is a vector of **constraint strengths**. Constraints can be represented as n-by-m Boolean arrays, where n is the number of environments (input conditions) described by the model, and m, the number of competing candidates:

(1) $C_l(i, j) = 1$ if and only if C_l is violated by the jth candidate in the ith environment.

Since constraints are assumed to be universal, the constraint set can be interpreted as a universal model of (some domain of) grammatical variation. **Constraint weights** W_i are independent normally distributed random variables W_i with mean values μ_i and identical standard deviations $\sigma_i = \nu$, interpreted as evaluation noise. Constraint strengths μ are parameters of the model, and their values are language-specific. A vector of values W_i of variables W_i determines a ranking of constraints from C: if $\mathrm{w}_k > \mathrm{w}_l$, then C_k is ranked higher than C_l, and a ranking determines the choice of the optimal candidate according to the standard OT evaluation procedure. A StOT model can be called **complete** if any ranking of constraints uniquely determines the optimal candidate for each environment. Obviously, a model is incomplete if and only if there exist at least two candidates that violate exactly the same set of constraints in at least one environment; in what follows, I assume that a StOT model must be complete.

Under these assumptions, the probability of a candidate being evaluated as optimal obviously does not depend on the absolute values of constraint strengths, but only on the differences between them. Accordingly, an r-constraint StOT model has no more than $r-1$ **degrees of freedom.** In what follows, it will be convenient to normalize any StOT model by setting the value of one constraint strength to 0 and the noise value to 1; in what follows, the normalizing constraint is denoted as C_0 (i.e. $\mu_0 = 0$).

The probability p_{ij} of candidate O_j occurring in a certain environment E_i can be represented as a function of language-specific constraint strengths μ under the universal conditions determined by the constraint set:

(2) $p_{ij} = \pi_c(\mu)$

Since the constraint weights are independent normally distributed random variables, their joint probability distribution function is the product of r normal distribution functions:

(3)

$$g(w_0, \ldots, w_{r-1}) = \prod_{k=0}^{r-1} \phi(w_k; \mu_k, 1)$$

Here $\phi(x; \mu, \sigma^2)$ denotes, as usual, the normal probability density function with mean value μ and standard deviation σ evaluated at x. The probability of each ranking ρ can be obtained by integration of this function over the corresponding domain:

(4)

$$p(\rho) = \int_\rho g(w_0, \ldots, w_{r-1}) dw_0 \ldots dw_{r-1}$$

Then, p_{ij} is the sum of probabilities of all rankings that select O_j as optimal in environment E_i. However, this direct approach can hardly be effective for actual computations, since it would require numerical integration over r variables (where r is the number of constraints). Presumably for this reason, the probability distributions predicted by StOT models are usually evaluated by running a computer simulation of the StOT grammar and counting the frequencies of different candidates in the generated "corpus". The goal of this section is to show that the function $\pi_c(\mu)$ can be considerably simplified, so that the computation of p_{ij} is reduced to integration over m or less variables (where m is the number of competing candidates); this would make the StOT-related computations simpler and more effective than simulations. Informally, the simplification in question is possible because the optimal candidate is determined only by the relation between **maximal** weights of constraints violated by different candidates. I will describe the proposed approach to computation of p_{ij} for the case of two competing candidates (which is not only the simplest one, but also the most common one in actual linguistic practice) and then outline its extension to the general case of competition between m candidates. In the rest of this section, I consider the distribution of candidates in one fixed environment; thus, the index specifying the environment is dropped in the notations, and p_i denotes the probability of the ith candidate.

In the case of two candidates, the set of relevant constraints includes only those constraints that are violated by exactly one of the candidates (if the constraint is violated by both candidates, it is irrelevant). Let C_i be the set of constraints violated by candidate O_i and W_i, the corresponding set of constraint weights. Let $M_i = \mathbf{max}(W_i)$. The maximum of several independent normally distributed random variables is a random variable with the following cumulative distribution function (simply put, this equation says that the maximum of several constraint weights is less than m if and only if each of these constraint weights is less than m):

(5)

$$F_{M_i}(m) = P(M_i \leq m) =$$
$$= \prod_{W_k \in W_i} P(W_k \leq m) = \prod_{W_k \in W} \Phi(m; \mu_k)$$

Here and below, $\Phi(x; \mu)$ denotes a cumulative normal distribution function with mean value μ and variance 1 evaluated at x. The corresponding probability density function is:

(6)

$$f_{M_i}(m) = F'_{M_i}(m) = \sum_{W_l \in W_i} [\phi(m; \mu_l) \prod_{W_k \in W_i, k \neq l} \Phi(m; \mu_k)]$$

The output of the competition is determined by the difference between M_i and M_j (where O_j is the other candidate). Setting $R = M_j - M_i$, the probability of O_i can be represented as the cumulative distribution function of R evaluated at zero (i.e. the probability that M_j is greater than M_i):

(7)

$$p_i = P(R < 0) = F_R(0) =$$
$$= \int_{-\infty}^{0} \int_{-\infty}^{\infty} f_{M_j}(t + r) f_{M_i}(t) dt dr = \int_{-\infty}^{\infty} f_{M_j}(t) F_{M_i}(t) dt$$

Substituting (5) and (6) in (7), we get the following expression for p_i as a function of constraint strengths:

(8)

$$p_i = \sum_{W_t \notin W_i} \int_{-\infty}^{\infty} \phi(m; \mu_t) \prod_{k \neq t} \Phi(m; \mu_k) dm$$

Simply put, we calculate the probability that some C_t violated by the **other** candidate outranks all other constraints, and then sum up these probabilities for all such constraints; the computation of p_i is thereby reduced to numerical integration over one variable.[2] Note that, for the purposes of actual computations, the integral boundaries can be safely defined as $\mu_t \pm 5\nu$ due to the properties of normal distribution. In the simplest case of a competition determined by interaction of exactly **two** constraints, R can be defined as the difference between two independent normally distributed variables (W_0 and W_1) and thus itself a normally distributed variable with mean value $\mu_i - \mu_j$ and variance $\sigma^2 = 2\nu^2 = 2$ (assuming, without loss of generality, that O_i violates C_i) Accordingly, equation (8) can be replaced by (9):

(9) $p_i = P(R < 0) = \Phi(0; \mu_i - \mu_j, 2)$

Here $\Phi(x; \mu, \sigma^2)$ denotes, as usual, the cumulative normal distribution function with the mean value μ and standard deviation σ evaluated at x.

In the general case of m candidates, the situation is complicated by the need to take into account possible overlaps between sets of constraints violated by O_i and some (but not all) other candidates. However, the computations can still be reduced to integration over $m - 1$ variables, since the conditions of optimality can be expressed in terms of relations between m or less sets of constraints. Let me briefly show how for the case of three candidates.

Let $C_{(i)}$ denote the set of constraints violated by all candidates specified by the indices and satisfied by all other candidates, e.g. C_1 is the set of constraints violated only by O_1 and C_{12} is the set of constraints violated by both O_1 and O_2. Then the rankings under which candidate O_1 is optimal fall into three subsets that can be described by the following conditions:

(10) a. $C_{23} \gg C_1, C_2, C_3, C_{12}, C_{13}$
b. $C_2 \gg C_3, C_{23} \gg C_1, C_{12}$ & $C_2 \gg C_{13}$
c. $C_3 \gg C_2, C_{23} \gg C_1, C_{13}$ & $C_3 \gg C_{12}$

[2] Since the normal probability density function and cumulative distribution function are standard functions, implementation of this formula should be a relatively simple task.

The first condition corresponds to the cases where the highest-ranking constraint penalizes two candidates, and so the remaining one emerges as the winner independently of how the other constraints are ranked. The other two conditions describe rankings with the highest-ranking constraint ruling out one candidate (e.g. O_2 in (10b)); the next relevant constraint is the highest-ranking constraint among those that distinguish between the two remaining candidates: in (10b), for O_1 to be optimal, this must be a constraint from C_3 or from C_{23}. These conditions are deliberately defined in such a way that the corresponding sets of rankings do not overlap, so that their probabilities can be summed up. The probability of a ranking belonging to the first set can obviously be defined in terms of competition between two constraint sets and thus calculated by using equation (8). The latter two sets of ranking can only be described in terms of competition between four constraint sets and thus will require integration over three variables to compute the corresponding probabilities. This approach can be easily extended to any number of candidates.

25.3 Language-specific applications: evaluation of parameters

Statistical datasets described by means of a specific StOT model can be represented as $n \times m$ matrices of integers, where rows correspond to different environments (inputs) and columns, to competing candidates; d_{ij} is the number of occurrences of candidate O_j in environment E_i. An example of such a dataset is given in Table 1.[3] This fragment of grammar can be described by a variety of different StOT models, one of which is shown in Table 2. Note that this constraint set does not distinguish between two environments with pronominal theme (E_1 and E_2). The first question to be answered is whether this set of constraints can account for English data, that is, whether there exists a vector of constraint strength that would predict probability distributions that are sufficiently close to the observed frequencies. This problem is usually solved by running the Gradual Learning Algorithm and finding out whether it converges to an appropriate vector of constraint strengths. However, the results described in Section 2 suggest a more reliable and computationally effective method.

As in the previous section, we normalize the model by setting $\mu_0 = 0$ and $\nu = 1$. Applying the results of Section 2, we get the follow-

[3]The dataset is based on the Switchboard corpus and has been kindly provided by Joan Bresnan for testing of the algorithm described here.

	Theme	Goal	O_1 = Theme *to* Goal	O_2 = Goal Theme	Total
E_1	Pro	NP	13	0	13
E_2	Pro	Pro	123	2	125
E_3	NP	NP	23	13	36
E_4	NP	Pro	16	242	258

TABLE 1 Dative shift vs. overt dative marking in English

Theme	Goal		C_0	C_1	C_2
E_1: Pro	NP	Pro *to* NP	*		
		NP Pro		*	*
E_2: PrO_1	PrO_2	PrO_1 *to* PrO_2	*		
		PrO_2 PrO_1		*	*
E_3: NP_1	NP_2	NP_1 *to* NP_2	*		
		NP_2 NP_1		*	
E_4: NP	Pro	NP to Pro	*		*
		Pro NP		*	

TABLE 2 A three-constraint StOT model for dative shift in English

ing expressions for probabilities of competing candidates in different environments:

(11) a.

$$p_{11} = p_{21} = \sum_{i=1,2} \int_{-\infty}^{\infty} \phi(m; \mu_i) \prod_{k \neq i} \Phi(m; \mu_k) dm$$

b.

$$p_{31} = \Phi(m; -\mu_1, 2)$$

c.

$$p_{41} = \int_{\infty}^{\infty} \phi(m; \mu_i) \prod_{k \neq 1} \Phi(m; \mu_k) dm$$

d.

$$p_{i2} = 1 - p_{i1} \qquad (i = 1, \ldots, 4)$$

Once the probabilities of candidates in different environments are expressed as functions of constraint strengths, our StOT model can be dealt with as any other parametric statistical model; in particular, we can use general statistical methods (for example, the method of maximum likelihood) to evaluate the values of relevant parameters (constraint strengths) for any dataset. The numbers of tokens of each structure occurring in a given environment follow the multinomial distribution, that is, the probability of a set of values $< d_{i1}, \ldots, d_{im} >$ for a given total number d$_i$ of occurrences of environment E_i is distributed as follows:

(12)

$$P(d_{i1}, \ldots, d_{im}) = \frac{d_i!}{d_{i1}! \ldots d_{im}!} \prod_{j=1}^{m} p_{ij}(\imath)^{d_{ij}}$$

where $p_{ij}(\imath)$ is the probability of candidate O_j occurring under conditions E_i. The corresponding log-likelihood function is:

(13)

$$L(\imath; D) = \sum_{i,j} d_{ij} \ln p_{ij}(\imath)$$

The optimal vector μ of constraint weights for the given dataset is the one that maximizes this function. According to my counts, $\mu = <0, 0.429, 2.572>$; the predicted probability distributions are shown in Table 3, along with the observed frequency distributions. According to χ^2-test, the dataset in Table 1 can be assumed to follow the predicted distributions, which means that the constraint set in Table 2 can satisfactorily account for English data. Note that the predicted probabilities most closely match the observed frequencies for the case of lexical Theme and pronominal Goal (E_4). This is because this is the most frequent environment; accordingly, the frequencies observed in this environment are supposed to approximate the underlying probabilities better and are therefore given more "weight" in the log-likelihood function.

	Frequency-based Estimates		Model predictions $\mu =< 0, 0.429, 2.572 >$	
	O_1	O_2	O_1	O_2
E_1	1.0	0.0	0.972	0.028
E_2	0.984	0.016	0.972	0.028
E_3	0.639	0.361	0.619	0.381
E_4	0.062	0.938	0.060	0.940

TABLE 3 Probabilities of overt dative marking (O_1) vs. dative shift (O_2)

To sum up, the results of Section 2 allow us to use general statistical methods to decide whether a given StOT model can account for the attested cross-linguistic variation and to find the corresponding vector of constraint strengths for each language under consideration without running the GLA (or any other learning algorithm, for that matter). Accordingly, the problem of **existence** of an appropriate vector of constraint weights for the observed dataset can be solved independently of the problems of convergence for learning algorithms. The proposed method of finding constraint strengths can also be thought of as a learning algorithm of another sort (based on the ability of a learner to memorize the frequencies of competing structures in the data).

25.4 Typological applications: StOT-specific predictions of StOT models

In what follows, I will distinguish between two multidimensional typological "spaces" defined by a StOT model. The dimensions of **primary space** correspond to constraints; the boundaries of this space are determined by a set of conditions like in (14), which define the maximum relevant difference between two constraint strengths and delimit the absolute values of constraint strengths by setting $\mu_0 = 0$:

(14)

$$\mu_0 = 0; \forall i = 0, \ldots, r, \exists j \neq i : |\ \mu_i - \mu_j\ | \leq 10\nu$$

The dimensions of the **secondary space** correspond to the predicted probabilities p_{ij} of competing candidates in different environments. Its "mathematical" boundaries are obviously defined by conditions (15).

(15)

$$\forall i, j\ 0 \leq p_{ij} \leq 1; \forall i \sum_{j=1}^{m} p_{ij} = 1$$

But the StOT model is generally supposed to define a narrower space, i.e. to impose additional linguistic conditions on the possible values of p_{ij} and their relations.

Informally, the primary typological space corresponds to the factorial typology of the standard version of OT (where different "points" correspond to different rankings), while the points of secondary space correspond to different types of distributions of candidates across inputs/environments. This difference is demonstrated in Table 4 for the constraint set of Table 2; the columns correspond to the points of secondary typological space.

It is the secondary space that constitutes testable typological predictions of an OT grammar. In our example, the standard OT prediction amounts to two implicational universals: if O_2 (=dative shift) is used in E_1 or in E_2, it is also used in all other environments; and if it is used in E_3, it also used in E_4. For the corresponding StOT model,

	$C_0 > C_1 > C_2$ $C_0 > C_2 > C_1$	$C_1 > C_0 > C_2$ $C_1 > C_2 > C_0$	$C_2 > C_0$ $> C_1$	$C_2 > C_1$ $> C_0$
E_1, E_2	O_2	O_1	O_1	O_1
E_3	O_2	O_1	O_2	O_1
E_4	O_2	O_1	O_2	O_2

TABLE 4 Primary vs. secondary typological space

this prediction transforms into the following statement about probabilities of dative shift in different environments, which imposes additional conditions on the secondary typological space:

(16) $p_{12} = p_{22} \leq p_{32} \leq p_{42}$

The predictions of the corresponding standard OT model are obviously entailed by (16): if $p_{12} = 1$ or $p_{22} = 1$, then the probability of dative shift equals 1 in all other environments; and if $p_{32} = 1$, then $p_{42} = 1$. However, the StOT version also accounts for non-categorical (stochastic) preferences and, accordingly, imposes additional conditions on the possible relations between probabilities of competing candidates.

It must be recognized, however, that a prediction like that in (16) does **not** depend on the specific StOT assumptions on the interaction of linguistic constraints. In particular, these (in)equalities would be the same independently of whether the combined weight of a set of cooperating constraints is defined as their maximum (as in StOT) or, for example, as their sum. For instance, p_{22} cannot be greater than p_{32} simply because the model contains no constraints that would penalize dative shift in absence of pronouns but not in the context of a pronominal theme. The specific mechanism of constraint interaction has nothing at all to do with this prediction. Accordingly, the ability of StOT to predict this sort of constraints on cross-linguistic variation cannot, in principle, corroborate its specific assumptions about constraint interaction. However, the StOT model in our example also entails some more subtle predictions, such as:

(17) If overt dative marking is preferred in constructions with two nominal objects, then the preference for dative shift for pronominal goals is weaker than the preference for overt dative marking in the context of pronominal theme, and vice versa.

This is because the preference for overt dative marking in absence of pronouns means that C_0 is weaker than C_1; accordingly, the combined effect of C_3 and C_0 against C_1 (in the context of pronominal goal) is bound to be weaker than the combined effect of C_3 and C_1 against C_0. What is essential is that a preference for overt dative marking or for dative shift in the absence of pronouns is **quantitatively** related to the difference between corresponding distributions for pronominal theme and pronominal goal, and this quantitative relation does prominently depend on the StOT mechanism of constraint interaction. A dataset can be in contradiction with the predictions of the model even if it is only slightly different from the English dataset in Table 1. Consider, for example, a made-up dataset in Table 5, where the number of tokens of overt dative marking in absence of pronouns is increased and all other numbers are the same as in Table 1, i.e. the preference for overt dative marking in absence of pronouns is supposed to be stronger, whereas the distributions for pronominal objects are exactly as in English.

	Theme	Goal	O_1	O_2	Total
E_1	Pro	NP	13	0	13
E_2	Pro	Pro	123	2	125
E_3	NP	NP	73	13	86
E_4	NP	Pro	16	242	258

TABLE 5 Dative shift vs. overt dative marking: a faux dataset

Following the procedure in Section 2, we can determine the best vector of constraint strengths for this dataset: $\mu =< 0, 0.570, 2.430 >$; the corresponding probabilities of dative shift are $p_{12} = p_{22} = 0.033$, $p_{32} = 0.343$, $p_{42} = 0.9125$. According to χ^2-test, the dataset in Table 5 cannot be assumed to represent this distribution; in other words, the model predicts that this combination of frequencies is impossible (it is outside the boundaries of secondary typological space defined by the model). Roughly speaking, the model predicts that if the combination of frequency distributions in the first three environments is as in Table 5, then the preference for dative shift in E_4 cannot be that strong (in fact, it is predicted to occur in about 70% of instances).

These observations are, of course, not intended as a claim that these predictions are "correct", i.e. that a structurally comparable grammatical variation in other languages will conform to these predictions; it may well turn out that this is not the case, which would mean that this particular constraint set just does not work as a partial universal grammar. The point is that these predictions are testable (that is, a comparable grammatical variation in other languages either can or cannot be described by the same constraint set with a different vector of constraint strengths) and the quantitative relations involved in these predictions directly depend on the StOT hypothesis on how linguistic constraints interact with each other. In other words, the predicted boundaries of secondary typological space for the same constraint set would differ depending on how exactly the combined weight of cooperating constraints is defined. Accordingly, we can hope to find cross-linguistic evidence for or against specific hypotheses about the mechanism of constraint interaction.

For Stochastic OT, the equations presented in Section 2 can be used to describe the predicted boundaries of secondary typological space, since they establish a correspondence between the points of primary and the secondary space: it suffices to perform the computations for a sufficient number of points in the primary space to determine the boundaries of the secondary one, and, consequently, the specific quantitative relations between the probabilities of candidates in different environments that have to be tested against cross-linguistic data to verify or falsify the model.

25.5 Non-redundancy meta-constraint on StOT grammars

As demonstrated in Section 4, the StOT mechanism of constraint interaction can entail non-trivial (StOT-specific) typological predictions in combination with **some** constraint sets. There also exist constraint sets that do not have this property; moreover, it can be shown that for any fragment of linguistic data (that is, for any set of candidates and any set of environments) there exists a StOT model that does not entail any typological predictions whatsoever; that is, for any mathematically possible point in the secondary typological space (as defined in (15)) there exists a corresponding point in the primary space (the appropriate vector of constraint strengths). Such StOT models can be called **trivial**.

A trivial StOT model can be built as follows: define one constraint violated by one candidate in all environments; for each other candidate and for each environment, define one constraint violated only by this candidate and only in this environment. It can be easily shown that such a model allows for any combination of probability distributions; for example, if there are two competing candidates, the values of constraint strengths can be directly calculated using equation (9): for each environment E_i, the strength of constraint violated by O_2 in this environment is the value of inverse normal distribution with mean value $\mu_0 = 0$ and variance 2 for the given probability of O_1 in this environment (assuming that O_1 violates C_0 in all environments). The triviality of such models is ensured by two properties: first, the only overlap between constraint sets relevant in any pair of environments is the normalizing constraint, which means that the distributions in different environments are determined by distinct sets of parameters and are therefore absolutely independent of each other; secondly, the sets of constraints violated by different candidates in any environment do not overlap at all, which ensures that their strengths can be adjusted to "predict" any probability distribution in this environment. Note that the required number of constraints in such a model is $r = n*(m-1)+1$, i.e. the number of degrees of freedom must equal (or exceed) the number of independent data points in any dataset. This property of a constraint set can be referred to as **redundancy**. Of course, whether or not a model is redundant depends on the number of constraints that actually affect the output of evaluation at least in some environments: if a constraint is violated by all candidates in all environments, it must be excluded from the consideration. If a model is non-redundant, some non-trivial overlaps between constraint sets relevant in different environments are bound to exist, which would entail some additional conditions on the secondary typological space.

Trivial redundant models seem to be widely used in actual linguistic applications of StOT, whereby typological predictions are expressed by external meta-constraints in the form of universal **partial rankings** of constraints. Obviously, such models cannot entail any StOT-specific typological predictions; as a matter of fact, the very need for meta-constraints can be viewed as a signal of the failure of OT as such to express typological generalizations. Moreover, in this class of applications Stochastic OT just provides a fancy — and rather complicated — way of "rewriting" attested frequencies in another form, since the number of independent parameters of the model equals the number of data points to be accounted for, and, under the conditions stated in (14), there exists a one-to-one correspondence between the vectors of parameter values and all possible sets of probability distributions.

Of course, a redundant model need not be trivial. As an example, consider the partial StOT grammar used by Clark (2004: 83-84) to describe the relative positioning of finite verb and medial adverbs in English; the crucial point is that the position of a verb depends on whether it is auxiliary or lexical: auxiliaries consistently precede adverbs, whereas the position of the lexical verb gradually changed in the course of history: in the 15th century, the verb preceded the adverb in ca. 64% percent of cases, and now it always follows the verb. Clark's model contains two constraints (C_0 and C_1 in Table 6) that penalize V-Adv and Adv-V orders respectively (independently of whether the verb is lexical or auxiliary) and an additional constraint (C_2) that penalizes V-Adv order for lexical verbs only. The syntactic change in question can be modeled as gradual strengthening of C_2. In Table 6, the constraint strengths for the periods 1425-75 and 1500-25 are those cited by Clark, but normalized according to conventions adopted here. The constraint strengths given for Modern English simply reflect the fact that the ranking of constraints does not vary: C_1 must always be ranked below C_0 (since adverbs cannot precede auxiliaries) and C_2 must always be ranked above C_1 (since lexical verbs cannot precede adverbs), i.e. there is no variation. In fact, the strength of C_1 could be set to -10 for the earlier periods as well without any difference for the predictions of the model.

		C_0 (*OB-HD(IP))	C_1 (*I)	C_2 (*Lex-in-I)
	1425-75	$\mu_0 = 0$	$\mu_1 = -18.3$	$\mu_2 = -0.5$
	1500-25	$\mu_0 = 0$	$\mu_1 = -24.95$	$\mu_2 = 1.05$
	Modern	$\mu_0 = 0$	$\mu_1 = -10.0$	$\mu_2 = 10.0$
E_1	O_1 = Adv V		*	
Aux	O_2 = V Adv	*		
E_2	O_1 = Adv V		*	
Lex	O_2 = V Adv	*		*

TABLE 6 A redundant non-trivial StOT model for verb positioning in English (Clark 2004).

This model is redundant: it has two degrees of freedom for two independent data points. However, it is non-trivial, since it imposes the following condition on the secondary typological space:

(18) $p_{12} \geq p_{22}$

As discussed in Section 4, such predictions are not StOT-specific: (18) would follow from this constraint set independently of how exactly the constraints interact, simply because there are no constraints that would penalize O_2 for auxiliaries but not for lexical verbs. Accordingly, the ability of StOT to "predict" any pair of distributions satisfying condition (18) cannot be considered as evidence in favor of the StOT mechanism of constraint interaction.

As it seems, redundant StOT models would generally entail no StOT-specific typological predictions, insofar as they minimize non-trivial overlaps between constraint sets relevant in different environments. Conversely, if the number of constraints is minimized, StOT-specific typological predictions are bound to be more significant. This implies that Stochastic OT can be considered as a plausible model of constraint interaction only insofar as linguistically plausible StOT partial grammars are non-redundant. In other words, if a certain type of grammatical variation can be described by a non-redundant StOT grammar (i.e. the typological predictions of such a grammar are not falsified by available cross-linguistic statistical data), this can be taken as evidence for the StOT mechanism of constraint interaction. Conversely, if the quantitative constraints on the secondary typological space imposed by **any** linguistically plausible and non-redundant set of constraints under the StOT assumptions on constraint interaction turn out to be too strong, this means that the StOT mechanism of constraint interaction does not work for the corresponding type of grammatical variation.

It seems worth noting that redundant models can also be ruled out on independent grounds. If the constraint set of a StOT model is thought of as a part of UG, then this part of UG is redundant in the sense that it does not reduce the amount of information to be learnt in the course of language acquisition by a single bit: formally, such "learning" is equivalent to memorizing frequencies of the candidates in the primary data, albeit in a non-direct way. If language learners can in some sense memorize $n * (m - 1)$ constraint strengths, they can just as well memorize n independent discrete probability distributions for m candidates and than randomly draw candidates from these distributions; in fact, both the learning process and the evaluation process would be considerably simplified. These considerations suggest that Stochastic OT, as a linguistic model of constraint interaction, must include a general meta-constraint prohibiting redundant grammars. A possible objection to this meta-constraint is that the linguistic constraints participating in partial StOT grammars usually come from an underlying linguistic theory and are motivated by other considerations as well. The existence of independent motivation means, however, that these constraints are also supposed to account for some other linguistic data, apart from the datasets under consideration. If so, then these other datasets must also be taken into account in establishing the values of constraint strengths, since the constraint strengths are supposed to be constant within a single language. This means that in order to find the appropriate values of language-specific parameters of the model we must consider a more comprehensive StOT grammar, which would account for all relevant pieces of statistical data. In this case, the non-redundancy meta-constraint applies to this more comprehensive model. If this model proves to be too complex to be dealt with in actual practice, the constraint weights can be established on the basis of a partial dataset and then tested against the other relevant data. In any event, the differences between strengths of shared constraints must be the same across all relevant datasets, which obviously reduces the actual number of degrees of freedom of each partial StOT grammar, so that the non-redundancy constraint is satisfied.

To sum up, the StOT assumptions about the mechanism of constraint interaction can but need not entail testable typological predictions depending on the structure of constraint sets involved in StOT grammars. In particular, these assumptions can be corroborated by cross-linguistic data only insofar as these data are described by a non-redundant StOT grammar.

References

Boersma, Paul and Bruce Hayes. 2001. Empirical tests of the gradual learning algorithm. *Linguistic Inquiry* 32(1):45–86.

Clark, Brady Z. 2004. *A Stochastic Optimality Theory Approach to Syntactic Change*. Ph.D. thesis, Stanford University.

26

Microvariation in LFG and OT

GUIDO SEILER

Microparametric syntax is a powerful tool, whose growth is perhaps to be compared with the development of the earliest microscopes. (Kayne 1996: xvii)

26.1 An empirical approach to syntactic microvariation

One of the most intriguing facts about language is its immense variability. Languages can be extremely different from each other, but crosslinguistic variation can be very subtle, too. Linguistic theory must be able to make explicit the similarities and differences in the structural organization of any two languages. It must be prepared to say something about both the full range of crosslinguistic variation as well as the smallest possible contrasts between grammars. The latter are the focus of the present paper.

The comparative investigation of very similar languages is the traditional domain of dialectology. Dialectologists have focused on pronunciation and vocabulary rather than on syntactic structure. On the other hand, syntactic theory has largely abstracted away spatial variation. However, in recent years the interest in dialect syntax has significantly increased in the contexts of linguistic typology (Kortmann 2002, 2004) and formal syntactic theory (Barbiers et al. 2002, Kayne 1996, Weiß 1998, Wurmbrand, to appear). Why? Of course, dialects are natural languages, too, and thus a legitimate object of linguistic investigation anyway. However, what makes dialectology a unique empirical source is

Architectures, Rules, and Preferences: Variations on Themes by Joan Bresnan.
Annie Zaenen, Jane Simpson, Tracy Holloway King,
Jane Grimshaw, Joan Maling, and Chris Manning, (eds.).

its appreciation of variation on the spatial dimension. Space, like time, is a continuum. If the spatial continuum (within a given area) is fully covered in our description, we might expect to observe the finest-graded transitions from one grammar to another. Therefore, dialectology provides the rare chance to uncover the minimal units of crosslinguistic variation.

Confronting syntactic theory with syntactic microvariation is an exciting enterprise the consequences of which are not fully predictable. From an empirical point of view, the study of microvariation brings in new empirical generalizations that are an interesting challenge for linguistic theory which needs to account for them. From a theoretical perspective, spatial syntactic variation can be seen as a 'laboratory' (Moulton 1962: 25) where hypotheses about the architecture of grammar can be assessed. In the present paper I will confront two phenomena of spatial syntactic variation, prepositional dative marking and clause final verb clusters, with LFG (Lexical-Functional Grammar, Bresnan 2001) and its optimization-based extensions. Why this choice of framework? LFG's architecture of parallel, imperfectly corresponding levels of structural representation is attractive because very often dialects slightly differ in their mappings between expressions and functional content. Furthermore, transitions in space sometimes are bit by bit, a fact which is in favor of OT (Optimality Theory) where constraints are positioned on a scale relative to other constraints. A very interesting property of OT is its aptitude to deal with variation, optionality, and preferences, which I believe to be an integrate part of speakers' knowledge of grammar.

The approach pursued in the present paper is empirical. I believe that a definition of microvariation remains circular as long as it is pre-empirical. Instead, facts about spatial variation will tell us what the minimal units of crosslinguistic variation are, and we as linguists then will have to make sense of them.

In section 2 I will make concrete what kind of data we have to expect when dealing with syntactic microvariation, and I will propose ways how the findings can be captured in an OT-LFG setting. The concluding section 3 arrives at a definition of the notion 'minimal contrasts between grammars', and argues why OT-LFG is well prepared for the empirical challenge.

26.2 Two case studies

In this section, I shall briefly discuss two representative case studies from Upper (i.e., Southern) German dialects. They are representative in two regards. On the one hand, they belong to quite different areas of syntax, case marking and word order. Due to the somewhat complementary character of the examples, we are able to demonstrate a relatively broad sample of the various problems we are faced with when dealing with microvariation. On the other hand, both are fairly typical insofar as similar problems arise in connection with many other phenomena that are not discussed in the present paper. Most of the data on prepositional dative marking are based on fieldwork with consultants from all parts of the Upper German language area, which includes the Alemannic dialects of Alsace (France), South-Western Germany, Switzerland, Piemonte (Italy), and the Bavarian dialects of South-Eastern Germany, Austria, South Tyrol (Italy). The data on verb clusters are due to the research project 'Dialect Syntax of Swiss German'.[1] The data are gained by means of written questionnaires sent to over 3000 consultants.

26.2.1 Prepositional dative marking

Upper German dialects distinguish three morphological cases: nominative, accusative, and dative. Case is inflectionally realized in determiners, whereas case inflection is almost absent in nouns. In several dialects dative DPs are preceded by a prepositional marker that is homophonous with the prepositions *a(n)* ('at, beside of') or *i(n)* ('in, into'):

(1) Bavarian, IN (Upper Inn Valley; Schöpf 1866: 286):
sàg's in der frau
say-it DM the:Dsf woman
'say it to the woman'

(2) Alemannic, AN (Glarus; Bäbler 1949: 31):
er git dr Öpfel a mir, statt a dir
he gives the apple DM me:D instead DM you:D
'he gives the apple to me, not to you'

I will call this construction 'prepositional dative marking' (PDM), the morphemes *an* or *in* 'dative markers' (DM). Used as dative markers, *i(n)* and *a(n)* are functionally equivalent; their distribution is geographically determined. In the following, I will first outline those properties of PDM which are shared among the different dialects, and then focus on some aspects of spatial variation. For all kinds of details I refer to Seiler (2003).

[1] University of Zurich, German Department. Project director: Elvira Glaser. Swiss National Science Foundation 1114-57121.99, (2000-2002), 1113-68244.02 (2003-2005).

The dative marker does not bear any lexical meaning, and it does not add anything to the meaning of the sentence. The examples above have exactly the same meanings as their equivalents in other Upper German dialects or in Standard German, where no dative marker occurs. Furthermore, PDM is possible with all thematic roles that are encoded by dative DPs in Upper German.

Note that in PDM the prepositional marker is combined with dative-inflected determiner forms, such that the dative is expressed twice. Since in many Germanic and Romance languages the emergence of prepositional encodings of the indirect object correlates with the loss of dative case inflection (English *to my mother*, French *à ma mère*), one might think that the erosion of case morphology is a necessary condition for the emergence of prepositional strategies. In Upper German PDM, however, prepositional markers occur although dative case morphology is fairly intact. Thus, PDM obviously is not a compensation of eroded case morphology, nor is it an avoidance strategy of dative inflections.

I analyze the dative marker as a preposition (one with some special properties, however).[2] The main argument lies in the fact that the dative marker and prepositions are in complementary distribution: The dative marker cannot be inserted if the dative DP is governed by a 'true' preposition. It therefore seems that that the dative marker is a dummy head of a PP that dominates dative DPs; P and DM are in complementary distribution because they occupy the same c-structural position (P^0):

(3) mit (*i) de muetter
with DM the:Dsf mother

However, note that the syntactic behavior of the dative marker differs from that of other prepositions in several ways. Special properties of the dative marker include the following:

The sequence dative marker–determiner cannot be interrupted (4). Other prepositions allow intervening material (5):

(4) daas schicke mer (*i) nume i zwöi lüüt
that send:1p we DM only DM two persons
'that we will send only to two persons'

[2]There are several proposals for a functional category K^0, e.g. Butt & King 2002 for an LFG analysis of Urdu case, or Bayer et al. 2001 for German (in a Principles-&-Parameters setting). The evidence provided by Upper German PDM does not justify the introduction of the category K^0. Of course, this does not say anything about evidence from other languages.

(5) i nume zwöi minuute
in only two minutes
'in only two minutes (...it was ready)'

In coordination, the dative marker must be repeated before the second conjunct (6). Ordinary prepositions can have scope over two conjuncts (7):

(6) i de Susi und *(i) de muetter
DM the:Dsf Susi and DM the:Dsf mother

(7) mit de Susi und de muetter
with the:Dsf Susi and the:Dsf mother
'with Susi and the mother'

Thus, the dative marker must, in contrast to other prepositions, immediately precede dative determiners. The observations question the c-structural position of the dative marker as a head of a PP. Rather, it is a nonprojecting head adjoined to the determiner it precedes. Further evidence can be found if we ask which component of grammar is responsible for dative marker insertion at all. The following data give us the relevant insights.

In Upper German (as in other non-standard varieties of German), a possessor can be expressed by an adnominal dative that precedes the 3rd person possessive pronoun:

(8) de muetter ires auto
the:Dsf mother her:Nsn car
'mother's car'

The adnominal dative DP can be introduced by the dative marker in PDM dialects:

(9) i de muetter ires auto
DM the:Dsf mother her:Nsn car

However, the dative marker is not inserted when the entire complex is dominated by a preposition:

(10) mit (*i) de muetter irem auto
with DM the:Dsf mother her:Dsn car
'with mother's car'

This fact is surprising since the preposition *mit* 'with' does not govern the dative DP *de muetter* 'the:Dsf mother' immediately, as it was the case in (3): P and DM exclude each other even if they certainly do not occupy the same c-structural position. Consequently, the complementary distribution of P and DM must be stated independently of their c-structural positions. These observations lead me to quite an unusual proposal. Neither the preposition vs. dative marker asymmetries in (4)–(7), nor the lack of PDM in (10) are predicted if PDM is analyzed as the requirement for dative DPs to be immediately dominated by a PP whose dummy head is the dative marker. Rather, the pure linear neighborhood of prepositions (including the dative marker) and dative forms of determiners plays a crucial role. PDM is a matter of possible environments of morphological dative forms. The explanation is to find in the realizational morphology of determiners.

Spencer's (2001) realization-morphological approach to analytic constructions is a model of imperfect correspondence between feature content and morphological means of expression. Spencer proposes a distinction between syntactic features (s-features) and morphological features (m-features). In an LFG setting, s-features can be identified with attribute–value pairs on f-structure. M-features specify only the shape of inflected word forms, but they are inherently meaningless. Realizational morphology maps s-features with m-features. PDM is thus a matter of how the s-feature CASE DATIVE of determiners is spelt out. CASE DATIVE is correctly realized if (i) inflectional m-dative forms of determiners are used, and (ii) if the determiner is preceded by a preposition:

(11) CASE DATIVE (Det) $\Longrightarrow$ P + Det
[m-case:dative]

In ordinary PPs, but also in (10), the realization of CASE DATIVE already is complete. However, a dummy preposition, the dative marker, is inserted if otherwise (11) would be violated. In other words, the dative marker is inserted as soon as dative forms of determiners otherwise are not linearly preceded by a preposition. (11) predicts not only the complementary distribution of P and DM in (3) but also in (10).

Further evidence that a realizational-morphological approach is on the right track is provided by the fact that in many dialects PDM is sensitive to different classes of determiners. Only in some PDM dialects can every determiner be combined with the dative marker (for instance, in Central Switzerland or in Central Alsace). But in other dialects, PDM occurs only with articles, or with articles and demonstrative pronouns, etc. If the insertion of the dative marker were not a direct consequence of environment restrictions on dative-inflected word forms, these facts would remain unexplained.

Whereas realizational morphology requires determiners to be preceded by a preposition, there is no evidence for the presence of a maximal projection PP. Instead, I assume that the dative marker is a nonprojecting prepositional head which is adjoined to the determiner. The inseparability of dative marker and determiner observed in (4)–(7) supports the head adjunction analysis. Furthermore, a full PP would violate Economy of Expression[3] (Bresnan 2001: 91).

My analysis of a dative DP such as *i de muetter* 'DM the:Dsf mother' is as follows:

(12) f-structure: c-structure:

$$\begin{bmatrix} \text{PRED} & \text{'mother'} \\ \text{NUM} & \text{SG} \\ \text{GEN} & \text{FEM} \\ \text{DEF} & + \\ \text{CASE} & \text{DATIVE} \end{bmatrix}$$

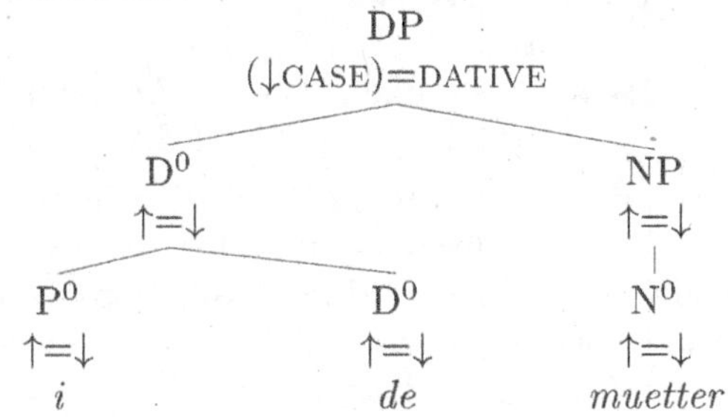

We are now ready to determine the lexical description of the dative marker. It is a member of the class {P}; it does not contain any lexical meaning (or a PRED feature, respectively); CASE of the dominating node is DATIVE:

(13) *i* : ∈ {P} (↑CASE)=DATIVE

In sum, the dative marker turned out to be a dummy prepositional 'satellite' of dative forms of determiners. It is a preposition structurally and a case marker functionally. The generalizations mentioned so far are valid for all PDM dialects. Let us now get into aspects of variation between different dialect grammars. In a few dialects (e.g. Muotathal valley, Central Switzerland), PDM is obligatory. That is, every dative is preceded by a preposition, either by a lexical preposition or by the dative marker. The above analysis is valid for these dialects without any further assumptions. In other dialects, more factors come into play which constrain dative marker insertion. The factors vary across the different dialects. I will focus on two of them: the role of information structure and inflectional morphology.

An influence of information structure on PDM is very common in German-speaking Switzerland. It is found, for instance, in Isenthal (Central Switzerland). Speakers tend to use PDM mainly if the da-

[3] "Economy of Expression: All syntactic phrase structure nodes are optional and are not used unless required by independent principles (completeness, coherence, semantic expressivity)" (Bresnan 2001: 91).

tive DP is focused. If the dative DP is not focused, the dative marker is not inserted:

(14) Dative ≠ Focus:
dasmal han ich etz dr Marte es BUECH gschänkt
this_time have I now the:Dsf Martha a book given
'this time, I gave Martha a BOOK' (Isenthal, Switzerland)

(15) Dative = Focus:
ich han s buech a dr MARTE ggëë
I have the book DM the:Dsf Martha given
'I gave the book to MARTHA' (Isenthal, Switzerland)

In these dialects, the dative marker at the same time expresses a case feature and a discourse function. In a parallel correspondence model of grammar, this overlap of functions can be represented in quite a straightforward way. In dialects with focus-sensitive PDM, the lexical description of the dative marker specifies that the dative marker is a part of an f-structure which is FOCUS of the superordinate f-structure (inside-out description, cf. Nordlinger & Sadler 2003):[4]

(16) i : ∈ {P} (↑CASE)=DATIVE
(FOCUS↑)

Dialects with focus-sensitive PDM differ from those where PDM is obligatory in the respective lexical entry of the dative marker, cf. (13) vs. (16). As for the dialects with focus-sensitive PDM, this difference has the consequence that in a sentence where the dative DP is not Focus the presence of the dative marker would create a Coherence violation (Bresnan 2001: 63).

In still other dialects, dative marker insertion interacts with a very different factor, namely inflectional morphology (whereas information structure is irrelevant). This is the case in South-Bavarian (Tyrol and Carinthia). In South Bavarian, the dative is morphologically distinct from nominative/accusative in feminine singular, but there are no morphological case distinctions in the plural. The dative marker is inserted exclusively or preferred before plurals:

[4]Instead of representing discourse functions on f-structure (Butt & King 1996), alternative proposals separate i(nformation)-structure from f-structure (Choi 1997, King 1997).

(17)

	Feminine singular:		Plural:
NOM	**d** frau		**di** fraun
ACC	**d** frau		**di** fraun
DAT	**da** frau	in +	**di** fraun
	'the woman'		'the women'

(South Bavarian)

Remember the constraint on the realization of CASE DATIVE (11). In South Bavarian, (11) applies to a more specific set of determiners than in other dialects. Only those determiners whose morphological dative form is not distinct from nominative/accusative forms are required to be preceded by a prepositional marker. As I mentioned above, it is a common property of PDM dialects that only a subset of determiner lexemes is subject to the realizational constraint (11) (one might think of these properties in terms of different inflectional classes the determiner lexemes belong to). In South Bavarian, however, dative forms of the same lexeme behave in different ways w.r.t. PDM, cf. (17).

The South Bavarian pattern reflects a much more general trait of the morphosyntax of German and its dialects which hardly can be accounted for as a lexical property of individual determiners without losing the relevant generalization: Datives (and, in Standard German, genitives) must be morphologically visible (cf. Bayer et al. 2001). It seems that PDM is used in South Bavarian only if it contributes something to morphological visibility of the dative.

The generalization can only be captured if we succeed in restricting (11) to those cases where PDM guarantees morphological visibility of the dative. In other words, (11) does not apply across the board in South Bavarian, but PDM is avoided as soon as the dative is distinctively expressed by means of inflectional morphology; it is 'more important' to avoid PDM than to obey the realizational constraint (11), but it is 'even more important' to insert the dative marker if that is the only way of keeping the dative visible.

At this point, an additional analytic device must be introduced which we have not referred to so far. The South Bavarian puzzle can only be solved if we accept that realizational-morphological, economical and visibility requirements partly are in conflict and cannot be satisfied all at the same time. An explicit format for generalizations of this type is the ranking of violable constraints: only if a higher ranked constraint is irrelevant a conflicting but lower ranked constraint becomes decisive. As for South Bavarian, visibility of the dative must be obeyed in all instances. If visibility is guaranteed by inflectional morphology anyway, PDM is avoided, which I attribute to the dominance of Economy of Expression over the morphological-realizational constraint (11); if visibility is not guaranteed, the dative marker is inserted. PDM thus violates Economy, but it satisfies the higher ranked principle of visibility. (18) proposes a formulation of the relevant principles as violable constraints, (19) demonstrates their interaction in South Bavarian:

(18) SHOW-CASE DATIVE: The realization of CASE DATIVE must be visible at the surface.

ECONOMY OF EXPRESSION: Avoid phrase structure nodes.

P+DATIVE: The s-feature CASE DATIVE of determiners is correctly realized if the determiner is preceded by a preposition.

(19) Candidate evaluation in South Bavarian ('woman'):

		SHOW-CASE DATIVE	ECO-NOMY	P+DAT-IVE
NUM SG, GEN FEM,	☞ *da frau*			*
DEF +, CASE DATIVE	*in da frau*		*!	
NUM PL, GEN FEM,	*di fraun*	*!		*
DEF +, CASE DATIVE	☞ *in di fraun*		*	

The difference between South Bavarian and dialects with obligatory PDM (e.g. Muotathal valley, Switzerland) can be understood as different relative ranking positions of ECONOMY OF EXPRESSION and P+DATIVE. In the Muotathal dialect, ECONOMY OF EXPRESSION is ranked below P+DATIVE, such that the more economical candidates without dative marker never win the against less economical PDM candidates.

Instead of going through other factors that come into play in other PDM dialects, I want to point on a more general aspect of PDM. It is often the case that there is no categorical grammaticality contrast between the two options bare dative vs. PDM, but rather a 'soft' preferential asymmetry. For instance, a speaker with focus-sensitive PDM finds the dative marker 'necessary' if the dative is focused and 'possible, but not required' if another constituent is focused. Others reject suggested PDM variants in a nonfocus context but accept both bare dative and PDM in a focus context. Our next case study, clause final verb clusters, will face us with very similar problems, and we will come back to the issue in greater detail soon.

To sum up, let us review which properties of PDM are constant across different dialects, and which are variable. Constant are the structural organization of the dative DP, and the syntactic category of the dative marker as a semantically empty, nonprojecting preposition. In terms of LFG, the constant properties are those of c-structure. The variable aspects of PDM are related to lexical properties of determiners, in particular their requirements of realizational morphology, and the lexical description of the dative marker, in particular its relation to information structure. This picture is quite symptomatic of microvariation. Frequently, the same c-structural expression options (such as bare dative vs. PDM) are arranged according to different lexical and functional requirements across different dialects. The intuition 'same expressions, different functions' is plausibly mirrored in LFG's architecture of parallel imperfect correspondance. The minimal contrasts between grammars thus are not only contrasts in the inventory of structural devices (e.g., whether there is PDM or not), but also differences in the functional properties of a given set of devices (if there are both bare datives and PDM: What is the functional arrangement between them?). The findings have interesting consequences for evolutionary models of diachronic change (see Seiler, to appear, for further discussion).

26.2.2 Clause final verb clusters

Not all microvariation phenomena have to do with different functional properties of structural devices. Clause final verb clusters are in a sense complementary to PDM since they display variation only on the level of c-structure. Nevertheless, they are a very typical representative of the nature of syntactic microvariation, too. In the first place, it is typical that major word order differences across Upper German dialects are found only within the narrow limits of verb clusters (and not, for instance, in the overall organization of the clause). However, that is not even the half of the issue. Rather, it is typical that a seemingly discrete distinction like the one between the orderings of two elements reveals much more and much subtler differences between the solutions found in the area than one would expect.

The data on verb clusters are based on preliminary results of the project 'Dialect Syntax of Swiss German' (see footnote 1). The goal of the research project is to explore the geographical distribution of syntactic construction types over German-speaking Switzerland. As of August 2004, 3196 consultants from 389 measuring points have been sent four written questionnaires containing translation tests, fill-in tests and multiple choice tests, 118 questions in total (see Bucheli Berger & Glaser 2002 for further details concerning the research design). A more detailed study on verb clusters in Swiss German is published in Seiler (2004).

In dialects of the Western periphery of German-speaking Switzerland, the finite auxiliary or modal verb precedes the nonfinite complement (Seiler 2004: 370–71):

(20) Guttannen (Bernese Highlands):

a. ...ob si das Auto schon **hed zahld**
whether she the car already has paid
'(I have no idea) whether she has already paid for the car'

b. ...ob är äis wil **hiraten**
whether he ever wants get_married
'(Well, I don't know) whether he ever wants to get married'

In Eastern dialects, the finite element follows:

(21) Thusis (Grisons district):

a. ...ob sie das Auto scho **zalt het**
whether she the car already paid has

b. ...ob är amal **hürata** **wetti**
whether he ever get_married wants

However, the geographical picture is much more complex than the examples suggest, as I will discuss shortly. Let me first make a brief note on the analysis of verbal periphrases in an LFG setting. It is controversial whether a finite auxiliary is to be represented as a predicate on f-structure which takes a nonfinite complement (XCOMP) or as a tense/aspect feature. The decision has to be made independently for each auxiliary or modal verb within each language (Dyvik 1999, Falk 2003). As for German, I assume that both auxiliaries and modal verbs are predicates, since their XCOMPs can be pronominalized:

(22) a. gestern habe ich den See überquert
yesterday have I the:Asm lake crossed
'yesterday I've crossed the lake'

b. das habe ich auch schon oft
that have I also already often
'I've already done that many times, too'

c. das will ich auch einmal
that want I also once
'I want to do that some time, too'

Consequently, the (simplified) f-structure of example (21)a is as follows:

(23) $$\left[\begin{array}{ll} \text{PRED} & \text{'AUX<XCOMP>SUBJ'} \\ \text{SUBJ} & \text{'she'} \\ \text{XCOMP} & \left[\begin{array}{ll} \text{PRED} & \text{'pay<SUBJ, OBJ>'} \\ \text{SUBJ} & \\ \text{OBJ} & \text{'the car'} \end{array}\right] \end{array}\right]$$

Let us now turn to the geographical facts (cf. Seiler 2004 and the maps therein). As the examples (20)–(21) above suggest, the general picture is a transition from Western ascending (finite–nonfinite) to Eastern descending (nonfinite–finite) ordering of elements. However, there is no clear-cut isogloss between the ascending and descending patterns. Instead, the transition is *gradual*. In the first place, auxiliaries and modal verbs behave differently. The switch from Western AUX–V to Eastern V–AUX is much farther in the West than the switch from MOD–V to V–MOD. We therefore find three basic patterns in our area (ascending patterns are bold):

(24)

Western	Central	Eastern
AUX–V	V–AUX	V–AUX
MOD–V	**MOD–V**	V–MOD

Thus, on the one hand, we have to construct (at least) three different grammars for the different areas. On the other hand, we want to make explicit the overall geometry the three grammars are parts of, i.e., the fact that the prominence of the descending pattern is relatively higher when moving from West to East. Optimality Theory is a promising instrument to fulfill both requirements: From one grammar to the next, it is always one constraint pair which is reranked. I propose the following constraints; (25)a–b are constraints on c-structure,[5] (25)c is a constraint on the correspondence between f- and c-structural elements (verbal PREDs and V^0 positions):[6]

[5] As for the c-structural realization of verb clusters, I assume (following Berman 2003: 38) that the involved verbs form a complex head at the right edge of the clause: $[_{V^0}\ V^0\ V^0]$.

[6] The purpose of the analysis presented here is mainly illustrational, but it is far from complete, since almost all possible complications are neglected. The picture gets much more complicated as soon as we are taking into account the behavior of three verb clusters, or the interaction of verb clusters with complements and adjuncts. See Seiler 2004 for a slightly more elaborate attempt, and Lötscher 1978 for the full range of empirical issues.

(25) a. AUX>V: Auxiliaries precede their complements.
b. MOD>V: Modal verbs precede their complements.
c. V_{NUC}-FIRST: The most embedded verbal PRED corresponds to the first V^0 of the verbal complex.

V_{NUC}-FIRST's ranking is lowest in the West and highest in the East. In the Central system, it is sandwiched between MOD>V and AUX>V, cf. (26).[7] The effects of the ranking valid in the Central system is illustrated in tableau (27):

(26) Western: {MOD>V, AUX>V} ≫ V_{NUC}-FIRST
Central: MOD>V ≫ V_{NUC}-FIRST ≫ AUX>V
Eastern: V_{NUC}-FIRST ≫ {MOD>V, AUX>V}

(27) Candidate evaluation in the Central system:[8]

		MOD>V	V_{NUC}-FIRST	AUX>V
PRED(1)=AUX, PRED(2)='pay'	*hät zalt*		*!	
	☞ *zalt hät*			*
PRED(1)='want', PRED(2)='marry'	☞ *wett hürate*		*	
	hürate wett	*!		

While the geographical picture of Western, Central, and Eastern systems is quite impressive – it is an idealization. It abstracts away subtler gradations in space which are revealed only at closer look. In order to answer the introductory question on the minimal contrasts between grammars it is necessary to weaken the idealizations. The design of the Zurich project on Swiss German dialect syntax makes possible generalizations on interpersonal and intrapersonal variation. An insight into interpersonal variation is possible because we have been working together with several consultants at each measuring point. The general picture — Western ascending order, Eastern descending order — is repeated on the quantitative dimension: The relative number of consultants who accept or prefer a descending variant gradually increases towards the East.[9] These findings are particularly interest-

[7] One might say that the ranking MOD>V ≫ AUX>V is constant whereas the position of V_{NUC}-FIRST is variable across our dialects. However, the mutual ranking of MOD>V and AUX>V cannot be determined on the basis of Western and Eastern data. Therefore, I dispense with explicitly ranking the two constraints in the Western and Eastern grammars.

[8] For reasons of space, I use abbreviated inputs instead of full f-structures, cf. (23).

[9] Map 3 in Seiler 2004 demonstrates that the measuring points where V–MOD is the preferred variant for the majority of consultants cluster in the easternmost areas.

ing from a sociolinguistic point of view since they demonstrate how a variant spreads across space and communities. However, as long as two competing variants are distributed over different groups of speakers, the individual competences of those speakers still can be accounted for within the simple model I introduced in (26) above. This is not the case with intrapersonal variation. We explicitly encouraged the consultants to indicate us the acceptable variants as well as their preferred ('most natural') variant. It turned out that it is not totally random in which areas a variant is judged as acceptable (though not preferred), preferred, or obligatory (i.e., alternative variants are rejected). Map 1 (section 26.4) shows the different prominences of V–MOD on the preferential dimension. Black dots represent measuring points where the majority of consultants judged V–MOD as obligatory. At grey places 50% or more of the consultants prefer V–MOD, but MOD–V is an option for them, too. White dots show the places where the majority of consultants accepts V–MOD, but prefers another variant (i.e., MOD–V). The black pinpoints are places where V–MOD is not acceptable. Despite some unavoidable noise (partly due to the highly structured topography of the country), the general picture is clear: Whereas in a relatively large area (excluding the West) V–MOD is acceptable, only in its easternmost parts is the variant preferred or even required. Thus, not only speakers' inventories of variants, but also their preferences for one or another variant are area-specific.

In (26), we have modeled the transition from MOD–V to V–MOD dialects as reversed rankings of V_{NUC}-FIRST and MOD>V. We now know that an abrupt switch from MOD–V to V–MOD is an idealization. In nature, the transition includes a designated area where a large number of speakers systematically allows both orderings. These speakers' competences are different from those with only one variant; therefore we must be able to model their knowledge of grammar. In terms of Optimality Theory, this means that their existence is not predicted by a simple ranking reversal of V_{NUC}-FIRST and MOD>V. Instead, in the area between the MOD>V $\gg$ V_{NUC}-FIRST and V_{NUC}-FIRST $\gg$ MOD>V dialects a grammar exists where the two crucial constraints are tied: {MOD>V, V_{NUC}-FIRST}. A constraint tie predicts variable outputs if (i) the tied constraints are in competition (i.e., violated by different sets of candidates), (ii) at least two candidates 'survive' the evaluation by higher ranked constraints, (iii) at least two candidates display the same number of violations of the tied constraints, (iv) this num-

They are surrounded by measuring points where less than 50% of the consultants prefer V–MOD. Farther westwards, V–MOD is not even preferred by a minority (instead, the consultants prefer MOD–V).

ber is greater than zero, and (v) no other candidate displays a lower number of violations. Following Anttila (2002: 231), I assume that a competence grammar containing tied constraints allows for all possible rankings of the tied constraints (with equal probability) in actual candidate evaluations.[10]

However, the overwhelming majority of our consultants is able not only to distinguish between (one or several) acceptable and unacceptable variants, but also to rank acceptable variants according to preference. As Map 1 (section 26.4) shows, preferences for a particular variant cluster in specific areas on the spatial continuum. How can these speakers' competences be mirrored in our model? So far, we have dealt with ranked constraints and with constraint ties, i.e., with constraints whose position on the constraint hierarchy totally overlaps. From here, it is a logical consequence to assume that partial overlaps of constraints are possible, too. Schematically:

(28) Ranked constraints: (C1) (C2)

Tied constraints: (C1, C2)

Partial overlap: (C1 () C2)

The idea of partially overlapping constraints has been elaborated in Stochastic Optimality Theory (Boersma 1997, Bresnan & Deo 2001, Bresnan, Dingare & Manning 2001) where constraints are ranked on a continuous scale of real numbers such that the distances between constraints may differ. At each evaluation there is a small amount of random perturbation such that the actual ranking value of a constraint is slightly above or below its mean ranking value. If the distance between the mean ranking values of two constraints C1 and C2 is rather small, reversed rankings are more likely to occur in actual evaluations. Although Stochastic OT is able to predict quantitative distributions of variants, the important aspect for present purposes is its qualitative statement: It takes seriously the fact that competing variants may coexist in one speaker's grammar whereby the choice between two available variants may be biased, and it models these facts in a very natural way, as an entirely expected thing.

26.3 Conclusion and outlook

After having examined two case studies, we now have a more concrete idea about the nature of syntactic microvariation.

[10] Therefore, lower ranked constraints are irrelevant as soon as the possible rankings of the tied constraints identify a winner candidate.

The first case study, prepositional dative marking, revealed that although the same set of expressional devices (bare datives and PDM) is found in a larger area, dialects differ in their functional arrangements between those devices. In order to capture the differences, we have employed many analytic instruments provided by the OT-LFG framework: the separation of c-structure from f-structure, lexical descriptions, realizational morphology, and constraint ranking. It turned out that the dialects differ in the lexical properties of the dative marker, the mapping between information structure and means of expression, and morphological requirements. The spatial variation involved in verb clusters is a matter of slightly different c-structural realizations. Not only have we revealed that auxiliaries and modal verbs behave in different ways. The gradual character of the transition from ascending to descending patterns raises unusual analytical problems. I have shown that the coexistence of options in one speaker's competence is an entirely expected fact which follows from the gradualness of spatial variation. Furthermore, dialects even may be different only in their preferences for one or another option. Since such dialects occupy a specific place on a consistent geographical picture, I conclude that it is part of the speakers' knowledge of grammar to be equipped with several available but more or less preferred variants. Optimality Theory, in particular its stochastic variant, is a promising model of such grammars, since it is able systematically to predict the occurrence of coexisting options and 'biased' choices between options. Whatever the internal architecture of a variable outputs grammar might be – there is no alternative to it. Sometimes optionality has been interpreted as the interplay of competing grammars in one speaker's mind (Kroch 2001: 720, Lightfoot 1999: 92). This approach models optionality as if it were something very different, namely diglossia. Despite the fact that the number of copresent grammars exponentially increases with each variable feature (Bresnan & Deo 2001: 39), the model is not able to say something substantial about the distribution of variants. This failure is particularly regrettable in cases when speakers 'softly' prefer one option according to functionally transparent patterns (as it is the case with PDM). I am convinced that it is the more productive way to derive variation from the internal structure of grammar itself. Moreover, I do not see a reason why a dialect with variable features should not deserve a grammar on its own, since it is this language that is acquired by the local speakers (although, of course, this grammar can be very similar to the neighbors' grammars).[11]

The minimal units of crosslinguistic variation, therefore, can be defined as differences in the functional or preferential arrangement of a set of options available in both of the compared languages. The framework of OT-LFG fulfills the unusually high requirements raised by spatial syntactic variation. Due to its relational architecture of imperfectly corresponding levels of structural representation, its appreciation of lexical properties, and its flexibility in dealing with coexisting variants, it is able explicitly to capture the subtlest similarities and differences between dialects. It is interesting to note that the framework has not been developed in order to account for dialect variation specifically.[12] The fact that it is capable to do so yet demonstrates its adequacy in an even more impressive way.

26.4 Map

[11] Having accepted that variation follows from the internal structure of a grammar (instead of being 'added' to a grammar), some unexpected consequences follow. In particular, this view changes the relationship of variation and linguistic change. As long as variation is seen as the synchronic reflex of ongoing change, the implict assumption is that change has a nonvariable state as its starting point and another nonvariable state as its target. However, if variation is taken to be the unmarked case, change appears to be an epidemical accumulation of variant choices by the speakers. This view is much more compatible with evolutionary conceptions of linguistic change, cf. Croft 2000, Haspelmath 1999, Kirby 1999, Seiler, to appear.

[12] This point might be an indication that wide-range typological variation and microvariation are not fundamentally different in nature. Rather, they operate on the basis of the same principles, though in different degrees.

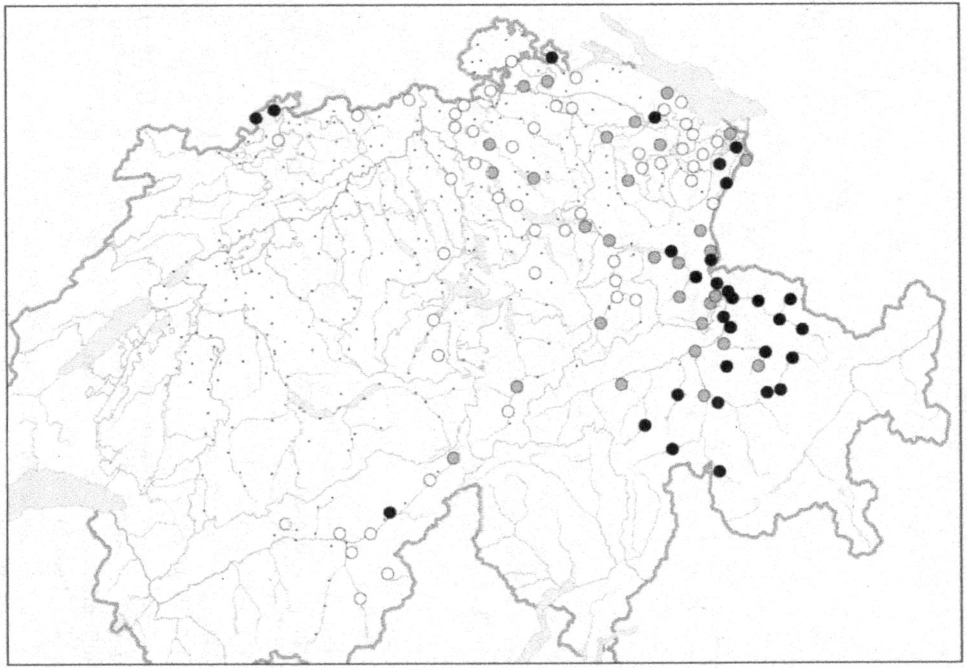

FIGURE 1 Map 1: V–MOD in German-speaking Switzerland. Black dots: V–MOD obligatory for $\geq$ 50%. Grey dots: V–MOD preferred by $\geq$ 50%. White dots: V–MOD accepted by $\geq$ 50%. ©Project 'Dialektsyntax des Schweizerdeutschen', SNF 1113-68244.02.

References

Anttila, Arto. 2002. Variation and phonological theory. In J. K. Chambers, P. Trudgill, and N. Schilling-Estes, eds., *The Handbook of Language Variation and Change*, pages 206–243. Oxford: Blackwell.

Bäbler, Heinz. 1949. *Glarner Sprachschuel*. Glarus: Verlag der Erziehungsdirektion.

Barbiers, Sjef, Leonie Cornips, and Susanne van der Kleij, eds. 2002. *Syntactic Microvariation*. Amsterdam: Meertens Instituut (Meertens Institute Electronic Publications in Linguistics).

Bayer, Josef, Markus Bader, and Michael Meng. 2001. Morphological underspecification meets oblique case: Syntactic and processing effects in German. *Lingua* 111:465–514.

Berman, Judith. 2003. *Clausal Syntax of German*. Stanford, CA: CSLI Publications.

Boersma, Paul. 1997. How we learn variation, optionality, and probability. *Proceedings of the Institute of Phonetic Sciences, University of Amsterdam* 21:43–58.

Bresnan, Joan. 2001. *Lexical-Functional Syntax*. Oxford: Blackwell.

Bresnan, Joan and Ashwini Deo. 2001. Grammatical constraints on variation: 'Be' in the survey of English dialects and (stochastic) Optimality Theory. Ms., Stanford University.

Bresnan, Joan, Shipra Dingare, and Christopher D. Manning. 2001. Soft constraints mirror hard constraints: Voice and person in Lummi and English. In M. Butt and T. H. King, eds., *Proceedings of the International Lexical-Functional Grammar Conference 2001 (LFG'01)*, pages 13–32. Hong Kong: CSLI Online Publications.

Bucheli Berger, Claudia and Elvira Glaser. 2002. The syntactic atlas of Swiss German dialects: Empirical and methodological problems. In S. Barbiers, L. Cornips, and S. van der Kleij, eds., *Syntactic Microvariation*, pages 42–74. Amsterdam: Meertens Instituut (Meertens Institute Electronic Publications in Linguistics).

Butt, Miriam and Tracy H. King. 1996. Structural topic and focus without movement. In M. Butt and T. H. King, eds., *Proceedings of the International Lexical-Functional Grammar Conference 1996 (LFG'96)*. Grenoble: CSLI Online Publications.

Butt, Miriam and Tracy H. King. 2002. The status of case. Ms., Universität Konstanz and Xerox PARC.

Choi, Hye-Won. 1997. Information structure, phrase structure, and their interface. In M. Butt and T. H. King, eds., *Proceedings of the International Lexical-Functional Grammar Conference 1997 (LFG'97)*. San Diego, CA: CSLI Online Publications.

Croft, William. 2000. *Explaining Language Change: An Evolutionary Approach*. Harlow: Longman.

Dyvik, Helge. 1999. The universality of F-structure: Discovery or stipulation? The case of modals. In M. Butt and T. H. King, eds., *Proceedings of the International Lexical-Functional Grammar Conference 1999 (LFG'99)*. Manchester: CSLI Online Publications.

Falk, Yehuda N. 2003. The English auxiliary system revisted. In M. Butt and T. H. King, eds., *Proceedings of the International Lexical-Functional Grammar Conference 2003 (LFG'03)*, pages 184–204. Albany, NY: CSLI Online Publications.

Haspelmath, Martin. 1999. Optimality and diachronic adaptation. *Zeitschrift für Sprachwissenschaft* 18(2):180–205.

Kayne, Richard S. 1996. Microparametric syntax: Some introductory remarks. In J. R. Black and V. Motapanyane, eds., *Microparametric Syntax and Dialect Variation*, pages ix–xxviii. Amsterdam: J. Benjamins.

King, Tracy H. 1997. Focus domains and information-structure. In M. Butt and T. H. King, eds., *Proceedings of the International Lexical-Functional Grammar Conference 1997 (LFG'97)*. San Diego, CA: CSLI Online Publications.

Kirby, Simon. 1999. *Function, Selection, and Innateness. The Emergence of Language Universals*. Oxford: Oxford University Press.

Kortmann, Bernd. 2002. New prospects for the study of English dialect syntax: Impetus from syntactic theory and language typology. In S. Barbiers, L. Cornips, and S. van der Kleij, eds., *Syntactic Microvariation*, pages 185–213. Amsterdam: Meertens Instituut (Meertens Institute Electronic Publications in Linguistics).

Kortmann, Bernd, ed. 2004. *Dialectology Meets Typology. Dialect Grammar from a Cross-Linguistic Perspective*, vol. 153 of *Trends in Linguistics: Studies and Monographs*. Berlin & New York, NY: Mouton de Gruyter.

Kroch, Anthony. 2001. Syntactic change. In M. Baltin and C. Collins, eds., *The Handbook of Contemporary Syntactic Theory*, pages 699–729. Oxford: Blackwell.

Lightfoot, David. 1999. *The Development of Language. Acquisition, Change, and Evolution*. Oxford: Blackwell.

Lötscher, Andreas. 1978. Zur Verbstellung im Zürichdeutschen und in anderen Varianten des Deutschen. *Zeitschrift für Dialektologie und Linguistik* 45:1–29.

Moulton, William G. 1962. Dialect geography and the concept of phonological space. *Word* 18:23–32.

Nordlinger, Rachel and Louisa Sadler. 2003. Tense beyond the verb: Encoding clausal tense/aspect/mood on nominal dependents. *Natural Language and Linguistic Theory* 22(3):597–641.

Schöpf, Johann B. 1866. *Tirolisches Idiotikon*. Innsbruck: Wagner.

Seiler, Guido. 2002. Prepositional dative marking in Upper German: A case of syntactic microvariation. In S. Barbiers, L. Cornips, and S. van der Kleij, eds., *Syntactic Microvariation*, pages 243–279. Amsterdam: Meertens Instituut (Meertens Institute Electronic Publications in Linguistics).

Seiler, Guido. 2003. *Präpositionale Dativmarkierung im Oberdeutschen*, vol. 124 of *Zeitschrift für Dialektologie und Linguistik, Beihefte*. Stuttgart: Steiner.

Seiler, Guido. 2004. On three types of dialect variation, and their implications for linguistic theory. In B. Kortmann, ed., *Dialectology meets Typology. Dialect Grammar from a Cross-Lunguistic Perspective*, vol. 153 of *Trends in Linguistics: Studies and Monographs*, pages 367–399. Berlin & New York, NY: Mouton de Gruyter.

Seiler, Guido. to appear. The role of functional factors in language change: An evolutionary approach. In O. Nedergaard Thomsen, ed., *Competing Models of Linguistic Change. Evolution and beyond*. Amsterdam & Philadelphia, PA: J. Benjamins. To appear.

Spencer, Andrew. 2001. The paradigm-based model of morphosyntax. *Transactions of the Philological Society* 99(2):279–313.

Weiß, Helmut. 1998. *Syntax des Bairischen*. Tübingen: Niemeyer. Studien zur Grammatik einer natürlichen Sprache.

Wurmbrand, Susi. 2004. West Germanic verb clusters: The empirical domain. In K. É. Kiss and H. van Riemsdijk, eds., *The Verb Cluster Sprachbund: Verb Clusters in Germanic and Hungarian*, pages 43–85. Amsterdam: J. Benjamins.

Zaenen, Annie and Ronald M. Kaplan. 1995. Formal devices for linguistic generalizations: West German word order in LFG. In M. Dalrymple, R. M. Kaplan, J. T. Maxwell III, and A. Zaenen, eds., *Formal Issues in Lexical-Functional Grammar*, pages 215–239. Stanford, CA: CSLI Publications.

Index